SIMULATORS VI

Titles in the *SIMULATION SERIES*

Vol. 1 No. 1 *Mathematical Models of Public Systems* George A. Bekey, Editor January 1971
Vol. 1 No. 2 *Systems and Simulation in the Service of Society* David D. Sworder, Editor July 1971
Vol. 2 No. 1 *The Mathematics of Large-Scale Simulation* Paul Brock, Editor June 1972
Vol. 2 No. 2 *Recent Developments in Urban Gaming* Philip D. Patterson, Editor December 1972
Vol. 3 No. 1 *Computer Simulation in Design Applications* Said Ashour and Marvin M. Johnson, Editors June 1973
Vol. 3 No. 2 *Simulation Systems for Manufacturing Industries* Marvin M. Johnson and Said Ashour, Editors December 1973
Vol. 4 No. 1 *Annotated Bibliographies of Simulation* Tuncer I. Ören, Editor June 1974
Vol. 4 No. 2 *Spanning the Applications of Simulation* Paul Brock, Editor December 1974
Vol. 5 No. 1 *New Directions in the Analysis of Ecological Systems: Part 1* George S. Innis, Editor June 1975
Vol. 5 No. 2 *New Directions in the Analysis of Ecological Systems: Part 2* George S. Innis, Editor December 1975
Vol. 6 No. 1 *Toward Real-Time Simulation (Languages, Models, and Systems), Part 1* Roy E. Crosbie and John L. Hay, Editors June 1976
Vol. 6 No. 2 *Toward Real-Time Simulation (Languages, Models, and Systems), Part 2* Roy E. Crosbie and John L. Hay, Editors December 1976
Vol. 7 No. 1 *An Overview of Simulation in Highway Transportation: Part 1* James E. Bernard, Editor June 1977
Vol. 7 No. 2 *An Overview of Simulation in Highway Transportation: Part 2* James E. Bernard, Editor December 1977
Vol. 8 No. 1 *Simulation of Energy Systems: Part 1* Kenneth E.F. Watt, Editor June 1978
Vol. 8 No. 2 *Simulation of Energy Systems: Part 2* Kenneth E.F. Watt, Editor December 1978
Vol. 9 No. 1 *Simulation in Business Planning and Decision Making* Thomas H. Naylor, Editor July 1981
Vol. 9 No. 2 *Simulating the Environmental Impact of a Large Hydroelectric Project* Normand Thérien, Editor July 1981
Vol. 10 No. 1 *Survey of the Application of Simulation to Health Care* Stephen D. Roberts and William L. England, Editors December 1981
Vol. 10 No. 2 *Computer Modeling and Simulation: Principles of Good Practice* John McLeod, Editor June 1982
Vol. 11 No. 1 *Peripheral Array Processors* Walter J. Karplus, Editor October 1982
Vol. 11 No. 2 *Computer Simulation in Emergency Planning* John M. Carroll, Editor January 1983
Vol. 12 No. 1 *Lumped-Parameter Models of Hydrocarbon Reservoirs* Ellis A. Monash, Editor March 1983
Vol. 12 No. 2 *Computer Models for Production and Inventory Control* Haluk Bekiroglu, Editor January 1984
Vol. 13 No. 1 *Aerospace Simulation* Monte Ung, Editor February 1984
Vol. 13 No. 2 *Simulation in Strongly Typed Languages: ADA, PASCAL, SIMULA . . .* Ray Bryant and Brian W. Unger, Editors February 1984
Vol. 14 No. 1 *All About Simulators, 1984* Vince Amico and A. Ben Clymer, Editors April 1984
Vol. 14 No. 2 *Peripheral Array Processors* Walter J. Karplus, Editor October 1984
Vol. 15 No. 1 *Emergency Planning* John M. Carroll, Editor January 1985
Vol. 15 No. 2 *Distributed Simulation 1985* Paul F. Reynolds, Editor January 1985
Vol. 16 No. 1 *Simulators* John S. Gardenier, Editor March 1985
Vol. 16 No. 2 *Aerospace Simulation II* Monte Ung, Editor January 1986
Vol. 17 No. 1 *Intelligent Simulation Environments* Paul A. Luker and Heimo H. Adelsberger, Editors January 1986
Vol. 17 No. 2 *Simulators III* Bruce T. Fairchild, Editor March 1986
Vol. 18 No. 1 *AI Applied to Simulation* E.J.H. Kerckhoffs, G.C. Vansteenkiste, and B.P. Zeigler, Editors February 1986
Vol. 18 No. 2 *Multiprocessors and Array Processors* Walter J. Karplus, Editor April 1987
Vol. 18 No. 3 *Simulation and AI* Paul Luker and Graham Birtwistle, Editors July 1987
Vol. 18 No. 4 *Simulators IV* Bruce T. Fairchild, Editor October 1987
Vol. 19 No. 1 *Methodology and Validation* Osman Balci, Editor January 1988
Vol. 19 No. 2 *Aerospace Simulation III* Monte Ung, Editor April 1988
Vol. 19 No. 3 *Distributed Simulation, 1988* Brian Unger and David Jefferson, Editors July 1988
Vol. 19 No. 4 *Simulators V* A. Ben Clymer and G. Vince Amico, Editors October 1988
Vol. 20 No. 1 *AI Papers, 1988* Ranjeet J. Uttamsingh, Editor January 1989
Vol. 20 No. 2 *Simulation in Emergency Management & Technology* Jim Sullivan and Ross T. Newkirk, Editors April 1988
Vol. 20 No. 3 *Simulation and AI, 1989* Wade Webster, Editor April 1988
Vol. 20 No. 4 *Advances in AI and Simulation* Ranjeet Uttamsingh and A. Martin Wildberger, Editors March 1989
Vol. 21 No. 1 *Multiprocessors and Array Processors V* Walter J. Karplus, Editor March 1989
Vol. 21 No. 2 *Distributed Simulation, 1989* Brian Unger and Richard Fujimoto, Editors March 1989
Vol. 21 No. 3 *Simulators VI* Ariel Sharon and Mohammad R. Fakory, Editors March 1989

SIMULATORS VI

Proceedings of the SCS Multiconference on
Simulators VI
28-31 March, 1989
Tampa, Florida

Edited by
Ariel Sharon
Fauske & Associates, Inc.
and
Mohammad R. Fakory
Computer Simulations Corporation

Simulation Series
Volume 21
Number 3
March 1989

A Society for Computer Simulation International (Simulation Councils, Inc.) publication
San Diego, California

P. O. Box 17900
San Diego, California

ISBN 0-911801-51-0

PRINTED IN THE UNITED STATES OF AMERICA

CONTENTS

CONTENTS

PREFACE

Simulators play an increasingly important role in today's industries. As industries become more complex and controls more sophisticated, demand for skilled operators is ever increasing. In this technological environment, simulators are vital.

While the first simulators in many industries were essentially basic training tools and were treated only as such, the vast expansion in computer resources allows the use of sophisticated dynamic models to extend the use of simulators. Simulators based on such advanced models can represent more complex transients and operations with much higher accuracy and fidelity. This has, of course, important implications for the quality of training. Moreover, different roles for simulators are emerging, making them much more versatile tools that can be used beyond just basic training.

The immediate benefit of a more accurate simulator is the ability to investigate system performance and controls. With reliable dynamic models it is possible to take the simulated system to its design limits and explore its dynamic behavior under such conditions. Improvement in the system design can be explored, operating instructions can be put to test, and the control functions as well as the use of emergency standby systems can be examined for plausible system conditions.

Man-machine interface research is another area that can be vastly improved with the use of simulators. The quality of the information displayed on the control panel can be examined. Is it sufficient for all cases? Which information is redundant? What is the critical information needed to diagnose unusual system behavior? Is the critical information clearly displayed? What is the best display arrangement? Answers to these questions are keys for improvements to existing systems that operate with a low frequency of accidents.

Of all industries the nuclear power industry has the most advanced plant simulators. Close scrutiny from the U. S. Nuclear Regulatory Commission (NCR) and within the industry itself by the Institute of Nuclear Power Operations (INFO) places stringent requirements on nuclear plant simulators. Sophisticated training centers with full-scope simulators dedicated to almost every plant type and site are now part of the successful operation of the many nuclear power plants across the U. S. A. Similar requirements and sophisticated simulators exist in virtually every country with nuclear power plants.

An increasing awareness of the role that simulators can have in assuring safe operation of the plants is apparent by the growing use of simulators and the constant upgrading of the simulators' hardware and software. While the automatic safety systems in the plants are designed to accommodate incredible accidents, it is the human operator that can mitigate an accident initiator and bring it to a controllable state or propel it to a large-scale accident. Indeed, human errors are cited as principle reasons for the two largest accidents in the nuclear history: Chernobyl and Three Mile Island. Operator errors during both accidents occured as results of both the lack of understanding of the plant dynamics under unusual conditions and from the insufficient display of the plant conditions in the control room. Both of these deficiencies – operator and designer understanding of the system dynamics and improvement in the control room data display and warning systems – can be remarkably improved by the use of simulators. Upgrades of the simulator computing capabilities can further enhance their use as a tool that deals with these deficiencies. Testing systems and control room response for beyond design base conditions is just one of the benefits of such upgrades.

Other industries, such as chemical, manufacturing, space, flight, marine and many others, are also expanding the roles of their simulators. Each industry with its own particular needs can only benefit from an accurate simulation facility where operators, system engineers and control designers can put their ideas to test. The simulator conference is the place to present and discuss these ideas, and how the use of simulators can be even further extended.

In this simulator conference various industries that are using and developing simulator technology are represented. Papers are presented on a large variety of topics that are state-of-the-art in simulator technology. Papers on physical modeling for simulators, and mathematical and computational tools are presented in seven sessions. Modeling of flow in porous beds with application to oil reservoirs are presented in two large sessions. Panel discussions and opinion papers on the certification of nuclear simulators and the research program on human factors are just some of the focal points of the nuclear simulator track. Other topics relevant to simulation and simulators in a large variety of industries and applications are also discussed. All of this unique collection of papers make the conference and its proceedings publication very valuable to those that want to keep up with the industry.

This conference was originated by many individuals that have one common cause: to promote the use and usefulness of simulators in the industries that they are involved in. Their voluntary effort and dedication have led to the successful program of this conference and its proceedings. On the behalf of all the participants and professional peers, I would like to thank all of the session, group and track chairpersons for their efforts.

Track Chairpersons: V. Amico, *Consultant*
M. Carpenter, *MITAGS*
F. S. Kovarik, *Petroleum Recovery Research Center*
A. Sharon, *Fauske & Associates, Inc.*
R. Shayam, *Autodynamics*

Group Chairpersons: L. Foulke, *Westinghouse Corporation, NSID*
S. Halverson, *Union Electric*
P. Kalim, *Wilkes College*
R. C. Kern, *Utility Associates International*

Session Chairpersons: J. Malcolm Black, *Northeastern Utilities*
A. Cheung, *Westinghouse*
A. Ben Clymer
B. Delamorton, *Virginia Power*
J. M. Doster, *North Carolina State University*
M. R. Fakory, *Singer-Link*
Y. A. Hassan, *Texas A&M University*
A. Hold, *Gessellschaft fur Reaktorsicherheit*
J. Luxat, *Ontario Hydro*
P. E. Meyer, *Westinghouse Electric Corporation*
J. Puglisi, *U.S. Merchant Marine Academy*
T. Suttner, *Singer-Link*
V. Tashjian, *Simulation Technologies Inc.*
B. L. Travis, *Los Alamos National Laboratory*
J. Wachtel, *Nuclear Regulatory Commission*

Thank you all.

Ariel Sharon, Ph.D
Chairman of the Simulator VI Conference
1989 Eastern Multiconference

Simulators VI

ISBN 0-911801-51-0

Communication: The key to understanding customer needs

John Davis
Science Applications International Corporation
3045 Technology Parkway
Orlando, Florida 32826-3299

ABSTRACT

This paper examines the problems involved in effectively communicating requirements for a simulator. Often, those wishing to have a simulator built do not have a background in computer simulation. Thus, the system manager and his software manager must be able to translate nebulous simulation needs into well defined requirements and be able to effectively communicate these requirements to the technical staff building the device. In this paper, the reasons for ineffective communications are examined first. This provides a basis for understanding why there are problems in this area. Next, the problems that occur when understanding between the parties involved is not reached are discussed to show the effects ineffective communication can have on a project. This is followed by the main portion of the paper, which is a set of rules and methods for improving the effectiveness of communicating technical data appropriate to simulator needs. Finally, a short synopsis of the benefits of improved communications capability to the finished system are covered. The viewpoint of this paper is that of a software manager trying to build a simulator to meet the needs of the end user.

INTRODUCTION

One wonders if the software management of simulator projects was what A. A. Milne was thinking about when he wrote the beginning of "Winnie The Pooh."

"Here is Edward Bear coming downstairs now, bump, bump, bump, on the back of his head, behind Christopher Robin. It is, as far as he knows, the only way of coming downstairs, but sometimes he feels that there really is another way, if only he could stop bumping for a moment and think of it."

Pooh couldn't communicate with Christopher Robin to effectively discuss the problem. Unfortunately, this seems to describe the feelings of many software managers, who spend their time beating their heads against a wall of frustration, because they don't have time to think of a better way to determine what the user really expects. This paper attempts to provide a better way for software managers to determine what the user really wants and needs. Since providing the user with a "good" viable system is the basis of any successful software simulation, the problem is how does one determine what the user requires for a "good" system.

This brings us to an area that could greatly aid in the software development of effective simulators: communication. Communication is the key to successfully understanding the needs of the customer and passing this information to the technical staff. The understanding of the requirements determines whether the project will succeed or not, since if the functionality of the completed simulator does not match what the user is expecting or needing, then the simulator will either require extensive rework or will be considered a failed project and not be used. The need for clear lines of communication is imperative! This is true whether the "customer" is part of the same organization as the developer or not. The two parties must come to an agreement as to what the reason is for the system and what functionality the completed system must display for it to meet the current need. The software manager must be able to discern between those capabilities that are necessary to accomplish the task, and those which are nice-to-have extras. The problems that occur and the need for understanding on the part of the software manager are basically the same on all simulation projects. A lack of understanding between the customer and the system and software managers leads to incomplete and/or insufficient design, resulting in a system that does not meet the needs of the customer. Therefore, it is imperative that the software manager understand the needs and wants of the customer (and the difference between the two). For the software manager to be able to understand what the wishes of the customer are, and to be able to do this effectively, he must be able to communicate clearly with the customer. Also, to translate between the imprecisely worded needs of the customer and the precise and exact requirements that are needed by the technical staff, then transmit them clearly to his development staff, the systems and software managers must be able to, with the aid of their technical staff, extract the requirements and define them clearly, completely and concisely. These requirements must be both technically feasible and meet the needs of the customer, while at the same time be affordable and accomplishable within the time span the customer allows. To accomplish all this, the system and software managers must be able to communicate as well as just understand the problem technically.

Reasons for Ineffective Communications in Defining Requirements

There are many reasons why communication between those involved with simulator development is not effective. First of all, the customer may not be sure of what it is he really wants developed or what capabilities are available. Also, the developer may not understand what the actual system needs are, at least not to the level of detail needed for the particular application.

Neither of these is helped by the fact that in many, if not most, cases the customer and developer speak a different language technically. Both may be perfectly clear in their own minds as to what they mean, but the same meaning may not be received by the other party since language is a template for communication. This misunderstanding is aggravated when the customer and developer use the same words but with different meanings. For example, consider what happened on the TACFIRE program. The system specification stated that the software shall select the "optimum" weapon yield, the system designers assumed the "optimum" meant the largest yield possible that would not harm our own troops. However, to the nuclear community, "optimum" yield is the smallest nuclear yield that will do the job. This difference was not found until the system had been designed and built and was in the process of being tested. Since the development effort had progressed to this stage, it cost hundreds of thousands of dollars to correct!

Another reason for the problems encountered in transmitting the requirements for a simulator is that customer and the developer look at the product from a different viewpoint. Often times to those not directly involved, it looks like the old Indian fable of the blind men and the elephant. The fable tells of six blind men, where each "saw" but a portion of an elephant; one felt the trunk and decided that an elephant is like a snake, one felt the side and decided that the elephant was like a wall, others felt an ear, leg, tail, tusk and assumed that the elephant was like a fan, tree trunk, rope and spear respectively. Even though none of them had the entire picture, each one was adamant about what an elephant looked like.

And, of course, there is the wants/needs conflicts of the customer. The customer is usually not just one individual, but a group of individuals, each of whom sees the problem and the solution from a slightly different perspective. Because of this, there may be conflicting and incompatible requirements which the software manager will then need to "work out" with the customer to insure that they are acceptable to the group before work is actually started. Also, if all the individuals of the customers requirements team are not consulted, the resulting system may not "look like" what is expected. Other want/need problems have to do with funding and scheduling. The needed system may be capable of being built with the amount of funds available, but the desire to have little extras or the latest and greatest system available may drive the cost too high. Worse is the case where the needed system cannot be built with the funds available and the decision must be made as to which features must be left out at the present time. Sometimes in this case it is better to just forget becoming involved with the project at all.

There is also the possibility that the system as wanted is not technically feasible or even possible. If this is the case, then the system manager must be able to determine how the requirements can be changed so the modified system can be built.

In all the above cases and those not mentioned, the system manager and his software manager must try to meet both the needs and the wants of the customer, and be able to direct the customer to the actual needs and the best overall system to meet those needs.

Problems Caused by Inadequate Requirements Definition

Unfortunately, the most common problem with simulation systems as delivered to the customer, is that they do not meet the customer's needs! This problem normally starts at the requirements analysis stage. With many systems, the requirements are not adequately understood by either the customer or the developer. When this happens, several problems occur that affect the developer. First and foremost is the loss of customer respect and trust that occurs when an inadequate system is delivered. This, in turn, leads to loss of future business. Secondly, there is the extra work required when portions of the effort are reaccomplished to correct inadequacies that are discovered during the development of the system. This redesign effort cuts into the developer's profit due to the additional costs incurred when unmet requirements are incorporated and/or inconsistencies are corrected. It also lessens the quality of the overall product when the redesign has to be forced to fit into an already designed structure. The extra time to incorporate these changes normally requires that development personnel work overtime to complete the project on time. This leads to overworked and unhappy employees who are more prone to make mistakes, which in turn leads to delays in the schedule.

A Set of Common Sense Rules for Improving Communications

The first question that must be answered before simulator requirements can be effectively communicated is "What is communication?" Communication is the transmission of information between individuals. It consists of four parts: the sender, the receiver, the message, and the medium. These four parts exist whether the communication is accomplished verbally over the phone or face to face or if written means are used.

The sender and receiver roles will alternate between the customer and the developer and although the software manager has no control over the capability of his customer, he does over himself, and his staff, and should attempt to use good communication practices whether or not the customer does.

The sender must translate his wants, ideas and questions into a form that can be understood by the receiver. Most people would consider you at least a little strange if you tried to pass information to them in Babylonian or Latin, yet these same people will use technical jargon which sounds like "Greek" to their listeners. So the first rule for improving communications is:

"Use language that is understandable to those to whom you are trying to communicate."

It is better to explain something in too much detail and have the other party tell you to go on, than to give too little explanation and have an inadequate system later. When relating specific needs and requirements, the sender must plan the wording so that it is not only understandable to those listening but also so that it is concisely worded using terminology that is common to the task. This is another rule of good communication:

"Use clear, concise and relevant terms."

Again, this information must be arranged in a clear and concise manner, and it must be presented in an understandable manner. One way to do this is to divide the total problem into smaller parts that are easier to understand and then treat one subject at a time. These ideas are defined in the following rules.

"Know what you are going to say before you say it."

"Stick to the subject."

"Divide the total problem into smaller parts that are easier to understand."

Silence is not necessarily the same as listening; daydreaming or even preparing a response to what is being said is not only not listening, it is counterproductive to understanding what is being said. Thus, the receiver also has an important part in facilitating communication. He must not be just a passive listener, but play an active part in the communication process. As the sender transmits information, it is the responsibility of the receiver to insure that he understands what is being stated. If there is any question at all in the receivers mind, he should ask for clarification. Of course, this implies that the receiver will be paying attention to what is said and not thinking about something different or planning his own reply instead. Good listening is learned and requires active participation.

Another important point is that when one person is speaking to another, the speaker needs signals back from the listener. The speaker wants to know if the message being sent is the same as the one being received. So, at times throughout the discussion, the listener needs to become the speaker and relate the main ideas and any questions he has back to the original speaker.

The manner in which this response is made is often crucial in solidifying the communications process. The response to a statement should be objective and information seeking, and not judgmental. "Why in the world would you want to do something like that?" is not a statement that is conducive to effective communications for it sets up a defensive posture on the part of the individual who originally made the statement.

Putting all this concisely, the rules for good listening are:

"Pay attention to what is being said."

"Allow the other person to do most of the talking."

"Restate the other's message until clear communication has been reached."

"Be descriptive and not judgmental in paraphrasing the other's message."

"Look at the problem from the other person's point of view."

You do not have to agree with a person or even like what they are saying to be able to listen effectively, that is, listening to understand.

If both parties involved concentrate on being good senders and good receivers, communication can be greatly facilitated.

Of course, there must also be some information to be passed between the sender and the receiver. The transmitting of information on what is expected of the simulator from the customer to the developer is essential to the creation of a successful simulator project. Again, this information must be well thought out, clear and definitive.

The medium is the fourth and final part of communication. The requirements for the simulator can be transmitted in oral or written form, by use of text or graphic representation or by a combination of these ways as will be explained in the next section.

A Methodology for Improving Requirements Definition

Definition of simulator requirements by the customer/user is central to the development of a properly functioning system. The standard method for doing this has been through the use of written systems requirements document, often times with no chance for the developer to ask questions of the right people as to what it is that is really wanted.

The methodology that has been found to greatly improve requirements definition is called Information Modeling. A high level overview of an improved methodology and specific rules for improving communication between people is given below. It is hoped that the following procedure and suggestions will aid in improving the general procedure for defining simulator system requirements, particularly software requirements.

At the beginning of the project, the system and software development managers must examine the customer's requirements with his senior staff. After this, representatives for the customer and the developer should meet and discuss the requirements and specification of the simulator. The format of the meeting should be that of an informal working meeting in which the customer restates verbally what it is that his group is expecting from the simulator. The software manager should then repeat the request in his own words, expanding the definition in complex areas or ones in which there is not clear understanding. The customer would then agree or clarify what is really wanted in areas where the software manager's assessment doesn't match the intended requirements. This should start at the top level - the goal or purpose - and be refined through successive decomposition of the system to its major functions.

The developer must then take the user's initial written requirements document, and with the additional information gained from the initial requirements meeting, write an expanded initial requirements document detailing the functions to be performed by the simulator and then prepare a presentation on the simulator and its capabilities to the customer. Senior personnel are given the customer's initial requirements document and from it devise a top-level functional design of the system that shows what functional areas will be used to meet each of the requirements. This specification should then be presented to the project, system, software and hardware managers in the form of a walk through. Once the specification is approved by management, the technical staff prepares the draft functional specification for the customer. Since this document is being written for non-software personnel, it should be written in a natural language such as English augmented with graphical representations. The Entity/Relation (E/R) diagrams and Data Flow diagrams (DFDs) can be used to graphically portray the functional requirement allocation. This system requirements document should consist of an introduction, system description, a list of requirements, and a summary as a minimum. A basic top-down breakout of the requirements into functional areas is better.

The introduction should state the purpose of the simulator. It should define what the problem is that the simulator needs to solve in a straightforward manner, such as "provide pilot training in basic procedures for the XH-F1 helicopter" or "provide a test area for ship hull design." A background of the problem should also be presented. This allows the user to have confidence in the design, as it shows that the developer's goal for the system matches his own, and it aids the detection of differences early in the project.

The next section gives the model of the solution. It provides an abstract description for the most important requirements. It also proposes the method of solving the problem.

The requirements section is used to explicitly define the requirements of the system. The requirements are itemized in this section, with only one function described in each paragraph. Each requirement should be stated in a manner such that it can be objectively tested. Thus, "the system must be user friendly" is not a requirement but a goal of the system. The term "user-friendly" is subjective. "Access to all functions in the system by the use of menus which can be accessed via keyboard or mouse" is a requirement that can be objectively tested, but is too broad. This broad requirement should be broken into smaller more easily tested pieces, such as: "the capability to insert simulator malfunctions shall be accessible by either keyboard or mouse input from the 'Malfunction Menu.'"

Both functional and non-functional requirements need to be included. Functional requirements are those which relate to the actual outputs of the system and are the ones on which interest is normally concentrated. However, the non-functional requirements, those relating to how the system works (maximum cost, minimum spare memory and timing, environmental requirements, response time, etc.), are equally important and need to be included in the documentation of the requirements from the beginning.

The summary concisely describes the simulator to be built, and lists areas that need clarification.

Other areas that may need to be included, depending on the size and formality of the project, are a cost/benefit analysis of optional features, a list of outputs, a list of inputs, a list of team members and resumes, and a list of systems and documents used in preparing the document.

As this document is created, it should be remembered that it is for the user and NOT for the programming staff. Every effort should be made to make the document readable and complete and to avoid any redundancies or ambiguities.

The developer should submit the written document, and after giving the user time to read and review the document, present the proposed simulator in a briefing, using oral and graphical forms in the briefing to supplement the written requirements document.

In this briefing the system manager describes the goal of the system and the software manager delineates the functions that the simulator will perform and the relationships between the functions. During the review, the system manager and the software manager discuss the chosen design, and take and answer questions from the customer. They also modify their concept of the design based on information gained from this discussion until the customer is happy with the initial concept. If the original design is significantly modified by the review, then a second review, to examine the redesign, would be needed.

One method that can be used to refine the definition of the system is that of rapid prototyping. Using this methodology, the developer puts together a simple system to demonstrate the requirements that are unclear, are innovative in character, or could cause special problems with the man-machine interface.

Throughout the above procedure, explicit communications is needed and it needs to be iterative. Too often requirements are established in one, or at most two, passes, and then not reviewed again until the time that the system is tested. There needs to be an ongoing refinement of the requirements throughout the requirements and specifications phases of the project.

Benefits of Improved Communication in Defining Simulator Requirements

First, the better defined that a system is prior to the actual implementation, the less rework will be needed during implementation and testing. The less extra work there is, the greater the profit, not only by saving money on the current project, but also by the earlier release of personnel to work on other projects.

Second, the better defined the system is, the more likely it is that the customer will be satisfied. This makes it more probable that the customer will use you to meet future needs, and will give other potential customers good reports of your work which can also lead to future projects.

And third, it will help keep good employees. It does this in several ways. With less rework, there is less overtime and overtime work is often a cause of dissatisfaction. Also, a successful project builds pride, pride in the company, pride in the team, and pride in each employee; pride that arises from a sense of accomplishment.

SUMMARY

The current capabilities of the simulator industry continue to improve: faster and cheaper hardware, structured and advanced programming techniques, more powerful languages and tools. The components to build more efficient and more effective simulators exist. However, the area of human interaction in defining the requirements for the simulator is very often ignored. It is hoped that by examining some of the reasons for ineffective communications and the problems that are caused by inadequate requirements definition, which are often caused by ineffective communications, that software managers will attempt to improve their ability to communicate in general and particularly in the area of software requirements definition. Significant increases in simulator capability will be obtained when software managers and software engineers develop the ability to communicate.

REFERENCES:

Augustine, N. R. 1980. "Augustine's Laws and Major Systems Development Programs." A Report compiled from Defense Systems Management Review, Defense Electronics, Astronautics & Aeronautics, The Washington Post.

Davis, J. and L. Fessenden. 1988. "Improving Software Management by the Application of Lessons Learned in Independent Software Verification and Validation." The Supplemental Proceedings of the 1988 Eastern Simulation Conferences: 65-68.

Hampton, D., C. Summer, and R. Webber. 1978. Organizational Behavior and the Practice of Management. Scott, Foresman and Company.

Milne, A. A. 1961. Winnie the Pooh. Dutton

Sommerville, I. 1985. Software Engineering. Addison-Wesley Publishing Company.

Simulators VI
© 1989 By The Society for Computer
Simulation International
ISBN 0-911801-51-0

A methodology for determining motion system requirements for a land vehicle simulator

C. S. Ernst
General Dynamics Land Systems
P.O. Box 2074
Warren, MI 48090-2074

and

J. B. Sinacori
J. B. Sinacori Associates
P. O. Box 360
Pebble Beach, CA 93953-0360

ABSTRACT

Presented here is a methodology for defining requirements for a six-degree-of-freedom synergistic motion base system. The system is to be used for simulating the motions of heavy land vehicles, including both tracked and wheeled vehicles, for the purpose of performing human factors testing, developing new design concepts, and conducting other analyses. The following analysis was founded on work presented in (Sinacori, 1973), in which an algorithm for motion cueing was described. The algorithm was intended to be programmed and used for driving a six-degree-of-freedom flight simulator. The adapted version used for this analysis takes angular velocities and specific forces and modifies the inputs in such a way as to recover (reproduce) these quantities as closely as possible within limits of position, velocity, and acceleration imposed by motion system hardware.

Three drive algorithm variations were analyzed for their abilities to recover the angular rates and specific forces produced by the vehicle traveling over a variety of terrains. The first version emphasized recovery of angular rates, the second emphasized recovery of specific forces; and the third was a hybrid logic aimed at reasonably good recovery of both. The best cases were chosen, and the resulting motion base angles and excursions defined the requirements for the simulator hardware.

MOTION SIMULATION BACKGROUND

The objective of simulating the motion of a land vehicle is to enhance the illusion of driving/riding in an actual vehicle. The simulator is moved in such a way as to create sensations in the crew that approximate those created in a real world situation. The human nervous system is highly adaptable, and is able to produce similar sensations of motion for stimuli of different magnitudes. Therefore, one-to-one correspondence between real world and simulated motions is not necessary, which is why motion simulation is possible.

The simulator crewstation ideally would move about in exact accordance with the motions produced by the vehicle. In reality, this is impossible because the simulator is constrained to move within limits of position, velocity, and acceleration. Thus, it is necessary to modify the inputs which drive the simulator, to avoid driving the motion system to its structural limits. These modifications are based on properties of the human vestibular system, in order to give the crew the correct perception of motion. While there is still much we need to learn about human motion perception, the things we do know lead to the assumptions that:

1) Spatial orientation is based on visually acquired data; and

2) Motion perception is based on data from the vestibular organs and skin and joint receptors. Motion perception data is used to complement visually acquired data.

The primary motion parameters sensed are angular velocity and specific force. These stimuli are perceived if their magnitudes exceed thresholds of perception, and if their frequencies fall within observable bands.

- Angular velocities can be sensed at frequencies between 0.5 rad/sec and 10 rad/sec.

- Specific forces are observable from 0 rad/sec to a very high frequency.

The term angular velocity is self-explanatory, but specific force requires some explanation. Specific force is the sum of the external forces on a body divided by the mass of the body, minus the components due to gravity. A man sitting in a chair feels a force pressing upwards on his body. This force is provided by the chair in reaction to the downward pull of the gravitational force. He does not actually feel the force of gravity. If the chair and the ground beneath him were removed, he would feel no force and would begin to fall. Specific force is what the man senses through deformation of different parts of his body while he sits in the chair. A linear accelerometer measures specific force.

The motion drive logic was formulated to modify the angular velocity and specific force inputs in such a way as to recover (reproduce) these quantities as closely as possible, within the limits of the abilities of the simulator. One of the most demanding motions to simulate is a long-duration specific force, because a great deal of platform travel is needed. One way to accomplish this with less demand on platform travel is with a "coordinating circuit". This type of circuit will use translational motion to simulate the onset of acceleration, then slowly tilt the platform to use the gravity vector to sustain the cue. The tilt angle must be achieved at a frequency below the perceptible level, in order to avoid giving a false rotational cue to the crew. In this way, translational and rotational motion of the simulator are coordinated to generate longitudinal and lateral specific forces.

MOTION DRIVE LOGIC

The inputs to the drive logic are produced by a mathematical model of the vehicle. The math model is a real-time program which accepts inputs from the terrain, steering mechanism, throttle, etc. The angular rates and specific forces at a reference point in the crewstation are calculated in the model, then used as inputs to the drive logic. The inputs are transformed to a reference point on the motion base. The point chosen as the simulator reference is shown in Figure 1. It is the centroid of the motion hardware; in this case it is a point located at the centroid of the upper triangle, slightly below the top of the platform.

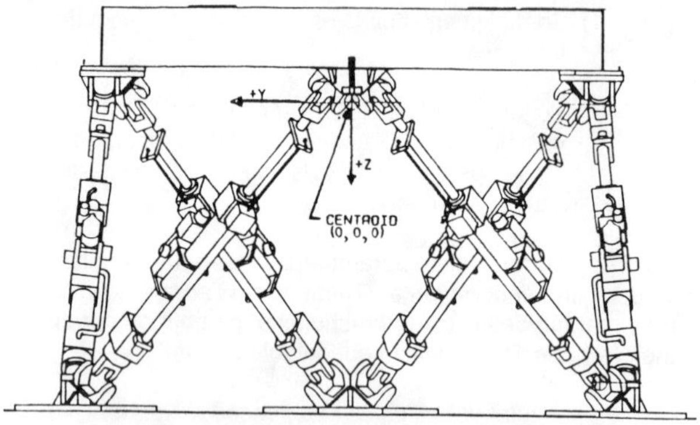

Figure 1. Motion Base Reference Point

The drive logic presented here is an adaptation of the one presented in (Sinacori, 1973). The block diagram (Figure 2) and a description of the algorithm are presented here for the sake of completeness.

The specific forces are high pass filtered to remove the low frequency portions, which are likely to cause the platform to exceed position limits. These filters are also referred to as "washout" filters because they tend to cause the platform to return to its reference position after the onset cue has been performed. The filtered specific forces are transformed to inertial axes and integrated twice to yield platform excursions. The double integraters are known as the inertial filters. The transformed specific forces are also used to calculate tilt rates for the coordinating function. Recall that coordinating involves using the gravitational component of platform tilt to achieve sustained specific forces. The tilt rates are calculated by taking the vector cross product of the specific force vector with the gravitational reaction vector. The shaping filters are useful for limiting platform excursions, but since these calculations are done in body axes, some translational drift is possible. The inertial filters are useful for final limiting of platform excursions. The [F] and [E] matrix expansions can be found in appendix C. [F] is a 3x3 matrix that transforms a vector in inertial space to crewstation space. [E] is a matrix that transforms Euler rates to body rates.

The angular rates are washed out in much the same way as the specific forces. The filtered rates are added to the coordinating tilt rates, then transformed to Euler parameters. The Euler rates are integrated to yield the platform Euler angles. The resulting specific forces and angular rates that are generated by the platform are calculated and compared to the inputs, to determine the quality of the recovery of the inputs.

The modifications to the original diagram occur at the points marked "A". Here, filters were added to simulate the effect of the lag introduced by the motion base hardware. Obviously, a motion system can not react instantaneously when commanded to move, so a lag is introduced into the system. It was assumed that the motion system lag could be approximated by a second order system with a critical frequency of 25 rad/sec and a 0.7 damping ratio.

The drive algorithm was programmed in Fortran on a Vax 11/780. The control filters were programmed using an algorithm which calculates a closed form solution for each integration step. The method is based on a Cauchy integral form, as shown in (Keith, 1969).

CHELSEA TEST

The existing vehicle models at General Dynamics Land Systems (GDLS) were somewhat limited in providing data for the drive algorithm, so a hardware test was run at the Chrysler Chelsea Proving Grounds (CPG) in Chelsea, Mi. The test was designed to generate motions that would be most difficult to simulate, i.e., motions that would drive requirements up. The main goal of the CPG runs was to generate sustained specific forces and combined motions in multiple degrees of freedom. Briefly, the test consisted of accelerometers and rate gyros mounted at the driver's and commanders seats, measuring angular rates and specific forces over bump course runs, cross country runs (with carefully designed off road areas), and several special maneuvers, such as pivot steer, hard braking and sharp turn/braking combinations.

TUNING PROCESS FOR DRIVE LOGIC

The use of a coordinating circuit can help extend the ability of the simulator to generate sustained accelerations, but the demanded motions may still exceed the performance limits of the simulator. And, if excessive tilts are used for low frequency specific force recovery, the angular rate recovery may be adversely affected. Therefore, the parameters of the filters must be tuned to give the best possible recovery while restraining the motion base to keep it within its limits. The algorithm may be tuned to provide very good angular recovery, or very good specific recovery; or a hybrid system may provide adequate recoveries of both (see Sinacori, 1973). A list of suggested values for the parameters can be found in Appendix B.

For angular recovery:

$$w_{4r} = w_{4p} = 0$$

This eliminates the coordinating effects. Thus, the angular rate recovery is not adversely affected by coordinating. The specific forces may be either restrained by the filters or set to zero at the inputs, in which case the gravity components due to platform tilts would drive the output specific forces.

For specific force recovery:

$$w_{4r} = w_{4p} = 1 \qquad z_{3r} = z_{3p} = 0.7$$
$$w_{1r} = w_{1p} = 0.266 \qquad w_{3r} = w_{3p} = 0.65$$

$k_{1r} = k_{1p} = 1$ $\quad$ $w_{2r} = w_{2p} = 0.65$

For hybrid recovery:

$w_{1p} = w_{2p} = 0$ $\quad$ $w_{3p} = w_{4p} = 0.25$

$k_{1p} = 1$ $\quad$ $z_{3p} = 0.7$

$w_{1r} = w_{2r} = 0$ $\quad$ $w_{3r} = w_{4r} = 0.25$

$k_{1r} = 1$ $\quad$ $z_{3r} = 0.7$

The shaping filters are replaced with a second order function that is intended to provide some coordinating, but not enough to adversely affect angular recoveries.

Four of the CPG runs were used for the analysis. The four courses were run through each of the three versions of the algorithm. The drive algorithm parameters were adjusted to give maximum recovery with minimum excursions.

RESULTS

Results of the twelve runs (four courses x three versions of the algorithm) were plotted as shown in Figures 3a-3f. The four CPG test runs were numbered and labeled BRK2, XCC1, XCC3, and BMP3. The graphs were designed to easily show the performance requirements, i.e. platform angles and excursions needed to perform each of the simulations. The pitch rate recovery graph will be described as an example to show how the plots were designed. The ordinate value represents the maximum platform pitch angle needed to perform a given simulation. The maximum pitch rate generated by the CPG test was plotted on the abscissa, along with the maximum pitch rate recovered by each of the three versions of the algorithm.

The graphs can be used to compare different commercially available motion systems. The performance characteristics of each system, in terms of maximum platform angles and excursions, would be plotted as vertical lines on the graphs to show which simulation runs are within the performance abilities of each system.

REFERENCES

Keith, S. 1969. "Documentation for MOPAS- Subroutine RIGID." Chrysler Space Division. TN-8-AP-69-408.

Peters, R. 1969. "Dynamics of the Vestibular System and Their Relation to Motion Perception, Spatial Disorientation, and Illusions." NASA Contract Report No. NAS 2-3650.

Sinacori, J. 1973. "A Practical Approach to Motion Simulation." In Proceedings of the AIAA Visual and Motion Simulation Conference (Palo Alto, CA, Sept. 10-12). AIAA, New York, N. Y. 73-931.

APPENDIX A

Additional uses for the algorithm include:

- motion system actuator length, velocity, and acceleration calculations.

- effects of different lag characteristics, i.e. size of simulator bandwidth, on recovery performance. This is another way to compare motion systems.

APPENDIX B

Coefficient	Units	Angular	Force	Hybrid
k_p		1.0	1.0	1.0
w_p	rad/sec	0.5	0.5	0.5
k_q		1.0	1.0	1.0
w_q	rad/sec	0.5	0.5	0.5
k_r		1.0	1.0	1.0
w_r	rad/sec	0.5	0.5	0.5
w_{1r}	"	0.266	0.266	0.0
w_{2r}	"	0.65	0.65	0.0
w_{3r}	"	0.65	0.65	0.25
w_{4r}	"	0.0	1.0	0.25
z_{3r}		0.7	0.7	0.7
w_{1p}	rad/sec	0.266	0.266	0.0
w_{2p}	"	0.65	0.65	0.0
w_{3p}	"	0.65	0.65	0.25
w_{4p}	"	0.0	0.65	0.25
z_{3p}		0.7	0.7	0.7
k_{1p}		1.0	1.0	1.0
k_{2r}		0.5	0.5	0.5
w_{7r}	rad/sec	0.0	0.0	0.0
w_{8r}	"	0.0	0.0	0.0
k_y		1.0	1.0	1.0
c_{1y}		0.1	0.1	0.1
c_{2y}		0.1	0.1	0.1
k_{2p}		0.5	0.5	0.5
w_{7p}	rad/sec	0.0	0.0	0.0
w_{8p}	"	0.0	0.0	0.0
k_x		1.0	1.0	1.0
c_{1x}		0.1	0.1	0.1
c_{2x}		0.1	0.1	0.1
k_{2z}		1.0	1.0	1.0
c_{1z}		0.01	0.01	0.01
c_{2z}		0.01	0.01	0.01
c_{3z}		1.4	0.0	0.7
c_{4z}		1.0	0.0	0.5
c_{5z}		0.3	0.0	0.0
k_z		1.0	1.0	1.0
k_ϕ		1.0	1.0	1.0
k_θ		1.0	1.0	1.0

k_ψ		1.0	1.0	1.0
w_{6r}	rad/sec	0.0	0.0	0.0
w_{6p}	"	0.0	0.0	0.0
w_{6y}	"	1.0	1.0	1.0

APPENDIX C

[F] and [E] Matrices

$$[F] = \begin{bmatrix} \cos\psi_m \cos\theta_m & \sin\psi_m & -\cos\psi_m \sin\theta_m \\ -\cos\phi_m \sin\psi_m \cos\theta_m + \sin\phi_m \sin\theta_m & \cos\phi_m \sin\psi_m & \sin\phi_m \cos\theta_m + \cos\phi_m \sin\psi_m \sin\theta_m \\ \sin\theta_m \cos\phi_m + \cos\theta_m \sin\phi_m \sin\psi_m & -\sin\phi_m \cos\psi_m & \cos\phi_m \cos\theta_m - \sin\theta_m \sin\phi_m \sin\psi_m \end{bmatrix}$$

$$[E] = \begin{bmatrix} 1 & \sin\psi_m & 0 \\ 0 & \cos\phi_m \cos\psi_m & \sin\phi_m \\ 0 & \sin\phi_m \cos\psi_m & \cos\phi_m \end{bmatrix}$$

$$[E]^{-1} = \begin{bmatrix} 1 & -\tan\psi_m \cos\phi_m & \tan\psi_m \sin\phi_m \\ 0 & \cos\phi_m \sec\psi_m & -\sin\phi_m \sec\psi_m \\ 0 & \sin\phi_m & \cos\phi_m \end{bmatrix}$$

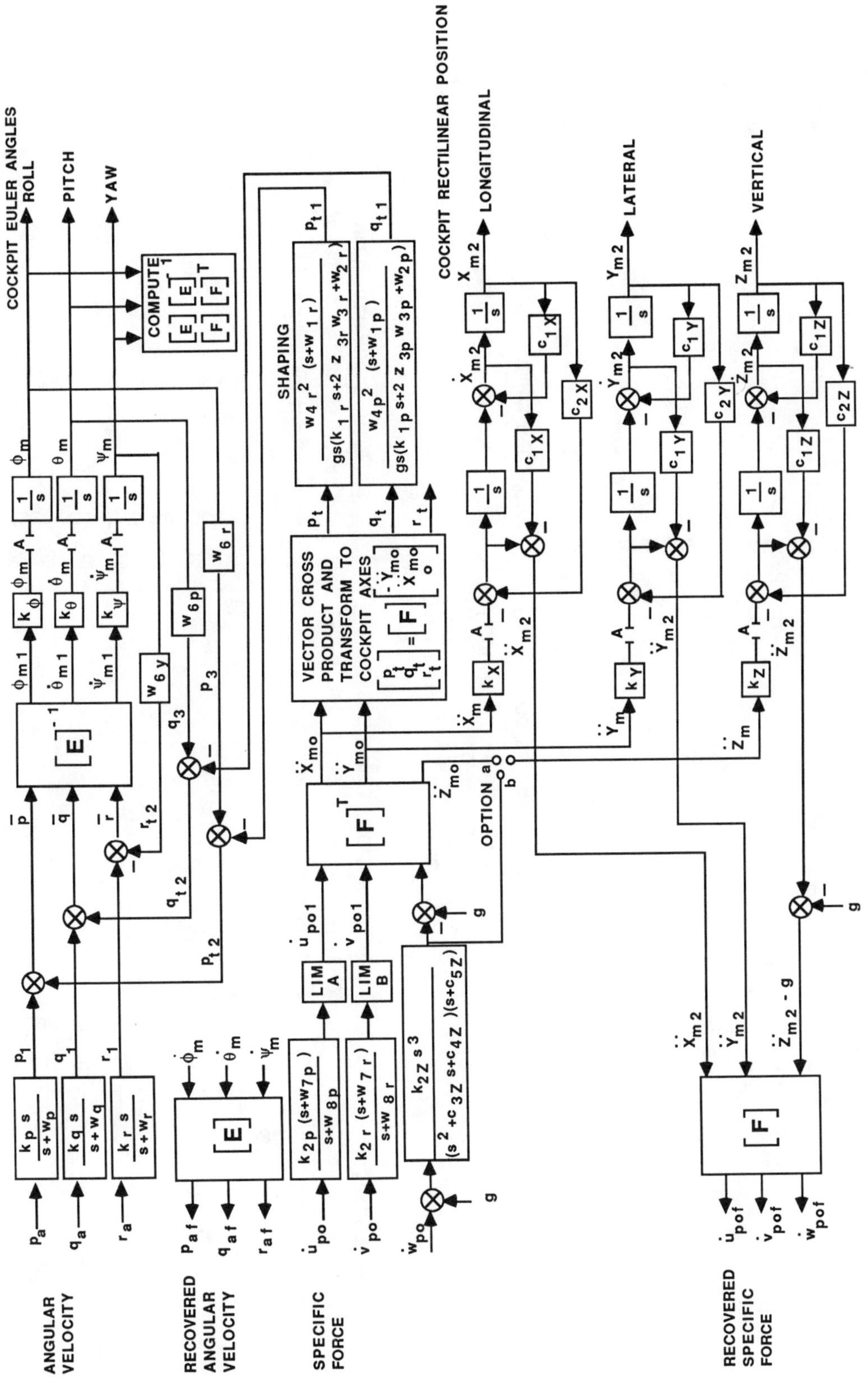

Figure 2. Motion Drive Algorithm Block Diagram

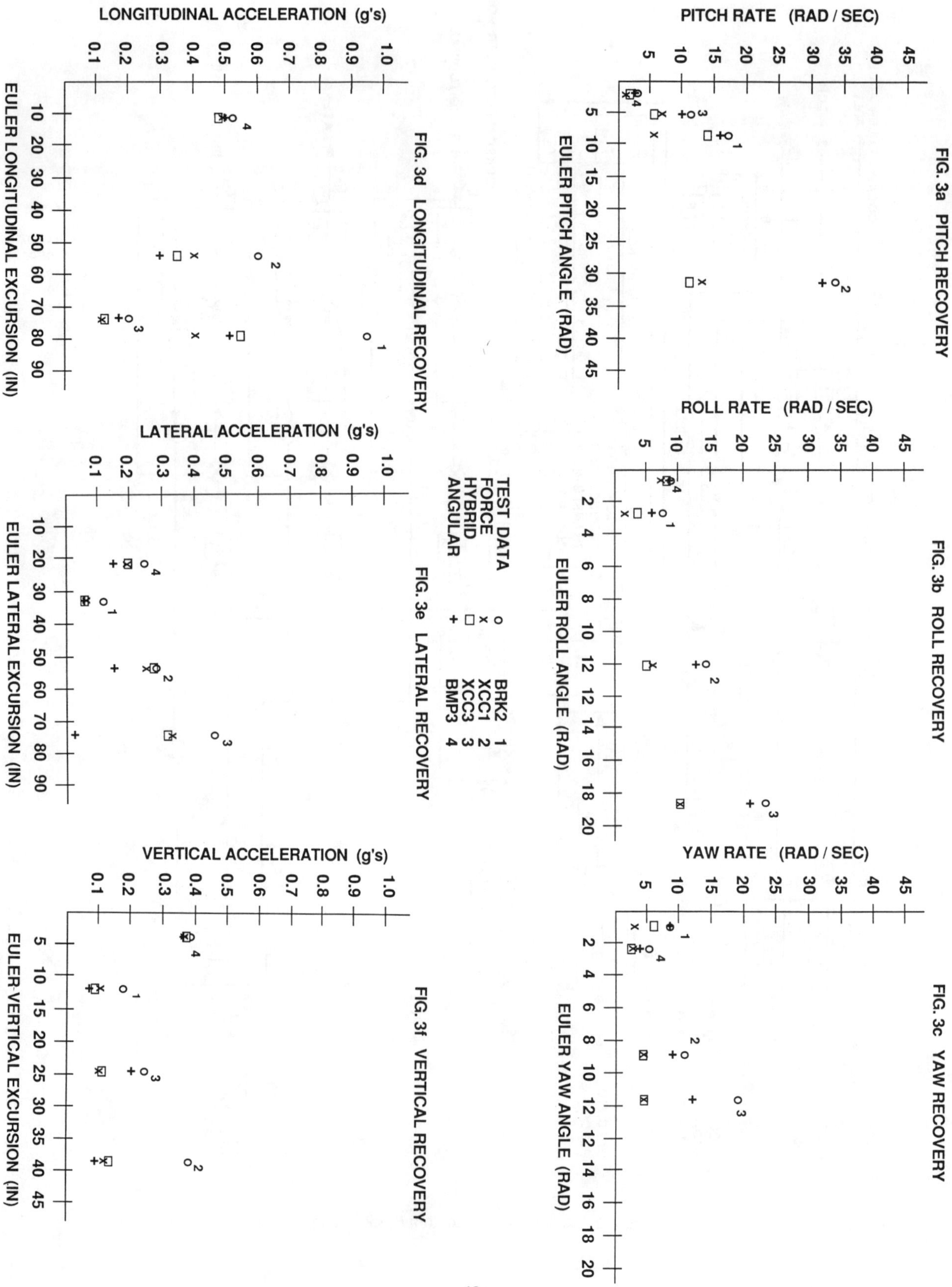
FIG. 3a PITCH RECOVERY
PITCH RATE (RAD / SEC)
EULER PITCH ANGLE (RAD)
FIG. 3b ROLL RECOVERY
ROLL RATE (RAD / SEC)
EULER ROLL ANGLE (RAD)
FIG. 3c YAW RECOVERY
YAW RATE (RAD / SEC)
EULER YAW ANGLE (RAD)
FIG. 3d LONGITUDINAL RECOVERY
LONGITUDINAL ACCELERATION (g's)
EULER LONGITUDINAL EXCURSION (IN)
FIG. 3e LATERAL RECOVERY
LATERAL ACCELERATION (g's)
EULER LATERAL EXCURSION (IN)
FIG. 3f VERTICAL RECOVERY
VERTICAL ACCELERATION (g's)
EULER VERTICAL EXCURSION (IN)
TEST DATA o BRK2 1
FORCE x XCC1 2
HYBRID □ XCC3 3
ANGULAR + BMP3 4

Simulators VI

ISBN 0-911801-51-0

How to document a simulator for everybody

James H. Bradley, Ph.D.
106 Portland Road
Atlantic Highlands, N.J. 07716

ABSTRACT

Well-designed, engineered and tested documentation devices for simulators are related to:
* instructional objectives, methods, and facilities;
* instructional, support, and modelling software;
* computer, interfacial, and stimulatory hardware;
* briefing, de-briefing and evaluatory hardware and software;
* stimulands, usually human trainees;
* and the specific or generic simulands.

The objectives are therefore:
* specification, development and delivery;
* teaching the use of the simulator;
* checkout and test;
* diagnosis and debugging;
* enhancements and modifications specific to the simulator;
* and keeping in step with (or ahead of) or enlarging the number of simulands and stimulands.

Teaching about the simulator (not the simuland) is:
* learning how to use the simulator;
* how the simulator works internally;
* reference materials.

Teaching about the simuland (not the simulator), where materials are provided by the simulator vendor (usually in generic or maintenance simulators) is:
* learning how to use the simuland;
* learning how the simuland works internally.

Available methods to emphasize the new and important and de-emphasize the commonplace and familiar include:
* graphical, tabular, database, and other basically non-textual approaches;
* several node-and-arc aids, decision tables, and sortable data bases;
* 2-page instructional spreads, and so on.

1. INTRODUCTION

The driver of a car differs from a mechanic and an automotive engineer. Difficulties with simulator documentation, however, include:

* teaching ***how things work*** instead of ***how to use them***,
* leaving out certain ***classes of user*** from the user-topic matrix,
* documenting ***internals and implementation details*** instead of ***intention*** (both are needed),
* ***reference*** instead of ***learning*** materials (both needed),
* unnecessarily requiring the ***simultaneous use of two documents*** (sometimes necessary, especially for development and upgrade staff),
* ***irrelevancies*** and poor ***signal-to-noise*** ratio, indicating a lack of storyboard layouts and walk-throughs,
* excessive ***jumps, loops, skips*** and references to materials which are ***not on two facing pages***,
* failure to distinguish ***various classes of necessity*** from ***conventions*** and ***semi-arbitrary decisions***,
* a lack of explanation of ***efforts to meet soft targets*** and ***matters which require R&D***,
* a ***lack of traceability*** of data sources and performance requirements,
* ***sequential access*** instead of ***random access*** materials, with inadequate ***indices***,
* no explanation of ***numerical methods***.

Diagrammatic and tabular materials should replace ***Victorian novels*** wherever possible; narrative specifications are usually ambiguous, incomplete, contradictory, unindexed, repetitious, ungrammatical, and full of claims or demands to do the impossible. They are hard to keep up to date. Information stored in several places independently (not by machine insertion) and cross-references (other than by machine) become obsolete, contradictory, and erroneous.

Preservation of some archival versions and a history of changes is usually necessary, but do not accept one of those configuration management systems from elementary data processing which is able to reconstruct every detail of every draft and every human error. Two advantages of machines are that they can check the spelling of individual words and can be used to check the existence of cross-references.

2. WHO, WHY, WHEN AND WHAT

Documentation must address who needs what information when, for what task, at the best reasonably attainable ***signal-to-noise ratio.*** However, all relevant facts or references to source materials should appear in the reference documentation or ***indices;*** if it is doubtful whether class *U* of user needs item *I* of information, at least put in a reference to where it can be found. Do not baffle the user with references and allusions to unnecessary things. Do not confuse the learner with functionless acknowledgements of the sources of information.

Remember that the maintenance and modification of the simulator will normally require someone else to repeat, or at least to understand the reasons for your decisions. If you needed information, or faced a decision, so will the system integrators and the modification engineers. Write down ***what*** you decided, ***why***, and ***what constraints applied.*** Distinguish largely ***arbitrary conventions*** just so that everybody does the same thing from ***necessities, technological constraints, and reflections of the simuland.*** Record the ***traceability*** of decisions to the simuland, or to the Request for Proposal, or to the semi-generic architectures of the simulator.

Examine through real examples ***bottom-up*** and record all ***generic aspects*** such that all modellers should use the same approach and numerical methods.

For every developer, user, maintainer, modification engineer, auditor, or license examiner the basic rule is that every working document or screen should be matched by at least one learning or reference aid, embedded if reasonable. The manuals on ***standards, guidelines, procedures, and conventions*** used by the developers are needed also for maintenance and modifications. The matrix of ***users and topics*** should cover these points.

3. OVERVIEWS FOR ALL USERS

Almost all users need a general idea of the internal workings of the simuland and the simulator. Therefore provide or acquire high-level block diagrams of both. A good many users will find it instructive and helpful to have block diagrams (or equivalently data flow diagrams; good block diagrams and DFD's differ only in rectangular versus circular boxes) one level lower in a hierarchy; such diagrams and lower-level documentation are needed for developers and modifiers in any case.

At this level the software architecture of the simulant (algorithmic model) may differ significantly from that of the simuland; for example, the simulator may have centralized handlers, logic and controls grouped by function, and so on. Except for models which have only a few data flows (most process models), the data flows must necessarily be grouped generically.

4. DOGWORK FIRST

Recognize basic skills which must be mastered before serious learning and work can begin. Teach the user how to insert a diskette ***generically***, apart from a particular use. Dogwork is like an academic discipline, taught separately from motivations for its use.

Development, test, integration and upgrade engineers in particular must learn the human interfaces and facilities of several pieces of support software such as the Multi-User Interactive Data Assignment and Retrieval Facility and the code pre-processor. They should be at ease with the procedural rules for linking, and so on.

5. GOOD PRACTICES

Judicious references are necessary in usable documentation. Their primary purposes are:

* traceability to the simuland, some statement of requirements, generic architecture, or decision;
* traceability to a reference work or publication for thermo-hydro-dynamic constants, rate constants, activation energies, and so on;
* usable cross-references through a hierarchy or network of teaching and reference materials.

References which are basically acknowledgements of the sources of ideas, or priorities in publication, have little place in simulators. Reprint rather than reference the main relevant ideas on numerical methods, computer science, laws of thermodynamics, and so on; supplement these reprints with ***clearly generic*** references to textbooks. The main question is ***why would a user consult the reference***; omit any reference which no user would need to consult or could not consult. Acknowledge personal communications, inaccessible project reports, and obscure brochures in the text rather than the bibliography.

If necessary, photocopy materials which are inconvenient to re-set. Use ***appendices*** for lengthy re-set or photocopied technical materials. Glossaries and appendices are for low-level material which must be mentioned in many places, or for lengthy reference materials. It is usually better to display a diagram twice than to have it invisible when it is discussed or referred to. Use sub-diagrams or highlights if necessary. Learning materials should normally appear as basic spreads on two facing pages; see Weiss (1985), pp.82-5 for some layouts.

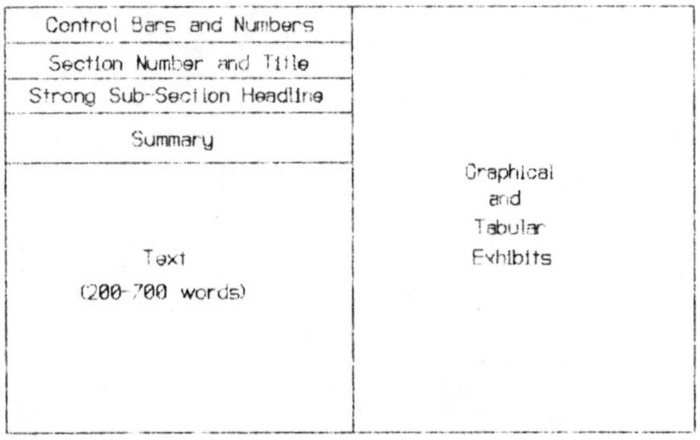

The basic "Hughes Aircraft" two-facing-page module

Try to separate the materials into groups which might change with varying probabilities on different time scales, and in a coordinated manner:

* Academic, well-established materials such as numerical methods for ordinary differential equations
* Materials about a generic simulator architecture
* Documentation of the particular simulator
* Generic principles of a class of simulands
* Specifics of a particular simuland.

Spell out synonyms; documentation should not be a job-security secret to exclude the uninitiated; for example, a Stieltjes matrix is often called an *S*-matrix, so give both names. Do not assume that the user knows that a positive semi-definite matrix is the same thing as a non-negative definite matrix. Jargon cannot be avoided altogether; one must require some prior knowledge of academic disciplines which are abstracted bottom-up to recognize genuine commonality, such as differential calculus. Make a list of all abbreviations, initials, and acronyms; include the place where they are defined, or the definition itself. Do not use acronyms before they are defined; do not hesitate to define them several times.

Although most narrative and semi-narrative documentation should be designed for ***random access*** via indices and/or alphabetization, subordinate material can be set off by smaller type or one- or two-sided indentation. Avoid merely different typefaces; the random-access user will not remember the conventions, and some books with four different typefaces get them out-of-step. Italics, hanging indentation, numbered or bulleted lists, judicious white space, and terminator bullets (often small filled or open squares) improve readability and ease of random access.

Indices and ***tables*** are key to good reference documentation and refresher learning materials. Check all *q.v.*, *see* and *see also* references by human use of a computer; index all possible synonyms. Indices should be prepared by a human, not a machine which lists words, and tested by:

* the preparer,
* an independent party,
* an expert in the subject matter,
* and a bunch of novices.

6. BAD PRACTICES

Among the bad practices implied above are:

* Jargon, abbreviations, acronyms, and initials, especially if the definitions are inaccessible
* Sequential access
* Useless, unnecessary and confusing references
* Conventions which the random access user does not remember and cannot easily consult
* Mingling instruction in dogwork with more serious learning.

Another bad practice is the display of the author's erudition at the expense of the user. Clearly distinguish the ***pre-requisites*** from incidental information which may interest the advanced student.

7. LEARNING TO USE THE SIMULATOR

One common, simple plan is a sequence of steps:

* State the objectives of the exercise (pre-brief)
* Briefly re-capitulate previous pre-requisites, and if appropriate compare and contrast some previous materials
* Demonstrate the lesson; the show part of ***show-and-tell***
* Have the students work the lesson
* Review and re-capitulate what was learned
* De-brief the students on difficulties in the material.

The objectives and re-capitulation can be in the opposite sequence; there can be various hierarchical and nested stages, each based on these rules. This basic outline can be elaborated in many ways. Another perspective is the idea of each hierarchically nested element as a ***stimulus-response*** unit; the instructor or the instructional materials apply successive and nested stimuli, each of which requires a response by the student.

A second simple plan is the ***two-page spread*** of Weiss (1985) illustrated above; the tutorial materials are basically self-pacing as are to some extent the reference materials. A complete (structured) view of the system is then decomposed into units which are expressed on two facing pages of written and exhibit material, a technique developed by Hughes Aircraft Co. Of course, he has to allow a nested hierarchy to some extent, and to recognize the need for dogwork first. The elements of pre-briefing, re-capitulation, demonstration, review, and de-briefing are largely left implicit or up to the student.

Weiss (1985) has many other good points and administrative schemes for people planning and preparing a set of essentially tutorial documentation. The principal changes needed from Weiss reflect his concern with users, not developers; also because a simulator is concerned with a simuland which has its own documentation, there are cases for instructors and even for trainees where it is not reasonable to reproduce all the information about the simuland within the documentation of the simulator.

Weiss (1983) and Sides (1984) discuss methods and forms of documentation appropriate for development and upgrade staff. See Kearsley (1983) for alternative terminologies for computer-based training.

8. LEARNING BY MEANS OF THE SIMULATOR

In some contracts the simulator vendor must also document the simuland or provide instructional materials. Notably this is so in:

* Generic simulators
* Basic-principles trainers, which tend to be generic
* Maintenance trainers
* Where the vendor of the simulator is the vendor of the real simuland, and in some contracts also the supplier of training services.

Self-paced instruction should follow the ideas set out above for learning how to use the simulator. Documentation for the simuland should be along the same lines as documentation for the simulator, but must recognize the differences between hardware in the simuland and software in the simulator.

As in the simulator, documentation is needed on both ***how to use the simuland*** and the largely ***motivational how the simuland works.*** The higher the degree of thinking and reasoning needed, the greater the emphasis on how the simuland works.

9. INTENTION VERSUS IMPLEMENTATION

Every resolved decision should be documented, and in many cases the basis for the decision. Purchased parts of hardware and software give the most trouble, but difficulties also arise in standard (library or off-the-shelf) and semi-generic components. The basis for decisions and the decisions themselves become lost behind a mere type number. Interfaces, failure modes, and features which are deemed immaterial are not recorded.

Nothing in a simulator should be treated as permanent and unchangeable. The aim is a service life of 40 years. Software in particular wears out rapidly when patches are put on top of patches. It is notorious that the embedded comments in code describe not what it does but ***what it used to do.***

One estimate, biased towards U.S. nuclear power plants and the larger U.S. military trainers, is that a simulator will undergo about 1000 changes during the development, another 1000 changes in the 1 to 2 year warranty period (partly because of incorrect information about the real simuland), and another 4000 changes in 20 years of useful life (including changes in the simuland, upgrades, and changes in instructional facilities).

10.CLASSES OF USER AND ITEM

1. Classes of user include:
   1: Specifiers: clients; purchasers
   2: Developers and deliverers
   3: Instructors
   4: Stimulands: human, software, hardware, systems
   5: Hardware and software maintenance engineers
   6: Hardware and software upgraders
   7: Auditors for owners and a regulatory agency
   8: Simuland modification engineers
   9: Forensic investigators

2. Classes of task include:
   1: Learning facilities and operations for work; largely procedural dogwork.
   2: Job exercises
   3: On-the-Job training
   4: Real work

3. Classes of material include:
   1: 2-page tutorial spreads and equivalents in computer-based training
   2: Reference
      a: Marked-up materials from the simuland
      b: Generic to the vendor line of simulators
      c: Specific to the particular simulator

4. Diagrammatic and tabular materials include:
   1: State, Logic and Discrete Control
      a: Marked up electrical elementary or control wiring diagrams
      b: State transition diagrams (STD), Augmented transition networks (ATN), and Recursive transition networks (RTN)
      c: State tables and State transition tables
      d: Event analyses: forwards and backwards
      e: Boolean diagrams and equations
      f: Decision tables
      g: Petri diagrams
   2: Continuous and quasi-continuous control
      a: Control charts: ISA forms
      b: Block diagrams

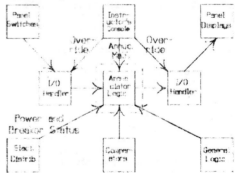

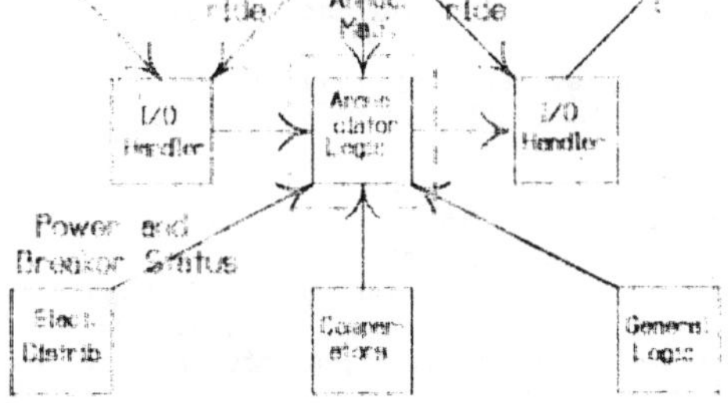

A Block or Data Flow Diagram for the Surroundings of Annunciator Logic

Signals across the dashed box are correct; others may be incomplete

3: Data flow and Antecedence
   a: Data flow diagrams (DFD) and Block diagrams
   b: Reduced context diagrams
   c: Event analyses: forwards and backwards
   d: Data dependency analyses
   e: Data dictionaries
   f: Definitions of what wrote/uses what
   g: Guardian abstract machines for data stores; see Bowen and Buhr (1980), for example.

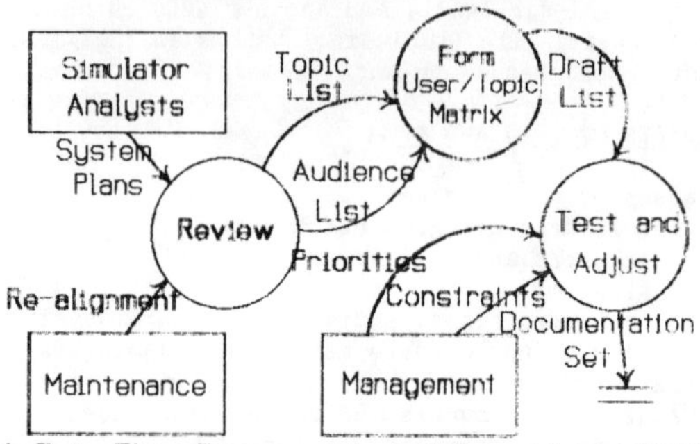

A Data Flow Diagram, adapted from Weiss (1985)

4: Conceptual
   a: Entity relationship diagrams (ERD) and semantic networks for the inter-relations of stored data
5: Invocation and Interaction
   a: Structure charts or compacted listings of what-calls-what under what circumstances
   b: Collaborating sequential processes
   c: Task spawning and object-oriented programming; see, for example, Andrews and Schneider (1983).
6: Temporal relations and sequence
   a: Flow charts
   b: Program design language (PDL)
   c: Timing diagrams
   d: Waveforms
7: Other
   a: Simulation diagrams: marked up Piping and Instrumentation Diagrams
   b: Block interface diagrams (BID)
   c: Causality diagrams and bond graphs
   d: Tables and tabular lists
   e: File layouts and definitions of access

Some of the tables are illustrated in the Appendices and Exhibits below. Distinctions among the graphical and textual tools are not rigorous; there exist intermediate forms and examples which fall in more than one class.

11. SIMULATOR GENERIC SOFTWARE

Generic and semi-generic software in simulators includes the following possible distinctions. Note that one basic but non-unique distinction is into classes of software which operate asynchronously, non-concurrently, or with merely apparent concurrency; in other words, into classes which are necessarily linked mainly or exclusively through data stored in fast or slow memories.

* Operating system and vendor utilities such as text editors, tape and file handlers, compilers, linkers, and so on;
* Support off-line software for configuration management, the definition of data structures, the code pre-processor, sorted listings of all data, and so on;
* Off-line software for instructional support and administration: lesson preparation, trainee records, trainee briefing and de-briefing, off-line trainee assessment, and so on;
* Real-time generic and semi-generic software such as simulation executives, linkage handlers, guardians of data stores to prevent conflicting access, etc.
* On-line and real-time software for instructional support: simulator checkout, malfunction processors, mode selections, menus, trainee guidance, trainee timing and sequence checks, the automated demonstrator, advisor, etc.
* On-line but not real-time utilities such as an interactive data assignment and retrieval facility;
* Library, mathematical and statistical software, some of which might be used on any time scale: square roots, coordinate transformations, least squares regression, statistics by the bootstrap method, analysis of variance, splines, tabular interpolation, etc.

Purchased software is often documented only through the vendor's user manuals; considerable supplementation and correction through experience is usually necessary. Cookbook recipes should be established for many tasks such as compilation, linkage, data base modification, and the output of listings laid out and sorted exactly as each engineer chooses for each task.

In-house software should be documented by ***judicious*** use of data flow diagrams (equivalent to good block diagrams, plus depictions of data stores), state transition diagrams (logic), and semantic networks for aspects which largely revolve around the roles of stored data; all of these are node-and-arc forms, potentially hierarchical, and need support by detailed text to add rigor to the ease of human comprehension. An elaborate version of these ***tools of structured analysis*** is given by Ward and Mellor (1985); note, however, that in practice it is rarely necessary or cost-effective to generate more than half the theoretically possible large volume of paper.

Other data bases and documentation in simulators may supplant some of the elements. Structure charts, which shows what-calls-what and the arguments passed, are relevant only to the instructional software of simulators. Many of the other recipes given in texts on structured analysis and structured design are obviously relevant only to very small systems is elementary data processing. For example, the idea that one should not group asynchronous signals leads to, say, 100,000 individually labelled directed arcs on one small sheet of paper. More detail, in need of some revisions is given by Bradley (1985).

Mathematical and library software must be documented mathematically, of course; the tools of structured analysis are hardly ever practically useful.

Some simulator systems have no clearly identifiable analog in the simuland. Generic signal handlers, valve drivers, and pump drivers should be defined in generic terms; they are essentially table-driven in the implementation.

12. SIMULATOR SPECIFIC SOFTWARE

Documentation of software and data structures specific to the simulator should include all the elements of the documentation of generic software, plus the following ***as appropriate***:

* Simulation diagrams: marked up Piping and Instrumentation diagrams, or equivalents
* Boolean diagrams, where logic has to be taken from relay contact ladders and other forms which express only implementation details, not intent as in any form of state transition representation
* Any other form of conventional engineering drawing
* Bond graphs and causality diagrams, which are popular with some simulationists
* Timing and waveform diagrams, judiciously
* Test plans and results, including but not limited to forwards and backwards event analyses, state tables, and state transition tables.

13. SIMULATOR HARDWARE

Documentation of simulator hardware has the following principal parts:

1: A statement of the overall requirements of the simulator: power, HVAC, temperature, humidity, weights, etc.
2: Major purchased functional units such as a computer complex; documentation and procedures are provided primarily by the original vendor, with supplementation according to options selected and any modifications made.
3: The interfaces among purchased components and devices, with the rationale for their choice, estimated operating margins, restrictions on operation, provisions for soft failure, and so on. For example, the rationale for uninterruptible power supplies and the various modes of degradation should be documented.
4: Devices which copy those in the real simuland, with references to the original source materials, purchase orders, explanations of type numbers, and so on. Any differences such as the remote detection of burned-out lamps should be recorded.
5: Custom fabricated or assembled units, with mechanical and electrical working drawings, procedures for scheduled and unscheduled maintenance, etc.
6: Tools and test devices, either standard commercial units or custom fabricated.
7: Procedures for diagnosis, maintenance access, and repair, including all safety precautions and necessary units such as cranes, hoists, or fork-lift trucks.
8: A list of recommended spare parts.
9: Interfaces to the architect of the building to house the simulator, including shipping sizes and weights.

14. TEST PLANS AND RESULTS

Errors in test plans are approximately as common as other mis-interpretations of the data from which they are derived. It is not necessary to archive every such error, only the accepted version and test results for most code; where the interfaces are complex and integration has been troublesome, some information about the difficulties may be helpful in the future detection of residual errors and in future modifications.

The Acceptance Test Plan in particular cannot cover every conceivable maneuver and sequence of events in the simulator. It depends heavily upon the reductionist hypothesis that parts which work separately will also work together, especially fully discrete aspects such as logic and electrical distribution; yet the Acceptance Test Plan also introduces secondary and tertiary effects and sequence-of-events which are very difficult to contrive solely by building models which meet the Acceptance Test Plan but nothing else. In other words the Acceptance Test Plan makes more significant use than other aspects of testing of ***known or provable properties which were not exploited in the implementation.***

15. DOCUMENTING SPAGHETTI CODE

The basic iterative steps in sorting out unstructured code are:

* Canonical flowcharts, with replicate code as needed
* Structure charts or what-calls-what lists
* Data flow diagrams to locate true sources and sinks of variables
* State transition diagrams
* Semantic networks, if appropriate
* Other graphical and tabular aids as needed.

Each step is iterative within itself and with all earlier steps. Do not worry about the size of essentially once-through top-to-bottom modules.

16. REFERENCES

Andrews, G. R. and F. B. Schneider, 1983. Concepts and Notations for Concurrent Programming. *Computing Surveys* 15, 3-43.

Bowen, B. A. and R. J. A. Buhr, 1980. *The Logical Design of Multiple-Microprocessor Systems.* Prentice-Hall, Englewood Cliffs, 306pp.

Bradley, J. H., 1985. Structured Methods in Semi-Repetitive Environments. Pages 110-115 in J. S. Gardenier, Ed., *Simulators: Proceedings of the Conference on Simulators.* Simulation Series, Volume 16, Number 1. Society for Computer Simulation (Simulation Councils, Inc.), La Jolla.

Kearsley, G. P., 1983. *Computer-Based Training.* Addison-Wesley, Reading, Mass., 204pp.

Sides, C. H., 1984. *How to Write Papers and Reports about Computer Technology.* ISI Press, Philadelphia, 142pp.

Ward, P. T. and S. Mellor, 1985. *Structured Development for Real-Time Systems.* Yourdon Press (now Prentice-Hall), New York, 3 vols.

Weiss, E. H., 1983. *How to Document a Computer System.* Prentice-Hall, Englewood Cliffs.

Weiss, E. H., 1985. *How to Write a Usable User Manual.* ISI Press, Philadelphia, 197pp.

APPENDICES AND EXHIBITS

Four Types of Event

External: incoming to the computer
  Binary input (DI) changes
  Instructor requests menu

Internal: inside the computer
  Comparator changes status
  End-of-file found

Relative Temporal
  25 minutes after engines started

Wall-clock Temporal
  Time for shift change

Three Cross Types: Control, Data, Mixed

Start button pushed; discrete control or logic
Setpoint changed; data
Trainee name entered: seek records; mixed

The following is a simple tabular form of Forward Event Analysis or Event List. Another method is to mark up data flow diagrams or state transition diagrams with colored pens or conventional symbols.In the absence of redundancy, every signal should have at least one event which gives rise to it in at least one mode of operation; this is Backward Event Analysis. In Forward Event Analysis every incoming signal should cause some response (if simulated) in at least one mode of operation.

Event or State	Action(s)
Maximum ratio and authorization entered	Store and use. Retain on loss of power.
Creek flow falls to zero	Close both control valves
Sampler inoperable	Close both control valves

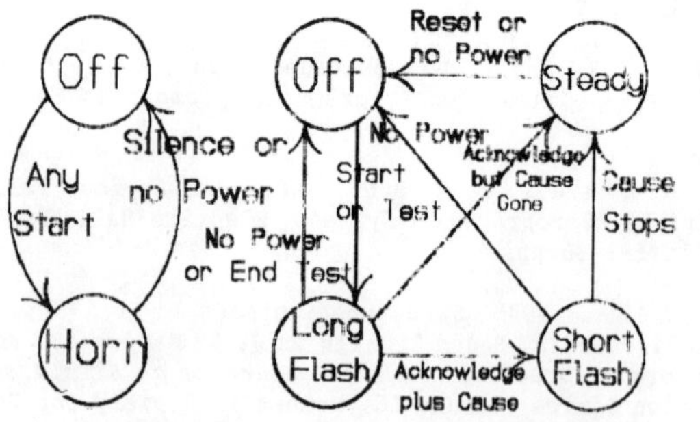

A Simple State Transition Diagram

A Boolean Diagram took 16 Hours!

A State Transition Table serving as a Test Plan for a Timed Sample-Collection System with 2 Jugs.

Event	Inputs			Memories			Outputs			Comment
	Jug Replaced	Actual Position	Pump Rotating	Current Jug Used	Other Used	Request Pending	Acknowledgement	Command to Switch	Request Replacement	
Reset	F	L	F	F	F	F	F	F	F	L = left
Time to Req.	-	-	-	-	-	-	-	-	-	Non-event
Time to Switch	-	-	-	-	-	-	-	-	-	No action
Pump Start	F	L	*T*	*T*	F	F	F	F	F	Jug now used
Pump Stop	F	L	*F*	T	F	F	F	F	F	Ital.= change
Time to Req.	F	L	F	T	F	F	F	F	F	No action
Time to Switch	F	*R*	F	*F*	*T*	F	F	*T**	F	* = momentary
Time to Req.	F	R	F	F	T	*T*	F	F	*T*	Req. change
Jug Replaced	*T**	R	F	F	*F*	*F*	*T**	F	F	
Time to Switch	F	*L*	F	F	F	F	F	*T**	F	Switch.
Pump Start	F	L	*T*	*T*	F	F	F	F	F	Flow present
Time to Req.	F	L	T	T	F	F	F	F	F	No action
Time to Switch	F	*R*	T	T	*T*	F	F	*T**	F	Switch
Time to Req.	F	R	T	T	T	*T*	F	F	*T*	Req. change
Time to Switch	F	R	*F*	T	T	T	F	F	T	Error cond.
Reset	F	R	F	*F*	*F*	*F*	F	F	*F*	Replace both

Many notations are possible for waveforms and actions which take a finite time. State Transition Tables apply to multiple-input systems as Specifications and Test Plans; only one input can change at a time. State Tables, in contrast, are described in the theory of single-input minimally-reduced finite state machines used as recognizers in computer science; the single input provides a string of characters.

A Simple Semantic Network

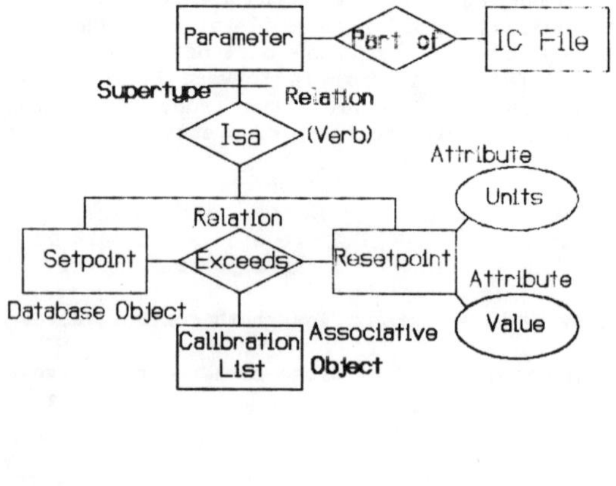

A Simplified Example of What-Calls-What.

What-calls-what allows for changeable arguments; it shows numbers, sequence and basic circumstances of calls. A Structure Chart shows only the existence of one-or-more calls and one fixed argument list.

```
The Main Program
PROGRAM DRYER: File DRYER.FOR
 CALL GETFIL
 CALL PHASE1
 CALL STARTI
 DO 1500 ITER = 1, NITER
  CALL HOOKS
  CALL ENTERI
  DO 1000 ITIME = 1,NSTEPS
   CALL ALGEB
   CALL FURIER (Q, MAUX, NDB-1, LWAVE)
   CALL MSUBT
    CALL SM1(MDOT,MAUX)
   ELSE
    CALL FURIER (MDOT, MAUX, NDB, LWAVE)
C   Put out true initial fluxes and tendencies if so
selected
   IF (ITIME .EQ. 1) THEN
C
C  Detailed Output
     IF (IDFIL .GT. 0) THEN
      CALL OUTPUT (IDFIL, IDFIL, IDFIL)
     ENDIF
C
C  Intermediate Output and End-of-Phase Output
C
    CALL OUTPUT (ITFIL, ILFIL, IVFIL)
C
    ENDIF
1000  TIME LOOP FOR PHASE
   IF (NITER. GT. 1) CALL NEXTIT
1500  PHASE ITERATION LOOP
     CALL RESTOR
2000  LOOP ON PHASES
```

****

Subroutines and Functions in alphabetical order by name

Check values permitted in the Phase or Block of Phases
SUBROUTINE CHECKP (FILARC, ICASE): File CHECKP.FOR
  CALL STORER(DT, DTB, NBLOCK)
  and many other calls to storing routines

Estimate the Drum equilibrium temperatures and cycle
SUBROUTINE DRUM: File ITER.FOR
No calls

Properties of air with injection of heat and water vapor
SUBROUTINE MIX (AIR, AIRT, MIXR, QTOT, MASS, ENTHAL, TE, CV): File ITER.FOR
No calls

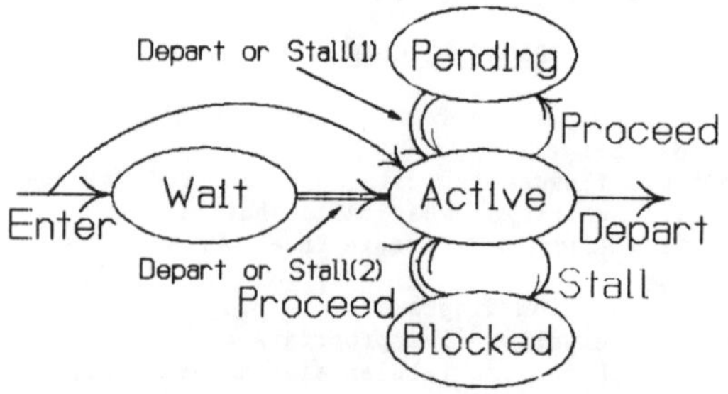

A Monitor of Type Mediator,
after Bowen and Buhr (1980).

Simulators VI

ISBN 0-911801-51-0

A tutorial review of acoustic synthesis techniques for simulator systems

Dr. L.S. Dooley
Dept. of Electrical Engineering
Polytechnic of Wales
Treforest, Mid Glamorgan, CF37 1DL.

ABSTRACT

This paper chronicles the various strategies which have evolved towards the artificial reproduction of ship-board generated sounds for Marine and Bridge Simulators. Analogue synthesis methods were the precursor, and while generally effective in creating an audible verisimilitude, they were very limited in their ability to synthesise rapidly changing sounds. Contemporary designs have concentrated upon using digital techniques, which afford a significantly greater degree of flexibility, together with an improved quality of acoustic faithfulness. The paper will describe the design rationale for a replete Digital Sound System, together with a synopsis of current research developments in this field.

INTRODUCTION

The essence of a Ship (Marine) Simulator is didactic, with Bridge and Engine Room crews having the opportunity to interact with a computer system, which accurately models the steering and handling characteristics of a vessel in various waterways, sea conditions and visibilities. There are four principal reasons for using simulators as a teaching aid:-

1. The saving in expenditure. Though initially expensive it is considerably cheaper than purchasing and maintaining a ship.
2. Conservation of time in performing training manoeuvres, with no necessity to divert other shipping from their normal route.
3. Environmental and mechanical conditions are entirely regulated by the instructor from his console, and may be easily duplicated or modified.
4. Finally and incontrovertibly, the paramount reason for simulation is that it is intrinsically safe, with crews being guided through exercises which would be completely inadmissable in the real world.

As ships represent one of the most complex Man-Machine interfaces in existance, it is paradoxical that the development of Nautical Simulators has been so tardy. The prerequisite for an authentic recreation of the atmosphere and action of a ship in today's Naval Simulators, has led to a considerable amount of research being undertaken, especially into advanced graphics systems to furnish daylight colour vision, as well as wide viewing angles. This is laudable if somewhat incongruous since the ears and feet of a mariner are as quintessential sensory receptors as the eyes. This lacunae in acoustic and motional simulation has recently been the catalyst for research to be pursued, with many diverse methodologies being investigated into procuring an accurate audible realism for contemporary Marine Simulators.

Philosophical Arguments

The principal aim of any simulator is not to supplant the "real thing" but to assist and hopefully teach both the novice as well as the experienced mariner. Seafarers are inherently sceptical of such an ethos, but as has been proven, difficult emergency procedures can be assimilated, accidents replayed and new diverse harbour topographies may be assessed prior to being constructed, all in complete safety. In supplying an acoustic facility to any simulator system, two main detractions are voiced; (i) the expense and (ii) the perforce. Although some systems are expensive to purchase as a single entity, in comparison with the capital outlay for a complete Marine Simulator, this argument appears somewhat flawed. Secondly, there is no overriding necessity for integrating a synthesiser into a simulator system, though when viewed pragmatically manifold epithets do accrue. Independent tests palpably reveal that the heart and pulse rates of simulator student's increase considerably when audio and visual aids are incorporated. This endorses the intuitive result that the greater the aura of authenticity, the more psychological pressure is applied to the student, which undoubtedly means that his ability can be more equitably appraised.

Finally, there are the subjective considerations which affect any sound system. Pitch and loudness for example, are both subjective quantities, so that any synthesiser design must afford the operator full control of such parameters, to maximise the flexibility to be engendered within the acoustic model.

OVERVIEW OF AUDIO SYNTHESIS METHODS

Though this paper will principally provide an overview of the many analogue and digital acoustic design implementations which have been employed for Ship Simulators, other techniques utilised in Aeronautical, Vehicle, Submarine and Weapon Simulation will also be delineated.

Analogue Techniques

Early design strategies adopted an analogue approach to marine sound simulation, generally using either a continuous loop variable-speed audio cassette or electromechanical techniques. The former approach, which was utilised at Warsash Naval College, Southampton (Longman et al. 1981) was only satisfactory for quasi-stationary mechanical sounds, while the latter technique generally required an inordinate amount of hardware. The synthesis supplied by using a tape recording was especially estimable for acoustic signals which were generated under quiescent speed and load conditions, particularly if the audio characteristics of the Simulator's Room were matched correctly. Subtle variations in the sounds could be achieved by flanging, which involved either manually or electrically varying the tape speed, though the degree of flanging was critical if the perceptual effect was to be maximised. One drawback of this closed-loop tape approach, was that the low frequency response tended to be circumscribed, so the quality of reproduction of the baseband Propeller Shafts resonances and the percussive Engine Room vibrations, could be poor. This was an important limitation for Marine Simulators, because this frequency region comprised the only major source of noise audible upon the Bridge of a ship. By comparison the electromechanical stragegy could synthesise low frequency signals very easily, as a large number of relays were used to switch in a bank of narrowband noise sources.The overall reproduction quality was however significantly inferior to that of the magnetic tape.

A disparate approach employed extensively upon early Aircraft simulators involved the use of wave-shaping analogue circuits to modulate a pure white noise source into the desired signal spectrum. Though efficacious for quiescent sounds, the technique was very consuming in terms of hardware,power and cost, and introducing any subtle changes to a synthesised sound was extremely intractable.

The one major drawback of all the aforementioned analogue methods was that they were totally unsuited to the reproduction of the fast changing non-stationary Start-up and Run-down procedures of machinery installations such as the Main Engines. This was ostensibly due to the natural mechanical percussive beat of the Engines slowing down significantly faster than the baseband resonances, during the Run-down routine and vice versa. Flanging the tape to synthesise this procedure, had the effect of slowing both of these components homologously, with the consequence that the perceived sound was distorted. With burgeoning technology however, digital designs began to be undertaken, aimed at improving both the quality of synthesis and alleviating some of the intrinsic constraints highlighted in the above systems.

Digital Techniques

In comparison with analogue methods, a digital solution affords a much greater degree of flexibility to the user, as well as providing the additional facility for incorporating subtle changes to a specific ship-board sound for differing environmental conditions, depth of water and Engine speed. The complex Start-up and Run-down routines of the Main Engines can also be efficaciously synthesised, because the percussive mid-band and sonorous baseband regions may be separately reproduced and subsequently remixed to provide the desired acoustic signals. Another important epithet which accrues from this stragegy, is that errors and faults within a particular mechanical installation may be audibly simulated, so complementing the visual information displayed by the simulator, to inculcate upon the user that there is perhaps malfunctioning machinery or that his perspicacity is impaired. The instructor can monitor from his console, the progress the user makes in diagnosing the fault and the corrective action that is taken.

With the recent advancement of VLSI technology, some very elegant methods of digital sound synthesis have evolved. A symbiosis has been forged with the speech processing area, with a number of real-time synthesis concepts being exploited with very propitious results. Most ship-board generated sounds under quiescent conditions may be broadly classified as time-invariant or quasi stationary. The strong underlying periodic component in most mechanical noise signals has lead to the extensive use of the memory based look-up table approach to reproducing particular sounds. One such design used a PDP11 minicomputer as a large storage database for digitised sound recordings for Submarine and Vehicle simulation. To recreate a sound, all that was required was to access the relevant data and reply it through an appropriate Amplifier, Mixer and Loudspeaker system. This strategy allowed the facile synthesis of both the Start-up and Run-down routines of machinery installations, though subtle nuances to a sound caused for instance by varying road conditions, could not be so readily simulated due to the access latency of the system. The overall sound quality was very good, though a large initial capital outlay was required and the system had bandwidth limitations.

Stand-alone units which facilitated easy interfacing to any simulator system quickly proceeded. The computer power of temporal microprocessors and the low cost of memory meant that 128Kbytes of data could be stored in a single EPROM and accessed at a speed enabling real-time audio reproduction. Although this approach generally required detailed signal processing to be undertaken to select and compress the segment of the signal which was to be stored, to minimise the data storage; provided this could be achieved, a very faithful reproduction of the original quiescent sound was obtained. This technique will be discussed more fully later in the paper.

The advent of programmable sound generator chips for home computer use, also pervaded into Acoustic Synthesisers, though these chips were very restrictive in the number of tones, the number of bits assigned to a noise source and the envelope facilities they afforded. Modern VLSI Digital Signal Processors (DSP) such as the TMS32020, have a much higher granularity, furnishing data throughputs which enable many algorithms to be implemented, which were previously not feasible for real-time synthesis. Short-Time Fourier Analysis and Synthesis, Walsh Functions and Spectral Estimation techniques such as Linear Predictive Coding (LPC), and the family of linear parametric models which include the Autoregressive (AR) and Moving Average (MA) approximations, have all been appraised as viable audio synthesis methods. The performance of the former method, which involved modelling a white noise source with an all-pole time-varying digital filter will be analysed in the course of the paper.

SOUND SYSTEM CONCEPTS

While a digital approach appears to provide many advantages, any design rationale must embody a number of important pragmatic considerations:-

1. Perfect digital audio reproduction cannot be achieved because the quantisation process inherently only approximates the original analogue signal. The proposed system should therefore aim to bestow naturalism to the simulator's surroundings.
2. As the majority of sounds contain a high random noise component superimposed upon the signal, the number of bits required for data

acquisition and reconstitution may be relaxed. Typically between 8 and 12 bits resolution is satisfactory, depending upon the spectral complexity of the signal and the amount of signal processing necessary.

3. The Sound Pressure Level (SPL) readings for certain space installations (notably the Main Engines and Propeller Shafts during cavitation) are inordinate and unrealistic for synthesis in either a laboratory or simulator environment. Some A-weighted SPL measurements for a Medium Speed Cross-Channel Ferry are given in Table 1.

Machinery Installation and location of each recording	SPL Reading dB(A)
Bridge Noise	65
Hydraulic Bow Thrusters	102
Control Room	84
Diesel Generator	112
Pump	89
Background Noise	89
Compressor	106
Turbocharger	111
Main Engines and Turbochargers	116
Propeller Shafts (during cavitation)	124

TABLE 1: A Synopsis of the Sound Pressure Measurements

4. The subjective control in an audio system of such parameters as loudness, pitch and timbre is paramount.
5. The heterogenous nature of the ship-board sounds generated at the three main noise locations - the Bridge, Engine Room and Control Room, means that they must be homogenised into their constituent primary noise sources.
6. Design flexibility, to expand the acoustic simulation to slow and fast as well as medium speed ships. The design strategy should also encompass vessels with divergent acoustic characteristics, and the complete system should be able to synthesise sounds either autonomously as a "stand-alone unit" or by interfacing to the Marine Simulator, via a proprietary-designed bus.

Hence, as the acoustic reproduction model is generally required to cover a wide and diverse gamut of ship-types (from frigate-class to slow-speed cargo carriers), a modular design has to be adopted. This enables the processing, reconstitution and simulation of the multifarious ship-board sounds, to be both facile and ingeminate.

A Digital Sound System Implementation

The following treatise refers to an acoustic synthesiser for a Medium Speed (Cross-Channel Ferry) Ship Simulator, which was implemented at the U.S. Maritime Research Centre, Toledo, Ohio, and has since been installed in a number of other Marine establishments in both Great Britain and Europe. The design has also been adapted for use in a Weapon Simulator to synthesise such sounds as a missile being launched and a gun being fired. Of paramount perceptual importance for this implementation was the Doppler Effect whenever a rocket was launched. All the essential criteria delineated in the preceding section are embraced in the system, with the synthesis and distribution of sounds accomplished using the following equipment.

1. A Digital Synthetic Sound Generation System. This comprises six independently controlled microprocessor boards that reproduce the sounds of the primary noise sources. The simulator can transfer data and information via a bi-directional General Purpose Input Output Bus (GPIO), to an appropriate sound card in the generation module. The selected board accepts the data, decodes it and takes remedial action. A typical generation unit would consist of six identical cards comprising the sounds of the Main Engines and Turbochargers, Propeller Shafts, Diesel Generators, Motor driven Pumps and Compressors, and Background Noise. The final board would be utilised to provide an authentic atmosphere when the students first enter the simulator room. The above configuration may be adapted for the simulation of other sounds such as Stern Thrusters and Auxiliary Engines by simply switching boards. No hardware or software modifications are perforce, because the design is completely modular. To reproduce the more muffled sounds heard on the Bridge and in the Control (Plant) Room, a filtered version of each primary noise provenance is available. Both the original and filtered synthesis signals are amplified prior to being fed to the distribution module.

2. A Distribution Unit. This has two functions, firstly to distribute AC main supply to the trio of mixer/amplifer units and secondly to direct the acoustic outputs from the generation unit to each mixer/amplifer module.

3. Mixer and Amplifier Module. This consists of a six channel audio mixer which aggregates the output from each sound board in the generation unit, using slider controls together with an overall volume control, to yield the requisite acoustic blend for the relevant ambience. A bargraph supplies a visual display of the signal level, while a plug-in headphone socket facilitates aural monitoring. The output of the mixer is subsequently ampified to drive three loudspeaker units. The amplifier is dual-channel, and furnishes a maximum output power of 100 Watts RMS per channel. Two amplifiers are used instead of a single wideband amplifier which covers the entire audio range, because each unit is only required to reproduce a particular spectral band. This Biamplification technique is achieved by splitting the audio spectrum into a bass and mid-range response, by using an active crossover network.

4. Loudspeaker Units. These are free standing units, which may be either floor or wall mounted. The system consists of a 15" Bass loudspeaker conjoint with two smaller hi-fi mid-range frequency units. The Bass speaker is a proprietary design, and has a maximum operating frequency of 250Hz, while the mid-band units cover the audio range up to 16KHz. This particular configuration covers the audible frequency span of all the machinery space installations on the model ship. For other ship types, an extension the top-end response up to and beyond 20KHz may be desirable, so provision exists within the Sound System for the integration of treble loudspeaker units.

The positioning of all three loudspeaker modules is an important aspect of the Digital Acoustic Synthesiser. The Bass speaker may be located anywhere in the simulator room, because of the omni-directional nature of the low frequency sounds, while the two mid-range speakers should be positioned to direct their sound towards the simulator user, to maximise the aura of a ship.

SOUND BOARD DESIGN

In designing a sound synthesis board, a thorough analysis of the characteristics and spectral composition of each sound must be procured. Concomitant with this signal processing, perceptual tests must be performed to asunder individual spectra into relevant bands to assist in the search for viable synthesis techniques and to afford an accurate empirical method of evaluating the audible bandwidth for each signal. A detailed description of such an analysis for the model ship may be found in (Dooley 1987) with the main corollaries epitomised as follows:-

1. The kernel conclusion was the paramount importance of the Propeller Shafts sound to the low frequency band; the Main Engines sound to mid-band frequencies and the Turbochargers to the top-end response.
2. The sound generated by all six primary noise sources under steady-state conditions, was classified as either stationary random or quasi-stationary.
3. The Start-up and Run-down procedures of the Main Engines, Diesel Generators and Turbochargers did not validate the classical time-invariant criterion of stationarity, though as with many signals whose characteristics are non-stationary, the time series was partitioned into short quasi-stationary segments in which the time variance was assumed to be small.
4. The Turbocharger noise spectrum possessed three extant harmonically related resonances, caused by the rotating Turbine blades. The analysis revealed that this signal could be very well approximated by a square wave.
5. The incommensurate SPL reading for the Pumps, Diesel Generators, Compressors and Background Noise in Table 1, does not preclude them from the acoustic synthesis model, because they are integral components in the heterogenous Engine Room noise produced when the ship is berthed.

Design Strategy

As alluded earlier, the strong periodic component on all the steady-state sounds, together with their stationary classification, motivated a cyclic loop-up table approach to the synthesis using an EPROM, a Digital to Analogue converter (DAC) and an interpolation filter. The EPROM stored the sampled form of one complete data frame representing a particular machinery space installation noise profile. This discrete data was then clocked from memory, and reconstituted into an analogue signal using a DAC and low-pass filter combination. The longevity of these frames was very important, because it determined the storage requirements necessary to faithfully reproduce the original signal, without a perceptible cyclic component due to end-effects, being superimposed upon the signal. This cyclic element is inherent in any system where quantised data is repetitiously replayed from memory, so the duration of the data frame had to be adapted to qualitatively essay the perceptual impact of this component. This concomitantly afforded an efficacious method of evaluating the minimum data storage requirements for each noise provenance. The discrete data frame representing each marine sound, was digitally filtered to remove artefactual noise and modulated by an exponential weighting function to expiate the end-effects in the replayed data. An exponential weighting function was chosen for two reason. Firstly, there was the intrinsic discontinuity in the reconstructed signal, generated between the end of the data frame and the beginning, which was manifest as a periodic audible click. Secondly, if the data segment was not sufficiently long, the cyclic component could become audible. This effect was perceived most prevalently with data frame lengths of less than two seconds, and was so objectionable for segment lengths of less than one second, to render the synthesis ineffectual. By weighting both ends of the stored signal, the cyclic component was attenuated significantly, as well as ensuring that the reconstituted signal was consistent, by constraining the data frame to contain either one complete cycle or multiple periods of the natural repetitious mechanical beat. A tabulation of the empirical and perceptual results derived for each ship-board acoustic signal is furnished in Table 2.

Machinery Space Installation	fs KHz	Min Frame Length before Processing	Min Frame Length after Processing
Main Engines	16	128 Kbytes	64 Kbytes
Prop Shafts	2	16 Kbytes	4 Kbytes
Diesel Gens	16	128 Kbytes	64 Kbytes
Compressors	16	128 Kbytes	48 Kbytes
Pumps	16	128 Kbytes	48 Kbytes
Turbochargers	32	256 Kbytes	96/2+ Kbytes
Background Noise	8	64 Kbytes	16 Kbytes
Main Eng.Start-Up	16	256 Kbytes	256 Kbytes

+ Square-Wave Approximation

Table 2. Empirical and Perceptual Observations upon the Data Segment Length required to derive a faithful reproduction of each Ship board sound.

This evinces the necessary sampling rate and storage requirements both prior to and following the processing of each sound. The comparison shows that a substantial data reduction ensued in the number of bytes necessary to derive a faithful reproduction quality for each noise source, when the exponential weighting function was applied to the data. The Turbocharger sound as mentioned above may be approximated by a square wave, so reducing the storage for this sound to 2Kbytes.

These analytical and perceptual conclusions formed the basis of the prototype sound synthesiser board shown in Figure 1 (Dooley 1988). The look-up table technique was implemented using an 8031 microprocessor to control the sampling rate. The 8031 also executed the control software for the GP10 bus interface, which facilitated fast communications with the Simulator. Due to the large processing overheads on the 8031 however, the maximum sampling frequency which could be realised was 8KHz, so the look-up table strategy had to be confined to the 4KHz baseband. To synthesise the percussive mid-band frequency range, a conventional sound generator chip (AY-3-8912) was utilised, with the various tone generators, envelope controls and noise sources, being adapted to furnish this important frequency band. As mentioned earlier however, the use of such chips was very restrictive in terms of signal resolution and flexibility, and this indubitably compromised the resultant synthesis quality. The high frequency Turbocharger sound was recreated by using a 16 bit counter to generate a variable frequency square wave, which aided in procuring an estimable reproduction quality for the fast changing Start-up and Run-down procedures of the Main Engines. The important low frequency and mid-band regions of these two utilities, were realised by using a Variable Sampling Rate (VSR) algorithm (Dooley 1987). This involved locking the cut-off frequency of an MF10 switch-capacitor filter to the current Nyquist sampling frequency, so that as the sampling period was either incremented or decremented (to impart the effect of either a decrease or increase in speed), the filter emandated all aliased components from the reconstituted signal. The output from the MF10 was subsequently added to the signal from the sound generator chip, prior to being filtered to acquire the requisite acoustic ambience. Subjective tests confirmed the efficacy of this VSR algorithm in simulating both the Start-up and Run-down Engine routines.

CURRENT DEVELOPMENTS

This final section presents a review of a contemporary design strategy which significantly improves certain aspects of the preceding design. The look-up table approach is retained since it proved very effective for the synthesis of the baseband sonority, but if this approach was utilised for the mid-band and high frequency reproduction, the data storage requirement could become unmanageable. Current research has therefore been concentrating upon both improving the overall quality of the mid-range percussive region and minimising data storage, by employing various spectral estimation and data compression techniques. These include the Periodogram, the time-varying all-pole AR and the pole-zero ARMA parametric models, while data compression methods include Vector Quantisation and Adaptive PCM. All the time varying estimates are realised by implementing various digital filter structures in software upon a TMS32020 Signal Processor. The filter modulates an internally generated binary random sequence, so that as the filter coefficients are periodically changed, so the output varies in accordance with the original signal. Figure 2 evinces a typical spectrum for an Engine noise, together with a 24 pole wideband AR estimate. The AR model is especially favourable for sounds which possess a large number of spectral peaks, because the estimate biases the poles (resonances) in the frequency response more heavily than the zeros (valleys), and subjectively the human ear perceives peaks much more readily than spectral troughs. The resultant estimate is acceptable in the regions of the Turbocharger resonances at 1.5KHz, 3.4KHz, and 5.8 KHz, but it is clear that the resolution in the remainder of the spectrum is very poor. In subjective testing, while the artificially generated percussive band was audible, a large rasping digital noise component was present upon the signal which rendered the synthesis very ineffective. To overcome this problem, the concept of narrowband spectral estimation was employed. Various proprietary algorithms were devised (Dooley 1987), which enabled selective frequency bands to be modelled, while the spectral vestige was ignored. Figure 3 shows a simulation upon the TMS32020 using a 20 pole AR model to synthesise the Main Engine's percussive frequency band between 3.5KHz and 9.5 KHz. Visually and mathematically, this approach provided a much better estimate than the wideband model, while perceptual tests corroborated the improvement in the quality of synthesis. In summarising, the use of spectral estimation has a number of important advantages:

1) High resolution synthesis may be obtained by modelling a selective portion of the spectrum with a large-order approximation. The remainder of the spectrum can be either ignored or approximated by a much lower order estimate.
2) Substantial reductions in memory capacity ensue, as the sound is now represented by a set of digital filter vectors rather than a data segment of the original signal. Typically between 120-140 filter coefficient frames were required for the quiescent Engine sound.
3) The calculation of only a narrowband AR estimate occurs at a significantly lower sampling rate than it's wideband counterpart, because all the processing is performed at baseband frequencies. This relaxes the processing constraints upon the TMS32020 considerably, enabling a higher order estimate to be realised. However, there is one major detraction, in that external heterodyning hardware in the form of an analogue multiplier and band-pass filter is required to translate the baseband estimate back to it's desired frequency band.

A new Acoustic Synthesiser development board based upon the TMS32020 and incorporating some of these signal processing concepts is shown in Fig. 4. It employs a look-up table for the low frequency band synthesis based around the 12bit AD7545 DAC and 27128 EPROM combination, with the sampling rate controlled by the 8254 Counter/Timer chip. The DSP calculates in real-time both the mid-band range and high frequency spectral estimates, with all the filter coefficients being loaded into fast static memory at power-up to minimise access times, so that the maximum data throughput is maintained. Bandwidths of up to 22 KHz have been achieved upon this board for a 16-pole AR approximation.

CONCLUSIONS

This paper has reviewed the bevy of diverse design strategies which have been developed in the pursuit of an efficacious acoustic synthesis facility for Marine Simulators. The merits and dermits of analogue methods were initially elucidated, however the advent of VLSI technology has meant that these have all been supplanted by digital methods. An overview of two disparate real-time digital designs is furnished, with the quantitative and subjective performance of both of these technique being examined.

REFERENCES

Longman M., Phelan C.N. and Hansford R.F., 1981, "Interactive Operation of Ship Simulators", Proc. of the 2nd International Conference on Marine Simulators MARSIM'81", (New York, June 1981), E3-1, E3-8.

Dooley L.S., 1987, "An Investigation of Sound Synthesis for Marine Simulators", Ph.D. Thesis, Univ. of Wales, Cardiff.

Dooley L.S. and Evans W.A., 1988 "Digital Synthesis of Ship-Board Generated Acoustics for Marine Simulators,", 12th IMACS World Congress on Scientific Computation, Paris, July 18-22.

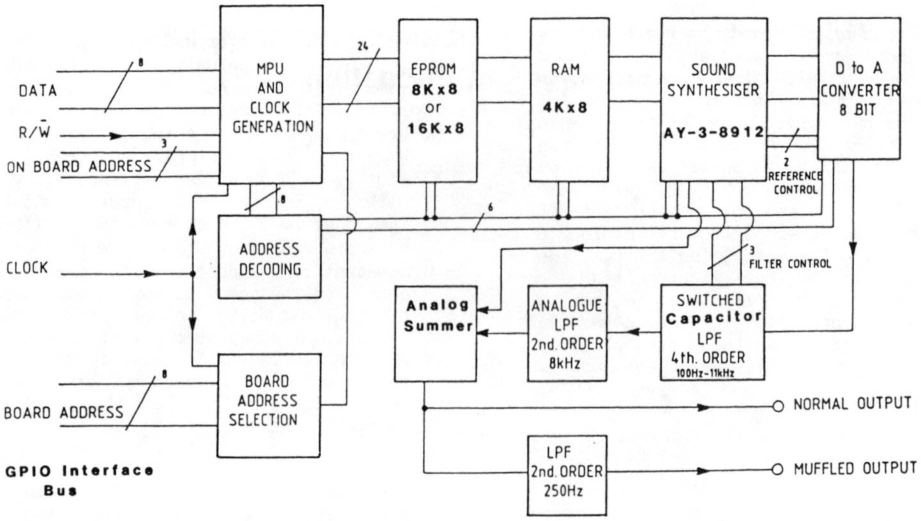

Figure 1 , Block Diagram of the Sound Synthesiser Board

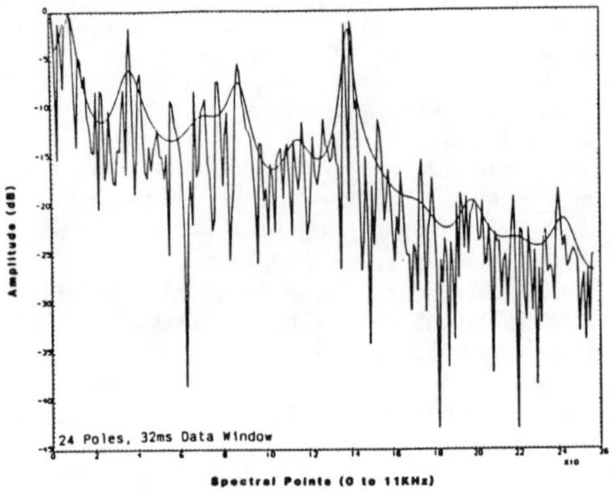

Figure 2, AR Wideband Estimate

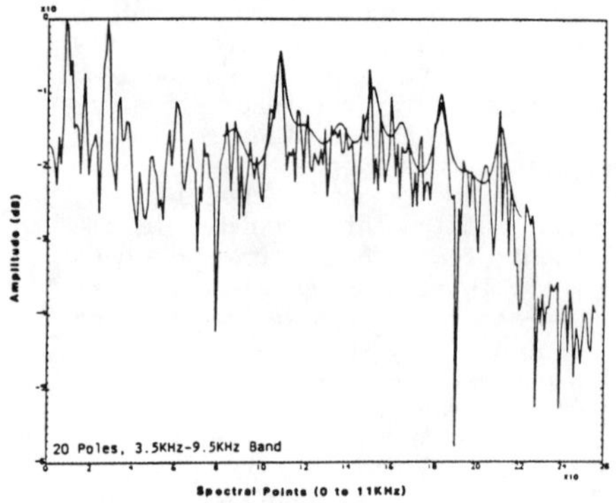

Figure 3, AR Narrowband Estimate

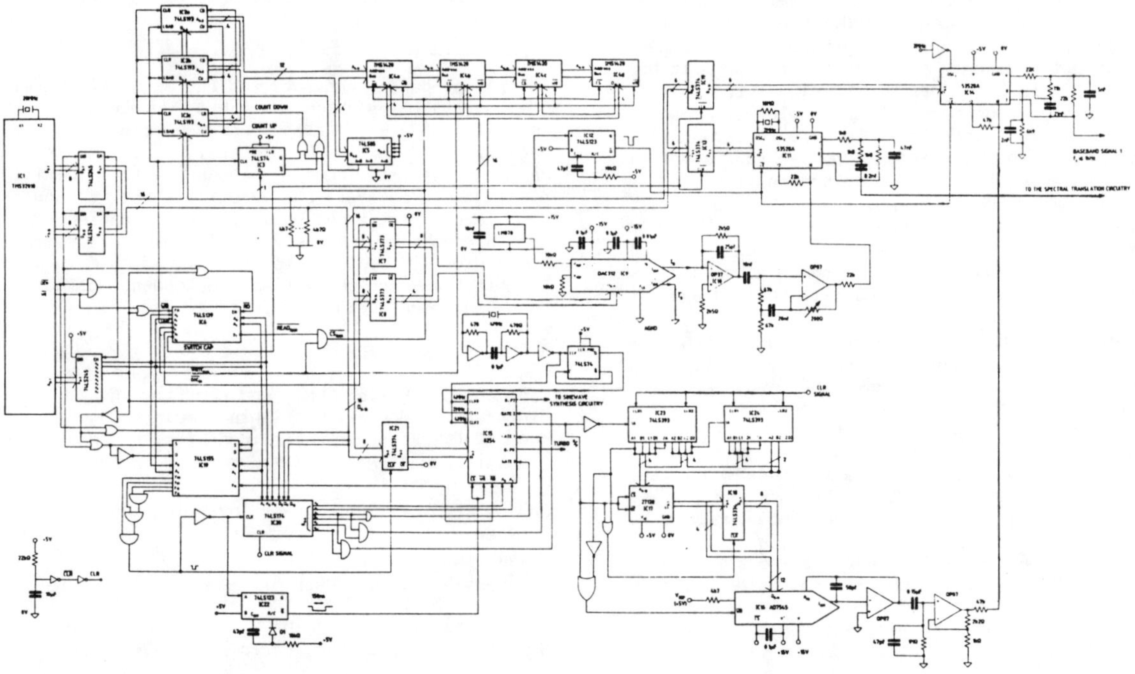

Figure 4, Sound Synthesis Prototype Board

Simulators VI

ISBN 0-911801-51-0

Fidelity rating of component modules for building distributed simulations in the national test bed

Kenneth L. Stanwood
Martin Marietta ISG
NTB Division
Falcon AFB, CO 80912-5000

ABSTRACT

The National Test Bed will provide the simulation capabilities necessary to support SDS decision makers. These capabilities will include distributed simulation to attain the level of computing power necessary to simulate the vast numbers of objects projected for SDS simulations. The distributed simulations are to be built out of building-block component modules modeling SDS elements, threats, environments, etc. A number of issues arise when trying to connect these component modules into a single, credible simulation. One of these issues is the fidelity of the component modules. This paper presents a method for describing the fidelity of these components so they may be appropriately pieced together into a distributed simulation.

INTRODUCTION

The National Test Bed (NTB) is being developed as a basis for providing and bringing together capabilities for simulating the various aspects of the Strategic Defense System (SDS). A proposed solution for providing the NTB's simulation capabilities is a distributed simulation framework, which will bring together the computing power necessary to simulate the vast numbers of objects and events involved in an SDS simulation.

Large distributed simulations will be varied to represent different candidate SDS architectures by swapping in and out simulation component modules which are themselves simulations of various candidate elements and functions of the SDS architectures. These component modules represent such architectural building blocks as weapons, sensors, communications systems, and battle management (BM) algorithms. Other simulation component modules which will be interchanged to produce variations in experiments are environments, phenomenology, and engagement models.

The component modules of a distributed simulation interact in a variety of ways. Many of these interactions can be ensured by enforcement of the simulation interface standards built into the NTB's simulation framework. For example, the simulation framework will require the use of Earth Centered Inertial (ECI) coordinates in position data crossing interfaces.

Other interactions are much harder to enforce. For example, the data received by a battle management (BM) routine doing cross-correlation of sensor data must come from sensor component modules using compatible algorithms and assumptions to ensure the BM routine produce valid results. For interactions such as the indirect interaction of the data from different sensor models, guidelines and procedures must be developed to help ensure the interoperability of the component module set chosen for a distributed simulation.

EFFECTS OF FIDELITY ON COMPONENT MODULE INTEROPERABILITY AND SIMULATION CREDIBILITY

To clarify what is presented below, this section starts with some definitions. The reference authority for each definition follows it in brackets.

a. accuracy -- the degree of conformity of a measure to a standard or a true value. [WOO]

b. aggregation -- the collecting of units or parts into a whole. [WOO]

c. compatibility -- two systems are deemed compatible if they are capable of exchanging data. [JCS]

d. detail -- a part considered or requiring to be considered separately from the whole. [WOO]

e. fidelity -- 1) accuracy in details [WOO]; 2) the degree to which a model reproduces the behavior of the modeled object. [MMC]

f. interoperability -- two systems are deemed interoperable if they are compatible and capable of mutually utilizing the data exchanged. [JCS]

g. precision -- 1) the accuracy (as in binary or decimal places) with which a number can be represented. [WOO]; 2) the degree of refinement with which an operation is performed or a measurement is stated. [WOO]

h. scope -- the extent of treatment, activity, or influence. [WOO]

From these definitions we can see that the scope of a component module determines what details it will include. The precision of inputs, outputs, and calculations affects its accuracy. The details included within its scope and the aggregation of those details determine its fidelity. Higher fidelity is expected to lead to higher accuracy, but must be verified to do so. Fidelity itself is relative and difficult to measure because there is no real-world SDS to compare against. Later in this paper we will present a method of describing the fidelity of simulation component modules.

Within the NTB, fidelity affects the credibility of a simulation even more than normal. The NTB will operate in an environment which allows a somewhat free exchange of standard component modules with hardware-in-the-loop (HWIL) and software-in-the-loop (SWIL) experiments. Component modules will be mixed and matched to achieve the configurations needed to support the particular experiments. Component module interoperability is essential for lessening the complexity of the verification and validation of simulations and experiments built by mixing and matching components. Component modules which are not appropriately matched may cause errors in design, assumption, and confidence. While properly matching component modules does not eliminate these problems, it lessens them.

The SDI effort must simulate the individual operations of architecture components and their interaction between themselves and other SDS elements. The key architectural components, and some of their fidelity considerations are:

a. Platforms -- A platform is a component on which one or more of the other elements can be placed. The manner in which power and other environmental attributes will be built into the platform will affect the number of elements which can be placed on the platform and the degree in which those elements can operate.

b. Sensors -- The sensor is the component which is used to sense or acquire a target. This acquisition can occur in either the pre-boost, boost, post-boost, mid-course or terminal phases. The accuracy of the sensor is affected by such things as the specific sensor type, sensor-target geometry, target background and other environmental characteristics.

c. Communications -- Once a sensor has located a target, data about that target may be passed to BM/C^2 modules, the central control center, and weapons. The ability of the sensors, weapons, and other control elements to communicate with one another is a major SDS interoperability issue. Types of antennae, signal propagation within space and space-to-ground, and the effects of jamming and nuclear detonation will all have to be analyzed and worked into the final simulation model.

d. Weapons -- Weapons are the components that engage threats. Once given a signal from the sensor and/or control center, weapons may have to point towards the target, fire, and assess whether a kill occurred (this may sometimes be a sensor function). Because of the different types of weapons, the number of controllers for a particular weapon, and the various distributions of functions to components, care must be taken to assure that interoperability between the weapon, the sensor and the controller is maintained.

e. Battle Management/Command, Control, and Communications (BM/C^2) -- BM/C^2 component modules perform the control of other component modules and process data received from the other component modules. In some instances, their functionality may be built into the other component modules rather than being modeled separately. BM/C^2 algorithms are the most likely piece of an architecture to be diversely emulated.

Another group of component modules provides the simulation services for the execution of end-to-end architecture simulations. This group includes such things as threat models, environmental models, scene generators, and engagement models.

A very high-fidelity presentation of the architecture of the defense system components would greatly increase the credibility of NTB results. However, very detailed simulations of some system components may be too time-consuming or resource consuming to be practically included in a full scale experiment, especially one with real-time HWIL or SWIL constraints. In these cases, a hierarchy of abstractions of models is needed for managing the complexity of the problem.

These models must be validated at their high-fidelity level. Once this is accomplished, higher level models may be built, abstracting the high-fidelity models while retaining sufficient accuracy. These higher level, lower fidelity models could then be used to reduce the cost of experiments. Since these models will not be as high-fidelity as their originating model, sensitivity analysis will need to be performed to determine the bounds within which they may be used without diminishing the credibility of the results obtained.

End-to-end simulations are simulations where an SDS architecture is developed out of architectural component modules (weapons, sensors, etc.), an environment is developed out of environmental component modules (threats, background environment, etc), and a simulation is run with all these components interacting. The SDS architecture designer creating an end-to-end simulation must properly balance the fidelity level of component modules used. For a given function, modules should use models of the same fidelity. Modules modeling the same function at differing fidelities could invalidate the results of the simulation. For example, a module that uses a very high-fidelity intercept algorithm to estimate where to aim a weapon at a target may cause the weapon to consistently miss, not because of an erroneous algorithm, but because the threat used a very simplistic trajectory algorithm and does not arrive quite when or where expected.

Similarly, accuracy and precision affect the interoperability of component modules. Two component modules may use the same algorithms, but if one is more precisely computed than the other, the results, especially cumulative results over time, may be incompatible. If one component module uses the results of another as its input, those results must be accurate enough for the second component module to produce valid, accurate results itself.

NTB COMPONENT MODULE FIDELITY STANDARDS

The proposed NTB Component Module Fidelity Standards provide a standard method for describing the fidelity of component modules used in simulations and experiments. This section describes this system and gives an example of its use.

Rationale

According to the NTB Technical Requirements Document [AFF], the number one threat to the NTB is anything that could compromise the technical credibility of the results of NTB simulations and experiments. If a simulation component module is labeled as high fidelity, it must be clear exactly what is meant by high fidelity for the component modeled. Exact definitions of fidelity levels and a procedure for precisely rating the fidelity of component modules is needed to help avoid attacks on the credibility of the NTB.

Method

Component modules may have some aspects that are modeled with high fidelity while simultaneously having other aspects that are modeled with much lower fidelity. Because of the need for component module interoperability, it is not descriptive enough to simply label a component module as high fidelity just because it has some high fidelity aspects, or as medium fidelity because it has both high and low fidelity aspects.

Fidelity ratings will be assigned to individual aspects of component modules so that users or automated decision aids can intelligently decide whether the pieces used to construct a simulation or experiment are interoperable with respect to fidelity. These detailed ratings provide users with a more precise rating of component module fidelity than would be attained with a single rating per component module. This, in turn, provides more credibility to the verification and validation analyses of simulations and experiments, and therefore, provides more credibility to the results of the NTB.

This proposed standard will:

a. Define standard fidelity levels and criteria for rating component modules.

b. Identify the aspects of component modules that can vary in fidelity independent of the rest of the module.

c. Provide a component module aspects versus fidelity levels matrix to be filled in with the fidelity of the various aspects of a component module.

d. Describe the criteria that the aspects identified by (b) must meet to attain each fidelity rating defined by (a).

Fidelity Rating System

For a given aspect of the world (physics, environment, etc), a component module of a simulation or experiment may:

a. Model that aspect of the world itself

b. Accept input from a component module that models that aspect, and model the effects of that aspect on the item it models

c. Totally ignore that aspect of the world.

Components must have fidelity ratings assigned to both their modeling and their use of various aspects of the world. The Fidelity Description Matrix will be structured to allow the rating of both the modeling and use. The following ratings will be used for stating the fidelity of the modeling or use of an aspect by a component:

a. E - Emulation,

b. H - High Fidelity,

c. M - Medium Fidelity,

d. L - Low Fidelity, and

e. N - Not considered by the component module.

For each aspect that can vary in fidelity, these ratings are being defined.

Aspects Varying in Fidelity

A component module may vary in fidelity in a number of aspects. These aspects are grouped into four categories:

a. Environmental Aspects

b. Physical Aspects

c. Operational Aspects

d. Mathematical/Statistical Aspects.

The Fidelity Description Matrix, shown in Figure A, shows the individual aspects that are grouped under each of these categories. This matrix is used to rate the fidelity of a component module in these individual aspects. The matrix has two sets of five columns. The first set of columns is used to rate the fidelity to which a particular aspect is modeled. The appropriate column is checked to indicate the fidelity to which the aspect is modeled. The second set of columns is used to specify the fidelity of input expected by the component module. The appropriate column is checked to indicate the fidelity to which a specific aspect must have been modeled to provide input information to the component module. For component modules that are able to accept input of varying fidelity for an aspect, these columns imply the fidelity at which the information is used.

It is expected that the fidelity ratings for component modules available to the NTB users will be stored in a tool called the Simulation Interoperability Database (SIDB) for on-line access by NTB users.

Example Criteria

Earth gravity is one aspect of the world that many component models will need to consider. For example, models calculating ballistic missile or satellite trajectories must take gravity into account. For some component models, a low fidelity earth gravity model may be adequate; while some component modules will need much higher fidelity models. [MIT] suggests four standard earth gravity models which we rate here.

a. Low : Spherical Earth -- This is the simplest earth gravity model and uses the spherically symmetrical earth gravity field. This is recommended for only low fidelity or model prototyping needs.

b. Medium : Oblate Earth -- Accounting for the oblateness of the earth produces the most pronounced variation from the spherical symmetry of the earth's gravitational field. The oblateness of the earth causes a dipole moment that can effect even low and medium fidelity calculations.

	Fidelity Modeled					Fidelity of Input Required				
Features	Emulation	High	Medium	Low	Not modeled	Emulation	High	Medium	Low	Not modeled
Environmental Aspects										
Gravity										
Nuclear Environment										
Atmospheric Conditions										
Magnetic Environment										
Propagation										
Atmospheric Effects										
Solar Radiation Effects										
Jamming										
Blasts										
Physical Aspects										
Trajectories										
Object Granularity										
Threat Aggregation										
Decoy Representation										
Footprint (signature)										
IR										
Visual										
Radar										
Effects of Obstacles										
Kill Assessment										
Damage Assessment										
Manuvering										
Hardening										
Weight										
Layout										
Operational Characteristics										
Battle Management Algorithms										
Standard Methods of Operation										
Implications of Damage										
Mathematical/Statistical Aspects										
Precision of Algorithms										
Probability of Occurrence of Non-deterministic Events										

Figure A: Fidelity Description Matrix

c. High : Few Moments -- The gravitational potential of the earth at a distance, r, from its center and at a geocentric latitude, ∂, and a geocentric east longitude, μ, is represented by the expression:

$$U = \frac{u}{r}\left\{ 1 + \sum_{n=2}^{\infty} \left(\frac{a_e}{r}\right)^n \sum_{m=0}^{n} P_{nm} (\sin \partial) [C_{nm} \cos m\mu + S_{nm} \sin m\mu] \right\}$$

∂ and μ are referred to the true equator and the Greenwich Meridian respectively. P_{nm} is the associated Legendre function (of the first kind) of degree n and order m. C_{nm} and S_{nm} are the harmonic coefficients for degree n and order m.

The NSSC geopotential models range from 6th to 16th order. Not all terms are significant for all satellites. For example, for satellite orbits in decay, the higher-order terms are masked by atmospheric density variations and attitude changes. [NTP]

d. Emulation : World Geodetic System ,1984 (WGS84) -- Standard geopotential models are provided by WGS84 which describe the gravitational potential of the earth. This is considered the highest fidelity earth gravity model currently available. Virtually every known variation in the earth's gravitational field is addressed in this model which extends the Few Moments model category to order 23. These higher-order coefficients do have uses (see [NTP]).

REFERENCES

[AFF] Air Force ESD; "Technical Requirements for the National Test Bed Integration Contract"; F19628-88-C-0012 Attachment 1; Nov 1987.

[JCS] Joint Chiefs of Staff; "Department of Defense Dictionary of Military and Associated Terms"; JCS-Pub-1; Government Printing Office; Jan 1972.

[MMC] Martin Marietta ISG; "NTB Interoperability Master Plan"; Aug 1988 (Preliminary Draft).

[MIT] MITRE Corp.; "NTB Interface Guidelines Whitepaper"; Feb 1988 (draft).

[NTP] North American Aerospace Command, SPADOC Computation Center; "Computer Program Product Specification Mathematical Foundation for SCC Astrodynamic Theory"; NORAD Technical Publication TP SCC 008; Apr 1982.

[WOO] Woolf, Henry Bosley; *Webster's New Collegiate Dictionary*; G. & C. Merriam Co.; Springfield, MA; 1979.

BIOGRAPHY

Mr. Stanwood received his M.S. in Computer Science from Stanford University in Dec '86 and his B.S. in Mathematical Sciences from Oregon State University in June '83. He has worked for Martin Marietta ISG on the National Test Bed integration contract since Feb '88. He has worked interoperability analysis for all aspects of the NTB and authored the NTB Interoperability Master Plan.

Prior to working for Martin Marietta, Mr. Stanwood spent 5 years with GTE Government Systems where he designed and implemented user interfaces for signal processing systems, performed modeling of signal processing and communications systems, and led research into the application of visual programming to simulation.

Mr. Stanwood has two previous papers published. Both deal with the application of graphics and visual programming to simulation. He has also participated as a session panelist to discuss the use of graphics workstations in the simulation of computer networks.

Simulators VI

ISBN 0-911801-51-0

A hydraulic transient analysis tool for power plant piping systems

Stephen R. Bonema, P.E.
Stoner Associates, Inc.
P.O. Box 86
Carlisle, PA 17013

and

Roger W. Young, P.E.
New York Power Authority
123 Main Street
White Plains, NY 10601

ABSTRACT

A hydraulic transient computer simulation procedure is presented which is capable of simulating the waterhammer response of power plant liquid piping systems under a variety of forcing functions. The procedure, which models most current pipeline hardware, is suitable for simulating events such as valve operation, pump start-up and shutdown, and the dynamic action of PID controllers.

Application of the procedure in an actual analysis of a condensate polisher and feedwater system is discussed. In addition to a presentation of simulation results, the following issues are covered:

1. Data acquisition and schematization of the system.
2. Simulation of waterhammer events in a non-uniform density liquid with a single-density computer procedure.
3. Model representation of various boundary conditions such as feedwater headers, polisher vessels, tanks, and steam generators.
4. Modeling of dynamic controllers which control valve operation and pump speed.

NOMENCLATURE

a	acoustic wavespeed
C_v	valve flow coefficient
C_{vo}	wide open valve flow coefficient
g	gravitational constant
ΔH	change in head
K	head drop coefficient
L	pipe length
N	number of pipe reaches
Q	volumetric flow rate
t_v	time from the initiation of check valve opening
V	fluid velocity
Δx	pipe reach length
z	elevation
ρ	fluid density
τ	dimensionless valve position, C_v/C_{vo}

INTRODUCTION

A hydraulic transient event occurs in a piping system whenever there is a sudden change in fluid velocity. The two most common causes of such an event are valve and pump operations. Considering the complexity of valving and pumps in power plant piping systems, it is no surprise that hydraulic transients and waterhammer are familiar terms to engineers who design and operate such systems. Much research and development has been done in the area of unsteady flow in recent years as the awareness about the damaging effects of hydraulic transients has increased among the power engineering community. From this work, sophisticated fluid flow simulation software has evolved which is being utilized by engineers to evaluate the effect of waterhammer on piping systems and to determine equipment and operations modifications to eliminate or minimize the effects of upset events.

One software product that is suited for the simulation of hydraulic transients in a complex system such as a feedwater system is LIQT® (LIQuid Transient). This general purpose procedure is capable of simulating unsteady flow behavior in single phase liquid piping systems comprised of pipes, valves, pumps, turbines, surge control devices, and dynamic controllers. Upset events such as valve operation, pump start and stops, and controller malfunction can be simulated in an interactive environment which allows the user to make observations and design and operations decisions as the simulation unfolds.

CASE STUDY

Presentation of the program's modeling capabilities is made in a discussion of a hydraulic transient analysis that was performed on the condensate polisher and feedwater systems in a nuclear power plant. The presentation of the modeling capabilities is complimented by a review of the modeling approach used in the analysis.

The analysis was performed as a means of determining potential surge pressures following several hypothetical upset events. A simplified line-circle schematic of the systems is presented in Figure 1. Listed on the schematic are the major components of the systems.

MODELING

Schematization

The solution procedure used by LIQT is based on the solution of the partial differential equations that govern unsteady fluid flow in pipelines. These equations are converted by the method of characteristics into ordinary differential equations which are integrated to yield finite differential equations. A complete treatment of the solution procedure is given by Wylie and Streeter (2). This widely used solution technique requires that all pipes in a hydraulic system model be divided into an integral number of reaches. Transient calculations are performed at each end of a reach at a specified time interval. The relationship between the time interval, which is common throughout the system, and a pipe reach length is:

$$\Delta t = \frac{\Delta x}{a} = \frac{L}{aN}$$

Selection of Δt and Δx requires careful consideration since the accuracy of the computer model is determined by the size of Δt and Δx. There are some general rules for the selection of Δt and Δx but there is no substitute for experience.

For the polisher and feedwater systems, a Δt = .005 seconds was selected. Since the computed acoustic wavespeeds ranged from 3500 ft/sec to 4500 ft/sec, the corresponding reach lengths varied from 17.5 to 22.5 ft. Obviously, the actual pipe runs are not integral multiples of the calculated reach lengths. There are a number of horizontal and vertical runs of pipes less than 20 ft in length which are separated by equipment such as tees, elbows, and valves. By equivalencing groups of pipes or equipment into single units, eliminating small pipe volumes and applying small adjustments to acoustic wavespeeds and pipe lengths, a simplified, economical, yet hydraulically representative model of the polisher and feedwater systems was constructed.

Fluid

The temperature of the water in the feedwater and polisher systems varies from 92°F at the condenser hotwell to 427°F at the steam generators. Along with this change in temperature is a variation in several liquid properties which are relevant to the transient behavior of the systems. These properties are density, vapor pressure, and the bulk modulus.

Different vapor pressures and acoustic wavespeeds (wavespeed is a function of bulk modulus and density) for a liquid can be specified with LIQT in different temperature zones; however, the program currently has two limitations that are important relative to the analysis.

One limitation is that LIQT considers only a single density value for all liquid in the modeled system. Webb and Caves (1) have shown that this limitation can be overcome by applying adjustments to model data. With this correction technique, a single density program such as LIQT can be used to accurately model systems where the density variations exist in space only. The adjustments applied cannot compensate for a temporal variation in density at a single point. Because of the rapid nature of hydraulic transients in the feedwater system analyzed, it was accepted that the temporal variation of fluid temperature during an upset event would have a negligible effect on the modeled transient response.

The correction technique first involves selecting a reference density (ρ') upon which the hydraulic calculations are to be based. In piping where the density (ρ), differs from ρ', the following adjustments are applied:

1. Elevation: $z' = z\rho/\rho'$
2. Pipe friction: $f' = f\rho'/\rho$
3. Valve loss coefficient: $K' = K\rho'/\rho$
4. Pump flow: $Q' = Q\rho/\rho'$
5. Pump head: $\Delta H' = \Delta H\rho/\rho'$

When the above corrections are applied, the volumetric flow rate computed at any location in the model can be multiplied by the reference density to obtain the true mass flow rate. The calculated pressures are the true pressures and, therefore, require no adjustment. To eliminate unnecessary confusion regarding the mass and volumetric flow rates, LIQT is capable of reporting both types of flow.

The second modeling limitation relates to the method used by the program for conditions where two phase flow (vapor-liquid) exists. LIQT computes the time varying size of a vapor cavity that exists when water pressure drops to vapor pressure and computes the pressure pulsation that occurs when the cavity collapses. However, in a situation involving distributed vaporous cavitation, the program does not account for the simultaneous flow of vapor and liquid nor the associated effects of such flow on density, friction, acoustic wavespeed, and momentum. In the program, vapor cavities are limited to discrete computational sections with pure liquid in the reaches. Realistic pressure and flow modeling can be achieved provided that the volume of vapor remains relatively small compared to the liquid volume in the reach.

Piping

Even though the pipe material and wall thickness varied throughout the systems, all the pipes were modeled as clean commercial steel pipe with an absolute roughness equal to .00015 ft and a Young's modulus of elasticity of 30×10^6 psi. The determination of roughness was based on visual inspection of the inside surfaces of pipes in several different locations.

Correct modeling of the piping material was important for several reasons. The pipe material and the wall thickness affect the elasticity of the pipe wall and thus affect the acoustic wavespeed. A higher wavespeed generally increases the magnitude of pressure surges. In addition, the smoother the pipe wall, the higher the fluid velocity will be for a given pressure drop across a pipe. The Darcy-Weisbach pipe friction model was used by LIQT to compute pipe friction loss. During the steady-state balance of the systems, LIQT developed pipe friction factors based on pipe roughness and the Reynolds number. These friction factors were used during the transient phase of the simulation.

Pumps

The polisher and feedwater systems contains four sets of pumps. These are the condensate, condensate booster, heater drain, and boiler feed pumps.

Pump head, flow, and efficiency data was obtained for forward flow/forward speed conditions. For pump data input, LIQT requires forward flow/forward speed, reverse flow/reverse speed, and forward flow/reverse speed data. Head-flow-torque-speed data for the two latter conditions are supplied by the program by substituting experimental data from a pump of similar specific speed. Results obtained during the time interval when a pump is experiencing reverse flow or speed are therefore based on the characteristics of a similar unit.

Valves

In complex piping systems such as the ones analyzed, the pressure losses associated with components such as elbows, tees, and valves can comprise a significant portion of the overall system pressure drop. In the analysis, substantial effort was made to ensure that all valves were accurately represented in the simulation model. There were two ways in which valves were represented in the model. The first was an explicit representation where a particular valve was modeled as a separate component. This was done for major valves such as check, relief, and feedwater regulating valves. Other groups of valves and pressure loss components were combined into minor loss elements which use the equation $\Delta H = KV^2/2g$ for pressure drop-flow computations.

The four feedwater regulating valves were modeled as ideal regulating valves which could change position instantaneously to maintain a specified flowrate even as the inlet pressure to the valves changed. Since the change in pressure was gradual in the simulations, the valve model was deemed appropriate.

Check valves were modeled to close in one computational time increment (.005 seconds) when flow through the valves reversed. If the flow direction turned positive again, a check valve would begin a .4 second opening. The valve position vs. time relationship used was:

$$\tau = (t_v/.4)^2$$

Polisher Vessels and Post Filters

Within the condensate polishing system there are two sets of polishing vessels: the Graver condensate polisher vessels and the post filters. The pressure-flow characteristics of these components were modeled with minor loss elements. Based on steady-state data obtained in the field, a C_v value was computed for each of the vessels. During a transient simulation, flow and pressure drop across each vessel were computed based on the C_v value.

Feedwater Heaters

The feedwater heaters in the feedwater system are U tube type heaters which consist of bundles of small diameter tubes. In the LIQT simulation model, each heater was modeled as a set of parallel tubes with an absolute roughness of .00015 ft and a wavespeed ranging from 3900 ft/sec to 4600 ft/sec.

Boiler Feed Pump Control System

The speed control system for the two turbine driven main boiler feed pumps (#31 and #32) consists of an electrical control system and an oil control system which operates the valves that control steam flow to the turbine drives. Because of the limited data availability for the oil system, this portion of the control system was not modeled. To compensate for the fluid inertia and servomotor response in the oil system, the time rate of change of output from the electrical system was limited.

Figure 2 is a schematic of the electrical control system. The prototype system, which consists of a series of transmitters and PID controllers, controls boiler feed pump speed to maintain a constant differential between the boiler feed pump discharge pressure and the main steam header pressure. Boiler feed pump suction pressure is also maintained. For the short transients analyzed it was assumed that main steam header pressure remained constant. Therefore, only boiler feed pump suction and discharge pressures were modeled as inputs to the boiler feed pump control system. In the model when the discharge pressure drops below the setpoint value, the speed of both pumps was increased. When suction pressure dropped below its setpoint for a particular speed, the pump speed was ramped down to bring the suction pressure back up.

To simplify the controller modeling process, several assumptions regarding steam flow were made:

1. The main steam header pressure remained constant during a short hydraulic transient event.
2. Main steam flow remained constant during such an event.
3. Main steam flow corresponded to 100% load.

The dynamic controller modeling capability within LIQT permitted an accurate representation of the electrical control system consisting of PID controllers with multiple input signals and low/high select switches.

Other Equipment

The steam generator blowdown heat exchanger was modeled as a minor loss element in a fashion similar to the polisher vessels. Because of their small size and relatively low flow rates, losses through the steam jet air ejector condensers and gland steam condenser were considered to be insignificant as were their volumes. They modeled only to accommodate nearby fitting losses.

Components containing significant liquid volumes were treated as constant pressure boundary conditions. It was assumed that the duration of the modeled transient events would be such that there would not be a large change in liquid volume during a particular event. Components falling under this category included the condensers, drains collecting tank, heater drain tank, and steam generators.

MODEL CALIBRATION

Following the completion of data acquisition, input data file preparation and a quality assurance review of the data collection process and related calculations, model calibration was performed. Calibration involved the adjustment of minor losses within the model to match the pressure-flow conditions observed by the client in the field for 100% load. Since the minor loss coefficients were obtained from handbooks and represented generic values, it was determined that the adjustment of these values would be the most logical approach in obtaining a close correlation of model-prototype pressure-flow data.

Calibration and a steady-state balance of the model were obtained using the steady-state front end capability in LIQT. Listed below are some of the steady-state conditions that were obtained:

Mass flowrate from condenser hotwells	=	10036605	lbs/hr
Mass flowrate from heater drain tanks	=	3460149	lbs/hr
Mass flowrate into steam generators	=	13452898	lbs/hr
Mass flowrate into seal water ducts on boiler feed pumps	=	43857	lbs/hr
Condensate pump suction pressure	=	-11.7	psig
Condensate pump discharge pressure	=	608	psig
Boiler feed pump suction pressure	=	360	psig
Boiler feed pump discharge pressure	=	1076	psig
Pressure drop across polisher vessels	=	33.7	psig
Pressure drop across post filters	=	41.4	psig
Pressure drop across the SGBHX-3	=	7.1	psig
Speed of BFP #31	=	4895	rpm
Speed of BFP #32	=	4850	rpm
Initial position of feedwater regulating valves	=	79%	open

HYDRAULIC TRANSIENT ANALYSIS

Several hydraulic transient simulations were made on the polisher and feedwater system to predict the unsteady flow response following hypothetical waterhammer events. Two of the simulations are discussed below.

Trip of Condensate Pump

The first simulation considered the trip of one of the two condensate pumps during 100% load operation. As the pump spun down, the drop in discharge pressure (Figure 3) caused the pump check valve to close at t = .7 seconds. At approximately the same time, a drop in discharge pressure at the boiler feed pumps occurred. The boiler feed pump control system responded by increasing the speed of both pumps (Figure 4). At t = 1.1 seconds, the low select feature of the boiler feed pump control system switched pump speed control to the low suction cutback controller as the suction pressure (Figure 5) dropped below the setpoint for the current pump speeds. Pump speed was reduced until the suction pressure was brought back up to a desirable value.

The drop in feedwater system pressure caused the feedwater regulating valves to open in an attempt to maintain the initial feedwater flowrate. The valves went fully open at 3.2 seconds.

Pressure throughout the system remained at or below the initial values.

Closure of Feedwater Regulating Valve and Trip of Boiler Feed Pumps

A 2.5 second closure of the feedwater regulating valves coupled with the trip of the boiler feed pumps was simulated. Flow through the pumps was sharply reduced within three seconds. The pressure pulse created by the valve closure and pump trip forced the heater drain pump check valves to close. The valves then reopened and closed several times (Figure 6).

The positive pressure wave created by the valve closure propagated back to the condensate pumps within a second of valve closure. The condensate and condensate booster pumps could not produce enough head to keep their check valves open. The valves lifted only slightly off their seats during the remainder of the simulation.

Between the condensate pumps and boiler feed pumps the peak pressure was 950 psig at the suction side at the boiler feed pumps (Figure 7). Between the boiler feed pumps and the steam generators, the peak pressure was 1635 psig near the feedwater regulating valves (Figure 8).

CONCLUSION

This analysis showed that a close correlation could be obtained between the results predicted by the LIQT simulation procedure and the pressure-flow values observed in the field. Attention to detail during model preparation and calibration of the piping system consisting of more than 6000 ft of pipe, over 500 minor loss components, and specialty equipments was the key to obtaining sound simulation results.

Accurate analysis of hydraulic transient events in a power plant piping system with an analysis procedure such as LIQT can be done but requires a thorough understanding of hydraulic transients, modeling practices, and program limitations by the engineer performing the analysis.

REFERENCES

1. Webb, S.W. and J.L. Caves. 1981. "Fluid Transient Analysis in Pipelines With Nonuniform Liquid Density." ASME Journal of Fluids Engineering (December): 423-428.

2. Wylie, E.B. and V.L. Streeter. 1982. Fluid Transients. FEB Press, Ann Arbor, MI.

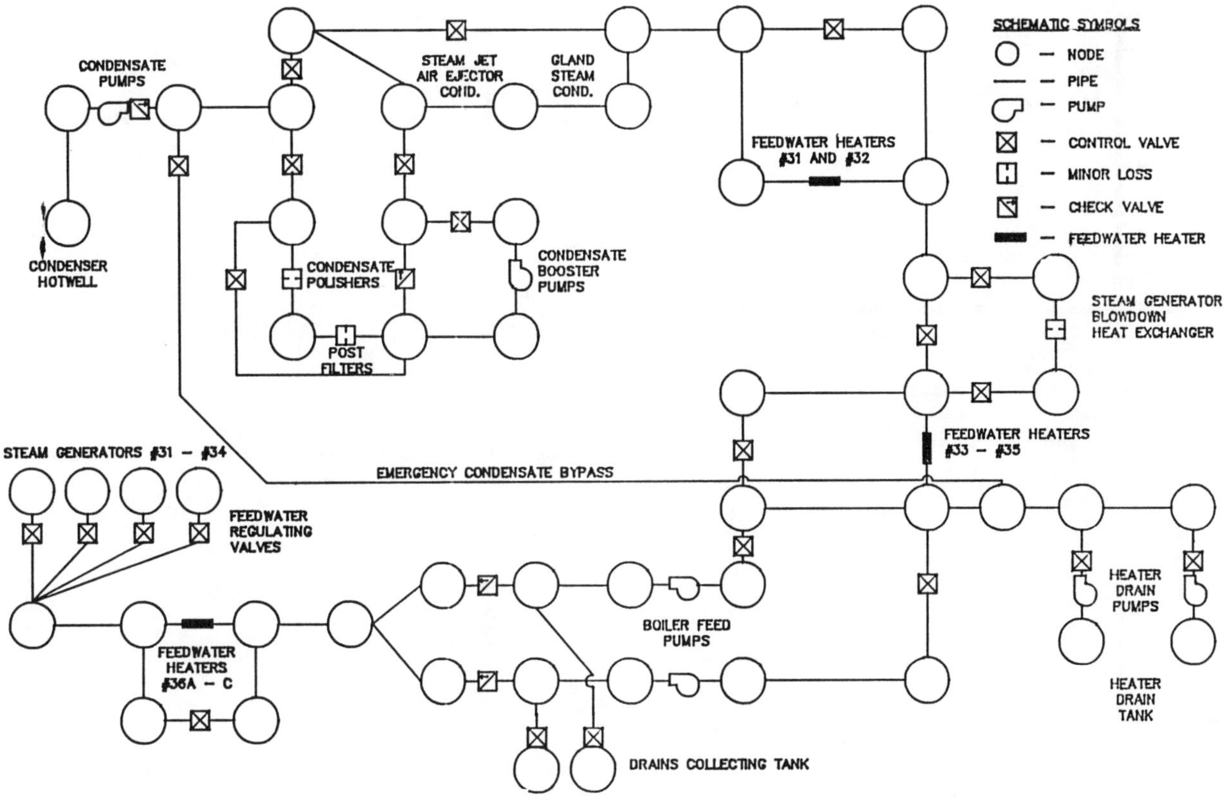

Figure 1 Condensate Polisher and Condensate Feedwater Systems Schematic

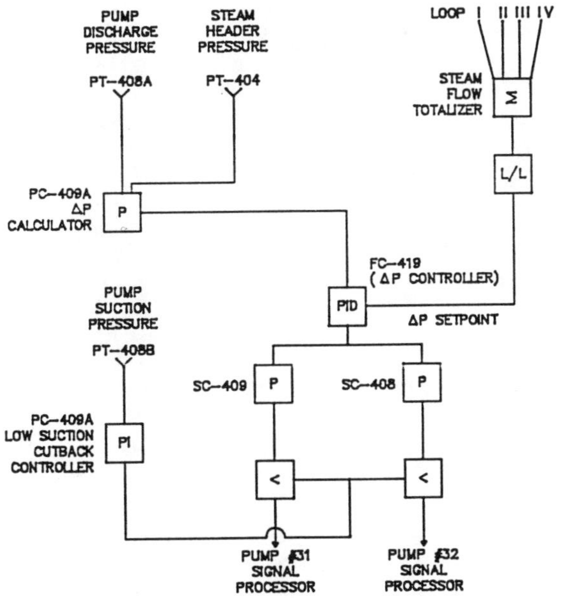

Figure 2 Boiler Feed Pump Electrical Control System Schematic

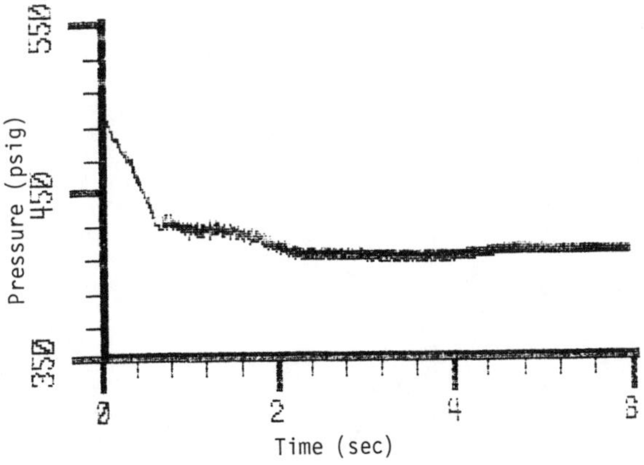

Figure 3 Condensate Pump Discharge Pressure

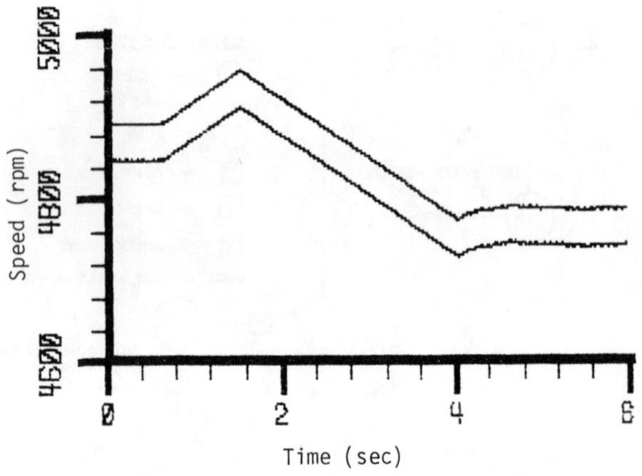

Figure 4 Boiler Feed Pump Speed

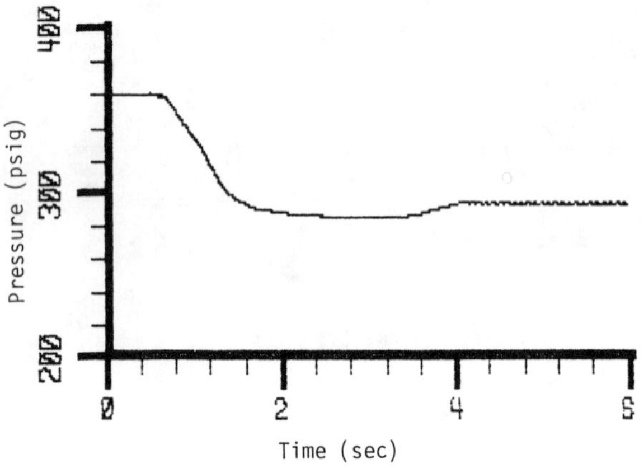

Figure 5 Boiler Feed Pump Suction Pressure

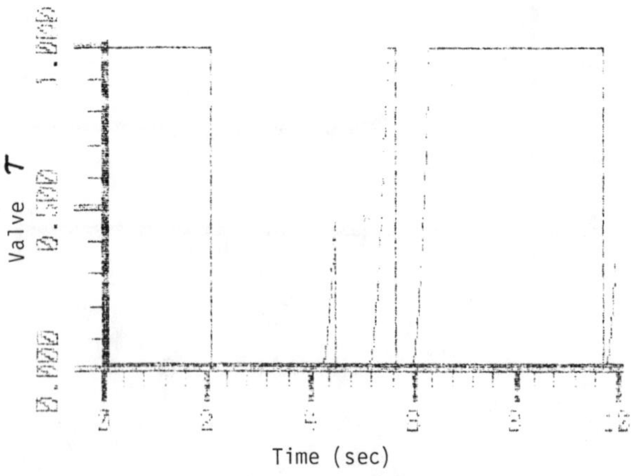

Figure 6 Heater Drain Pump Check Valve Behavior

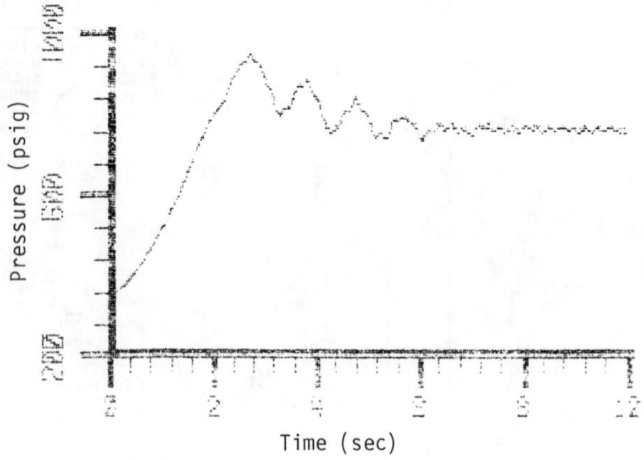

Figure 7 Boiler Feed Pump Suction Pressure

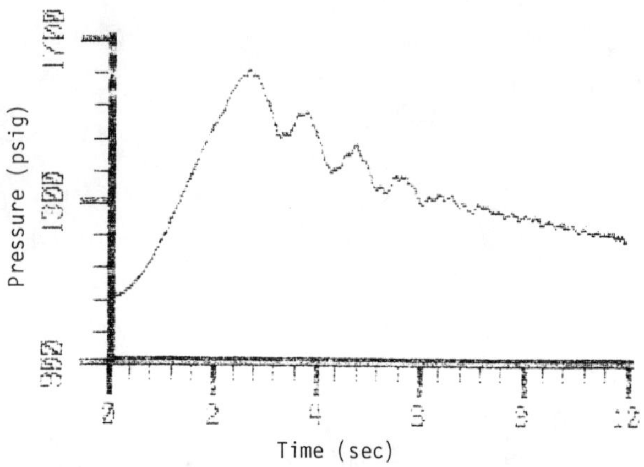

Figure 8 Pressure at Feedwater Regulating Valves

Simulators VI

ISBN 0-911801-51-0

An EPRI methodology for determining and monitoring simulator operating limits

R. Eichelberg, M. Pellechi, B. Wolf
General Physics Corporation
6700 Alexander Bell Drive
Columbia, Maryland 21046

and

Robert Colley
Electric Power Research Institute
3412 Hillview Avenue
Palo Alto, California 94303

This paper is extracted from an Electric Power Research Institute sponsored report to be published in 1989.

Abstract

Of paramount concern to nuclear utilities today, is whether their plant-referenced simulator(s) comply with ANSI/ANS 3.5-1985.Of special interest is Section 4.3 of the Standard which requires, in part, "that a means be provided to alert the instructor when certain parameters approach values indicative of events beyond the implemented model or known plant behavior". EPRI established Research Project 2054-2 to develop a comprehensive plan for determining, monitoring, and implementing simulator operating limits.

As part of the project, a survey was conducted to identify the current/anticipated approach each of the sampled utilities was using to meet the requirements of Section 4.3. A preliminary methodology was drafted and host utilities interviewed. The interview process led to redefining the methodology.

The scope of this paper will cover the objectives of the EPRI project, survey responses, overview of the methodology, resource requirements and conclusions. It will also provide readers with a discussion of considerations when using the EPRI-sponsored methodology.

INTRODUCTION

Nuclear power plant training simulators have received increased attention in the last few years because of the number of nuclear power plant simulators in operation and because of regulatory concern about the fidelity of these simulators when used in operator licensing tests. Revisions to 10 CFR 55.45 (1) require operator licensing tests to be conducted in a simulation facility approved by the Nuclear Regulatory Commission (NRC). Regulatory Guide 1.149, Nuclear Power Plant Simulation Facilities for Use in Operator License Examinations (2), effectively endorses the requirements of ANSI/ANS-3.5-1985, Nuclear Power Plant Simulators for Use in Operator Training (3), as one method acceptable to the NRC staff for obtaining approval of a simulation facility for use in operator licensing tests.

Of paramount concern to utilities is whether their simulator(s) comply with ANSI/ANS-3.5-1985. Of special interest is Section 4.3 of ANSI/ANS-3.5-1985 which states, "Mathematical equations may be simplified to meet real time simulation requirements. In addition, it is sometimes possible to create events on a simulator which progress beyond design limits. Examples of such events include primary containment failure, gross core damage, and reactor coolant system two-phase flow." The Standard also requires, in part, "that a means be provided to alert the instructor when certain parameters approach values indicative of events beyond the implemented model or known plant behavior".

Past EPRI projects have developed a methodology and plan for simulator qualification, and a method for prioritizing simulator discrepancies. To aid utilities in meeting the NRC requirements for notifying the simulator instructor when the simulator is approaching its operating limits (as expressed in Section 4.3 of ANSI/ANS-3.5-1985) EPRI established Research Project 2054-2 to develop a comprehensive plan for determination of simulator operating limits.

OBJECTIVES

The overall objective of the Simulator Operating Limits Methodology Program was to provide procedures detailing an efficient methodology for implementing the requirements of Section 4.3 of ANSI/ANS-3.5-1985 for Simulator Operating Limits.

This objective was satisfied by:

- o Providing guidelines for alerting the simulator instructor of the simulator approaching a Simulator Operating Limit.
- o Providing guidelines for implementing the Simulator Operating Limits.
- o Providing forms for documenting the Simulator Operating Limits, method(s) used to monitor, and method(s) used to alert the instructor.

The project was performed as a joint effort with Georgia Power Company, Northeast Utilities Service Company, and Washington Public Power Supply System. The research was initiated by sending survey forms to approximately 20 utilities requesting their current/anticipated approach to meeting the requirements of Section 4.3 of ANSI/ANS-3.5-1985. A preliminary methodology was drafted and sent to three host utilities for their review/comment. After visiting three host utilities (four simulator groups) it became apparent that modifications to the procedures would be necessary to make them more usable. Recommendations were made and discussed with the host utilities. The procedures were re-written to ensure compatibility with current utility practices.

OVERVIEW OF SIMULATOR OPERATING LIMITS

Simulator Operating Limits are limitations placed on simulator operations to prevent exceeding a plant design or simulator model limit. Imposition of these limitations may be by computer software or administrative procedures.

Simulator Operating Limits may be imposed based on plant design limits. A plant design limit is a restraint placed on a plant system or component to maintain that system or component within its design boundaries. An example would be a BWR Reactor Coolant System pressure that should not exceed 1325 psig. Simulator Operating Limits may also be imposed due to model limits. A model limit is a restraint placed on a system or component replicated by a math-based software program (model) due to restrictions, simplifications, or deficiencies in the software program. An example is that melting of the fuel is not currently simulated.

The discussion of simulator operating limits is divided into four sections corresponding to the following major areas:

- o Rationale for the Imposition of Simulator Operating Limits
- o Determination of Simulator Operating Limits
- o Monitoring Simulator Operating Limits
- o Alerting the Instructors

RATIONALE FOR THE IMPOSITION OF SIMULATOR OPERATING LIMITS

Simulator Operating Limits are required by Section 4.3 of ANSI/ANS-3.5-1985; which states, "In order to avoid negative training...administrative controls or other means shall be provided to alert the instructor when certain parameters approach values indicative of events beyond the implemented model or known plant behavior." Thus, simulator operating limits are imposed to avoid the negative training which could result from simulator operations during events which progress beyond plant design limits and/or model limits. For example, after an instructor inserts a malfunction, an operator performs an evolution on the simulator which results in reactor pressure exceeding the plant design limit. The operator then recovers the plant (simulator) from this condition to a steady state condition. Exceeding a plant design limit does not necessarily indicate that plant component will actually fail. It is simply a limit placed on the component by the manufacturer which specifies the design capacity. Exceeding the limit would result in a prolonged analysis to determine the decrease in useful plant life or may actually cause a failure and be unrealistic. If the operator believes his actions and the simulator response to be correct, then negative training has occurred. This is because the operator, using what he has learned from the training session, may perform the same evolution in the plant believing he can allow reactor pressure to exceed plant design pressure and carry out the actions that he performed on the simulator without adverse effects.

Simulator Operating Limits may also be imposed to avoid a reduction in credibility of the simulator. A simulator which is allowed to operate beyond the plant design limits for the reference plant provides little confidence to the operators (with respect to the credibility of the simulator). Any question of simulator credibility detracts from the practical training an operator receives. For example, if an the operator sees the simulator perform in a manner he knows the reference plant cannot due to plant design limits, then his belief in the expected simulator response to his actions is diminished. The simulator may in fact respond correctly and provide proper indications for the actions taken because the plant may be capable of surviving conditions beyond the guaranteed design conditions. The problem is due to the lack of confidence in the simulator. The operator does not believe what he is seeing during the training evolution and therefore does not learn from the training session.

DETERMINATION OF SIMULATOR OPERATING LIMITS

Simulator operating limits could be imposed on all plant design limits. This approach would appear to be a very easy and cost effective method for determining the limits. Therefore, one might conclude that this is the best approach.

However, when one considers all plant design limits, a different conclusion may be drawn. First, to impose all plant design limits places limitations on the scope of simulation. For example, imposing a simulator operating limit based on the design pressure of the turbine lube oil piping when the turbine lube oil piping is not simulated would place a limitation on the ability to make simplifications to the turbine lube oil model. Secondly to impose simulator operating limits on all plant design limits may require extensive modeling of plant systems that are not used or required to meet the needs of a utility's licensed operator training program.

Simulator operating limits could be imposed only on those items listed in Section 4.3 of ANSI/ANS-3.5-1985, "Conditions to be considered are:

1) Primary Containment pressure greater than design limit;
2) Reactor coolant system pressure greater than design limit;
3) Fuel temperature histories indicative of gross fuel failure;
4) Reactor coolant system pressure versus temperature relationship indicative of gross voiding;
5) BWR suppression pool temperature greater than the highest value at which condensation instability is known not to occur".

However, by imposing only those limits listed in Section 4.3 of ANSI/ANS-3.5-1985, events which progress beyond other plant design limits or model limits may occur providing negative training or a reduction in simulator credibility.

Determination of simulator operating limits may effectively be accomplished by evaluating the simulated systems. The systems mainly of interest here are those which maintain the integrity of the radioactive material barrier, prevent the release of radioactive material, are essential to core cooling, are essential to containment pressure suppression, and are vital auxiliaries necessary to support the above. These systems can be summarized as all safety-related systems. An example of each is given below:

- o Radioactive material barrier - Reactor Core (Cladding)
- o Prevent the release of radioactive material-Primary Containment
- o Essential to core cooling - High Pressure Coolant Injection
- o Containment Pressure Suppression-Containment Spray
- o Vital Auxiliaries - Diesel Generators

Reviewing each system, using the appropriate reference material (i.e., Technical Specifications, Plant Procedures, etc.), the plant design and model limits for each system may be identified. If the identified limit may be exercised during any training session used for Reactor Operator and Senior Reactor Operator license certification and requalification training and audit examinations, it should be included for further evaluation. This further evaluation may address such concerns as reaching this limit is prevented by an automatic system response which is simulated.

MONITORING SIMULATOR OPERATING LIMITS

One approach to monitoring simulator operating limits is to have a software program that executes periodically and compares selected parameters with the appropriate simulator operating limits. The program could identify when a simulator operating limit would reach or approach a setpoint (Critical Action Value) to indicate when certain events occurred during an evolution. The program would need to be capable of identifying not only when the simulator operating limits are exceeded, but also on the approach to the simulator operating limits. This applies to not only directly observable parameters, but also those parameters that are critical but not directly observable in the control room (break flow, pressure/temperature relationships).

The software program could be designed to execute periodically on the simulator computer and run during available spare time. Once the program identifies when the simulator is approaching an operating limit (i.e., reaches a CAV), a warning indicator would alert the instructor. The software implementation requires consideration of 1) the expertise and availability of Software Engineers, 2) the availability of spare memory and time in the instructor station computer, and 3) the availability of display systems.
Another approach to monitoring simulator operating limits is via the instructor. In order for the instructor to effectively monitor simulator operating limits, he needs to be aware of which plant design limits and model limits are likely to be exceeded during a training session. The instructor guides could point out specific operator actions, events, parameters, or indications to be visually monitored by the instructor for the specific plant design limit and/or model limit associated with the training session. By being aware of which operator actions, events, parameters, and indications to watch out for, the instructor can intervene to prevent operation of the simulator beyond the plant design or model limits. Consideration of the increased instructor knowledge and qualification requirements are concerns that should be addressed by the individual utility when deciding whether or not to use the above approach.

ALERTING THE INSTRUCTORS

As stated earlier, Simulator Operating Limits may be imposed to prevent negative training or loss of simulator credibility. Negative training or loss of simulator credibility may occur by allowing events to progress beyond simulator operating limits. To prevent simulation parameters from approaching values indicative of events beyond the implemented model or known plant behavior, the instructor must have early warning of the progression of simulation to the simulator operating limits.

To provide this early warning, simulator instructors need to be informed of the possibility of an event occurring (i.e., of a simulator operating limit being reached) during the performance of a training scenario. Several methods to accomplish this early warning are discussed below. In deciding which of the methods the utility should use, several considerations need to be addressed by the individual utility. These considerations include, but are not limited to;

1) the capability of the simulator computer and instructor station (lack of available memory space, execution time, etc.),

2) the characteristics of the simulator operating limit (boolean verses analog), and

3) the increased knowledge and qualification requirements for simulator instructors.

One method of accomplishing this is to administratively have all training scenarios which could provide the possibility of entering any condition beyond plant/model design include precautions. These precautions could be placed at points in the scenario where exceeding an operating limit is likely to occur. The precautions would key the instructor to observe selected operator actions and intervene wherever such actions would place the simulator beyond plant design limits or model limits.

Due to the nature of some simulator operating limits, and the time required for instructor intervention, some limits should be afforded additional means of preventing the simulator from entering the realm beyond plant/model design. Accomplishment of this may be through the use of several software programming techniques. One is a warning indicator at the instructor station to inform the instructor that a simulator operating limit has been reached. The software program used for monitoring the operating limits would identify when the simulator reaches or approaches the respective CAV. The program could then activate a warning indicator at the instructor station. If the utility were to choose to alert the instructor via a CRT, the minimum information that should be presented to the instructor is the responsible parameter, a brief description of the operating limit, the value of the CAV, and the current parameter value.

In the situation where there is only one instructor during a training session, the use of an inconspicuous annunciator in the simulator control room may be a second and more appropriate software technique. An inconspicuous annunciator is an annunciator light that is out of the operator's normal line of sight. When actuated, the light would come on solid. No alarm horn or flashing would be associated with the annunciator to alert the operators. Upon receiving the annunciator, the instructor would proceed to the instructor's station to activate a CRT tableau or printer that provides information on what the responsible parameter is, what the corresponding plant or model limit is, what the value of the CAV is, and what the current parameter value is. Actions could then be taken by the instructor to prevent negative training or a reduction in simulator credibility.

For some simulator operating limits, there may not be enough time to allow the instructor to intervene. For these limits a freeze of the simulator may be a third and more appropriate technique. This could be a soft or a hard freeze. A soft freeze allows the instructor to override the freeze and continue to run. This would allow the instructor to continue on with the training session. A hard freeze requires the simulator to be reinitialized.

There is however, a potential drawback to using the above software programming approaches. The inconspicuous annunciator or freezing of the simulator can be used to prevent exceeding plant and/or model design limits. However, they themselves present an aspect of negative training in that a question of simulator credibility by the operator may arise if the simulator reaches the operating limits during many of the training scenarios.

RESULTS

The purpose of this EPRI research project was to develop cost-effective guidelines for implementing and documenting simulator operating limits which would meet the requirements of Section 4.3 of the ANSI/ANS-3.5-1985 standard to the satisfaction of the Nuclear Regulatory Commission (NRC). It is felt that the guidelines/procedures given in the report will meet those objectives.

Responses to the survey were received from twelve domestic utilities representing sixteen simulators, one foreign utility and one non-utility (Westinghouse Hanford). Of the sixteen domestic power plant simulators, only six currently had an operating limit plan implemented. Most of the remaining ten simulator owners were still considering options and formulating plans.

It is estimated that the procedures can be implemented within 200 man-hours plus the time required to generate any necessary software and enter precautionary comments in the training guides. This effort is split amongst senior reactor operator simulator instructors, experienced simulator software engineers, nuclear power plant operations experts, and the simulator supervisor. Most of the procedures have been reduced to simply filling in the forms supplied herein. Examples are given for all forms. It is felt that this approach is the most cost-effective while ensuring the thorough identification of all simulator operating limits which could provide negative training.

CONCLUSION

The EPRI guidelines for determining and monitoring simulator operator limits represent a comprehensive and efficient program for documenting the method(s) used to prevent a simulator from exceeding its operating limits. Due to the differences in physical and functional fidelity among simulators, the procedures were written to be general with the recommendation to tailor the guidelines to the specific simulator prior to implementation. While the guidelines include considerations that need to be addressed when evaluating the mechanism(s) for monitoring the limits and alerting the instructor, no discussion of how to interact with the students once the limit(s) are reached is given. Each utility must evaluate how best to proceed once an operating limit has been approached or exceeded. It is evident to the authors that further discussion on this subject is necessary among the nuclear utilities.

REFERENCES

1. Title 10, Code of Federal Regulations, Part 55.45 "Operating Tests" as described in FRN - 52 FR 9453, 25 March, 1987.

2. U. S. Nuclear Regulatory Commission. Nuclear Power Plant Simulation Facilities For Use In Operator License Examinations. April 1987. Regulatory Guide 1.149. as described in FRN - 52 FR 16007, 1 May, 1987.

3. American National Standards Institute. American National Standard: Nuclear Power Plant Simulators for Use in Operator Training. Illinois: 1985. ANSI/ANS-3.5-1985.

4. Electric Power Research Institute. Simulator Qualification Plan EPRI NP-5504. November 1987.

Simulators VI
© 1989 By The Society for Computer
Simulation International
ISBN 0-911801-51-0

Modeling of cooling water system for thermal power plants

Pradip Som
Industrial Engineering
Texas A & M University
College Station, TX 77840

and

Suresh K. Khator
Industrial & Mgmt Syst Engineering
University of South Florida
Tampa, FL 33620

ABSTRACT

The paper presents optimization of Cooling Water (C.W.) System for thermal power plants using simulation modeling. Various factors of the C.W. system, viz., cooling tower characteristics, wet bulb temperature variation, turbine characteristics, etc. are modeled and integrated through discrete event simulation. The optimization of C.W. system is arrived at a specific design wet bulb temperature of the cooling tower. Contrary to the industrial practice of selecting the desing wet bulb temperture for cooling tower as the heighest of summer months, the paper indicates that optimum system is arrived at a moderate design wet bulb temperture. Prudent selection of design wet bulb temperature strikes proper balance between total power generation and the cost of the cooling water system installed leading to optimized C.W. System.

INTRODUCTION

A thermal power plant which operates on the principle of the Second Law of Thermodynamics has the following three basic modules:

i) Boiler - the heat source
ii) Steam Turbine - the heat engine
iii) Condenser - the heat sink.

In modern thermal power plant, the high pressure, high temperature steam produced by the boiler is expanded through the turbine to generate power. The steam is condensed in the condenser where it rejects its latent heat to the cooling water which flows through the condenser. Input to the condenser is cold water while output from the condenser is hot water. The hot water, in turn, rejects the gained heat to the atmosphere by various means. Thermal power plants generally operate at 40% efficiency level which means nearly 60% of the heat input to the system has to be rejected. While 15% of the heat is lost in the plant up the stack and in the ash, about 45% of the heat output is required to be removed by some external means (Jimeson and Adkins 1975). This establishes a need for an efficient cooling water (C.W.) systems for thermal power plants. The cooling system employing wet cooling tower as the major heat rejection device is considered for modeling in this paper.

In wet-tower cooling, the cooling tower tries to cool the hot water up to the atmospheric wet bulb temperature. But due to the inefficiency in the system, there remains an 'approach' between the temperature of the cold water outlet from the cooling tower and the wet bulb temperature. The saturation temperature of steam, which depends on the temperature of water outlet from the cooling tower, is obtained as follows:

Saturation Temperature = Wet Bulb Temperature + Approach + Range + TTD

where,

Approach: The difference between the cooling tower outlet temperature and the wet bulb temperature.

Range: The difference between the hot water temperature and the cold water temperature.

TTD: Terminal Temperature Difference - the difference between the saturation steam temperature and the condenser outlet temperature.

The turbine exhaust pressure as well as the turbine output are dictated by the corresponding saturation temperature of the steam. The saturation steam temperature, in turn, depends on the design of the cooling water system. Most cooling water systems are compared on the reference frame of one year operating costs on the basis of a set of fixed design conditions, i.e., dry and wet bulb air temperature, turbine back pressure, heat load and power load. The fixed design conditions are usually chosen using "rules of thumb" which are dependent on extreme conditions, e.g., constant turbine load throughout the year or maximum summer time temperatures. While all cooling towers are purchased to function at 100% of capability in accordance with the required design conditions, in actual on-stream employment, the level of operation is many times lower, downward to as much as 50% (Burger 1984). This sometimes leads to the selection of a C.W. system of larger capacity than required.

A C.W. system requires power to operate its components. Mechanical draft cooling towers require fans to move air along with pumps to drive water through the condenser and lift it to the top of the tower packing. The cooling system total cost (capital cost and operating cost) depends on the total water flow, approach to wet bulb, range, power consumption, increased fuel consumption and loss of capability due to inefficient C.W. system design (Campagne and McDonough 1984). The idea behind the optimization of a cooling water system is to minimize the total cost function considering the fluctuation of the operational mode of the power plant and the variations in the weather condition. The total cooling water system may be simulated for the complete power plant life to arrive at the optimum design conditions.

SYSTEM INTEGRATION

An inefficient cooling system has multiple effects on the overall power plant operation. In general, an inefficient cooling water system results in the following problems:

i) With the increased condenser cooling water temperature, turbine exhaust pressure is increased leading to decreased turbine performance.

ii) In-plant power requirement, for system operation, is increased with more water pumping through a piping network having high frictional head.

iii) More fuel (coal or gas) is consumed to produce a unit of electricity at a given turbine generator output.

iv) Loss of power generation capability will occur at full load when the condenser temperature increases beyond a certain level.

A schematic diagram of the cooling water system is shown in Figure 1. The cooling water pumps deliver cold water through the condenser where heat exchange takes place between the exhaust steam and the cooling water. The cold water, collected at the cooling tower basin, is recirculated by the C.W. pumps. For different combinations of cooling water flow, condenser heat exchanger area and cooling tower design wet bulb temperature, three different cases may occur:

i) Optimum steam turbine performance when required cold water temperature is achieved.

ii) Better steam turbine performance when lower cold water temperature is achieved.

iii) Inferior steam turbine performance when higher cold water temperature is achieved.

With lower cold water temperature there may be some higher percentage of power generation while with higher cold water temperature, turbine performance drops down leading to loss of capability. During the low power generation period, the deficit power may be compensated by buying from alternative source. Otherwise, a penalty may have to be paid for low generation.

The efficiency, performance and operation variability of the cooling water system depends on the efficient integrated operation of the cooling tower, the condenser, the turbine and C.W. pumps.

Therefore the optimization problem can be formulated as:

Minimize [C.W. system capital cost + C.W. system operating cost + cost due to loss of generation]

considering the optimization of the integrated system behavior.

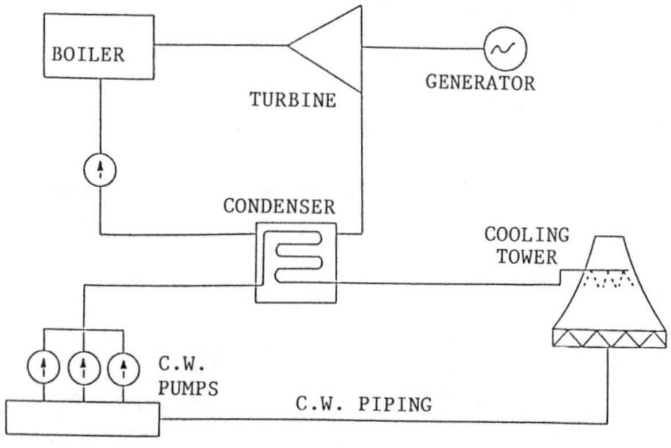

Figure 1. Schematic Diagram of Power Plant Cooling Water System

Steps Towards System Integration

To arrive at an optimized C.W. system for thermal power plant, following steps are considered.

1. Determination of the temperature of water outlet from the cooling tower for a given wet bulb temperature and approach. Merkel's equation, which is well documented in literature (Kolfat 1974; Lichenstein 1943; Merkel 1925) is solved to arrive at the outlet water temperature.

2. The atmospheric wet bulb temperature change, during an entire year, generally follows a set pattern. Determination of the underlying distribution of the wet bulb temperature is the second step.

3. Optimization of piping system leads to minimization of non-linear cost function C with pipe diameter d as a variable. The problem is viewed as a case of constrained non-linear optimization and is solved for the optimum pipe diameter d.

4. In the final step a simulation model of the C.W. system for the power plant is developed. The model generates different cold water temperature from the cooling tower depending on varying wet bulb temperature throughout the range of plant operation. Moreover, the model integrates the turbine performance, the condenser performance and the cooling tower performance to determine output power at differing working conditions.

5. To determine the optimum cooling water system, a reference tower (Clark 1980) is selected based on atmospheric data, power demand and manufacturer's recommendation. Then different tower ratings are chosen above and below the reference tower and the power outputs for different tower designs are determined. The economics for system optimization has been developed which gives net gain from increased power generation against the extra cost needed to install the cooling water system.

The model is verified using actual atmospheric wet bulb temperature variation, and the performance curves of the cooling tower and steam turbine from Big Bend Station of Tampa Electric Company (TECO) Florida. Economic calculations have been made to arrive at the most cost-effective C.W. system.

DEVELOPMENT OF MODELS

For the purpose of simulating the behavior of the power plant C.W. system, the following components are modeled:

i) Cooling Tower,
ii) Saturation Pressure vs. Temperature Relationship,
iii) Turbine Characteristics,
iv) Meteorological Conditions,
v) Integration of Component Models,
vi) Optimized Pipe Diameter.

A brief discription of these component models follows:

i) Model for Cooling Tower

Model for the Cooling Tower finds out the cold water temperature at the outlet of the cooling tower from the given inlet hot water temperature, ambient wet bulb temperature and design set points for the cooling tower.

Mechanical draft cooling tower with cross flow air-water interface has been chosen for development of the model. Finite difference approximation method has been used to find the integral for Merkel's Equation. The model uses tower characteristics (KaV/L) and liquid to air ratio (L/G) which are obtained from the cooling tower characteristic curves (Cooling Tower Institute 1967).

ii) Model for Saturation Pressure vs. Temperature Relationship

The cold water temperature in the condenser determines the back pressure at which the steam turbine should operate during power generation. It is assumed that in the main condensing section of the condenser only saturated steam and condensation will take place at constant temperature. The saturation vapor pressure can be found out from the Psychometric Chart (Meyer et.al.).

For the purpose of utilization of the temperature vs. saturation pressure data from Psychometric Chart, attempt has been made to develop an equation for certain portion of the data. From experience, it is found that for power plant operation, the saturation temperatures generally vary between 60°F to 130°F. The saturation pressures corresponding to these temperatures are observed and non-linear regression technique has been used for curve fitting. The following is the best fit model:

$$y = -0.7112 - 0.002865x + 0.1177\, e^{0.02407x} \quad \text{.... (1)}$$

Where, y = Pressure in psi, x = Temperature in °F.

The pressure estimates corresponding to different temperatures in the 60°F to 130°F range were made using the model. The comparison of the actual pressure vs. estimated pressure showed a maximum variation of .025 psi which results in less than 1.25% error indicating a very close fit.

iii) Model for Turbine Characteristics

Power generation output depends on the turbine exhaust pressure. The lower the exhaust pressure, the higher the output for same input parameters of steam in the turbine. The exhaust pressure vs. output curve is known as Turbine Characteristics. Turbine Characteristics vary from manufacturer to manufacturer with change in design of turbine parts. Therefore no effort has been made to develop a generalized equation for turbine characteristic to fit all sorts of curves and manufacturers data have been used to develop the model. The turbine data, obtained from the Tampa Electric Co., Tampa, Florida are used for modeling:

Turbine Make: General Electric Company,
Schnectady, N.Y.
Rating: 444.464 MW
Initial Steam Pressure: 2400 psig.
Initial Steam Temperature: 1000 deg.F
RPM: 3600

To develop a model for the turbine characteristic, curve fitting of data by non-linear regression technique has been used. From the normal drooping nature of the turbine characteristic curve, a negative exponential fit has been presumed. Various non-linear models have been tried to fit the data and the best fit model appears as follows:

$$y = \frac{1152}{2.074 + 0.087x + 0.505e^{-0.245x}} \quad \text{.... (2)}$$

The power output estimates were made for different exhaust pressure using this model. The actual and estimated outputs, as shown in Figure 2, varied not more than 0.65 MW which corresponds to less than 0.15% error indicating an excellent fit.

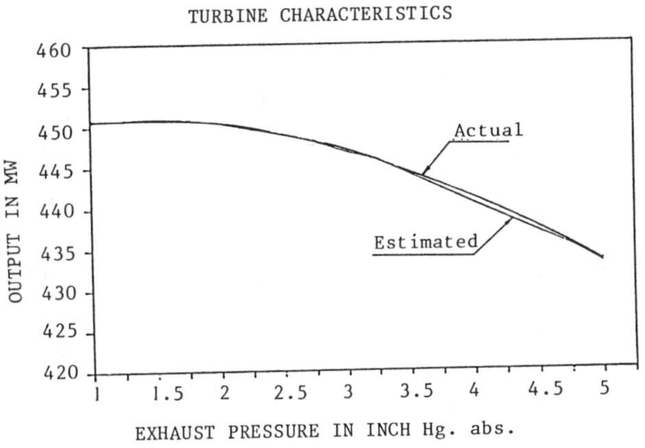

Figure 2. Exhaust Pressure vs. Turbine Output

iv) Model for Meteorological Conditions

Meteorological conditions play an important role in thermal power generation. The factor that determines the heat rejection capacity of a mechanical draft cooling tower is atmospheric wet bulb temperature. Hence attention has been given to develop a model to capture the atmospheric wet bulb temperature (WBT) variation. Half-hourly data have been collected for every day for a whole year (1985) for the purpose of development of the model.

Scrutinizing the data, it appears that WBT in a month, in general, follows a probability distribution. The probability distribution with estimated parameters from the given data can be used to model wet bulb temperature variation for any month.

Every four hourly data for the entire month, starting from January to December, have been considered to determine the distribution. Various distributions have been tried to fit the data. Chi-square tests were conducted with each distribution to check whether we can accept the hypothesis or not. It appeared that Normal and Weibull distributions very closely approximate the distribution of WBT for most of the months in a year. As an illustration, histogram for the month of January is presented in Figure 3. The annual variation of the Wet Bulb Temperatures is presented in Figure 4.

v) Integration of Component Models

The final model integrates the models for meteorological condition, cooling tower characteristic, saturation pressure vs. temperature and turbine characteristic. The inter-relationships between wet bulb temperature, condenser exhaust pressure and output power is presented in Figure 5.

The probabilistic nature of the wet bulb temperature variation deters the accurate prediction of WBT at any specific point in time and hence the corresponding power output. To capture this probabilistic nature, discrete event simulation has been sought for to determine the final power output. Since the WBT distribution varies from month to month considerably, the model is developed for finding monthly power generation.

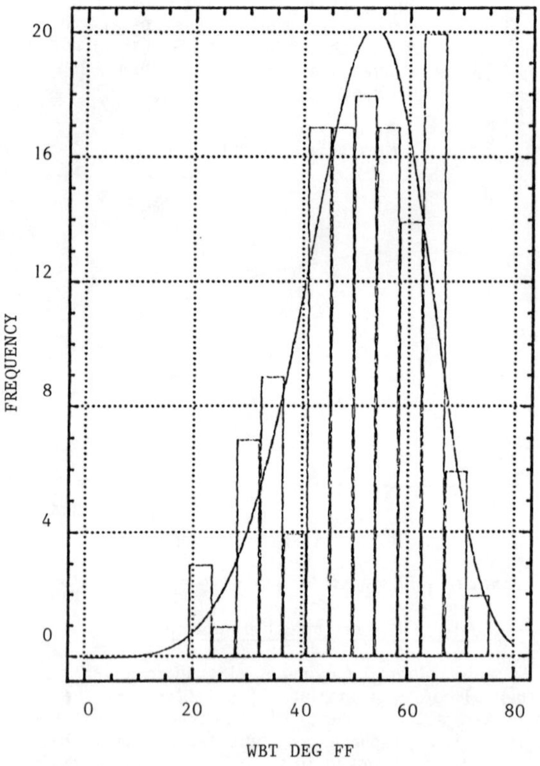

Figure 3. Frequency Histogram - Jan85 Weibull

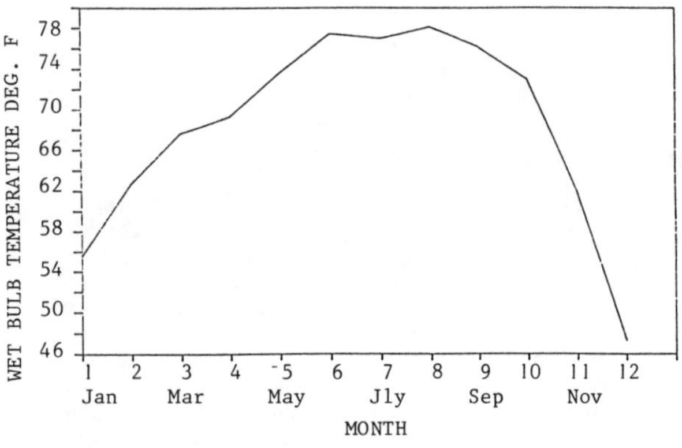

Figure 4. Annual Wet Bulb Temperature Variation

The discrete event simulation model uses SIMAN simulation language for system integration. Simulation begins by taking a sample of wet bulb temperature for a 4-hour interval from the wet bulb temperature distribution. Inlet hot water temperature is then estimated by adding range to the outlet water temperature (initially assumed as 85°F). The model then calls a subroutine (CALC) to calculate power output. This subroutine in turn calls another subroutine (OUTEMP) to calculate the outlet water temperature from the cooling tower characteristics. Subroutine CALC then progressively calculates the saturation pressure from the hot water temperature and the final power output. Complete listing of the simulation model and other subroutines are given elsewhere (Som 1988).

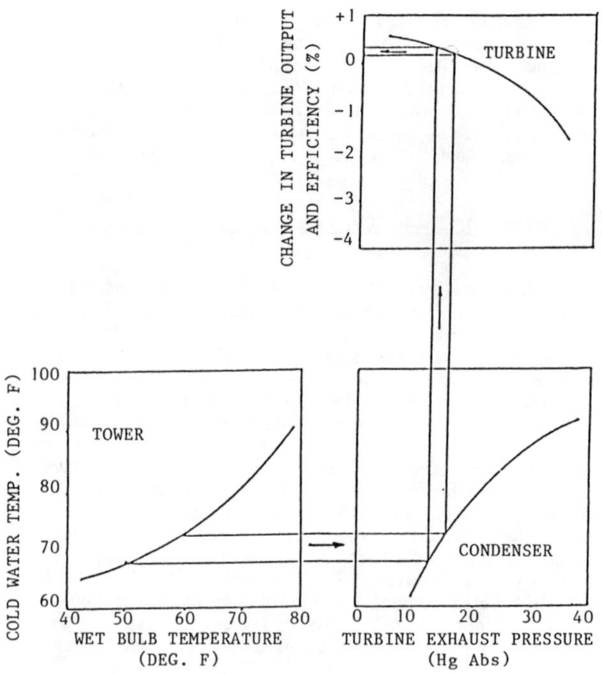

Figure 5. Effect of Wet Bulb Temperature on Turbine Performance

To find the saturation pressure, the input needed is the saturation temperature. The saturation temperature is determined from the hot water temperature as follows:

Saturation temperature = Hot water temperature + TTD = Cold water temperature + Range + TTD

In normal thermal power plant practice: Range = 20°F, TTD = 5°F.

Hence, Saturation temperature = Cold water temperature + 25°F.

The saturation pressure corresponding to the saturation temperature is determined from the saturation pressure vs. temperature Equation (1). The power output is determined from the saturation pressure using Equation (2).

After determining the output power, the control is returned to the main model. The model collects statistics on the wet bulb temperature (used for validation), the cold water temperature and the output power. The simulation clock is advanced by four hours to simulate the next interval. The program stops after 720 hours of simulation representing one month data. This program can be run with different monthly wet bulb temperature distribution to simulate the entire year's operation of the power plant.

vi) Model for Pipe Diameter Optimization

The total cost function C in terms of the pipe diameter d is described as follows:

Total cost = Capital cost + Operational cost

$$C = \pi d l C_2 + \frac{S(\pi/4)d^2 \, (h_s + K_1/d)^5 \, C_1 K_3 \gamma}{K_2 \eta}$$

Where,

- C = Total cost
- C_1 = Cost of unit power, \$/KWH
- C_2 = Cost of pipe per foot length per sq.ft. + excavation, backfilling and coating cost per foot per sq.ft., \$
- d = diameter of the pipe, ft.
- l = length of pipe line, ft.
- S = velocity of water flow, ft/sec.
- h_s = static head, ft.
- γ = specific weight of water, lb/cu. ft.
- η = efficiency of pump
- $K_1 = \frac{flW^2}{2gd}$ = a system constant
- W = cooling water flow rate, ft^3/sec.
- f = friction loss co-efficient, ft/100 ft.
- g = acceleration due to gravity, ft/sec^2
- K_2 = power conversion factor (Metric to British)
- K_3 = present worth factor (depends on interest rate)

In normal power plant practice, the amount of cooling water flow is a fixed quantity as that determines the selection of cooling water pump parameters. The pumps run continuously 24 hours a day with fixed water delivery volume. The flow quantity is determined from required heat rejection and condenser characteristics. Hence in the present case, the cooling water flow rate is considered as a parameter of system and is assumed to be constant.

The cost function then looks like

$$C = \pi d l C_2 + \frac{W(h_s + K_1/d^5)C_1 K_3 \gamma}{K_2 \eta}$$

Where, $W = S(\pi/4)d^2$ = Water flow rate.

The optimum pipe diameter is given by

$$d = (5WK_1C_1K_3\gamma/K_2\eta\pi l C_2)^{1/6}$$

It is important to note that in determining pipe diameter d by the above method, velocity of water through pipe should lie between 2 ft./sec. and 8 ft./sec.

The cost model as developed is not a monotonic function of diameter d and the optimum diameter lies between the upper and lower limits of constraints. The pipe diameter vs. total cost relationship, obtained from the actual data is presented in Figure 6.

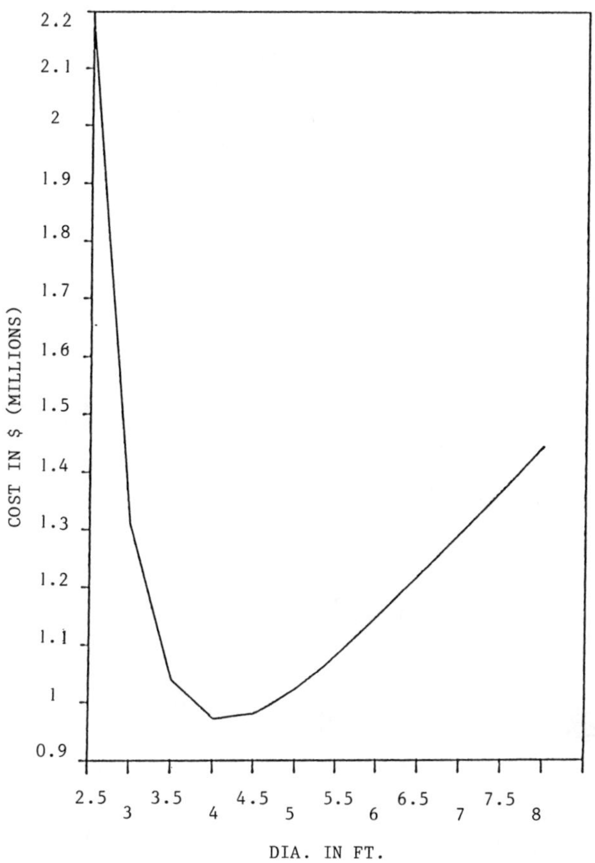

Figure 6. Diameter vs. Cost Relationship (Low Flow)

SIMULATION RESULTS

The following input data are considered for the purpose of simulating the C.W. system:

Plant generation capacity = 444 MW
L/G = 1 (standard cooling tower practice)
Range = Temperature rise through condenser = 20°F
TTD = Terminal Temperature Difference = 5°F

The cooling water system is simulated for three different design wet bulb temperatures: T_1 = 80°F, T_2 = 70°F, T_3 = 65°F.

The objective is to determine at which level of design wet bulb temperature, the C.W. system incurs minimum cost.

The number of tower units, NTU, varies for different design wet bulb temperatures.

At 80°F design WBT, 3°F approach is considered. When 65°F, 70°F and 75°F design WBT are considered, the equivalent approaches are 6.2°F, 5°F and 4°F respectively.

The following values of NTUs are used:

Design Wet Bulb	NTU
80°F	2.9
70°F	2.0
65°F	1.5

The above values were obtained from Cooling Tower Performance Curves (Cooling Tower Institute 1967).

The system is simulated to collect data on wet bulb temperature, hot water temperature input to the system, cold water temperature output from cooling tower and power generation. The simulation run is made for one complete year. To indicate the variation of power generation with atmospheric wet bulb temperature, plot for the month of January using 1.5 NTU is shown in Figure 7. The plots for different NTUs indicate that power generation varies considerably with atmospheric wet bulb temperature as well as design wet bulb temperature of the cooling tower.

Analysis of Results

For the purpose of analyzing the results of the simulation run, the following cooling tower specification has been chosen:

Type: Induced Draft Counterflow
Nos.: Six (6)
Flow Rate: 30,000 GPM
Design Wet Bulb Temperature: 80°F
Range: 20°F

The following reference case has been considered for subsequent optimization of the system:

Flow rate = 30,000 GPM
Design Wet Bulb = 80°F
Approach = 8°F
L/G = 1
Fan BHP = 370 HP
Basin Area = 144 x 36 = 5184 ft²
Cost of cooling tower = $505,000
Cost of power = $72 per KW-yr
Capitalization factor = 11.786
Cost of Basin = $30 per ft²

The objective of the analysis is to obtain differential cost at different design WBT and approach from the reference case and determination of the optimum.

Table 1. Cost Comparison of Different Cooling Towers

	Design WBT 80°F	Design WBT 70°F	Design WBT 65°F
Extra Cost from reference tower	$4,391,448	$2,088,625	$1,178,193
Gain from extra power*	(451.616-X) x (848592)	(450.56-X) x (848592)	(449.169-X) x (848592)
Net Gain	$-1,406,710	Base	$-269,960

* Where, X is the average power generation in the reference case.

From the above table it appears that at design wet bulb temperature of 70°F, the total cost incurred becomes lower compared to 80°F and 65°F WBT.

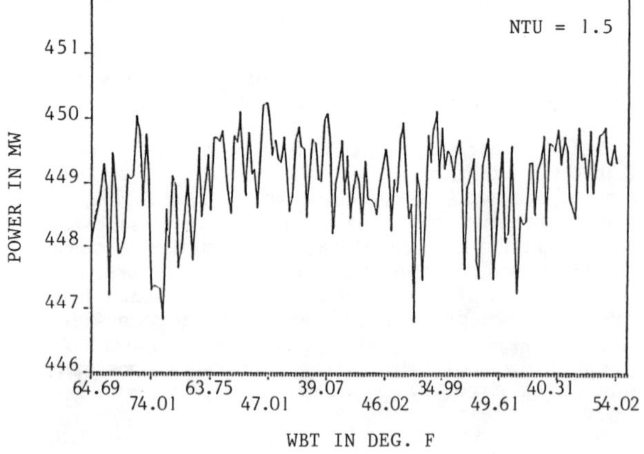

Figure 7. Wet Bulb Temperature vs. Power - January

CONCLUSION

The above analysis indicates that at lower design wet bulb temperature, the plant generation virtually suffers in the hotter months (at high WBT) and the plant penalty is severe in terms of total cost. The usual practice is to set the design WBT at the highest level, considering summer months, so that power generation is never hampered. However, the paper shows that fixing design WBT at the highest level also does not lead to optimality. Here plant penalty in terms of higher fixed and operational cost exceeds the gain from more power generation. At design WBT of 70°F, which is well below the maximum WBT during the year, the cost function becomes optimized. For a very small portion of the year, the atmospheric wet bulb temperatures reach the highest level which may lead to less power generation. But the proportion of less power generation time to the time during which the system remains unutilized (when a very high design WBT is considered), is very low. Therefore, it appears that power generation to the rated capacity may be sacrificed for a small portion of time of the year considering the total plant economics. The shortage in power can be met by buying the differential amount from an outside agency. Diesel generator set may also be used to supplement the power shortage which does not take very high installation cost. The judicious selection of design WBT should lead to least cost compared to other alternatives.

REFERENCES

Burger, R. 1984. "Cooling Tower: Energy Conservation Strategies." Energy Engineering: Journal of the Association of Energy Engineers. 81(4), June-July, 53-64.

Campagne, W.V.L. and L.J. McDonough. 1984. "How Cooling Towers Affect Process Energy Savings." Hydrocarbon Processing. 63(6), June, 103-107.

Clark, S.D. 1980. "Sizing Cooling towers to Optimize Plant Performance." Journal of the Cooling Tower Institute. 1(1), June, 15-23.

Cooling Tower Institute. 1967. Cooling Tower Performance Curves. Houston, TX.

Jimeson, R.M. and G.G. Adkins. 1975. "Waste Heat Disposal in Power Plants." Cooling Towers, Chemical Engineering Progress - AIChE. 1.

Kolfat, T.D. 1974. "Cooling Tower Practices." Power Engineering. Jan., 32-39.

Lichenstein, J. 1943. "Performance and Selection of Mechanical-Draft Cooling Towers." Transactions of the ASME. 65, Oct., 779-787.

Meyer, C.A. et.al. Thermodynamics and Transport Properties of Steam Comprising Tables and Charts for Steam and Water. ASME, New York, NY 10017.

Merkel, F. 1925. "Verdunstungskulung." VDI Forschungsarbeiten, No. 275, Berlin.

Som, P. 1988. Optimization of Cooling Water System for Thermal Power Plants. Unpublished Master's Thesis, University of South Florida, Tampa, Florida, December.

Simulators VI
© 1989 By The Society for Computer
Simulation International
ISBN 0-911801-51-0

Modelling and simulation of large-scale multiparameter computer aided dynamical control systems

John Jones, Jr.
Department of Mathematics and Computer Science
Air Force Institute of Technology
Wright-Patterson AFB OH 45433

ABSTRACT

Dynamical systems of the form:

$$E(\theta)\dot{x}(t,\theta) = A(\theta)x(t,\theta) + B(\theta)u(t,\theta);$$

$$y(t,\theta) = C(\theta)x(t,\theta) + D(\theta)u(t,\theta);$$

$$t \geq 0$$

$$\dot{x}(t,\theta) = \frac{dx(t,\theta)}{dt}, \quad t \geq 0$$

are considered.

The elements of the matrices, $E(\theta)$, $A(\theta)$, $B(\theta)$, $C(\theta)$, $D(\theta)$ belong to the ring of polynomials $\mathbf{R}[\theta]$ where $\theta=(\theta_1,\theta_2,\theta_3,\ldots,\theta_p)$ is a multiparameter and the coefficients of the polynomials belonging to $\mathbf{R}[\theta]$ have elements belonging to the field $\mathbf{C}$ of complex numbers, or the elements of such mutliparameter matrices may be of the form $f(\theta) = a(\theta)|b(\theta)$ where the polynomials $a(\theta)$, $b(\theta) \in \mathbf{R}[\theta]$, for $b(\theta) \neq 0$. $E(\theta)$ may be a singular matrix for possible parameter values of θ. The parameter θ may also be a holomorphic function of a single complex variable z for z belonging to simply-connected bounded regions in the complex z-plane. The basic questions of stabilization, controllability, observability, etc., in the presence if changes in subsystems as regards the overall dynamical system needs to be treated in reponse to changing parameters in subsystems.

INTRODUCTION

Modelling and Simulation of large-scale multidimensional multiparameter dynamical systems require the use of large-scale computers to generate feed-back control laws especially when model uncertaintities exist. Now robust control theory is concerned with the problem of analyzing and synthesizing control systems that provide an acceptable level of performance where many model parameters or uncertainties may exist since mathematical models of physical systems are usually never exact due to the presence of such parameters.

The need to be able to design robust feed-back control laws is very important in such systems. Usually a physical model will have significant structural information about the interconnection of components and subsystems but less information concerning their integrated system performance. Hence, many variations of parameters must be carried out on super-computers in order to determine the more significant and sensitive parameters which must be adjusted very rapidly to accomplish a desired level of performance.

Fast numerical methods requiring parallel processing are necessary to compute adjustments as time t changes. Transfer function matrices, controllability matrices, observability matrices, feed-back and control laws need to be recomputed as parameters change. Such matrices may be multiparameter matrices and may allow for improvement of control laws such as in cases where $E(\theta)$ may become a singular matrix and the dynamical systems require considerable fast changes in feed-back control laws.

Use is made of recent results of J. Jones, Jr., concerning generalized inverses of such multiparameter matrices to aid in computer aided changes to carry out modeliing and simulation and analysis of such dynamical systems.

Results of work obtained in this paper may also be applied to cases of more general nonlinear dynamical systems described by the following nonlinear equations:

$$\begin{cases} \dot{z}(t) = p(z(t),u(t)) \\ y(t) = q(z(t),u(t)) \end{cases}$$

where $z(t) \in R^{nx1}$ is the state vector, $u(t) \in R^{px1}$ is the input vector and $y(t) \in R^{mx1}$ is the output vector where $m \leq p$.

The basic problems of considering the stabilization, controllability, observability, feed-back control laws, etc. will be considered for such type systems. Inverse systems of such nonlinear dynamical systems are considered. Such an approach allows the use of iterative techniques and requires the usage of supercomputer technology for the carrying out of parallel processing methods and implemented such as in pipeline structure.

This work will consider both numerical techniques and mathematical methods of establishing properties of such nonlinear dynamical solutions. Numerical examples will be given to illustrate the theory developed and the accuracy of the approach to such problems. Applications of such dynamical systems occur in the area of nonlinear control theory, robotics, nonlinear differential equations and elsewhere.

NONLINEAR DYNAMICAL SYSTEMS

In a detailed treatment of large nonlinear dynamical systems several steps are necessary to successfully be carried out in detail. The first stage of handling such a large problem consists of problem formulation, i.e., the detailed mathematical description of the nonlinear differential system of equations which describe the dynamic problem. In most cases the system of nonlinear equations cannot be solved directly and numerical methods must be used to obtain a solution or solutions. Usually the solutions are such that they have properties which are undesirable, that is, they may be unstable in some sense. Hence, a knowledge of the solutions alone of the dynamical system is not sufficient for the actual modelling and simulation of the physical problem associated with the mathematical model. Thus the important phase of stabilization of the dynamical system must be carried out. This is done by constructing a feed-back and also a feed-forward phase of the problem.

Once the stabliization phase has been accomplished, the basic controllability problem must be considered. Next the observability criteria must be examined in order to satisfy observability conditions. Next feed-back laws need be computed in order to control such a dynamical system. The system with its many parameters must be simulated on large-scale computers using parallel processing to obtain critical parameters of the system. In the computer simulation phase of the dynamical system a comparison of the discretized problem solution versus that of continuous solutions, if available, need be made. After a running solution of the system is made possible, many replications of possible modes of the system are needed to anticipate undesirable states of the system and possible computer-aided changes throughout to enhance reliability and robustness of controls in case of failures of some of the components. In order to incorporate artificial intelligence and have an expert system analysis must be continuously carried out to actually monitor the state of the system and predict possible corrective measures needed in various component sub-systems as quickly as possible, large-scale computers having a parallel programming capability is required. Such systems must be expert systems for mapping applications to parallel architectures and support parrallel processing and advisory expert systems for generalized purpose scientific dynamic sofware libraries, and sophisticated user interfaces for such scientific and engineering systems overall operation. Finally, a continuous monitoring of the overall system in operation is thus necessary throughout the entire operation of the system modelling and simulation.

Example Of A Nonlinear Dynamical System

In this section as an example of a nonlinear dynamical system will be treated to illustrate the approach established in the later sections of this paper.

Consider the following nonlinear system of differential equations:

$$\begin{cases} \dot{x}(t) = y(t)z(t) - x^2(t) \\ \dot{y}(t) = z(t)x(t) - y^2(t) \\ \dot{z}(t) = x(t)y(t) - z^2(t) \end{cases}$$

which may be written as follows:

$$\begin{pmatrix} \dot{x}(t) \\ \dot{y}(t) \\ \dot{z}(t) \end{pmatrix} = \begin{pmatrix} -x(t) & 0 & y(t) \\ 0 & -y(t) & x(t) \\ y(t) & 0 & -z(t) \end{pmatrix} \begin{pmatrix} x(t) \\ y(t) \\ z(t) \end{pmatrix}$$

or

$$\begin{pmatrix} \dot{x}(t) \\ \dot{y}(t) \\ \dot{z}(t) \end{pmatrix} = \begin{pmatrix} -x(t) & z(t) & 0 \\ z(t) & -y(t) & 0 \\ 0 & x(t) & -z(t) \end{pmatrix} \begin{pmatrix} x(t) \\ y(t) \\ z(t) \end{pmatrix}$$

or

$$\dot{x}(t) = A(x(t))\, x(t)$$

Einstein's law of gravitation is expressed by a system of ten partial differential equations of the second order. It can be shown that a special case of these equations reduce to the above systems of three ordinary nonlinear differential equations. Thus matrices containing variable elements can be used to represent nonlinear operators on a vector whenever the elements of the matrix contain components of the vector on which it is operating as shown above.

Let

$$\begin{pmatrix} u \\ v \\ w \end{pmatrix} = \begin{pmatrix} 1 & 1 & 1 \\ 1 & \omega & \omega^2 \\ 1 & \omega^2 & \omega^4 \end{pmatrix} \begin{pmatrix} x \\ y \\ z \end{pmatrix} = \begin{pmatrix} 1 & 1 & 1 \\ 1 & \omega & \omega^2 \\ 1 & \omega^2 & \omega \end{pmatrix} \begin{pmatrix} x \\ y \\ z \end{pmatrix} = \Omega \begin{pmatrix} x \\ y \\ z \end{pmatrix}$$

where $\omega^3 = 1$, or $\omega^3 - 1 = 0$, or $(\omega-1)(\omega^2 + \omega + 1) = 0$.

Then:

$$\begin{aligned} uv: &\ = 1x^2 + \omega y^2 + \omega^2 z^2 - \omega^2 xy - 1yz - \omega zx \\ vw: &\ = 1x^2 + 1y^2 + 1z^2 - 1xy - 1yz - 1zx \\ wu: &\ = 1x^2 + \omega^2 y^2 + \omega z^2 - \omega xy - 1yz - \omega^2 xz \end{aligned}$$

Multiply differential equations above by $\begin{pmatrix} 1 \\ \omega \\ \omega^2 \end{pmatrix}, \begin{pmatrix} 1 \\ \omega^2 \\ \omega^4 \end{pmatrix}$

and adding we get:

$$\begin{pmatrix} \dot{u} \\ \dot{v} \\ \dot{w} \end{pmatrix} = \begin{pmatrix} \underline{0} & \underline{0} & \underline{-v} \\ \underline{-v} & \underline{0} & \underline{0} \\ \underline{0} & \underline{0} & \underline{-u} \end{pmatrix} \begin{pmatrix} u \\ v \\ w \end{pmatrix} = \begin{pmatrix} 0 & -w & 0 \\ -v & 0 & 0 \\ 0 & 0 & -u \end{pmatrix} \begin{pmatrix} u \\ v \\ w \end{pmatrix} \text{ or } \begin{cases} \dot{u} = -vw \\ \dot{v} = -uv \\ \dot{w} = -wu \end{cases}$$

The last pair of equations imply that $\frac{dv}{v} = \frac{dw}{w}$

which imply that $V = k^2 w$, when k^2 is an arbitrary constant written in this form for convenience and the above system is equivalent to the following:

$$\begin{cases} \dot{u} = -k^2 w^2 \\ \dot{w} = -w\,u \\ \dot{v} = k^2 w \end{cases}$$

Eliminating u from the first pair of equations above we get by taking the second derivative of

$\dot{w} = -wu$ to get:

$$\begin{cases} \ddot{w} = -\dot{w}u - w\dot{u} \\ \dot{u} = (-)k^2 w^2 \end{cases}$$

and

$$\ddot{w} = -\dot{w}\left(\frac{-\dot{w}}{w}\right) - w(-k^2 w^2)$$

$$w\ddot{w} = \frac{(\dot{w})^2}{w} + k^2 w^3$$

$$w\ddot{w} = (\dot{w})^2 + k^2w^4$$

$$w\ddot{w} - (\dot{w})^2 = k^2w^4$$

Let

$$p = \dot{w}\ ;\ \ddot{w} = p\left(\frac{dp}{dw}\right)$$

then

$$wp\frac{dp}{dw} - p^2 = k^2w^4$$

and

$$2wp\frac{dp}{dw} - 2p^2 = 2k^2w^4$$

or

$$\left[\frac{2p\left(\frac{dp}{dw}\right) - \left(\frac{2}{w}\right)p^2}{w^2}\right] = 2k^2w$$

$$\frac{w^2}{w^2}\cdot\left[\frac{2p\left(\frac{dp}{dw}\right) - \left(\frac{2}{w}\right)p^2}{w^2}\right] = 2k^2w$$

$$\left(\frac{\begin{matrix} w^2 \\ 2w^2p\frac{dp}{dw} - 2wp^2\end{matrix}}{w^4}\right) = 2k^2w$$

$$2p\left(\frac{dp}{dw}\right) - \left(\frac{2}{w}\right)p^2 = 2k^2w^3$$

and

$$\left(\frac{p^2}{w^2}\right)' = 2k^2w$$

so

$$\frac{p^2}{w^2} = k^2w^2 - c^2$$

whenever the constant of integration is taken to be $-c^2$. If the constant of integration is taken as $+c^2$ the resulting solution will involve hyperbolic-functions instead of circular functions.

Next solving for $p = \frac{dw}{dt}$, separating variables, and integrating again, we obtain

$$\frac{dw}{w\sqrt{k^2w^2-c^2}} = \pm\, dt$$

or

$$\frac{1}{c}\sec^{-1}\left(\frac{kw}{c}\right) = \pm(t+b)$$

so

$$w = \frac{c}{k}\sec c(t+b)$$

Substituting the w in the last of the pair of equations above, which give v, u:

$$\begin{cases} v = (ck)\sec c(t+b) \\ u = (-c)\tan c(t+b)\end{cases};\quad \begin{pmatrix}u\\v\\w\end{pmatrix} = \begin{pmatrix}1&1&1\\1&\omega&\omega^2\\1&\omega^2&\omega^4\end{pmatrix}\begin{pmatrix}x\\y\\z\end{pmatrix}$$

Now for

$$\begin{cases} x = 1/3(u+v+w)\\ y = 1/3(u+\omega^2v+\omega w)\\ z = 1/3(u+\omega v+\omega^2 w)\end{cases};\quad \begin{pmatrix}x\\y\\z\end{pmatrix} = 1/3\begin{pmatrix}1&1&1\\1&\omega^2&\omega\\1&\omega^4&\omega^2\end{pmatrix}\begin{pmatrix}u\\v\\w\end{pmatrix}$$

imply that

$$\begin{cases} x = \left(\frac{k^2+1}{3k}\right) c\sec c(t+b) - \frac{c}{3}\tan c(t+b)\\ y = \left(\frac{\omega^2k^2+\omega}{3k}\right) c\sec c(t+b) - \frac{c}{3}\tan c(t+b)\\ z = \left(\frac{\omega k^2+\omega^2}{3k}\right) c\sec c(t+b) - \frac{c}{3}\tan c(t+b)\end{cases}$$

where k, b, c are arbitrary constants, and x(t), y(t), z(t) represent the general solution of the orginial nonlinear dynamical set of equations.

GENERALIZED INVERSE OF MULTIPARAMETER MATRICES

Example. Given the multiparameter matrix:

$$A(x,y) = \begin{pmatrix} x & x^2+1\\ x^2y & x^3y+xy\end{pmatrix}$$

Making use of the method of J. Jones, Jr. we first compute the various generalized inverses of A(x,y). Making use of elementary row and elementary column operations we have the following:

$$A(x,y) = \begin{pmatrix} x & x^2+1\\ x^2y & x^3y+xy\end{pmatrix} \rightarrow \left(\begin{array}{cc|cc} x & x^2+1 & 1 & 0\\ x^2y & x^3y+xy & 0 & 1\\ \hline 1 & 0 & & \\ 0 & 1 & & \end{array}\right) \rightarrow$$

$$\left(\begin{array}{cc|cc} x & x^2+1 & 1 & 0\\ 0 & 0 & -xy & 1\\ \hline 1 & 0 & & \\ 0 & 1 & & \end{array}\right) \rightarrow \left(\begin{array}{cc|cc} x & 1 & 1 & 0\\ 0 & 0 & -xy & 1\\ \hline 1 & -x & & \\ 0 & 1 & & \end{array}\right) \rightarrow \left(\begin{array}{cc|cc} 1 & x & 1 & 0\\ 0 & 0 & -xy & 1\\ \hline -x & 1 & & \\ 1 & 0 & & \end{array}\right) \rightarrow$$

$$\left(\begin{array}{c|c|cc} 1 & 0 & 1 & 0\\ \hline 0 & 0 & -xy & 1\\ \hline -x & 1+x^2 & & \\ 1 & -x & & \end{array}\right) \rightarrow \left(\begin{array}{c|c|cc} 1 & 0 & \frac{1}{x^2+y^2+1} & \frac{xy}{x^2+y^2+1}\\ \hline 0 & 0 & -xy & 1\\ \hline -x & 1+x^2 & & \\ 1 & -x & & \end{array}\right) \rightarrow$$

$$\left\{\begin{array}{c|c||cc} 1 & 0 & \frac{1}{x^2y^2+1} & \frac{xy}{x^2+y^2+1} \\ \hline 0 & 0 & -xy & 1 \\ \hline \frac{x}{(x^2+1)^2+x^2} & \frac{x^5+3x^3+2x}{(x^2+1)^2+x^2} & & \\ \frac{x^2+1}{(x^2+1)^2+x^2} & \frac{x^4-2x^2}{(x^2+1)^2+x^2} & & \end{array}\right\}$$

Now:

$$A_1(x,y) = \begin{pmatrix} -x \\ 1 \end{pmatrix} (1 \quad 0) = \begin{pmatrix} -x & 0 \\ 1 & 0 \end{pmatrix}; \; A_2(x,y) =$$

$$A_1(x,y) = A_{1,2}(x,y)$$

$$A_{1,2,3} = \begin{pmatrix} -x \\ 1 \end{pmatrix} \begin{pmatrix} \frac{1}{x^2+y^2+1} & \frac{xy}{x^2+y^2+1} \end{pmatrix} =$$

$$\begin{pmatrix} \frac{-x}{x^2+y^2+1} & \frac{-x^2y}{x^2+y^2+1} \\ \frac{1}{x^2y^2+1} & \frac{xy}{x^2+y^2+1} \end{pmatrix}$$

$$A_{1,2,4} = \begin{pmatrix} \frac{x}{(x^2+1)^2+x^2} \\ \frac{x^2+1}{(x^2+1)^2+x^2} \end{pmatrix} (1 \quad 0) = \begin{pmatrix} \frac{x}{(x^2+1)^2+x^2} & 0 \\ \frac{x^2+1}{(x^2+1)^2+x^2} & 0 \end{pmatrix}$$

$$A_{1,2,3,4} = \begin{pmatrix} \frac{x}{(x^2+1)^2+x^2} \\ \frac{x^2+1}{(x^2+1)^2+1} \end{pmatrix} \begin{pmatrix} \frac{1}{x^2+y^2+1} & \frac{xy}{x^2+y^2+1} \end{pmatrix}$$

The flow chart for parallel computation is as follows:

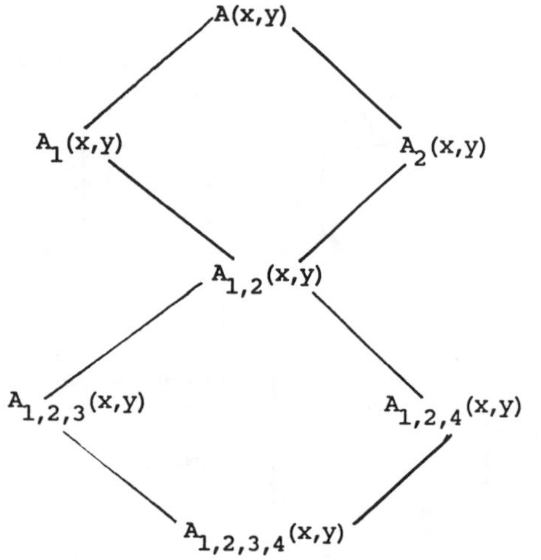

MATHEMATICAL MODELLING AND SIMULATION OF LARGE MULTIPARAMETER DYNAMICAL SYSTEMS

Various inverse systems associated with nonlinear systems of the form $E(\theta)\dot{x} = A(\theta)x+B(\theta)u$, $y = C(\theta)x + D(\theta)u$ are considered where the matrices $E(\theta)$, $A(\theta)$, $B(\theta)$, $C(\theta)$, $D(\theta)$ are multiparameter matrices. Use is made of recent results of J. Jones, Jr. (1,2,3) concerning generalized inverses of such multiparameter matrices and a fundamental theorem of linear algebra for such matrices.

In this paper nonlinear multiparameter multidimensional dynamical systems of the form

$$\begin{cases} E(\theta)\dot{x} = A(\theta)x + B(\theta)u & (1.1) \\ y = C(\theta)x + D(\theta)u & (1.2) \end{cases}$$

for $t \geq 0$ will be considered where x is an r-vector of internal variables, u is an m-vector of control inputs or functions and y is a p-vector of outputs. The multiparameter matrices $A(\theta)$, $E(\theta)$, $B(\theta)$, $C(\theta)$, $D(\theta)$ belong to various vector spaces. Let $C^{mxn}(\theta)$ denote the vector space of all mxn matrices whose elements belong to the ring of polynomials of several parameters denoted by $(\theta_1, \theta_2, \ldots, \theta_r) = \theta$ and have coefficients belonging to the field C of complex numbers or the ratio of such polynomials $p(\theta)/q(\theta) \neq 0$. Also these coefficient matrices may be allowed to have holomorphic functions of a single complex variable z for z belonging to simply-connected bounded regions R of the z-plane.

The matrices above belong to the following vector spaces: $A(\theta)$, $E(\theta)$ ε $C^{nxn}(\theta)$, $B(\theta)$ ε $C^{nxp}(\theta)$, $C(\theta)$ ε $C^{mxn}(\theta)$, $D(\theta)$ ε $C^{mxp}(\theta)$, $(m \leq p)$. Also suppose that $D(\theta)D^-(\theta) = I_m$ for any 1-generalized inverse $D^-(\theta)$ of $D(\theta)$ holds where $D(\theta)D^-(\theta)D(\theta) = D(\theta)$ and $D^-(\theta)$ ε $C^{pxm}(\theta)$. It will also be assumed that $E(\theta)E^-(\theta)A(\theta) = A(\theta)$ and $E(\theta)B(\theta)D^-(\theta) = B(\theta)D^-(\theta)$ for any 1-generalized inverse of $D^-(\theta)$, $E^-(\theta)$.

The main purpose of this work is to first obtain inverse-systems of the form:

$$\begin{cases} \dot{x} = A_1(\theta)x + B_1(\theta)u & (1.3) \\ u = C_1(\theta) + D_1(\theta)u & (1.4) \end{cases}$$

for $t \geq 0$ associated with (1.1), (1.2) above and then make use of the multiparameters of the inverse system (1.3), (1.4) and the various 1-generalized inverses od $D(\theta)$, $E(\theta)$ to modify or choose appropriately in an attempt to obtain stabilization, controllability, and observability properties of the inverse systems (1.3), (1.4) obtained. Thus computer simulation allows the adjustment of these arbitrary available parameters to obtain more desirable responses of such large dynamical systems in modelling and simulation and obtain information concerning integrated system response which is not always obtained from detailed information concerning subsystems alone. Also, parameters not considered prior to integrated operation may be adjusted in the computer modelling and simulation process.

In systems modelled by (1.1), (1.2) the matrix $E(\theta)$ can easily become singular or bifurication points in the parameter-space may exist, in which case the solutions of the system may become chaotic or not even exist at all, or have mixed impulsive and other types of responses. This occurs when subsystems fail and the effect is reflected throughout the entire system. Robust control feedback-laws are needed in such cases. Results obtained generalize the classical case where the coefficient matrices above were constant matrices.

In section II the case of the multiparameter coefficient matrices will be considered and in section III the case where matrices A,B,C,D have elements which are continuous functions of t will be considered.

MULTIPARAMETER DYNAMICAL SYSTEMS

Associated with the multiparameter system (1.1), (1.2) above is the following matrix $S(\theta) \epsilon C^{(m+n)x(n+p)}C(\theta)$:

$$S(\theta) \stackrel{\Delta}{=} \begin{bmatrix} E(\theta) & -B(\theta) \\ 0 & D(\theta) \end{bmatrix} \qquad (1.5)$$

In this section various inverse systems of (1.1),(1.2) will be established. We have the first result.

Theorem 1. The matrix given above in (1.5) has a 1-generalized inverse given ny

$$S(\theta)^{-} = \begin{bmatrix} E^{-}(\theta) & B(\theta)D^{-}(\theta) \\ 0 & D^{-}(\theta) \end{bmatrix} \qquad (2.1)$$

whenever $E(\theta)E^{-}(\theta)B(\theta) = B(\theta)$, $E(\theta)B(\theta)D^{-}(\theta) = B(\theta)D^{-}(\theta)$ hold.

Proof. Consider the following:

$$\begin{bmatrix} E(\theta) & -B(\theta) \\ 0 & D(\theta) \end{bmatrix} \begin{bmatrix} E^{-}(\theta) & B(\theta)D^{-}(\theta) \\ 0 & D^{-}(\theta) \end{bmatrix} \begin{bmatrix} E(\theta) & -B(\theta) \\ 0 & D(\theta) \end{bmatrix} \qquad (2.2)$$

$$= \begin{bmatrix} E(\theta)E^{-}(\theta) & E(\theta)B(\theta)D^{-}(\theta)-B(\theta)D^{-}(\theta) \\ 0 & D(\theta)D^{-}(\theta) \end{bmatrix} \begin{bmatrix} E(\theta) & -B(\theta) \\ 0 & D(\theta) \end{bmatrix}$$

$$= \begin{bmatrix} E(\theta)E^{-}(\theta)E(\theta) & -E(\theta)E^{-}(\theta)B(\theta)+E(\theta)B(\theta)D^{-}(\theta)-B(\theta)D^{-}(\theta)D(\theta) \\ 0 & D(\theta)D^{-}(\theta)D(\theta) \end{bmatrix}$$

$$= \begin{bmatrix} E(\theta) & -B(\theta) \\ 0 & D(\theta) \end{bmatrix} = S(\theta)$$

Thus $S(\overline{\theta})$ is a 1-generalized inverse of $S(\theta)$ above, i.e., $S(\theta)S^{-}(\theta)S(\theta) = S(\theta)$.

Theorem 2 - The matrix $S^{-}(\theta)$ given in (2.1) above is also a 2-generalized inverse of $S(\theta)$ given in (1.5) above whenever $E^{-}(\theta)E(\theta)B(\theta)D^{-}(\theta) = E^{-}(\theta)$ $B(\theta)D^{-}(\theta)$ and $E^{-}(\theta)E(\theta)E^{-}(\theta) = E^{-}(\theta)$, $D^{-}(\theta)D(\theta)D^{-}(\theta) = D^{-}(\theta)$ hold, $(E^{-}(\theta), D^{-}(\theta))$ are 2-generalized inverses of $E(\theta)$, $D(\theta)$).

Proof - Consider the following:

$$\begin{bmatrix} E^{-}(\theta) & B(\theta)D^{-}(\theta) \\ 0 & D^{-}(\theta) \end{bmatrix} \begin{bmatrix} E(\theta) & -B(\theta) \\ 0 & D(\theta) \end{bmatrix} \begin{bmatrix} E^{-}(\theta) & B(\theta)D^{-}(\theta) \\ 0 & D^{-}(\theta) \end{bmatrix} \qquad (2.3)$$

$$= \begin{bmatrix} E^{-}(\theta)E(\theta) & -E(\theta)B(\theta)+B(\theta)D^{-}(\theta)D(\theta) \\ 0 & D^{-}(\theta)D(\theta) \end{bmatrix} \begin{bmatrix} E^{-}(\theta) & B(\theta)D^{-}(\theta) \\ 0 & D^{-}(\theta) \end{bmatrix}$$

$$= \begin{bmatrix} E^{-}(\theta)E(\theta)E^{-}(\theta) & E^{-}(\theta)E(\theta)B(\theta)D^{-}(\theta)-E(\theta)B(\theta)D^{-}(\theta)+B(\theta)D^{-}(\theta)D(\theta)D^{-}(\theta) \\ 0 & D^{-}(\theta)D(\theta)D^{-}(\theta) \end{bmatrix}$$

$$= \begin{bmatrix} E^{-}(\theta) & B(\theta)D^{-}(\theta) \\ 0 & D^{-}(\theta) \end{bmatrix}$$

Thus $S^{-}(\theta)S(\theta)S^{-}(\theta) = S^{-}(\theta)$ and $S^{-}(\theta)$ is a 2-generalized inverse of $S(\theta)$.

Theorem 3 - The system (1.1),(1.2) may be written as follows:

$$\begin{bmatrix} E(\theta) & -B(\theta) \\ 0 & D(\theta) \end{bmatrix} \begin{bmatrix} \dot{x} \\ u \end{bmatrix} = \begin{bmatrix} A(\theta)x \\ y-C(\theta)x \end{bmatrix} \qquad (2.4)$$

A solution $\begin{bmatrix} \dot{x} \\ u \end{bmatrix}$ of equation (2.4) exists if and only if the equation holds:

$$\begin{bmatrix} E(\theta) & -B(\theta) \\ 0 & D(\theta) \end{bmatrix} \begin{bmatrix} E(\theta) & -B(\theta) \\ 0 & D(\theta) \end{bmatrix}^{-} \begin{bmatrix} A(\theta)x \\ y-C(\theta)x \end{bmatrix} = \begin{bmatrix} A(\theta)x \\ y-C(\theta)x \end{bmatrix} \qquad (2.5)$$

Proof. If equation (2.4) has a solution $\begin{bmatrix} \dot{x} \\ u \end{bmatrix}$ then

$$\begin{bmatrix} E(\theta) & -B(\theta) \\ 0 & D(\theta) \end{bmatrix} \begin{bmatrix} E(\theta) & -B(\theta) \\ 0 & D(\theta) \end{bmatrix}^{-} \begin{bmatrix} A(\theta)x \\ y-C(\theta)x \end{bmatrix} \qquad (2.6)$$

$$= \begin{bmatrix} E(\theta) & -B(\theta) \\ 0 & D(\theta) \end{bmatrix} \begin{bmatrix} E^{-}(\theta) & B(\theta)D^{-}(\theta) \\ 0 & D^{-}(\theta) \end{bmatrix} \begin{bmatrix} A(\theta)x \\ y-C(\theta)x \end{bmatrix}$$

$$= \begin{bmatrix} E(\theta)E^{-}(\theta) & E(\theta)B(\theta)D^{-}(\theta)-B(\theta)D^{-}(\theta) \\ 0 & D(\theta)D^{-}(\theta) \end{bmatrix} \begin{bmatrix} A(\theta)x \\ y-C(\theta)x \end{bmatrix}$$

$$= \begin{bmatrix} E(\theta)E^{-}(\theta) & 0 \\ 0 & D(\theta)D^{-}(\theta) \end{bmatrix} \begin{bmatrix} A(\theta)x \\ y-C(\theta)x \end{bmatrix}$$

$$= \begin{bmatrix} (E(\theta)E^{-}(\theta)A(\theta)x \\ D(\theta)D^{-}(\theta)(y-C(\theta)x) \end{bmatrix} = \begin{bmatrix} A(\theta)x \\ I_m(y-C(\theta)x) \end{bmatrix} = \begin{bmatrix} A(\theta)x \\ y-C(\theta)x \end{bmatrix}$$

and equation (2.5) follows:

Proof. Conversely, if equation (2.5) holds then (2.4) has a solution of the form:

$$\begin{pmatrix}\dot{x}\\ u\end{pmatrix}=\begin{pmatrix}E(\theta) & -B(\theta)\\ 0 & D(\theta)\end{pmatrix}^{-}\begin{pmatrix}A(\theta)x\\ y-C(\theta)x\end{pmatrix} = \text{solution}$$

Since

$$\begin{pmatrix}E(\theta) & -B(\theta)\\ 0 & D(\theta)\end{pmatrix}\begin{pmatrix}\dot{x}\\ u\end{pmatrix}=\begin{pmatrix}E(\theta) & -B(\theta)\\ 0 & D(\theta)\end{pmatrix}\begin{pmatrix}E(\theta) & -B(\theta)\\ 0 & D(\theta)\end{pmatrix}^{-}$$

$$\begin{pmatrix}A(\theta)x\\ y-C(\theta)x\end{pmatrix}=\begin{pmatrix}A(\theta)x\\ y-C(\theta)x\end{pmatrix} \qquad (2.7)$$

However the general solution of (2.5) under these consistency of conditions is of the following form:

$$\begin{pmatrix}\dot{x}\\ u\end{pmatrix}=\begin{pmatrix}E(\theta) & -B(\theta)\\ 0 & D(\theta)\end{pmatrix}^{-}+\left[I-\begin{pmatrix}E(\theta) & -B(\theta)\\ 0 & D(\theta)\end{pmatrix}^{-}\right.$$

$$\left.\begin{pmatrix}E(\theta) & -B(\theta)\\ 0 & D(\theta)\end{pmatrix}\right]Z(\theta)$$

for arbitrary $Z(\theta)$ of appropriate size. This representation of $\begin{pmatrix}\dot{x}\\ u\end{pmatrix}$ is the general solution as is seen by choosing $Z(\theta)$ appropriately. Let $\begin{pmatrix}\dot{x}\\ u\end{pmatrix}_0$ by any be any solution of $S(\theta)$ $\begin{pmatrix}\dot{x}\\ u\end{pmatrix}_0=\begin{pmatrix}A(\theta)x\\ y-C(\theta)x\end{pmatrix}$,

$Z(\theta)=\begin{pmatrix}\dot{x}\\ u\end{pmatrix}_0$ and using (2.8) we see that

$$\begin{pmatrix}\dot{x}\\ u\end{pmatrix}=\begin{pmatrix}E(\theta) & -B(\theta)\\ 0 & D(\theta)\end{pmatrix}^{-}\begin{pmatrix}A(\theta)x\\ y-C(\theta)x\end{pmatrix}+\begin{pmatrix}\dot{x}\\ u\end{pmatrix}_0-\begin{pmatrix}E(\theta) & -B(\theta)\\ 0 & D(\theta)\end{pmatrix}^{-}$$

$$\begin{pmatrix}E(\theta) & -B(\theta)\\ 0 & D(\theta)\end{pmatrix}\begin{pmatrix}A(\theta)x\\ y-C(\theta)x\end{pmatrix} \qquad (2.9)$$

and finally:

$$\begin{pmatrix}\dot{x}\\ u\end{pmatrix} \quad \begin{pmatrix}\dot{x}\\ u\end{pmatrix}_0$$

Hence any inverse system of (1.1), (1.2) can now be written:

$$\begin{pmatrix}\dot{x}\\ u\end{pmatrix}=\begin{pmatrix}E^{-}(\theta) & B(\theta)D^{-}(\theta)\\ 0 & D^{-}(\theta)\end{pmatrix}\begin{pmatrix}A(\theta)x\\ y-C(\theta)x\end{pmatrix}+$$

$$(2.10)$$

$$\left[\begin{pmatrix}I_p & 0\\ 0 & I_p\end{pmatrix}-\begin{pmatrix}E^{-}(\theta) & B(\theta)D^{-}(\theta)\\ 0 & D^{-}(\theta)\end{pmatrix}\begin{pmatrix}E(\theta) & -B(\theta)\\ 0 & D(\theta)\end{pmatrix}\right]Z(\theta)$$

or as below:

$$\begin{cases}\dot{x}=[E^{-}(\theta)A(\theta)-B(\theta)D^{-}(\theta)C(\theta)]x+[B(\theta)D^{-}(\theta)]y+\\ \qquad [I_p-B(\theta)D^{-}(\theta)D(\theta)]h\\ u=[-D^{-}(\theta)C(\theta)]x+[D^{-}(\theta)]y+[I_p-D^{-}(\theta)D(\theta)]h\end{cases} \qquad (2.11)$$

where h is an arbitrary px1 matrix. The consistency condition is satisfied by any choice of the (p-m) arbitrary elements of the px1 matrix

$(I_p-D^{-}(\theta)D(\theta))h$.

If $D^{-}(\theta)$ is any 1-generalized inverse of $D(\theta)$, then the general form of all 1-generalized inverses of $D(\theta)$ satisfies the following:

$$Z(\theta)=D^{-}(\theta)+K(\theta)-D^{-}(\theta)D(\theta)K(\theta)$$

where $K(\theta)$ is an arbitrary (pxm) matrix. Thus, any choice of the matrix $K(\theta)$ will give an inverse system of (1.1),(1.2); however, properties of the inverse system will depend upon the particular choice of $K(\theta)$.

EXAMPLE OF A SINGULAR SYSTEM

Consider the following example of a singular system (1.1),(1.2):

$$\begin{cases}E\dot{x}=Ax+Bu\\ y=Cx+Du\end{cases}$$

where

$$E=\begin{pmatrix}1&0&0\\0&1&1\\1&0&0\end{pmatrix};\ A=\begin{pmatrix}1&0&1\\0&1&0\\1&0&1\end{pmatrix};\ E^{-}=\begin{pmatrix}1&0&0\\0&1&0\\0&0&0\end{pmatrix}$$

$$EE^{-}A=\begin{pmatrix}1&0&1\\0&1&0\\1&0&0\end{pmatrix}\begin{pmatrix}1&0&1\\0&1&0\\1&0&1\end{pmatrix}=A;\ B=\begin{pmatrix}0&1\\1&-2\\0&0\end{pmatrix};$$

$$C=\begin{pmatrix}1&0&0\\0&0&0\\0&0&0\end{pmatrix};\ D=\begin{pmatrix}0&1\\0&0\\0&0\end{pmatrix}$$

First computing a 1-generalized inverse of D by the method of John Jones, Jr. (2):

$$\left(\begin{array}{cc|ccc}0&1&1&0&0\\0&0&0&1&0\\0&0&0&0&1\\ \hline 1&0&&&\\0&1&&&\end{array}\right)\rightarrow\left(\begin{array}{c|c|ccc}1&0&1&0&0\\ \hline 0&0&0&1&0\\0&0&0&0&1\\ \hline 0&1&&&\\1&0&&&\end{array}\right),\ D^{-}(\theta)=\begin{pmatrix}0\\1\end{pmatrix}$$

$$(1\ \ 0\ \ 0)\Rightarrow\begin{pmatrix}0&0&0\\1&0&0\end{pmatrix}$$

Now any 1-generalized inverse of D is of the form Z, for arbitrary K.

$$Z = \begin{bmatrix} 0 & 0 & 0 \\ 1 & 0 & 0 \end{bmatrix} + \begin{bmatrix} k_{11} & k_{12} & k_{13} \\ k_{21} & k_{22} & k_{23} \end{bmatrix} - \begin{bmatrix} 0 & 0 & 0 \\ 1 & 0 & 0 \end{bmatrix} \begin{bmatrix} 0 & 1 \\ 0 & 0 \\ 0 & 0 \end{bmatrix} \begin{bmatrix} k_{11} & k_{12} & k_{13} \\ k_{21} & k_{22} & k_{23} \end{bmatrix}$$

$$Z = \begin{bmatrix} 0 & 0 & 0 \\ 1 & 0 & 0 \end{bmatrix} + \begin{bmatrix} k_{11} & k_{12} & k_{13} \\ k_{21} & k_{22} & k_{23} \end{bmatrix} - \begin{bmatrix} 0 & 0 \\ 0 & 1 \end{bmatrix} \begin{bmatrix} k_{11} & k_{12} & k_{13} \\ k_{21} & k_{22} & k_{23} \end{bmatrix}$$

$$Z = \begin{bmatrix} 0 & 0 & 0 \\ 1 & 0 & 0 \end{bmatrix} + \begin{bmatrix} k_{11} & k_{12} & k_{13} \\ k_{21} & k_{22} & k_{23} \end{bmatrix} - \begin{bmatrix} 0 & 0 & 0 \\ k_{21} & k_{22} & k_{23} \end{bmatrix}$$

$$Z = \begin{bmatrix} k_{11} & k_{12} & k_{13} \\ 1 & 0 & 0 \end{bmatrix} = \text{arb. } D^{-}, \text{ for any } k_{11}, k_{12}, k_{13}.$$

Next to compute E^{-} for E given above

$$\left[\begin{array}{ccc|ccc} 1 & 0 & 0 & 1 & 0 & 0 \\ 0 & 1 & 1 & 0 & 1 & 0 \\ 1 & 0 & 0 & 0 & 0 & 1 \\ \hline 1 & 0 & 0 & & & \\ 0 & 1 & 0 & & & \\ 0 & 0 & 1 & & & \end{array}\right] \rightarrow \left[\begin{array}{ccc|ccc} 1 & 0 & 0 & 1 & 0 & 0 \\ 0 & 1 & 1 & 0 & 1 & 0 \\ 0 & 0 & 0 & -1 & 0 & 1 \\ \hline 1 & 0 & 0 & & & \\ 0 & 1 & 0 & & & \\ 0 & 0 & 1 & & & \end{array}\right] \rightarrow$$

$$\left[\begin{array}{cc|c|ccc} 1 & 0 & 0 & 1 & 0 & 0 \\ 0 & 1 & 0 & 0 & 1 & 0 \\ \hline 0 & 0 & 0 & -1 & 0 & 1 \\ \hline 1 & 0 & 0 & & & \\ 0 & 1 & -1 & & & \\ 0 & 0 & 1 & & & \end{array}\right]$$

$$E^{-} = \begin{bmatrix} 1 & 0 \\ 0 & 1 \\ 0 & 0 \end{bmatrix} \begin{bmatrix} 1 & 0 & 0 \\ 0 & 1 & 0 \end{bmatrix} = \begin{bmatrix} 1 & 0 & 0 \\ 0 & 1 & 0 \\ 0 & 0 & 0 \end{bmatrix}$$

$$EE^{-} = \begin{bmatrix} 1 & 0 & 0 \\ 0 & 1 & 1 \\ 1 & 0 & 0 \end{bmatrix} \begin{bmatrix} 1 & 0 & 0 \\ 0 & 1 & 0 \\ 0 & 0 & 0 \end{bmatrix} = \begin{bmatrix} 1 & 0 & 0 \\ 0 & 1 & 0 \\ 1 & 0 & 0 \end{bmatrix}; \; EE^{-}A = A$$

Now any 1-generalized inverse of E is of the form Z for arbitrary K.

$$Z = \begin{bmatrix} 1 & 0 & 0 \\ 0 & 1 & 0 \\ 0 & 0 & 0 \end{bmatrix} + \begin{bmatrix} k_{11} & k_{12} & k_{13} \\ k_{21} & k_{22} & k_{23} \\ k_{31} & k_{32} & k_{33} \end{bmatrix} - \begin{bmatrix} 1 & 0 & 0 \\ 0 & 1 & 0 \\ 0 & 0 & 0 \end{bmatrix} \begin{bmatrix} 1 & 0 & 0 \\ 0 & 1 & 1 \\ 1 & 0 & 0 \end{bmatrix} \begin{bmatrix} k_{11} & k_{12} & k_{13} \\ k_{21} & k_{22} & k_{23} \\ k_{31} & k_{32} & k_{33} \end{bmatrix}$$

$$Z = \begin{bmatrix} 1 & 0 & 0 \\ 0 & 1 & 0 \\ 0 & 0 & 0 \end{bmatrix} + \begin{bmatrix} k_{11} & k_{12} & k_{13} \\ k_{21} & k_{22} & k_{23} \\ k_{31} & k_{32} & k_{33} \end{bmatrix} - \begin{bmatrix} 1 & 0 & 0 \\ 0 & 1 & 1 \\ 0 & 0 & 0 \end{bmatrix} \begin{bmatrix} k_{11} & k_{12} & k_{13} \\ k_{21} & k_{22} & k_{23} \\ k_{31} & k_{32} & k_{33} \end{bmatrix}$$

$$Z = \begin{bmatrix} 1 & 0 & 0 \\ 0 & 1 & 0 \\ 0 & 0 & 0 \end{bmatrix} + \begin{bmatrix} 0 & 0 & 0 \\ -k_{31} & -k_{32} & -k_{33} \\ k_{31} & k_{32} & k_{33} \end{bmatrix} = \begin{bmatrix} 1 & 0 & 0 \\ -k_{31} & 1-k_{32} & -k_{33} \\ -k_{31} & -k_{32} & -k_{33} \end{bmatrix} \text{(for arbitrary k's)}$$

For a given $S(\theta)$ associated with a dynamical system, consider the following method due to J. Jones, Jr. (1,2,3).

$$S(\theta) \rightarrow \left[\begin{array}{c|c} E(\theta) & -B(\theta) \\ \hline 0 & D(\theta) \end{array}\right] = \left[\begin{array}{ccc|cc} 1 & 0 & 0 & 0 & -1 \\ 0 & 1 & 1 & -1 & 2 \\ 1 & 0 & 0 & 0 & 0 \\ \hline 0 & 0 & 0 & 0 & 1 \\ 0 & 0 & 0 & 0 & 0 \\ 0 & 0 & 0 & 0 & 0 \end{array}\right] \rightarrow \left[\begin{array}{ccc|cc|c} 1 & 0 & 0 & 0 & -1 & \\ 0 & 1 & 1 & -1 & 2 & \\ 1 & 0 & 0 & 0 & 0 & \\ 0 & 0 & 0 & 0 & 1 & I \\ 0 & 0 & 0 & 0 & 0 & \\ 0 & 0 & 0 & 0 & 0 & \\ \hline & I & & & & \end{array}\right]$$

$$\left[\begin{array}{ccc|cc|cccccc} 1 & 0 & 0 & 0 & 0 & 0 & 0 & 1 & 0 & 0 & 0 \\ 0 & 1 & 0 & 0 & 0 & -1 & 0 & 1 & 0 & 0 & 0 \\ 0 & 0 & 1 & 0 & 0 & 2 & 1 & -2 & 0 & 0 & 0 \\ \hline 0 & 0 & 0 & 0 & 0 & 1 & 0 & -1 & 1 & 0 & 0 \\ 0 & 0 & 0 & 0 & 0 & 0 & 0 & 0 & 0 & 1 & 0 \\ 0 & 0 & 0 & 0 & 0 & 0 & 0 & 0 & 0 & 0 & 1 \\ \hline 1 & 0 & 0 & 0 & 0 & & & & & & \\ 0 & 0 & 1 & -1 & 1 & & & & & & \\ 0 & 0 & 0 & 1 & 0 & & & & & & \\ 0 & 0 & 0 & 0 & 1 & & & & & & \\ 0 & 1 & 0 & 0 & 0 & & & & & & \end{array}\right] \rightarrow \left[\begin{array}{c|c|c} I_r & 0 & T \\ \hline 0 & 0 & M \\ \hline S & N & 0 \end{array}\right]$$

which yields

$$S_{1,2}(\theta) = ST = \begin{pmatrix} 1 & 0 & 0 \\ 0 & 0 & 1 \\ 0 & 0 & 0 \\ 0 & 0 & 0 \\ 0 & 1 & 0 \end{pmatrix} \begin{pmatrix} 0 & 0 & 1 & 0 & 0 & 0 \\ -1 & 0 & 1 & 0 & 0 & 0 \\ 2 & 1 & -2 & 0 & 0 & 0 \end{pmatrix}$$

$$\begin{pmatrix} 0 & 0 & 1 & 0 & 0 & 0 \\ 2 & 1 & -2 & 0 & 0 & 0 \\ 0 & 0 & 0 & 0 & 0 & 0 \\ 0 & 0 & 0 & 0 & 0 & 0 \\ -1 & 0 & 1 & 0 & 0 & 0 \end{pmatrix}$$

where

$$S_{1,2}(\theta)S(\theta)S_{1,2}(\theta) = S_{1,2}(\theta);\ S_{1,2}(\theta)S(\theta) = S(\theta)$$

hold. Then inverse systems of the orginial singular system exist. A treatment of the stabilization, controllability, observability, etc. will appear elsewhere.

REFERENCES

1. Jones, John Jr., "Solutions of Matrix Equations Containing Parameters in Multidimensional Systems Simulation", IEEE Computer Society, Vol. I, 1985, pp. 253-263.

2. Jones, John Jr., "Multidimensional and Multiparameter Systems Theory and Supercomputers", International Supercomputing Institute, Inc., Vol. II, 1987, pp. 461-470.

3. Jones, John Jr., Supercomputing Simulation and Mathematical Modelling of Large Linear Multi-dimensional Multiparameter Dynamical Systems", International Supercomputing Institute, Inc., Vol. III, May 1988.

Simulators VI
© 1989 By The Society for Computer Simulation International
ISBN 0-911801-51-0

Conservation equations in multiphase flows

J. Michael Doster
Nuclear Engineering Department
North Carolina State University
Box 7909
Raleigh, NC 27695-7909

ABSTRACT

The conservation equations that describe mass, energy and momentum transport in a multiphase flow system can be rigorously derived from the classic Navier-Stokes equations for single-phase flows. This paper provides a review of the derivation of these equations. Area averaged tube-stream forms of the phasic conservation equations (six equation models) are presented. The origins of interfacial interaction terms are explicitly shown. Simplifications of the six equation model, including five equation models, Drift Flux models and Homogeneous Equilibrium Mixture (HEM) models are shown to be linear combinations of the more general six equation model.

INTRODUCTION

The mathematical modeling of many industrial processes, including those in the chemical and nuclear industries, requires the description of multiphase flow systems. Of particular interest, particularly in the nuclear industry, are two-phase, vapor/liquid (steam/water) systems. Systems of this type are complicated by phase change processes at the vapor/liquid interface. The conservation equations that describe the mass, energy and momentum transport in a multiphase flow system can be rigorously derived from the classic Navier-Stokes equations for single-phase flows (Ishii 1975, Delhaye et al. 1981). This paper provides a review of the derivation of these equations. While it is possible to develop both volume averaged and area averaged forms of the phasic conservation equations (six equation models), we concentrate here on the area averaged tube-stream (one-dimensional) form which provides the basis for most current reactor analysis codes. The flow geometry is illustrated in Figure 1. Phase change is assumed to occur at both the fixed surfaces and the interface between phases. This leads to terms in the phasic conservation equations which represent mass, energy and momentum transfer at the interface. Uncertainties in these interfacial interaction terms and computational difficulties associated with the full six equation model has led to the development of simpler models which include five equation, Drift Flux and Homogeneous Equilibrium Mixture (HEM) models. These simplifications can be shown to be linear combinations of the more general six equation model. As each of these models has been used in the in the simulation of nuclear power systems their derivation is presented here along with a discussion of their limitations.

FLUID CONSERVATION EQUATIONS

The area averaged, multiphase flow equations are derived from the differential form of the fluid conservation equations presented here without derivation:

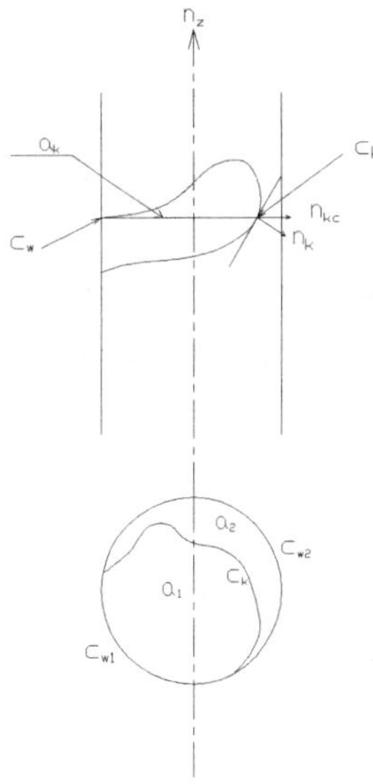

Figure 1 Flow geometry showing phase boundaries and vector notation [from Delhaye et al. 1981]

Continuity

$$\frac{\partial \rho}{\partial t} + \nabla \cdot (\rho \mathbf{v}) = 0$$

Momentum

$$\frac{\partial}{\partial t}(\rho \mathbf{v}) + \nabla \cdot (\rho \mathbf{v}\mathbf{v}) + \nabla \cdot \mathcal{T} - \rho \mathbf{g} = 0$$

Total Energy

$$\frac{\partial}{\partial t}[\rho(u + 1/2\ \mathbf{v}\cdot\mathbf{v})] + \nabla\cdot[\rho(u + 1/2\ \mathbf{v}\cdot\mathbf{v})] + \nabla\cdot[\mathbf{q} + \mathcal{T}\cdot\mathbf{v}] - Q_g - \rho\mathbf{g}\cdot\mathbf{v} = 0$$

Other useful forms of the energy equation include the

Kinetic Energy Equation

$$\frac{1}{2}\frac{\partial}{\partial t}(\rho \mathbf{v}\cdot\mathbf{v}) + \frac{1}{2}\nabla\cdot[(\rho\mathbf{v}\cdot\mathbf{v})\mathbf{v}] = -\nabla\cdot P\mathbf{v} + P\nabla\cdot\mathbf{v} + \nabla\cdot\sigma\cdot\mathbf{v} - \sum_{j=1}^{3}\sum_{i=1}^{3}\sigma_{ij}\frac{\partial}{\partial x_j}v_i + \rho\mathbf{g}\cdot\mathbf{v}$$

which is derived directly from the Momentum Equation, and the

Internal Energy Equation

$$\frac{\partial}{\partial t}(\rho u) + \nabla\cdot(\rho u \mathbf{v}) + \nabla\cdot\mathbf{q} - Q_g = -P\nabla\cdot\mathbf{v} + \sum_{j=1}^{3}\sum_{i=1}^{3} \sigma_{ij}\frac{\partial}{\partial x_j} v_i .$$

The Internal Energy Equation is obtained by subtracting the Kinetic Energy Equation from the Total Energy Equation and may be used in place of the Total Energy Equation without loss of generality. In addition to its simpler form, the Internal Energy Equation has computational advantages and will be used in all further discussions here.

AREA AVERAGED MULTIPHASE FLOW EQUATIONS

The conservation equations for a particular phase in a multiphase flow system are obtained by averaging the differential form of the conservation equations (given above) over the cross sectional flow area occupied by that phase. While the development is general and may be applied to flow systems with multiple components and/or multiple phases, the discussion here will be restricted to single component two-phase systems (steam/water) typical of those found in nuclear power systems. Examine first the Continuity Equation applied to an arbitrary phase k.

Continuity Equation

$$\frac{\partial}{\partial t}\rho_k + \nabla\cdot(\rho_k \mathbf{v}_k) = 0$$

Integrate over area a_k.

$$\int_{a_k} \frac{\partial}{\partial t}(\rho_k)ds + \int_{a_k} \nabla\cdot(\rho_k \mathbf{v}_k)ds = 0$$

To evaluate the integrals, we make use of limiting forms of Leibniz Rule and Gauss Theorems (Delhaye et al. 1981).

Leibniz Rule

For an arbitrary function ψ

$$\frac{\partial}{\partial t}\int_{a_k} \psi(r,t)\, ds = \int_{a_k} \frac{\partial\psi}{\partial t} ds + \int_{c} \psi \mathbf{v}_i\cdot\mathbf{n}_k \frac{dc}{\mathbf{n}_k\cdot\mathbf{n}_{kc}} .$$

Gauss Theorems

(i) Vector Fields

$$\int_{a_k} \nabla\cdot\mathbf{B}\, ds = \frac{\partial}{\partial z}\int_{a_k} \mathbf{B}\cdot\mathbf{n}_z\, ds + \int_{c} \mathbf{B}\cdot\mathbf{n}_k \frac{dc}{\mathbf{n}_k\cdot\mathbf{n}_{kc}}$$

Note: If $\mathbf{B} = \mathbf{n}_z$

$$\int_{a_k} \nabla\cdot\mathbf{n}_z\, ds = \frac{\partial}{\partial z}\int_{a_k} ds + \int_{c} \mathbf{n}_z\cdot\mathbf{n}_k \frac{dc}{\mathbf{n}_k\cdot\mathbf{n}_{kc}}$$

$$\int_{a_k} \frac{\partial}{\partial z}(1)\, ds = \frac{\partial}{\partial z} a_k + \int_{c} \mathbf{n}_k\cdot\mathbf{n}_k \frac{dc}{\mathbf{n}_k\cdot\mathbf{n}_{kc}}$$

$$\frac{\partial}{\partial z} a_k = -\int_{c} \mathbf{n}_z\cdot\mathbf{n}_k \frac{dc}{\mathbf{n}_k\cdot\mathbf{n}_{kc}}$$

which is a result which will prove useful later.

(ii) Tensor Fields

$$\int_{a_k} \nabla\cdot\mathcal{M}\, ds = \frac{\partial}{\partial z}\int_{a_k} \mathcal{M}\cdot\mathbf{n}_z\, ds + \int_{c} \mathcal{M}\cdot\mathbf{n}_k \frac{dc}{\mathbf{n}_k\cdot\mathbf{n}_{kc}}$$

Applying the above to the Continuity Equation gives

$$\frac{\partial}{\partial t}\int_{a_k} \rho_k\, ds + \frac{\partial}{\partial z}\int_{a_k} (\rho_k \mathbf{v}_k)\cdot\mathbf{n}_z\, ds + \int_{c} \rho_k(\mathbf{v}_k - \mathbf{v}_i)\cdot\mathbf{n}_k \frac{dc}{\mathbf{n}_k\cdot\mathbf{n}_{kc}} = 0.$$

Define the area averaged parameter $\langle\psi_k\rangle_2$

$$\langle\psi_k\rangle_2 \equiv \frac{1}{a_k}\int_{a_k} \psi_k\, ds$$

such that

$$\frac{\partial}{\partial t} a_k\langle\rho_k\rangle_2 + \frac{\partial}{\partial z} a_k\langle\rho_k \mathbf{v}_k\cdot\mathbf{n}_z\rangle_2 + \int_{c} \rho_k(\mathbf{v}_k - \mathbf{v}_i)\cdot\mathbf{n}_k \frac{dc}{\mathbf{n}_k\cdot\mathbf{n}_{kc}} = 0.$$

We further define

$$\rho_k(\mathbf{v}_k - \mathbf{v}_i)\cdot\mathbf{n}_k \equiv \Gamma_k$$

where Γ_k is the flow rate per unit area of phase k into the phase boundary and represents the evaporation /condensation rate of phase k. It should be noted, that Γ_k has a component due to phase change on the fixed boundaries of a_k as well as a component due to interfacial mass transfer.

$$\int_{c} \Gamma_k \frac{dc}{\mathbf{n}_k\cdot\mathbf{n}_{kc}} = \int_{c_w} \Gamma_k \frac{dc}{\mathbf{n}_k\cdot\mathbf{n}_{kc}} + \int_{c_k} \Gamma_k \frac{dc}{\mathbf{n}_k\cdot\mathbf{n}_{kc}}$$

For

$$\int_{c} \Gamma_k \frac{dc}{\mathbf{n}_k\cdot\mathbf{n}_{kc}} \equiv \delta_k$$

$$\int_{c_w} \Gamma_k \frac{dc}{\mathbf{n}_k\cdot\mathbf{n}_{kc}} \equiv \delta_{wk}$$

$$\int_{c_k} \Gamma_k \frac{dc}{\mathbf{n}_k\cdot\mathbf{n}_{kc}} \equiv \delta_{ik}$$

$$\delta_k = \delta_{wk} + \delta_{ik}$$

where the individual δ's represent the total phase change rate per unit length, the phase change rate per unit length on the fixed boundaries and the phase change rate per unit length at the phasic boundary of k respectively. If we let $\mathbf{v}_k\cdot\mathbf{n}_z = v_k$ and $a_k = \alpha_k A_x$, then the area averaged phasic continuity equation is

$$A_x \frac{\partial}{\partial t} \alpha_k\langle\rho_k\rangle_2 + \frac{\partial}{\partial z} \alpha_k\langle\rho_k v_k\rangle_2 A_x + \delta_k = 0$$

Momentum Equation

The momentum equation applied to phase k is

$$\frac{\partial}{\partial t}(\rho_k \mathbf{v}_k) + \nabla\cdot(\rho_k \mathbf{v}_k \mathbf{v}_k) + \nabla\cdot\mathcal{T}_k - \rho_k \mathbf{g} = 0.$$

The momentum equation as written is a vector equation. To convert the vector equation into a scalar equation in the direction of interest, we project the momentum equation along the tube axis by dotting against the unit vector $\mathbf{n}_z$.

$$\frac{\partial}{\partial t}(\rho_k v_k \cdot n_z) + \nabla \cdot (\rho_k v_k v_k) \cdot n_z + \nabla \cdot \mathcal{T}_k \cdot n_z - \rho_k g \cdot n_z = 0$$

or

$$\frac{\partial}{\partial t}(\rho_k v_k) + \nabla \cdot (\rho_k v_k v_k) + \nabla \cdot \mathcal{T}_k \cdot n_z - \rho_k g_z = 0$$

Integrate over a_k.

$$\frac{\partial}{\partial t} \int_{a_k} \rho_k v_k \, ds + \frac{\partial}{\partial z} \int_{a_k} (\rho_k v_k v_k) \cdot n_z \, ds$$
$$+ \int_c \rho_k v_k (v_k - v_i) \cdot n_k \frac{dc}{n_k \cdot n_{kc}} = - \frac{\partial}{\partial z} \int_{a_k} \mathcal{T} \cdot n_z \cdot n_z \, ds$$
$$- \int_c \mathcal{T} \cdot n_k \cdot n_z \frac{dc}{n_k \cdot n_{kc}} + \int_{a_k} \rho_k g_z \, ds$$

Rewrite the surface stress tensor in terms of its normal and shear stress components. In terms of area averaged notation, the momentum equation is

$$\frac{\partial}{\partial t} a_k \langle \rho_k v_k \rangle_2 + \frac{\partial}{\partial z} a_k \langle \rho_k v_k v_k \rangle_2 + \int_c \Gamma_k v_k \frac{dc}{n_k \cdot n_{kc}} =$$
$$- \frac{\partial}{\partial z} \int_{a_k} (P_k \mathcal{I} - \sigma_k) \cdot n_z \cdot n_z \, ds - \int_c (P \mathcal{I} - \sigma_k) \cdot n_k \cdot n_z \frac{dc}{n_k \cdot n_{kc}}$$
$$+ a_k \langle \rho_k g_z \rangle_2 .$$

The remaining integrals are evaluated as follows:

(a) $$\int_c \Gamma_k v_k \frac{dc}{n_k \cdot n_{kc}} \equiv \delta_k \hat{v}_k$$

where $\hat{v}_k$ is defined to be the <u>intrinsic velocity</u> associated with momentum transfer at the phase boundary during phase change.

(b) $$\int_{a_k} (P_k \mathcal{I}) \cdot n_z \cdot n_z \, ds = \int_{a_k} (P_k) \, ds = a_k \langle P_k \rangle_2$$

(c) $$\int_{a_k} (\sigma_k) \cdot n_z \cdot n_z \, ds = \int_{a_k} (\sigma^k_{zz}) \, ds = a_k \langle \sigma^k_{zz} \rangle_2$$

This term represents the fluid-to-fluid shear stresses acting on a_k and is normally neglected; i.e.

$$a_k \langle \sigma^k_{zz} \rangle_2 \cong 0 .$$

(d) $$\int_c (P \mathcal{I}) \cdot n_k \cdot n_z \frac{dc}{n_k \cdot n_{kc}} \cong \langle P_k \rangle_2 \int_c n_k \cdot n_z \frac{dc}{n_k \cdot n_{kc}}$$

for P_k assumed constant on c. Recall

$$\frac{\partial}{\partial z} a_k = - \int_c n_z \cdot n_k \frac{dc}{n_k \cdot n_{kc}}$$

such that

$$\int_c (P \mathcal{I}) \cdot n_k \cdot n_z \frac{dc}{n_k \cdot n_{kc}} \cong - \langle P_k \rangle_2 \frac{\partial}{\partial z} a_k .$$

(e) $$\int_c (\sigma_k) \cdot n_k \cdot n_z \frac{dc}{n_k \cdot n_{kc}} = \int_{c_w} (\sigma_k) \cdot n_k \cdot n_z \frac{dc}{n_k \cdot n_{kc}}$$
$$+ \int_{c_k} (\sigma_k) \cdot n_k \cdot n_z \frac{dc}{n_k \cdot n_{kc}}$$

Examine:

$$\int_{c_w} (\sigma_k) \cdot n_k \cdot n_z \frac{dc}{n_k \cdot n_{kc}}$$

This term represents the wall shear forces acting on phase k per unit length and may be written as

$$\int_{c_w} (\sigma_k) \cdot n_k \cdot n_z \frac{dc}{n_k \cdot n_{kc}} = - \langle \tau_{wk} \rangle_1 P_{wk} .$$

Note: The (-) sign accounts for wall forces acting to oppose the flow.

Similarly,

$$\int_{c_k} (\sigma_k) \cdot n_k \cdot n_z \frac{dc}{n_k \cdot n_{kc}} = \langle \tau_{ik} \rangle_1 P_{ik}$$

represents the interfacial shear acting on phase k. This term may act to aid or oppose the motion of phase k depending on the relative flow directions and velocities.

Therefore:

$$\int_c (\sigma_k) \cdot n_k \cdot n_z \frac{dc}{n_k \cdot n_{kc}} = - \langle \tau_{wk} \rangle_1 P_{wk} + \langle \tau_{ik} \rangle_1 P_{ik} .$$

Expressing a_k in terms of the area fraction of phase k, the area averaged phasic momentum equation is then

$$A_x \frac{\partial}{\partial t} \alpha_k \langle \rho_k v_k \rangle_2 + \frac{\partial}{\partial z} \alpha_k \langle \rho_k v_k v_k \rangle_2 A_x = - \alpha_k A_x \frac{\partial}{\partial z} \langle P_k \rangle_2$$
$$- \langle \tau_{wk} \rangle_1 P_{wk} + \langle \tau_{ik} \rangle_1 P_{ik} - \delta_k \hat{v}_k + \alpha_k \langle \rho_k g_z \rangle_2 A_x .$$

<u>Internal Energy Equation</u>

The Internal Energy Equation for phase k is

$$\frac{\partial}{\partial t} (\rho_k u_k) + \nabla \cdot (\rho_k u_k v_k) = -P_k \nabla \cdot v_k - \nabla \cdot q$$

where the viscous work term has been neglected. Integrate over a_k.

$$\frac{\partial}{\partial t} \int_{a_k} \rho_k u_k \, ds + \frac{\partial}{\partial z} \int_{a_k} \rho_k u_k v_k \cdot n_z \, ds$$
$$+ \int_c \rho_k u_k (v_k - v_i) \cdot n_k \frac{dc}{n_k \cdot n_{kc}} = - \int_{a_k} P_k \nabla \cdot v_k \, ds$$
$$- \frac{\partial}{\partial z} \int_{a_k} q_k \cdot n_z \, ds - \int_c q_k \cdot n_k \frac{dc}{n_k \cdot n_{kc}}$$

The integral

$$\int_{a_k} q_k \cdot n_z \, ds$$

represents the heat transfer rate through a_k in the flow stream direction and is predominantly due to conduction. In highly convective flows, typical of reactor systems, this term can be neglected.

We again assume P_k constant on a_k such that

$$\int_{a_k} P_k \nabla \cdot v_k \, ds \cong \langle P_k \rangle_2 \int_{a_k} \nabla \cdot v_k \, ds$$

and rewrite the area integral as

$$\int_{a_k} \nabla \cdot v_k \, ds = \frac{\partial}{\partial z} \int_{a_k} v_k \cdot n_z \, ds + \int_c v_k \cdot n_k \frac{dc}{n_k \cdot n_{kc}}.$$

The Internal Energy Equation may then be written in the more conventional notation

$$\frac{\partial}{\partial t} a_k \langle \rho_k u_k \rangle_2 + \frac{\partial}{\partial z} a_k \langle \rho_k u_k v_k \rangle_2 + \int_c \Gamma_k u_k \frac{dc}{n_k \cdot n_{kc}} =$$

$$- \langle P_k \rangle_2 \frac{\partial}{\partial z} a_k \langle v_k \rangle_2 - \langle P_k \rangle_2 \int_c v_k \cdot n_k \frac{dc}{n_k \cdot n_{kc}}$$

$$- \int_c q_k \cdot n_k \frac{dc}{n_k \cdot n_{kc}}.$$

The remaining integrals are then evaluated as follows:

$$\int_c q_k \cdot n_k \frac{dc}{n_k \cdot n_{kc}} = \int_{c_w} q_k \cdot n_k \frac{dc}{n_k \cdot n_{kc}} + \int_{c_k} q_k \cdot n_k \frac{dc}{n_k \cdot n_{kc}}.$$

Define

$$\int_{c_w} q_k \cdot n_k \frac{dc}{n_k \cdot n_{kc}} \equiv - q'_{wk}$$

where q'_{wk} is the heat transfer rate per unit length from the fixed boundaries to phase k and

$$\int_{c_k} q_k \cdot n_k \frac{dc}{n_k \cdot n_{kc}} \equiv - q'_{ik}$$

where q'_{ik} is the interfacial heat transfer rate per unit length to phase k.

Therefore

$$\int_c q_k \cdot n_k \frac{dc}{n_k \cdot n_{kc}} = - q'_{wk} - q'_{ik}.$$

Examine next the integral

$$\langle P_k \rangle_2 \int_c v_k \cdot n_k \frac{dc}{n_k \cdot n_{kc}}.$$

Note:

$$\int_c v_k \cdot n_k \frac{dc}{n_k \cdot n_{kc}} = \int_c \frac{\rho_k (v_k - v_i) \cdot n_k}{\rho_k} \frac{dc}{n_k \cdot n_{kc}}$$

$$+ \int_c v_i \cdot n_k \frac{dc}{n_k \cdot n_{kc}}$$

$$\int_c v_k \cdot n_k \frac{dc}{n_k \cdot n_{kc}} = \int_c \frac{\Gamma_k}{\rho_k} \frac{dc}{n_k \cdot n_{kc}} + \int_c v_i \cdot n_k \frac{dc}{n_k \cdot n_{kc}}$$

In addition,

$$\langle P_k \rangle_2 \int_c v_i \cdot n_k \frac{dc}{n_k \cdot n_{kc}} = \frac{\partial}{\partial t} a_k \langle P_k \rangle_2 - a_k \frac{\partial}{\partial t} \langle P_k \rangle_2$$

such that

$$\langle P_k \rangle_2 \int_c v_k \cdot n_k \frac{dc}{n_k \cdot n_{kc}} = \langle P_k \rangle_2 \int_c \frac{\Gamma_k}{\rho_k} \frac{dc}{n_k \cdot n_{kc}} + \langle P_k \rangle_2 \frac{\partial}{\partial t} a_k.$$

The phasic form of the Internal Energy Equation is then

$$\frac{\partial}{\partial t} a_k \langle \rho_k u_k \rangle_2 + \frac{\partial}{\partial z} a_k \langle \rho_k u_k v_k \rangle_2 + \int_c \Gamma_k u_k \frac{dc}{n_k \cdot n_{kc}} =$$

$$- \langle P_k \rangle_2 \frac{\partial}{\partial z} a_k \langle v_k \rangle_2 - \langle P_k \rangle_2 \int_c \frac{\Gamma_k}{\rho_k} \frac{dc}{n_k \cdot n_{kc}}$$

$$- \langle P_k \rangle_2 \frac{\partial}{\partial t} a_k + q'_{wk} + q'_{ik}.$$

If we define the enthalpy of phase k associated with phase change as

$$\hat{h}_k \equiv u_k + \langle P_k \rangle_2 / \rho_k$$

then the final form of the area averaged Internal Energy Equation is

$$A_x \frac{\partial}{\partial t} \alpha_k \langle \rho_k u_k \rangle_2 + \frac{\partial}{\partial z} \alpha_k \langle \rho_k u_k v_k \rangle_2 A_x + \delta_k \hat{h}_k =$$

$$- \langle P_k \rangle_2 \frac{\partial}{\partial z} \alpha_k \langle v_k \rangle_2 A_x - \langle P_k \rangle_2 A_x \frac{\partial}{\partial t} \alpha_k + q'_{wk} + q'_{ik}.$$

JUMP CONDITIONS

Coupling of phases across the phase boundary is formulated in terms of interfacial balance equations called jump conditions.

Continuity

If c_k is the interface between phases a and b, then mass conservation at the interface requires

$$\rho_a (v_a - v_i) \cdot n_a = - \rho_b (v_b - v_i) \cdot n_b$$

or

$$\Gamma_a = - \Gamma_b.$$

By noting

$$\frac{dc}{n_a \cdot n_{ac}} = \frac{dc}{n_b \cdot n_{bc}}$$

we have

$$\int_{c_k} \Gamma_a \frac{dc}{n_a \cdot n_{ac}} = - \int_{c_k} \Gamma_b \frac{dc}{n_b \cdot n_{bc}}$$

which in terms of previously defined integral properties gives

$$\delta_{ia} = - \delta_{ib}.$$

A similar arguement can be used to show

$$\delta_{wa} = - \delta_{wb}.$$

Momentum

Momentum conservation at the interface requires

$$\left[\rho_a v_a (v_a - v_i) + P_a \mathcal{I} - \sigma_a \right] \cdot n_a =$$

$$- \left[\rho_b v_b (v_b - v_i) + P_b \mathcal{I} - \sigma_b \right] \cdot n_b.$$

Project along the flow direction $\mathbf{n}_z$

$$\Gamma_a v_a \cdot n_z + P_a \mathcal{I} \cdot n_a \cdot n_z - \sigma_a \cdot n_a \cdot n_z = - \Gamma_b v_b \cdot n_z - P_b \mathcal{I} \cdot n_b \cdot n_z + \sigma_b \cdot n_b \cdot n_z$$

and integrate over the interface c_k.

$$\int_{c_k} \left\{\Gamma_a v_a + P_a \mathcal{I}\cdot n_a\cdot n_z - \sigma_a\cdot n_a\cdot n_z\right\} \frac{dc}{n_a\cdot n_{ac}} = - \int_{c_k} \left\{\Gamma_b v_b + P_b \mathcal{I}\cdot n_b\cdot n_z - \sigma_b\cdot n_b\cdot n_z\right\} \frac{dc}{n_b\cdot n_{bc}}$$

$$\delta_{ia}\hat{v}_a + \int_{c_k} P_a \mathcal{I}\cdot n_a\cdot n_z \frac{dc}{n_a\cdot n_{ac}} - \langle\tau_{ia}\rangle_i P_{ia} = - \delta_{ib}\hat{v}_b - \int_{c_k} P_b \mathcal{I}\cdot n_b\cdot n_z \frac{dc}{n_b\cdot n_{bc}} + \langle\tau_{ib}\rangle_i P_{ib}$$

If we again assume P_k constant on c_k

$$\delta_{ia}\hat{v}_a + (\langle P_a\rangle_2 - \langle P_b\rangle_2) \int_{c_k} n_a\cdot n_z \frac{dc}{n_a\cdot n_{ac}} - \langle\tau_{ia}\rangle_i P_{ia} = - \delta_{ib}\hat{v}_b + \langle\tau_{ib}\rangle_i P_{ib}.$$

If we further assume that $\langle P_a\rangle_2 = \langle P_b\rangle_2 = P$, we obtain the usual momentum jump condition

$$\delta_{ia}\hat{v}_a - \langle\tau_{ia}\rangle_i P_{ia} = - \delta_{ib}\hat{v}_b + \langle\tau_{ib}\rangle_i P_{ib}.$$

Internal Energy

The Internal Energy Equation was obtained by subtracting the Kinetic Energy Equation from the Total Energy Equation, and as a result, while interfacial balance equations exist for both Total Energy and Momentum no formal interfacial balance equation exists for Internal Energy. The following derivation however leads to simple jump conditions which are often posed for the Internal Energy Equation. The Total Energy and Momentum Jump Conditions are

$$[\rho_a e_a(v_a - v_i) + q_a + \mathcal{T}_a\cdot v_a]\cdot n_a = - [\rho_b e_b(v_b - v_i) + q_b + \mathcal{T}_b\cdot v_b]\cdot n_b$$

where $e_k = u_k + 1/2\ v_k\cdot v_k$

and

$$[\rho_a v_a(v_a - v_i) + P_a \mathcal{I} - \sigma_a]\cdot n_a = - [\rho_b v_b(v_b - v_i) + P_b \mathcal{I} - \sigma_b]\cdot n_b.$$

In more compact form

$$\Gamma_a e_a + q_a\cdot n_a + \mathcal{T}_a\cdot v_a\cdot n_a = - \Gamma_b e_b - q_b\cdot n_b - \mathcal{T}_b\cdot v_b\cdot n_b$$

and

$$\Gamma_a v_a + \mathcal{T}_a\cdot n_a = - \Gamma_b v_b - \mathcal{T}_b\cdot n_b.$$

Dot the momentum jump condition with v_i

$$\Gamma_a v_a\cdot v_i + \mathcal{T}_a\cdot n_a\cdot v_i = - \Gamma_b v_b\cdot v_i - \mathcal{T}_b\cdot n_b\cdot v_i$$

and subtract from the total energy jump condition.

$$\Gamma_a(e_a - v_a\cdot v_i) + q_a\cdot n_a + \mathcal{T}_a\cdot(v_a - v_i)\cdot n_a = - \Gamma_b(e_b - v_b\cdot v_i) - q_b\cdot n_b - \mathcal{T}_b\cdot(v_b - v_i)\cdot n_b$$

Separate the stress tensor into its normal and viscous components.

$$\Gamma_a(e_a + P_a/\rho_a - v_a\cdot v_i) + q_a\cdot n_a - \sigma_a\cdot(v_a - v_i)\cdot n_a = - \Gamma_b(e_b + P_b/\rho_b - v_b\cdot v_i) - q_b\cdot n_b + \sigma_b\cdot(v_b - v_i)\cdot n_b$$

This equation may be rearranged to give

$$\Gamma_a h_a + q_a\cdot n_a + \Gamma_a\left\{\frac{1}{2} v_a\cdot v_a - v_a\cdot v_i\right\} - \sigma_a\cdot(v_a - v_i)\cdot n_a = -\Gamma_b h_b - q_b\cdot n_b - \Gamma_b\left\{\frac{1}{2} v_b\cdot v_b - v_b\cdot v_i\right\} + \sigma_b\cdot(v_b - v_i)\cdot n_b.$$

We next assume the kinetic energy exchange is balanced by the viscous forces such that

$$\Gamma_a h_a + q_a\cdot n_a = -\Gamma_b h_b - q_b\cdot n_b$$

and

$$\Gamma_a\left\{\frac{1}{2} v_a\cdot v_a - v_a\cdot v_i\right\} - \sigma_a\cdot(v_a - v_i)\cdot n_a = - \Gamma_b\left\{\frac{1}{2} v_b\cdot v_b - v_b\cdot v_i\right\} + \sigma_b\cdot(v_b - v_i)\cdot n_b.$$

Take the simple thermal balance equation

$$\Gamma_a h_a + q_a\cdot n_a = -\Gamma_b h_b - q_b\cdot n_b$$

as the Internal Energy Jump Condition. Integrate over c_k

$$\int_{c_k} \Gamma_a h_a \frac{dc}{n_a\cdot n_{ac}} + \int_{c_k} q_a\cdot n_a \frac{dc}{n_a\cdot n_{ac}} = - \int_{c_k} \Gamma_b h_b \frac{dc}{n_b\cdot n_{bc}} - \int_{c_k} q_b\cdot n_b \frac{dc}{n_b\cdot n_{bc}}$$

which gives for the integrated jump condition

$$\delta_{ia}\hat{h}_a - q'_{ia} = -\delta_{ib}\hat{h}_b + q'_{ib}.$$

A similar procedure may be followed to develop the interface conditions at the fixed surfaces. We assume phase a to be incident on the fixed surface resulting in the production of phase b on the surface. Again using a simple thermal balance at the fixed (wall) surface gives

$$\Gamma_{wa} h_a + q_a\cdot n_a = - \Gamma_{wb} h_b - q_w\cdot n_w$$

where q_w is defined to be the outward directed wall heat flux. Integrating over c_w produces the wall condition

$$\delta_{wa}\hat{h}_a - q'_{wa} = -\delta_{wb}\hat{h}_b - q''_w P_{wa}.$$

APPLICATIONS TO LIQUID/VAPOR SYSTEMS

The phasic conservation equations and jump conditions derived in the previous sections my be applied directly to the description of two-phase liquid/vapor systems such as those found in nuclear power systems. We make the following additional assumptions

$$\langle AB \rangle \cong \langle A \rangle \langle B \rangle = A \cdot B$$

and

$$\langle P_a \rangle_2 = \langle P_b \rangle_2 = \langle P \rangle_2.$$

Continuity

Liquid Phase

$$A_x \frac{\partial}{\partial t} (\alpha_1 \rho_1) + \frac{\partial}{\partial z} (\alpha_1 \rho_1 v_1) A_x + \delta_1 = 0$$

Vapor Phase

$$A_x \frac{\partial}{\partial t} (\alpha_g \rho_g) + \frac{\partial}{\partial z} (\alpha_g \rho_g v_g) A_x - \delta_1 = 0$$

Momentum

Liquid Phase

$$A_x \frac{\partial}{\partial t} (\alpha_1 \rho_1 v_1) + \frac{\partial}{\partial z} (\alpha_1 \rho_1 v_1 v_1) A_x = - \alpha_1 A_x \frac{\partial}{\partial z} P$$
$$- \langle \tau_{w1} \rangle_1 P_{w1} + \langle \tau_{i1} \rangle_1 P_{i1} - \delta_{i1} \hat{v}_1 - \delta_{w1} \hat{v}_1 + \alpha_1 \rho_1 g_z A_x$$

Vapor Phase

$$A_x \frac{\partial}{\partial t} (\alpha_g \rho_g v_g) + \frac{\partial}{\partial z} (\alpha_g \rho_g v_g v_g) A_x = - \alpha_g A_x \frac{\partial}{\partial z} P$$
$$- \langle \tau_{wg} \rangle_1 P_{wg} - \langle \tau_{i1} \rangle_1 P_{i1} + \delta_{i1} \hat{v}_1 + \delta_{w1} \hat{v}_g + \alpha_g \rho_g g_z A_x$$

Internal Energy

Liquid Phase

$$A_x \frac{\partial}{\partial t} (\alpha_1 \rho_1 u_1) + \frac{\partial}{\partial z} (\alpha_1 \rho_1 u_1 v_1) A_x + \delta_{i1} \hat{h}_1 + \delta_{w1} \hat{h}_1 =$$
$$- P \frac{\partial}{\partial z} (\alpha_1 v_1) A_x - P_1 A_x \frac{\partial}{\partial t} (\alpha_1) + q'_{w1} + q'_{i1}$$

Vapor Phase

$$A_x \frac{\partial}{\partial t} (\alpha_g \rho_g u_g) + \frac{\partial}{\partial z} (\alpha_g \rho_g u_g v_g) A_x - \delta_{i1} \hat{h}_1 - \delta_{w1} \hat{h}_g =$$
$$- P \frac{\partial}{\partial z} (\alpha_g v_g) A_x - P_g A_x \frac{\partial}{\partial t} (\alpha_g) + q'_{wg} - q'_{i1}$$

where the jump conditions have been used to eliminate some of the interfacial terms.

Mixture Equations

A convenient form of the conservation equations may be obtained by adding the phasic equations to obtain the so called Mixture Equations.

Continuity

$$A_x \frac{\partial}{\partial t} (\alpha_1 \rho_1 + \alpha_g \rho_g) + \frac{\partial}{\partial z} (\alpha_1 \rho_1 v_1 + \alpha_g \rho_g v_g) A_x = 0$$

Momentum

$$A_x \frac{\partial}{\partial t} (\alpha_1 \rho_1 v_1 + \alpha_g \rho_g v_g) + \frac{\partial}{\partial z} (\alpha_1 \rho_1 v_1 v_1 + \alpha_g \rho_g v_g v_g) A_x =$$
$$- A_x \frac{\partial}{\partial z} P - \langle \tau_{w1} \rangle_1 P_{w1} - \langle \tau_{wg} \rangle_1 P_{wg} + \delta_{w1} (\hat{v}_g - \hat{v}_1)$$
$$+ (\alpha_1 \rho_1 + \alpha_g \rho_g) g_z A_x$$

Internal Energy

$$A_x \frac{\partial}{\partial t} (\alpha_1 \rho_1 u_1 + \alpha_g \rho_g u_g) + \frac{\partial}{\partial z} (\alpha_1 \rho_1 u_1 v_1 + \alpha_g \rho_g u_g v_g) A_x =$$
$$- P \frac{\partial}{\partial z} (\alpha_1 v_1 + \alpha_g v_g) A_x + q''_w P_w$$

We further define the mixture properties:

$$\rho \equiv \alpha_1 \rho_1 + \alpha_g \rho_g$$
$$\rho v \equiv \alpha_1 \rho_1 v_1 + \alpha_g \rho_g v_g$$
$$\rho u \equiv \alpha_1 \rho_1 u_1 + \alpha_g \rho_g u_g$$
$$v \equiv \rho v / \rho$$
$$\langle \tau_w^{2\phi} \rangle_1 P_w \equiv \langle \tau_{w1} \rangle_1 P_{w1} + \langle \tau_{wg} \rangle_1 P_{wg}$$

and assume $\hat{v}_g = \hat{v}_1$

such that the mixture equations may be written as

Continuity

$$A_x \frac{\partial}{\partial t} (\rho) + \frac{\partial}{\partial z} (\rho v) A_x = 0$$

Momentum

$$A_x \frac{\partial}{\partial t} (\rho v) + \frac{\partial}{\partial z} (\alpha_1 \rho_1 v_1 v_1 + \alpha_g \rho_g v_g v_g) A_x = - A_x \frac{\partial}{\partial z} P$$
$$- \langle \tau_w^{2\phi} \rangle_1 P_w + \rho g_z A_x$$

Internal Energy

$$A_x \frac{\partial}{\partial t} (\rho u) + \frac{\partial}{\partial z} (\alpha_1 \rho_1 u_1 v_1 + \alpha_g \rho_g u_g v_g) A_x =$$
$$- P \frac{\partial}{\partial z} (\alpha_1 v_1 + \alpha_g v_g) A_x + q''_w P_w$$

The convective terms in both the Internal Energy Equation and the Momentum Equation are of the form

$$\alpha_1 \rho_1 \phi_1 v_1 + \alpha_g \rho_g \phi_g v_g.$$

If we let

$$\rho \phi = \alpha_1 \rho_1 \phi_1 v_1 + \alpha_g \rho_g \phi_g v_g$$
$$\rho \phi v = (\alpha_1 \rho_1 \phi_1 v_1 + \alpha_g \rho_g \phi_g v_g) \cdot v$$

it can be shown (with some manipulation) that

$$\alpha_1 \rho_1 \phi_1 v_1 + \alpha_g \rho_g \phi_g v_g = \rho \phi v + \frac{\alpha_1 \rho_1 \alpha_g \rho_g}{\rho} (\phi_g - \phi_1)(v_g - v_1).$$

such that the Mixture Equations can be written in the more convenient form:

Continuity

$$A_x \frac{\partial}{\partial t} (\rho) + \frac{\partial}{\partial z} (\rho v) A_x = 0$$

Momentum

$$A_x \frac{\partial}{\partial t} (\rho v) + \frac{\partial}{\partial z} (\rho v v) A_x = - A_x \frac{\partial}{\partial z} P - \langle \tau_w^{2\phi} \rangle_1 P_w$$
$$+ \rho g_z A_x - \frac{\partial}{\partial z} \left\{ \frac{\alpha_1 \rho_1 \alpha_g \rho_g}{\rho} (v_g - v_1)^2 A_x \right\}$$

Internal Energy

$$A_x \frac{\partial}{\partial t} (\rho u) + \frac{\partial}{\partial z} (\rho u v) A_x = - P \frac{\partial}{\partial z} (v A_x) + q''_w P_w$$
$$- P \frac{\partial}{\partial z} \left\{ \frac{\alpha_1 \rho_1 \alpha_g \rho_g}{\rho} (u_g - u_1)(v_g - v_1) A_x \right\}$$
$$- P \frac{\partial}{\partial z} \left\{ \frac{\alpha_1 \alpha_g}{\rho} (\rho_1 - \rho_g)(v_g - v_1) \right\} A_x$$

Fluid models based on six conservation equations (one for each phase) are referred to as "six equation" models. While a number of six equation models exist, all are based on some linear combination of the phasic equations given here. For example, an equivalent system would consist of three phasic equations (one each for continuity, energy and momentum) and three mixture equations. In later discussions it will be understood that references to two phasic equations is equivalent to one phasic and one mixture equation. It should be noted that though the six equation models are the most general, they require detailed information on complex interfacial phenomena which may be difficult or impossible to obtain. In addition to the interfacial phenomena and wall interaction terms (drag, heat transfer, etc.), the unknowns in the six equation model are:

$$\alpha_l, \alpha_g, \rho_l, \rho_g, v_l, v_g, u_l, u_g, P \Rightarrow 9.$$

This requires the six conservation equations, the definition

$$\alpha_l + \alpha_g = 1$$

and state relationships of the form

$$\rho_l = \rho_l(u_l, P)$$
$$\rho_g = \rho_g(u_g, P)$$

to achieve closure.

ALTERNATIVES TO THE SIX EQUATION MODEL

Simplifications to the Six Equation Model can be obtained by utilizing a single mixture equation in place of two phasic equations.

Five Equation Models

Five equation models employ four phasic and one mixture equation to describe the two-phase system. As an example, consider a five equation model utilizing two phasic continuity equations, two phasic momentum equa-tions and the mixture internal energy equation. It should be obvious that we have reduced our number of equations by one while maintaining the same number of unknowns. To achieve closure, we must therefore pose some constraint on the condition of the fluid. This can be accomplished by forcing one phase (usually the least massive) to be at saturation, effectively replacing an energy equation by a state relation of the form

$$u_b = u_b^s(P).$$

An advantage of this model is that all interfacial heat transfer terms have been eliminated. Accuracy is lost however if highly nonequilibrium flows are to be described, such as might be found in modeling rapid depressurization events in a reactor Loss Of Coolant Accident (LOCA). Models of this type provided the basis for the RELAP5/Mod1 code series (Ransom et al. 1982).

An alternative five equation model can be constructed utilizing two phasic continuity equations, two phasic internal energy equations and a mixture momentum equation. To achieve closure we again must assume something about the state of the fluid. In choosing a mixture momentum equation, we have lost information concerning the individual phase velocities. The simplest choice is to assume homogeneous flow, i.e.

$$v_l = v_g = v.$$

Under this assumption the mixture equations reduce to forms which are identical to single-phase equations. A more satisfying approach is to assume some phenomenologically based empirical model for the relative phase velocities. The Drift Flux model is a highly successful model based on this concept.

Drift Flux Models

Define the following local parameters:

$$j_k \equiv \alpha_k v_k$$
$$j \equiv j_l + j_g$$

where j_k is the superficial velocity of phase k and j is the mixture flux. Write the following identity

$$v_g = j + (v_g - j)$$

and multiply by α_g

$$\alpha_g v_g = \alpha_g j + \alpha_g (v_g - j)$$

or

$$j_g = \alpha_g j + \alpha_g (v_g - j).$$

Note: In any given flow channel, the velocity and void vary with location. As we are interested in area averaged parameters, average the above over the channel cross section

$$\langle j_g \rangle_2 = \langle \alpha_g j \rangle_2 + \langle \alpha_g (v_g - j) \rangle_2.$$

As our fluids models only predict average quantities, rewrite the above as

$$\langle j_g \rangle_2 = \frac{\langle \alpha_g j \rangle_2}{\langle \alpha_g \rangle_2 \langle j \rangle_2} \langle \alpha_g \rangle_2 \langle j \rangle_2 + \langle \alpha_g \rangle_2 \frac{\langle \alpha_g (v_g - j) \rangle_2}{\langle \alpha_g \rangle_2}$$

Define the following parameters:

$$C_o \equiv \frac{\langle \alpha_g j \rangle_2}{\langle \alpha_g \rangle_2 \langle j \rangle_2}$$

$$V_{gj} \equiv \frac{\langle \alpha_g (v_g - j) \rangle_2}{\langle \alpha_g \rangle_2}$$

Substituting for C_o and V_{gj} gives

$$\langle j_g \rangle_2 = C_o \langle \alpha_g \rangle_2 \langle j \rangle_2 + \langle \alpha_g \rangle_2 V_{gj}$$

C_o is defined to be the Concentration Parameter and quantifies the effect of radial void and velocity distribution. V_{gj} is the Drift Velocity and is closely related to the terminal rise velocity of the vapor phase through the liquid. Both the concentration parameter and the drift velocity are determined empirically as a function of flow regime.

Examine:

$$\langle \alpha_g \rangle_2 V_{gj} = \langle \alpha_g (v_g - j) \rangle_2$$

which may be rewritten as

$$\langle \alpha_g \rangle_2 V_{gj} = \langle \alpha_l \alpha_g (v_g - v_l) \rangle_2 \equiv j_D^G.$$

The parameter j_D^G is called the Drift Flux and provides the necessary relationship between the relative velocity and the drift velocity.

Advantages of the five equation drift flux model include elimination of interfacial momentum transfer terms while allowing for nonhomogeneous, nonequilibrium flows. The model is limited however by the accuracy of the drift flux correlations used to predict the relative phase velocities. A five equation drift flux model provided the basis for the early TRAC code series (TRAC-P1 1978).

Four Equation Models

Four equation models are based on the combination of two phasic and two mixture equations and thus require two additional constraints on the fluid state to achieve closure. For example, consider a four equation model consisting of mixture continuity, mixture energy and phasic momentum equations. No information is available from this equation set to specify the state of either phase without requiring both phases to be at equilibrium. An additional disadvantage is the presence of interfacial momentum transfer terms. Consider next a four equation model consisting of phasic continuity equations, mixture energy and mixture momentum equations. This equation set has the advantage of requiring no interfacial terms other than the evaporation/condensation rate. Closure is obtained by specifying one phase be at saturation and assuming a drift flux model for the relative phase velocities (Liles and Reed 1978).

Three Equation Models

Three equation models are based solely on the mixture equations and require both phases to be at saturation. The simplest three equation models assume homogeneous flow as well such that the two-phase equations differ from single phase equations only in equations of state and constituitive equations for wall drag and heat transfer. While the simplest of the two-phase models, these Homogeneous Equilibrium Mixture (HEM) models are also the least accurate. Drift flux models can be used to relax the homogeneous flow assumption.

CONCLUSIONS

Conservation equations for multiphase flow systems can be rigorously derived from the classic Navier-Stokes equations for single-phase flows. The area averaging process results in integral parameters which represent mass, energy and momentum transfer between phases and between the phases and the fixed surfaces. These integral parameters represent such macroscopic properties as wall drag, wall heat transfer, interfacial drag, interfacial heat transfer and evaporation and condensation rates at both fixed and interfacial surfaces. While no discussion of these parameters is given here, they are usually determined empirically and correlated in terms of the area averaged properties. Simplifications to the more general six equation model can be obtained directly in terms of linear combinations of the phasic equations. This results in loss of information however concerning the state of the fluid or relative velocities between the individual phases. Simplifying assumptions are necessary to achieve closure which may be invalid for a given flow situation.

REFERENCES

Delhaye, J.M., M. Giot and M.L. Riethmuller. 1981. *Thermohydraulics of Two-Phase Systems for Industrial Design and Nuclear Engineering*. Hemisphere, Washington, D.C.

Ishii, M. 1975. *Thermo-Fluid Dynamic Theory of Two-Phase Flow*. Eyrolles, Paris.

Liles, D.R. and W.H. Reed. 1978. "A Semi-Implicit Method for Two-Phase Fluid Dynamics," *Journal of Computational Physics* **26**, 390-407.

Ransom, V.H., R.J. Wagner, J.A. Trapp, K.E. Carlson, D.M. Kiser, H. Kuo, H. Chow, R.A. Nelson, S.W. James. 1982. RELAP5/MOD1 Code Manual, Volume 1: *Systems Models and Numerical Methods*. NUREG/CR-1826 EGG-2070.

TRAC-P1 1978: An Advanced Best Estimate Computer Program for PWR LOCA Analysis: 1. *Methods, Models, User Information and Programming Details*, NUREG/CR-0-63.

NOMENCLATURE

a_k = Area occupied by phase k
A_x = Cross sectional flow area
$\mathbf{B}$ = Arbitrary vector function
c = Circumference of a_k
c_k = Circumference of a_k associated with the phase boundary
c_w = Circumference of a_k in contact with the fixed surfaces
C_o = Concentration parameter
dc = Differential length
ds = Differential area
$\mathbf{g}$ = Gravitational vector
h = Enthalpy
$\mathcal{I}$ = Unit tensor
j = Mixture flux
j_D^G = Drift flux
j_k = Superficial velocity of phase k
$\mathcal{M}$ = Arbitrary tensor function
$\mathbf{n}$ = Unit outward normal vector
P = Pressure
$\mathbf{q}$ = Heat flux
q' = Heat transfer rate per unit length
q" = Heat flux
Q_g = Volumetric heat generation rate
t = time
$\mathcal{T}$ = Surface stress tensor
u = specific internal energy
$\mathbf{v}$ = Velocity vector
v_i = Velocity of the interface
$\hat{v}$ = Intrinsic velocity
V_{gj} = Drift velocity
z = Flow direction

Greek Symbols

α = Area fraction
δ = Phase change rate per unit length
Γ = Phase change rate per unit area
ρ = density
σ = Shear stress tensor
τ = Shear stress

Subscripts

a = Phase designation
b = Phase designation
g = Vapor phase
i = Interface
i,j = Coordinate directions
k = Arbitrary phase notation
l = Liquid phase
w = Wall
z = Flow direction

Simulators VI
© 1989 By The Society for Computer
Simulation International
ISBN 0-911801-51-0

Numerical solutions of multiphase flow problems

J. Michael Doster
Nuclear Engineering Department
North Carolina State University
Box 7909
Raleigh, NC 27695-7909

ABSTRACT

This paper reviews time and spatial discretization schemes commonly used in modeling heat transfer and fluid flow in nuclear reactor systems. Area averaged single-phase equations are used to develop and illustrate time and spatial discretization schemes. The same discretization techniques however are directly applicable to two-phase systems as is demonstrated for a three equation Drift Flux model. Stability implications and accuracy of the individual methods are discussed. These techniques usually result in large sparse matrix equations which must be solved at each time step in the simulation. Implementation on parallel computers is discussed as a means to reduce computational time.

INTRODUCTION

The dynamic simulation of nuclear power systems requires solution of the conservation equations for mass, energy and momentum transport in a two-phase system. These equations are highly nonlinear and numerical solution techniques are required. This paper reviews time and spatial discretization schemes commonly used in modeling heat transfer and fluid flow in nuclear reactor systems. To illustrate the various time and spatial discretization schemes, consider the area averaged fluid conservation equations for a single-phase fluid.

Continuity

$$A_x \frac{\partial}{\partial t}(\rho) + \frac{\partial}{\partial z}(\rho V) A_x = 0$$

Momentum (Conservative Form)

$$\frac{\partial}{\partial t}(\rho V) + \frac{1}{A_x}\frac{\partial}{\partial z}(\rho VV) A_x = -\frac{\partial}{\partial z} P - \frac{K\rho|V|V}{2} + \rho g_z$$

Momentum (Nonconservative Form)

$$\rho \frac{\partial}{\partial t}(V) + (\rho V)\frac{\partial}{\partial z}(V) = -\frac{\partial}{\partial z} P - \frac{K\rho|V|V}{2} + \rho g_z$$

Internal Energy

$$A_x \frac{\partial}{\partial t}(\rho u) + \frac{\partial}{\partial z}(\rho u V) A_x = -P\frac{\partial}{\partial z}(VA_x) + q_w'' P_w$$

where the wall shear stress term has been assumed to take the form

$$\frac{K\rho|V|V}{2} \equiv \frac{\langle\tau_w\rangle_i P_w}{A_x}$$

The absolute value sign accounts for potential changes in flow direction. It is often more convenient to work with the nonconservative form of the momentum equation and it will serve as the basis for all further discussions. The single-phase equations are used to develop and illustrate various time and spatial discretization schemes. These techniques however are directly applicable to two-phase systems as will be demonstrated for a three equation Drift Flux model. While the numerical solution techniques to be developed are relatively independent of computer architecture, it has been shown that many aspects of reactor thermal-hydraulic calculations are inherently parallel and can benefit from implementation on parallel computer architectures (Doster et al. 1988). With the increased availability of mini supercomputers employing parallelism through multi-CPU's and/or vector pipelines, this technology could play an important role in power plant simulation. Implementation on parallel machines is discussed as appropriate.

SPATIAL DISCRETIZATION

A number of spatial discretizations are possible based on standard differencing schemes. Consider first a central difference scheme about a computational node i. Assume for simplicity a constant area channel with uniform spacing.

Continuity

$$\left.\frac{\partial\rho}{\partial t}\right|_i + \frac{(\rho V)_{i+1} - (\rho V)_{i-1}}{2\Delta z} = 0$$

Momentum

$$\rho\left.\frac{\partial(V)}{\partial t}\right|_i + (\rho V)_i \frac{(V_{i+1} - V_{i-1})}{2\Delta z} = -\frac{(P_{i+1} - P_{i-1})}{2\Delta z} - \left.\frac{K\rho|V|V}{2}\right|_i + \rho_i g_z$$

Internal Energy

$$\left.\frac{\partial(\rho u)}{\partial t}\right|_i + \frac{(\rho u V)_{i+1} - (\rho u V)_{i-1}}{2\Delta z} = -P_i\frac{(V_{i+1} - V_{i-1})}{2\Delta z} + \left.\frac{q_w'' P_w}{A_x}\right|_i$$

This central difference is second order correct and at first glance would appear to be an acceptable scheme. Examine the behavior of this discretization however as applied to the pressure distribution illustrated in Figure 1. The indicated spatial discretization implies a zero pressure gradient and would clearly lead to unphysical results.

The saw-toothed pressure distribution can be easily eliminated by forward differencing the field equations from point i.

Continuity

$$\left.\frac{\partial\rho}{\partial t}\right|_i + \frac{(\rho V)_{i+1} - (\rho V)_i}{\Delta z} = 0$$

Momentum

$$\rho \frac{\partial(V)}{\partial t}\Big|_i + (\rho V)_i \frac{(V_{i+1} - V_i)}{\Delta z} = - \frac{(P_{i+1} - P_i)}{\Delta z} - \frac{K\rho|V|V}{2}\Big|_i$$
$$+ \rho_i g_z$$

Internal Energy

$$\frac{\partial(\rho u)}{\partial t}\Big|_i + \frac{(\rho u V)_{i+1} - (\rho u V)_i}{\Delta z} = - P_i \frac{(V_{i+1} - V_i)}{\Delta z}$$
$$+ \frac{q''_w P_w}{A_x}\Big|_i$$

Similar results can be obtained by backward differencing. Both the forward and backward difference schemes are first order correct. In addition, care must be taken in the direction of differencing relative to the flow direction to maintain numerical stability. However the forward and backward difference schemes are viable methods.

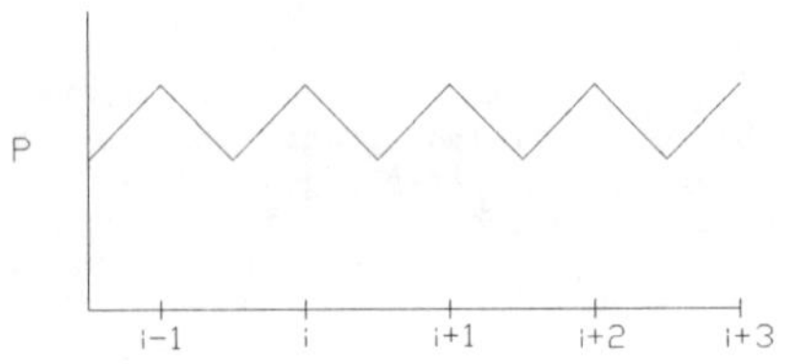

Figure 1: Illustrative pressure distribution

Consider next a central differenced scheme obtained by integrating the scalar equations (continuity and internal energy) over the volume centered at i and bounded by $i \pm 1/2$ and the vector (momentum) equation over the volume centered at $i+1/2$ and bounded by $i \pm 1$ as illustrated in Figure 2.

Continuity

$$\frac{\partial \rho}{\partial t}\Big|_i + \frac{(\rho V)_{i+1/2} - (\rho V)_{i-1/2}}{\Delta z} = 0$$

Momentum

$$\rho \frac{\partial(V)}{\partial t}\Big|_{i+1/2} + (\rho V) \frac{\Delta V}{\Delta z}\Big|_{i+1/2} = - \frac{(P_{i+1} - P_i)}{\Delta z}$$
$$- \frac{K\rho|V|V}{2}\Big|_{i+1/2} + \rho_{i+1/2}\, g_z$$

Internal Energy

$$\frac{\partial(\rho u)}{\partial t}\Big|_i + \frac{(\rho u V)_{i+1/2} - (\rho u V)_{i-1/2}}{\Delta z} =$$
$$- P_i \frac{(V_{i+1/2} - V_{i-1/2})}{\Delta z} + \frac{q''_w P_w}{A_x}\Big|_i$$

By offsetting the momentum control volume, the field equations are said to be integrated over a "staggered spatial mesh". As written, the staggered mesh scheme is second order correct and yields physically meaningful results. Complications arise however in the momentum flux term and in the convective terms where cell centered values (ρ, ρu) are now required at cell boundaries. These complications aside, the staggered mesh scheme provides the basis for most current reactor analysis codes.

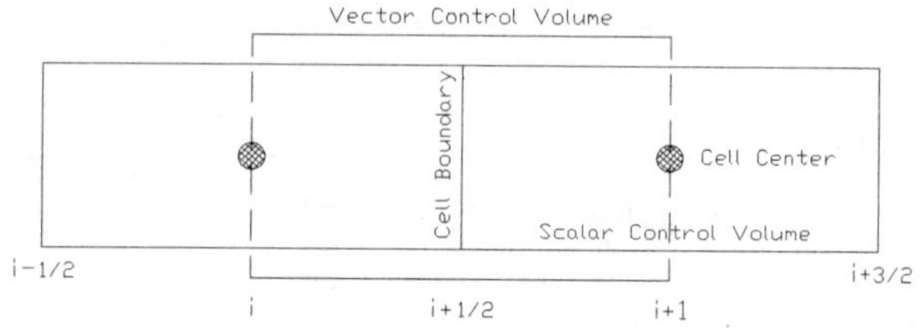

Figure 2: Control volumes for a staggered spatial mesh

Convective terms in the staggered mesh scheme are usually determined by "donor cell" averaging, which for a convected property ψ may be written

$$\psi_{i+1/2} = \begin{cases} \psi_i & V_{i+1/2} > 0 \\ \psi_{i+1} & V_{i+1/2} < 0 \end{cases}$$

or analytically

$$\psi_{i+1/2} = \frac{1}{2}(\psi_{i+1} + \psi_i) + \frac{1}{2}\frac{|V_{i+1/2}|}{V_{i+1/2}}(\psi_i - \psi_{i+1}).$$

The donor cell scheme is first order correct. If the remaining spatial difference in the momentum flux term is approximated by a standard central difference

$$\frac{\Delta V}{\Delta z}\Big|_{i+1/2} = \frac{V_{i+1} - V_i}{\Delta z}$$

undefined velocities are introduced at the cell centers. An alternative approach is to "upwind difference" the spatial derivative (TRAC-BD1/MOD1 1984)

$$\Delta V_{i+1/2} = \begin{cases} (V_{i+1/2} - V_{i-1/2}) & V_{i+1/2} > 0 \\ (V_{i+3/2} - V_{i+1/2}) & V_{i+1/2} < 0 \end{cases}$$

which again may be expressed analytically as

$$\Delta V_{i+1/2} = \frac{1}{2}\big((V_{i+1/2} - V_{i-1/2}) + (V_{i+3/2} - V_{i+1/2})\big)$$
$$+ \frac{1}{2}\frac{|V_{i+1/2}|}{V_{i+1/2}}\big((V_{i+1/2} - V_{i-1/2}) - (V_{i+3/2} - V_{i+1/2})\big).$$

An alternate formulation of the momentum flux term is obtained by taking advantage of the equality

$$\rho V \frac{\partial V}{\partial z} = \frac{1}{2}\rho \frac{\partial V^2}{\partial z}$$

such that

$$\rho \frac{\partial V}{\partial t} + \frac{\rho}{2}\frac{\partial V^2}{\partial z} = - \frac{\partial P}{\partial z} - \frac{K\rho|V|V}{2} + \rho g_z$$

or in discretized form

$$\rho \frac{\partial(V)}{\partial t}\Big|_{i+1/2} + \frac{1}{2}\frac{\rho_{i+1/2}}{\Delta z} V^2\Big|_{i}^{i+1} = -\frac{(P_{i+1} - P_i)}{\Delta z}$$

$$- \frac{K\rho|V|V}{2}\Big|_{i+1/2} + \rho_{i+1/2}\, g_z .$$

Note: This formulation also requires values of V^2 at cell centers.

The V^2 terms can be evaluated by assuming a donor like approach (RELAP5/MOD2. 1985).

Assume

$$(V^2)_{i+1} = \overset{\circ}{V}V_{i+1}$$

with V_{i+1} as of yet undefined and

$$(\overset{\circ}{V}A)_{i+1} = \begin{cases} (VA)_{i+1/2} & V_{i+1} > 0 \\ (VA)_{i+3/2} & V_{i+1} < 0 \end{cases}$$

which expressed analytically is

$$(\overset{\circ}{V}A)_{i+1} = \frac{1}{2}\left\{ (VA)_{i+1/2} + (VA)_{i+3/2} \right\} + \frac{1}{2}\frac{|V_{i+1}|}{V_{i+1}}\left\{ (VA)_{i+1/2} - (VA)_{i+3/2} \right\}$$

or

$$\overset{\circ}{V}V_{i+1} = \frac{V_{i+1}}{2}\left\{ V_{i+1/2}\frac{A_{i+1/2}}{A_{i+1}} + V_{i+3/2}\frac{A_{i+3/2}}{A_{i+1}} \right\} + \frac{|V_{i+1}|}{2}\left\{ V_{i+1/2}\frac{A_{i+1/2}}{A_{i+1}} - V_{i+3/2}\frac{A_{i+3/2}}{A_{i+1}} \right\}.$$

Define V_{i+1} such that

$$V_{i+1} \equiv \frac{1}{2}\left\{ V_{i+1/2}\frac{A_{i+1/2}}{A_{i+1}} + V_{i+3/2}\frac{A_{i+3/2}}{A_{i+1}} \right\}$$

and

$$\overset{\circ}{V}V_{i+1} = V^2_{i+1} + \frac{|V_{i+1}|}{2}\left\{ V_{i+1/2}\frac{A_{i+1/2}}{A_{i+1}} - V_{i+3/2}\frac{A_{i+3/2}}{A_{i+1}} \right\}.$$

The expression

$$\frac{|V_{i+1}|}{2}\left\{ V_{i+1/2}\frac{A_{i+1/2}}{A_{i+1}} - V_{i+3/2}\frac{A_{i+3/2}}{A_{i+1}} \right\}$$

acts as an additional viscous term. It should be noted, that in the RELAP5 documentation this expression is given as

$$\frac{|V_{i+1}|}{2}\left\{ V_{i+1/2} - V_{i+3/2}\frac{A_{i+3/2}}{A_{i+1/2}} \right\}.$$

The reason for this discrepancy could not be determined. This formulation for the cell center squared velocity is assumed to hold in both single and two phase flows.

Loss coefficients are in general a function of the flow direction. For example, consider the flow geometry illustrated in Figure 3. For flow from node i to node i+1 the fluid experiences a sudden expansion at junction i+1/2. Similarly, for reverse flow the

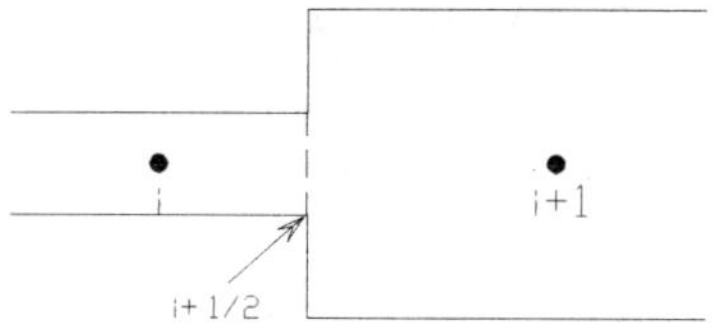

Figure 3: Flow junction for a sudden expansion/sudden contraction

fluid experiences a sudden contraction. The nonconservative form of the momentum equation at junction i+1/2 is identical to that for a constant area straight pipe section except in the wall shear stress term.

$$\rho \frac{\partial(V)}{\partial t}\Big|_{i+1/2} + (\rho V)\frac{\Delta V}{\Delta z}\Big|_{i+1/2} = -\frac{(P_{i+1} - P_i)}{\Delta z}$$

$$- \frac{K\rho|V|V}{2}\Big|_{i+1/2} + \rho_{i+1/2}\, g_z$$

where the loss coefficient is

$$K_{i+1/2} = \begin{cases} K_{exp} & V_{i+1/2} > 0 \\ K_{cont} & V_{i+1/2} < 0. \end{cases}$$

This can be generalized to an arbitrary flow obstruction at i+1/2 with the loss coefficient a function of direction.

$$K_{i+1/2} = \begin{cases} K^+_{i+1/2} & V_{i+1/2} > 0 \\ K^-_{i+1/2} & V_{i+1/2} < 0 \end{cases}$$

The selection of the appropriate loss coefficient can then be expressed as a donored property in the form

$$K_{i+1/2} = \frac{1}{2}(K^+_{i+1/2} + K^-_{i+1/2}) + \frac{1}{2}\frac{|V_{i+1/2}|}{V_{i+1/2}}(K^+_{i+1/2} - K^-_{i+1/2}).$$

The TRAC formulation for the momentum flux term has the advantage of requiring no assumptions concerning cell centered velocities and will give the correct pressure drop across a sudden expansion without additional local loss coefficients. For steady-state incompressible flows, the RELAP formulation reduces directly to Bernoulli's Equation with no ambiguity as to applications of loss coefficients, even in branching flows where application of the upwind differencing scheme becomes less clear.

Extension of the staggered mesh scheme to unevenly spaced systems with arbitrary flow area is straight forward and yields

Continuity

$$\mathcal{V}_i \frac{\partial \rho}{\partial t}\Big|_i + (\rho VA)_{i+1/2} - (\rho VA)_{i-1/2} = 0$$

Momentum

$$\Delta z\, \rho \frac{\partial(V)}{\partial t}\Big|_{i+1/2} + (\rho V)\frac{\Delta V}{\Delta z}\Big|_{i+1/2} \Delta z_{i+1/2} = -\left(P_{i+1} - P_i\right)$$

$$- \frac{K\rho|V|V}{2}\Big|_{i+1/2} \Delta z_{i+1/2} + \rho_{i+1/2}\, g_z\, \Delta z_{i+1/2}$$

Internal Energy

$$V_i \frac{\partial(\rho u)}{\partial t}\Big|_i + (\rho u VA)_{i+1/2} - (\rho u VA)_{i-1/2} =$$

$$- P_i \left\{(VA)_{i+1/2} - (VA)_{i-1/2}\right\} + \dot{q}_{wi}$$

Averaging and differencing schemes other than those discussed here may be possible, though the donor cell and upwind differencing schemes have stablity characteristics which are relatively well understood.

Branch Nodes

The discretization schemes discussed here for flow volumes with a single inlet and a single outlet can be easily extended to flow geometries with multiple inlets and outlets. The continuity and internal energy equations for a general flow volume are

Continuity

$$V_i \frac{\partial \rho}{\partial t}\Big|_i + \sum_{exits} (\rho VA)_{exit} - \sum_{inlets} (\rho VA)_{inlet} = 0$$

Internal Energy

$$V_i \frac{\partial(\rho u)}{\partial t}\Big|_i + \sum_{exits} (\rho u VA)_{exit} - \sum_{inlets} (\rho u VA)_{inlet} =$$

$$- P_i \left\{ \sum_{exits} (VA)_{exit} - \sum_{inlets} (VA)_{inlet} \right\} + \dot{q}_{wi}$$

Momentum

The nonconservative form of the momentum equation

$$\rho \frac{\partial V}{\partial t} + \frac{\rho}{2}\frac{\partial V^2}{\partial z} = -\frac{\partial P}{\partial z} - \frac{K\rho|V|V}{2} + \rho g_z$$

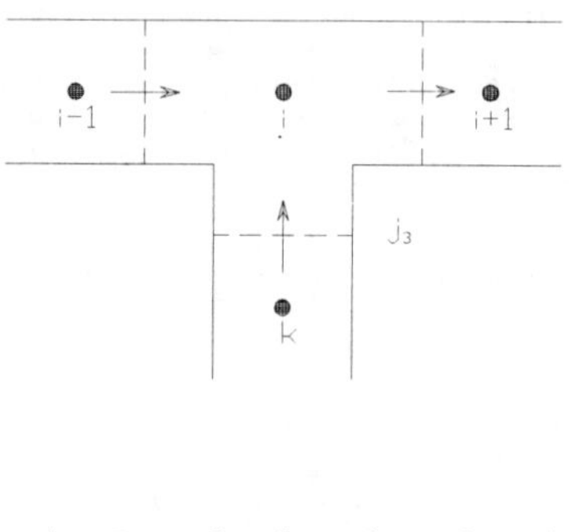

Figure 4: Control volume for a branch node

can be applied directly to each junction of a multiple-inlet/multiple-outlet flow volume and differs from that for a single-inlet/single-outlet volume only in the definition of the cell centered velocities and in formulation of the loss coefficients. For example, for the branching volume illustrated in Figure 4, the momentum equations are:

Junction 1

$$\rho_1 \frac{\partial V_1}{\partial t} + \frac{\rho_1}{2}\left\{\frac{(V^2)_i - (V^2)_{i-1}}{\Delta z_1}\right\} = -\left\{\frac{P_i - P_{i-1}}{\Delta z_1}\right\}$$

$$- \frac{K_1 \rho_1 |V_1| V_1}{2} + \rho_1 g_z$$

Junction 2

$$\rho_2 \frac{\partial V_2}{\partial t} + \frac{\rho_2}{2}\left\{\frac{(V^2)_{i+1} - (V^2)_i}{\Delta z_2}\right\} = -\left\{\frac{P_{i+1} - P_i}{\Delta z_2}\right\}$$

$$- \frac{K_2 \rho_2 |V_2| V_2}{2} + \rho_2 g_z$$

Junction 3

$$\rho_3 \frac{\partial V_3}{\partial t} + \frac{\rho_3}{2}\left\{\frac{(V^2)_i - (V^2)_k}{\Delta z_3}\right\} = -\left\{\frac{P_i - P_k}{\Delta z_3}\right\}$$

$$- \frac{K_3 \rho_3 |V_3| V_3}{2} + \rho_3 g_z$$

Specification of the loss coefficients at each junction is complicated by their dependence not only on the flow direction at that specific junction but also on the flow direction at all other junctions associated with the volume.

TIME ADVANCEMENT

A high degree of nonlinearity exists even in the simplest set of conservation equations. Most time advancement schemes are formulated so as to minimize or eliminate these nonlinearities.

Explicit Time Advancement

The simplest and most obvious time advancement scheme is to forward difference the time derivatives to give

Continuity

$$V_i \left(\frac{\rho_i^{n+1} - \rho_i^n}{\Delta t} \right) + (\rho VA)^n_{i+1/2} - (\rho VA)^n_{i-1/2} = 0$$

Momentum

$$\Delta z\, \rho^n_{i+1/2} \left(\frac{V^{n+1}_{i+1/2} - V^n_{i+1/2}}{\Delta t} \right) + (\rho V)\frac{\Delta V}{\Delta z}\Big|^n_{i+1/2} \Delta z_{i+1/2} =$$

$$- \left(P_{i+1} - P_i\right)^n - \frac{K\rho|V|V}{2}\Big|^n_{i+1/2} \Delta z_{i+1/2}$$

$$+ \rho^n_{i+1/2}\, g_z\, \Delta z_{i+1/2}$$

Internal Energy

$$V_i \left(\frac{(\rho u)^{n+1}_i - (\rho u)^n_i}{\Delta t} \right) + (\rho u VA)^n_{i+1/2} - (\rho u VA)^n_{i-1/2} =$$

$$- P^n_i \left\{(VA)_{i+1/2} - (VA)_{i-1/2}\right\}^n + (\dot{q}_{wi})^n$$

The explicit approach allows direct advancement of all variables except pressure (P_i) to the new time level. Advancement of pressure requires the state relationship

$$\tilde{\rho}_i^{n+1} = \rho\left(u_i^{n+1},\ P_i^{n+1}\right)$$

where

$$u_i^{n+1} = (\rho u)_i^{n+1}/\rho_i^{n+1}.$$

The state relationship is in general nonlinear in P and thus requires an iterative solution. An alternative is to form the linearized state relation

$$\rho_i^{n+1} = \tilde{\rho}_i^n + (u_i^{n+1} - u_i^n)\left.\frac{\partial\rho}{\partial u}\right|_i^n + (P_i^{n+1} - P_i^n)\left.\frac{\partial\rho}{\partial P}\right|_i^n$$

and solve for P_i^{n+1} directly. It is important to note that the past time density is the "true" density from the full state relationship and not the past time solution density. If a Newton-Raphson approach is used to iterate on pressure, the linearization above is equivalent to a single pass through the Newton-Raphson iteration.

The explicit algorithm is first order correct in time and as with all explicit algorithms is conditionally stable. The stability criterion for this method is

$$\Delta t < \min_i \left\{\frac{\Delta z_i}{c_i}\right\}$$

where

$$c_i = \sqrt{\frac{dP_i}{d\rho_i}}$$

is the sonic velocity in the fluid. This time step size is prohibitively small for most reactor applications.

Semi-Implicit Time Advancement

The sonic time step limit in the explicit scheme can be traced to the explicit time advancement of pressure in the momentum equation and velocity in the convective terms of the continuity and internal energy equations. To ease the stability criterion associated with the explicit scheme, terms necessary to eliminate the sonic time step limit, and phenomena known to have small time constants are evaluated at the new time level (implicitly). In addition, time level specification is usually based on preserving a high degree of linearity and producing matrices of desirable structure. The equation set for the semi-implicit scheme is then:

Continuity

$$V_i\left[\frac{\rho_i^{n+1} - \rho_i^n}{\Delta t}\right] + (\rho^n\, V^{n+1}\, A)_{i+1/2}$$

$$- (\rho^n\, V^{n+1}\, A)_{i-1/2} = 0$$

Momentum

$$(\Delta z\, \rho^n)_{i+1/2}\left[\frac{V_{i+1/2}^{n+1} - V_{i+1/2}^n}{\Delta t}\right]$$

$$+ (\rho V)\left.\frac{\Delta V}{\Delta z}\right|_{i+1/2}^n \Delta z_{i+1/2} = -\left(P_{i+1} - P_i\right)^{n+1}$$

$$- \left.\frac{K^n\, \rho^n\, |V^n|\, V^{n+1}}{2}\right|_{i+1/2} \Delta z_{i+1/2} + \rho_{i+1/2}^n\, g_z\, \Delta z_{i+1/2}$$

Internal Energy

$$V_i\left[\frac{(\rho u)_i^{n+1} - (\rho u)_i^n}{\Delta t}\right]$$

$$+ (\rho u)^n\, V^{n+1}\, A\Big|_{i+1/2} - (\rho u)^n\, V^{n+1}\, A\Big|_{i-1/2} =$$

$$- P_i^n\left\{(VA)_{i+1/2} - (VA)_{i-1/2}\right\}^{n+1} + (\dot{q}_{wi})^{n'}$$

The velocities in the pressure work term can be evaluated explicitly, however the time level specification indicated results in smoother behavior, is consistent with the philosophy of specifying convective velocities at new time and results in the convection of enthalpy like terms across flow boundaries. The time level specification (n') for the wall heat transfer rate can be explicit, implicit or mixed depending on the application and time constant associated with heat transfer.

Equation of State (Linearized)

$$\rho_i^{n+1} = \tilde{\rho}_i^n + (u_i^{n+1} - u_i^n)\left.\frac{\partial\rho}{\partial u}\right|_i^n + (P_i^{n+1} - P_i^n)\left.\frac{\partial\rho}{\partial P}\right|_i^n$$

The internal energy equation still contains a nonlinearity in the ρu term. This nonlinearity can be eliminated by linearizing the product ρu about past time values of ρ and u or more simply by modifying the state relationship to be of the form (RELAP5/MOD1 1982)

$$\rho_i^{n+1} = \tilde{\rho}_i^n + (\rho u_i^{n+1} - \rho u_i^n)\left.\frac{\partial\rho}{\partial \rho u}\right|_i^n + (P_i^{n+1} - P_i^n)\left.\frac{\partial\rho}{\partial P}\right|_i^n.$$

The semi-implicit method is first order correct and conditionally stable with the stability criterion being

$$\Delta t < \min_i \left|\frac{\Delta z_{i+1/2}}{V_{i+1/2}}\right|$$

i.e., the time step must be less than the material transport time across any computational cell. This stability criterion is usually referred to as the material Courant limit and is much less restrictive than the sonic transport limit of the explicit scheme.

The semi-implicit scheme given here is linear in the new time variables ρ, ρu, P, and V. If applied to a flow system with N computational nodes, the matrix equation resulting from this discretization is of order 4N x 4N. This may be reduced algebraically to an N x N system in pressure by the following procedure.

(a) The momentum equation is used to eliminate velocities in favor of pressure in the continuity and internal energy equations.

(b) The linearized state relation is substituted for density in the continuity equation, eliminating density in favor of internal energy and pressure.

(c) The internal energy and continuity equations can then be combined to yield one linear equation in the spatial pressure distribution of the form

$$b_i P_{i-1}^{t+\Delta t} + a_i P_i^{t+\Delta t} + c_i P_{i+1}^{t+\Delta t} + \sum_j d_j P_j^{t+\Delta t} = S_i^t \qquad \text{(a)}$$

The first three terms in this equation represent the pressure distribution in the major flow direction. The summation terms result from nodes representing Tees or other branching volumes. The remaining systems variables ρ, ρu, and V may be obtained directly from the pressure solution through equations of the form

$$L_v \, V = S_v \, (P) \qquad (b)$$

$$L_\rho \, \rho = S_\rho \, (P) \qquad (c)$$

$$L_{\rho u} \, \rho U = S_{\rho u} \, (P) \qquad (d)$$

It should be noted that the evaluation of local thermodynamic and fluid properties is inherently parallel as these parameters depend only on local variables and are uncoupled from neighboring computational nodes. In addition, given **P** from (a), Equations (b), (c), and (d) are independent and therefore could be executed in parallel on modern computer architectures with multiple computational units and/or vector pipelines. For the time discretization shown here L_v, L_ρ and $L_{\rho u}$ are diagonal matrices and therefore their inversion is also highly parallel.

A typical two-loop PWR nodalization is illustrated in Figure 5. The matrix structure resulting from applying Equation (a) to this nodalization is shown in Figure 6. As can be seen, the matrix is large, sparse, primarily tridiagonal with off-diagonal elements scattered above and below the main tridiagonal bands. The off-diagonal elements result from connections of one-dimensional piping segments at Tee or other branching nodes. The location of these off-diagonal elements is therefore a function of the geometry modeled and in general the numbering scheme chosen. These matrices have the properties, that (a) the values of the nonzero elements are time dependent and therefore the matrices must be inverted at each time step, and (b) while the positions of the nonzero elements are symmetric, the numerical values of the elements are not equal such that in general $\mathbf{L} \neq \mathbf{L}^T$ and each element of **L** must be stored and eliminated during the inversion. While matrix structures of this type usually suggest solution by some matrix iterative technique, direct solution schemes have been found to be superior in time dependent fluids problems due to the sensitivity of the iterative schemes to the convergence criterion and corresponding matrix solution error inherent to these algorithms (Sills and Doster 1986). The direct solution scheme presented here is the TR Algorithm (Sills and Doster 1986) developed specifically for matrices of the structure shown in Figure 5. The TR Algorithm is similar to Porsching's block elimination technique (Porsching 1971) and though developed for application to parallel computer architectures has been shown to give good performance on scalar computers.

<u>TR Algorithm</u>

The NxN system represented by Equation (a) can be expressed as

$$\mathbf{L} \; \mathbf{P} = \mathbf{S}.$$

Split **L** into a tridiagonal matrix **T** plus a remainder matrix **R**, where **R** has m columns containing nonzero elements:

$$\mathbf{L} = \mathbf{T} + \mathbf{R}$$

such that

$$(\mathbf{T} + \mathbf{R}) \; \mathbf{P} = \mathbf{S}.$$

The value of m is roughly twice the number of computational volumes which represent branching components and in general is much less than N. Invert **T** and multiply by $\mathbf{T}^{-1}$

$$(\mathbf{I} + \mathbf{T}^{-1} \, \mathbf{R}) \; \mathbf{P} = \mathbf{T}^{-1} \, \mathbf{S} \qquad (e)$$

It can be shown that the rows of Equation (e) corresponding to the nonzero columns of **R** produce an mxm system of equations which may be solved directly for the corresponding elements of **P**. The remaining values of **P** are then given explicitly in terms of these elements through Equation (e).

Many variations on the semi-implicit scheme have been proposed (TRAC-P1 1978, Liles and Reed 1978, RELAP5/MOD1 1982) though most result in either increased numbers of nonlinear terms or a degradation in the matrix structure. In LOCA calculations where choked flow exists in the vicinity of the break, the fluid velocity approaches the sonic velocity and time step sizes are reduced to those of explicit schemes. To overcome this limitation, Courant violating schemes have been developed.

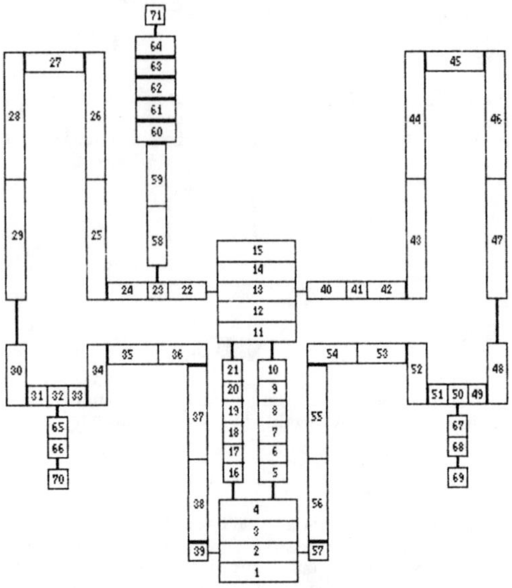

Figure 5: Typical PWR nodalization

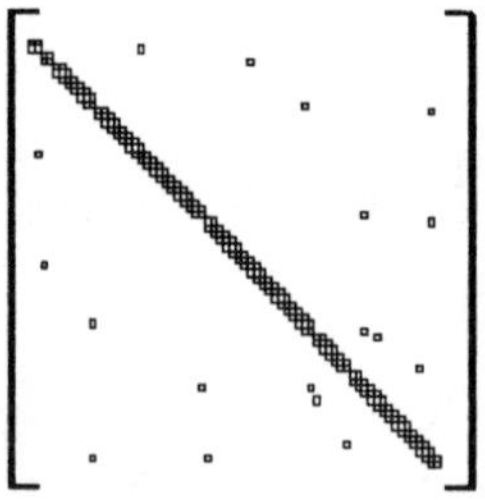

Figure 6: Matrix structure for PWR nodalization

COURANT VIOLATING METHODS

Fully Implicit Time Advancement

Fully implicit schemes are obtained by backward differencing the conservation equations to obtain

Continuity

$$V_i \left(\frac{\rho_i^{n+1} - \rho_i^n}{\Delta t} \right) + (\rho VA)_{i+1/2}^{n+1} - (\rho VA)_{i-1/2}^{n+1} = 0$$

Momentum

$$\Delta z\, \rho_{i+1/2}^n \left(\frac{V_{i+1/2}^{n+1} - V_{i+1/2}^n}{\Delta t} \right) + (\rho V) \left. \frac{\Delta V}{\Delta z} \right|_{i+1/2}^{n+1} \Delta z_{i+1/2} =$$

$$- \left(P_{i+1} - P_i\right)^{n+1} - \left. \frac{K\rho|V|V}{2} \right|_{i+1/2}^{n+1} \Delta z_{i+1/2}$$

$$+ \rho_{i+1/2}^{n+1} g_z \Delta z_{i+1/2}$$

Internal Energy

$$V_i \left(\frac{(\rho u)_i^{n+1} - (\rho u)_i^n}{\Delta t} \right) + (\rho uVA)_{i+1/2}^{n+1} - (\rho uVA)_{i-1/2}^{n+1} =$$

$$- P_i^{n+1} \left((VA)_{i+1/2} - (VA)_{i-1/2}\right)^{n+1} + (\dot{q}_{wi})^{n+1}$$

The fully implicit scheme is unconditionally stable, however it results in nonlinear systems of equations which must be solved by iterative methods. The matrix associated with the iterative solution is very large, sparse and block structured.

Multi-Step Methods

Multi-step methods have been developed in an effort to reduce the computational effort associated with the fully implicit schemes while maintaining the advantages of larger time step sizes (Mahaffy 1982, RELAP5/MOD2 1985). While these methods vary somewhat in their application, most are based on a semi-implicit like first step, followed by a stabilizing step and are very much like Predictor-Corrector algorithms commonly used in the solution of ordinary differential equations. For example the Stability- Enhancing Two-Step (SETS) method developed at Los Alamos (Mahaffy 1982) follows a semi-implicit time advancement, very much like the semi-implicit scheme developed in the previous section, by stabilizing mass and energy equations of the form

Stabilizing Mass Equation

$$V_i \left(\frac{\rho_i^{n+1} - \rho_i^n}{\Delta t} \right) + (\rho VA)_{i+1/2}^{n+1} - (\rho VA)_{i-1/2}^{n+1} = 0$$

Stabilizing Internal Energy Equation

$$V_i \left(\frac{(\rho u)_i^{n+1} - (\rho u)_i^n}{\Delta t} \right) + (\rho uVA)_{i+1/2}^{n+1} - (\rho uVA)_{i-1/2}^{n+1} =$$

$$- P_i^{n+1} \left((VA)_{i+1/2} - (VA)_{i-1/2}\right)^{n+1} + (\dot{q}_{wi})^{n+1}$$

The stabilizing equations are identical in form to the mass and energy equations from the fully implicit scheme. The velocities and pressures used here however are those calculated from the semi-implicit step. The stabilizing equations are independent linear equations in the density and energy distributions with the same matrix structure as the original pressure equation. These equations may be solved directly utilizing the matrix techniques discussed earlier. Multi-step methods, while not unconditionally stable, give enhanced stablility for much larger time steps than the normal semi-implicit techniques.

EXTENSIONS TO MULTIPHASE SYSTEMS

The numerical techniques discussed here for single-phase flows can be directly applied to multiphase systems. As an example, consider the three equation drift flux model

Continuity

$$A_x \frac{\partial}{\partial t} (\rho) + \frac{\partial}{\partial z} (\rho V) A_x = 0$$

Momentum (Nonconservative Form)

$$\rho \frac{\partial}{\partial t} (V) + (\rho V) \frac{\partial}{\partial z} (V) = - \frac{\partial}{\partial z} P - \frac{K\rho|V|V}{2}$$

$$+ \rho g_z - \frac{1}{A_x} \frac{\partial}{\partial z} \left\{ \frac{\rho_l \rho_g}{\rho} \frac{1}{\alpha_l \alpha_g} j_D^{G2} A_x \right\}$$

Internal Energy

$$A_x \frac{\partial}{\partial t} (\rho u) + \frac{\partial}{\partial z} (\rho uV) A_x = - P \frac{\partial}{\partial z} (VA_x) + q_w'' P_w$$

$$- P \frac{\partial}{\partial z} \left\{ \frac{\rho_l \rho_g}{\rho} (u_g - u_l) j_D^G A_x \right\}$$

$$- P \frac{\partial}{\partial z} \left\{ \frac{(\rho_l - \rho_g)}{\rho} j_D^G \right\} A_x$$

where we have defined the mixture variables

$$\rho \equiv \alpha_l \rho_l + \alpha_g \rho_g$$

$$\rho V \equiv \alpha_l \rho_l V_l + \alpha_g \rho_g V_g$$

$$\rho u \equiv \alpha_l \rho_l u_l + \alpha_g \rho_g u_g$$

$$V \equiv \rho V / \rho$$

$$j_D^G \equiv \alpha_l \alpha_g (V_g - V_l)$$

$$\frac{K\rho|V|V}{2} \equiv \frac{<\tau_w^{2\phi}>_l P_w}{A_x}$$

Though more sophisticated two-phase models exist, the time and spatial discretization schemes are identical. In addition, solution of the Drift Flux equations requires much of the same work as the more sophisticated models and result in matrix equations of the same structure. Integrate over a staggered spatial mesh and assume a semi-implicit time advancement for the temporal terms.

Continuity

$$V_i \left(\frac{\rho_i^{n+1} - \rho_i^n}{\Delta t} \right) + (\rho^n V^{n+1} A)_{i+1/2}$$

$$- (\rho^n V^{n+1} A)_{i-1/2} = 0$$

Momentum

$$(\Delta z\, \rho^n)_{i+1/2} \left(\frac{V_{i+1/2}^{n+1} - V_{i+1/2}^n}{\Delta t} \right)$$

$$+ (\rho V) \left. \frac{\Delta V}{\Delta z} \right|_{i+1/2}^n \Delta z_{i+1/2} = - \left(P_{i+1} - P_i\right)^{n+1}$$

$$- \left. \frac{K^n \rho^n |V^n| V^{n+1}}{2} \right|_{i+1/2} \Delta z_{i+1/2} + \rho_{i+1/2}^n g_z \Delta z_{i+1/2}$$

$$+ \frac{1}{A_x} \left. \left\{ \frac{\rho_l \rho_g}{\rho} \frac{1}{\alpha_l \alpha_g} j_D^{G2} A_x \right\} \right|_{i+1/2}^n$$

$$- \frac{1}{A_x} \left. \left\{ \frac{\rho_l \rho_g}{\rho} \frac{1}{\alpha_l \alpha_g} j_D^{G2} A_x \right\} \right|_{i-1/2}^n$$

Internal Energy

$$\mathcal{V}_i \left(\frac{(\rho u)_i^{n+1} - (\rho u)_i^n}{\Delta t} \right)$$

$$+ (\rho u)^n V^{n+1} A\Big|_{i+1/2} - (\rho u)^n V^{n+1} A\Big|_{i-1/2} =$$

$$- P_i^n \left\{ (VA)_{i+1/2} - (VA)_{i-1/2} \right\}^{n+1} + (\dot{q}_{wi})^{n'}$$

$$- P_i^n \left\{ \frac{\rho_l \rho_g}{\rho} (u_g - u_l) j_D^G A_x \right\}_{i+1/2}^n$$

$$+ P_i^n \left\{ \frac{\rho_l \rho_g}{\rho} (u_g - u_l) j_D^G A_x \right\}_{i-1/2}^n$$

$$- P_i^n \left\{ \frac{(\rho_l - \rho_g)}{\rho} j_D^G A_x\Big|_{i+1/2} - \frac{(\rho_l - \rho_g)}{\rho} j_D^G A_x\Big|_{i-1/2} \right\}^n$$

Equation of State (Linearized)

$$\rho_i^{n+1} = \tilde{\rho}_i^n + (\rho u_i^{n+1} - \rho u_i^n) \frac{\partial \rho}{\partial \rho u}\Big|_i^n + (P_i^{n+1} - P_i^n) \frac{\partial \rho}{\partial P}\Big|_i^n .$$

The drift flux equations are linear in the new time variables ρ, ρu, V and P and may be solved directly using the techniques discussed for single-phase flow. The remaining system variables are obtained as

$$\rho_l = \rho_l^s(P)$$
$$\rho_g = \rho_g^s(P)$$
$$u_l = u_l^s(P)$$
$$u_g = u_g^s(P)$$

$$\alpha_g = \frac{(\rho - \rho_l)}{(\rho_g - \rho_l)} = 1 - \alpha_l$$

completing the time advancement (with the exception of the constituitive relations).

SUMMARY AND CONCLUSIONS

The dynamic simulation of nuclear power systems requires solution of the conservation equations for mass, energy and momentum transport in a two-phase system. These equations are highly nonlinear and numerical solution techniques are required. Stable time and spatial discretization schemes can be developed to model heat transfer and fluid flow in flow networks typical of nuclear reactor simulations. These discretization techniques lead to large sparse matrix equations which must be solved at each time step in the simulation. As the solution of these matrices can become prohibitively time consuming, efficient matrix inversion schemes are required, particularly in real time applications. While the numerical solution techniques presented are general and relatively independent of computer architecture, it has been shown that many aspects of reactor thermal-hydraulic calculations are inherently parallel and can benefit from implementation on parallel computer architectures. With the increased availability of mini supercomputers employing parallelism through multi-CPU's and/or vector pipelines, this technology could play an important role in power plant simulation.

REFERENCES

Doster, J.M., J.A. Turner and E.D. Sills. 1988. "Applications of advanced computer architectures to the thermal-hydraulic simulation of nuclear power systems," *Simulators V 1988*, Society for Computer Simulation, 97-102.

Liles, D.R. and W.H. Reed. 1978. "A Semi-Implicit Method for Two-Phase Fluid Dynamics," *Journal of Computational Physics* **26**, 390-407.

Mahaffy, J.H. 1982. "A Stability-Enhancing Two-Step Method for Fluid Flow Calculations," *Journal of Computational Physics* **46**, 329-341.

Porsching, T.A., J.H. Murphy, and J.A. Redfield. 1971. "Stable Numerical Integration of Conservation Equations for Hydraulic Networks," *Nuclear Science and Engineering* **43**, 218-225.

RELAP5/MOD1 1982: Code Manual, Volume 1: *Systems Models and Numerical Methods.* NUREG/CR-1826 EGG-2070.

RELAP5/MOD2 1985: Code Manual, Volume 1: *Code Structure, Systems Models, and Solution Methods.* NUREG/CR-4312 EGG-2396.

Sills, E.D and J.M. Doster. 1986. "Evaluation of Algorithms for the Solution of the Drift-Flux Equations on Advanced Computers." In *Proceedings of the 2nd International Conference on Simulation Methods in Nuclear Engineering.* (Montreal, Canada, Oct. 14-16). CNS/ANS, Toronto, Ontario, 678-699

TRAC-BD1/MOD1 1984: An Advanced Best Estimate Computer Program for Boiling Water Reactor Transient Analysis, Volume 1: *Model Description*, NUREG/CR-3633 EGG-2294.

TRAC-P1 1978: An Advanced Best Estimate Computer Program for PWR LOCA Analysis: 1. *Methods, Models, User Information and Programming Details*, NUREG/CR-0-63.

NOMENCLATURE

A = Cross sectional flow area
A_x = Cross sectional flow area
$\mathbf{g}$ = Gravitational vector
j_D^G = Drift flux
K = Loss coefficient per unit length
P = Pressure
P_w = Wetted Perimeter
q' = Heat transfer rate per unit length
q'' = Heat flux
t = time
u = specific internal energy
V = Velocity
$\mathcal{V}$ = Volume
z = Flow direction

Greek Symbols

α = Area fraction
ρ = density
τ = Shear stress

Subscripts

g = Vapor phase
l = Liquid phase
w = Wall
z = Flow direction

Superscripts

n = Time level
s = Saturation
2ϕ = Two phase

Simulators VI
© 1989 By The Society for Computer
Simulation International
ISBN 0-911801-51-0

Simulation of a marine guidance and expert collision aviodance system

R. S. Burns, G. K. Blackwell and K. M. Miller
Ship Control Group, Plymouth Polytechnic,
Plymouth, Devon, U.K.

ABSTRACT

One of the major problems that stands in the way of the fully automated ship is that of safe guidance in and out of port. This paper addresses the problem of automatic guidance and collision avoidance, and draws upon the work undertaken over a number of years by the Ship Control Group at Plymouth Polytechnic, U.K., in terms of simulation, prototype model testing and full-scale system implementation.

Techniques to model and simulate the dynamic behaviour of a surface vessel are presented, together with simulated and actual results of an optimal ship guidance system. The problem of collision avoidance in port approaches is tackled using an expert system. Simulaltion results from a prototype system are given. Finally, the paper considers the need for an expert controller to provide integrated automatic guidance and collision avoidance.

INTRODUCTION

Although overall standards of safety at sea are very good, the approaches to a port, where traffic density is intense, may be considered a high risk area. It has been shown for example (Coldwell 1981) in the Humber Seaway, where there are 100 traffic movements per day, that there is at least one collision or grounding per week. In addition, there is the human element to consider. It has been highlighted (Panel on Human Error 1976) that 85 percent of all marine collisions and groundings are due to human error.

This suggests that there is a need for automatic guidance and collision avoidiance systems for marine vehicles in confined waters. As electronic navigation aids become more sophisticated and on-board computer systems become more available, the concept of the fully automatic ship becomes a tangible reality, and it is predicted that above 50 percent of the world`s shipping will be fully automated by the turn of the century.

The work presented in this paper is concerned with the simulation of a marine guidance and collision avoidance system. A ship is considered to be a multivariable system that may be controlled by formulating an optimal policy that seeks to maximise the return from the system for a minimum cost. The optimal guidance system therefore controls simultaneously the position, heading and speed of the vessel. In addition, a rule-based expert system is simulated to handle sensory data input, and to make collision avoidance decisions based upon the International Regulations for preventing Collisions at Sea (1981).

SHIP MATHEMATICAL MODEL

All moving rigid bodies contain six degrees of freedom. In this paper the ship is considered to be a rigid body with three degrees of freedom, namely surge, sway and yaw. Ship motions in heave, pitch and roll are considered small enough to be neglected. It is convenient to describe the motion in terms of a moving system of axes coincident with the mass centre of the hull, which gives rise to an Eulerian set of equations of motion.

It is necessary to obtain the hydrodynamic surge and sway forces together with the yaw moments acting on the hull. These may be considered as functions of:

(i) Properties of the ship e.g. length and hull geometry.

(ii) Properties of motion e.g. velocity.

(iii) Properties of the fluid e.g. density of sea water.

These may be reduced to a useful mathematical form by the use of Taylor`s expansion for a function of several variables (Abkowitz 1964). It has been shown (Burns et al. 1985) that taking only the linear terms from the expansion is insufficient to define the ship accurately. Non-linear terms that give rise to more than 10% of the global force or moment were considered of major importance, and included in the equation set.

The state vector $x(t)$ chosen to represent the vessel contains the following state variables:

1. Actual rudder angle
2. Actual engine speed
3. Forward position
4. Forward velocity
5. Lateral position
6. Lateral velocity
7. Heading
8. Yaw rate

The forcing vector $u(t)$ contains the following variables:

a. Demanded rudder angle
b. Demanded engine speed
c. Component of current speed in surge direction
d. Component of current speed in sway direction
e. Component of wind speed in surge direction
f. Component of wind speed in sway direction

From these eight states a set of first-order differential equations can be used to define the ship.

$$\dot{x}(t) = F(t)x(t) + G(t)u(t) \tag{1}$$

It is convenient to partition G matrix into the control forcing functions G_c and the disturbance forcing functions G_D.

$$\dot{x}(t) = F(t)x(t) + G_c(t)u(t) + G_D(t)w(t) \tag{2}$$

The corresponding discrete time solution is:

$$x(k+1) = A(k,k+1)x(k) + B(k,k+1)u(k) + C(k,k+1)w(k) \tag{3}$$

Equation (3) may be used in a recursive manner to simulate the passage of a vessel when the control vector u(k) and the disturbance vector w(k) are known.

Figure 1 shows a turning circle simulation of a fast cargo ship of displacement 17,100 tonnes. In the simulation the speed of approach is 15 knots and 20 degrees of starboard rudder has been applied.

function or performance index. This is based upon the summation of the weighted errors over some time interval, say, the time to complete the pilotage phase of the voyage. In addition to minimizing the errors in the output parameters, the optimal controller attempts to minimize also the control effort, i.e. to keep to a minimum the rudder and engine activity. The cost function is usually stated in the following quadratic terms:

$$J = \int_{t_0}^{t_1} \{(x-r)^T Q(x-r)+u^T Ru\}\, dt \tag{4}$$

Q and R are usually diagonal matrices and the values of the individual elements reflect the importance of the parameter being controlled. For example, in a track changing manoeuvre, large course errors will be incurred. If the track-keeping elements in the Q matrix are weighted more heavily than the course-keeping terms, then the majority of the control effort will be expended in reducing the track error, at the expense of the course deviation.

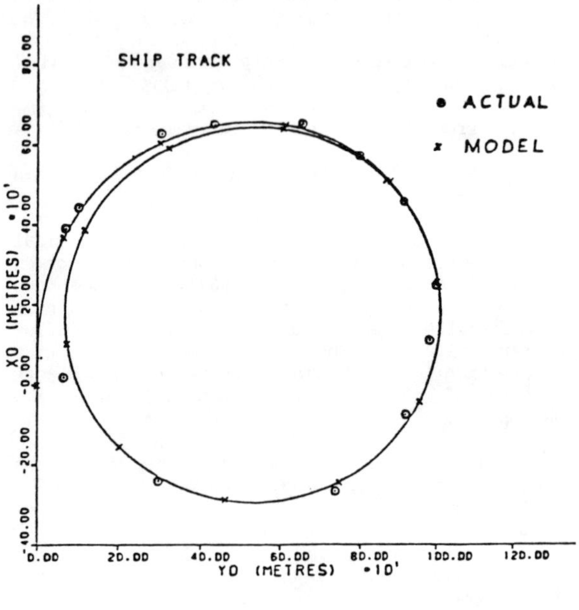

Figure 1

Turning Circle - Fast Cargo Ship

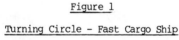

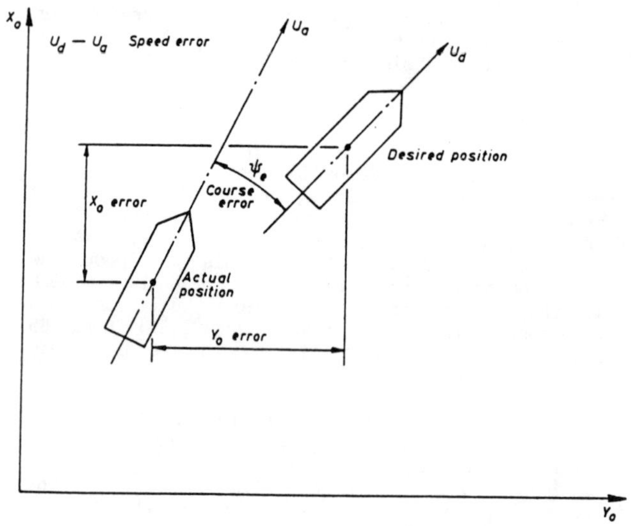

Figure 2

The Multivariable Control Problem

THE SHIP GUIDANCE PROBLEM

Multivariable Control

The guidance of a ship into the approaches to a port is a multivariable control problem.

The deviation from the desired position, course and speed, as shown in Figure 2 must be corrected for by operation of the rudder(s) and main engine(s). A feature of an optimal system is that it will seek to minimize a global parameter J, called the cost

Figure 3 shows a simulation of a full-size car ferry in the approaches to Plymouth. Here, the track-keeping is most heavily weighted, followed by the heading and forward speed. If the reduction in forward speed during a tight manoeuvre can be tolerated, the speed control loop may be dispensed with altogether.

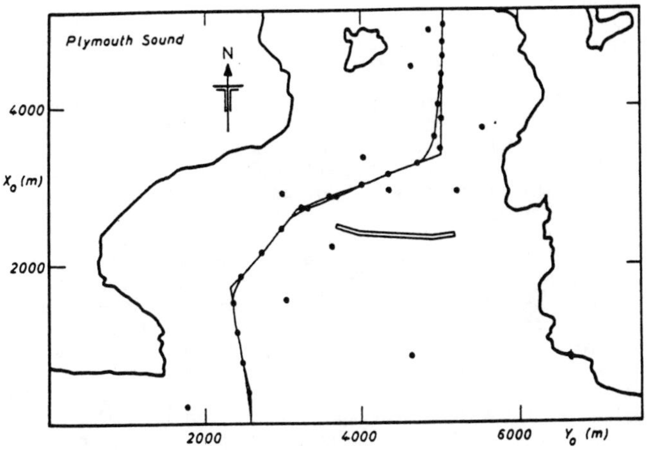

Figure 3

Computer Simulation - Approaches to Plymouth

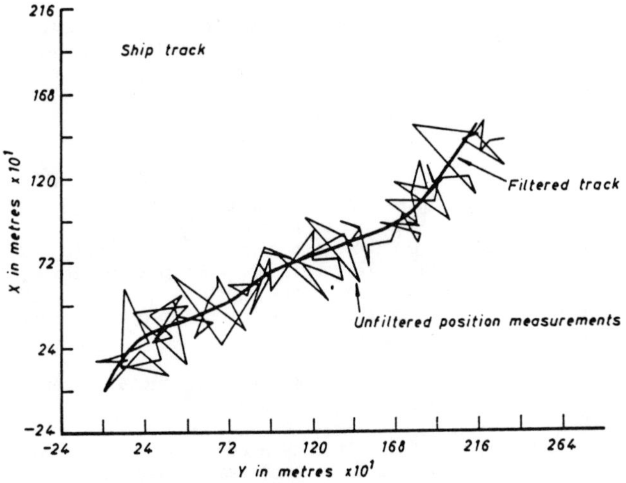

Figure 4

Filtered Track at Night

Measurement and State Estimation

In Figure 3 it is assumed that all the state variables can be measured with complete accuracy. All navigational instruments contain measurement errors and a best estimate can be obtained by incorporating a minimum variance or Kalman-Bucy filter. These have been developed extensively for aerospace, and latterly marine navigation (Dove et al. 1985)

The Kalman filter is a recursive computational algorithm which works in a predictor-corrector manner. The current best estimate of the state vector x(k) is used to drive the mathematical model of the ship in real time to predict the state of the vessel at time (k+1). The predictions are compared with the measurements and multiplied by the Kalman gain matrix to obtain the best estimate x(k+1).

In determining the value of the gain matrix, consideration has to be given to measurement errors. These are assumed to be random with a Gaussian distribution, and are stated in terms of a co-variance matrix.

Figure 4 shows the simulation of a typical passage into the port under night-time conditions. The simulation assumes that positional data is being received from a Decca Navigator using a standard deviation of 200 m. It is seen that the true and filtered tracks are almost coincident.

THE COLLISION AVOIDANCE PROBLEM

A rule-based approach is an essential pre-requisite to the task of collision avoidance at sea, whether or not computers are involved in the process. At first sight, it might seem that a simple procedural application of a standard set of rules, with consequent actions, would cover all requirements; indeed, all mariners are expected to abide by just such a set of rules.

Such a procedural approach has been used most effectively in computer simulation of marine traffic flow and collision avoidance. (Colley et al. 1984) The effects of changes (e.g. in traffic volume) in high-density traffic lanes have been highlighted by such a model, and the technique has also been used to good effect in training mariners. However, this approach takes no account of the need for experience and common sense in aplying these rules and, as such, is not a practical option in real-world situations.

The International Regulations for Preventing Collisions at Sea, although quite specific as far as they go, do not in themselves give rigorous definitions of preconditions and consequent actions. It is left to the mariner to decide such details as timing, clearances, and suitable course alterations; such discretion comes with years of accumulated experience and wisdom. One must also consider `non-standard` situations, particularly those involving more than two vessels which could not all be adequately covered by any reasonable reference guide.

Clearly, it is possible to provide `rules of thumb` for specific types of situation, and to add supplementary rules for variations in these situations. Such a rule structure would be founded on the previously mentioned anti-collision regulations, would incorporate the accumulated wisdom of expert mariners and would, presumably, also be tailored to reflect the response characteristics of the system operating that rule structure - speed of response, breadth of information available to the system and possible consequence of misjudgement (confidence limits).

An expert system as described would require access to two types of information, static and dynamic. Static information relates to fixed characteristics of the vessel - length, beam, maximum speed, minimum turning circle, safe clearing distance, and a variety of technical data (some possibly specific to current voyage). Dynamic information, to be constantly updated, would include such considerations as current speed and course, plus data on position, speed and course of any potential hazards in the vicinity. Such information must, by its nature, be input to the system directly via a range of sensors, including such instrumentation as radar.

Such an intelligent response system should be capable of evaluating an encounter between two or more vessels from the standpoint of an experienced mariner, and taking (or advising) appropriate action. On being provided with the information normally available on the bridge of a well-equipped ship, this system should be capable of:

(a) Recognising an encounter (potential hazard) situation in good time;

(b) Identifying the type of encounter and the status of one`s own vessel (own-ship) in that encounter, according to the International Regulations for Preventing Collisions at Sea - such status would normally be either `stand-on` (having right of way) or `give-way`, according to one`s position relative to the other vessel (subject to types of vessel involved, fishing vessels and deep-draught vessels having right of way in many circumstances);

(c) Choosing a course of action which combines a sensible safety margin with the least practicable inconvenience (where own-ship is judged to be stand-on, this will - initially at least - mean no alteration of course);

(d) Maintaining a watching brief on the other vessel(s) in the encounter, and being ready to take avoiding action if necessary, should the situation change - it is not unknown for `rogue` vessels to disregard the regulations and plough straight on when they should give way, or even to turn into danger.

COLLISION AVOIDANCE SIMULATION

The simulation package in current use is at the `second prototype` stage. The package comprises a simulator module, driving each of two vessels (own-ship and hazard vessel) independently on the knowledge bases for each of the two vessels. At 20 second intervals, ship time (simulated by 1/2 second intervals in real time) the following sequence is carried out:

(a) Certain minimal information, as would be available via instrumentation (speed, course, relative position) is communicated from the knowledge base of each ship to the knowledge base of the other;

(b) The expert system module considers the current state of each vessel independently, setting status indicators for consequent action, to be carried out by the simulator module;

(c) The simulator module updates the position, speed, and course information for each vessel in turn, with due regard for the `recommendations` of the expert system with respect to that vessel;

(d) The screen display is updated to show the new current situation.

The first prototype (Blackwell et al. 1987) contained the decision-making logic for the expert system module in such a form that the rules were `hard-wired` into the program code. Whilst adequate for an initial test-bed, this approach was unsuited to a flexible, expanding rule base as envisaged at the outset of this paper. The second prototype incorporates a content-free `inference engine` actioning a set of rules which form a `decision network` - see Figure 5. These rules are held as a set of nodes, or objects, each comprising a simple boolean decision function, pointers to two other nodes, and six other relevant parameters defining consequent action. The most significant of these are the two flags, one for each of the `child nodes`, indicating whether that node is to be actioned immediately or at the next time-step (solid and dotted lines respectively in Figure 5). This form of structure allows for the inference/decision network to be expanded and enriched to any degree of sophistication. A simple extension will also permit `backtracking` to explain the decision process at any stage, and parallel processing is a clear possibility without major changes.

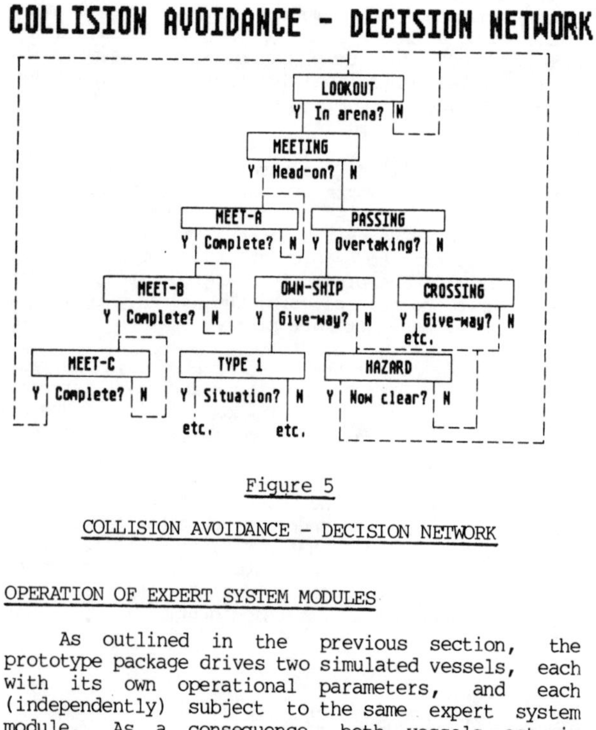

Figure 5

COLLISION AVOIDANCE - DECISION NETWORK

OPERATION OF EXPERT SYSTEM MODULES

As outlined in the previous section, the prototype package drives two simulated vessels, each with its own operational parameters, and each (independently) subject to the same expert system module. As a consequence, both vessels act in accordance with the anti-collision regulations, and there is no likelihood of one vessel having to take evasive action at a late stage to deal with non-co-operation by the other. In the near future, it is intended to model the two ships on separate computers, interacting via a communications link; an additional feature of such a system would be the provision of a manual override on one of the ships - the hazard - to enable testing of an extension of the rule base to handle `rogue` behaviour.

At the present phase of development, the rule base consists of rules for:

1. Identifying the presence of a potential hazard, and assessing the degree of threat in terms of expected time to infringement of the domain - this time factor is central to the decision on when to take avoiding action, if necessary.

2. Identifying the type of encounter, including several variants in some cases (the primary types of encounter being head-on, crossing and overtaking), and fixing the status of own-ship and the perceived status of hazard-ship in the encounter.

3. Negotiating the stages of the encounter, with due regard for appropriate safety margins.

SIMULATION RESULTS

Figure 6 shows a completed head-on encounter. Note that the status of own-ship is known in detail, but hazard ship is known only to be changing course.

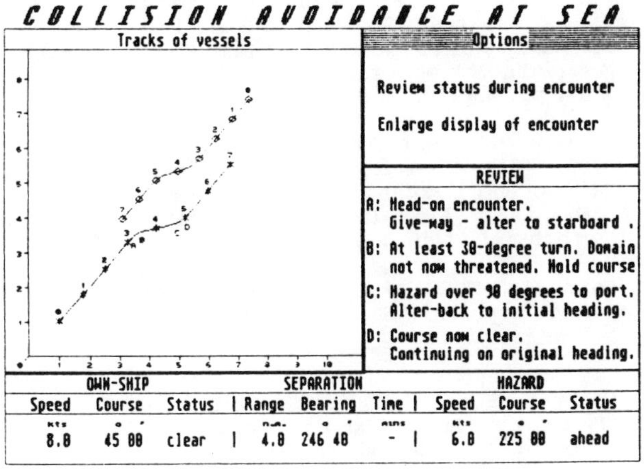

Figure 6

Example of a Completed Head-on Encounter

Figure 7 shows an overtaking manoeuvre when own-ship is to starboard of hazard vessel. Here own ship turns starboard on the same heading, but parallel track of the hazard ship, and then turns to port on original course, passing ahead of hazard vessel.

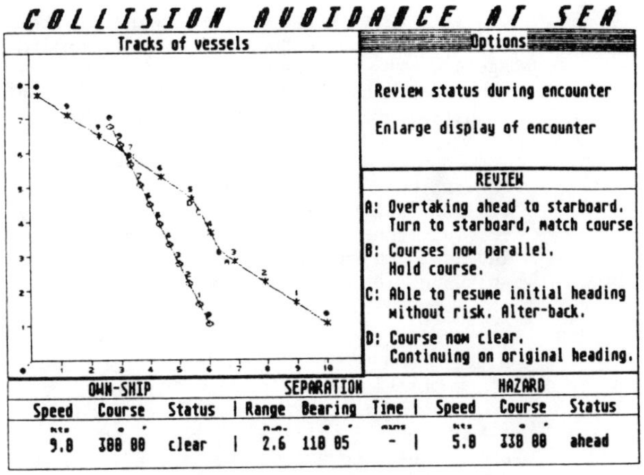

Figure 7

Own Ship being Overtaken by Hazard Vessel

ANALYSIS OF SIMULATION RESULTS

The effectiveness of the present rule structure has been evaluated by a multiple run of 500 simulated encounters. The results of this exercise are shown in the bar chart in Figure 8.

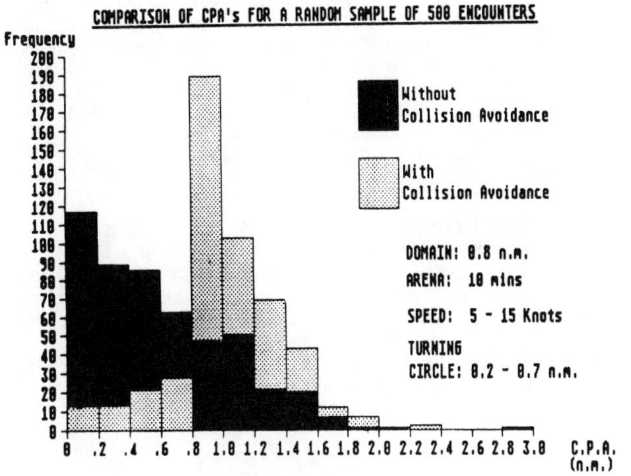

Figure 8

Comparison of CPA`s for a Random Sample of 500 Encounters

The results of this multiple simulation illustrate that, in the large majority of cases, potential domain violations were avoided by the expert system invoking appropriate collision avoidance strategies; moreover, the manoeuvres involved did not, in the main, involve excessive course alterations - closest point of approach (CPA) separations for these manoeuvres are clearly bunched just outside the domain boundary. However, a small number of the encounters still show CPA`s within the domain boundary - this is clearly unacceptable. The reasons for this are considered to be threefold:

1. The rule base in the initial expert system module was shown to have certain `blind spots`, in which each vessel assessed the other as the give-way vessel, and the required avoidance action was not taken;

2. In using a fairly simple model for generation of simulated vessels, some realism was lost - vessels with unlikely combinations of characteristics were involved in a number of the offending encounters;

3. A small number of these simulations highlighted the need for an increased level of sophistication in the strategy for recognising and handling encounter situations. Specifically, the fixed look-ahead, used to assess the time to initiate avoidance manoeuvres, appeared inadequate in certain cases; an ongoing look-ahead, extrapolating at regular intervals from current status, seemed indicated to ensure action at the optimum time. This is considered to be the most important development to arise from the multiple simulation exercise, and will form a central feature of future developments.

AUTOMATIC GUIDANCE AND COLLISION AVOIDANCE

At present, the collision avoidance system described in this paper acts as an expert advisor. The next stage of development is to link the guidance and collision avoidance systems together to form an expert controller. The advent of such systems should be viewed along-side recent advances in Vessel Traffic Systems (VTS). Discussions in the International Maritime Organisation (IMO) and the European Economic Community (EEC) have contributed to a global dialogue on the future aims and objectives of VTS.

The challenge facing the maritime world over the next decade will be the implementation of VTS in all major ports, using advanced surveillance and communication techniques, together with shipborne automatic guidance and collision avoidance systems. Such systems will increase the efficiency of port operation and at the same time improve safety levels, particularly in poor weather conditions.

NOMENCLATURE

Matrices and Vectors

A	Discrete State Transition Matrix
B	Discrete Control Matrix
C	Discrete Disturbance Matrix
F	Continuous Time System Matrix
$G, G_C G_D$	Continuous Time Forcing Matrices
Q	State Error Weighting Matrix
R	Control Weighting Matrix
r	Desired State Vector
u	Control Vector
w	Disturbance Vector
x	Ship Related State Vector

Scalar Symbols

J	Cost Function or Performance Index
k	Integer Counter
t	Continuous Time
t_o, t_1	Initial and Final Times
u_a, u_d	Actual and Desired Forward Velocity
X_o, Y_o	Earth Co-ordinate System
ψ_e	Course Error

REFERENCES

Abkowitz, M. 1964. "Lectures on Ship Hydrodynamics, Steering and Manoeuvrability." Hy-A Report, Hy, 5., Denmark.

Blackwell, G.K., R.S. Burns and C.T. Stockel. 1987. "An Expert System Approach to Collision Avoidance." Proceedings of Summer Computer Simulation Conference, Montreal. Society for Computer Simulation, July, 1987, pp. 43-48.

Burns, R.S., M.J. Dove, T.H. Bouncer, C.T. Stockel. 1985. "A Discrete, Time Varying, Non-linear Mathematical Model for the Simulation of Ship Manoeuvres." First International Maritime Simulation Symposium, Munich, June 1985.

Coldwell, T.G. 1981. "Marine Traffic Flow and Casualties on the Humber." Journal of Navigation, Volume 34,000.

Colley, B.A., R.G. Curtis, C.T. Stockel, 1983. "Manoeuvring Times, Domains and Arenas." Journal of Navigation. Volume 36, pp 324-328.

Dove, M.J., R.S. Burns, C.T. Stockel, T.H. Bouncer. 1985. "Simulation of a Digital Filter/Estimator for the Navigation of Large Ships in Confined Waters." Proc. First Intercontinental Symposium on Maritime Simulation, Control Data Corporation. Schliersee, W. Germany, pp 147-160.

International Marine Organisation, 1981. "International Regulations for Preventing Collisions at Sea."

Panel on Human Error in Merchant Marine Safety. 1976. "Human Error in Merchant Marine Safety." National Academy of Science, Washington D.C.

Simulators VI
© 1989 By The Society for Computer Simulation International
ISBN 0-911801-51-0

Simulation of the manoeuvring and powering characteristics of marine vehicles in calm water and in a seaway

R. S. Burns
Ship Control Group, Plymouth Polytechnic,
Plymouth, Devon, U.K.

ABSTRACT

It is well known that a ship sailing in a seaway requires more power to maintain a given speed than when it is in calm water. This is due to the added resistance which results mainly from the motion of the ship, particularly in pitch and heave, when excited by waves.

Multivariable system theory has in the past been used to model the manoeuvring characteristics of surface ships in calm water. This paper considers the extension of such a model to include added resistance effects so that trans-oceanic passages may be simulated. It is shown that average added resistance can be found using a mean response curve together with the energy spectrum of the sea. A real-time simulation is undertaken to demonstrate the effect of moving from calm water into a seaway of gradually increasing wave height.

INTRODUCTION

A ship may be considered to be a multivariable system as shown in Figure 1. Inputs to the system are the control variables (propeller and rudder) and the disturbance variables (wind, tide and waves). If the dynamic behaviour of the ship can be modelled accurately, then its response, in terms of a state variable set, may be predicted.

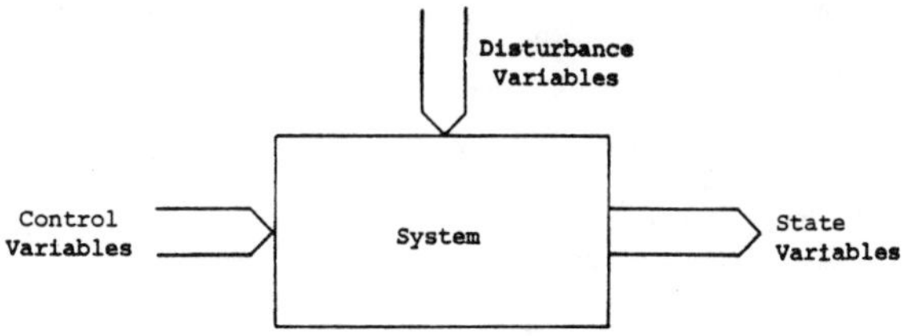

Figure 1

A Multivariable System

Multivariable system theory is employed to construct a calm water model based upon eight state variables, namely forward and lateral position and velocity, heading, yaw-rate, rudder angle and engine speed. The model has two deterministic inputs - demanded rudder and engine plus four stochastic disturbance inputs in the form of wind and current vectors.

This model is then extended to include the added resistance in waves. The parameters that affect the added resistance have been shown (Strom-Tejsen 1973) to be:

1. Added wind resistance on superstructure and hull.
2. Added resistance due to the motion of the ship, in particular pitch and heave.
3. Added resistance caused by wave reflection on the hull.
4. Added resistance due to yaw and sway.
5. Reduction in propulsive efficiency.

Items 1 and 4 are taken into account in a discrete, time-varying non-linear calm water model, and item 2 is considered as an extension to the model. Item 3, which is generally considered to be small, and item 5 are not considered in this presentation.

CALM-WATER SHIP MATHEMATICAL MODEL

Equations of Motion

The ship is considered to be a rigid body with three degrees of freedom, in surge, sway and yaw. Ship motions in the other three degrees of freedom, roll, pitch and heave are neglected. The motion is described by a moving system of axes coincident with the mass centre of the hull. The equations of motion may be written in the form:

$$m\dot{u} - mrv = X$$
$$m\dot{v} + mur = Y$$
$$I_z\dot{r} = N \qquad (1)$$

A Taylor series expansion (Abkowitz 1964) is employed to obtain expressions for hydrodynamic forces and moments. For applications such as course-keeping, where changes in rudder and heading angles do not usually exceed five degrees, a linear approximation, using only the first order terms in the expansion, is normally quite adequate. In a track-keeping situation where large changes in heading can be expected, it becomes necessary to include second and third order expansion terms.

Surge Equation

The complete surge equation in dimensionalised form is:

$$m\dot{u} - mrv = X_{\dot{u}}\dot{u} + X_u(u+u_c) + \overline{X}_{uu}u^2 + \overline{X}_{uuu}u^3 + \overline{X}_{vv}v^2$$

$$+ \overline{X}_{rr}r^2 + \overline{X}_{\delta\delta}\delta^2_A + \overline{X}_{un}un_A + \overline{X}_{nn}n^2_A$$

$$+ X_{ua}\,u_a \qquad (2)$$

In the above equation a shorthand subscript and bar notation has been adopted, for instance:

$$X_u = \frac{\partial X}{\partial u}, \quad \overline{X}_{uu} = 1/2\, X_{uu} = 1/2\frac{\partial^2 X}{\partial u^2}$$

The dimensionalised hydrodynamic coefficients are obtained from the non-dimensional values in the usual manner:

$$X_u = (1/2\,\rho\, L^2\ \ U)X_u'$$

Sway and Yaw Equations

The dimensionalised sway and yaw equations are:

$$m\dot{v} + mur = Y_{\dot{v}}\dot{v} = Y_v(v + v_c) + Y_{\dot{r}}\dot{r} + Y_r r + \overline{Y}_{nn}n^2_A$$

$$+ \overline{Y}_{vvv}v^3 + \overline{Y}_{rvv}rv^2 + \overline{Y}_{nn\delta}n^2_A\,\delta_A + \overline{Y}_{nn\delta\delta\delta}n^2_A\,\delta^3_A$$

$$+ \overline{Y}_{\delta vv}\,\delta_A v^2 + Y_{va}v_a \qquad (3)$$

$$I_z\dot{r} = N_{\dot{v}}\dot{v} + N_v(v + v_c) + N_{\dot{r}}\dot{r} + \overline{N}_{nn}n^2_A + \overline{N}_{vvv}v^3$$

$$+ N_r r + \overline{N}_{rvv}rv^2 + \overline{N}_{nn\delta}n^2_A\,\delta_A + \overline{N}_{nn\delta\delta\delta}n^2_A\,\delta^3_A$$

$$+ \overline{N}_{\delta vv}\,\delta_A v^2 + N_{va}v_a \qquad (4)$$

Steering Gear and Main Engine

These are both modelled by first order linear differential equations.

$$\dot{\delta}_A = \frac{1}{T_R}\,\delta_D - \frac{1}{T_R}\,\delta_A \qquad (5)$$

$$\dot{n}_A = \frac{1}{T_N}\,n_D - \frac{1}{T_N}\,n_A \qquad (6)$$

Where δ_D and n_D are the demanded rudder angle and demanded engine speed respectively.

State Space Formulation

Much attention was devoted to the choice of state variables and the state vector was finally based on the ship body axes.

$$X^T = (\,\delta_A\ \ n_A\ x\ u\ y\ v\ \psi\ r) \qquad (7)$$

This state is affected by the forcing vector:

$$U^T = (\,\delta_D\ n_D\ u_c\ v_c\ u_a\ v_a) \qquad (8)$$

Equations (5), (6), (2), (3) and (4) can be arranged in the following matrix form:

$$\dot{X}(t) = F(t)X(t) + G_C(t)U(t) + G_D(t)W(t) \qquad (9)$$

The corresponding discrete solution is:

$$X((K + 1)T) = A(T, KT)X(KT) + B(T, KT)U(KT)$$

$$+ C(T, KT)W(KT) \qquad (10)$$

where:

$$A(T, KT) = e^{F(t)T}$$

$$B(T, KT) = (e^{F(t)T} - I)\ F(t)^{-1}G_C(t)$$

$$C(T, KT) = (e^{F(t)T} - I)\ F(t)^{-1}G_D(t) \qquad (11)$$

Study Vessel

Manoeuvring simulations were undertaken on a vessel with a Mariner hull form. A complete set of linear and non-linear hydrodynamic coefficients for a vessel of this class are available (Chislett and Strom-Tejsen 1965). The model was validated (Burns, 1985) by undertaking a comparative evaluation with full-scale measurements taken on the USS Compass Island (Morse and Price 1961).

Study Vessel Particulars

Length	:	160.9 m
Draught	:	9.07 m
Beam	:	23.17 m
Block Coefficient	:	0.6
Displacement	:	17,062.9 tonnes
No. of Propellers	:	1
Diameter	:	6.706 m
Rotation	:	Right Handed

Calm Water Simulations

Figure 2 shows the surge dynamics of the study vessel. In the uper curve, the ship is accelerated, with a constant propeller speed of 102 rev./min., from rest up to the operating speed of 7.717 m/s (15 knots). In the lower curve, the propeller speed is 23 rev./min., and the vessel achieves 2.572 m/s (5 knots) after 500 seconds has elapsed.

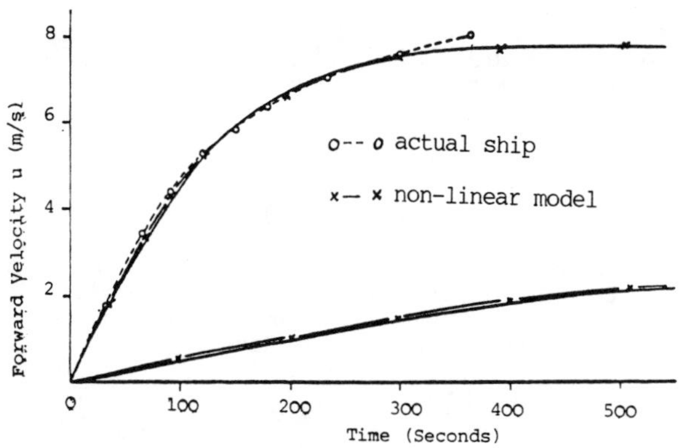

Figure 2

Surge Dynamics of Study Vessel

Figure 3 illustrates the effect of sway and yaw on the forward velocity, when the vessel is turning with 20 degrees starboard rudder. The Morse-Price data is shown for comparison.

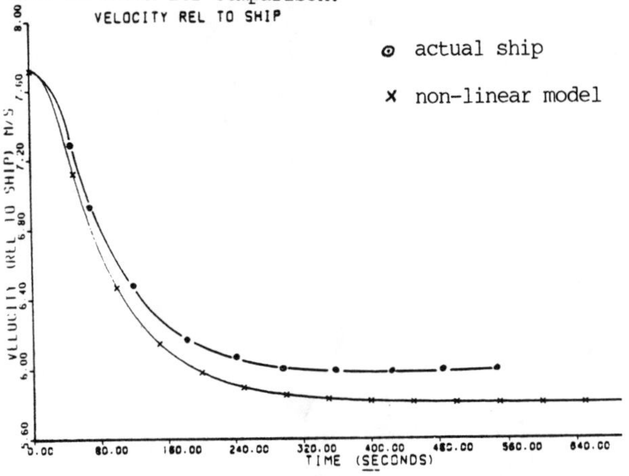

Figure 3

Effect of Sway and Yaw on Forward Velocity

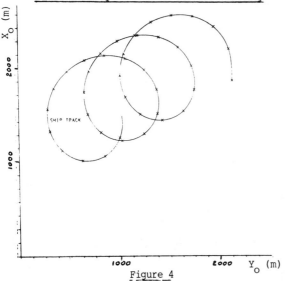

Figure 4

Turning Manoeuvre with Wind and Tide

In Figure 4, the ship is performing turning circles with the action of starboard rudder, whilst under the influence of south-easterly tide and wind.

SHIP MATHEMATICAL MODEL IN A SEAWAY

Regular Waves

The velocity V_W of a sinusoidal wave of wavelength L_W and circular frequency W_W is given by:

$$V_W = \frac{L_W W_W}{2\pi} \qquad (12)$$

where, for deep water,

$$W_W = \sqrt{\frac{2\pi g}{L_W}} \qquad (13)$$

The equation of a sinusoidal wave of amplitude ζ_A is:

$$\zeta = \zeta_a \sin (kx - W_W t) \qquad (14)$$

where k is the wave number:

$$k = \frac{2\pi}{L_W} \qquad (15)$$

A ship heading directly into waves (in a head sea) will meet successive waves more quickly, and the waves will appear to have a higher frequency and shorter wave length. For a ship travelling with forward velocity u, the circular frequency of encounter W_e is given by:

$$W_e = W_W \left(1 + \frac{W_W u}{g}\right) \qquad (16)$$

Irregular Waves

In practice, seaways are very irregular and consist of a complex wave pattern, which may be assumed to consist of a large number of sinusoidal waves of different wavelengths and heights, all superimposed on each other. These may be described by the energy or wave spectrum of the sea.

The variance of the wave spectrum function m_o is given by the area under the curve:

$$m_o = \int_o^\infty S_\zeta (W_W)\, dW_W \qquad (17)$$

where S_ζ is the spectral density. The significant wave height $h_{1/3}$ of an irregular seaway at any given time and location is the arithmetic mean of the heights of the one-third highest waves recorded.

The standard wave spectrum recommended by the International Towing Tank Conference is the Pierson-Moskowitz sea spectrum:

$$S_\zeta(W_w) = \frac{A}{W_w^5} e^{-B/W_w^4} \tag{18}$$

where, in SI units, $A = 0.0081\, g^2$

$$B = \frac{3.11}{h_{1/3}} \tag{19}$$

Figure 5 shows a Pierson-Moskowitz spectrum for a significant wave height of 4.573 m (15 feet). The x-axis is expressed in terms of W_e, the frequency of encounter for a vessel travelling at 7.717 m/s (15 knots) into a head sea.

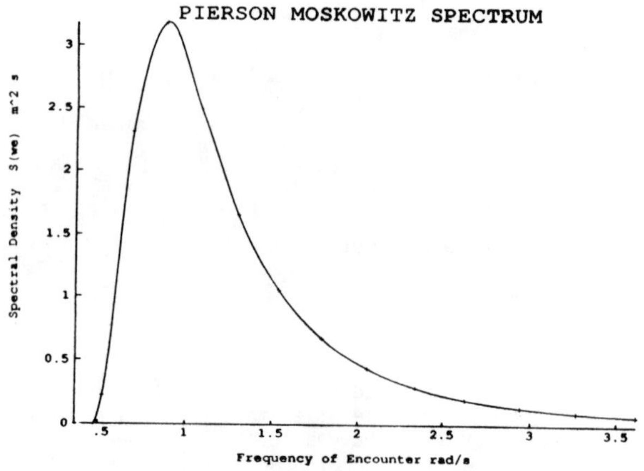

Figure 5

Pierson-Moskowitz Spectrum

Added Resistance in Regular Waves

Early equations that give a first approximation to the added resistance (Havelock 1958, Joosen 1966) are of the form:

$$R_{AW} = \frac{W_e^3 \left(b_z Z_a^2 + b\theta_a^2\right)}{2g} \tag{20}$$

where Z_a and θ_a are the heave and pitch amplitudes. Equations of this nature pose a problem for 3-degree of freedom models, which do not include these axes.

An alternative approach is to construct a mean added resistance response curve from either an experimental programme or a theoretical relationship. Added resistance has been found to be proportional to the square of wave height, so a non-dimensional added resistance coefficient may be expressed as:

$$\sigma_{AW} = \frac{R_{AW}}{\rho g \zeta_a^2 (B^2/L)} \tag{21}$$

Using regular waves, the added resistance R_{AW} can be measured using model tests for a number of different wave encounter frequencies using a response amplitude operator (RAO) of the form:

$$R(W_e) = R_{AW} / \zeta_a^2 \tag{22}$$

Figure 6 shows an experimentally derived mean added resistance response curve for a Series 60, C_B = 0.6 vessel, which is similar in size and shape to the Mariner hull. The added resistance coefficient σ_{AW} is plotted against non-dimensional frequency of encounter μ_e where,

$$\mu_e = W_e \sqrt{\frac{L}{g}} \tag{23}$$

The curve corresponds to a Froude number of 0.194, which is equivalent to 7.717 m/s for the study vessel.

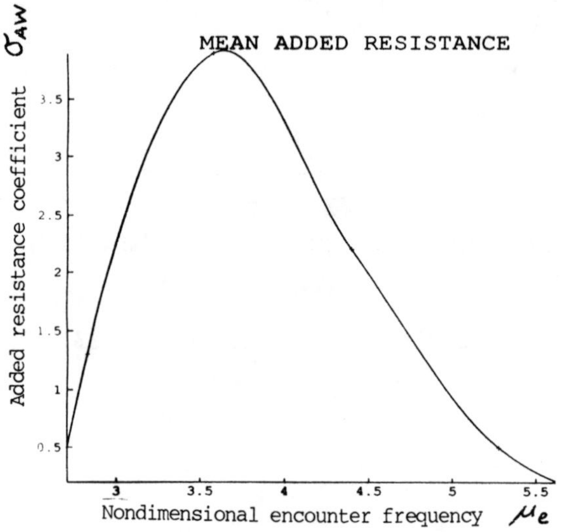

Figure 6

Mean Added Resistance

Added Resistance in Irregular Waves

The added resistance of a ship in an irregular seaway can be obtained by using the principle of linear superposition:

$$\overline{R_{AW}} = 2\int_0^\infty S_\zeta(W_e) R(W_e)\, dW_e \tag{24}$$

Performing this integration for a spectral density function relating to a particular significant wave height will result in an average added resistance corresponding to that sea state and Froude number. If the integral is evaluated for a range of significant wave heights and Froude numbers, a family of average added resistance curves will result. Figure 7 shows such a family emperically derived for the Mariner hull.

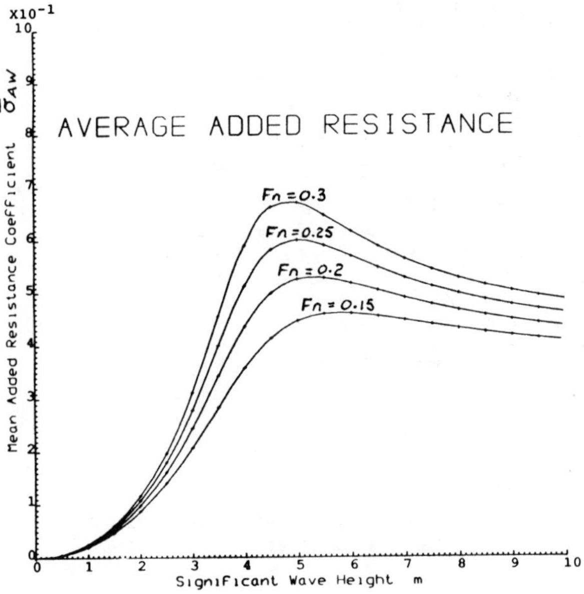

Figure 7

Average Added Resistance

The emperical relationship is:

$$\overline{\sigma}_{AW} = \frac{0.0186\ (1 + 1.33\ F_n)\ h_{1/3}^{\ 2}}{\sqrt{(1 - 0.0625\ h_{1/3}^{\ 2})^2 + 0.0375\ \frac{h_{1/3}}{F_n}}} \qquad (25)$$

Using this relationship, when the significant wave height is 4.573 m and the Froude number is 0.194, the average added resistance for the study vessel is 348.5 kN.

SIMULATION IN AN IRREGULAR SEAWAY

Representation of Sea State

It can be assumed that the sea state consists of the $h_{1/3}$ significant wave height together with either:

(a) a superimposed random variation

(b) selected components from the wave spectra

(c) a random variation filtered by the wave spectra

In the simulation results presented here, method (b) was chosen. The instantaneous wave amplitude is therefore given by:

$$\zeta_a = h_{1/3}(1 + A_1 \sin W_{e1}\ t + \ldots\ldots + A_n \sin W_{en}\ t) \qquad (26)$$

The amplitudes $A_1 \ldots A_n$ have been restricted to a maximum of 20% of the significant wave height. Five frequencies have been employed based upon the wave spectrum given in Figure 5, namely W_e = 0.5, 0.7, and 0.9, 1.3 and 1.7 rad/s.

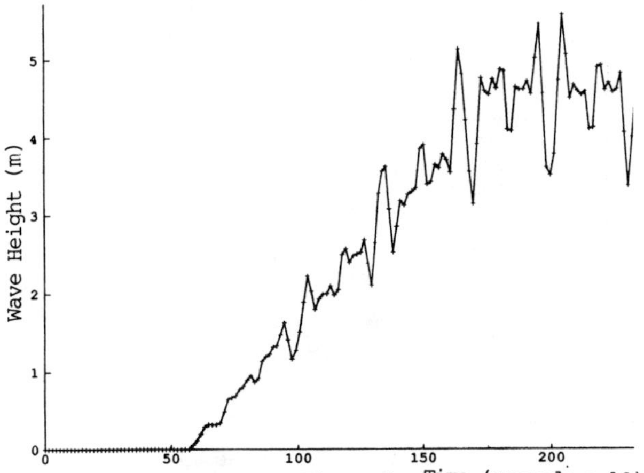

Figure 8

Wave Height Time History

Figure 8 shows the time history of the wave heights used in the simulation. The graph consists of three time domains:

Domain	Sea State
0 - 600 seconds	Calm Water. It is assumed in this period that the vessel is in calm water such as may be experienced in port approaches.
600 - 1800 seconds	Developing Seas. As the vessel heads towards the open seas, the wave amplitudes progressively increase according to the relationship given in equation (25).
1800 - 2400 seconds	Fully Developed Seas. The vessel is now travelling in fully developed seas with a significant wave height of 4.573 m.

Vessel Response

The surge response of the study vessel to the seas described above is shown in Figure 9. Under calm water conditions it maintains a constant forward velocity of 7.717 m/s. As the seas develop, the speed gradually drops, and in the fully developed seas the vessel maintains an average speed of approximately 6 m/s.

There is good correlation between Figures 8 and 9, for example, when t = 1600 seconds the instantaneous wave height exceeds 5 m, and there is a corresponding (but delayed) fall in speed.

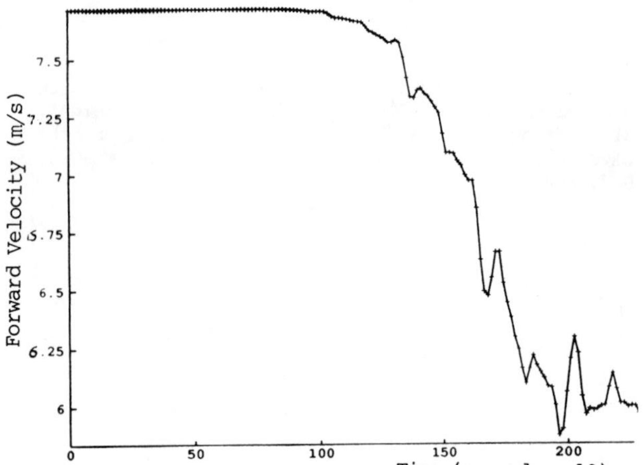

Figure 9

Vessel Response in Calm, Developing and Developed Seaways

CONCLUSIONS

It has been demonstrated that added resistance due to waves can be included within a 3-degree of freedom model that does not include heave or pitch. The average added resistance compares favourably with values computed by Strom-Tejsen (1973) for various 190 m vessels in a head sea using a Pierson-Moskowitz spectrum with significant wave height 4.573 m.

Ship Type	Speed (m/s)	Added Resistance (kN)
Mariner C_B = 0.6	7.717	348.5
Series 60 C_B = 0.6	11.47	371.9
Series 60 C_B = 0.75	7.717	320.7
Destroyer	8.643	251.3
	15.125	351.8

The average speed loss of 22% is slightly less than computed by other methods for similar wave heights. Townsin (1982) gives 31%, Calvert (1988) 26% but James` (1955) speed loss curves gives 17.6%. These results, however, are for a variety of hull forms and should not be compared too closely.

The techniques described in this paper still require refinements in the following areas:

(a) extension to include beam and following seas,
(b) reduced propulsive efficiency in a seaway,
(c) modelling of pitch, heave and roll (i.e. full 6-degree of freedom).

NOMENCLATURE

Matrices and Vectors

A,B Discrete State and Control Transition Matrices
C Discrete Disturbance Matrix
F Continuous Time System Matrix
G_C, G_D Continuous Time Forcing Matrix
U Control Vector
W Disturbance Vector
X Ship Related State Vector

Scalar Symbols

B Beam
g Acceleration due to gravity
$h_{1/3}$ Significant wave height
I_z Moment of inertia about z axis
K Interger counter
k Wave number
L Length of ship
L_w Wave length
m Mass of ship
n_A, n_D Actual and demanded engine speeds
R_{AW} Added resistance due to waves
$R(W_e)$ Response amplitude operator
S_ζ Spectral density
T_n, T_R Time constants for main engines and rudder
u Forward velocity of ship
u_a, u_c Forward components of wind and current velocities
V_w Wave length
v Lateral velocity of ship
v_a, v_c Lateral components of wind and current velocities
W_w Wave circular frequency
W_e Circular frequency of encounter
x,y,z Ship related orthogonal co-ordinates
δ_A, δ_D Actual and demanded rudder angles
ρ Density of sea water
ζ, ζ_a Wave height and amplitude
σ_{AW} Added resistance coefficient
μ_e Non-dimensional frequency of encounter
ψ Heading of ship

REFERENCES

Abkowitz, M. 1964. "Lectures on Ship Hydrodynamics, Steering and Manoeuvrability". Hy-A Report, Hy 5., Denmark.

Burns, R.S., M.J. Dove, T.H. Bouncer and C.T. Stockel 1985. "A Discrete, Time Varying, Non-Linear Mathematical Model for the Simulation of Ship Manoeuvres". First International Maritime Simulation Symposium, Control Data Corporation, Munich, W. Germany.

Calvert, S. 1988. "Optimal Weather Routeing Procedures for Vessels on Trans-Oceanic Voyages". CNAA Transfer Report, Plymouth Polytechnic.

Chislett, M.S., and J. Strom-Tejsen, 1965. "Planer Motion Mechanism Tests and Full-Scale Steering and Manoeuvring Predictions for a MARINER Class Vessel". International Shipbuilding Progress, Vol. 12, pp 201-224.

James, R.W. 1955. "Application of Wave Forecasts to Marine Navigation". U.S. Naval Oceanographic Office, SP-1.

Joosen, W.P.A. 1966. "Added Resistance of Ships in Waves". Proc. 6th Symposium on Naval Hydrodynamics, Washington D.C.

Morse, R.V. and D. Price. 1961. "Manoeuvring Characteristics of the MARINER Type Ship (USS Compass Island) in Calm Seas". Sperry Palaris Management, Sperry Gyroscope Company, New York.

Strom-Tejsen, J., H.Y.H. Yeh and D.D. Moran. 1973. "Added Resistance in Waves". Trans. SNAME, Vol. 81, pp 109-143.

Townsin, R.L. 1982. "Approximate Formulae for the Speed Loss due to Added Resistance in Wind and Waves." Trans. RINA, Vol. 129, pp 199.

Simulators VI
© 1989 By The Society for Computer Simulation International
ISBN 0-911801-51-0

A dynamic model for a pressurizer

A. Sharon
Fauske & Associates, Inc.
16W070 West 83rd Street
Burr Ridge, Illinois 60521

ABSTRACT

A lumped parameter dynamic model for a pressurizer in a PWR is presented. The model is applicable for a large range of transients initiating from full power operating conditions. It takes advantage of the the thermal equilibrium conditions between water and steam that are expected to be valid under those conditions.

An implicit solution to the surge line flow is presented for various transients and geometry conditions. This solution can be used to explain "unexpected" behavior of the pressurizer during the TMI-2 accident.

The model is fully implicit and can be used for any real-time applications on a training simulator.

INTRODUCTION

A Pressurized Water Reactor (PWR) is a power plant in which the thermal energy generated from the nuclear fuel is transferred to water that serves as a coolant. The water flows in closed primary system loops containing the reactor core, where it receives the heat, several steam generators, where the heat is rejected, and several coolant pumps that provide forced circulation in the loops. PWRs are designed to operate with subcooled water and no bulk boiling of the coolant is permitted. A schematic description of a PWR Plant is shown in Figure 1.

To enable high thermodynamic efficiency of the plant and prevent bulk boiling of the coolant, the primary system is pressurized to high pressure, typically of the order of 150 bars (2200 psia). This high pressure is maintained and controlled by a pressurizer vessel.

The pressurizer vessel is connected to one of the primary system pipes that carries the coolant from the core to the steam generator (hot leg). It contains water and steam in thermodynamic equilibrium, such that the pressure in the vessel is the water vapor pressure corresponding to the water temperature inside the pressurizer. Schematic illustration of a pressurizer is provided in Figure 2.

The pressure is controlled by several systems inside the pressurizer:

- Heaters are submerged in the water pool and are activated when the system pressure is too low. Steam that is generated from the pool accumulates in the gas space of the pressurizer and increases the system pressure.
- A spray line at the top of the pressurizer is connected to the discharge pipe from a main coolant pump (cold leg). If the pressure is too high, valves in this line will open and spray colder water into the pressurizer gas space. Steam condensation around the colder water droplets will reduce the system pressure.

In addition to these two main pressure controlling systems, the surge line that connects the pressurizer to the hot leg allows for continuous flow communication between the pressurizer and the primary system so as to equivibrate the pressure in both systems. Any temperature surges in the primary system will cause flow of excess coolant into the pressurizer. On the other hand, if the primary system temperature drops, the priamry coolant will shrink and hot water from the pressurizer will fill the system. Flow will also be directed into the pressurizer, regardless of the water temperature, if water is injected into the primary system. In contrast, in case of a break in the primary system, water will drain from the pressurizer and replace the fluid lost through the break.

To prevent the system from over-pressurizing, the pressurizer is equipped with safety valves and power operated relief valves (PORV) mounted on its top. These valves are designed to open when the pressure is higher than a maximum safe pressure. When these valves are opened and the pressure decreases below a predetermined set point, the valves will close.

The dynamics of the pressurizer are therefore very important for simulating the power plant behavior. A realistic, yet simple model is required when the system simulation has to be performed in real time. A model is proposed here that is suitable for small perturbation from full power operation and under various accident conditions starting from full power operation. Advantage of thermodynamic equilibrium condition is taken to simply the physical models. Lumped parameter approach is also used hence assuming perfect mixing in the pressurizer and the primary system. This assumption is valid during most full power operating conditions and accident conditions involving relatively large flows and hence good mixing in both systems. Again, these accident conditions are applicable to most anticipated transients that are used on training simulators.

The Dynamic Model

For a vessel containing a fluid which is pressurized by its own vapor pressure, the dynamic equation for the system pressure is given in Reference [1] as:

$$\frac{dP}{dt} = \frac{\left[\sum_{j=1} Q_j - \sum_{i=1} W_i \, (h_i - \lambda) \right] h_{fg}}{MC^* \, T \, v_{fg} \, (1-\gamma)} \qquad (1)$$

where

$\sum_{j=1}^{\kappa} Q_j$ - is the heat generation in the vessel from κ different sources or sinks,

W_i - is the mass flow through link i into or out of the vessel,

h_i - is the enthalpy associated with link i flow,

n - number of flow links,

λ - is the fluid specific internal energy:

$$\lambda = h - \frac{v}{v_{fg}} h_{fg}, \quad (2)$$

h - enthalpy of the fluid in the vessel,

h_{fg} - latent heat of vaporization,

M - mass of fluid (liquid + vapor) in the vessel,

T - system (saturation) temperature,

v_{fg} - difference between gas and liquid specific volume,

C* - the fluid mixture specific heat along the saturation line:

$$C^* = \frac{de_\ell}{dT} + \chi \frac{de_{fg}}{dT}, \quad (3)$$

e - internal energy (ℓ - liquid, fg - change of phase),

χ - gas quality (Mg/M),

$$\gamma = \frac{e_{fg}\phi}{\nu_{fg}C^*} \quad (4)$$

and

$$\phi = \frac{dv_\ell}{dT} + \chi \frac{dv_{fg}}{dT} \quad (5)$$

Equation (1) is derived from a lumped parameter mass and energy balances on a fixed control volume (dV/dt=0) assuming thermodynamic equilibrium between the phases. The system mass, which is the second dynamic variable, is simply calculated by the following dynamic equation:

$$\frac{dM}{dt} = \sum_{i=1}^{n} W_i \quad (6)$$

In applying equations (1) and (6) to a pressurizer, three flow links are considered:

- the surge line (W_{sr}),
- the spray line (W_{sp}), and
- the relief valve (W_{rv}).

These flows are shown in Figure 2.

The net heat generation in equation (1) is the difference between the heater's power (Q_h) and the heat losses through the pressurizer walls (Q_ℓ).

For a dynamic simulation of the power plant, the surge line and the relief valves flow require additional attentions. The spray flow and the net heat generation can be considered as constants whenever the controllers turn those systems on.

Flow Through the Relief Valves

Once the relief valves are open the flow out of the pressurizer has a strong influence on the system pressure. This flow is normally choked due to the large pressure differential between the pressurizer pressure and the discharge pressure (normally atmospheric). To calculate the flow rate W_{rv} and the enthalpy associated with that flow, the location of the two-phase water level relative to the valve is required. If the valve is above that level, only steam is discharged. In this case, the critical gas flow is used in determining the flow rate, and the steam enthalpy of the pressurizer is h_{rv}. In this case fast reduction in the system pressure is typically observed. On the other hand, if the two-phase level is all the way at the top of the pressurizer, two-phase is discharged through the valve. In the event that high, cold safety injection flows are introduced to the primary system, it is possible that the pressurizer becomes full and water is discharged through the relief valve. In both cases large losses of coolant will occur but the pressure will decrease slowly.

A simple, yet accurate way to calculate the two-phase level location is by performing a mass balance over the gas phase of the pressurizer, ignoring secondary effects (gas density changes, etc.). As recommended in Reference [1] this yields

$$\frac{dh_m}{dt} = \frac{v_{fg}(\chi W)_{rv}}{A} - j_g(\alpha) \qquad h_o < h_m < h_{pz} \quad (7)$$

where

h_m - mixture two-phase level,

$(\chi W)_{rv}$ - steam flow rate out of the relief valve,

A - pressurizer cross sectional area,

j_g - steam superficial velocity leaving the mixture pool,

α - void fraction in the pool,

h_o - collapsed liquid level, and

h_{pz} - height of the pressurizer.

The gas superficial velocity depends on the two-phase flow regime inside the pressurizer. For cases where the relief valves are open, a churn-turbulent flow regime is expected in which

$$j_g = \frac{U_\infty \alpha}{1 - C_o \alpha} \quad (8)$$

where U_∞ is the bubble rise velocity (~0.19 m/s) and C_o is a constant parameter ~1.2). Equation (7) implies that swelling can occur only when the relief valves are opened and maximum swelling will be achieved as the steam flux from the relief valve equals that from the pool. As the void fraction in the pool becomes higher, j_g exceeds the steam relief valve flux, and the swell level will decrease. Since the main significance of the swell level is to determine its location relative to the relief valve, this method is adequate for all training applications and due to its simplicity is adequate for real-time modeling.

Flow Through the Surge Line

Under full power operating conditions, the primary system is subcooled and flow communication through the surge line is in response to the thermal expansion of the coolant in the primary system. A lumped parameter primary sytem model can be used in this case to determine the flow rate through the surge line.

A mass balance on the primary system requires that

$$\frac{dM_{ps}}{dt} = W_s - W_{sr} \tag{9}$$

where W_s is the net flow source to the primary system (injection - leakage). An energy balance requires that

$$\frac{dT}{dt} = Q_s - a\, W_{sr} \tag{10}$$

where

Q_s = net temperature sources including convective energies through injection and leakage, and

a = net enthalpy carried through the surge line divided by the primary system heat capacity.

Since the primary system volume is constant, dV/dt=0, and therefore from equation (9)

$$-\frac{M_{ps}}{v}\frac{dv}{dT}\frac{dT}{dt} = \frac{dM_{ps}}{dt} = W_s - W_{sr} \tag{11}$$

Equation (10) and (11) can now be solved directly for W_{sr}:

$$W_{sr} = \frac{M_{ps}\beta\, Q_s - W_s}{1 - M_{ps}\beta\, a} \tag{12}$$

where β is the water thermal expansion

$$\beta = \frac{1}{v}\frac{dv}{dT} \tag{13}$$

This procedure is valid for as long as the primary system is subcooled. When the PORV is stuck open the pressure will decrease and the primary system will become saturated. In this case flow may be directed to the pressurizer due to bubble formation (flashing) in the primary system rather than thermal expansion.

The flow through the surge line can be calculated for a saturated primary system by requiring that both the primary system and the pressurizer will depressurize at the same rate, such that their pressures should be equal. For a saturated primary system, equation similar to equation (1) can be written such that

$$\left(\frac{dP}{dt}\right)_{ps} = \dot{P}_{ps} + b_{ps} W_{sr} \tag{14}$$

In equation (14) $\dot{P}_{ps}$ and b_{ps} are calculated by direct substitution in equation (1). Similar relation can be written for the pressurizer

$$\left(\frac{dP}{dt}\right)_{pz} = \dot{P}_{pz} + b_{pz} W_{sr} \tag{15}$$

Hence,

$$W_{sr} = \frac{\dot{P}_{ps} - \dot{P}_{pz}}{b_{ps} + b_{pz}} \tag{16}$$

When the primary system void fraction becomes large or if the PORV is finally closed, liquid will drain from the pressurizer into the primary system. This drainage would occur only if the surge line is straight and stable water-gas interface cannot exist in the surge line. In this case however, shown in Figure 3, internal flooding in the surge line will limit the drainage of the pressurizer. Appropriate flooding correlations such as in Reference [3] should be used for the gas and water flow rates through the surge line.

On the other hand, if the surge line contains a loop seal such as shown in Figure 4, drainage of the pressurizer would not occur strictly due to gravity.In this case a stable steam-water interface is established and equation (16) would continuously apply. The flow will be directed into the pressurizer (W_{sr}>0) as long as $\dot{P}_{ps} > \dot{P}_{pz}$. In other words, as long as the primary system pressurization rate exceeds that of the pressurizer, the pressurizer will not be drained.

This condition is applicable to the TMI-2 accident in which the PORV was stuck open. The TMI-2 has a loop seal in the surge line. Due to the lack of sufficient cooling in the steam generators during the accident, the primary system pressure continuously increased but the pressurizer did not drain into the primary system. Drainage of the pressurizer would have terminated the accident and would have prevented fuel melting. This condition follows directly from equation (16) and can be accurately simulated with this model.

REFERENCES

1. A. Sharon and M. Grolmes, 1985. "A Dynamic Model for a Saturated Vessel", Simulators IV, Vol. 18, No.4.

2. M. Grolmes, A. Sharon, C. S. Kim, R. E. Pauls, 1986. "Level Swell Analysis of the Marviken Test T-11." Nuclear Science and Engineering: 229-239.

3. G. B. Wallis. 1969. One Dimensional Two-Phase Flow. McGraw-Hill.

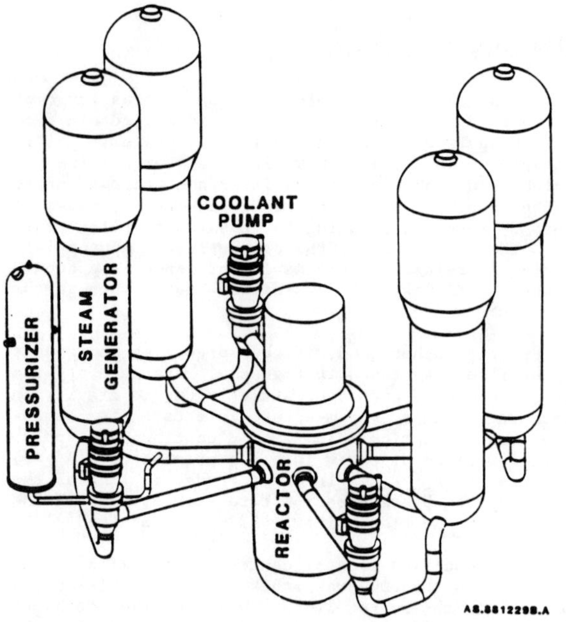

Figure 1: Schematic description of 4 loop pressurizer water reactor.

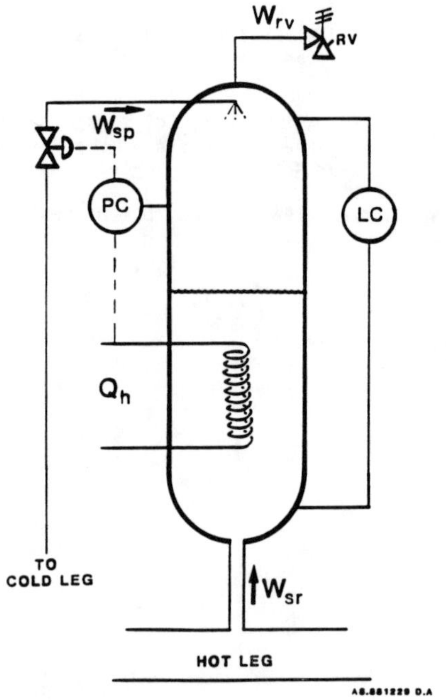

Figure 2: Schematic description of a pressurizer.

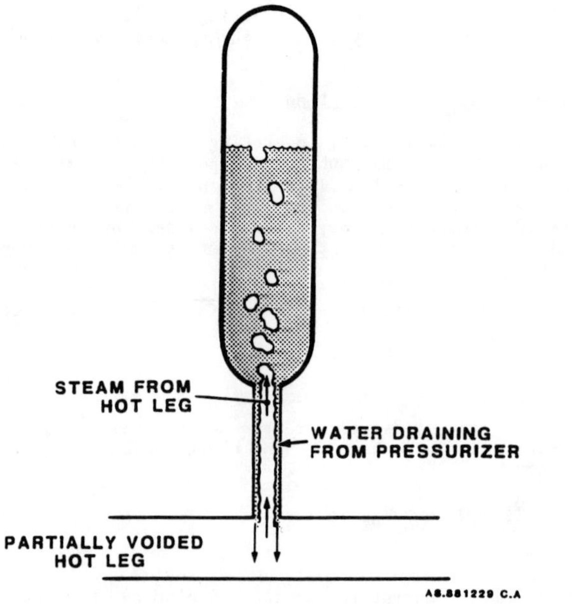

Figure 3: Drainage from a pressurizer when the surge line has no loop seal.

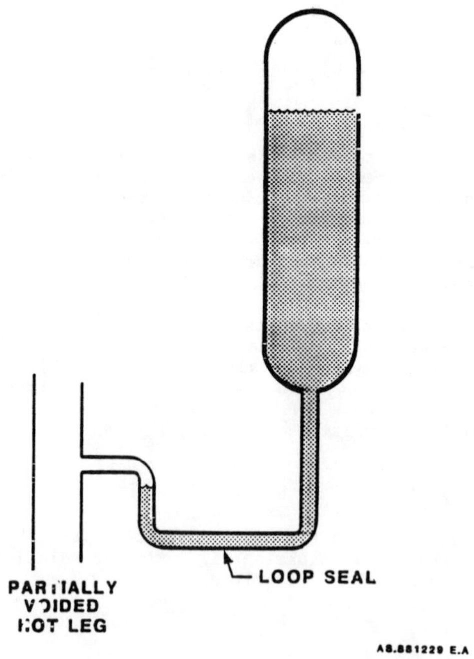

Figure 4: Schematic configuration of the water in a surge line with a loop seal when the hot leg is partially voided (as in the TMI-2 accident).

Simulators VI

ISBN 0-911801-51-0

Thermal-hydraulic oscillations at LaSalle

M. Wayne Hodges
Reactor Systems Branch
Office of Nuclear Reactor Regulation
Nuclear Regulatory Commission

ABSTRACT

On March 9, 1988, LaSalle, Unit 2 underwent a dual recirculation pump trip event. Trip of the recirculation pumps resulted in a flow decrease to natural circulation flow. As a consequence of the rapid power decrease which accompanied the flow decrease, the feedwater heater level control system began isolating extraction steam from the heaters. The cooler feedwater led to an increase in power and transition into a region of thermal-hydraulic instability. Approximately five minutes after the recirculation pump trip, large (25 percent peak-to-peak) neutron flux oscillations were observed. The oscillations increased in magnitude until a reactor trip occurred on high average power range neutron flux at 118 percent of full power. Although no fuel thermal or mechanical limits were exceeded during the event, the event caused concern relative to the adequacy of licensing analyses and potential violation of safety limits. The NRC and the BWR Owners' Group have sponsored analyses which generally show present practice to be adequate but which show the potential for violation of safety limits if due caution is not exercised.

INTRODUCTION

This paper describes the thermal-hydraulic instability event which occurred at LaSalle, Unit 2 and some of the analyses which have been performed to better understand the event and its implications. The analyses are ongoing; therefore, the results are incomplete. However, enough has been learned to make decisions about the adequacy of continued operation. Recommendations for avoiding instabilities and actions to take if instabilities occur have been developed. Core wide oscillation, as observed at LaSalle, are the most likely mode of oscillation but other modes have been observed in some foreign reactors and can be modeled using three-dimensional neutronics and thermal-hydraulics.

EVENT DESCRIPTION

On Wednesday, March 9, 1988, LaSalle, Unit 2, underwent a dual recirculation pump trip event. The reactor was operating at steady-state conditions at approximately 84 percent power with 76 percent rated core flow using both recirculation pumps and with the control rods withdrawn to the 99 percent flow line. Feedwater temperature was 402 deg.F. A valving error during instrument surveillance caused a pressure pulse in the reference leg of the water level instrumentation. This pulse gave a low level signal and actuated the recirculation pump trip which is part of the Anticipated Transient Without Scram (ATWS) protection.

The two pump trip caused a large and rapid power decrease to about 45 percent of full power as a result of the flow reduction to natural circulation conditions. The large drop in power caused a large change in extraction steam flow and pressure. Extraction steam supplies the heating to the feedwater heaters. The change in extraction steam caused perturbations in the feedwater heater level control system due to water flashing to steam from lower shell pressures, reduction in shell side input from reduced steam flow, and changes in condensing rate. The feedwater level control tripped the extraction steam input to the heaters in order to prevent induction of water into the main turbine.

The securing of steam heating to the feedwater heaters resulted in cooler feedwater being supplied to the reactor. The feedwater temperature dropped about 45 deg F in four minutes. This reduction in feedwater temperature caused an increase in reactor power because of the negative moderator temperature coefficient.

Between four and five minutes into the event, the Average Power Range Monitor (APRM) indications were observed by the operators to be oscillating between 25 percent power and 50 percent power every two to three seconds and the Local Power Range Monitor (LPRM) down scale alarms began to annunciate and clear. Attempts to restart a recirculation pump in order to increase flow were unsuccessful and the decision was made to manually scram the reactor. About seven minutes into the event, and prior to a manual scram, the reactor automatically scrammed on high neutron flux as seen by the APRMs (118 percent of full power).

POTENTIAL IMPLICATIONS OF EVENT

Boiling water reactors have long been known to be less stable than pressurized water reactors. Instabilities have been observed on several occasions, but most of the known cases of instability were a result of deliberate testing. The instabilities that were observed exibited small amplitude oscillations. In addition, methods for predicting instabilities had been validated against in-reactor data and uncertainty bounds established. LaSalle, Unit 2 had been analyzed and a large margin to instability calculated. Because of the calculated stability margin, LaSalle had no procedures for dealing with instabilities initiated from two pump operation.

No fuel thermal limits or mechanical limits were violated during the event; however, the event caused concern for several reasons. These are: 1) Licensing analyses for LaSalle had indicated considerable margin to thermal-hydraulic instability. Should we continue to use the licensing analyses? 2) The magnitude of the oscillations was much larger than expected or previously experienced. How large could the oscillations grow prior to reactor trip? Could the oscillations grow large enough to cause fuel damage? 3) The oscillations at LaSalle were core wide. Would localized, out-of-phase, oscillations result in fuel damage? 4) Recirculation pump trip is used to minimize the heat input to the heat sink (suppression pool) for ATWS events. Is this still the appropriate action?

RESULTS OF PRELIMINARY ANALYSES

Soon after the event, General Electric (GE) reanalyzed LaSalle with their stability method. They were able to show that they could calculate the instability if actual plant conditions were input to the code and more detailed noding were used. The licensing stability method is accurate if enough detail is provided for actual plant conditions. The most bounding conditions are difficult to define in advance because of the large number of variables and the sensitivity to small changes to such variables as axial and radial power distribution. Thus, the licensing stability methods are of qualitative benefit for predicting onset of instability and are sufficiently accurate to use for predicting changes in stability margin.

Licensing stability codes are phase-plane codes and are useful only for predicting stability margin or onset of instability. Prediction of amplitude of oscillations requires time-domain analyses. The BWR Owners' Group contracted with General Electric to perform analyses with the GE version of the TRAC code. TRAC is a very sophisticated thermal-hydraulics code that can use three-dimensional thermal-hydraulics and neutronics. Analyses of core wide oscillations were performed with the reactor scram function disabled. Analyses of regional oscillations were also performed with the power shapes being forced and the thermal-hydraulics calculated by TRAC. The Nuclear Regulatory Commission (NRC) contracted with Brookhaven National Laboratory (BNL) to perform analyses with the RAMONA code. RAMONA also calculates three-dimensional thermal-hydraulics and neutronics. Generally, the RAMONA code has better neutronics models than TRAC and TRAC has better thermal-hydraulic models than RAMONA. Both codes are capable of simulating oscillations. TRAC is very expensive to run. RAMONA is less expensive but cannot accurately model very low or reverse two-phase flow.

Although only one unconstrained TRAC analysis was performed, the results provide a strong indication that, for core wide oscillations, reactor trip will occur on high neutron flux prior to reaching oscillations of sufficient magnitude to violate critical power limits. For regional oscillations, GE calculated one case, at the extreme of the maximum extended operation domain (initial point at 75 percent flow and 100 percent power and critical power ratio at the operating limit) prior to the two pump trip which resulted in the probable violation of the critical power limit. Although the safety limit could be violated, there is sufficient time between the time of pump trip and the onset of instability to manually trip the reactor and prevent violation of the safety limit.

The RAMONA analyses verified that core wide oscillations are more likely than regional oscillations. RAMONA also prepicted both radial and side-to-side oscillations. The mode of oscillation appears to be dependent on control rod pattern. Regional oscillations appear to be driven by a few bundles and suppression of the oscillations appears to be dependent upon suppression of oscillations in those bundles. RAMONA was unable to calculate oscillations larger than about 200 percent peak-to-peak because of the low flow limitation. RAMONA calculated reverse flow for the very large oscillations and the calculations could not be completed.

Both TRAC and RAMONA results indicate the the average power does not increase for increasing oscillations other than the increase that would be expected from the decrease in feedwater enthalpy. As the feedwater temperature decreases, the power increases due to the negative temperature coefficient of reactivity. With water level controlled by the feedwater controller, the reactor average power is controlled by the feedwater flowrate and the feedwater enthalpy. Additional analyses to investigate the effect of reduced water level are needed to encompass ATWS conditions but these preliminary analyses support more simplistic reasoning that says the power should be controlled by the feedwater conditions.

Thermal-hydraulic oscillation period is controlled by the transit time of voids through the flow channels. For BWR natural circulation conditions, the transit time is two to three seconds and the oscillation periods observed in reactors and analyses are two to three seconds. The fuel has a large thermal inertia. The thermal time constant for the fuel ranges from about six to eight seconds. Therefore, the fuel temperature and heat flux oscillations are greatly damped. Neutron flux oscillations of 100 percent peak-to-peak result in heat flux oscillations of about 10 percent peak-to-peak. These factors explain how very large neutron flux oscillations can occur without violating critical power or heat flux limits.

Although neutron flux oscillations can reach a large magnitude (About 300 percent peak-to-peak calculated for the TRAC region wise oscillations and up to 200 percent peak-to-peak with RAMONA), both codes tend to show that the magnitude of the oscillations is limited by void and doppler feedback with void being the most effective. No means of establishing an upper bound on the magnitude has been found and there is no reason to assume that the 300 percent value is the largest that could be experienced.

RAMONA results show that oscillations grow quickly once oscillations begin if the oscillations are prone to grow. Some oscillations will reach a limit cycle at a low peak-to-peak value; other oscillations will grow to much larger limit cycle values in 10 to 15 cycles (on the order of 30 seconds). These oscillations start following the two pump trip and a transition period which leads into the unstable conditions. At LaSalle, this transition period lasted several minutes.

INTERIM CONCLUSIONS

Thermal-hydraulic instabilities, as occurred at LaSalle, can occur under low flow, high power conditions. The full scope of conditions which will lead to instabilities are not amenable to prior analysis. Instabilities have been shown to be readily suppressed by flow increase or insertion of control rods. Avoidance of low flow, high power regions of operation should preclude reoccurrence of instabilities. For two pump trip events, instabilities can be avoided by timely scram of the reactor.

Approved licensing models for stability analyses still provide useful insights and guidance for defining regions of potential instability. The decay ratios calculated with these models are subject to question but the models should be reliable for calculating changes from known conditions. A combination of analyses and startup tests to verify analyses for a particular core configuration should be very reliable.

The magnitude of oscillations cannot be predicted apriori but the magnitude is limited by void and doppler feedback. The magnitude can be quite large but no fuel limits should be exceeded for core wide oscillations with scram systems operable. For regional oscillations, violation of critical power limits is possible but not likely. Manual scram of the reactor on trip of both recirculation pumps should provide adequate protection against violation of critical power limits. Automatic scram, as exists at some plants, should also provide adequate protection although the scram signal would initiate on something other than loss of pumped flow.

Recirculation pumps are tripped and water level lowered for ATWS events in order to reduce reactor power. This power reduction is necessary to assure availability of the primary heat sink (suppression pool). Thermal-hydraulic instabilities are likely to occur during an ATWS event (although the ATWS event itself is very rare). Although these instabilities are undesirable, they are considerably more desirable than the loss of heat sink and potential core melt. Thus recirculation pump trip is still appropriate for ATWS events.

Violation of the critical power limit does not of itself mean fuel or cladding failure. Violation of the critical power limit simply means that, likely, some fuel will experience film boiling rather than nucleate boiling. The rapidity with which the heat flux changes would probably mean that film boiling would be experienced followed by rewetting; the time in film boiling would not be sufficient to allow extensive heatup of the cladding. In addition, BWR fluid conditions are normally high void annular flow; the difference between nucleate and film boiling heat transfer is not as large as for PWR fluid conditions and even steady-state film boiling will not always lead to extensive cladding heatup. Thus, the likelyhood of cladding or fuel failure resulting from thermal-hydraulic instabilities is very small.

Simulators VI

ISBN 0-911801-51-0

Treat simulation of two steam generator tube rupture events

E. R. Frantz, A. C. Cheung, R. N. Lewis
Westinghouse Electric Corporation
P.O. Box 355
Pittsburgh, PA 15230

R. F. Anderson
North Anna Power Station
P.O. Box 402
Mineral, VA 23117

ABSTRACT

The general objectives of the recovery actions following a steam generator tube rupture (SGTR) are to minimize the radiological releases from the ruptured SG and to equalize reactor coolant system (RCS) pressure with the ruptured SG pressure to stop the primary to secondary leakage. Although these basic objectives are the same for all SGTR events, there can be significant differences in the plant response due to differences in plant design, equipment availability, and operator actions taken during the recovery. This paper provides the simulations and plant data comparisons for two SGTR events - the Ginna SGTR of January 25, 1982 and the North Anna Unit 1 SGTR of July 15, 1987. The simulations were performed using TREAT (Transient Real-time Engineering Analysis Tool), a Westinghouse-developed interactive computer program that models the important features of the primary and secondary systems of a Pressurized Water Reactor (PWR). The similarities and differences between the two SGTR cases and the thermal hydraulic phenomena important to SGTR simulations are discussed.

SGTR RECOVERY ACTIONS IN WESTINGHOUSE PLANTS

An important feature of the SGTR event is the number and comparatively rapid pace of operator actions geared at limiting the releases from the ruptured SG. Whereas a loss of reactor coolant or secondary break accident are traditionally analyzed to be "walk away" safe for 30 minutes or more following the accident, SGTRs typically assume a number of operator actions in addition to all the automatic actions during this time frame. These actions are contained in and dictated by the plant's Emergency Operation Procedures (EOPs). Actions characteristic of SGTR recovery in a Westinghouse PWR are described here.

The EOPs applicable to Westinghouse PWRs are generally structured consistent with the Westinghouse Owner's Group (WOG) Emergency Response Guidelines (ERGs). One version of the ERGs is presented and summarized in the references (ERGs 1983; Surman et al. 1983). These guidelines have been revised several times since the general EOP upgrade required following the March 1979 accident at Three Mile Island Unit 2. However, the basic recovery technique used following a SGTR has not changed significantly since the early 1980s (although there has been an increased awareness and more specialized training on the SGTR within the last several years).

For SGTR recovery, the operator is first directed to the EOP patterned after the ERG E-0, "Reactor Trip and Safety Injection." In E-0, proper operation of safeguards equipment is first verified in a number of immediate action steps. Various symptoms are then checked to determine the type of accident. After diagnosis of a SGTR based on abnormal secondary radiation indication (condenser air ejector, main steamline, or SG blowdown), a transition is made to E-3, "Steam Generator Tube Rupture." The major actions performed in E-3 include the following:

1. identification of the ruptured SG
2. isolation of the ruptured SG
3. initial cooldown of the RCS using the intact SG(s)
4. depressurization of the RCS
5. termination of safety injection flow

These major steps summarize the recovery actions taken to stop the primary to secondary leakage and place the plant in a stable condition prior to the post-SGTR cooldown and depressurization.

The ruptured SG may be known (or suspected) early in the transient. In E-3, the ruptured SG is confirmed by an abnormal radiation indication unique to the specific SG (SG sample, steamline, or blowdown line) or by an unexpected narrow range level increase due to the primary to secondary break flow, which will become more apparent as the auxiliary feedwater (AFW) flow to the SG is reduced. After the ruptured SG is identified, all steam and feed flow to the SG is isolated to limit the radioactive releases.

Steam is then dumped from the intact SGs to cool the RCS to a temperature of approximately 500°F (the pressure in the ruptured SG is used to determine the exact temperature to be achieved during the initial cooldown). The intent of the initial cooldown is to keep the RCS subcooled following the subsequent depressurization to the ruptured SG pressure. The condenser would be used for steam dump, if available; otherwise, the SG atmospheric relief valves would be operated.

Following the initial cooldown, the RCS is depressurized to minimize the break flow and refill the pressurizer. The depressurization is stopped when one of three conditions is met - (1) the RCS pressure is less than the ruptured SG pressure and pressurizer level is on span, or (2) the pressurizer fills to a high level (e.g., 80%), or (3) the RCS subcooling becomes less than uncertainties. If the reactor coolant pumps (RCPs) are operable, normal pressurizer spray is used for the depressurization. If normal spray is not available, one pressurizer power-operated relief valve (PORV) (or auxiliary spray) is operated to complete the depressurization.

Finally, after the RCS depressurization is complete, safety injection flow is terminated and normal inventory and pressure controls (i.e., charging, letdown, and pressurizer heater operation) are established. After SI termination, the RCS pressure would be approximately the same as the ruptured SG pressure and the primary to secondary leakage would be minimal. A post-SGTR recovery procedure (e.g., ES-3.1, "Post-SGTR Cooldown Using Backfill") is then followed to cooldown and depressurize the plant to cold shutdown conditions.

SIMULATION OF THE GINNA AND NORTH ANNA SGTR EVENTS

The recovery actions outlined above were, for the most part, followed without exception in the SGTR events at Ginna and North Anna 1. In many respects, the two events are very similar. However, underlying differences in the high-pressure SI systems cause some significant differences in plant parameters and in the recovery actions taken by the operators. In this section, the two events are compared "side-by-side" to accentuate these similarities and differences. The two SGTR events studied are described in more detail in the references (Ginna 1982; NRC 1982; North Anna 1987; NRC 1987).

Simulations of both events were performed using TREAT, a real-time interactive computer program developed at Westinghouse, originally for application to reactor transients requiring operator actions and advanced two-phase flow thermal hydraulic predictions. TREAT has been used for a number of generic and plant-specific applications including long term cooling and recovery analysis for small LOCAs and secondary breaks, recovery analysis for fire hazards and safety grade cold shutdown, safety parameter display system (SPDS) validation, input for plant emergency drills, and development of ERG training materials for inadequate core cooling and loss of secondary heat sink transients. A non-condensible version (TREAT-NC) has also be used to analyze loss of decay heat removal scenarios during mid-loop operation (performed in response to NRC Generic Letters 87-12 and 88-17). In this paper dealing with SGTR events, phenomena considered in the simulation of the SGTR transients are pointed out. These are then used to test the adequacy of TREAT in predicting the proper plant response for SGTR simulations.

Table 1 compares the Ginna and North Anna 1 SGTR events and the plant parameters important in describing the resulting plant responses. At North Anna, the failure was verified to be double-ended, based on inspections after the accident. At Ginna, the failure could be considered double-ended since the fish-mouth opening was large (compared to the tube area) and this prevented any flow communication between the two tube sections. For both events, the break flow from either tube side was sub-critical for the duration of the transient. (Note, however, that for a break located close to the exit on the cold side, the flow from the short tube section will initially be critical. Thus, the capability for modeling choked and unchoked flow conditions is important.)

In addition to the break flow (or break area), the capacity of the high-pressure SI system determines the stabilization pressure early in the transient. These factors account for the significant difference in the post-trip RCS pressures for the two cases (i.e., 1300 psig at Ginna versus 1800 psig at North Anna). Due to the reduced pressure, the Ginna operators were instructed to trip the RCPs early in the transient. Thus, the reduced shutoff head pressure of the high-pressure SI pumps indirectly complicated the Ginna recovery. With the resulting trip of the RCPs, the depressurization had to be performed with a pressurizer PORV (or auxiliary spray) instead of normal spray. In addition, natural circulation (versus forced circulation) was required for decay energy removal. Loss of natural circulation in the inactive loop with the ruptured SG also caused a minor pressurized thermal shock concern due to the addition of the cold SI water to the relatively stagnant cold leg of this loop.

Table 2 presents a condensed time table of events for the two SGTR cases. Time zero was determined based on available indications for a number of parameters, primarily pressurizer level and pressure. Increased condenser air ejector radiation was also observed at Ginna. At North Anna, the condenser air ejector grab samples were taken periodically (approximately once per shift) since this radiation monitor was out of service at the start of the accident. Although these samples were not frequent enough to pin-point the start time of the accident, other measurements (steamline radiation and on-line secondary chemistry indications), were available. These latter measurements (conductivity and pH) showed slight departures from normal conditions at approximately 6:24 a.m.; however, more rapid changes were noted roughly 6 minutes later (at the assumed 6:30 start of the accident).

Most of the times noted in Table 2 are accurate only to within about one minute. These times were determined primarily from plant logs and operator interviews after the accident. As evident from the table, however, certain events were recorded with more precision by the plant computer. These include the reactor trip time, SI actuation time, and (for Ginna) the times during which the pressurizer PORV was operated. Times for the actual plant transients are reported in Table 2. The TREAT times for the Ginna reactor trip and SI actuation are about 10 seconds later than those listed in Table 2. The TREAT times are otherwise the same as those given in Table 2 since most of the events listed were manual actions.

Prior to reactor trip, the operator and plant responses for both SGTR events were very similar, very rapid, and feature some very good tests for the simulation model and some of the control systems. At North Anna, power was reduced at a rate of about 2% per minute until the reactor was tripped. The rate for Ginna was considerably faster. In both cases, the power reduction was a manual action performed by reducing the steam demand on the secondary side. When in automatic control, the control rods automatically move into the core in response to the increased temperature.

The pre-trip charging flow for both events was controlled partly by automatic and partly by manual action. In the case of North Anna, the flow from one (of two) comparatively high capacity centrifugal charging pumps (approximately 250 gpm capacity at the nominal pressurizer pressure of 2235 psig) automatically increased based on the decreasing pressurizer level. One of the operators then took manual control of the system, set the charging flow control valve to full open, and subsequently realigned the pump suction to the refueling water storage tank (RWST). At Ginna, two (of three) smaller capacity (60 gpm) positive displacement charging pumps were initially operating, one in manual and one in automatic mode. The speed controller increased the flow from the pump in auto-control to near maximum flow, the same as the flow from the pump in manual control. At approximately 140 seconds, the third charging pump was manually started.

The last pre-trip action noted in Table 2 is letdown isolation. At Ginna, this occurred several seconds before reactor trip when pressurizer level reached the low level setpoint (10.6%). At North Anna, letdown isolation was performed manually, as directed by the shift supervisor.

Since full charging flow (for both cases) was not able to keep up with break flow, pressurizer pressure and level continued to decrease and eventually the reactors were tripped. In the case of Ginna, the power had been reduced to about 70% and reactor trip occurred automatically (based on compensated pressurizer pressure) when the pressurizer pressure was less than 1900 psig and level was less than 10%. At North Anna, the charging pump flow was more comparable to the break flow (roughly half, i.e., 250 versus 500 gpm), so the trip time is expected to be later. When the decision was made to manually trip the reactor, the pressurizer pressure was approximately 2100 psig and level was about 45%.

In both cases, post-trip shrink caused a further reduction in the RCS pressure and SI was actuated about 10 seconds after trip when pressurizer pressure reached the respective SIAS setpoints (1723 psig for Ginna and 1765 psig for North Anna).

The remainder of actions listed in Table 2 were explained briefly in the previous section on SGTR recovery actions. Additional details are provided below where the response of several specific parameters of interest are discussed.

RCS Pressure - TREAT solves for a global system pressure, so RCS and pressurizer pressure are one and the same. Plant data is based on a composite of the narrow range pressurizer pressure and wide range RCS pressure taken from various sources (usually plant computer output or strip chart recorders). Comparison plots of these parameters are presented in Figures 1a (Ginna) and 1b (North Anna).

After reactor trip and SI actuation, three high-pressure SI pumps begin to inject and maintain RCS pressure at about 1300 psig during the initial period of the Ginna transient (prior to the RCS depressurization). At North Anna, the two higher capacity centrifugal charging pumps realign to the SI mode (injecting through the boron injection tank) and pressure recovers to approximately 1800 psig. During this phase of the accident, the SI flows are slightly higher than the break flows since they make up for some cooldown shrink and still cause both pressurizers to begin to refill. Predictions for the SI flows during this phase are 50 lbm/sec (360 gpm) for Ginna versus 70 lbm/sec (500 gpm) for North Anna.

The North Anna event features an initial cooldown (1140-1440 sec) that is more rapid and has a more pronounced effect on RCS pressure than the slower more progressive cooldown at Ginna. In the North Anna transient, the pressurizer empties during this initial cooldown (due to shrink) and this causes a slight change in slope in the pressure response as the surge line vents to the rest of the RCS. After the initial cooldown is over, pressure recovers due to the additional SI and reduced break flow. In the Ginna event, a slight repressurization is also evident between 2300 and 2400 seconds after charging flow (which was stripped on the SI signal) is re-established.

For the RCS depressurization phase, it can be noted that the pressurizer PORV (used at Ginna) results in a depressurization several times faster than normal spray (used at North Anna). The difference is attributable to the different processes involved, i.e., direct removal of steam from the vapor region of the pressurizer through the PORV versus condensation on the spray droplets. The spray is also noted to be most effective near the beginning of the depressurization when the temperature difference between the steam and incoming spray water is the large. The TREAT predictions for these two phenomena agree quite well with plant data.

The target pressure for both RCS depressurization actions was approximately 1000 psig (i.e., the ruptured SG pressure). In the Ginna event, the PORV did not reseat upon demand following the fourth opening. However, the operator quickly isolated the PORV with the block valve to limit the depressurization. As a result of the extended depressurization, however, some upper head voiding was predicted. The cold leg temperature in the ruptured loop also dropped as the flow in this loop essentially stagnated and the SI flow increased.

In the North Anna SGTR, safety injection was immediately terminated following the RCS depressurization with normal spray. As reported in the references (North Anna 1987; NRC 1987), the operator also augmented the RCS depressurization at approximately 2040 seconds by opening one pressurizer PORV until RCS pressure dropped about 40 psi. RCS pressure then stabilized at about 1000 psig (i.e., the ruptured SG pressure) at the end of the transient modeled. At Ginna, pressure was allowed to recover for a brief period of time. After 4300 seconds, SI was terminated and pressure also dropped to about 1000 psig.

Pressurizer Level - The pressurizer level comparison plots for the Ginna and North Anna events are presented in Figures 2a and 2b, respectively. Up to the point of RCS depressurization, the pressurizer level response is similar to the RCS pressure response. In the Ginna event, pressurizer level goes off-span (low) following reactor trip but is predicted to remain above the actual bottom of the pressurizer. At approximately 2000 seconds, level does return on-span. For the corresponding period at North Anna, level stabilizes at about 5% and slowly increases to about 10% by 1000 seconds. This slight increase is most likely due to a reduction in the post-trip cooldown shrink due to the AFW flow reduction and isolation of steam flow from the ruptured SG. During the rapid cooldown at 1140-1440 seconds, however, pressurizer level goes off-span (low) and the pressurizer was predicted to completely empty. However, level was soon re-established after the cooldown was stopped and the RCS was depressurized.

During the depressurization, the increased SI flow and reduced break flow caused the pressurizer level to increase. At North Anna, level continues to slowly increase to about 85% after the depressurization was stopped. Letdown was later established at 2340 seconds; two minutes later, pressurizer level peaked at 88% and then began to decrease.

Due to the extended opening of the pressurizer PORV at Ginna, pressurizer level reached 100% during the depressurization. Level remained at 100% for the duration of the transient presented here. The TREAT response shows a similar trend as the plant data, however, there is one important discrepancy in the analysis that should be mentioned to explain the difference in the level response after SI termination. In the TREAT analysis, the pressurizer heaters were inadvertently left in automatic mode and were therefore, actuated when level exceeded the low-level setpoint of 10.6% (at approximately 2000 sec). This heat input to the pressurizer water raised its temperature to near saturation following SI termination. In the actual Ginna event (see NRC 1982), the pressurizer heaters did not automatically energize upon reaching the low-level setpoint (note: the backup heaters did energize at North Anna). Instead, the Ginna heaters were manually energized at 10:42 (4600 sec) and the steam bubble started to form about one hour later. Thus, the simulation of the early pressurizer heatup in TREAT accounts, at least partially, for the level deviation after SI termination. The TREAT prediction is, otherwise, in reasonable agreement with the plant data.

Narrow Range Level in Ruptured SG - The final set of comparison plots shown in Figures 3a and 3b features the narrow levels in the ruptured SGs. This level (in percent) is an indication of the SG water level in the 12 foot span just above the top of the SG U-tubes. Initial water levels for the two cases were about 50% (Ginna) and 45% (North Anna). During the initial pre-trip period, these levels increased only slightly (several percent) as the feedwater controllers attempted to keep levels at the programmed values. Following reactor trip, the levels decreased to near the bottom of the span due to the post-trip shrink and void collapse. Several minutes later, level indication returned to about 20% (both cases) due to the AFW and break flow additions. In the North Anna event, AFW flow to the ruptured SG was stopped at about this time (i.e., at 960 sec), however, level continued to increase due to break flow until the RCS and ruptured SG pressures were made equal. At approximately 2000 seconds, this condition was achieved and the level peaked at about 60%. As noted in the comparison, TREAT predicts the correct trend for the SG level reasonably well. It should also be noted that this is one of the more difficult parameters to predict accurately since the span covers only a fraction of the SG height. In addition, the levels and SG masses predicted before and after trip are also dependent on accurate models for the SG void fraction and recirculation flow rates.

In the Ginna event, level also continued to increase after AFW to the ruptured SG was stopped. However, since the break was comparatively large and RCS pressure remained high for a longer period of time, the level in the ruptured SG continued to rise to the top of the narrow range span and eventually filled the SG steam dome. Some water was also carried over into the steamlines, however, this proved to not be a serious problem, both from the structural as well as the radiological standpoints. This overfill prediction is difficult to predict with certainty since plant instrumentation was not originally designed to track this occurrence. A simple "leaky SG safety valve" model, however, was reasonably successful at predicting the RCS and ruptured SG pressure during the end period of the transient where SG overfill was suspected. The TREAT comparison for the Ginna ruptured SG pressure is shown in Figure 4.

In addition to the parameters previously described, a number of others are important and have been compared for the TREAT SGTR simulations. These include cold leg temperature in the ruptured loop; in the Ginna transient, this temperature decreased to less than 300°F during the RCS depressurization and later increased to about 400°F following SI termination. Core exit and upper head temperatures were also checked to confirm the expected natural circulation delta-T and to indicate the approach to saturation in the upper head. Other "traditional" parameters (flows, temperatures, etc.) readily available to the operator (plus some not available such as break flow) were also studied for the simulation assessment.

SUMMARY AND CONCLUSIONS

TREAT has been used to simulate two steam generator tube rupture events - the Ginna SGTR of January 25, 1982 and the North Anna Unit 1 SGTR of July 15, 1987. Although many similarities between these two cases exist, a number of thermal hydraulic phenomena unique to each event have been identified.

Similarities include some of the very rapid pre-trip actions. This initial phase of the SGTR transient also provides some good tests for many of the simulator model control and protection systems. The basic recovery techniques used in the two cases were also similar since the actions taken for both events were based on those prescribed in the Westinghouse Owners Group ERGs.

Significant differences arise in the post-trip response. In particular, the RCS stabilization pressure several minutes after trip is significantly higher for the North Anna case (1800 psig versus 1300 psig). This is mainly due to the higher pressure injection capability of the charging/SI pumps at North Anna and the lower shut-off head pressure (1500 psig) of the Ginna high-head SI pumps. Due to the reduced pressure at Ginna, the RCPs were tripped and this action had an impact on some of the major recovery actions taken. Specifically, the two events featured different modes for RCS depressurization - i.e., operation of the pressurizer PORV at Ginna versus normal pressurizer spray at North Anna. The decay heat removal mechanisms (i.e., forced versus natural circulation) were also different between the two cases.

In view of the differences noted for the two SGTR events, it is considered that the unique features for both events will provide an appropriate test of the simulator model capability to predict the proper plant response for SGTR events. The TREAT model predictions were found to agree reasonably well with the actual plant data for both SGTR events that were simulated.

ACKNOWLEDGMENTS

The authors would like to acknowledge Mr. Robert Eliasz of Rochester Gas and Electric for his review and help with the Ginna transient. We would also like to thank Mr. Richard Ofstun of Westinghouse for all the help he has provided in performing the TREAT simulations.

REFERENCES

Cheung, A. C., at al. 1985. "The Westinghouse Transient Real Time Engineering Analysis Tool," Proceedings of the Specialists Meeting on Small Break LOCA Analyses in LWRs, Pisa, Italy (June 23-27).

ERGs. 1983. "Westinghouse Owners Group Emergency Response Guidelines," Rev. 1 (Sept.).

Ginna. 1982. "Incident Evaluation of the Ginna Steam Generator Tube Failure Incident of January 25, 1982," R. E. Ginna Nuclear Power Plant Event Report, Docket No. 50-244 (April 12).

North Anna. 1987. "North Anna Unit 1 July 15, 1987 Steam Generator Tube Rupture Event Report," Virginia Electric and Power Company Report, Rev.0-A (Aug. 17).

NRC. 1982. "NRC Report on the January 25, 1982 Steam Generator Tube Rupture at R. E. Ginna Nuclear Power Plant," NUREG-0909 (April).

NRC. 1987. "NRC Augmented Inspection Team Report Nos. 50-338/87-24 and 50-339/87-24," NRC Report on the North Anna Unit 1 SG Tube Rupture of July 15, 1987 (Aug.).

Surman, R. C., et al. 1983. "Guidance for Control Room Emergency Operations," Proceedings of the ANS Topical Meeting on Anticipated and Abnormal Plant Transients in Light Water Reactors, Jackson, WY (Sept.).

Table 1

Comparison of Ginna and North Anna 1 SG Tube Rupture Events

	R. E. Ginna	North Anna 1
Type of Plant	W 2-Loop PWR	W 3-Loop PWR
Date of Accident	January 25, 1982	July 15, 1987
Description and Shape of Failure, Location of Failure, Initial Break Flow	Large Fish Mouth Near Hot Leg 700-800 gpm	Double-Ended Near SG U-Bend 550-637 gpm
Pre-trip Actions Performed	Increase Charging, Isolate Letdown Reduce Power	Same
Type of Reactor Trip	Automatic Low Pzr Pressure	Manual
Type of SI Actuation	Low Pzr Pressure	Same
Shut-off Head Pressure of High-Pressure SI Pumps	1500 psig	2500 psig
RCS Stabilization Pressure Several Minutes After Trip	1300 psig	1800 psig
Reactor Coolant Pump Status Several Minutes after Trip	All Tripped	All Left Running
Initial Cooldown	One Intact SG Dump to Condenser	Two Intact SGs to Condenser
Method of RCS Depressurization	One Pressurizer PORV	Normal Pzr Spray
RCS Coolant Circulation	Natural Circulation Flow Stagnates in Ruptured Loop	Forced Flow for all Loops

Table 2

Time Table of Events - Ginna and North Anna 1 SGTR Events

Event	Time of Event (seconds) Ginna	North Anna 1
Full Power Operation, Assumed Start of SGTR Failure	0 (9:25:10 a.m.)	0 (6:30 a.m.)
Pre-Trip Actions:		
Charging Flow Increased (Max)	0-140	0-120
Power Reduced	80	180
Letdown Isolated	180	180
Reactor Trip Followed by Turbine Trip	183 (auto)	324 (manual)
SIAS on Low Pzr Press (auto) (Full AFW Flow by One Min. Later)	190	341
RCPs Tripped	240	---
Brief Initial Cooldown Using All SGs	770-830	---
Ruptured SG Isolated (MSIV Closed)	890	960
Initial Cooldown Using Intact SGs (to Less Than 500°F)	900-1200	1140-1440
RCS Depressurization (with Normal Spray-North Anna) (with One Pzr PORV-Ginna) (Note: block valve used to isolate PORV for last PORV cycle at Ginna)	2530-2535 2550-2557 2604-2612 2630-2680	1620-2160
Pressurizer Heaters Energized	2000-end (TREAT) 4600-end (actual)	1800-1860
Safety Injection Terminated, Normal Charging Established	4310	2040
End of Transient Modeled	5060	2200

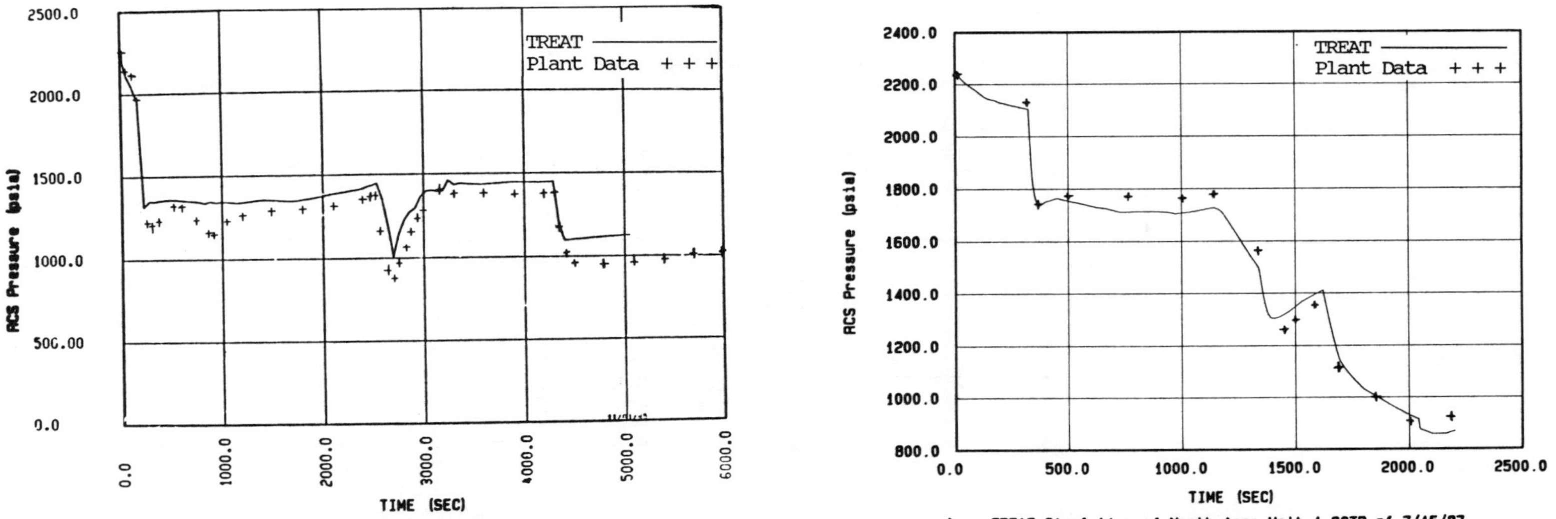

a. TREAT Simulation of Ginna SGTR of 1/25/82

b. TREAT Simulation of North Anna Unit 1 SGTR of 7/15/87

Figure 1. RCS/Pressurizer Pressure Response for Two SGTR Events

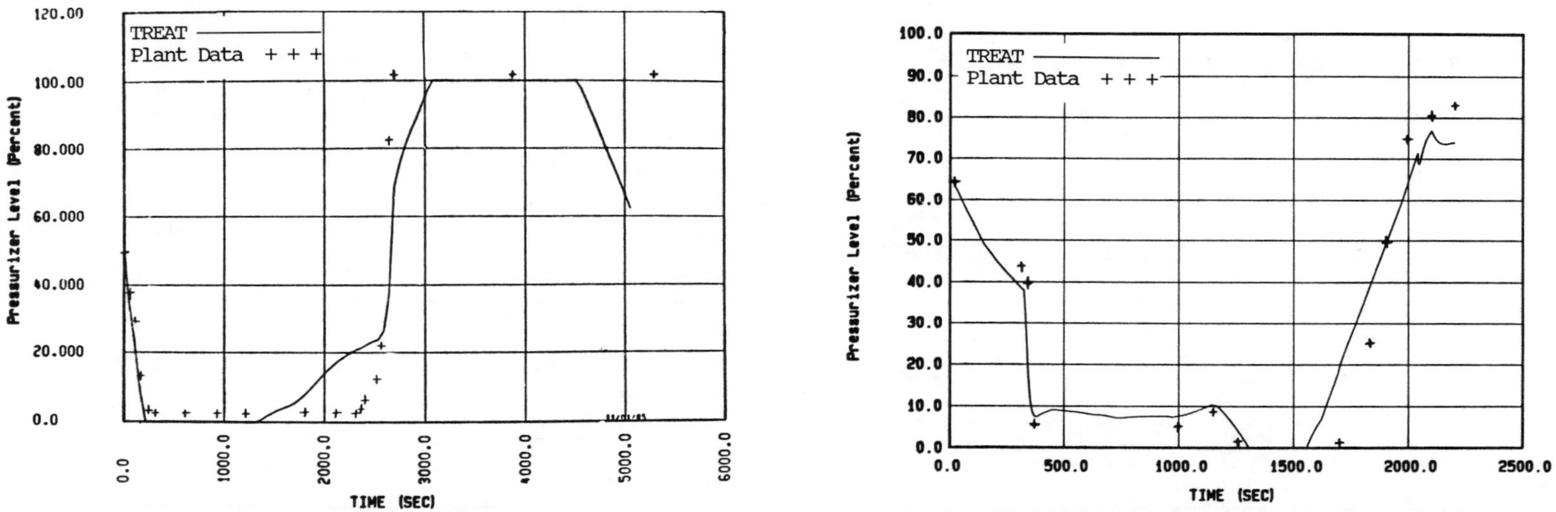

a. TREAT Simulation of Ginna SGTR of 1/25/82

b. TREAT Simulation of North Anna Unit 1 SGTR of 7/15/87

Figure 2. Pressurizer Level Response for Two SGTR Events

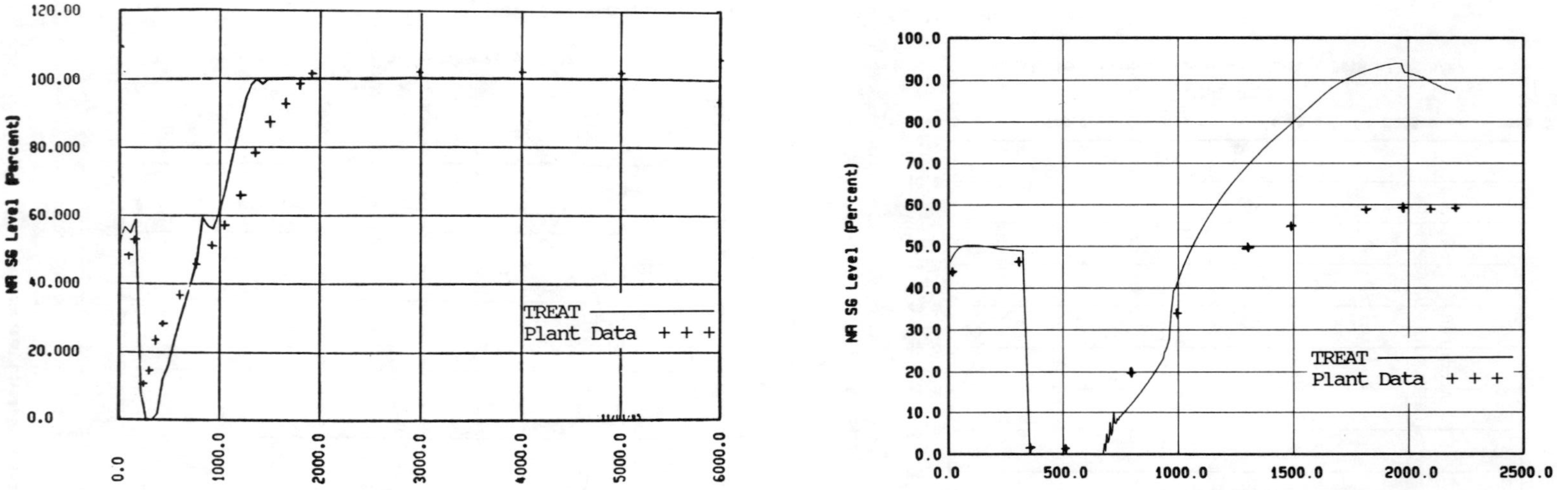

a. TREAT Simulation of Ginna SGTR of 1/25/82

b. TREAT Simulation of North Anna Unit 1 SGTR of 7/15/87

Figure 3. Narrow Range SG Level Response in Ruptured SG for Two SGTR Events

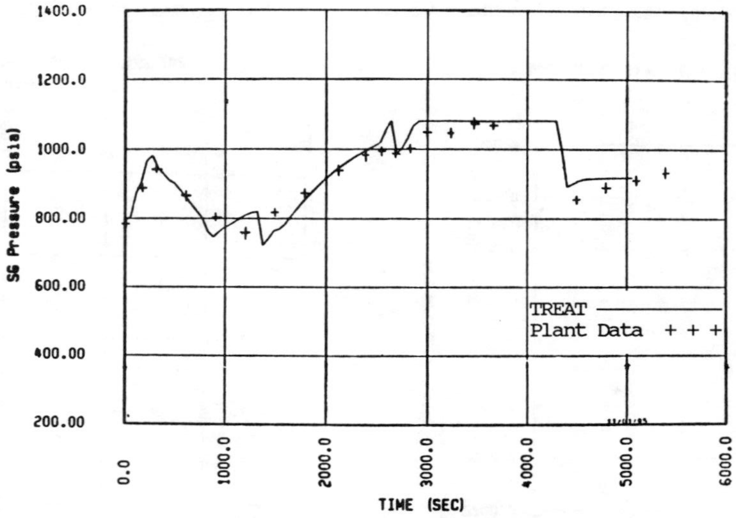

TREAT Simulation of Ginna SGTR of 1/25/82

Figure 4. Ruptured Steam Generator Pressure Response for Ginna SGTR Event

Simulators VI
© 1989 By The Society for Computer
Simulation International
ISBN 0-911801-51-0

Application of a qualified RETRAN model to plant transient evaluation support

P.G. Sedano, P. Mata
UITESA
Serrano 41
Madrid, SPAIN

and

F. Alcantud, J. Serra
HIDROELECTRICA ESPAÑOLA
Hermosilla 3
Madrid, SPAIN

ABSTRACT

This paper presents the applicability and usefulness of a complete and well qualified plant transient code and model to support in depth evaluation of anomalous plant transients. Analyses of several operational and abnormal transients occurred during the first three cycles of Cofrentes (BWR-6) NPP are presented. This application remarked the need of a very detailed and adjusted simulation of the control systems as well as the convenience of having an as complete as possible data adquisition system.

INTRODUCTION

A qualified best-estimate RETRAN-02 model is available for Cofrentes Nuclear Power Plant. Cofrentes is a BWR-6 with a rated power of 2894 MW (thermal) presently uprated to 2952 MW. A plant model has been developed for the RETRAN-02 code, and an extensive qualification has been made with seven different preoperational tests and transients.

The model is at present being used to support and complete the evaluation of real plant transients. The usefulness of the model in this area can be focused in the following subjects:

1 Assessment and complementation of ERIS (Emergency Response Information System) signals taken during the transient.

2 Assessment of manual actions taken during the transients.

3 Evaluation of possible transient alternatives and improvements suggestion.

4 Better knowledge of transients evolution and plant behaviour.

APPLICATION TO PLANT TRANSIENTS

Evaluation of operational transients is a rather complex matter due to the fact that not always the systems respond as they are supposed to, and actual plant process is not always exactly recorded.

A working group has been created with personnel from Hidroeléctrica Española (Cofrentes utility) and Uitesa (support engineering), for the systematic analysis of Cofrentes plant transients (operational and abnormal) during cycles 1, 2 and 3.

The transients analyzed include:

- Load rejection with anomalous turbine bypass behaviour.
- Fast closure of 1 MSIV with flux scram.
- Inadvertent initiation of HPCS at full power.
- Loss of feedwater with scram.
- Load rejection with anomalous behaviour of several control systems.
- Feedwater controller failure with scram.

The analyses of the first three transients are presented in this paper.

ANALYSES RESULTS

- LOAD REJECTION WITH ANOMALOUS BYPASS

In this transient an electrical disturbance caused a load rejection as well as the loss of voltage of several a.c. buses, which resulted in the misbehaviour of several control systems and appearance of spurious recorded signals.The RETRAN model through repeated executions of the transient, has been used to assess the real systems actuation and to determine the correct signals.

The analyses showed the following conclusions:

- There was a real malfunction in the bypass but not so much as the bypass position indicated. In Figure 1 the ERIS bypass position signal and the real actuation (as deducted with RETRAN using bypass demand signal) are shown. In Figure 2 the pressure evolutions using the different bypass signals are shown.

- Retran analyses indicated than 12 SRV´s were actuated (instead of 9 as ERIS indicated). Also all the SRV´s were closed at 23 s. (instead of 38 s. indicated by ERIS SRV´s position signals).

- Recirculation valves runback did not happen in the transient, according to RETRAN analyses. This was a real malfuction properly registered by ERIS FCV position signals.

- Other real malfuctions corroborated with RETRAN analyses were the asymmetrical behaviour of recirculation pumps, the 10 s delay in feedwater pump trip and the anomalous level setpoint step.

- FAST CLOSURE OF 1 MSIV

In this transient a fast closure of 1 MSIV ocurred. Although the pressure control system tried to recover the steam flow drop through the TCV´s, there was a dome pressure excursion which resulted in a high neutron flux (118%) scram signal.

The RETRAN model was used to estimate the real MSIV closure time as well as to determine the plant behaviour should neutron flux scram have not occurred.

- The adequate response of the model, as well as the calculated evolution in case of no flux scram is shown in Figure 3.

- In Figure 4 the different evolutions of reactor power for different MSIV closure times are presented (flux scram precluded). As can be seen the flux scram signal could be avoided for the closure of 1 MSIV if the closure time is larger than 3 seconds.

- HPCS INITIATION

In this transient an inadvertent initiation of the HPCS at full power occurred. The HPCS cold water injection resulted in a dome pressure drop and in a vessel level rise that almost caused a high level (L8) scram signal. Manual actions were taken by the operator to reduce feedwater flow at 40s of transient and to shutdown HPCS at 39s, and scram was prevented.

The RETRAN model was used to analyze the efficiency of the manual actions taken, and to propose automatic and manual alternative options.

- The adequate response of the model can be observed in the comparisons of Figures 5 and 6.

- The analysis shows that the manual reduction of feedwater flow is effective to prevent the scram signal, only if made before 30 seconds from transient beginning, as deducted from Figure 6. In this Figure the different level evolution with and without manual FW reduction is shown. The automatic level controller was lowering the FW flow by the time the manual action was taken and so that measure did not affect the maximum level reached.

- The sudden shutdown of HPCS system causes a short term level rise, which could result in a scram signal, although the long term effect is a level reduction. In Figure 7 the different level evolution with and without manual HPCS shutdown is presented. The HPCS shutdown is not recommendable if the level is close to the scram setpoint, due to the effect mentioned before.

- As a general conclusion, the automatic level control system would be adequate to prevent the scram signal in the case of inadvertent HPCS initiation, with no need of manual actions. Only in the case of a very low master level controller gain the system could not have fast enough response to prevent the scram signal. In Figure 8 the different vessel level evolutions are shown for different controller gains, actual plant gain (K=1.1), design gain (K=4.17) and an intermediate gain (K=2.5), with no manual action or HPCS shutdown.

CONCLUSIONS

This paper shows the applicability of a complete and well qualified plant transient model to calculate and support in depth evaluation of plant transients. This application remarked the need of a very detailed and adjusted simulation of the control systems as well as the convenience of having an as complete as possible data adquisition system.

REFERENCES

1. J.J. MARTINEZ, P.G. SEDANO "Qualification of a Retran-02 Model for Cofrentes NPP" presented at 5th Int. Retran Meeting, Boston, USA, Nov. 1.987.

2. "Estudio Final de Seguridad" Cofrentes NPP.

3. J.H. McFADDEN et al, "RETRAN-02 - A Program for Transient Thermal-Hydraulic Analysis of Complex Fluid Flow Systems", Vols 1 to 5, NP-1850-CCM, Energy Inc. (May 1.981).

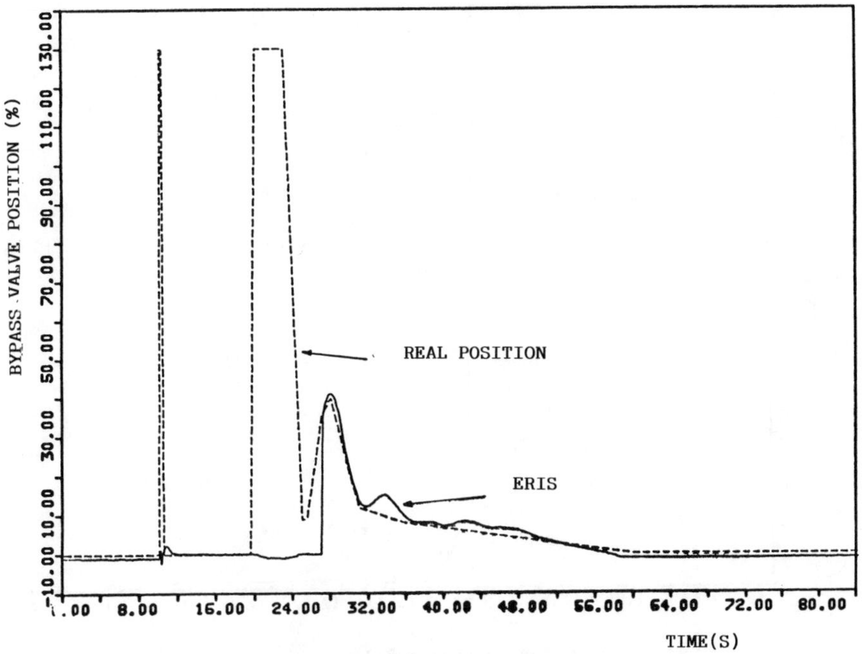

FIG. 1. LOAD REJECTION WITH ANOMALOUS BYPASS.
BYPASS POSITION VS. TIME.

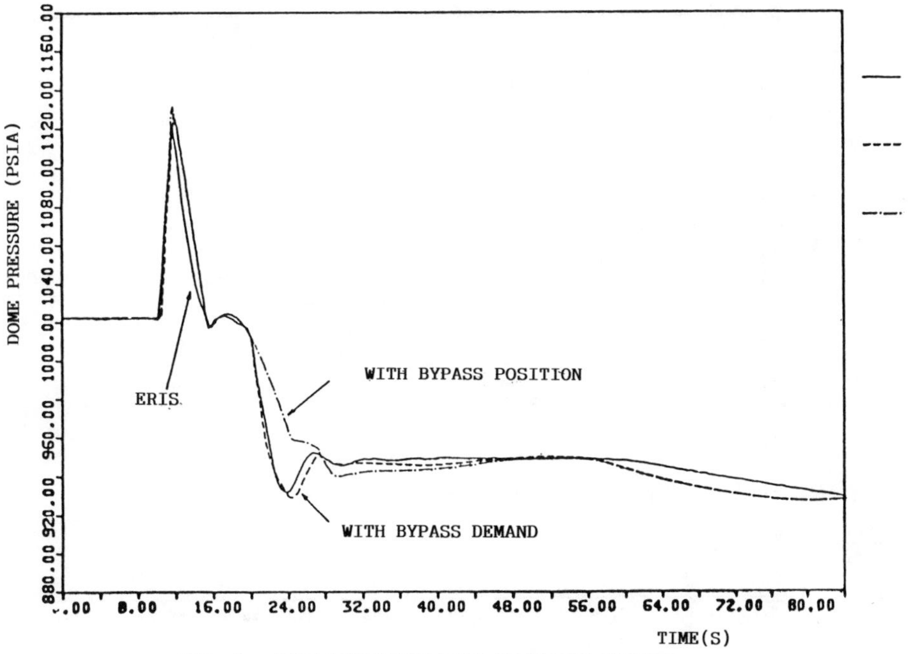

FIG. 2. LOAD REJECTION WITH ANOMALOUS BYPASS.
PRESSURE VS. TIME.

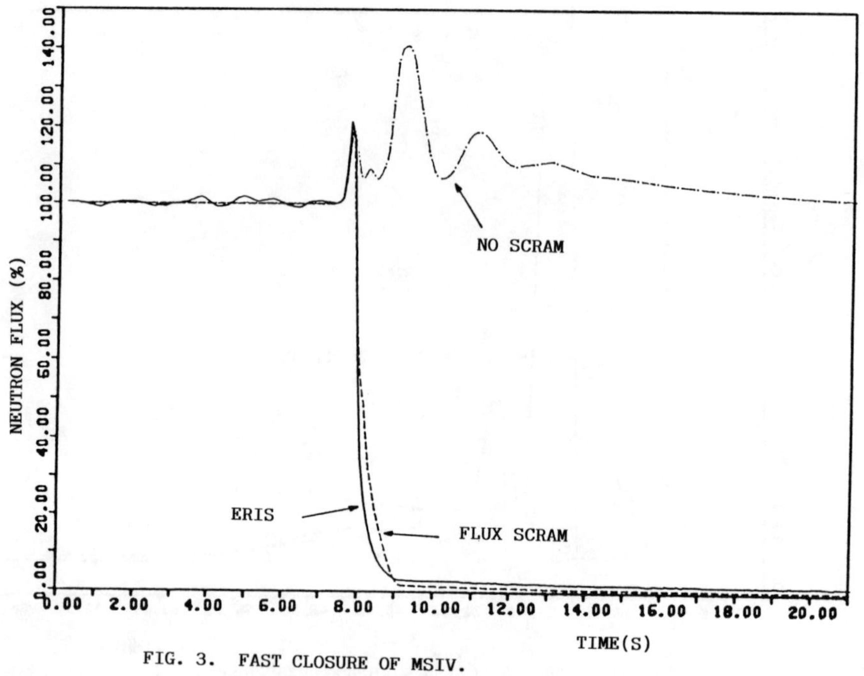

FIG. 3. FAST CLOSURE OF MSIV.
NEUTRON FLUX WITH AND WITHOUT SCRAM

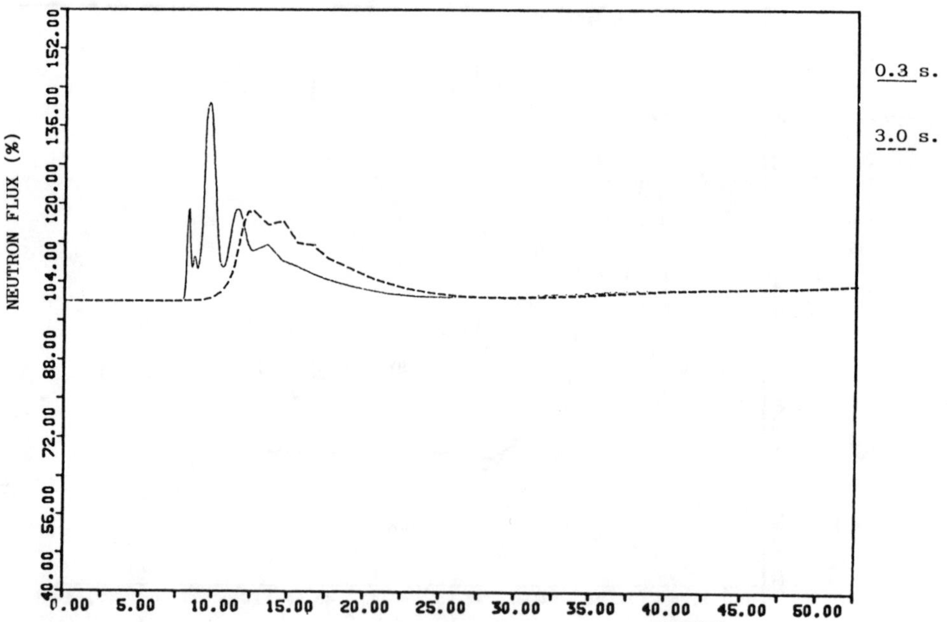

FIG. 4. FAST CLOSURE OF MSIV.
NEUTRON FLUX FOR DIFFERENT MSIV CLOSURE TIMES.

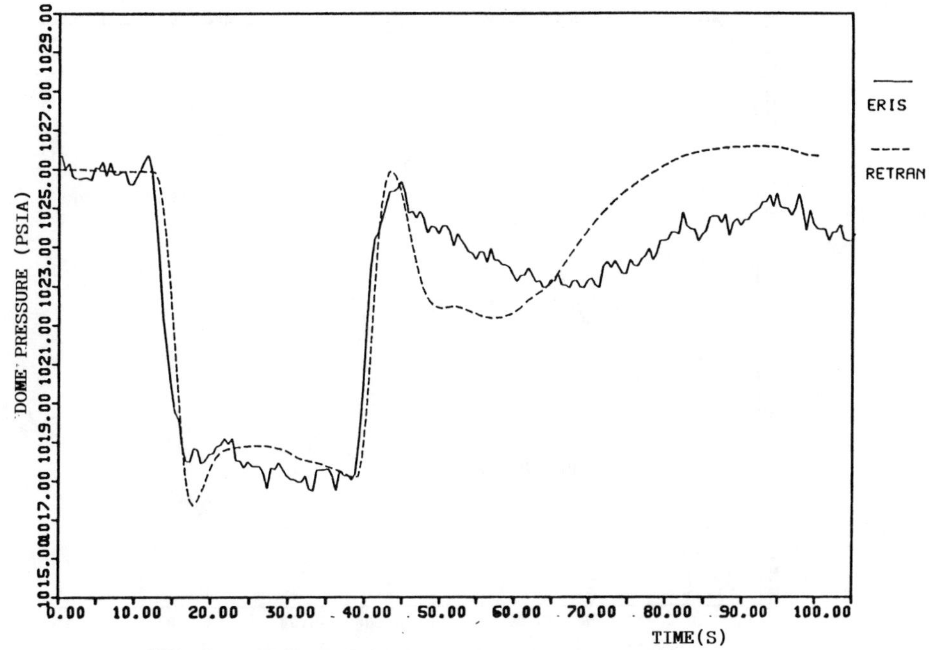

FIG. 5. HPCS INITIATION. DOME PRESSURE VS. TIME

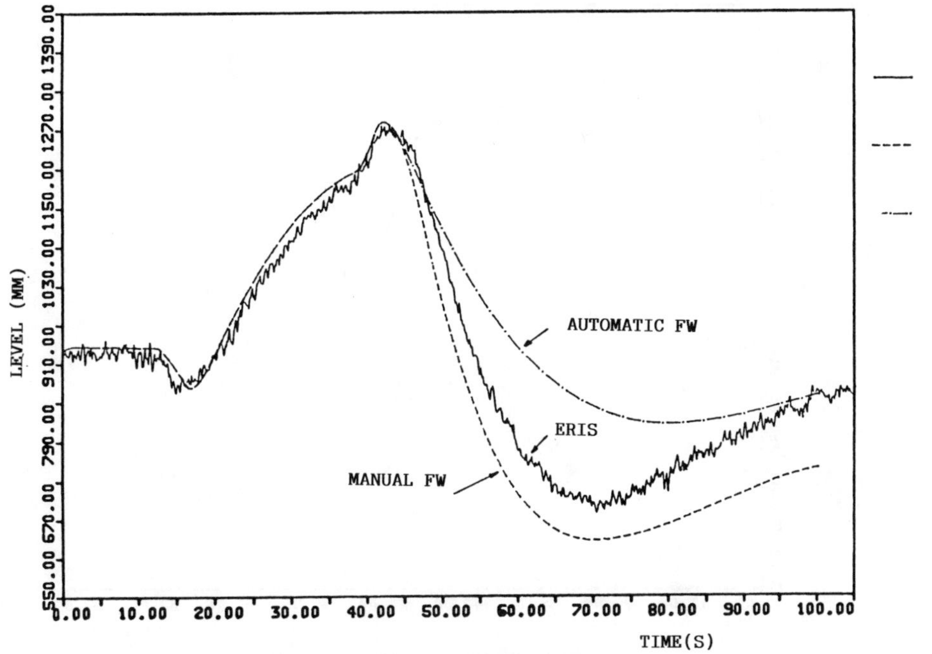

FIG. 6. HPCS INITIATION. LEVEL EVOLUTION
WITH AND WITHOUT MANUAL FW CONTROL.

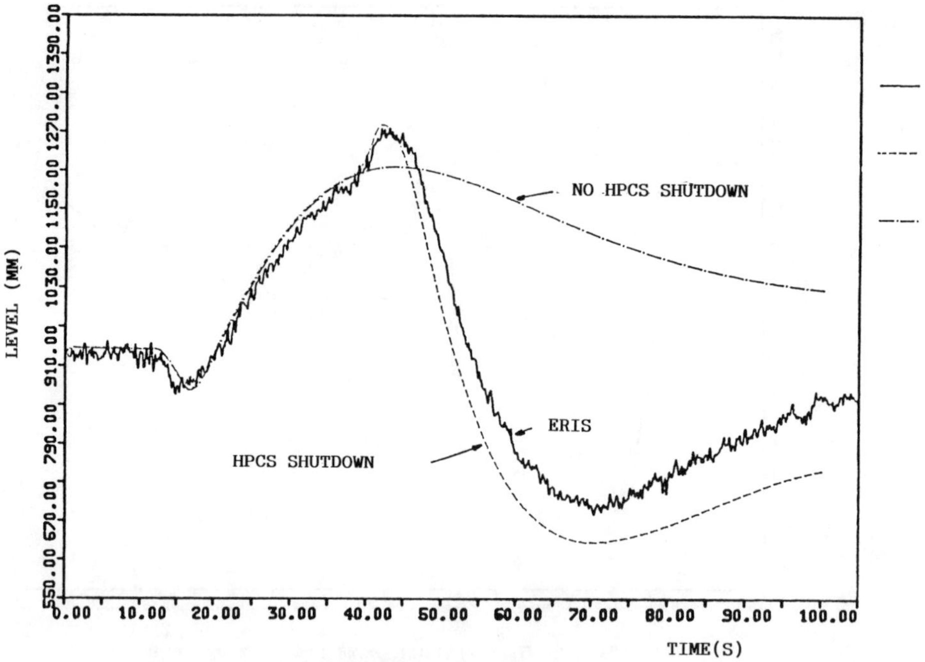

FIG. 7. HPCS INITIATION. LEVEL EVOLUTION WITH AND WITHOUT HPCS SHUTDOWN.

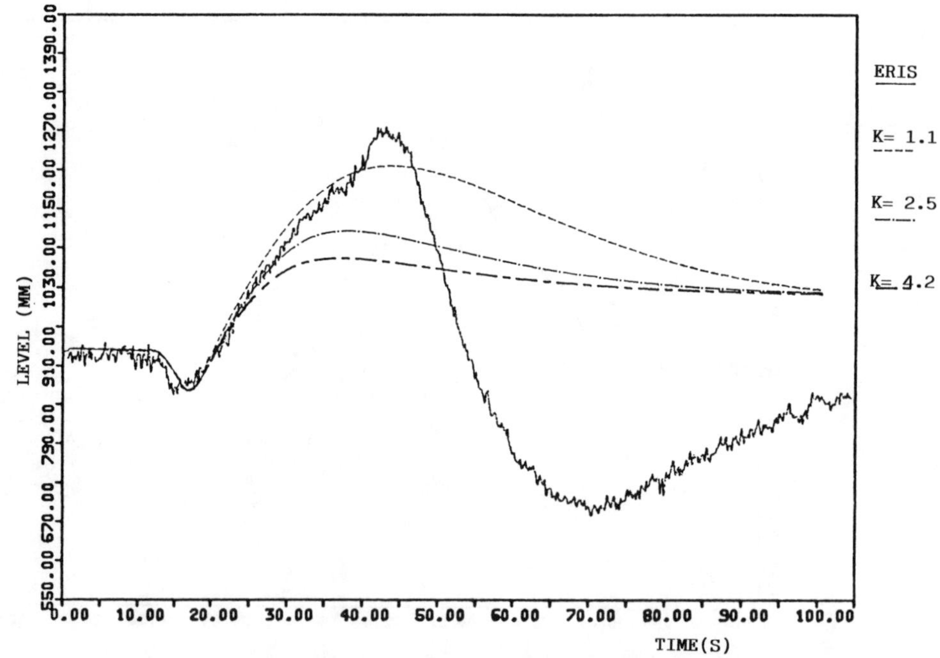

FIG. 8. HPCS INITIATION. LEVEL EVOLUTION WITH DIFFERENT LEVEL CONTROLLER GAINS AND NO HPCS SHUTDOWN.

Simulators VI

ISBN 0-911801-51-0

Phased usage of a training simulator for a nuclear power plant

Paul G. Scharold
Westinghouse Hanford Company
P. O. Box 1970
Richland, Washington 99352
(509) 376-9578

David W. Fraley
Boeing Computer Services, Richland
P.O. Box 300
Richland, Washington 99352

ABSTRACT

The benefits of staged delivery of a nuclear power plant control room simulator are presented and examined. The particular simulator analyzed is unique; however, the methods of determining the training value of incremental deliverables may be applicable to other simulator projects.

INTRODUCTION

The U.S. Department of Energy (DOE), through an operations contractor, developed a full-scope simulator for the Hanford Site N Reactor. The N Reactor is a 4,000-MW (thermal), graphite-moderated, pressurized water reactor that was operated for the DOE. The N Reactor Operator Training Simulator is a facility that was used to train and evaluate personnel in the safe, efficient operation and maintenance of N Reactor.

The Simulator Development Program differed from other integrated hardware and software development efforts. The program was divided into phases to make the simulator available for training with partial capability while the development continued. As such, training requirements played a significant role in defining releases produced in the interim and establishing internal schedules. In addition to assessing the impacts of providing interim training, it is important to estimate the merits of having this capability.

The benefit of a nuclear plant simulator is difficult to measure. In addition to safe operation, simulator training helps operating personnel to correctly and promptly respond to plant emergencies. The U.S. Nuclear Regulatory Commission (NRC) recognizes the value of simulators by requiring all commercial plants to provide full-scope simulator experience to control room operators. The high DOE standards and emphasis on safe operation also dictate the need for simulator training.

The methodology that is being used to estimate the relative "value" of interim simulator training is presented. In the approach, the specific training activities provided by the simulator are first categorized. These are then ranked and given weightings based on relative importance. The method then compares the relative contribution of each intermediate release product to the overall training value.

For optimum training benefit, simulator products were released in five phases prior to the final, full-scope product release. Many factors were considered in establishing how many intermediate products would be released, when they would be released, and what training capability each would provide. The completion dates for each phase were established to coincide with previously set training schedules, allowing enough lead time for training personnel to become familiar with each product. The capabilities provided at each phase were determined by how the hardware and software development schedules could be arranged to provide incremental increases in capabilities that the training personnel would find valuable and would use.

SIMULATOR

The N Reactor Operator Training Simulator was used to provide initial certification and periodic requalification of reactor operators and supervisors. It was designed with sufficient fidelity to allow N Reactor personnel to conduct team training and to develop and verify operating procedures independent of actual reactor operation.

On completion, the simulator included a complete set of operator panels, an instructor's console, an electronic interface, a computer complex, and a full complement of software. The operator panels are duplicates of those in the N Reactor control room to the extent necessary to provide training in the operators' plant control activities. The instructor's console allows initiation, monitoring, and control of training sequences. The electronic interface links the computer to the instrumentation of the operator panels. Software models unique to the simulator replicate plant operation.

The simulator provided reactor certification training equivalent to that provided by private industry. The NRC and American Nuclear Society requirements, used as functional guidelines, are met, or exceeded where possible. These requirements include definitions for the hardware fidelity, normal plant fidelity, simulated malfunction training capabilities, performance criteria, and updating of requirements.

TRAINING ACTIVITIES

The first step in the evaluation was to characterize the specific training activities provided by the simulator. These are, in effect, the objectives of the simulator. Ten specific categories of training were identified as follows:

1. Control Chain Manipulations--Controlling plant systems directly using control room instrumentation and indirectly via communication to operators stationed throughout the plant

2. Abnormal Plant Transients/Analysis--Controlling systems within desired parameters to lessen the severity of the transient. Analyzing the transient cause and taking actions to mitigate its effects

3. Plant Startup and Power Ascension--Manipulating plant equipment during power ascension from zero power to equilibrium using the appropriate procedures

4. Normal Shutdown--Bringing the reactor to zero power

5. Standard Operating Procedures--Using procedures to change system configuration

6. Administrative Controls--Instruction on when and how to use administrative controls such as the Equipment Status Control System, Lock and Tag System, and the Yellow Identification Tag System

7. Communications--This training emphasizes formality of communications between control room operators and outer building personnel, utilizing the various communication equipment available in the control room

8. Equipment Maintenance Standards--Performing maintenance on various pieces of equipment and recording the results

9. Panel/Console Familiarization--Relating Plant Systems to the console and panel locations in the control room by which they are controlled

10. Special Procedures--Training on procedures such as special cooling in which reactor cooling is switched from the Primary System to the Graphite and Shield Cooling System.

Training Activity Weights

The next step of the method is to assign a relative weighting to the training activities. To establish this weighting, simple pairwise comparisons are made. Weights are established in the following manner.

1. Rank the training activities in order of importance. The ten activities given above are in order of priority. That is, training on control chain manipulations is the most important.

2. Using pairwise comparisons (contiguous pairs only), assign a percentage representing the importance weight of the second activity relative to the first activity in the pair. For example, the relative importance of training on abnormal plant transients (priority No. 2) is compared to the importance of training on control chain manipulations (priority No. 1). In our assessment, training on abnormal plant transients was determined to be 90 percent as important as training on control chain manipulations. This process is then repeated for each prioritized pair. Training on startup and power ascension is next compared to that on abnormal plant transients, etc. For example:

Priority	Activity	Weighting factor (%)
1	Control chain manipulations	100
2	Abnormal plant transients	90
2	Abnormal plant transients	100
3	Startup and power ascension	50

3. Once the pairwise comparison is completed, the relative importance weights are then normalized on a percentage basis. Again, as in the above example, control chain manipulations are first given a value of 100, and abnormal plant transients, rated at 90 percent as important, are given a value of 90 (90 percent of the value of 100). This process is repeated for all activities. For example, startup and power ascension, rated at 50 percent as important as abnormal plant transients, is given a 45 (50 percent of the value of 90 assigned to abnormal plant transients). These values are then normalized as a percentage. For example:

Priority	Activity	Weighting factor (%)
1	Control chain manipulations	100
2	Abnormal plant transients	90
3	Startup and power ascension	45

Table 1 gives the results of this comparison. Notice, for example, that training activities No. 4 and 5, normal shutdown and standard operating procedures, are given equal relative value. Similarly, activities No. 6 and 7, administrative controls and communications, are also given equal relative value. The last column of Table 1 gives the normalized training value as a percentage.

Intermediate Releases

The next step in assessing the "training value" of the simulator products was to determine the amount of training available at each release point. For the initial release training course, the simulator had the following capabilities:

- Primary and secondary control chain training
- System parameter interrelationships
- Limited malfunctions
- Limited control logic.

The 42 hours of simulator training used in the course included the following major areas:

- General system review
  - System layouts and flowpaths
  - Major component description
  - Interlocks
  - System lineup for normal operation
- Control chains
  - Sensor to control device logic, interlocks, and component failure alarms
- Console familiarization
- Annunciator responses
- Malfunctions
  - Cause and effect
  - Indicators and operator actions.

The initial release capabilities were measured relatively on the basis that the complete, full-scope simulator provides 100 percent training activities. For example, the initial training provided approximately 60 percent of the control chain manipulation training as that to be provided by the full-scope simulator. Similarly, 70 percent of the full-scope capabilities training on panel/console familiarization was available for training at the first release point. Using this process, the relative training value of each of the training activities at each of the intermediate release points was estimated as shown in Table 2.

Using the relative training capability in combination with the relative values of each of the training activities, it is possible to determine a single measure of the "training value" at each release point. For example, in the first release it is shown that approximately 60 percent of the total capability is available for training on control chain manipulations. Calculation of the "training value" for this activity for the first release is based on the following:

- 25 percent of total training value
- 60 percent available at first release point
- Contribution
- Thus, 0.25 x 0.60 = 15 percent of total.

Table 3 shows this calculation for the "training value" of the initial release of simulator products.

Table 1. Relative Training Value Methodology.

Priority	Simulator training activities	Pairwise comparisons (%)		Training value (%)	
				Relative	Normalized
1	Control chain manipulations	100	100	100	25.2
2	Abnormal plant transients/analysis	90	100	90	22.7
3	Plant startup and power ascension	50	100	45	11.3
4	Normal shutdown	75	100	33.8	8.5
5	Standard operating procedures	100	100	33.8	8.5
6	Administrative controls	80	100	27	6.8
7	Communications	100	100	27	6.8
8	Equipment maintenance standards	50	100	13.5	3.4
9	Panel/console familiarization	100	100	13.5	3.4
10	Special cooling	--	100	13.5	3.4

Table 2. Relative Capability at Intermediate Points.

Priority	Simulator training activities	% of full scope at release (No.)					
		1	2	3	4	5	6 (full scope)
1	Control chain manipulations	60	60	65	80	90	100
2	Abnormal plant transients/analysis	5	12	12	12	12	100
3	Plant startup and power ascension	0	0	20	80	90	100
4	Normal shutdown	0	0	50	90	98	100
5	Standard operating procedures	3	3	3	26	38	100
6	Administrative controls	20	40	50	100	100	100
7	Communications	15	15	15	50	50	100
8	Equipment maintenance standards	0	0	0	52	73	100
9	Panel/console familiarization	70	70	80	90	100	100
10	Special cooling	0	0	0	0	0	100

Table 3. Initial Release Simulator Training Value.

Priority	Simulator training activities	Training capability	Activity weight	= Value
1	Control chain manipulations	60	25.2	15.1
2	Abnormal plant transients/analysis	5	22.7	1.1
3	Plant startup and power ascension	0	11.3	0
4	Normal shutdown	0	8.5	0
5	Standard operating procedures	3	8.5	0.3
6	Administrative controls	20	6.8	1.4
7	Communications	15	6.8	1.0
8	Equipment maintenance standards	0	3.4	0
9	Panel/console familiarization	70	3.4	2.4
10	Special cooling	0	3.4	0
--	Total training value	--	--	21.3

Repeating the calculation shown in Table 3 at each of the intermediate release points for simulator products yields the following estimates of relative value:

Intermediate release	Release date	Relative training value (%)
1	8/83	21
2	4/84	24
3	8/84	33
4	12/84	57
5	8/85	63
6 (full scope)	4/86	100

These are shown as a plot on Figure 1.

SUMMARY

It is important to keep in mind that the "training value" of a simulator is strictly a function of its use as a training tool. A simulator's value does not increase as intermediate products are completed. Its value increases only as people are trained in greater depth.

This paper has shown how intermediate releases were assessed relative to the completion of a total product. Because plant control rooms are regularly being changed, it also provides a method to help assess the need for upgrading fully operational simulators.

The decision to train with intermediate releases while conducting a development program is not uncommon. There are, however, a number of trade-offs that require consideration in making this decision. On the negative side, the release of intermediate products may cause some overall schedule delays and associated cost impacts. Lesson plans and acceptance test procedures also must be prepared and conducted at each point. Allowing for training while continuing development also stresses computer resources and access to the facility.

The limited training afforded by releasing intermediate products allowed productive use of the simulator almost 2 years before its scheduled completion. This approach forced more communication and evaluation of the simulator that allowed improvement of the final product. It has also provided the development staff with near-term milestones and an effective way of measuring progress. The value of a simulator is in its effective use as a training tool. This simple method is one way to help assess its value during the development process.

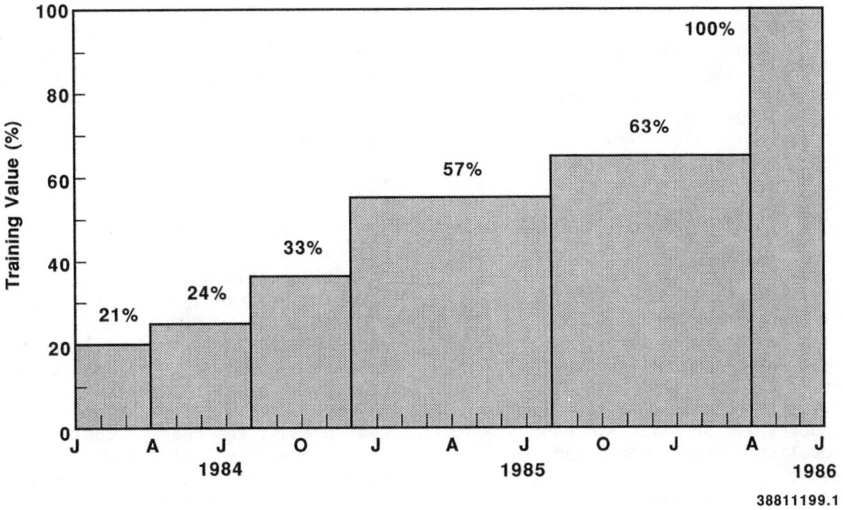

Figure 1. Simulator Training Value versus Time.

Simulators VI

ISBN 0-911801-51-0

Qualification of a loss of recirculation flow model for jet pump BWR's

R. C. Kern
Utility Associates International
6003 Executive Blvd.
Rockville, MD 20852

ABSTRACT

Best estimate analysis capability for Boiling Water Reactors (BWR's) is important for the support of plant operations, since it is necessary to establish realistic response characteristics during normal and anticipated transient conditions. Prior to usage, it is necessary to qualify the model by comparisons with measured data. This paper represents one such qualification for analysis of loss of recirculation flow events.

The best estimate model is based on the DYNODE-B computer program which simulates the transient response of the nuclear steam supply system of a BWR for all transients other than design basis LOCA's. The qualification is based on a startup test performed on the Susquehanna Steam Electric Station Unit 2 involving the trip of one recirculation pump.

Comparisons of the calculated and measured key system parameters and loop flow rates show excellent agreement. The major notable difference is in the untripped drive line flow. A sensitivity study demonstrated that improvement in this parameter can be achieved by adjusting the drive line hydraulic characteristics such that a smaller flow increase is sufficient to produce the increased driving head.

INTRODUCTION

Best estimate analysis capability for Boiling Water Reactors (BWR's) is important for the support of plant operations, since it necessary to establish realistic response characteristics during normal and anticipated transient conditions. This capability can be used to support startup and periodic tests, emergency planning, operating procedures, load changes, equipment qualification, control and protective system setpoint changes, and simulator validation. Prior to usage, it is necessary to qualify the model by comparisons with measured data. This paper presents one such qualification for analysis of loss of recirculation flow events. First, descriptions of the plant and test are provided; then the model is described. Comparisons between the model predictions and measurements are presented. The results of sensitivity studies are discussed. The summary reviews the major conclusions.

PLANT AND TEST DESCRIPTIONS

Susquehanna Steam Electric Station (SSES) Units 1 and 2 are nearly identical GE BWR4 units. This design contains two external recirculation drive lines each of which has one recirculation pump and each feeds 10 internal jet pumps. Variable speed M/G sets provide power to the recirculation pumps and are used for flow control. The nuclear boiler rated power of each unit is 3293 Mwt and the rated core flow is 12600 kg/s (100 Mlb/hr).

The startup test program for each unit consisted of a number of steady-state and transient tests which span a wide range of conditions for normal operations and anticipated transients. These tests provide an excellent source of data which can be used to qualify best estimate models of the plant.

One of these tests on Unit 2 consisted of a loss of flow transient in which the power to one recirculation pump was tripped. This test was performed at near rated power and flow conditions with the reactor initially operating in an equilibrium state. All control systems with the exception of the flow controller were in automatic. No manual intervention was expected for this test.

MODEL DESCRIPTION

The best estimate model used in the current work was developed from information provided by Roscioli. This model is based on the DYNODE-B computer program (Kern et al. 1983) which simulates the transient response of the nuclear steam supply system for all non-design basis LOCA's. For the current analysis, the following options were selected: the point-kinetics model was used with 6 delayed neutron and 11 decay heat groups; the reactor coolant system (RCS) flow rate was calculated with the homologous pump model; the M/G flow and feedwater control systems were explicitly modeled; and a profile-fit model was used to compute the core void fraction distribution. In addition, since this analysis was being performed to qualify the hydraulic models of the recirculation flow system, the transient reactor vessel dome pressure and main steam flow were forced based on the measured data. The transient began as a Drive Motor Trip (M/G motor), and the test data indicated that at 22 seconds a Recirculation Pump Trip occurred with possible attendant closure of the recirculation discharge valve in this drive line. Thus the model was set up in this manner. Input parameters relating to initial conditions were also based on the measurements.

RESULTS

Comparisons of the calculated and measured key system parameters and loop flow rates are shown in Figs. 1 and 2, respectively, for the base case. In general, these comparisons show excellent agreement. The major notable difference is in the untripped drive line flow. A sensitivity study demonstrated that improvement in this parameter can be achieved by adjusting the drive line hydraulic characteristics such that a smaller flow increase is sufficient to produce the increased driving head.

SUMMARY

In summary, this paper presents the qualification of a best estimate loss of recirculation flow model for jet pump BWRs by comparions between calculation and plant test measurements. Results of a sensitivity study are also discussed.

REFERENCES

Kern, R. C., et al. 1983. "DYNODE-B Version 5.4 - Boiling Water Reactor Simulator", Topical Report UAI 83-51, Rev. 0 Utility Associates International, Rockville, MD. (November 1).

Roscioli, A. J. of Pennsylvania Power and Light. Personal communication of information including system design and operational data and plant transient measurements.

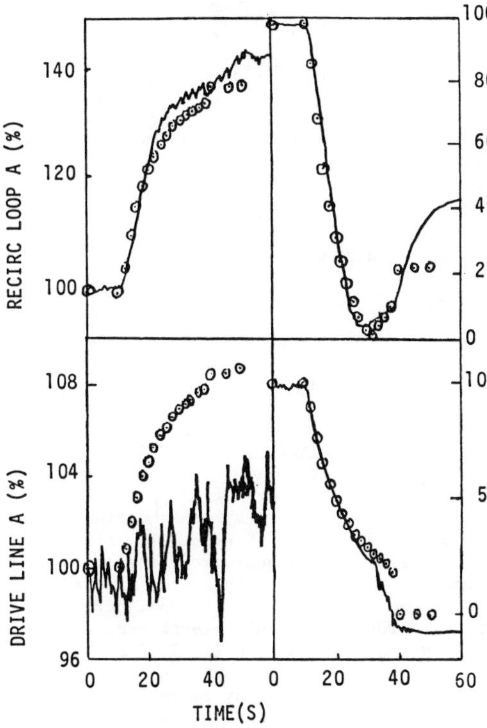

FIGURE 2. COMPARISONS OF LOOP FLOW RATES

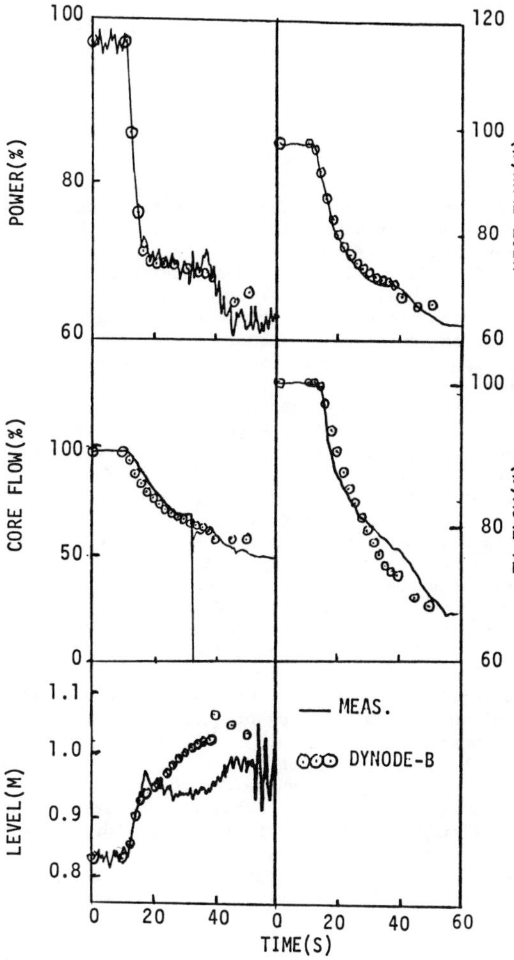

FIGURE 1. COMPARISONS OF SYSTEM PARAMETERS

Simulators VI

ISBN 0-911801-51-0

Dynamic response of gas fired industrial boilers to demand changes

A. Korving and J.M.P. van der Looij
Laboratory for Thermal Power Engineering
Delft University of Technology
P.O. Box 5037, 2600 GA Delft
The Netherlands

ABSTRACT

This paper investigates the dynamic behaviour of a typical gas fired industrial boiler by comparing various transients obtained using a detailed non-linear dynamic model developed at the authors' laboratory, to those obtained from a commercially available, internationally marketed modular program suite capable of dynamically modeling various types of power plants and their components, including boilers. Section 2.1 briefly discusses features of the first model believed to be of general interest, e.g. the solution method and the arguments for distributed parameter modeling of the evaporator. Contrary to the authors' program which is written in FORTRAN, the latter program suite, described in section 2.2, makes use of the ACSL block-oriented simulation language and has been developed to suit a wide range of users, emphasizing versatility, graphics output and user friendliness. Based on a comparison of the results and of the computational and engineering manpower required to obtain them, conclusions will be drawn concerning the impact on boiler dynamics of the various physical assumptions investigated and impressions will be given on the relative advantages of general and special purpose programs by designers and plant owners.
In search of reduced order and therefore simplified modeling, a singular value decomposition of the Hankel matrix of the model impulse response is used in section 3 to obtain an initial guess of the minimum model order. A sensitivity analysis is used to determine the cause of the principal dynamics, giving rise to using additional simplifying assumptions.

1. INTRODUCTION

The ability of boilers to accommodate large and steep changes in demand, occurring e.g. in certain process plants, is primarily determined by their thermal capacitance. This is notably true for the ability of natural circulation boilers to sustain sudden rises in demand without risking local overheating of evaporator tubes due to temporary interruption of the circulation flow. The prediction of operating limits imposed by such considerations, previously based on empirical data specific to certain boiler designs, has been greatly facilitated by the advent of computer simulation models based on the solution of the set of time dependent conservation equations describing a boiler's dynamic behaviour. The attention has since focussed on the degree of refinement incorporated in these models and the various physical assumptions underlying them. In these areas a certain discrepancy exists between the needs of designers wishing to know the effects of detailed design changes on a boiler's dynamic behaviour and those of plant owners looking for unsophisticated, user friendly software enabling them to set or adjust practical operating limits for existing boilers, notably in the event of plant changes.

2. MODEL DESCRIPTIONS

The basic characteristics and a schematic of the boiler modeled in this paper can be found in table 1 and figure 1, respectively. Although in reality the boiler under consideration delivers part of its steam production to a process, we assume for the sake of simplicity that all of the steam is fed directly to the turbine throttle valve. This assumption is of no importance with respect to the objective of this paper.

Thermal power	105	MW
Operating pressure	10.1	MPa
Live steam temperature	800	K
Steaming rate	32	kg/s

TABLE 1. Full load conditions of the gas fired boiler modeled.

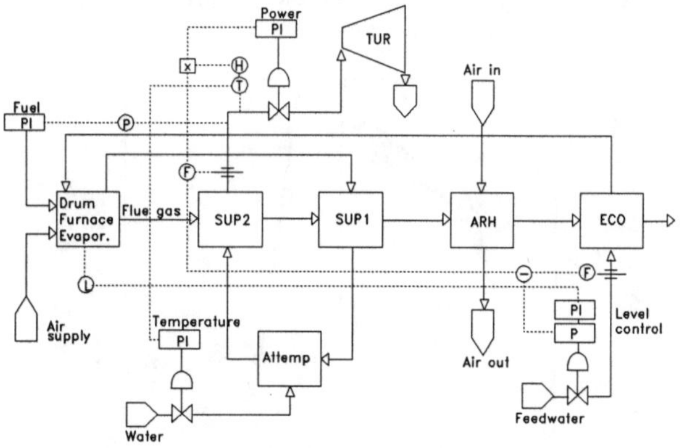

FIGURE 1. Schematic of the boiler modeled.

2.1. DYPFIB Model Description

The DYPFIB (DYnamic model of a pulverized coal FIred Boiler) model derives from the fluidized bed boiler model developed by VAN DER LOOIJ (1988). The fluidized bed and the freeboard are replaced by a gas fired furnace. The present paper is limited to a summary treatment. For a detailed description the reader is referred to the aforementioned reference. The model was implemented on a IBM 3083-JX1 mainframe computer and validated with respect to steady state and dynamic characteristics by comparison of simulation results with values found in practice.

2.1.1. Model Components

The furnace sub-model derives from HOTTEL and SAROFIM (1967). Quasi steady state is assumed for the flue gases. The flue gases are assumed to be in plug flow and radiative heat transfer is calculated using an average flue gas and pipe wall temperature.

The flue gas duct sub-model describes heat transfer from the flue gas to the superheaters and economizer. Both radiative and convective heat transfer are taken into account. The former is modeled using the zone-method approach, HOTTEL and SAROFIM (1967).

The drum model, based on the pressurizer study by GOEMANS (1972), consists of two control volumes: a water and a steam volume. The water is assumed to remain saturated by condensation and evaporation.

The evaporator model, based on that derived by BRUENS (1981), includes slip between the gas and liquid phases and neglects acceleration and dissipation effects.
The single phase heat exchanger models (superheaters and economizer) mentioned above derive from the two-phase evaporator model.

To limit the use of computing time for the numerous water/steam properties needed in the simulations cubic and bi-cubic splines were used.

2.1.2. Discretization And Solution Procedure

The model describing the dynamic behaviour of the gas fired boiler contains a large number of partial differential equations describing energy transport. In order to limit the number of iterations needed in the computer program we choose an explicit scheme for discretization of these balances. The choice of the order of the scheme is a trade-off between accuracy, which is low for low order schemes, and numerical problems such as numerical oscillations which are introduced by higher order terms. Here we select a second order scheme and use monotonocity factors to avoid numerical oscillations, see VAN LEER (1974).
The ordinary differential equations are solved using first order schemes.
With respect to the solution of the various algebraic relations, partial and ordinary differential equations the following is worth noting. Due to the physical coupling between mass, momentum and energy balances their solution is cumbersome. Frequently an initial estimate of mass flow and pressure profile is used to compute the energy balance, followed by an update of the former two variables. This procedure generally leads to a large number of iterations and thereby consumes the major part of the computing time. In the present solution procedure this was avoided through the following approach. The momentum balance can be written as:

$$p_i - p_{i-1} = C_1 \dot{m}^2 + C_2 \dot{m} + C_3 \qquad (1)$$

where the index i refers to space step i. The boundary condition for the momentum balance follows from:

$$p_{out} - p_{in} = \Sigma\, [p_i - p_{i-1}] = D_1 \dot{m}^2 + D_2 \dot{m} + D_3 \qquad (2)$$

where C and D are coefficients which are only slightly flow- and pressure dependent. The mass flow $\dot{m}$ is a characteristic mass flow for the system considered, e.g. that at the entrance. Substitution of (1) into (2) yields a second order polynomial which results in good initial estimates of the mass flow $\dot{m}$. In practice only two to four iterations are needed to account for mass flow and pressure dependence of the coefficients C and D.

2.2. MMS Model Description

The Modular Modeling System (MMS 1985) code developed under the auspices of EPRI and used here for developing an alternative dynamic model of the above boiler, consists of a library of pre-programmed modules representing power plant components. The user interconnects these modules and inserts its parameters into the modules according to a prescribed methodology to make them represent the components of a particular plant. Each module represents a specific component such as an attemperator, a pump or a valve. The MMS makes use of the simulation language ACSL (Advanced Continuous Simulation Language 1986). Steam properties and additional support subroutines are linked with ACSL. The code may be implemented on main-frame computers as well as on minicomputers and PC's. The underlying model is represented by a set of 32 first order non-linear differential equations and accompanying algebraic relationships and is running on a PC-AT system.
The components used are shown in figure 1. Furnace, drum and evaporator are combined in one MMS module. The physical modeling of the furnace follows the same principles as applied in DYPFIB. There are options which modify the flow of combustion gases and heat transfer in the furnace to adjust the heat flow entering the duct.
The drum features perfect separation of steam and water and includes the effects on the water level of shrinks and swells due to pressure and heat absorption changes in the boilers saturated water inventory.
The evaporator is modeled as a single downcomer riser loop. The natural circulation driving head calculations include the effect of variable two- phase slip. Except for the consistent application of spatial lumping (versus distributed parameter modeling of the superheaters and the economizer in DYPFIB), the lumping of tube wall and water energy storage capacities*) and representation of the airheater as a simple heat sink, the single phase heat exchanger and attemperator models are sufficiently similar to those of DYPFIB to refer the reader to this latter model for further details.
To simulate a realistic power demand behaviour a high-pressure turbine, including the turbine valves, module is connected to the model. The module is based on the conservation equations including the Stodola relation.
Control loops for steam temperature, steam pressure and drum level, featuring PI controllers and actuators, may be added to the model as required by the user.

---

* it should be noted that this assumption, while permissible for the steady state, may not hold during some transients (as noted in the MMS manual); its impact will be closely examined in section 2.4.

2.3. Comparison Of MMS And DYPFIB Modeling Approaches

Apart from the differences noted in the foregoing the modeling approaches of DYPFIB and MMS differ in the following aspects:

- The spatially lumped approach, leading to non-linear ordinary differential equations, throughout MMS versus the use of partial differential equations in the model of DYPFIB. It should be noted that this difference has significant impact on computing time.
- In MMS drum, downcomer and evaporator are treated as a single vessel containing steam and water where as each of these components is modeled separately in DYPFIB. It stands to reason that the recirculation ratio (i.e. the inverse value of exit steam quality) is poorly predicted in MMS.
- As a result of the detailed modeling of DYPFIB its solution procedure is far from straightforward and requires many iterations and therefore extensive computing time. By contrast the MMS code tries to minimize the number of iterations (algebraic loops in ACSL) by various assumptions.
- The steady state is computed separately in the DYPFIB code, while in the MMS code the boiler is directed to its desired operating point by adjusting/tuning parameters such as heat transfer coefficients, until certain data such as pressures or temperatures equal known steady state values for the boiler under consideration. While the additional simulation time required for this purpose is hardly relevant in the light of the afore mentioned difference in computing time between MMS and DYPFIB the need for apriori knowledge of steady state data must be considered an inherent drawback of MMS.
- It follows from the foregoing that the validity of heat transfer and pressure drop data in MMS is limited to heat transfer and flow regimes corresponding to those prevailing under steady state conditions. Extrapolation beyond these conditions as required e.g. for large transients, may result in discrepancies for MMS models as opposed to DYPFIB which uses widely valid correlations taken from literature.
- The MMS code is accompanied by a user-friendly code generator which greatly facilitates its use. The DYPFIB code on the other hand, like most detailed computer codes, is far from user-friendly. While simple changes in geometry are easily introduced in both codes, the addition of e.g. an extra superheater requires in DYPFIB a significant amount of FORTRAN programming.

This foregoing comparison emphasizes that the MMS code is more user-friendly while DYPFIB is more detailed. A comparison between the two codes should therefore primarily give an impression as to whether the MMS results are sufficiently accurate.

2.4. Comparison Of Simulation Results From MMS And DYPFIB

Transients typical of industrial boiler operation were selected for comparison of the open loop responses predicted by the two codes. Small step (+1%) transients on both the turbine valve and the fuel mass flow were first applied in order to avoid the effects of excessive extrapolation in MMS mentioned in section 2.3, subsequently a large transient (-15%) is applied on the turbine valve to bring out the effects of extrapolation and of non-linear system behaviour. It was found in all cases that the models possess a physically unstable operating mode, as evidenced (e.g. in figure 2) by the response of the drum level to a step change in turbine valve position. Linear analysis in the discrete time domain revealed a positive eigenvalue of the system just outside the unit circle, which points to the presence of a pure integrator. This mode should be associated with the overall boiler mass balance: changes in steaming rate caused by changes of turbine valve position are not matched by corresponding changes in feed water mass flow, which is kept constant. This results in a continuous change in drum level.

2.4.1. Positive 1% step change in turbine valve

The responses predicted for this transient are shown in figure 2 and give rise to the following comments.

The differences in static gain predicted by DYPFIB and MMS for pressure and temperatures are attributed to inadequacies in the parameter adjustment approach required for the MMS steady state computations (adjustments to the point where the differences in static gain become zero would require excessive iteration time) as mentioned in section 2.3.

The difference in dynamic behaviour predicted for the turbine inlet temperature can be explained by the MMS approximation of lumping the tube wall and water/-steam energy storage capacities, as pointed out in section 2.2. The impact of this approximation is underscored by the DYPFIB simulation, also shown in figure 2, of pipe wall temperatures at the outlet of the second superheater.

The decline in these pipe wall temperatures corresponds to an extra heat flow to the steam leading to a faster response in the steam temperature after approximately 150 seconds, as indicated by the dashed line for turbine inlet temperature.

While the gradient in drum level obtained after a few minutes from both DYPFIB and MMS corresponds to the change in steady state steam mass flow, the predictions for the preceding transients response differ markedly for the two codes. This has two reasons. First the larger pressure decline in the DYPFIB response will cause an additional fall in drum level decline. This effect, however is not sufficient to explain all of the difference. The second effect results from the inclusion in DYPFIB of condensation on the water surface and metal walls in the steam space of the drum. This condensate is continuously discharged into the water volume of the drum except

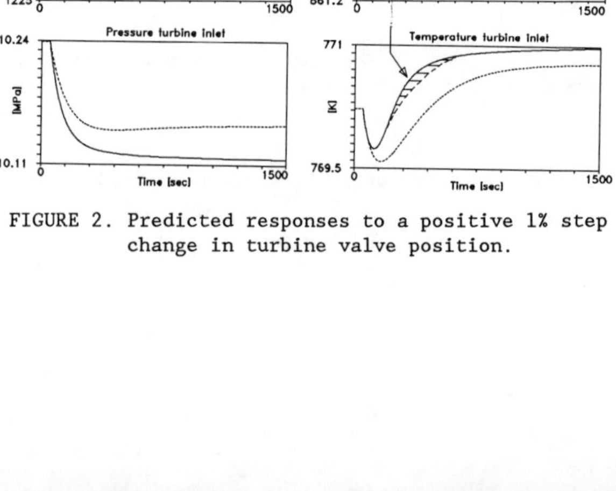

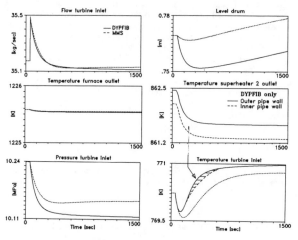

FIGURE 2. Predicted responses to a positive 1% step change in turbine valve position.

after sudden pressure decreases such as the one occurring in the present transient. This condensate mass flow causes an extra steam mass flow generation in the evaporator leading to a larger steam quality in evaporator and riser. The interruption of this condensate flow causes an additional lowering of the drum water level.

2.4.2. Positive 1% step change in gas mass flow

Figure 3 again indicates good agreement of the predicted turbine steam mass flows.
The temperature transient in the flue gas leaving the furnace bears witness to the differences in radiative heat transfer modeling between the two codes. The MMS model transfers less heat to the furnace, hence the resulting steam pressure will be somewhat lower. The difference in the transient response predicted for the turbine inlet temperature has been explained in section 2.4.1., as has the difference in drum level behaviour.

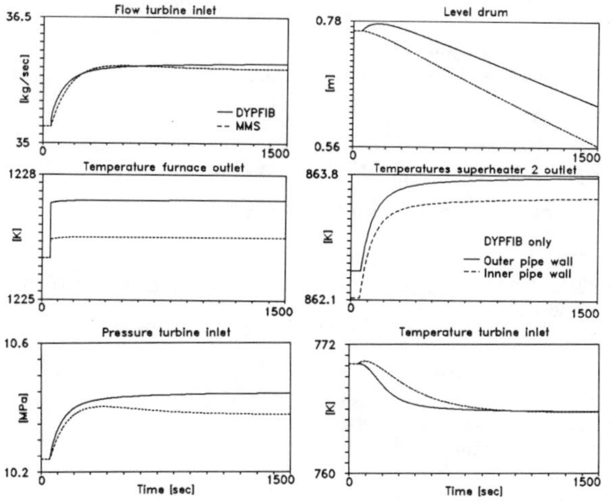

FIGURE 3. Models' responses to a positive 1% step change in gas mass flow.

2.4.3. Negative 15% step change in turbine valve

The responses predicted for this transient are shown in figure 4 and indicates the same behaviour as for the 1% transients. The differences in the transient responses are explained in section 2.4.1.. This leads to the conclusion that the simplifying assumptions, as discussed in section 2.3, in MMS are justified.

3. MODEL ORDER REDUCTION

The transient responses of the boiler models shown in the preceding section suggest that further model reduction beyond MMS might be possible, without unduly compromising the accuracy of the predicted responses. To obtain some quantification of the minimum order required we applied a singular value decomposition (SVD) of the Hankel matrix H, i.e. a matrix consisting of the model impulse responses:

$$H = \begin{vmatrix} M(1) & M(2) & \circ & \circ & & M(p) \\ M(2) & M(3) & \circ & & & \\ \circ & \circ & \circ & & & \circ \\ & & & \circ & & \\ & & & & \circ & \\ & & & & \circ & \circ \\ & & & & & M(2p-1) \end{vmatrix} \qquad (3)$$

where M(i) represents the i-th point of the impulse responses. As indicated by several authors, e.g. VAN ZEE (1981), the pattern of the singular values of the Hankel matrix provides a sound basis for the selection of the model order.
Figure 5 presents the singular value pattern based on the responses of {live steam temperature, steam

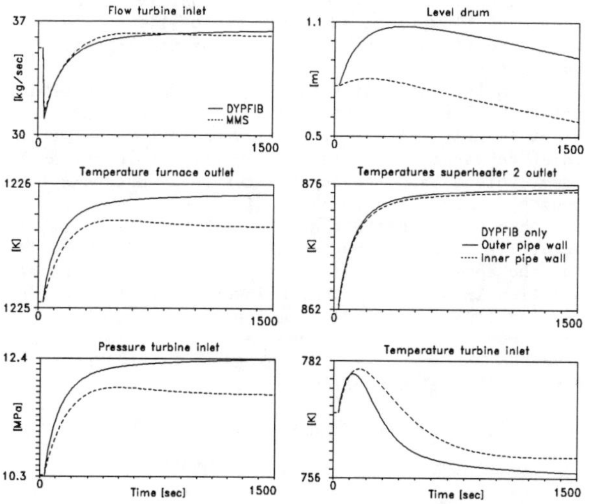

FIGURE 4. Predicted responses to a negative 15% step change in turbine valve position.

pressure, steaming rate, drum level} to an impulse change in {gas mass flow, feed water mass flow, spray water mass flow, turbine valve opening}. The singular values decrease rather steeply with increasing number till approximately number 16, after which the decrease starts to level off. A comparison between the step responses of the non-linear model and those of a linear model of varying order derived from the aforementioned impulse responses by approximate realization, showed no visible differences for model orders 16 and higher. This implies that order reduction, i.e. model simplification, might be possible down to an order of approximately 16.

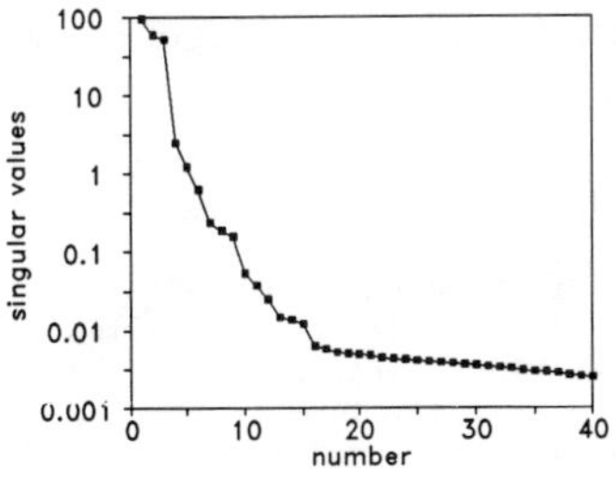

FIGURE 5. Singular value pattern.

4. SENSITIVITY ANALYSYS

MMS modeling is very well suited to study the effect of variations in parameters, notably when using Gear's Stiff integration method and interactive handling of ACSL commands.
Sensitivity analyses were carried out for the following parameter changes:

- A drum volume increase of 50%
- A drum metal mass increase of 50%
- A superheater 1 metal mass decrease of 50%
- A superheater 1 pipe length increase of 50%
- An economizer metal mass decrease of 50%
- An economizer pipe length increase of 50%

The same steady state conditions were used for all these geometric variations.
The transients applied were a positive 1% step in fuel mass flow and a positive step of 1% in turbine valve position. Open loop responses were obtained in both cases.
The simulations indicated that turbine flow, turbine inlet pressure and flue gas temperature are not significantly affected. The drum level and turbine inlet temperature are rather sensitive to changes in drum volume and to superheater metal mass and tube length, as is illustrated in figure 6.
It should be noted that the high frequency effects occurring early in the transients are not sensitive to the applied parameter changes, confirming the assumption in section 3 that a lower order model can be applied (apart from the drum level effects). The high frequency effects are determined by the mass- and momentum balances, while the energy balance accounts for the thermal capacitance effects.

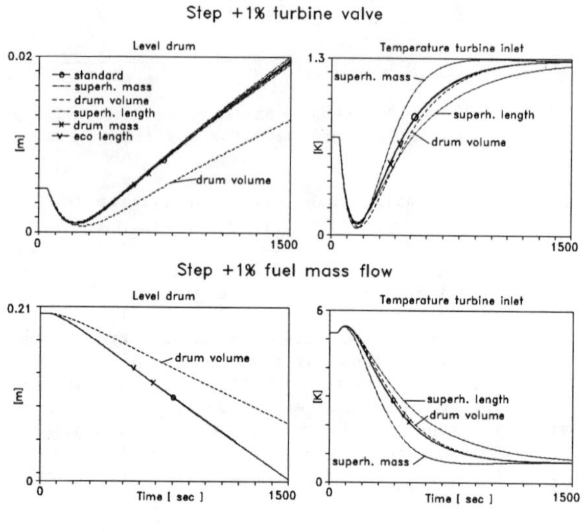

FIGURE 6. Effect of some geometric parameters.

5. CONCLUSIONS AND RECOMMENDATIONS

- MMS yields significant reductions in computing time with respect to the far more detailed DYPFIB code. E.g. a transient lasting 1500 plant seconds MMS requires a simulation time of about 3 minutes on a PC-AT system, as compared to about 90 minutes for the DYPFIB simulation on a mainframe.
- Responses obtained from MMS are generally, except for the drum level response, in fair agreement with those predicted by DYPFIB. Further improvement may be possible by improved steady state tuning of MMS.
- It is recommended that the foregoing conclusion be verified for different boiler designs and fuels.
- In case of a positive outcome of the foregoing recommendation possibilities for further simplification (order reduction) of MMS should be investigated for scoping and in-plant applications.
- On the other hand the incorporation of more detailed component modules (e.g. for evaporator and superheaters) into MMS might be considered for applications requiring a high degree of accuracy of the responses, as e.g. predicting metal temperatures. Such improved modeling appears indispensable for drum level studies.

ACKNOWLEDGEMENT

The authors wish to thank prof. ir. D.G.H. Latzko for his assistance in preparing this paper.

REFERENCES

BRUENS, N.W.S. (1981).
PWR plant and steam generator dynamics.
Ph.D Thesis, Delft University of Technology.

GOEMANS, T. (1972).
Mathematical modelling of pressurizer thermodynamics.
Ph.D Thesis, Delft University of Technology.

HOTTEL, H.C. and SAROFIM, A.F. (1967).
Radiative transfer. Mc Graw-Hill.

LEER, B. van, (1974).
Towards the ultimate conservative scheme. II. Monotonicity and conservation combined in a second order scheme.
Journal of computational physics, 14, 361/370.

LOOIJ, J.M.P. van der (1987).
Dynamic modeling and control of coal fired fluidized bed boilers.
Ph.D Thesis, Delft University of Technology.

MITCHEAL and GAUTHIER
Advanced Continuous Simulation Language,
User Guide/Reference Manual
Fourth Edition, 1986

Modular Modeling System (1985).
A code for the Dynamic Simulation of Fossil and Nuclear Power Plants.
Babcock & Wilcox Co. Theory Manual, 1st Edition, Volume 1,2, Lynchburg, VA

ZEE, G.A van, (1981).
System identification for multivariable control.
Ph.D. Thesis, Delft University Press, Delft.

Simulators VI
© 1989 By The Society for Computer
Simulation International
ISBN 0-911801-51-0

Updating the emergency coolant injection system model for the Pickering NGS A simulator

K.C. Goel, K.S. Lee, R.M. Davis
Instrumentation and Control Department
Design and Development Division - Generation, Ontario Hydro
700 University Avenue Toronto, Ontario M5G 1X6 CANADA

ABSTRACT

Many major modifications are being made to the older nuclear generating stations either to meet improved safety standards or for plant life extension. There is also an ever increasing reliance for operator training on the full scope replica simulators. As a result major updates will be required to many older simulators. However, updating some old simulators poses a great challenge, particularly if their computer systems are obsolete and have limited CPU time and memory to accommodate the updated software. In addition, the simulation software of an old simulator might have already undergone many revisions over the several years of its operation without corresponding updates to the documentation, thereby making it difficult to determine its existing status for the purpose of planning the update work.

This paper describes the approach used in updating the ten-year old Pickering A Simulator which is used to train operators for Ontario Hydro's 4 x 540 MW(e) Pickering Nuclear Generating Station A. The update was performed to reflect the extensive modifications made to the station to improve its Emergency Coolant Injection system. The update work was completed in January 1987 even before the station modifications which were completed on the first unit in April 1987.

INTRODUCTION

Ontario Hydro has four nuclear generating stations already in operation and a fifth one is soon to be in operation. All five of these stations consist of four units of the CANDU Pressurized Heavy Water Reactor (PHWR) design with each unit's capacity ranging from 540 to 880 MW(e). Generally two stations are built at each site, e.g., the Pickering A and B stations are built side by side on the same site and share some major equipment such as the ECI water storage tank, high pressure pumps, Containment vacuum building, etc.

For each of its five nuclear generating stations, Ontario Hydro has a full scope operator training simulator.

The Pickering A Simulator was the first Ontario Hydro simulator and it went in service in 1976. It is a full scale replica of the Unit 1 portion of the Pickering A control room. The simulation software includes models for all the station systems such as the Reactor, Moderator, Heat Transport, Steam, Electrics, Common Processes, Control Computers, etc. (Chou, Stokes and Bereznai 1976). All the software is programmed in Assembler language for the Texas Instruments TI980A computers.

Ontario Hydro updates its simulators regularly to reflect on-going station changes so that operator training is provided on up-to-date simulators. Recently, one of the major modifications made to the Pickering A simulator was the updating of the Emergency Coolant Injection system model.

This paper describes the planning and development of the simulation software for the Pickering A ECI system updates. The difficulties and problems encountered in the various phases of the update work are particularly described. In addition, the approach used in achieving a trouble free integration of the updated software with the rest of the simulator is also described.

Overview of the ECI System Modifications

The ECI system is designed to provide make-up cooling water to the Heat Transport system in the event of a major break in the Heat Transport System piping. Its successful operation is of prime importance to maintain or restore cooling of the fuel, thereby preventing fuel bundle failures due to overheating.

The original ECI system at Pickering A has been vastly modified to improve system availability, effectiveness and operability. [Figure 1].

The old ECI System was designed to inject heavy water from the Moderator System to the Heat Transport System by means of the Moderator System pumps via the Recovery Injection valves.

The new ECI System is designed to inject light water from an elevated ECI water storage tank by means of three 100 percent duty high pressure pumps via the Station Interface Isolation valves and the H_2O injection valves. The ECI storage tank and the three 100 percent high pressure pumps are the same as those used for the twin station Pickering B. Therefore, most of the control for these (including the pump testing facilities) is provided in the Pickering B control room. However, equipment status indication is provided in the Pickering A control room also.

The major instrumentation in the old ECI System was triplicated whereas it is quadruplicated in the new system for sufficient availability. In addition, instrumentation for the detection of in-core breaks (i.e., breaks inside the reactor core, called the Calandria) has been added to improve system effectiveness. The system operation is now fully automatic, whereas manual operator intervention was required to operate the old ECI System after the initial automatic operation for a short period of time.

The ECI System requires periodic testing to ensure that it always meets its design target availability. The testing operations for the new system are more complicated than for the old system. Therefore, simulator training plays a more important role for the new system.

PLANNING

Many difficulties were evident at the very beginning of the project. The major ones are:

(a) Clear description of the scope of the station design changes was not available at the beginning of the update work. This is because the simulator updates were made even before the station modifications were completed so that the simulator could be used to train the operators for commissioning the station modifications.

(b) The simulator software documentation was obsolete because the ten year old model reports were never updated. The only up-to-date source of information available to the modellers was the program listing, which also happened to be in the Assembler language.

(c) Very limited computer memory and execution time was available to accommodate the new software.

(d) None of the people directly involved in the project had previously worked on the Pickering A Simulator. This was a major problem because the modelling practices employed on the Pickering A Simulator are unique and quite different from the modern Ontario Hydro simulators. For example, all other Ontario Hydro simulators are based on Fortran programming on the DEC/VAX-11/785 computers or GOULD/SEL-32 computers. The problem was further compounded because some of the modellers had no prior knowledge of the Assembler language. Of course none of the modellers had any knowledge of the TI specific Assembler language. In addition very limited expertise was available to train and coach the modellers during the course of the project. Thus the modellers had to rely heavily on self study to familiarize themselves with the necessary information, which too, had to be obtained by digging out old memorandums and reports, some of which were also obsolete.

Due to the above difficulties, extreme care was taken in planning the update work. Several meetings of all the people involved in the project were held to define (a) the scope of work, (b) the simplifications required to meet the CPU memory and time constraints, and (c) the division of work responsibilities between the four modellers involved in the development and integration of the updated software. As a result of these meetings, two documents, namely a Model Development Plan and Functional Specifications were prepared which formed the basis for all the development work. These are described below.

Model Development Plan

The Model Development Plan is basically a detailed list of all the station changes which were incorporated in the simulator. It contained a total of 44 design change entries. Due to space limitations, only a sample page of the model development plan is shown in Table 1. In addition to the list of station changes, the model development plan also identified a number of new modules to be created. A very important feature of the model

TABLE 1

Pickering NGS A Simulator ECI Update

A Sample List of Station Design Changes

1. Moderator System

S.No.	Change Made To	Brief Description of Major Changes	Modules	References
M1	Calandria Inlet Valves 3211-CV48, 50, 54, 55	- Added logic to auto close on recovery signal	MV	CD#NA44-3G-63335-155 -157
		- Added PB45 and 47 D, E, F, S on panel 7C and accompanying logic to allow testing of the auto closure logic.	HL	CD-D-44N-63240-1 Sections 4.4, 8.2.11 of (2)
M2	Calandria Outlet Valves 3211-CV2, 4, 26, 27	- Deleted logic to auto open on LOCA	MV	CD#NA44-3G-63335-166
		- Added controller 63210-L1-LIC2 and a control loop selector HS on panel 4D and accompanying logic to facilitate on-power testing of valve controllability.	MV	CD-D-44N-63210-4 Sections 5.3, 8.2.12 of (2)
		- Deleted handswitch 3211-CV2-HS1 used previously for dump port level control during emergency injection. (Panel 4D)	MV	
		- Increased valve status indicating lights on panel 4D	MV	
M3	Dump Tank Outlet Valves 3211-MV9, 10	- Added logic to annunciate "Off-Normal HS" alarm when the valve HS position is turned to "AUTO".	CZ	CD-D-44N-63210-5, 6 Section 5.4 of (2)

development plan is that it also identifies the specific modules (including both new and existing modules) in which each and every station change will be incorporated.

The model development plan was found to be very useful for subsequent discussions and responsibility identification among modellers in the development phase. It was also useful in monitoring the status of the update work at any given time and provided a convenient checklist before starting the integration phase.

Functional Specifications

Due to the limited CPU time and memory available to accommodate the updated software, it was necessary to make some major modelling simplifications without adversely limiting the training capabilities of the simulator. For this purpose, functional specifications were prepared at the beginning of the update work which provided the following information to the modellers:

(a) the major assumptions to be used in modelling;

(b) instructor controlled malfunctions and manipulation to be incorporated in the model to meet the training requirements;

(c) available CPU time and memory including the number of spare locations available in the cross reference (or common database); and

(d) documentation and coding standards required to be consistent with the existing practice for the Pickering A simulator.

Development Facility

Due to limited accessibility to the software development facility at the simulator site, a surplus TI980A computer was acquired from an external vendor and used for developing the new software modules. This temporary development facility was found to be very convenient to the modellers both for familiarizing with the TI operating system and for developing and debugging the new software modules.

MODEL DEVELOPMENT

The model development plan discussed in Section 2.0 identified that 3 new modules had to be created and about 20 existing modules had to be updated. Since the modelling methodologies for the process hydraulics and the control logic are quite different, they are described separately below.

Process Modelling

The process flow diagrams were simplified into a simple schematic diagram [Figure 2] based upon the assumptions given in the functional specifications. This schematic diagram was marked with all the cross-reference labels. In addition tables of input and output labels were prepared. The hydraulics were modelled using the pressure integration method. Then a pseudo code was prepared which could be programmed in the Assembler language. Since the TI980A computer does not directly allow floating point arithmetic, scaling techniques were employed to deal with decimal numbers. Furthermore, since the TI980A is only a 16 bit machine and the use of double precision had to be minimized to conserve computing resources, the scaling technique had to be applied very judiciously to compromise between round-off errors and running the risk of overflows and underflows. This is important because underflows and overflows are not flagged by the operating system during execution and, therefore, can be quite a nuisance to debug. For this purpose, the range of values any variable can take under all conceivable operating conditions, had to be properly estimated for all the variables prior to writing the Assembler code. If the estimated range is too narrow, then underflows and overflows will be encountered during execution. On the other hand, too wide a range will cause large round off errors and may result into other indirect problems such as oscillations and instability. In order to minimize the use of CPU resources, the execution time required by the various Assembler instructions was kept in mind all the time and the use of extended format was minimized. This required the coding to be arranged in a way which does not necessarily follow the rules of structured programming in Fortran.

For offline testing of the new process module, a Fortran program was also prepared and tested on the VAX computer. This is because few tools for testing are available on the TI980A system. This resulted in a considerable saving of the scarce simulator time during testing of the integrated software.

Logic Modelling

Based upon the list of station changes, the corresponding elementary wiring diagrams (EWD's) were marked up to identify the changes. The modules in which the changes were incorporated and the labels which were used in the coding were also marked up on the EWD's. The identification of the labels on the EWD's was important because it provided a clear picture of the grouping of the bit parallel variables which were used extensively to save CPU time and memory. It also facilitated communication among the different modellers so that missing or duplicate labels during integration could be minimized. Our past experience (Davis and Webb 1988; Langan and Poon 1988) shows that an update job of this size creates a lot of problems during integration if the modellers do not communicate frequently during the development phase. Thus, ongoing discussions and regular meetings among the modellers were held throughout the development phase. This type of excellent co-operation among the modellers is considered to be a major factor in achieving a trouble free integration.

After collection of the data, pseudo code was prepared which was then programmed in the Assembler language. To save execution time and memory space, bit parallel logic was used to solve symmetrical logical equations. For bit parallel logic to be used effectively, the equations must be symmetric in form and aligned to corresponding bits. Hence, for equations which were not fully symmetrical, the differences were calculated before the bit parallel operation and dummy variables used to align them symmetrically. Indexed schemes were extensively used in conjunction with bit parallel operations since the three out of four logic used at the Pickering A station falls naturally into this category.

The testing of the logic modules was also done both on the VAX computer in Fortran and on the TI computer in Assembler. This was because the delivery of the TI hardware for testing purposes was delayed considerably. Therefore, to meet the overall schedule, the testing time on the TI system was minimized by doing preliminary testing on the VAX computer which was easily available. Very powerful testing facilities are available on the VAX computer which is a byproduct of our later simulators. In addition, off line testing of the logic modules was also done by integrating all the three new modules.

INTEGRATION AND TESTING

For testing and/or commissioning of the integrated software, Detailed Commissioning Specifications (DCS) and Detailed Commissioning Procedures (DCP) were prepared. The DCP is simply a set of objectives for the operational performance of the ECI system. For the updated software to be in-service all the objectives must be met within the scope of the frozen data and the functional specifications.

The commissioning procedures included testing of all the standard and non-standard operating procedures relevant to the ECI system such as the routine component and logic testing for reliability purposes, the Loss-of-Coolant Accident, the Steam Line Break etc. A total of 72 tests were performed. Any unexpected simulator response during these tests was identified as a "snag".

Due to the care taken in planning the update work and detailed module testing during the development phase, very few snags were encountered during integration of the updated software with the full simulator software and hardware. Most of the snags were of a minor nature and were corrected quickly during the course of testing. Only a few snags requiring tuning of the hydraulic constants required a significant amount of simulator time to be cleared. This was expected since the TI system had no facilities for off-line testing of the hydraulic system. However, due to excellent co-operation among the modellers, even the time required for tuning the hydraulic constants was quite small.

CONCLUSION

Updating the ten year old Pickering A simulator to reflect the ECI system changes at the station even before the changes were implemented at the station was found to be a complex and challenging task. Several problems such as incomplete system design data, obsolete simulator documentation, limited CPU time and memory available to accommodate the updated software, limited software development expertise etc. were encountered. Nevertheless, due to meticulous planning and excellent team co-operation, the project was successfully completed within the specified budget and schedule, with minimum simulator downtime required for installation of the updated software.

ACKNOWLEDGEMENTS

The authors wish to thank the management of Ontario Hydro's Design and Development - Generation Division for their support in the preparation of this paper. The contributions of our colleagues in the Instrumentation and Control Department, the Simulator Services Department and the Eastern Nuclear Training Centre are also gratefully acknowledged.

REFERENCES

Chou, Q.B.; H.W. Stokes; and G.T. Bereznai. 1976. "Modelling and Dynamic Performance of the Pickering Training Simulator". Presented at IAEA/NPPCI Specialists' Meeting on Simulators for Training of Nuclear Power Plant Operators and Technical Staff. Studswick, Sweden.

Davis, R.M. and N.J. Webb. 1988. "Updating a Nuclear Training Simulator". Presented at Summer Computer Simulation Conference, Orlando, Florida, USA.

Langan, M.D. and K.L. Poon. 1988. "Modelling and Commissioning an Emergency Coolant Injection Retrofit of the Bruce A Simulator". Presented at Summer Computer Simulation Conference, Orlando, Florida, USA.

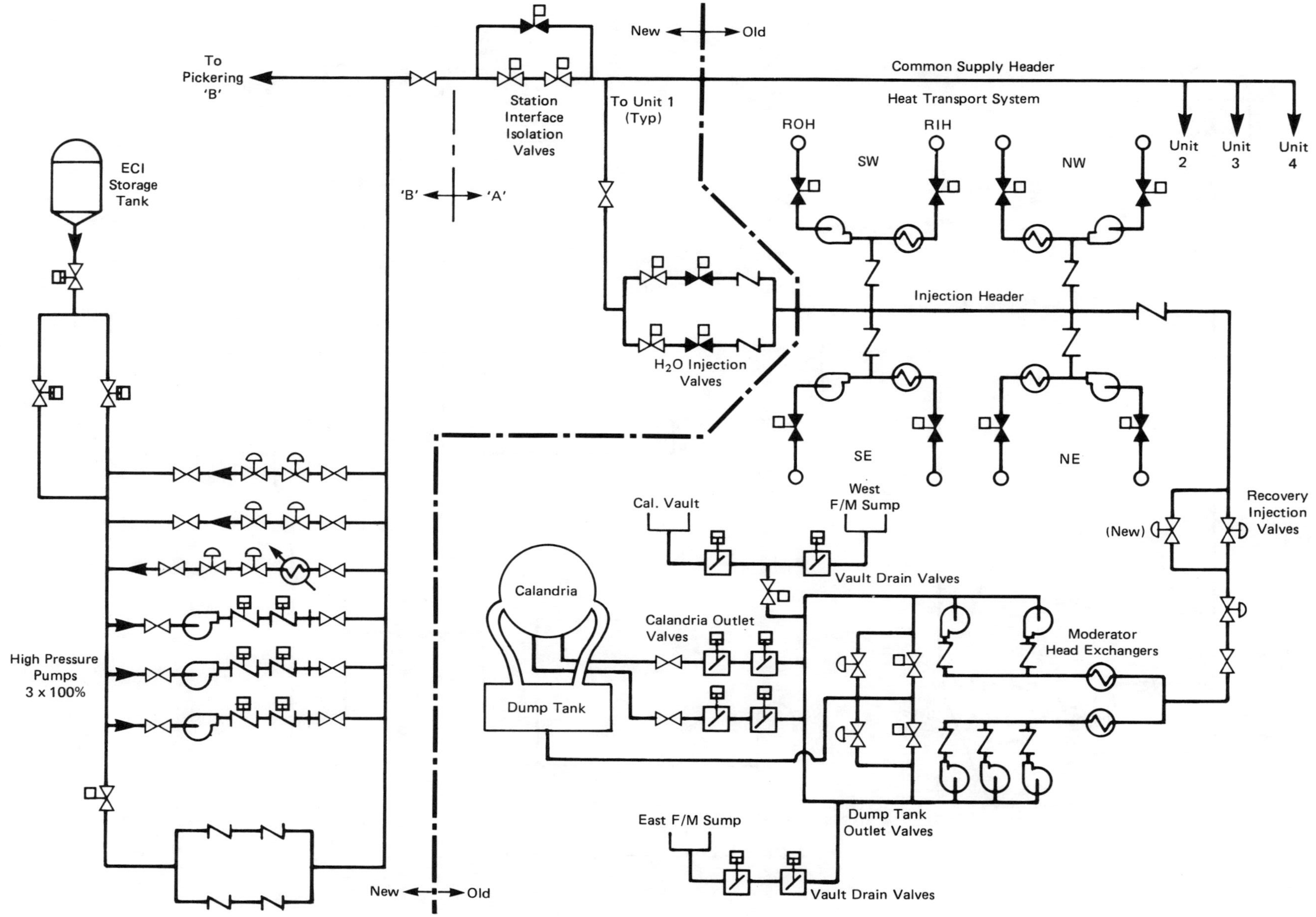

FIGURE 1: Overview of the ECI System Updates

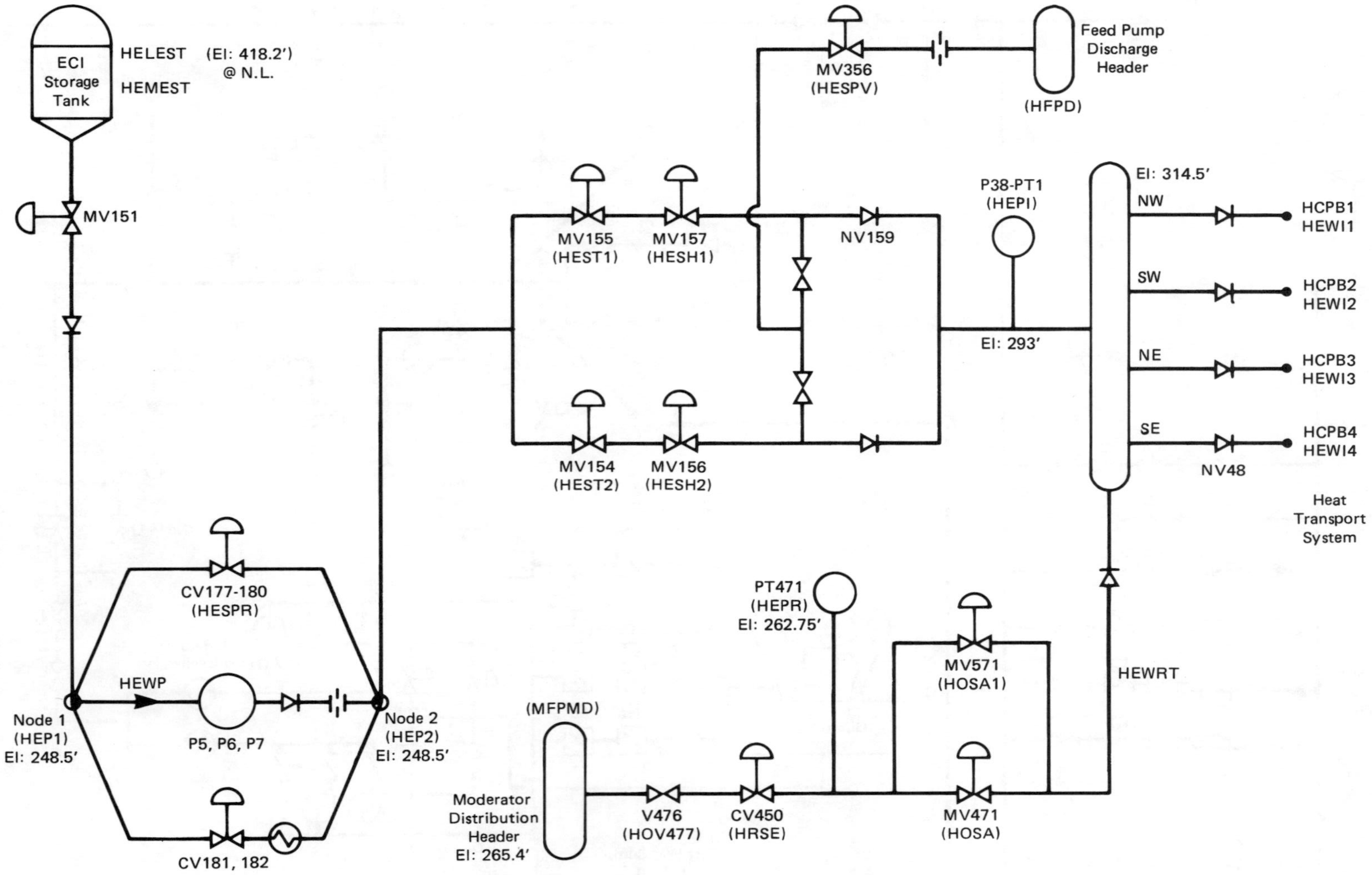

FIGURE 2: Model Schematic Diagram of the ECI System

Simulators VI

ISBN 0-911801-51-0

Engineering simulator development at the Idaho National Engineering Laboratory

E. T. Laats, J. R. Venhuizen, H. Makowitz, D. L. Rittenhouse,
J. D. Burtt, D. G. Bannister, G. L. Mortensen
Idaho National Engineering Laboratory,
EG&G Idaho, Inc.
P.O. Box 1625
Idaho Falls, Idaho 83415-2407 USA

ABSTRACT

The Idaho National Engineering Laboratory (INEL) is pursuing the development of engineering simulator capabilities for use by several agencies of the U.S. Government. These simulators, which are part of the INEL Engineering Simulation Center, provide the highest fidelity simulation for studying augmented nuclear reactor operator training, and for advanced concepts testing as applicable to control room accident diagnosis and management. Two simulator development activities are the subject of this article.

INTRODUCTION

The INEL Engineering Simulation Center was established in April 1988. The goal is to provide a modern, flexible, state-of-the-art simulation facility by unifying the computational simulation hardware and software, the experimental hardware, and the many years of related staff expertise at the Idaho National Engineering Laboratory (INEL). These capabilities have been developed over the past 35 years while designing, building and testing some 52 nuclear reactors at the INEL for the U.S. Government.

These hardware and software technologies are being merged to develop "first-of-its-kind" simulation capabilities. The initial applications of these capabilities are being focused on two areas. First, recent events in the nuclear industry are demanding that the technical community pursue a higher degree of realism from nuclear power plant training simulators within their current limits of applicability, and also that their limits of applicability be extended to simulate severe accident scenarios. This tool will greatly augment the training of plant operators in the recognition and mitigation of accidents. Second, to support the operator in making the most appropriate decisions under extreme stress, emphasis is also being placed on developing techniques that reduce the operator's burden when responding to an event.

This paper will present an overview of the INEL Engineering Simulation Center and discuss two unique simulators being developed to address the two key applications areas.

ENGINEERING SIMULATION CENTER COMPONENTS AND STATUS

The INEL Engineering Simulation Center consists of numerous components, illustrated in Figure 1. The Center consolidates these numerous components that are located at the INEL and other facilities nationwide.

*Work supported by the U. S. Department of Energy, Under Department of Energy contract No. DE-AC07-76ID01570.

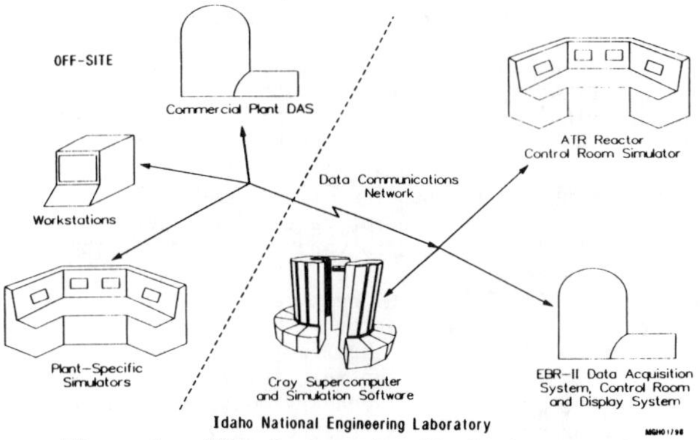

Figure 1. INEL Engineering Simulation Center.

The basic components located at the INEL include

- o the CRAY X-MP/24 supercomputer with its associated software and hardware systems,
- o the Reactor Control Room Simulator at the Advanced Test Reactor (ATR),
- o the Experimental Breeder Reactor-II (EBR-II) with its associated control and monitoring systems, and
- o the INEL site-wide data communications network that ties the INEL components together and provides the high speed links to the off-site components.

The off-site components identified as workstations and plant-specific simulators are located at NRC facilities throughout the U.S.

The Center's supporting staff expertise includes the following areas:

- o thermal hydraulic systems,
- o control and instrumentation systems,
- o operator training and examinations,
- o human factors,
- o probabilistic risk assessment,
- o data communications,
- o simulation hardware,
- o artificial intelligence, and
- o nuclear plant operations.

Taken collectively, these components provide a true engineering simulation testbed.

The hardware within the INEL components is now operational. The data communications networks between the CRAY X-MP/24 and the ATR Reactor Control Room Simulator, and the CRAY X-MP/24 and the EBR-II data acquisition and display system are also operational. All of the simulation and development software systems have progressed at least to the beta testing phase and many are production systems that have been operational for about six years.

TWO KEY APPLICATIONS OF THE INEL ENGINEERING SIMULATION CENTER

The remainder of this article will be devoted to describing two simulator development activities being pursued under the auspices of the INEL Engineering Simulation Center. The first project is an upgrade of the ATR plant simulator into an engineering simulator. The second project is a coupled simulation code/safety parameter display system/expert system for testing the latest advanced reactor controls concepts for the EBR-II.

ATR Reactor Control Room Simulator Upgrade.

The Advanced Test Reactor (ATR), located at the Idaho National Engineering Laboratory (INEL), has been in operation for over 20 years. Since construction in the mid 1960s, this test reactor has been continually used for materials irradiation research with major shutdowns only for scheduled maintenance. Its unique design makes it possible for up to nine experiments at one time to be subjected to very intense radiation for days to months at a time. The ATR is a low temperature (<240°F), low pressure (<390 psig) light water cooled, nuclear reactor with a maximum thermal power of 250 MW. This unique facility has three control rooms to handle the reactivity changes, the flow in the primary and secondary coolant loops, and the nine experiment loops, respectively.

The important role that the ATR fulfills for the U.S. Department of Energy is projected to be required for at least another 20 years. Modernization of various components of the plant is required to provide higher reliability systems for the additional years of operation.[1] The reactor operator's control console and annunciator system are the first components to be redesigned and replaced supporting the updated requirements. A sequence of events recorder is also being added to monitor the status of the plant protection system.

The control room upgrade project created the requirement for a new control room simulator. Since 1966, the ATR reactor operators have had a training simulator available for practicing normal operations such as start-up, shutdown and routine power maneuvers. This simulator, using an analog computer system, was operational until early 1988. A totally new simulator facility was recently completed that is a "face front" duplicate of the updated reactor control room. The new simulator facility was designed to provide the same functionality as the actual control room. Figure 2 shows the new simulator panels currently operational, which will be an exact duplicate of the upgraded control room.

Since the analog computer in the original simulator was also obsolete, the decision was made to use digital computers exclusively, in the new simulator. The simulator uses the same display techniques as the actual control room without the redundant host computer. In addition, an interface computer and physics model computer are used for their respective operations.

The control room simulator was ready for system operational testing in April 1988, some twelve months prior to the scheduled reactor change out, providing necessary operator training and debugging of the new systems. In addition, the simulator provided a test bed for the new displays created for the control room redesign.

The mathematical models being used for the ATR control room simulator are basically the same simplified models used in the previous simulator, i.e., the basic hydraulic requirement is that the coolant remain liquid (no two phase flow phenomena), and the core inlet conditions are input functions (no feedback from core outlet to core inlet through the plant heat exchangers). Single point reactor kinetics with six delay groups are used to calculate the reactor power. An average temperature is computed for each of five lobes (lumped coolant channels) in the core, and combined appropriately for the total reactor outlet temperature. Core pressure drops and quadrant water powers are computed for display purposes only. Rod withdrawal permissive logic and plant protective system logic are simulated on the interface computer. The automatic power control system and sequence of events recorder uses actual hardware for their functions. These models are adequate for normal operational transient training (start-up, shutdown, and power maneuvers).

Recent events in the nuclear industry (e.g., Three Mile Island, Chernobyl) indicate the importance of training operators with a high degree of realism for severe accident scenarios. To provide the range of fidelity required for this training, the ATR simulator software for the core thermal hydraulics and nuclear power calculation was replaced by the world renowned RELAP5 simulation code[2]. The RELAP5 code resides on the CRAY X-MP/24 super-computer located some 50 miles from the simulator. The current data link is via a statistical multiplexer over telephone lines (9600 baud), with plans for a fiber optic link in the early summer of 1989.

The real genius in this hardware strategy comes from using the ATR reactor control room simulator to handle all of the operator input, output and display (graphics) tasks, and using the RELAP5 code on the CRAY supercomputer only for the thermal-hydraulic model solutions. This technique presently requires the amount of data exchanged between the CRAY supercomputer and the simulator to be only a few variables, i.e., the RELAP5 code gets the net reactivity due to control rod motion from the simulator and outputs the power and core thermal-hydraulic conditions to the simulator. These data are exchanged ten times per second. This configuration was demonstrated in September 1988. The goal for the final operational system is to provide full operator controls and greatly enhanced ATR Simulator/RELAP5 data exchanges by September 1989. Only then will the system have reached its full potential.

Limited benchmark studies have been conducted using this simulation environment, which included normal operational transients. With no "fine tuning" of the RELAP5 model, the timing and magnitude of the older simulator's predictions have been overlaid by RELAP5. This result adds considerable confidence to the RELAP5 prediction since the older simulator has been continuously benchmarked over the past 20 years for these operational transients.

EBR-II Advanced Reactor Control Systems Simulation.

A cooperative project is underway between EG&G Idaho and Argonne National Laboratory - West (ANL-W) to demonstrate a futuristic simulation capability. A tightly coupled transient analysis system is being developed that consists of four major components: the Experimental Breeder Reactor - II (EBR-II), the DSNP simulation code[3] as it is used to model the EBR-II,

Figure 2. New ATR Control Room Simulator.

an expert system and other A/I tools being developed for recognition of accidents in the EBR-II, and an advanced safety parameter display system.

Figure 3 illustrates the present coupling of the components. The two simulation codes (DSNP and the expert system) reside on the two processor CRAY X-MP/24 computer, which provides a faster-than-real-time simulation and concurrently a situation diagnosis capability. The safety parameter display system resides on a Sun Microsystems workstation that has local compute and color graphics output capabilities. These systems are then coupled with the EBR-II data acquisition system that provides real-time plant data to the simulation and display systems. In return, the coupled system provides feedback to the control room operators and the workstations at the EBR-II.

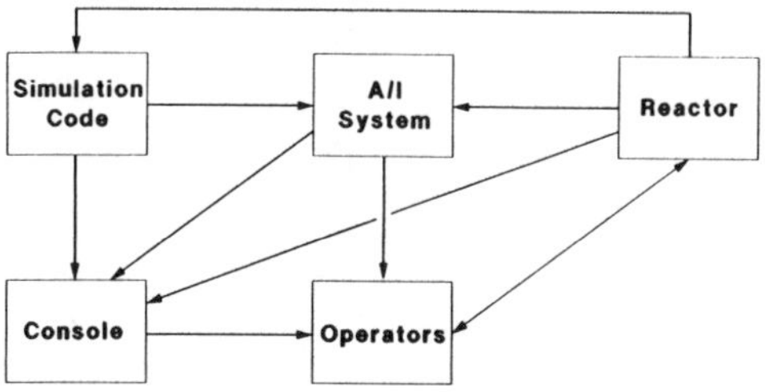

Figure 3. EBR-II Advanced Reactor Controls Systems Development Testbed Prototype.

SUMMARY

The need to increase the realism of nuclear power plant simulators and to reduce reactor operator burden has led to the establishment of the INEL Engineering Simulation Center in April 1988. Two major activities reported in this article are well underway that include the ATR simulator upgrade project and an advanced plant control systems development project. Both projects demonstrate prototype "first-of-its-kind" simulation tools.

NOTICE

ACKNOWLEDGMENTS

This paper represents the diligent work of many people from many organizations, in particular, the U.S. Department of Energy, the Argonne National Laboratory - West, and EG&G Idaho, Inc. The authors wish to gratefully acknowledged these people for their contributions to the establishment of the INEL Engineering Simulation Center.

REFERENCES

1. J. R. Venhuizen and E. T. Laats, "Development Of A Full Scope Reactor Engineering Simulator," Proceedings of the 1988 Summer Computer Simulation Conference, Seattle, Washington, July 25-28, 1988.

2. V. H. Ransom, et al., "RELAP5/MOD2 Code Manual," NUREG/CR-4312, August 1985.

3. D. Saphier, "The Simulation Language of DSNP: Dynamic Simulation for Nuclear Power-plants (User Manual)," ANL-CT-20, Rev. 3.4, December 1983.

Simulators VI
© 1989 By The Society for Computer
Simulation International
ISBN 0-911801-51-0

Engineering simulator applications to emergency response training*

R. J. Beelman M. A. King F. S. Jaggar
Idaho National Engineering Laboratory
EG&G Idaho, Inc.
Idaho Falls, Idaho

G. W. Bethke
COMEX Corporation
Olalla, Washington

ABSTRACT

The Idaho National Engineering Laboratory has recently conducted three comprehensive severe accident drill scenarios at the U.S. Nuclear Regulatory Commission Operations Center in Washington, D.C. Developed on a RELAP5 based engineering simulator, each scenario resulted in severe core damage with significant offsite release. During each scenario actual emergency procedures were implemented in a representative fashion and realistic complications consistent with the initiating events were introduced. The drill controllers fulfilled all licensee, federal, state and local counterpart functions and also simulated political, media and public affairs liaison. These technically demanding drills are clearly beyond the capability of present day replica simulators and have been instrumental in enhancing the technical support capability and overall emergency response preparedness of the Nuclear Regulatory Commission.

INTRODUCTION

In response to its legislative mandate to ensure the public safety by providing technical support backup and oversight to U.S. nuclear plant licensees during abnormal transients, the U.S. Nuclear Regulatory Commission (USNRC) periodically conducts training exercises to evaluate and enhance its emergency response preparedness. In the aftermath of the Three Mile Island accident the need to expand the scope of training to encompass "beyond" design basis accidents (DBAs) was apparent. The Idaho National Engineering Laboratory (INEL) has recently conducted three technically demanding beyond DBA drills at the USNRC Operations Center in Washington, D.C. The purpose was to assist the NRC in its continuing effort to upgrade its ability to respond to such emergencies. The scenarios were developed using the RELAP5 engineering simulator capability on the INEL Nuclear Plant Analyzer (NPA) [1,2,3].

The three scenarios consisted of an unisolable main steam line break (MSLB) with progressive steam generator tube rupture (SGTR) in a Babcock and Wilcox (B&W) design, a loss of feedwater (LOFW) anticipated transient without scram (ATWS) in a Westinghouse design, and a turbine header break with failure to isolate in a Combustion Engineering (CE) design. During each scenario actual emergency procedures were implemented in a representative fashion and realistic complications consistent with the initiating events were introduced. Each succeeding scenario escalated in severity, resulting in successively more severe core damage with significantly greater offsite releases, in order to progressively challenge the organizational, procedural and technical interdependence of the NRC support teams. Information relative to plant status was taken from a computer graphic display and communicated to the NRC Operations Center in a manner identical to that employed by nuclear plant licensees during an actual event. The drill controllers, consisting of a thermal-hydraulic analyst, an operator licensing examiner, a radiological consultant and several support personnel, all former operators, fulfilled all licensee, federal, state and local counterpart functions, and also simulated congressional, gubernatorial and public affairs interface and news media liaison functions. Actual emergency plans were followed using prevailing real time plant meteorological data. These technically demanding drill scenarios are clearly beyond the capability of present day replica simulators. This paper describes the application of an engineering simulator to the development and conduct of technically accurate severe accident scenarios for emergency response training.

*Work supported by the U.S. Nuclear Regulatory Commission, Office of Nuclear Regulatory Research, under DOE Contract No. DE-AC07-76ID01570.

ENGINEERING SIMULATOR DESCRIPTION

The distinguishing characteristic of an engineering simulator is the ability to mechanistically predict with high fidelity the phenomena based response of a reactor plant over the range of plant conditions expected during both anticipated and abnormal transients for any arbitrary set of initial and time varying boundary conditions. At the heart of the INEL engineering simulator is the ability to interact online with the advanced RELAP5 thermal-hydraulic computer code, while observing simulated plant response via a color graphic display schematic. This capability allows online imposition of component failures and interactive simulation of corresponding operator actions thereby enabling the development of high fidelity emergency response training scenarios.

Unlike a replica simulator which is plant specific, the RELAP5 based INEL engineering simulator allows transient simulation of any reactor plant for which a valid RELAP5 input model exists. The code models multiphase flow of fluids in piping networks; heat transfer between the fluid, the fuel, heat exchangers and structural components; reactivity feedback effects between the fuel, the fluid, control rods and boron in the reactor core; and control system interactions with system components. RELAP5/MOD2 [3], the latest released version, solves coupled transient two-phase hydrodynamic, multi-region heat conduction and space-independent neutronic equation sets formulated on a one-dimensional, two-velocity, nonequilibrium flow model. The hydrodynamic model also transports and accounts for the effects of noncondensibles and boron solute. The constitutive package uses mechanistic correlations for interphase mass, energy and momentum transfer, convective heat transfer, wall drag, form induced head loss and hydrodynamic choking.

The code provides process component input models for modelling piping networks, plenums, pumps, valves, tees, turbines, accumulators, steam separators, point reactor kinetics, control systems, actuation signals and structural component mass. The code also allows interactive manipulation of process component models enabling automatic or manual rate-actuation-modulation-override online control of simulated reactor plant components to the same extent provided an operator in a reactor plant control room. Additionally, this capability allows the user to introduce simulated malfunctions online. Interactive RELAP5 input models have been developed for each of the major U.S. pressurized water-cooled nuclear reactor (PWR) designs.

NUCLEAR PLANT ANALYZER DESCRIPTION

The RELAP5 transient simulation results are displayed in a coherent graphical fashion on the Nuclear Plant Analyzer (NPA). The NPA is a computer graphics based reactor safety analysis tool developed at the INEL to assist an analyst in simulating and evaluating the transient behavior of nuclear power plants [5]. The NPA integrates advanced reactor safety codes with online computer graphics routines allowing interactive reactor plant transient simulation and online analysis of results, or replay of past simulations, by means of graphic displays. NPA interactive simulation allows the user to view the results of a RELAP5 calculation online and to simultaneously exercise user provided interactive input modelling features to affect the course of the simulation as the calculation advances. The replay capability allows the user to review the results of a previous calculation by redisplaying the data at a user selectable rate, equal to, faster or slower than real time, and allows him to move forward or backward in the calculation at will. Both modes allow online plotting of parameters.

The results of the thermal-hydraulic calculation are superimposed on a static plant display schematic which is animated by online color-graphic processing techniques. User selectable color-graphic display techniques have been developed to illustrate process instrumentation readouts and safety parameter display systems (SPDS), void profile and mass distribution, hydrodynamic flow regime, fluid thermodynamic state (i.e., subcooled, saturated, superheated), fuel rod status and stored energy, collapsed and two-phase mixture levels, and simulated plant component status. These color-graphic schemes are overlaid on a static schematic derived from the corresponding input model nodalization. The juxtaposition of calculated process parameter readouts and color-graphically illustrated thermal-hydraulic conditions allows the user to introduce malfunctions interactively, observe and interpret simulated plant response online, and implement emergency procedures interactively, as the calculation advances, based upon analogous information available to a reactor plant operator under similar circumstances [6]. This capability enables the development of high fidelity emergency response training scenarios.

SCENARIO DEVELOPMENT

Once a candidate nuclear power plant has been identified, actual plant specific emergency operating procedures (EOPs) are acquired. A review of the applicable Final Safety Analysis Report (FSAR), Licensee Event Reports (LERs) and EOPs ensues from the perspective of the degree of core damage desired to identify limiting safety analysis concerns, plant specific performance peculiarities, and procedural interface considerations. A plausible initiating event is then selected and scoping calculations are undertaken to simulate best estimate plant response. Challenges to engineered safety features (ESFs), quantification of safety margins, and reliance on operator intervention are assessed. An analysis of the extent to which ESFs need to be compromised to achieve the desired plant vulnerability is completed. The transient simulation is then begun in earnest on the NPA. Procedural deficiencies, operator errors, equipment availabilities, malfunctions and power outages are exploited during the transient simulation in introducing complications consistent with the initiating event as a means of effecting the multiple failures necessary to penetrate the safety in depth provided by the design basis envelope. Once completed, the thermal-hydraulic calculation provides the source term and event sequence to develop the radiological scenario.

For the scenario to be realistic and proceed as planned, eventualities arising from NRC inquiries and recommendations must be anticipated and explanations for simulated course of action must be justifiable. Sensitivity studies are undertaken to formulate advance response contingencies in order to avoid introducing artificialities. Painstaking research and frequent controller collaboration are required during scenario development to ensure fidelity.

CONDUCT OF EXERCISE

For the purpose of conducting a drill, an NPA workstation, linked by high speed telecommunications to a mainframe computer at the INEL, is set up in an isolated area of the Operations Center complex in Washington, D.C., rife with phone circuits. The previously calculated scenario is then played back in real time and viewed by the controllers on the NPA display, which serves as the focal point of drill coordination efforts. Initial Operations Center notification of the simulated licensee unusual event is communicated to the drill Duty Officer over a local phone circuit bridged to the Emergency Notification System (ENS) switchboard. After an initial briefing by the drill Duty Officer, the technical support teams establish counterpart communications with the drill control center over the ENS circuit and Health Physics Network (HPN). Each of the three key controllers assumes responsibility for all licensee, federal, state or local counterpart functions within his area of expertise, armed with a prepared and rehearsed script and advance technical information. In response to NRC inquiries concerning plant status or radiological consequences, calculated process parameter values are read from the NPA display, depicting the course of the transient, and dose rates are taken from dispersion charts appropriate to the prevailing site winds and stability class. The data are then relayed over the ENS or HPN circuit in a manner identical to that employed by licensees during an actual event. NPA color graphic display depictions enable capsule analyses simulating licensee technical support activities. In responding to NRC inquiries during the exercise controllers improvise background information, drawing from their extensive operations backgrounds and previous drill experience, adding realism to the scenario. Support personnel inject preplanned political and media commentary during the scenario appropriate to the event sequence.

SCENARIO DESCRIPTION

The three severe accident drill scenarios consisted of an unisolable MSLB with progressive SGTR in a B&W design, a LOFW-ATWS in a Westinghouse design and a turbine header break with common mode failure to isolate in a CE design. Abbreviated event sequences for the three scenarios are provided in Tables 1, 2 and 3.

Table 1. EVENT SEQUENCE FOR JANUARY 1986 EXERCISE

Vendor: Babcock & Wilcox
Type: 177 FA class PWR (2x4)

Event: unisolable MSLB outside containment with progressive SGTR

Initial conditions:
full power operation

Equipment status:
1 HPI pump out of service

Time	Event Description	Comments
0:00:00	MSLB with SGTR in SG-A	1 tube ruptured
0:00:03	SLBIC actuation; SCRAM	Main condenser isolated, SG-B relieves through ADVs to atmosphere.
0:00:18	Turbine EFW actuation	3 tubes ruptured
0:00:54	Manual SI actuation	(P_{RCS} < 1800 psig) 1 HPIP fails to start 1 HPIP remaining
0:02:25	All diesels started and ready	SG-B at low level limit 5 tubes ruptured
0:03:20	Pressurizer empty	Upper head starts to void
0:05:00	Operator trips one RCP per loop	2 min trip window exceeded
	"ALERT" declared	
0:09:20	Primary saturated	
0:10:00	"SITE AREA EMERGENCY" declared	10 tubes now broken.
0:25:00	Drawing main condenser vacuum	15 tubes now broken
0:30:00	Emergency cooldown begun (250F/hr)	SG-B TBV in manual
0:38:20	Accumulators isolated	Isolation valve closed. Breaker relocked open
0:40:00	Normal cooldown begun (100F/hr)	P_{RCS} < 500 psi
0:48:20	Running "B" RCP seizes cracking HPI injection nozzle	high loop void fraction
1:00:00	Loss of offsite power	No RCPs
	Vital bus powering only available HPIP grounded	No HPI pumps
1:20:00	Operator throttles EFW	SG depressurizing
1:21:40	Core heatup begins	
1:26:40	"GENERAL EMERGENCY" declared	
1:30:00	PORV and high point vents opened; RCS depressurizes	CETC > 1200 F
1:45:00	LPI injection; PORV closed	CETC < 700 F
2:00:00	Reflood complete	Transition to DHRS. 5% cladding oxidation

Table 2. EVENT SEQUENCE FOR APRIL 1987 EXERCISE

Vendor: Westinghouse
Type: 3-loop PWR

Event: LOFW-ATWS

Initial conditions:
- full power operations
- SG levels low in the programmed band due to feedwater transient
- Rod control system in MANUAL for surveillance testing

Equipment status:
- Turbine AFW pump down for maintenance
- One charging pump down for maintenance

Time	Event Description	Comments
0:00:00	Both MFPs trip; MDAFPs start	Heater drain pumps cavitating
	Turbine trip but no Rx SCRAM	ATWS - SCRAM brks. don't open
0:00:30	ATWS recognized by operator	
0:01:00	SGs noted to be dry	AFW cannot makeup demand
	RO begins driving rods in manually	
	Both diesels start	
0:01:30	Primary "solid"	insufficient TBV capacity
	Primary pressure offscale high	
0:02:00	Rx SCRAM	Rod drive MG sets de-energized P_{RCS} > 3200 psig T_{RCS} = 656 F
	Containment radiation alarm	Quench tank blow out
	RO isolates SG-B	SG-B PORV fails to close
	All SGs depressurizing (dry)	TBV in T_{AVE} control mode
	SGTR in SG-A	1 tube; > 2800 psid
	Fuel clad rupture	1% gap release
0:02:08	RCPs tripped	Lack of adequate subcooling
	SI actuation (high Rx bldg P)	P_{RCS} > HPI shutoff head
	CCP aligned to borate primary	Bad valve lineup
0:02:45	FW throttled to 100 gpm each to SG's A and C	dry SG criteria
0:05:00	MSIV-A closed	SG-A tube rupture detected
	Pressurizer SRV leaking	Valve fails to reseat
	"SITE AREA EMERGENCY" declared	re: "Release path to atmosphere"
0:14:00	1 charging pump fails	Improper alignment earlier
0:15:00	Cooldown begun(>100 F/hr)	200 gpm to SG-C 100 gpm to SG-A
0:26:00	Core heatup begins	
0:30:00	Loss of Off-Site Power	1 MDAFP; no CCPs P_{RCS} > HPI shut off head
	DG-A powering Bus E-1 DG-B repulsed from Bus E-2	grounded bus

Time	Event Description	Comments
0:36:40	CSF yellow path (core cooling)	CETC > 700 F
0:45:00	Core heatup abated	AFW maximized
1:00:00	STATION BLACKOUT	Bus E-1 fire racking in HPIP bkr.
1:06:40	"GENERAL EMERGENCY" declared	Second core heatup begins
1:30:00	Gas turbine generator on Bus E-2	MDAFW-B and 1 CCP available
	High containment H_2	Cladding oxidation
	Feeding SG-C at 400 gpm	RCS depressurizes rapidly
1:33:20	HPI injection begins	1 HPI train
1:40:00	Core exit T/C > 1500 F	Substantial core damage
1:41:40	Core quench	Vessel inventory increasing
1:46:40	100 F/hr cooldown in progress	
3:00:00	Exercise completed	15% Zr oxidized; massive releases

Table 3. EVENT SEQUENCE FOR MAY 1988 EXERCISE

Vendor: Combustion Engineering
Type: 2700 MW class PWR (2x4)

Event: Unit 1 - Turbine header break with failure of MSIVs to close
Unit 2 - Loss of main feedwater due to Unit 1 steam line break

Initial conditions:
Units 1&2 at full power

Equipment status:

HPI pump 13 out of service	-motor rewind
CCP 13 out of service	-seal replacement
1 PORV (ERV-404) out of service	-leaking -block valve tagged shut
AFW pump 23 out of service	-wearing ring maintenance -Unit 2 in 72 hr action statement

Time	Event Description	Comments
0:00:00	Turbine header break	MSIVs intermediate Both SGs blow down
0:00:05	SGIS actuation	MFPs trip insufficient steam pressure to run turbine driven AFPs
0:00:15	SI actuation	1710 psig CCPs, HPI & LPI pumps start letdown isolates
0:00:24	Unit 1 HPI injection starts	1250 psig
0:01:20	Unit 1 accumulators inject	200 psig
	Unit 1 recriticality	approx. 10% full power CCP suction shifted to BAST cladding failure due to DNB 2-3% FP gas release
0:02:00	Flooding in the turbine building	cooling water line break
0:03:00	Unit 2 LOFW	both MFPs trip
0:07:00	Unit 1 subcritical	

Time	Event Description	Comments
0:16:00	Fire in vital bus 11(ZA)	bus grounded; deenergized neither PORV operable 1 CCP, 1 HPI available no AFP available
	"ALERT" declared	
0:20:00	Unit 1 "solid"	SRV begins cycling
0:30:00	"SITE AREA EMERGENCY" declared	AFP 21 fails

****

1:00:00	Operations Center manned	Duty Officer Briefing

****

1:05:00	Flooding controlled	
	Unit 2 cooldown commenced	Rescue party enters turbine building 3 trapped under wreckage 12 fatalities
1:30:00	Vital bus 11(ZA) restored	CCPs 11 & 12 operational
	Unit 1 once-thru-cooling initiated	PORV 402 opened PORV 404 fails to open Unit 1 depressurizes to sat'n, then repressurizes above HPI shut off head
2:00:00	Operator fails to switch Unit 1 CCP suction from BAST	Both CCPs fail
	Unit 1 repressurizes to 2400 psig	
	"GENERAL EMERGENCY" declared	containment leak detected
3:00:00	MSIV 12 closed	
	Degraded AFW initiated to SG 12	AFP 13 damaged due to runout Unit 1 depressurizes rapidly
3:10:00	Unit 1 core heatup begins	core uncovers resulting in 20-30% core damage
3:30:00	Unit 1 HPI injection starts	core quench causes repressurization above HPI shutoff head
4:00:00	Drill terminated	40-50% core damage

SUMMARY AND CONCLUSIONS

A means of developing and conducting technically accurate severe accident scenarios for emergency response training has been demonstrated. These challenging engineering simulator scenarios are clearly beyond the capability of present day replica simulators. This capability has been developed to assist the USNRC in its continuing effort to upgrade its emergency response preparedness. Future development will extend the capability into the realm of accident management.

ACKNOWLEDGMENTS

The authors wish to gratefully acknowledge Messrs. Ray Priebe, John Hickman and Don Marksberry of the USNRC for their continuing support of this effort. We also wish to thank Mr. Tom Laats of EG&G Idaho for his administrative and logistical support.

NOTICE

REFERENCES

1. "Engineering Simulator for Nuclear Reactor System Analysis", D. G. Hall, F. Aguilar, R. J. Beelman, R. J. Wagner, Computers in Engineering 1983, ASME International Computers in Engineering Conference, Chicago, IL, August, 1983, American Society of Mechanical Engineers, New York, N.Y.

2. E. T. Laats, et al, User's Manual for the U.S. Nuclear Regulatory Commission's Nuclear Plant Analyzer, EGG-RTH-7515, February 1987, EG&G Idaho, Inc., Idaho Falls, Idaho.

3. "The Nuclear Plant Analyzer - A Proven Engineering Simulator", R. J. Beelman, E. T. Laats, R. J. Wagner, Transactions of The 1985 Summer Computer Simulation Conference, Chicago, Illinois, July 22-24, 1985, Society for Computer Simulation, San Diego, CA.

4. V. H. Ransom, et al., RELAP5/MOD2 Code Manual, NUREG/CR-4312, EGG-2396, August 1985, EG&G Idaho, Inc., Idaho Falls, Idaho.

5. "Nuclear Plant Simulation Using the Nuclear Plant Analyzer," R. J. Beelman, E. T. Laats and R. J. Wagner, Proceedings Of The International Conference On Power Plant Simulation, Cuernavaca, Mexico, November 1984.

6. "Interactive Operator Guideline Evaluation Using RELAP5", R. J. Beelman and J. N. Curtis, Transactions of the American Nuclear Society, 45, 1983 ANS Winter Meeting, San Francisco, CA, November 1983, American Nuclear Society, La Grange Park, IL.

Simulators VI
© 1989 By The Society for Computer
Simulation International
ISBN 0-911801-51-0

Modular high-temperature gas-cooled reactor core heatup accident simulations

S. J. Ball and J. C. Conklin
Oak Ridge National Laboratory
Oak Ridge, Tennessee 37831-6010

ABSTRACT

The design features of the modular high-temperature gas-cooled reactor (HTGR) have the potential to make it essentially invulnerable to damage from postulated core heatup accidents. Simulations of long-term loss-of-forced-convection (LOFC) accidents, both with and without depressurization of the primary coolant and with only passive cooling available to remove afterheat, have shown that maximum core temperatures stay below the point at which fuel failures and fission product releases are expected. Sensitivity studies also have been done to determine the effects of errors in the predictions due both to uncertainties in the modeling and to the assumptions about operational parameters.

INTRODUCTION

This paper describes analyses of postulated long-term core heatup scenarios for which no active cooling systems are used to remove afterheat following the accidents. The simulation models the U. S. Department of Energy (DOE) reference design of a standard modular HTGR (MHTGR). This work, sponsored by the Nuclear Regulatory Commission (NRC) to assist in the preliminary determinations of licensability of the design, included a detailed review and appraisal of the DOE Preliminary Safety Information Document (PSID) for the MHTGR. More details on ORNL code development and analysis descriptions may be found in a supporting report (Ball and Conklin, 1989). The purpose of this paper is to give an overview of the code and the methodology used and to describe the significant features and consequences of the postulated accident sequences.

MODULAR HTGR DESCRIPTION

The design features of the MHTGR are shown in Fig. 1. Each of four reactor modules consists of a tall cylindrical ceramic core with a thermal power rating of 350 MW, and a single once-through steam generator with a superheater to provide high-temperature (538 °C, 1000 °F) steam to a steam header and turbine plant common to all four modules. The rated output of the four-module plant is 540 MW(e), with a net thermal efficiency of 39%. The high-pressure helium coolant is driven downward through the core by a single motor-driven circulator. A smaller-capacity circulator-heat exchanger loop, the shutdown cooling system (SCS) located within the reactor vessel, is used for decay heat removal during maintenance. In cases for which neither the main nor the SCS loop is available, afterheat is removed by the passive, safety-grade air-cooled reactor cavity cooling system (RCCS), which is in operation at all times, and which does not require any operator or automatic actuation. There is no conventional containment building, since the multilayered silicon carbide coatings on the microscopic fuel particles are claimed by DOE to be a sufficient containment barrier.

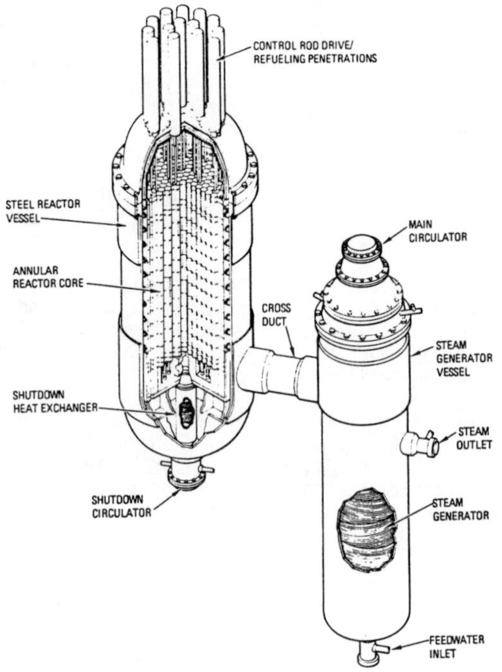

Fig. 1. MHTGR nuclear steam supply module.

MORECA CODE DESCRIPTION

The MORECA code was developed at ORNL to perform independent analyses for the NRC of a broad range of MHTGR long-term core heatup accident scenarios. MORECA is an outgrowth of an earlier NRC/ORNL code (ORECA) which has been in use at ORNL and elsewhere since 1975 (Ball, 1976). ORECA has been utilized in accident studies requiring core thermal analysis of the Fort St. Vrain (FSV) HTGR, the 2240-MW(t) HTGR design by DOE, and several other HTGR designs. ORECA-FSV has been partially verified by comparisons with operating data and benchmark calculations with similar codes developed by General Atomics (GA, the vendor). Verification of other versions of ORECA has been limited to comparisons with GA and Brookhaven National Laboratory (BNL) code calculations. These activities are continuing to verify model applicability to wider classes of transients and accidents.

The MORECA model for the core conduction and convection heat transfer uses a point heat capacity node for each of the 66 fuel and 139 reflector elements (vs one node per 7-element region in ORECA) in each of the 14 axial regions. The core is thus represented by 2870 nodes. This fine structure is required for accurate predictions of fuel failure because of the high sensitivity of low fuel failure rates to time-at-temperature transients near 1600 °C, which is a nominal limit set for maximum core temperatures. This structure also allows for investigations of azimuthal asymmetry, a feature that other current MHTGR core dynamics codes do not have.

Variable core thermal properties supplied by GA were used for the reference case calculations. These properties are functions of both temperature and irradiation. Fully-irradiated thermal properties are used for the fuel, the inner reflector, and the ring of outer reflector elements adjacent to the fuel. Currently, the MORECA model does not include effects of annealing, which increases the thermal conductivity of the fuel and adjacent reflectors as the core heats up during hypothetical accidents.

Coolant flow in the core is modeled over the full ranges expected in both normal operation and accidents, including pressurized and depressurized, forced and natural circulation, upflow and downflow, and turbulent and laminar flow. Flow in each of the fuel elements is modeled explicitly. Flow in the inner and outer reflectors is assumed to be uniformly distributed in the spaces between blocks.

Other major features of the current MORECA model are as follows:

1) The core barrel and vessel are each represented by 7 axial and 4 radial (quadrants) nodes, plus nodes corresponding to the regions opposite the inlet and outlet plenums. Coverplate failure is not an issue here as it was in earlier HTGR designs because the shields are made of the high-temperature material Alloy 800 instead of carbon steel. Insulation resistance and radiation shielding of the upper plenum insulation cover area is also modeled. The safety issue of interest here is the tradeoff for LOFC accidents between the needs to remove afterheat from the core through the vessel, primarily by radiation to the RCCS, and to keep the vessel temperatures below ASME code limits. Optimum placement of insulation is complicated by the fact that the maximum temperatures during postulated heatup accidents are in different regions for the pressurized and depressurized heatups.

2) The reactor cavity cooling system (RCCS) model incorporates detailed heat transfer and natural circulation cooling calculations for panel nodes corresponding to adjacent vessel nodes. Since the RCCS simulation is unique, it is described in more detail in the next section.

3) A model for the shutdown cooling system (SCS) is included in MORECA but is not used in the core heatup scenarios presented here. Use of the SCS model is of particular interest for investigating scenarios in which forced circulation flow is restored following long heatup periods during which no circulation is available. Typically in HTGR designs, flow restart scenarios can become operation limiting situations for fear of damage to components downstream of the hot core outlet gases. While the SCS inlet path has been designed to withstand high temperatures, detailed calculations are needed to determine safety margins.

REACTOR CAVITY COOLING SYSTEM

Description

For all reactor operating conditions, the reactor vessel (RV) will transfer heat by radiation and natural convection through the reactor cavity to the RCCS panels (Fig. 2), where the heated air flow inside these panels is induced by buoyant forces (the chimney effect). The RCCS has no moving parts.

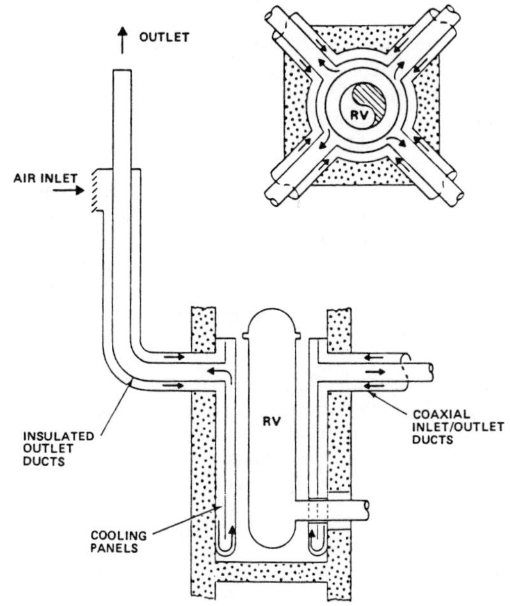

Fig. 2. Passive air-cooled RCCS.

There are four quadrants of RCCS panels each with an active heat transfer length of approximately 17 m. There also are four inlet/outlet structures with coaxial ducts, where the inner duct carries the hotter air from the reactor cavity and the outer duct carries the cooler ambient air. The height of the inlet/outlet ducts is approximately 33 m above the panels. Redundancy is provided by interconnecting ducts and plenums to ensure that a natural convection flow of ambient air is available at all times.

Analysis

The equations governing the air flow and the air heat transfer in the RCCS are coupled. Further coupling via radiation and convection occurs by the transfer of heat from the outer surface of the RV to the outer surface of the RCCS panels. For dynamic modeling of the heat transfer process, the simplifying assumption is made that there is negligible thermal and mass inertia on the air side relative to the thermal inertia of the metal panels. The use of this "quasi-static" assumption greatly simplifies the analysis and can be rigorously justified (Conklin 1986). The same assumption is made for the primary coolant in the core.

The conservation of energy equation for each of the nine RCCS panel nodes is a simple heat balance of the heat transferred by radiation and natural convection from the vessel and the heat convected to the air flowing upward in the channel.

The flow of air through the RCCS ductwork, including the hot riser section of the panels, is modeled with the one-dimensional momentum equation adapted by Ball (1976) for the core cooling channels. The outlet air temperature from each node is computed using the exponential approach model, which is an exact solution of the differential equation for conservation of energy where the panel temperature is uniform over the node length, the air transit time is negligible, and the air thermophysical properties are constant. Thermal radiation heat transfer from the front face to the sides or back of the internal hot riser channel is neglected. The convective heat transfer from the side walls to the flowing air is modeled as an extended surface (Gebhart 1973). The back face of the panel duct is treated as an adiabatic surface. The computed heat transfer to ambient conditions was found to be insensitive to the value of the heat transfer coefficient on the air side of the RCCS panels.

The heat transfer process inside the reactor cavity from the uninsulated outer wall of the RV to the RCCS hot riser panels consists of natural convection and thermal radiation. Participating media thermal radiation heat transfer in the annular space between the RV and the RCCS panels is neglected in the analyses presented here but is being considered for postulated accidents in which steam or aerosols are present.

The net heat transferred by radiation from the RV to the RCCS panels is modeled with the assumption that all surfaces are gray, i.e., the emissivities are independent of wavelength. Natural convection of heat across the cavity is also modeled, but is much less than the radiant heat transfer across the annulus.

For natural-convection flow analysis, the conservation of energy and momentum equations for the fluid are coupled so that simultaneous solution is usually required. However, because the dynamics of the RCCS panel are much slower than the dynamics of the air, values of the air temperatures and flows will not appreciably change over a reasonably short time step. Therefore, panel temperatures from a previous time step are used in the equation to compute air flow.

SUMMARY OF MORECA CODE RUNS AND FINDINGS

In two classes of heatup accidents that were studied, it was assumed that the RCCS was operational. In the first, there was a rapid depressurization and immediate LOFC with scram, with no subsequent primary coolant system forced cooling. In the reference case (Fig. 3), peak temperatures are reached after 4 to 5 days.

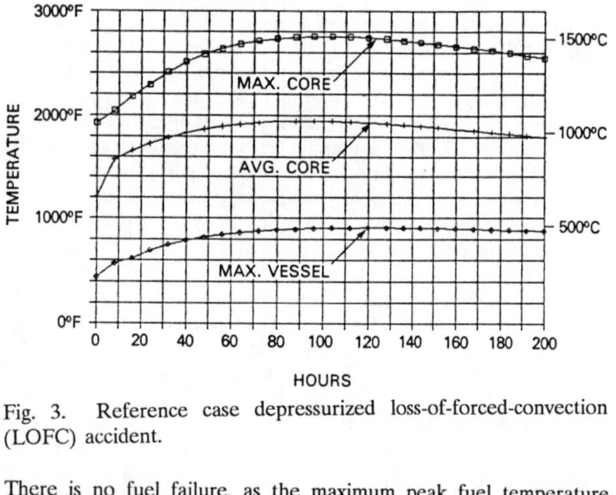

Fig. 3. Reference case depressurized loss-of-forced-convection (LOFC) accident.

There is no fuel failure, as the maximum peak fuel temperature (1482 °C, 2699 °F) is well below the 1600 °C nominal "limit." The maximum vessel temperature (478 °C, 893 °F) is below the 1000 °F extended code limit for a depressurized vessel. These results are generally in good agreement with DOE PSID values except for vessel temperatures, where the PSID maximum was less than 427 °C (800 °F). Reasons for this discrepancy are being investigated

Results of the second class of heatup accident with RCCS operational, the pressurized LOFC with scram, are shown in Fig. 4. The maximum fuel temperatures predicted are even lower than those in the depressurized LOFC case, so there is no concern about fuel damage. The primary concern is that the vessel temperature (maximum 469 °C, 876 °F) exceeds the 800 °F extended ASME code limit for a pressurized vessel. The corresponding PSID prediction, using the GA PANTHER code, was 400 °C (750 °F). Some of the discrepancies were found to be due to simplifications in the PANTHER code that GA plans to address in the next stages of the design; however, others have not yet been resolved.

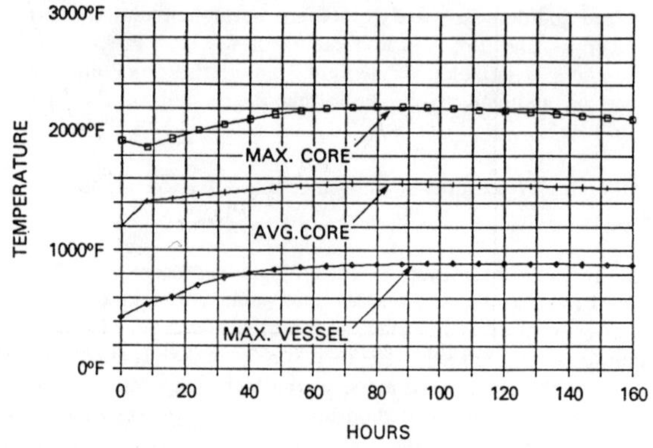

Fig. 4. Reference case pressurized LOFC accident.

The MORECA prediction of maximum primary system pressure (7.05 MPa, 1022 psia) was not high enough to actuate the relief valve (7.18 MPa, 1041 psia); however, assumptions governing steam generator cavity temperatures, which have a significant effect on pressure, were simplified and arbitrary. The extent of the overtemperature at pressure predicted here would not cause a vessel failure; however, considering the uncertainties involved in the temperature predictions, we recommend that means should be provided to depressurize and to monitor vessel temperature. Monitoring would provide a basis to judge if restart following an LOFC should be allowed.

SENSITIVITY STUDIES

Variations of these two classes of accidents were studied to observe sensitivities of the severity of the predicted results to both parametric (modeling) and operational assumptions.

Three parametric variations of the reference depressurized and pressurized LOFC cases had major significance in predictions: (1) fuel and reflector thermal conductivities; (2) use of the conservative (PSID) afterheat relationship vs best-estimate values; and (3) variations in assumed RCCS performance, including effects of assumed emissivity values that have a direct effect on transfer of heat from the core blocks to the RCCS panels.

In the reference cases, the fuel and nearby regions of the reflector were assumed to be irradiated, with a corresponding large reduction in thermal conductivity. However, for the case of relatively unirradiated (or annealed) elements, the thermal conductivities would be considerably higher. Further uncertainties are due to the fact that data on effective fuel and graphite conductivities are difficult to obtain because of effects of impurities, geometries, gaps, thermal radiation effectiveness, and annealing that may take place during measurements. Hence there may be wide variations in core conductivity values because of data uncertainties and actual changes based on operating history.

Typically, increasing the fuel and outer reflector conductivities will enhance heat transfer to the RCCS heat sink in LOFC heatup accidents and result in lower peak fuel temperatures. Several-hundred-degree variations in peak fuel temperatures were possible because of reasonable variations in assumed conductivities. While low values of conductivity were used in the reference case (resulting in acceptable peak fuel temperatures for the limiting-case depressurized LOFC), it is essential that thermal conductivity values be carefully verified to provide assurance of negligible fuel failure.

Maximum vessel temperature predictions are also affected by core thermal conductivity assumptions. While it was expected that increased core conductivities would result in higher peak vessel temperatures, in fact the opposite was true, at least for the cases in which the axial conductivity was assumed to increase along with the radial. Increased conductivities (favorably) changed the times at which the peak temperatures occurred and made the temperatures more axially and circumferentially uniform, thus reducing the gradients.

Use of a best estimate afterheat curve results in predicted peak fuel temperatures about 150 to 250 °C lower than those of the reference case for the depressurized LOFC (depending on other parameter assumptions). There is less of an effect for the pressurized cases. Peak vessel temperatures for the best-estimate afterheat cases are typically about 50 °C lower. Use of the Fort St. Vrain Final Safety Analysis Report afterheat curve gives results nearly identical with analyses using the more conservative PSID values.

While the performance of the RCCS during postulated heatup accidents has relatively little effect on peak fuel temperatures, it has a significant effect on peak vessel temperatures. For example, a depressurized LOFC case in which the RCCS was assumed to be failed totally for a one day period after the LOFC and scram predicted a maximum fuel temperature increase of less than 20 °C over the case of no RCCS failure. Assuming emissivity values of 0.5 (vs 0.8 in the reference case) for the RCCS panels and vessel walls increases the predicted peak fuel temperature in depressurized LOFCs by only about 30 °C, but the peak vessel temperature increases by about 120 °C. Hence it is important that the critical emissivity values be maintained at ~0.8. In depressurized LOFC cases in which one of the four quadrant RCCS panels is substantially blocked, the maximum fuel temperature goes only about 10 °C higher than without the blockage. The vessel temperature opposite the failed panel, however, exceeded its design limit in 1 to 2 days. Hence, RCCS performance should be monitored such that partial RCCS failures, especially during pressurized LOFCs, could be detected so that suitable corrective actions such as depressurization could be taken.

Besides the three major (important) variations noted, many other variations were studied, and these were all shown to have less significant effects on the safety-related outcome of the accidents:

(1) An arbitrary forced-convection cooldown period following the scram, which makes the effective "initial condition" temperatures of the core lower, had only a relatively small effect on maximum fuel temperatures.

(2) Variations in the assumed initial reflector bypass flow fraction. In calculations of pressurized LOFCs in which thermal insulation in the upper vessel region was reduced, a large (~10%) assumed bypass flow resulted in significantly higher maximum vessel temperatures, compared with assuming no bypass flow, which was done in the PSID. However, after adding insulation (per current design), the maximum vessel temperatures for the pressurized LOFC appeared in the area adjacent to the fuel, and assumed bypass flow fraction variations had little effect on maximum vessel temperature.

(3) Variations in the assumed initial and shutdown power peaking factors. These changes address differences between the power distribution during operation and after shutdown. The post-shutdown power distribution should be "smeared" out considerably to more realistically model post-scram gamma heating. An interesting aspect of this particular sensitivity study was that in the pressurized LOFC case, for which a uniform post-scram radial power distribution was assumed, the nonuniform azimuthal temperatures persisted throughout the accident as a result of the initial nonuniform fuel temperatures and the natural convection flow patterns set up at the start.

(4) Variations in RCCS flow loss coefficients (i.e., for increased friction factors or partial blockage) and air side heat transfer coefficients. Variations over relatively wide ranges had minor effects on RCCS heat removal performance.

(5) Variations in outdoor temperature (RCCS inlet air temperature). The reference case assumed 29 °C (85 °F), while the maximum design temperature is 43 °C (110 °F). Peak vessel temperatures increase about one degree for every two degree rise in ambient.

COMPLETE RCCS FAILURE

A "complete" long-term failure of the RCCS is currently considered as a nonmechanistic failure, since no reasonable mechanisms have been postulated to cause such failures, assuming that the RCCS is built to the proposed quality specifications. In the postulated failure calculation, the RCCS structure with its insulation between the riser and downcomer is assumed to be in place, but there is no air flow. Conduction and thermal radiation to the concrete silo are modeled simplistically, and credit is taken for the concrete heat capacity. No credit is taken for heat losses to the upper and lower heads. The results are shown in Fig. 5. Although the peak fuel temperature of 1606 °C (2923 °F) exceeds the 1600 °C limit, the predicted fuel failure was insignificant. The vessel temperature, however, exceeds ASME code values in about one day, and in two to four days, temperatures reach the point were possible concrete degradation and vessel support failures would make it difficult to define recovery action alternatives.

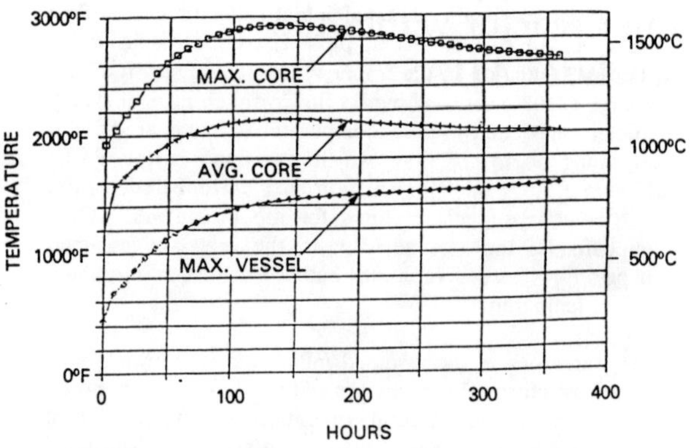

Fig. 5. Response to complete RCCS failure (depressurized LOFC).

CONCLUSIONS

LOFC heatup accident analyses show that the current MHTGR design is not susceptible to significant fuel failure from postulated accidents with very low probabilities, and even from certain drastic, nonmechanistic events. This conclusion is based on the assumption that the R&D work planned by DOE is successful in confirming certain key design characteristics assumed in our models. The ORNL results generally corresponded well with independent calculations by DOE contractors and by BNL. Considering that these are calculations of the most serious types of accidents that can be reasonably postulated, the fact that there is such good agreement indicates that the analyses are relatively straightforward and therefore credible. One major concern is the possibility of reactor vessel overheating, and that would not be considered as an immediate safety concern unless RCCS or partial RCCS long-term failures occurred. Sensitivity studies showed that the most crucial safety-related parameters or operational uncertainties were the core thermal conductivities, the afterheat curve, and the effective RCCS heat removal performance.

REFERENCES

Ball, S. J. and J. C. Conklin. 1989. *Modular HTGR Heatup Accident Analyses*, ORNL/TM report to be published, Oak Ridge National Laboratory, Oak Ridge, Tennessee.

Ball, S. J. 1976. *ORECA-I: A Digital Computer Code for Simulating the Dynamics of HTGR Cores for Emergency Cooling Analyses.* ORNL/TM-5159, Oak Ridge National Laboratory, Oak Ridge, Tennessee.

Conklin, J. C. 1986. *Scaling Analysis of the Coupled Heat Transfer Process in the High-Temperature Gas-Cooled Reactor Core.* ORNL/TM-10099, NUREG/CR-4649, Oak Ridge National Laboratory, Oak Ridge, Tennessee.

Gebhart, B. 1973. *Heat Transfer*, Second Edition. McGraw-Hill, New York, Chapters 5 and 11.

Simulators VI
© 1989 By The Society for Computer
Simulation International
ISBN 0-911801-51-0

Modelling of a pressurized water reactor within the German nuclear plant analyzer ATLAS*

H. Austregesilo, Z. Jakubowski, J.E. Miró and T. Voggenberger
Gesellschaft für Reaktorsicherheit (GRS) mbH
Forschungsgelände, D-8046 Garching
Federal Republic of Germany

ABSTRACT

The basic process model of the nuclear plant analyzer ATLAS is the thermalhydraulic computer code ATHLET. In this paper, the simulation of a Pressurized Water Reactor using the fast running options of ATHLET and some additional Balance of Plant (BOP) models is described. Furthermore, an evaluation of the overall performance of the process software from the point of view of an advanced plant analyzer is given. Improvements required in the process software are identified in the areas of modelling capabilities, numerics and program structure.

INTRODUCTION

The nuclear power plant analyzer ATLAS (ATHLET Analysis Simulator) is a joint project between Gesellschaft für Reaktorsicherheit (GRS) and Siemens (Beraha et al. 1988). The objective of this project is to simulate a reference nuclear power plant, basically a German KONVOI-PWR, but in future also other reactor designs and types (e.g. BWR). The purpose of the simulation is to analyze the response of the plant against perturbations and during accidents in order to, e.g. evaluate the overall safety, help to develop measures for the prevention of accidents and the mitigation of their consequences and complement plant personnel training. According to that, it can be classified as an engineering simulator requiring different attributes than training simulators: a wider spectrum of events has to be covered and complex thermalhydraulic phenomena have to be simulated more accurately but real time simulation is not compulsory for all applications. The development of ATLAS has been started in 1985, much later than similar projects at INEL, BNL or CEA but will continue over the next years in order to improve the present capabilities specially by extending the simulation range (coupling of models for containment, 3-D neutron kinetics, core degradation and core meltdown) and by increasing the speed of computation. This paper concentrates on the modelling aspects of a PWR within ATLAS, evaluating the overall performance of the process software when applying fast running models and pointing out where improvements are to be achieved in the next future.

ATLAS is described in every detail in a separate paper in these proceedings, so that here no further information concerning graphics or hardware will be given.

* Work sponsored by the German Federal Ministry for Research and Technology

MODELS USED WITHIN ATLAS

The basic process model is the thermalhydraulic computer code ATHLET (Analysis of Thermalhydraulics of Leaks and Transients). This computer program has been developed at GRS (Wolfert et al. 1988) and includes the models of ALMOD for transient analysis (Schaefer et al. 1983), DRUFAN for blowdown analysis (Steinhoff 1982) and FLUT for refill and reflood analysis (Hora et al. 1983). ATLAS can also run with the program TRAC/PF1. However due to its need of large computation effort and due to the fact that the ATHLET code is being further developed and can be adapted to the ATLAS requirements by a code developers team in close connection with the ATLAS team, the latter constitutes an advantageous option as far as the capabilities of the former are not needed.

The Thermalhydraulic Computer Code ATHLET

The basic features of the computer code ATHLET are given in the following. The models of the contributing codes ALMOD, DRUFAN and FLUT have been described according to a unified scheme in Forge et al. 1988.

Code Structure. The code is composed by the basic modules:

Thermo-Fluiddynamics	(TFD)
General Control Simulation	(GCSM)
Heat Conduction	(HECU)
Neutron Kinetics	(NEUKIN)

Other independent modules (e.g. large models with own time-integration procedure) can be coupled without structural changes by means of a general interface.

For the representation of a TFD-System, a modular network approach is provided. By con-catenation of basic TFD-elements, here called "Objects", a given configuration can be simu-lated. There are several object types, each of them applying for a certain TFD-Model. All object types are classified into three basic categories

- pipe-objects: apply for a one-dimensional TFD-Model with partial differential equations describing the transport of fluid
- branch-objects: apply for any TFD-Model defined by a set of ordinary differential equations or algebraic equations.
- special objects: used for component with complex geometry (e.g. cross connection of pipes within a multichannel model).

Thermo-Fluiddynamic Models. There are several options in ATHLET/Mod1 concerning fluiddynamic simulation. The most detailed one (coming from the DRUFAN code) is a 4 equation model. It consists of the conservation laws for vapour mass, liquid mass, mixture energy and mixture momentum in differential form (the non-dominant phase being considered at saturation). The relative velocity between vapour and liquid is calculated by means of a full-range drift-flux model (cocurrent and countercurrent flow in vertical and horizontal geometries with consideration of CCFL). Another important feature of this model is the mixture level tracking. The equations are formulated in terms of the finite volume spatial approximation technique.

Furthermore, a simplified 3 equation model (coming from ALMOD) is available. The mixture equations are discretized in space using the Asymmetric Separated Region Weighted Residual (ASWR) method with split-matrix or the Integrated Mass and Momentum Balance (IMMB) method (elimination of pressure waves). The latter constitutes a fast running simulation option applicable to the calculation of anticipated and abnormal plant transients.

At present, work is being carried out in order to include the 6 equation model of FLUT in ATHLET as an additional fluiddynamic option.

Models for Components and Processes. The simulation of the heat conduction in structures, fuel rod and electrical heaters is performed within the basic module HECU.

The nuclear heat generation can be modelled by a point or a one-dimensional kinetics model. A multidimensional simulation of the reactor vessel fluiddynamics can be performed in an approximated way by a multichannel approach.

Major components (e.g. pressurizer, steam generators) can be modelled by connecting TFD-objects. Simplified, compact models for those components are also available as special branch objects.

Additional models are available for the simulation of valves, pumps, accumulators, steam separators, single ended breaks, double ended breaks, fills and leaks, boundary conditions for pressure and enthalpy. A 1-D thermal-non-equilibrium discharge model is also available.

Time Integration. Time integration is performed with the FEBE (Forward-Euler, Backward-Euler) method (Hofer 1981). For most applications the fully implicit option of FEBE is chosen. The linearization of the implicit system is done numerically by calculation of the Jacobian matrix. A block sparse matrix package (FTRIX) is available in order to reduce the effort in solving the equation system. A rigorous error control is performed basing on an extrapolation technique. According to the error bound specified by the user, the time step and the order of the method (>2) are determined for every integration step.

General Control Simulation Module (GCSM). A dedicated high level simulation language is provided by the basic module GCSM for the flexible description of control, trip and auxiliary systems (Balance of Plant systems). By connecting basic functional blocks (see table 1) within the input deck, the user can model the desired control circuit or fluid system as a block diagram. The process variables can be input to a user defined block diagram. Output signals are for instance rod position, valve cross sectional area or boundary conditions for mass or heat addition rate, pressure and temperature.

Table 1: Basic Blocks of GCSM

SWITCH	two-step-switch with hysteresis
ADDER	signal adder
FUNGEN	function generator
OR	logical or
AND	logical and
LAG	low pass filter 1. order (PT1)
LIMITER	signal limiter
INTE	integrator
DIF	differentiator
SORT	signal sorting
DELAY	dead time element
MULDIV	signal multiplier/divider
SOLAG	low pass filter 2. order (PT2)
EXPONENT	exponential function
SIGN	signum/absolute value
NOT	logical not
SINUS	sinus-generator
TSSWITCH	three-step-switch
SQRT	square root
LOG	logarithm function
PROP	thermodynamic properties (SI units)
NPA	interface to specific BOP models

Specific Balance of Plant (BOP) Models

A special group of BOP models are models with fixed structure, offering a very detailed simulation (programmed in FORTRAN 77). In contrast to models constructed on the basis of GCSM, changes in these models can not be performed just at the input level.

A library with a set of approximately 40 specific BOP models for the reference plant has been developed and made available by Siemens. There are models for technological components (turbine, condenser, emergency feedwater system etc.) as well as for control systems (reactor power control, pressurizer pressure control, condensate flow control, feedwater flow control etc.). Some of the models from this library have been integrated already into ATLAS, after successful testing. Redundancies in systems are only taken into account as far as required by functionality. The simulation range is limited in the way that no leaks can be assumed in these systems.

The specific BOP models are coupled with ATHLET by a special interface, which consists in a set of subroutines that have following tasks:

- transfer of data between BOP models and process model (ATHLET)
- synchronization of the integration procedures in BOP and process models.

The second task, also called numerical coupling, is a rather delicate one because the BOP models use the explicit technique with fixed time steps and the fluiddynamics the implicit technique with variable time steps. The problem is to preserve the degree of accuracy of the fluiddynamics solution dictated by the user requirements without having to reduce the time step of the fuiddynamics which in turn would lead to excessive computation times. In some cases a strong coupling is needed which links the solution of the BOP models to the error control mechanism of the fluiddynamics solution increasing the computation effort per time step but leading to the desired accuracy. Also, the discontinuities in the solution caused by the BOP models (e.g. opening of a valve) have to be treated in a special way (the discontinuity causes the beginning of a new time step for the fluiddynamics) as implicit methods are not suitable for integrating accross discontinuities.

MODELLING OF A PWR

Four basic types of processes have to be simulated: nuclear fission, heat transfer and heat conduction, fluiddynamics and control. Fig. 1 depicts in a compact way the different components and systems that have been considered within the plant analyzer. An important feature is that the nodalization of the plant can be changed for a certain application by just changing the ATHLET input deck.

The primary system with the steam generators secondary side has been simulated by means of the thermalhydraulic models of ATHLET. The figure shows the division in fluiddynamic objects and cells. The shaded components have been simulated by specific models developed outside the ATHLET code (turbine, feedwater line and pumps). Left on the picture (framed) the simulated control and BOP systems are listed indicating the type of modelling tools used.

In the figure, the interaction points between the thermalhydraulic models and the other models simulating control, protection and auxiliary systems are indicated by arrows. A summary of the main modelling assumptions is given in the following.

Primary System

As mentioned above, several fluiddynamic models are available within the ATHLET code. Up to now two generic ways of simulating a PWR have been successfully applied within ATLAS using:

i) 4 equation models (DRUFAN models) with different assumptions concerning kinematic non-equilibrium and mixture level tracking for the different plant components.

ii) 3 equation models (ALMOD models) for the simulation of the coolant transport and dedicated models for the pressurizer and steam generator secondary side.

The first type of models offers the possibility of accurate prediction of the two-phase flow phenomena during LOCA transients but the computational effort required does not allow calculations in real time even for non-LOCA-transients. The second type of models offers this capability but is not suitable for the calculation of large and medium LOCAs or situations where thermal non-equilibrium is relevant.

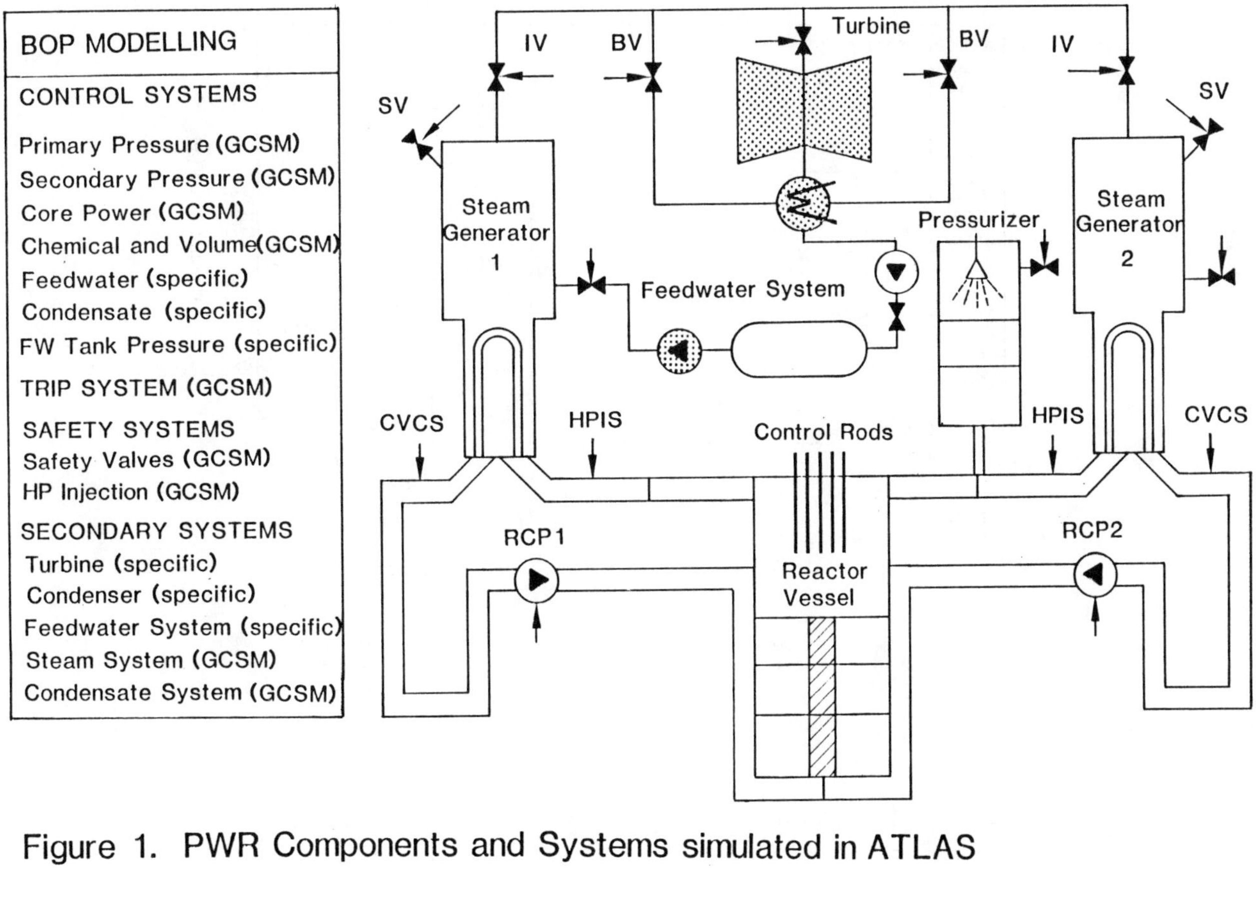

Figure 1. PWR Components and Systems simulated in ATLAS

The simulation of a PWR using the models of the second type, also called "fast running" models is the one this paper focuses on. It is to be pointed out that these models are not simplifications of other reference models made specially to meet the requirements of a plant analyzer, but these options are the basis of the transient analysis code ALMOD.

For the representation of the core dynamics, the point kinetics option has been chosen. The fuel rod is represented by using the general heat conduction module. This module can also be used for considering the thermal interaction between coolant and structure.

Secondary System.

Almost the whole secondary side (shown in Fig. 2) is modelled with the GCSM basic blocks and specific BOP models. Only the feedwater tank is modelled as an ATHLET fluiddynamic object.

The main steam system includes the turbine valves, relief and safety valves, turbine with reheater, header and turbine-bypass. The turbine with reheater is modelled in a detailed way within a specific BOP model whereas the other elements are modelled in a quasi-stationary way with GCSM. The turbine inlet steam flow is approximated by a function of the turbine valve position and the pressure at turbine inlet. In an analogous way, the mass flow rates through the bypass station, relief and safety valves are calculated as linear functions of valve position and steam pressure. The header pressure is calculated considering dynamic pressure losses from the main steam line to the header. Additionally, an equalization mass flow between loops is calculated when the pressures in the loops are different from each other.

The main condensate system and the feedwater system are modelled as simple as possible. The first of these systems is modelled with the GCSM and the second as specific BOP system. Parallel pumps of these systems are represented by a common characteristic (dischange pressure as a function of the feedwater flow). The control valves are described by a variable flow resistance. Mass flows are calculated solving the momentum balance equation; in the feedwater system an iterative procedure is applied for this purpose.

The secondary control systems are simulated with the GCSM as well as with specific BOP models. For example, the feedwater control system whose structure is shown in Fig. 3, is represented as specific BOP model. The controllers and logic part of this system are simulated in a rather detailed way. A full three-component structure, with PI-controllers and taking into account different load levels has been modelled.

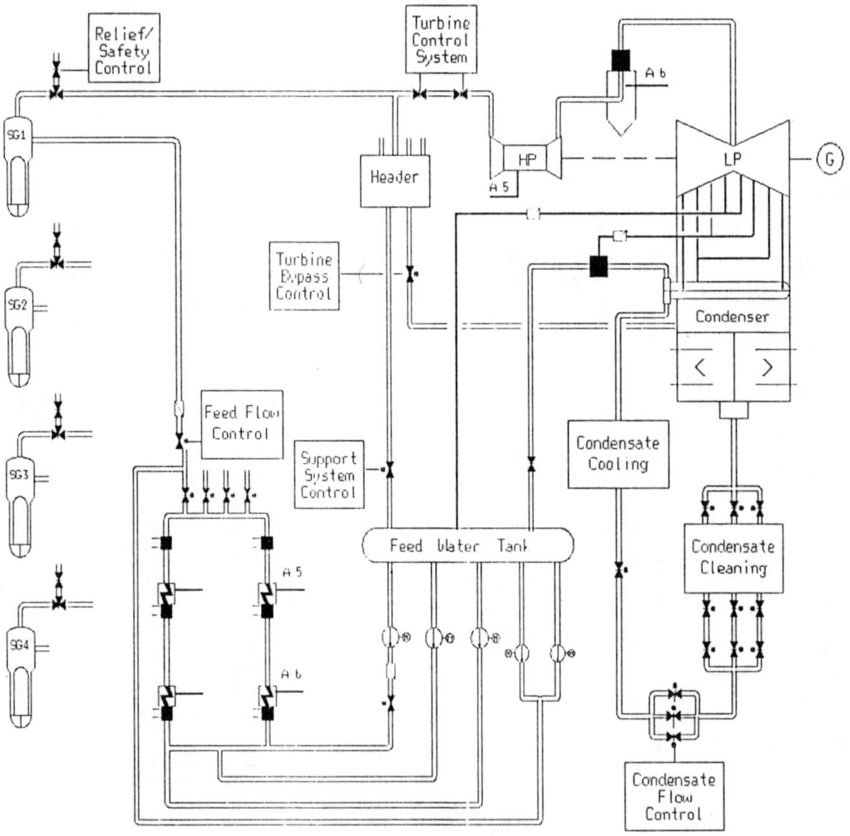

Figure 2 Secondary Side Representation in ATLAS

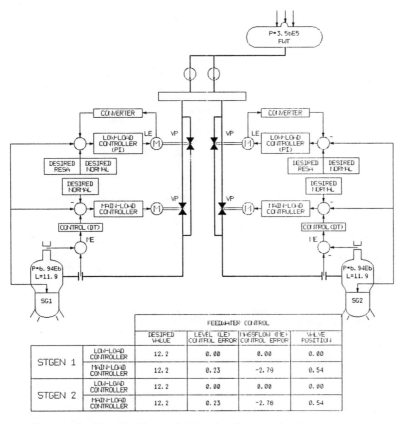

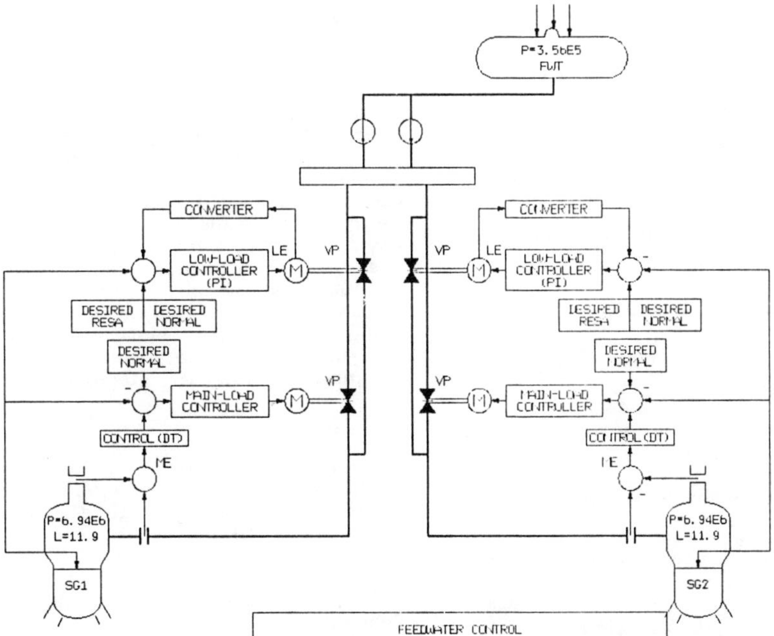

		FEEDWATER CONTROL			
		DESIRED VALUE	LEVEL (LE) CONTROL ERROR	MASSFLOW (ME) CONTROL ERROR	VALVE POSITION
STGEN 1	LOW-LOAD CONTROLLER	12.2	0.00	0.00	0.00
	MAIN-LOAD CONTROLLER	12.2	0.23	-2.79	0.54
STGEN 2	LOW-LOAD CONTROLLER	12.2	0.00	0.00	0.00
	MAIN-LOAD CONTROLLER	12.2	0.23	-2.78	0.54

Figure 3 Simulation of the Feedwater System

EVALUATION OF THE PERFORMANCE

First, it has to be pointed out that the validity range of the models evaluated here is limited to anticipated and abnormal transients excluding large and medium LOCAs and situations with strong phase separation in the primary system (other ATHLET models could be applied for the evaluation of those phenomena).

Nevertheless, a rather comprehensive simulation of control and auxiliary systems has been selected in order to obtain an accurate description of the influence of BOP systems on the overall plant response.

Concerning verification it has been already mentioned that the ATHLET-models used have been verified in the code ALMOD for many years and are being further verified in the ATHLET code as they are not only being used within ATLAS but also as reference transient analysis tool in several German and foreign institutions.

The overall computation time can be splitted according to the different tasks:

t/ATHLET Computation time of the standard ATHLET models

t/BOP Computation time for the BOP outside ATHLET

t/I Computation time spent for accomplishing the malfunction and interactive capability

t/I/O Computation time needed for handling special restart and plot files

t/GRAPH Computation time needed for graphic display

t/TA Turnaround time

All these computation times (the graphics are computed in parallel) contribute to the total simulation time that appears on the screen together with the problem time and the time dependent ratio of both.

The computation time of the ATHLET models is by far the most important contribution to the simulation time. Nevertheless, the BOP models can also contribute considerably to the overall computation time of the process software (t/ATHLET + t/BOP) due to the numerical coupling of both model packages. t/I and t/I/O are negligible in general. t/GRAPH is about Ø.5 s per display and t/TA results from the fact that several jobs are running simultaneously on the mainframe computer.

For most applications t/ATHLET can be kept below real time in average. The fact that an implicit method with variable time step is used, needing a rather high computational effort for the calculation of the Jacobian matrix implies that real time computation can not be reached at all time points during the simulation. Time integration using an "unexpensive" explicit algorithm is being considered in order to reach even lower computation times for the process software.

PRESENT AND FUTURE WORK

As it can be derived from the previous evaluation, the improvement of the process software has to proceed in order to meet the requirements of an advanced plant analyzer. The necessary tasks can be classified into three major areas:

Modelling Capabilities

Here, ATLAS will benefit from the developmental work being carried out at present within the project ATHLET

- Severe accidents capability (version ATHLET-SA)
- Implementation of a second energy balance in the four-equation model.

Other developments in progress in ATHLET are directed specially to the application within ATLAS, like the implementation of a fast 3D-Core model for a more detailed description of operational transients.

Another capability relevant for the ATLAS project is the possibility of coupling to ATHLET software packages developed independently without making structural changes every time a new package is added. This has been accomplished for several types of BOP models by means of a general interface as mentioned before. An extension of this capability in order to couple even more complex models (e.g. steam generator secondary side, fuel rods, containment) is underway.

Finally, the applicability field of the fast running ATHLET options has to be extended by improving the existing models specially for two-phase flow simulation and by adding new ones, e.g. Boron concentration model in order to keep well verified, unexpensive simulation capabilities available.

Numerics

The improvements in numerics have to be directed towards two objectives:

One objective is to reduce the effort necessary for the time integration of the fluiddynamic equations in order to obtain computation times well below real time during the whole simulation. The implicit technique has shown to be very efficient for the process model when applied by itself. However, when applied within ATLAS, the calculation of the Jacobian and the variable time step cause a large distortion of the computation time versus real time which in turn restricts the fulfillment of the permanent real time requirement. If a constant time step is forced the advantages of an implicit method against an explicit one reduce considerably.

The other objective is that the coupling of the different time integration algorithms (fluiddynamics, control systems, BOP systems, independent modules) does not lead to accuracy losses or to extremely high computation times (small time steps).

Code Structure

In order to reduce drastically the computation time for the process software the use of adequate hardware is obligatory, specially if the range of simulated systems and phenomena is to be extended in the future. Here, the adaptation of the process software to advanced computer architectures (parallel processing) is indicated.

CONCLUSIONS

The simulation of the response of a PWR (Siemens type KONVOI) during LOCAs, anticipated and abnormal transients taking into account all relevant BOP systems and using well verified process models is available within ATLAS. Nevertheless, real time simulation, in an average sense, is only reached by certain modelling options whose applicability field is restricted to transients. In order to accomplish the envisaged objectives concerning the spectrum of events covered including severe accidents and high computational speed, improvements of the process software have to continue in three basic areas: modelling capabilities, numerical techniques for time integration and adaptation of the code structure to advanced computer architectures.

REFERENCES

Beraha, D.; Lerchl, G.; and Voggenberger, T. 1988. Analysesimulator, ein Werkzeug zur Beurteilung schutzzielorientierter Maßnahmen". In proceedings of the GRS-Fachgespräch 1988. (Cologne, 3-4 Nov.)

Forge, A.; Pochard, R.; Porracchia, A; Miró, J.; Sonnenburg, H.G.; Steinhoff, F. and Teschendorff, V. 1988. Comparison of Thermal-Hydraulic Safety Codes for PWR Systems. Commission of the European Communities. Graham & Trotman, London/Dorchecht/Boston.

Hofer, E. 1981. "An A(α)-stable variable order ODE-solver and its application as advancement procedure for simulations in thermo- and fluiddynamics". In proceedings of the International Topical Meeting on Advances in Mathematical Methods for the Solution of Nuclear Engineering Problems (Munich).

Hora, A.; Michetschläger, C.; Sonnenburg, H.G.; and Teschendorff, V. 1983. "Analysis of Reflood Phenomena by the Two-Fluid Code FLUT". In Proceedings of Advances in Two-Phase Flow and Heat Transfer, M. Nijhoff Publ. (The Hague).

Schaefer, A.; Miró J.E.; Höppner, G.; Frisch, W.; Meissner, R.; and Gaal, U. 1983. "ALMOD4 Advanced PWR Transient Analysis Code". In proceedings of the ANS Topical Meeting on Anitcipated and Abnormal Plant Transients in Light Water Reactors. (Jackson, USA, 26-29 Sept.).

Steinhoff, F. 1982. "DRUFAN 02, Interim Program Description". GRS Reports. Part 1: GRS-A-685, March 1982, Part 2: GRS-A-714, May 1982.

Wolfert, K.; Lerchl, G.; Miró, J.E.; and Sonnenburg H.G. 1988. "The GRS Thermalhydraulic System Code ATHLET for PWR and BWR Analyses". In Proceedings of 3rd International Topical Meeting on Nuclear Power Plant Thermalhydraulics and Operation (Seoul, Corea, 14-17 Nov.)

Simulators VI
© 1989 By The Society for Computer
Simulation International
ISBN 0-911801-51-0

Software standardizes signal scaling

Scott Crawford
Westinghouse Electric Corporation
Engineering and Instrumentation Services Division
Applied Technology Services
Post Office Box 105547
Atlanta, GA 30348-5547

ABSTRACT

The necessary scaling of large-sized process control systems has always been a complex, time consuming, and costly operation, requiring many hours of manual computation and careful application of the process and module equations before proper voltage values of gain and bias are obtained. INCAS (an acronym for Integrated Computer-Aided Scaling) was developed to address several of the long-standing problems associated with scaling and testing protective and control systems at nuclear power plants. The system is a unique self-contained hardware/software package specifically designed to perform the complex scaling computations on customer identified control loops with efficacy and consistency. Using the system to standardize the scaling of large process control systems provides a cost effective solution to the problems associated with scaling.

INTRODUCTION

Until now, the scaling of large-sized process control systems has been a complex, time consuming, and costly operation. Nuclear power plants have complicated control and protection loops which have many modules (control cards) in cascade (series). Adjustments made in one module will affect other modules that follow along the signal path. Also, since some loops supply signals to other loops (branch out), a change in process parameter can affect the way that many of the modules must be adjusted.

Traditionally, scaling required many hours of manual computation and careful application of the process and module equations before the proper voltage values of gain and bias could be obtained. If a particular process value were changed, recalculation of the voltage values for all modules affected was necessary, requiring additional hours of calculation and extra care to ensure that no modules requiring recalculation were missed. The potential for human error is apparent.

The INCAS system was developed to address several of the persistent problems associated with scaling and testing protective and control systems at nuclear power plants. It is a unique computer-aided process control instrumentation scaling and troubleshooting system specifically designed to perform the complex scaling computations on customer identified control loops with efficiency and consistency. Combining state-of-the-art hardware and software, the system can be customized for any control configuration and includes all proof testing, documentation, and training of customer personnel.

SENSOR SETPOINT SCALING SUMMARIZED

Sensor setpoint scaling is the design problem of determining the relationship between process values (engineering units) and module analog signals (voltages or currents), and then calculating or selecting module settings (gain and bias) necessary so that appropriate system indication, control, and protection functions can be accomplished within a process system.

Scaling can be defined as the design and mathematical conversion operation for developing process variable to analog signal relationships and determining necessary instrumentation module settings so that the appropriate system indication, control, and protection functions are performed within a control system.

The instrumentation modules in a process control system interpret the information provided by field mounted sensors so that the appropriate system indication, control, and protection functions can be accomplished. The process variables (flow, pressure, temperature, etc.) monitored by the field mounted sensors must first be converted into equivalent analog voltage or current signals. Any required signal modifications or calculations are then accomplished by adjusting the instrumentation module settings. Consequently, to ensure that the appropriate system indication, control and protection outputs are achieved, the process variable to analog signal relationship must be developed and the necessary instrumentation module settings determined. (See Example 1.)

Actual settings for each module must be calculated by using information from the following sources:

(A) Precaution Limitations and Setpoint (PLS) Document. (This provides ranges and setpoint in process units, i.e. PSI, FPM, degrees Fahrenheit.)

(B) As-built drawings on flow element diameters to determine the differential pressure relationship to flow.

(C) As-built drawings showing dimensions and instrument installation, e.g., elevations of reference legs for differential pressure (d/p) transmitter, tap to tap distances, etc.

(D) Process equations developed from plant design concepts which describe the process in mathematical terms.

(E) Technical information on the instrumentation to establish: (1) a module equation for each type module used; (2) the limits for the input and output values for each module; (3) and the limits for the gain and bias for each module.

(F) Loop drawings showing interconnection between modules.

(g) Technical specifications giving protection setpoints for safe plant operation.

Scaling Method

The usual method of scaling is to take specific information (as described above) and calculate the gain and bias for each module. After many hours of computation, carefully applying the process equations and module equations, the proper voltage values of gain and bias can be obtained. (See Example 2.) With plant start-up, some of the process values must be changed for better operation. Changing a particular process value requires recalculation of the voltage values for all affected modules and hours of calculation and extra care so that no modules requiring recalculations are misssed.

After learning the basics of process control and then the plant, an engineer could spend another year or more learning scaling methodology. Consistency in the scaling method used becomes critical to plant operating efficiency.

Scaling Standardization Solutions

Using the INCAS system to standardize the scaling of large process control systems provides a cost effective solution to the problems associated with scaling. The system is a self-contained hardware/software package designed to provide the operator with a wide range of scaling related capabilities. These capabilities include:

(1) Automatic scaling value generation on an overall instrument loop basis.

(2) Simulation of control loop responses to theoretical input changes.

(3) User friendly system and subsystem graphics.

(4) System troubleshooting.

(5) Dynamics testing.

(6) File generation and mangement.

The hardware portion of the system consists of four main components. These are the main computer unit, nineteen inch color monitor, printer, and keyboard.

The main computer unit includes a permanently installed hard disk drive unit and one 3-1/2 inch diskette drive. The hard disk within this unit contains the entire software package and thus precludes the need for storage and loading of many floppy disks. Therefore, the use of the hard disk simplifies the overall process of system start-up and operation. The 3-1/2 inch diskette drive is used primarily to make backup copies of the program or to load the program in the event of a hard disk drive malfunction.

The system's software is a plant specific, customized menu driven, user friendly, hard disk operating entity. Each menu, graphic, or tabular listing presented on the monitor provides the operator with a complete set of options and prompts which enable him to access adjacent menus or enter available modes such as graph plotting or loop parameter revision. (See Example 3.) In addition, the system is provided with fail-safe features that prevent the inadvertent erasure of modified loop parameter files and help the operator correct erroneous or out-of-tolerance entries.

Consistent In Change Capability

Consistency of method is a key feature of the software package. This feature abolishes the problems associated with the application of different scaling methods to the same loop because the scaling methods used remain constant. Such problems can arise when a person other than the originator rescales a part of a loop. Since he did not perform the original scaling, he does not realize the effect that the use of a dissimilar scaling method will have on other loops.

Many options are available when scaling a loop. Three people may scale the same loop in three unlike ways, all of which will be correct. As overall loop gain may be distributed over several modules, each scaler may choose a different combination of module gains to obtain the same total gain. Also, when the signal path branches off to another loop from one of the intermediate modules, the gain to this point can be different and different gains mean different signal value to process value ratios (such as volts per degree Fahrenheit or volts per PSIG). Such ratio differences require the branch loop scaling to be different. The software puts an end to the problems and potential errors connected with changing scaling methods since all the modules which require rescaling are rescaled automatically by the system's routines, utilizing the same method, thereby "standardizing" scaling procedures.

The system's software has all the required process, voltage, and module equations built into its programs. This assures that the proper equation will be used to rescale.

Control loop responses to user determined process value changes are simulated by the system. This greatly enhances plant efficiency since operating personnel can determine the reaction of the process to any given process value change by simulation rather than by physical implementation.

Process parameter changes to be entered are limited to safe operating ranges because the system's programs will not permit unsafe values to be entered. In addition, new process values that affect more than one loop can only be changed at the beginning of the program, preventing the use of different values in different loops. New values and test reports (data sheets) are calculated instantly upon new process value entry thus saving hours of engineering time previously expended manually.

Graphic display may be drawn showing the effects of new process value entry. Dynamic module graphics show the effects of time constant changes providing assistance in developing scaling data for a desired module time response.

Block diagrams of actual plant loop configurations along with current scaling data are graphically displayed. Such block diagrams are valuable training tools and troubleshooting guides for maintenance, engineering, and operations personnel, providing a straight forward approach to integrated control loop configuration.

SUMMARY AND CONCLUSIONS

This unique system provides solutions to many of the long-standing problems that accompany scaling and testing protective and control systems. It incorporates the latest innovations in hardware and software and can be customized for any control configuration.

To reiterate, a key feature of the system is consistency of method. Precise scaling values are generated instantly, saving hours of engineering time and eliminating the possibility of mathematical error due to the extensive complex calculations associated with scaling.

All required process, voltage, and module equations are built into the system's programs thus removing the possibility of improper scaling since scaling is addressed on an overall instrument loop basis. Further, unsafe process parameter changes cannot be entered. The system also enhances plant efficiency by simulating control loop responses to user determined process value changes.

New test reports (data sheets) and values are instantly calculated by the system upon entry of a new process value. Detailed graphics display the effects of new process value entry, time constant changes, and block diagrams of loop configurations along with current scaling data.

The scaling of process control systems is necessary to ensure that appropriate system indication, control and protection functions are accomplished. Use of the INCAS system to standardize the scaling of large process control systems provides a cost effective and practical means of solving the problems encountered with this intricate, time consuming and costly activity.

EXAMPLE 1

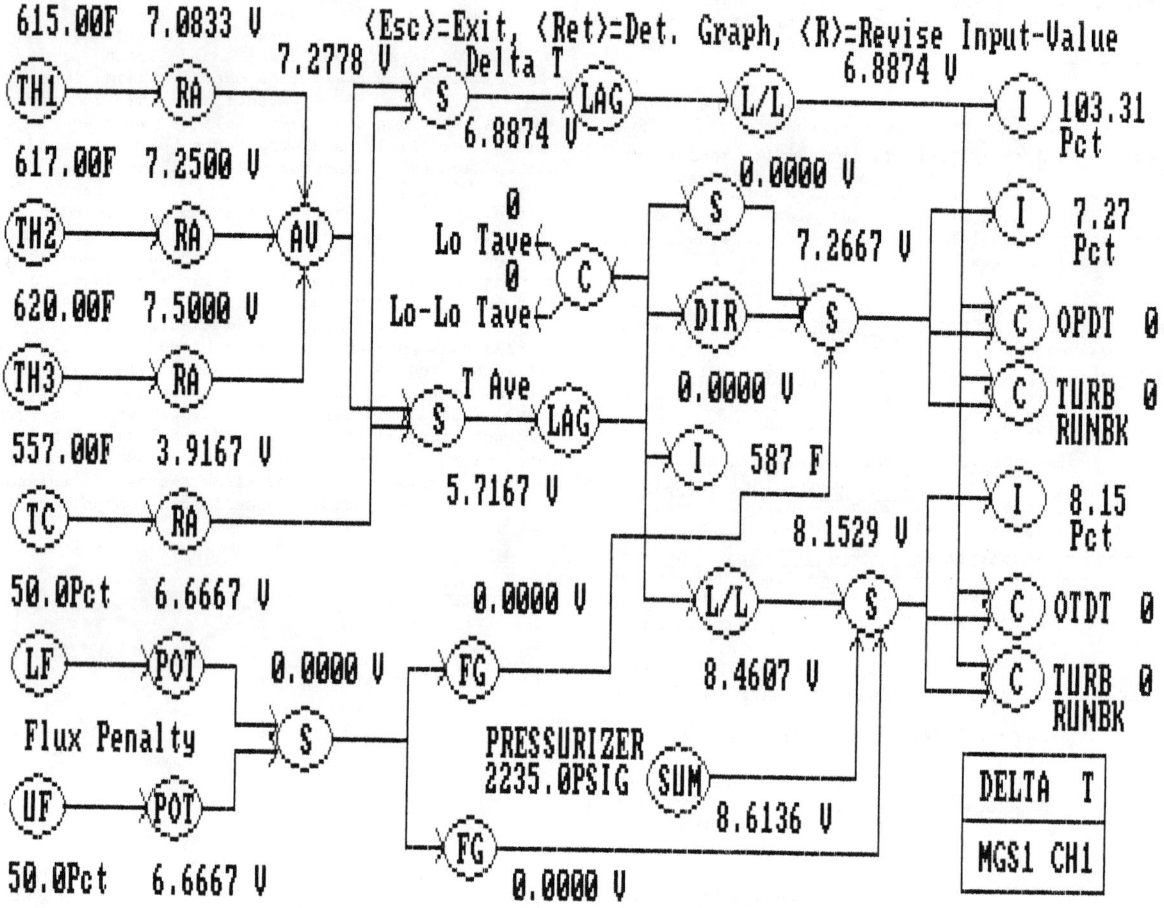

Delta T-T Average System Block Diagram

Example 2

Module Transfer Functions

Integral	$1/\tau_I S$
Lag	$1/(1 + \tau_\ell s)$
Rate	$\tau_r S/(1 + \tau_\ell s)$

Where: τ_I = integral time constant

τ_ℓ = lag time constant

τ_r = rate time constant

Lead/Lag is derived by adding lag and lead:

$$1/(1 + \tau_\ell s) + \tau_r s/(1 + \tau_\ell s) = (1 + \tau_r s)/(1 + \tau_\ell s)$$

Proportional plus integral:

$$1 + (1/\tau_I s)$$

Proportional plus integral plus derivative:

$$1 + (1/\tau_I s) + [s/\ (1\tau_D + \tau_D s/10)]$$

Unit Step Input to Lag

$$E_o = \frac{1}{s} G \left(\frac{1/T_L}{s - (-1/T_L)}\right)$$

$$\mathcal{L}^{-1}\ \frac{1}{s} \left\{\frac{1/}{s - (-1/\ )}\right\} = \int_o^T \left(\frac{1}{T_L} e^{-T/T_\ell}\right) dt =$$

$$e^{-T/T_L} \Big|_t^o = 1 - e^{-t/T_L}$$

$$E_o = G\ (1 - e^{-t/})$$

Unit step input to Lead (rate or derivative)

$$E_o = \frac{1}{s} G \left(\frac{\left(\frac{T_R}{T_L} S\right.}{s - (-1/T_L)}\right) = G \left(\frac{\frac{T_R}{T_L} S}{s - (-1/T_L)}\right)$$

$$\mathcal{L}^{-1} \left\{\frac{\frac{T_R}{T_L}}{s - (-1/T_L)}\right\} = \frac{T_R}{T_L} e^{-t/T_L}$$

$$E_o = G \frac{T_R}{T_L} e^{-t/T_L}$$

Unit step input to Lead/Lag

$$E_o = \frac{1}{s} G\left(\frac{T_R S + 1}{T_L S + 1}\right) \text{ or } E_o =$$

$$G\left[1 + \left(\frac{T_R}{T_L} - 1\right) e^{-t/T_L}\right]$$

Ramp input to Lag

$$E_o = 1/S^2\ GR \left(\frac{^1/T_L}{s - (-1/T_L)}\right)$$

$$\mathcal{L}^{-1} \left\{\frac{1}{S^2} \frac{1/T_L}{S - (-1/T_L)}\right\} = \int_o^t \int_o^T \frac{R}{T_L} e^{-\lambda/T_L} dT =$$

$$R \int_o^t e^{-\lambda/T_L} \Big|_o^t dT = R \int_o^t (1 - e^{-T/T_L})\ dT =$$

$$R\ [T + T_L e^{-T/T_L}\ ]_o^t = R\ [t - T_L(1 - e^{-t/T_L})]$$

$$E_o = GR[t + T_L\ (e^{-t/T_L} - 1)]$$

Ramp input to Lead

$$E_o = \frac{1}{s^2} GR \left(\frac{T_D/T_L\ S}{S - (-1/T_L)}\right)$$

$$\mathcal{L}^{-1} \left\{\frac{R}{S} \frac{T_D/T_L}{S - (-1/T_L)}\right\} = \frac{G\ T_R\ R}{T_L} \int_o^t e^{-T/T_L} dT$$

$$T_R\ GRE^{-T/T_L} \Big|_o^t = GRT_R\ (1 - e^{-t/T_L})$$

$$E_o - GRT_R\ (1 - e^{-t/T_L})$$

Ramp input to Lead/Lag

$$E_o = \frac{RG}{s^2} \left(\frac{T_R\ S + 1}{T_L\ S + 1}\right) \quad \text{or}$$

$$E_o = GR\ [t + (T_R - T_L)(1 - e^{-t/T_L})]$$

Controller - PID

$$E_o = G\left[1 + \frac{1}{T_I\ S} + \frac{T_D\ S}{1 + T_D/_{10} S}\right]$$

Unit step input

$$E_o = \mathcal{L}^{-1} \left\{\frac{1}{s} G\left[1 + \frac{1}{T_I\ S} + \frac{T_D\ S}{1 + \frac{T_D}{10} S}\right]\right\} =$$

$$\mathcal{L}^{-1} \left\{G\left[\frac{1}{s} + \frac{1}{T_I\ S^2} + \frac{T_D}{1 + \frac{T_D}{10} S}\right]\right\} =$$

$$\mathcal{L}^{-1} \left\{G\left[\frac{1}{s} + \frac{1}{T_I\ S^2} + \frac{10}{s - (-10/T_D)}\right]\right\} =$$

$$G\left[1 - \frac{t}{T_I} + 10e^{-10t/T_D}\right]$$

EXAMPLE 3

SYSTEM MAIN MENUS

****** NUCLEAR POWER PLANT ******

```
****** Delta T, T Average Main Menu ******

1. - System Input Values
2. - Delta T-T Average System
3. - Flux Axial Imbalance System
4. - Overtemperature Setpoint System
5. - Overpower Setpoint System
6. - System Block Diagrams
7. - File Manager (for Scaling Mode Only)
```

Use arrows for selection then press <RETURN>
<ESC> to exit, <?> for HELP

Simulators VI

ISBN 0-911801-51-0

Qualification of a model for Once Through Steam Generator loss-of-feedwater transients

Richard C. Kern
Utility Associates International
6003 Executive Boulevard
Rockville, Maryland 20852

ABSTRACT

Steady state and transient loss-of-feedwater tests have been performed at the Babcock and Wilcox Alliance Research Center on a 19-tube model of a once through steam generator (OTSG). This paper describes best estimate analyses and sensitivity studies of the transient tests using the DYNODE-P computer program.

The comparison of the measured and calculated steam flows for the tests was the parameter used to assess the adequacy of the computational model. The results obtained for the OTSG with recirculation tests indicate excellent agreement between calculation and measurement. The results for the IEOTSG test showed that it was necessary to represent low flow heat transfer properly in the subcooled region to obtain this same excellent agreement.

INTRODUCTION

Steady-state and transient loss-of-feedwater (LOFW) tests have been performed at the Babcock and Wilcox (B&W) Alliance Research Center on a 19-tube model of a once-through steam generator (OTSG). The test results and comparisons to calculations made with RELAP5/MOD1 are reported by Hassan and Morgan (1983). This paper describes best estimate analyses of the transient tests using the DYNODE-P computer program (Kern et al. 1983). Results from appropriate sensitivity studies are included.

OTSG DESCRIPTION

An OTSG is a single-pass counterflow, vertical straight tube and shell heat exchanger used to transfer the heat generated in B&W pressurized water reactors (PWR) from the primary (tube) side to the secondary (shell) side. The feedwater on the secondary side enters at the bottom as liquid and is heated to superheat steam conditions by the time it exists at the top. There are two basic B&W OTSG designs. The earlier design has a recirculation feature in which a small amount of steam is bled from the boiler section into the downcomer annulus to heat the feedwater to saturation before it enters the boiler section. The new design, Integral Economizer OTSG (IEOTSG), does not have this feedwater pre-heat feature, so that the feedwater enters the tube region in the subcooled state.

TEST RIG DESCRIPTION

The 19-tube bundle model can be operated in either the recirculation or integral economizer mode. The tube length is 15.9m and the Inconel tubes have a 1.394 cm ID and a 1.587 cm OD with a 2.22 cm triangular pitch. For the loss-of-feedwater tests, steady-state conditions were established prior to initiating the transient. During the tests, measurements were made of feedwater and steam flows as well as primary and secondary fluid temperatures and pressures.

SIMULATION MODEL DESCRIPTION

The DYNODE-P computer program simulates the transient response of the nuclear steam supply system (NSSS) of a PWR. DYNODE-P has the capability to represent any of the current PWR designs via geometry input options. Thus, either OTSG design can be modeled relatively easily by proper selection of the input option variables. Also, DYNODE-P can be used to simulate a variety of transients which include a loss-of-feedwater transient. For the current analysis, the model for the remainder of the NSSS was set up to maintain a constant primary system boundary condition for the tube inlet temperature and flow as existed during the test. It should be noted that DYNODE-P self-initializes all parameters based on the required input boundary condition parameters to facilitate usage of the program.

The input for the DYNODE-P OTSG model was derived as follows. The information given by Hassan and Morgan was used to calculate the geometric data. The initial power was obtained from the measured initial feedwater flow and inlet and exit temperatures. The initial lengths of the subcooled and saturated regions were obtained from the initial measured secondary side temperature profile. The measured transient feedwater flow was imposed as the boundary condition of the secondary side.

COMPARISONS

Figure 1 shows the comparison of the measured and calculated steam flows for the two tests which was the parameter used to assess the adequacy of the computational model. For the IEOTSG test, the initial calculation (Labeled DYNODE-1) was performed assuming that the subcooled heat transfer mode is forced convection (Dittus-Boelter heat transfer coefficient). In this case, since the coefficient is proportional to the $Re^{0.8}$, heat transfer to the subcooled fluid is lost when the feedwater flow ceases resulting in a significant decrease in the heat input to the secondary side. This reduction in heat load causes the secondary pressure and hence steam flow to decrease too rapidly. The second calculation (labeled DYNODE-2) assumed that the subcooled heat transfer coefficient was constant. These results show a significant improvement. A third case (not shown) using the low-flow heat transfer coefficient model from RELAP5/MOD1 (Ransom et al. 1981) as the lower limit for the subcooled region produced results similar to the DYNODE-2 results.

The results shown for the OTSG with recirculation test indicate excellent agreement between calculation and measurement. Note that the discrepancy in the IEOTSG comparison discussed above did not enter in this case, since there is no subcooling in the tube bundle region.

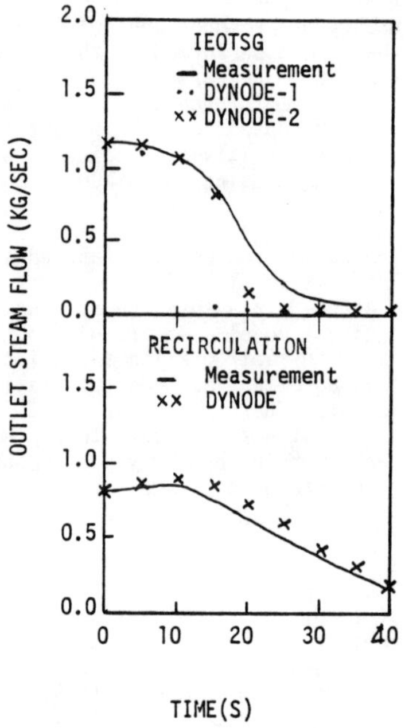

FIGURE 1. OUTLET STEAM FLOW COMPARISONS

SUMMARY

In summary, the comparisons between measured and calculated transient steam flows under loss-of-feedwater transient conditions have provided a significant qualification of DYNODE-P for analysis of this type of event in PWR's with OTSG's. This work has identified the importance of the subcooled heat transfer regime for the IEOTSG design during a LOFW event.

REFERENCES

Hassan, Y. A. and C. D. Morgan. 1983. "Steady-State and Transient Predictions of a 19-Tube Once-Through Steam Generator Using RELAP5/MOD1," **Nuclear Technology**, No. 60 (Jan.): 143.

Kern, R. C., et al. 1983. "DYNODE-P Version 5.4 - A Nuclear Steam Supply System Transient Simulator for Pressurized Water Reactor - User Manual", Topical Report UAI 83-49. Utility Associates International, Rockville, MD. (Nov.)

Ranson, V. H., et al. 1980. "RELAP5/MOD1 Code Manual - Volume 1: System Models and Numerical Methods." EG&G Idaho, Inc., Idaho Falls, ID (Nov.)

Simulators VI
© 1989 By The Society for Computer
Simulation International
ISBN 0-911801-51-0

Importance of momentum effects in BWR reactor vessel modeling

R. C. Kern
Utility Associates International
6003 Executive Blvd.
Rockville, MD 20852

ABSTRACT

The most severe class of events (other than design-basis LOCAs) for Boiling Water Reactors (BWR's) entails rapid pressurization of the Reactor Vessel (RV) due to rapid valve closures in the main steamlines. The severity of these events is caused by the fact that the pressurization of the core results in a rapid decrease in the core void fraction and, coupled to a strong negative void coefficient of reactivity, in a rapid power increase if the reactor protective system is slow in responding.

The DYNODE-B program models the Nuclear Steam Supply System of BWR's. Early versions only explicitly calculated the RV dome pressure. The latest version permits optional explicit calculation of the dome, core outlet, and core average pressures. The use of the new option has shown the influence of the two-phase momentum effects on the core pressure and flow transients resulting from pressure wave reflections at the liquid (incompressible) core inlet region.

INTRODUCTION

For Boiling Water Reactors (BWR's), rapid pressurization of the Reactor Vessel (RV) caused by rapid valve closures in the main steamlines; such as Main Steamline Isolation or turbine stop/control valves; results in a relative severe transient. The severity of these events is the result of pressurization of core which causes a collapsing of the voids in this region coupled with a strong negative void coefficient of reactivity. Thus, the core power increases rapidly due to the addition of positive reactivity, if the reactor protective system (RPS) is slow to respond thereby resulting in a slow negative reactivity insertion by the control rods.

Data taken at the Peach Bottom Unit 2 plant during turbine trip testing with delayed RPS response (Carmichael and Niemi 1978) indicated that the RV dome and core pressure transients are similar in nature and the only major difference was a time delay associated with the sonic pressure wave traveling between these two regions. The true detailed nature of the two pressure responses however is obscured by high frequency oscillations caused by the sensing lines which cannot be numerically filtered out easily.

The Peach Bottom tests have been successfully modeled with the DYNODE-B computer program (Kern et al. 1981). In early versions of DYNODE-B, the only pressure which was explicitly calculated in the RV was the dome pressure; the core pressure was taken as the dome pressure with an appropriate time delay. The results obtained with this version did not show any significant core flow increase which was indicated from the core pressure drop measurements. A revised code version (Kern 1988) in which the dome, core outlet, and core average pressures are explicitly calculated has been developed and shows the influence of the two-phase momemtum effects on the core pressurization and flow transients which result from the pressure wave propagation through the core and reflection at the solid core inlet region.

MODEL DESCRIPTIONS

The early versions of DYNODE-B (Old Model) calculate the RV dome pressure based on the conservation of mass and energy in this region of the system. The recirculation flow used for the boundary conditions on this region are obtained from solving the overall loop momentum equation in which the fluid acceleration between the core outlet and dome inlet is obtained from the core inlet flow acceleration. This assumption is equivalent to assuming fluid incompressibility in the two-phase core and core outlet regions.

The latest version of DYNODE-B (New Model) calculates the RV dome, core outlet, and core average pressures along with the associated connecting flow rates by simulataneously solving conservation of mass, energy, and momentum. The recirculation boundary flows at the core inlet and dome outlet are obtained from the overall loop momentum equation which has been modified to account for the fluid acceleration at the core outlet. This model accounts for the momentum effects within the RV caused by changes in the boundary steam flows.

RESULTS

To determine the influence of the RV momemtum effects on a severe overpressurization transient, a typical BWR plant was modeled for a turbine trip transient. In this case, the turbine stop valves close in 0.1 sec. The sonic wave transit time from the stop valve to the RV inlet is an additional 0.11 sec. The RPS scram signal occurs at 0.27 sec.

The comparisons of the results obtained with the two different models are shown in Figures 1 through 3 for the RV dome and core average pressures and the core inlet flow. The three cases presented are denoted as: 1 (Old Model); 2a (New Model-Nominal Core Outlet Inertia); and 2b (New Model - 1/2 Nominal Core Outlet Inertia).

As seen from these results, the models predict similar pressure references but the new model yields higher core pressures. The influence of the core outlet inertia is evident in these results. The smaller inertia case (2b) results in a faster initial pressurization of the core as expected but allows the reflected pressure wave at the core inlet to pass more effectively back into the dome as evidenced by the comparison at 0.6 sec. In effect, the larger inertia bottles the pressure in the core region and results in a more severe transient.

The core inlet flow response between cases 1 and 2 are significantly different and illustrate the impact of the equivalent assumption of incompressibility in the Old Model. The larger inertia case (2a) results in a stiffer coupling of the dome and core pressures thereby causing a higher initial acceleration of the core inlet flow and subsequent higher peak (0.4 sec). The core inlet flow response in both cases is a damped oscillation with a similar frequency for the dominant harmonic. The smaller inertia case appears to have several harmonics.

SUMMARY

The comparisons of models for calculating the pressurization of BWR reactor vessels resulting from rapid reductions in the boundary steam flow have demonstrated the impact of two-phase momentum effects in the core region on the core pressure and flow responses.

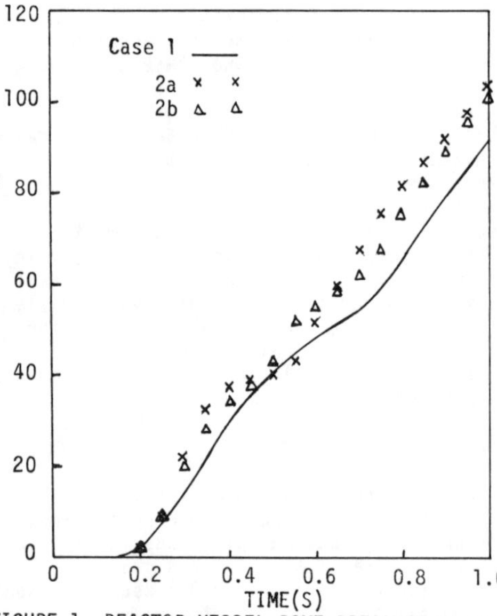

FIGURE 1. REACTOR VESSEL DOME PRESSURE RESPONSE

REFERENCES

Carmichael, L. A. and R. O. Niemi. 1978. "Transient and Stability Tests at Peach Bottom Atomic Power Station Unit 2 at End of Cycle 2", Topical Report EPRI NP-564. Electric Power Reserch Institute, Palo Alto, CA. (June)

Kern, R. C., et al. (1981). "Qualification of an Advanced BWR Transient Model for Pressurization Transients", In **Transactions of the American Nuclear Society**, No. 39 (San Francisco, CA, Nov. 29-Dec. 4) 629-630.

Kern, R. C. (1988). "DYNODE-B Version 6.0 - Boiling Water Reactor Simulator", Topical Report UAI 88-11. Utility Associates International, Rockville, MD (July).

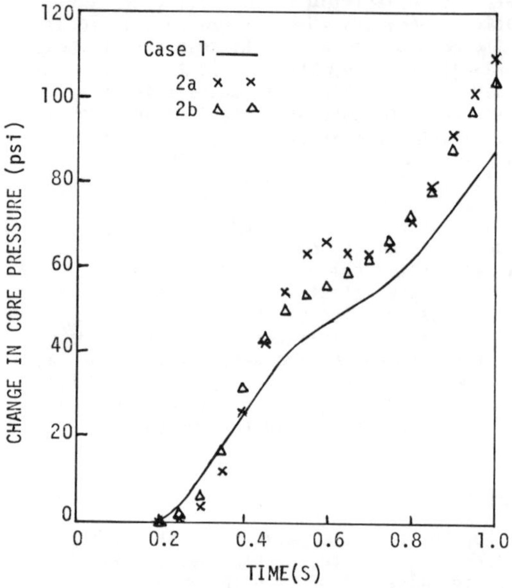

FIGURE 2. CORE AVERAGE PRESSURE RESPONSE

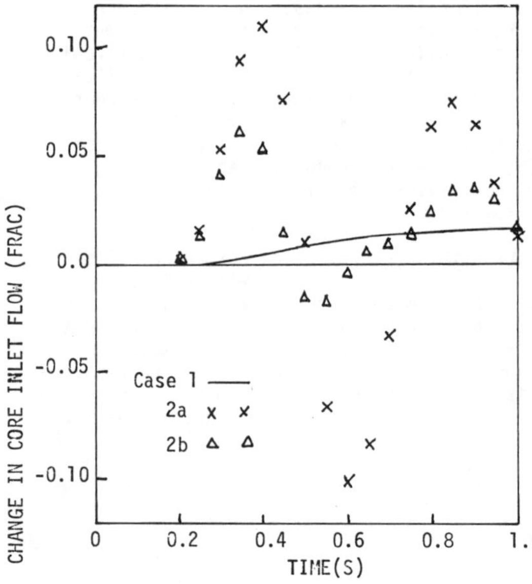

FIGURE 3. CORE INLET FLOW RESPONSE

Simulators VI

ISBN 0-911801-51-0

A nuclear power plant certification test plan and checklist

Scott M. Halverson
Union Electric Company
Callaway Plant
P.O. Box 620
Fulton, Missouri 65251

ABSTRACT

Regulations within the nuclear industry are requiring that all reference plant simulators be certified prior to or during 1991. A certification test plan is essential to ensure that this goal is met. A brief description of each step in the certification process will be provided in this paper, along with a checklist to help ensure completion of each item. Detailed requirements and additional guidance is found in the following documents:

10 CFR Part 55 Operators' Licenses

NRC FORM-474 Simulator Facility Certification

REGULATORY GUIDE 1.149 Nuclear Power Plant Simulation Facilities for Use in Operator License Examinations

NUREG-1258 Evaluation Procedure for Simulation Facilities Certified Under 10 CFR 55

NUREG-1262 Answers to Questions at Public Meetings Regarding Implementation of Title 10, Code of Federal Regulations, Part 55 on Operator's Licenses

ANSI/ANS-3.5-1985 Nuclear Power Plant Simulators for Use in Operator Training

INTRODUCTION

Prior to attempting certification of the reference plant simulator, a review of all the above documents should be completed. A list of work items should be prepared to include: identification of software modifications, hardware modifications, the plant data to be obtained, initial conditions to be stabilized, tests to be performed, and the documentation required. A basic outline of the certification project should be established and a milestone schedule should be developed by the simulator supervisor. A checklist should be drafted to be sure that all items are included on the schedule.

A manpower estimate must then be completed to determine if the present staff can achieve all of the items in the time period allowed. Once the project plan, schedule, and manpower estimate are completed, a presentation should be made to management for approval of the project.

CONFIGURATION CONTROL

A Configuration Control process is assumed to be in place at the simulation facility. Plant modification data must be readily available to the simulator group. The plant data is used as the database for the simulator. This data is reviewed, evaluated, and implemented in the form of simulator modifications, matching the simulator to the reference plant. Student and instructor feedback is used to initiate simulator modifications, based on training needs. Configuration Control Tests are required to verify proper completion of the modifications on the simulator. A tracking mechanism is needed to document the configuration control process.

TEST PLAN

The tests required for Certification of the Simulator will be discussed here. Keep in mind that the Certification effort is not complete without an in-place Configuration Control process and a method to control software and hardware implementation. The certification process involves testing in four basic categories:

1. Annual Tests - Tests conducted each year to certify the overall operability of the simulator and hardware fidelity

2. 25% Test - Malfunction and Surveillance Procedure Tests performed during the four year cycle, at a rate of 25% each year, to validate simulation support of the examination process for Senior Reactor Operator and Operator License Applicants

3. Random Tests - Tests of the instructor interface system that are performed on a random basis to ensure operability of the various instructor commands to support training needs

4. Configuration Control Tests - Tests conducted to verify the accuracy and functionality of all modifications made to the simulator during the previous year

A Certification Testing Plan should include the following testing items:

ENVIRONMENTAL VALIDATION

Control Room

The reference plant control room and the simulator control room must be evaluated. Specifically, the "at-the-controls" area at both locations must be as close as is reasonable and practical. Methods used in the comparison could include: review of floor plans, plant control room tours, and operator feedback. The major concerns are that the same number of panels are present and the panel layout is similar to the reference plant. Differences must be corrected or justified.

The purpose of matching the control room and the simulator control room is to train in an environment that closely matches the plant. This should reduce the possibility of errors made due to changes in the environment. The NRC also uses the simulator as an examination tool and allows use of a reference plant simulator instead of conducting tests in the actual plant control room. The examiners require that the license examination candidates take the same actions in the simulator as those expected to be observed in the real plant.

Control Panels

The control panels that are simulated must look, feel, and respond like the reference plant control panels. Typically, slides, pictures, or video tapes are made of both the main control room panels and the simulator panels. An engraving list comparison could also be used to identify items that are difficult to see on the slides. Particular attention should be paid to locations, types/styles, and color of controls and indications simulated.

For panels not simulated and not having controls added, a picture should be placed on the panel front to display what the controls look like.

Special Features

Explain all items that are present in the simulator that are not required but enhance the training process. Items that may be present include:

Video tape equipment
Microphones
Emergency telephone equipment
Instructor booth
Viewing area
Panels simulated that are not in the "at-the-controls" area

REAL TIME VERIFICATION

A method must be available to compare simulation time to real time, to verify that the simulator is still running in real time. Central processing speed, memory size, and individual task modules may slow down simulation. Typical measuring techniques include a software resource monitor program or a hardware add-on board. A combination of observation of simulator operations and monitoring of the computer time may be desirable.

STEADY STATE OPERATIONS

Initial Conditions

Operators expect the simulator indications to match the plant. Prior to operation of the simulator, the initial conditions must be established. The initial conditions on the simulator should match possible plant conditions. One method to establish a known baseline condition is to obtain technical specification logs in the plant and compare these to logs taken on the simulator. Adjust the simulator to match the known plant conditions. This will validate that the simulator matches the plant at the first instant in time.

Examples of possible choices for initial conditions:

Ready to withdraw shutdown bank rods - BOL
Ready to withdraw control bank rods - BOL
1% steady state power - BOL
10% steady state power - BOL
20% steady state power - BOL
50% steady state power - BOL
80% steady state power - BOL
100% steady state power - BOL
100% steady state power - Middle of Life
100% steady state power - End of Life

Steady State Stability

The simulator is run for a period of 60 minutes at the beginning of life 100% steady state power level condition. Indications (Analog outputs) are recorded during the test. Indications on the simulator can be compared to the initial snapshot condition to validate stability. An automatic printout can be used to display those indications exceeding a change of more than the allowed value. The present requirements are a 2 percent change for critical parameters and a 10 percent change for other parameters. The full scale value of the indication is defined as 100 percent.

This technique can also be used to verify stability of initial conditions at other than 100% power by running the stability tests for shorter periods of time.

NORMAL OPERATIONS

Daily Operations

Daily simulator operations include a heatup from cold shutdown conditions followed by a reactor startup and power operations. Load changes are conducted during power operations. A plant shutdown is conducted followed by cooldown of the simulator to cold shutdown conditions. Typically these normal operations are performed during the initial operator training simulator courses. Documentation must show that these evolutions were completed and a feedback mechanism is available to correct any discrepancies noted during the training scenario.

Surveillance Procedures

Surveillance procedures on safety related systems that can normally be conducted from the control room, with control room indications available, should be capable of being performed on the simulator.

TRANSIENTS

The ten transients listed in Appendix B of ANSI/ANS-3.5-1985 should be run and graphed for evaluation. The parameters to graph are clearly stated for each transient. The time period of the graph, starting from 100 seconds prior to the event until 600 seconds following the event, will usually plot the transient to a stable condition. Plotting the graph at 1 second intervals provides a good resolution.

Be aware that the data is required to be recorded at one half second intervals by the ANSI standard.

SIMULATOR OPERATING LIMITS

The simulator must be capable of alerting the instructor if operating limits are being approached. If a Safety Parameter Display System is available messages will automatically be available, in many cases, if parameters approach off-scale readings. If two instruments in the same channel approach off-scale readings, a FAIL message is printed on the screen. An alternate method to indicate operating limits is to print messages on the instructor console if predesignated setpoints are exceeded.

INSTRUCTOR INTERFACE

Malfunctions

Specific malfunctions are required to be available on the simulator. Twenty-five percent of all malfunctions must be tested annually. Include items monitored such as annunciators, meters, and controllers. Also include the expected plant response and the actual simulator response. Documentation must show that each test was completed with satisfactory results. A testing "abstract" has been required by the NRC.

Local Operator Actions

Local Operator Actions (LOAs) are provided to allow the instructor to simulate taking actions that would in reality be performed by operators outside the control room (normally at the direction of Control Room personnel). To ensure the adequacy of the currently available LOAs on the reference plant simulator, a random selection of LOAs is normally tested. This testing can be accomplished during the performance of surveillance procedures on the simulator. When a surveillance procedure requires the assistance from the operators, remote from the control room, the appropriate LOA is used and tested concurrently with the surveillance procedure.

Plant Parameters

During the course of training on the simulator, situations may develop which necessitate the changing of a particular plant parameter which varies a system operating characteristic. These items are not normally controlled or changed quickly by an operator, (e.g., specific levels in certain tanks, boron concentrations, temperatures, grid voltage and frequency, etc.). To allow the instructor control over items of this nature, a plant parameter interface is available.

Random selection testing of the plant parameters ensures that this function is available to the instructor. This function often is used to force students to refill a tank or perform a surveillance procedure.

Bistables

Setpoints for the various controllers and alarms are adjusted via the bistable instructor command. Bistables can also be turned off or on by the instructor. Testing should include verification that bistables can be placed in each of these conditions.

Many of the plant protective actions are initiated by bistables when a given setpoint is exceeded. Occasionally these bistables must be manually changed (setpoint adjusted, manually tripped, etc.) because of abnormal plant conditions. These bistables may also, on occasion, fail to perform correctly; either failing as they are or actually initiating a protective action when actual plant conditions do not warrant such action.

Annunciators

Annunciators can be failed in the "on" condition, the "off" condition, or "as-is" condition. Annunciators can easily be tested by an automatic program which tests logic in a controlled manner. The setpoints of the annunciator inputs are tested via the bistable tests.

Component Override

During the normal training session, the instructor may desire to initiate an event on the main control board for which no other instructor interface (Malfunction, Bistable, etc.) exists. Any light, switch, meter, controller, recorder, annunciator, or item on the main control board may be overridden into a desired condition. This could represent a switch failure at the zero position. To ensure that the instructor can accomplish this on any one of the myriad of control board components, the instructor interface Component Override exists.

SIMULATOR CERTIFICATION REVIEW GROUP

A group of personnel from Operations, Engineering, Licensed Training, and Simulator Group should review all Configuration Control Tests and Certification Tests and provide final acceptance. This review should include both random retesting on the simulator and a detailed review of the documentation.

ANNUAL REPORT

An annual report should be prepared to describe the status of the Reference Plant Simulator. The report should include a general description of the simulator and provide a brief overview of all tests performed. Attachments should include a four year summary of work items prior to the date of the report, the summary of all tests conducted during the year, and a schedule indicating how open items will be corrected in the future. The initial report is forwarded to the NRC accompanied by a NRC Form-474. All reports following the initial report are retained on-site as a four year retention required record.

References:

1987 Callaway Plant Simulator Initial Certification Report

1988 Callaway Plant Simulator Annual Recertification Report

John Oakes, Engineer-Simulator Support
Callaway Plant Simulator

Norm Reed, Engineer-Simulator Support
Callaway Plant Simulator

REFERENCE PLANT SIMULATOR
CERTIFICATION
CHECK LIST

1.0 ENVIRONMENTAL VALIDATION

1.1 CONTROL ROOM

____1. Obtained latest revision copy of Reference Plant control room floor plan. Obtained drawing of Reference Plant Simulator control room floor plan. A comparison of the floor plans was completed. A list of differences is available for inspection.

____2. Compared lighting in the plant and simulator control rooms. A list of differences is available for inspection.

____3. Communications systems available in the plant and simulator control rooms have been compared. A list of differences is available for inspection.

____4. Furnishings in the plant and the simulator have been reviewed. A list of differences is available for inspection.

1.2 CONTROL PANELS

____1. Pictures of the Reference Plant main control boards have been taken. Pictures of the Reference Plant Simulator main control boards have been taken. A comparison of the pictures was completed. The pictures are available for inspection.

____2. The control panels have been verified to be correct as compared to the plant engraving list. The engraving list is available for inspection.

____3. The simulator will support the plant computer keyboard functions identified on the attached list.

____4. The simulator will support the plant computer displays identified on the attached list.

____5. The simulator will support plant computer trending capabilities identified on the attached list.

____6. The simulator will support the plant computer alarm displays identified on the attached list.

1.3 SPECIAL FEATURES

____1. Special features available on the Reference Plant Simulator are indicated on the attached list.

2.0 REAL TIME VERIFICATION

____1. The simulator runs in real time.

3.0 STEADY STATE OPERATIONS

3.1 INITIAL CONDITIONS

____1. For each initial condition to be certified, technical specification logs have been compared and are available for both the plant and the simulator.

____2. Heat Balances have been performed at 20%, 50%, 80% and 100% steady state of power beginning of life initial conditions.

3.2 STEADY STATE STABILITY

____1. Stability tests have been performed at 20%, 50%, 80%, and 100% steady state of power beginning of life initial conditions.

4.0 NORMAL OPERATIONS

____1. Normal plant operations are performed during the control board certification course. Problems identified via feedback from instructors and students are either corrected or indicated on the attached list.

____2. All applicants surveillance procedures were performed on the simulator. Problems identified via feedback from instructors and students are either corrected or indicated on the attached list.

5.0 TRANSIENTS

____1. Transients listed in Appendix B of ANSI/ANS-3.5-1985 have graphed on the simulator. The tests have been reviewed by a committee with members from Operations, Engineering and Training. Problems identified have either been corrected or are identified on the attached list.

6.0 SIMULATOR OPERATING LIMITS

____1. When parameters monitored on the SPDS panel are exceeding the expected values an amber light is displayed on the panel warning operators that an unusual condition exists and that indications can no longer be relied upon.

7.0 INSTRUCTOR INTERFACE

7.1 MALFUNCTIONS

____1. All malfunctions listed in ANSI/ANS-3.5-1985 have been tested. The tests have been reviewed by a committee with members from Operations, Engineering and Training. Problems identified have either been corrected or are identified on the attached list.

7.2 LOCAL OPERATOR ACTIONS

____1. Random selection testing has been conducted to validate the operability of local operator actions. The tests have been reviewed by a committee with members from Operations, Engineering and Training. Problems identified have either been corrected or are identified on the attached list.

7.3 PLANT PARAMETERS

____1. Random selection testing has been conducted to validate the operability of plant parameters. The tests have been reviewed by a committee with members from Operations, Engineering and Training. Problems identified have either been corrected or are identified on the attached list.

7.4 BISTABLES

____1. Random selection testing has been conducted to validate the operability of the bistables. The tests have been reviewed by a committee with members from Operations, Engineering, and Training. Problems identified have either been corrected or are identified on the attached list.

7.5 ANNUNCIATORS

____1. An automatic testing sequence has been conducted to validate the operability of the annunciators. The tests have been reviewed by a committee with members from Operations, Engineering, and Training. Problems identified have either been corrected or are identified on the attached list.

7.6 COMPONENT OVERRIDE

____1. Random selection testing has been conducted to validate the operability of component override. The tests have been reviewed by a committee with members from Operations, Engineering, and Training. Problems identified have either been corrected or are identified on the attached list.

Simulators VI
© 1989 By The Society for Computer
Simulation International
ISBN 0-911801-51-0

Accurate predictions of steam generator bundles using new heat transfer correlations and flow regime maps

Thomas Blanchat and Yassin Hassan
Department of Nuclear Engineering
Texas A&M University
College Station, Texas 77843-3133

ABSTRACT

A RELAP5/MOD2 computer code model for a Once Through Steam Generator has been developed. Parametric studies were conducted on aspirator placement, code-allowed junction geometry options, tube heat structure surface area, tube hydraulic diameter, and feedwater temperature. The calculated heat transfer in the nucleate boiling flow was underpredicted as shown by a predicted superheat of only 11°C (20°F), whereas plant values range from 22–30°C (40–60°F). Existing heat transfer correlations used in thermal-hydraulic computer codes do not provide accurate predictions of the measurement-derived secondary convective heat transfer coefficients for steam generators because they were developed for flow inside tubes, not tube bundles. A new flow regime map for flow across bundles has been developed and implemented in the code. This new flow regime map predicts better transition criteria between bubbly-to-slug and slug-to-annular flow. Consequently, improved saturated conditions for the fluid flow at the entrance to the boiler were obtained. A new Chen-type correlation was developed to predict the boiling heat transfer for steam generator tube bundle geometries. This new correlation predicts better superheat.

INTRODUCTION

The steam generator is a major component in pressurized water reactors (PWR). Predicting the response of a steam generator during both steady-state and transient conditions is essential in studying the thermal-hydraulic behavior of a nuclear reactor coolant system. Therefore, extensive analytical and experimental research has been performed to investigate the thermal-hydraulic behavior of the steam generators during operational and accident transients. The objective of this study is to predict the behavior of the secondary side of the Once Through Steam Generator (OTSG), using the RELAP5/MOD2 computer code and, in particular, to obtain a better prediction of heat transfer coefficients in bundles.

The RELAP5/MOD2 code is a new version of the RELAP5 thermal-hydraulic code series (Ransom et al. 1978)(Ransom et al. 1982)(Ransom et al. 1985). This light water reactor transient analysis code was developed for the United States Nuclear Regulatory Commission, to provide an advanced best-estimate predictive capability for use in a wide spectrum of applications in support of the regulatory evaluation and licensing process. The principal new feature of RELAP5/MOD2 is the use of the full six-equation, two-fluid, nonequilibrium, and nonhomogenous model.

There is abundant information available on boiling in tubes, but unfortunately, information on flow boiling in tube bundles is scarce. This study focused on the flow regime map and the heat transfer correlations for tube bundles. Steady-state conditions were predicted with the current version of the RELAP5/MOD2 (cycle 36.05) code, and compared with experimental plant data. The code predictions consistently underpredict the degree of superheat. With no code modifications, the code currently predicts a 11°C (20°F) superheat. The goal is to predict a 22–33°C (40–60°F) superheat (as suggested by test data), through modifications of flow regime maps and heat transfer correlations. The cause for the inaccurate OTSG predictions is that "tube bundle" flow differs from "tube" flow. A steam generator is composed mainly of tube bundles; however, the code currently uses round tubes or pipes as component volumes in addition to using round tube thermal-hydraulic correlations in calculations.

RELAP5/MOD2 COMPUTER CODE DESCRIPTION

The principal objective of the RELAP5 code is to provide the U.S. Nuclear Regulatory Commission (USNRC) with a fast running and user convenient light water reactor system transient analysis code for use in rule making, licensing audit calculations, evaluation of operator guidelines, and as a basis for a nuclear plant analyzer (Ransom et al. 1985). The code is used extensively at the Idaho National Engineering Laboratyory (INEL) for experiment planning, pretest prediction, and posttest analysis in support of the Semiscale, LOFT, and Power Burst Facility (PBF) LWR research projects. A secondary objective is to provide advanced analysis capability to other nuclear power organizations for use in design, safety analysis, and licensing application work.

The goal of the code has been to establish a reliable analytical capability for use in the nuclear power industry. The approach has been to rely on first principles modeling where possible and thus reduce empiricism. The RELAP5/MOD2 two-phase flow model provides a significantly improved capability over RELAP5/MOD1 and represents an enhanced understanding of the underlying physics of two-phase flow.

An additional goal of the code has been to provide a more comprehensive and generic modeling of the complete nuclear steam supply system including turbines, generators, condensers, feed systems, and plant controls. The code includes many generic component models from which general systems can be simulated. The component models include pumps, valves, pipes, annuli, branches, single volumes, single junctions, heat structures, reactor point kinetics, electric heaters, jet pumps, turbines, separators, accumulators, and control system components. In addition, special process models are included for effects such as form loss, flow at an abrupt area change, branching, choked flow, boron tracking, and a noncondensible gas. The highly generic modeling capability of the code also permits it to be used in many nonnuclear applications of steam-water systems. The PWR applications for which the code is intended include large and small break loss-of-coolant accidents, operational transients, such as anticipated transients without SCRAM, loss of feed, loss-of-offsite power, loss of flow, and over cooling transients. The system behavior can be simulated up to the point of fuel damage. Fuel cladding ballooning and/or rupture with metal-water reaction are not modeled.

Each version of the code reflects the increased knowledge and new simulation requirements from both large and small scale experiments, theoretical research in two-phase flow, numerical solution methods, computer programming advances, and the increased size and speed of computers. The principal new feature of the RELAP5 series is the use of a two-fluid nonequilibrium nonhomogeneous hydrodynamic model for transient simulation of the two-phase system behavior. RELAP5/MOD2 employs a full nonequilibrium, six equation, two-fluid model. The use of the two-fluid model eliminates the need of the RELAP4 submodels, such as the bubble rise and enthalpy transport models, which were necessary to overcome the limitations of the single fluid model.

RELAP5/MOD2 can also be used for analysis of the transient behavior of piping systems containing steam/water, such as for estimating hydraulic loads on relief valve discharge lines.

ONCE THROUGH STEAM GENERATOR

The B&W Once Through Steam Generator (OTSG), is a vertical, straight-tube, straight-shell, counter-current flow heat exchanger with shell-side boiling. Figure 1 shows the OTSG fluid flow paths. Primary reactor coolant enters the steam generator through a nozzle in the upper level, flows down through more than 15,000 Inconel-600 alloy tubes, and exits at the bottom head through two outlet nozzles. On the secondary side, subcooled feedwater is sprayed downward into the annulus between the shell and the tube-bundle shroud, where it is heated to saturation by direct contact with steam aspirated from the tube bundle. The saturated feedwater enters the bottom of the tube bundle where nucleate boiling begins. After reaching 100% quality at about the mid-bundle elevation, the steam is superheated in the upper half of the bundles, flows down through the steam annulus, and exits through two steam outlet nozzles. The tubes are located on a triangular pitch, and the spacing between tubes is maintained along the length of the bundle by the tube support plates (TSP). The plates support each tube at equally spaced points around the circumference, while allowing most of the tube surface to be contacted by the secondary fluid. It should be noted that there is approximately a 50% reduction in flow area at the TSP in the tube bundle region. In addition, the subcooled feedwater should reach a saturated condition at approximately a mid-level position in the feedwater downcomer.

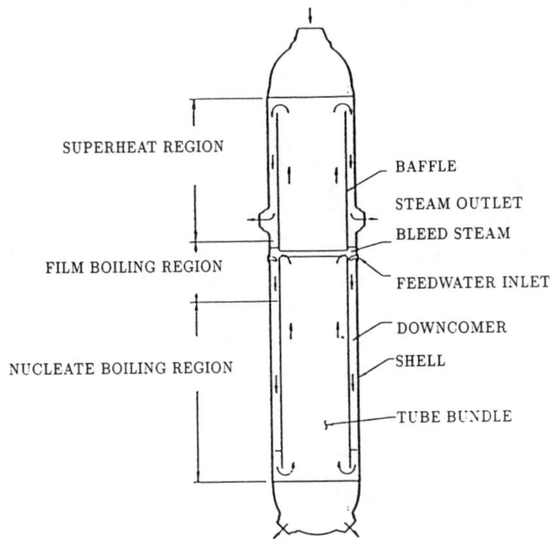

Figure 1 Once Through Steam Generator Flow Schematic

The RELAP5/MOD2 model of the OTSG depicting main components and flow paths is shown in Figure 2. The primary side of the steam generator was modeled by a pipe component consisting of twenty hydrodynamic volumes (700) and sixteen heat structures. The inlet to the primary was modeled, using a time-dependent volume (100) and junction (110), which forced the primary mass flow at 15.22 MPa (2,208 psia) and 316°C (601°F) in the steam generator inlet plenum. The primary coolant from the outlet plenum was discharged to a time-dependent volume (200) at 15.17 MPa (2,200 psia). The tube heat structure dimensions were based on 15,531 tubes with an inner diameter of 1.4147 cm (0.0464 ft) and a wall thickness of 0.0864 cm (0.0028 ft).

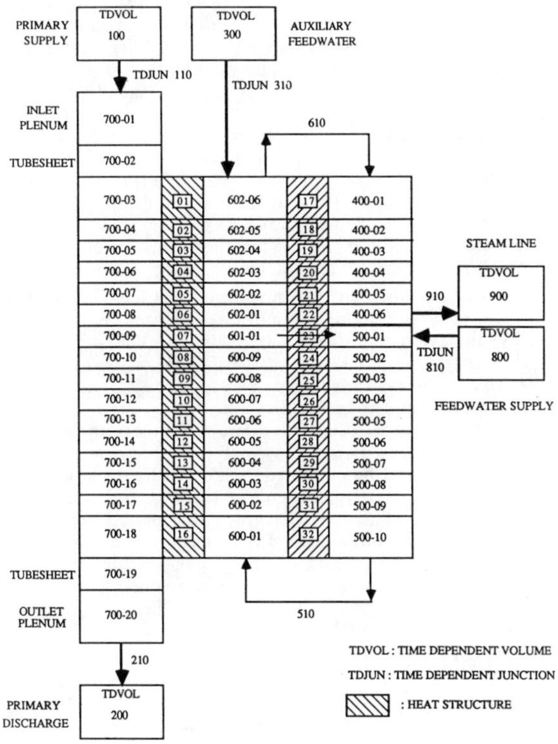

Figure 2 RELAP5/MOD2 Once Through Steam Generator Nodalization

The secondary side of the steam generator is divided into three major regions; the incoming feedwater annulus (500) (pipe component with ten hydrodynamic volumes), the tube bundle or "boiler" region, and the steam outlet annulus (400) (pipe component with six hydrodynamic volumes). The tube bundle region consists of two pipe components (600 & 602) and a branch component (601), for a total of sixteen hydrodynamic volumes. This allows the placement of fifteen reduced internal junction flow areas which model the internal tube support plates (TSP). In addition, the branch component is necessary to model an aspirator flow from the tube bundle region to preheat the incoming subcooled feedwater. An additional sixteen heat structures are used to model the vertical cylindrical baffle which connects the tube bundle region to the feedwater annulus and the steam outlet annulus.

The feedwater supply is modeled with a time-dependent junction (810) and volume (800). In addition, at steady state conditions, the steam exits the steam annulus through a single junction component to a time-dependent volume (900). The steam outlet time-dependent volume pressure is adjusted to maintain a pressure of 6.45 MPa (925 psia) in the steam annulus.

A time-dependent junction (310) and volume (300) is connected to the top of the tube bundle region to model the auxiliary feedwater connections for later transient analysis. No flow is allowed through this junction during the steady-state analysis.

The resulting model is initialized to a steady-state condition based on 100% load parameters.

TUBE BUNDLE FLOW REGIME MAP

In gas-liquid flow, the two phases can distribute in the conduit in a variety of ways. These distributions can vary when changes take place in flow rates, fluid properties, or conduit shape. In these distributions, it has been observed that natural groupings or patterns occur. It is expected that pressure drops, void fractions, heat transfer rates, and other parameters of interest will behave differently as the flow pattern changes (Dukler and Taitel 1986). Early work in this field showed that the use of empherical correlations that were different for each flow pattern, improved the comparison between calculated and measured pressure drops in horizontal pipes (Baker 1958). Currently, it is believed that it will be necessary to predict the flow pattern that exists in the system of interest to provide accurate predictions of the flow related phenomena.

Very few studies have appeared dealing with flow pattern transitions in a geometry different from a round pipe. However, a review of the literature pertaining to gas–liquid flow pattern transitions for vertical rod bundles has shown that geometry does affect the flow pattern transition points. Experiments using a 24–rod circular bundle with air–water systems have shown that bubble rise velocities in tube bundles are greater than those in tubes (Venkateswararao 1981). In addition, Venkateswararao finds that the trend of rise velocity with bubble size, when the bubbles rise in the restricted space of a four rod cell, is different than that for an infinite medium.

Venkateswararao also observed two types of slug flow patterns in tube bundles. In one, Taylor bubbles occupy the space in a four rod cell and flow upward, while the liquid flows down as a film along the rods. The cap of the bubble is not penetrated by the rod. This flow pattern is designated "cell type" slug flow. In the second, a large Taylor bubble is formed which spans a number of rods, with each rod penetrating the cap of the bubble. This Taylor bubble can be large enough to occupy the entire test section cross–sectional area. This slug pattern is designated "shroud" slug flow.

Currently, the RELAP5/MOD2 code chooses the bubble–to–slug transition (α_{B-S}) criteria as

$$\alpha_{B-S} = 0.25 \text{ MIN}\left[1.0, \left(\frac{D^*}{22.2}\right)^8\right] \tag{1}$$

for low mass fluxes (G $\leq$ 2000 kg/m^{2}s). D^* is the limiting dimensionless tube diameter allowing the presence of bubbly flow:

$$D^* = D_h\left[\frac{g}{\sigma}(\rho_f - \rho_g)\right] \tag{2}$$

where g is the gravitational constant and σ is the surface tension. This is the criteria that RELAP5/MOD2 has been choosing, since the mass flux is approximately 190 kg/m^{2}s for the OTSG model. This transition equation does not work for tube bundles. D^* for the OTSG is approximately 12, this corresponds to $\alpha_{B-S} = 0.002$ by Equation 2. This implies that any void fraction formation immediately places the flow into a slug regime.

Venkateswararao has developed a new theoretical bubble–to–slug transition equation

$$\alpha_{B-S} = 0.25\frac{\left[\sqrt{2}\left(\frac{P_t}{D_{tube}}\right) - 1\right]^2}{\frac{4}{\pi}\left(\frac{P_t}{D_{tube}}\right)^2 - 1} \tag{3}$$

where P_t is the tube pitch and D_{tube} is the tube outer diameter. Dispersed bubbles are never observed in the space directly between two rods, but are concentrated in the open space defined by the four rod cell. Bubbles which originate in the gap between two rods migrate to the open region as a result of the pressure driving force that exists due to the lower velocity that occurs between adjacent rods as compared to the open area. It is suggested that the transition flow in a bundle array takes place when the "local" voids of the open region reach 0.25. However, the calculated "average" voids at the transition will be lower and will depend on pitch–to–diameter ratio (P_t/D_{tube}). Equation 3 suggest that the bubble–to–slug transition for the OTSG bundle configuration should occur at

$$\alpha_{B-S} = 0.1604 \tag{4}$$

for the OTSG values of P_t and D_{tube}. This is lower from the conventional bubble–to–slug transition value of 0.25 for flow inside tubes.

A modified version of RELAP5/MOD2 was created to check the utilization of the two new words, pitch and tube o.d., and also Equation 3. The steam exit annulus, feedwater downcomer annulus, and primary tube volume's pitch and tube o.d. were set to 0.0 and the secondary tube bundle region's pitch and tube o.d. were set to 2.221 cm (0.072 feet) and 1.774 cm (0.052 feet), respectively. If RELAP5/MOD2 determined that a volume's pitch was equal to 0.0, then the bubble–to–slug transition (α_{B-S}) criteria was chosen as before with no modification. If RELAP5/MOD2 determines that a volume's pitch is not equal to 0.0, then the code chooses Equation 3 as the new bubble–to–slug transition criteria. However, little difference was noted in the secondary temperature profile since this transition occurs in the first "tube bundle " volume.

The literature review also suggests churn–to–annular transition for tube bundles occurs at a lower value than that for a circular tube geometry (Venkateswararao 1981, Collier 1981, Carey et al. 1986). The RELAP5/MOD2 computer code combines the churn regime with the slug regime. It uses a slug–to–annular transition α_{S-A} based on the critial vapor velocity required to suspend a liquid droplet developed by Taitel and Dukler (Ransom et al. 1982).

$$\alpha_{S-A} = \text{MAX}\left\{0.75, 1.4\frac{\left[\sigma g(\rho_f - \rho_g)\right]^{\frac{1}{4}}}{V_g\rho_g^{\frac{1}{2}}}\right\} \tag{5}$$

It also places a limit on the range of the slug–to–annular transition.

$$0.75 \leq \alpha_{S-A} \leq 0.96 \tag{6}$$

Two points need to be made. First, the coefficent 1.4 was chosen since it gave better code results to experimental data for "tube" geometry. Second, the same reason was used to place a lower limit (0.75) on the slug–to–annular transition point. Experiments show that churn–to–annular transition for vertical rod bundles occurs at values of α_g less than that for tube geometry (Venkateswararao 1981). Venkateswararao has determined that the theoretical churn–to–annular transition for flow in vertical rod bundles occurs at lower values of the gas superficial velocity than for pipe flow. His experimental results for flow in rod arrays also shows that the transition occurs at lower void values for low liquid flow rates. Venkateswararao has also shown that his theory shows reasonable agreement with data from other experimenters (Bergles et al. 1968, Williams and Peterson 1978).

Jones and Zuber have examined this transition for various geometries. The recommended equation for churn–to–annular flow transition uses a factor which takes into account the hydraulic equivalent diameter for a rod bundle (Collier 1981). It can be shown that use of this factor reduces the transition point below that for a tube geometry.

Another study on annular film–flow boiling in a vertical channel with offset strip fins (geometry similar to tube bundles) also concludes that the transition occurs at a value of void fraction below that for tubes (Collier 1981, Carey and Mandrusiak 1986). In terms of the parameter j_g^* (nondimensional superficial gas velocity) defined by Wallis, the transition occurred at j_g^* equal to 0.5, whereas Wallis suggested a value of j_g^* equal to 0.9 for normal tube geometries (Collier 1981).

$$j_g^* = 0.9 = U_g\ \alpha_{S-A}\ \rho_g^{\frac{1}{2}}\ \left[gD(\rho_f - \rho_g)\right]^{-\frac{1}{2}} \tag{7}$$

The following theoretical equations have been developed for predicting void fractions in the churn regime (α_{churn}) based on the holdup model, and in the annular regime (α_{ann}) based on an overall force balance on the gas and liquid flowing in a four rod cell (Venkateswararao 1981). The void fraction in the churn regime is given by

$$\alpha_{churn} = \frac{U_{gs}}{1.15(U_{gs} + U_{ls}) + U_0} \tag{8}$$

where U_{gs}, U_{ls}, and U_0 are superficial vapor velocity, superficial liquid velocity, and stagnant liquid bubble rise velocity, respectively. The void fraction in the annular regime is given by

$$\alpha_{ann} = 1 - \frac{\frac{.0025}{CD_{tube}\alpha_{ann}^{3}}\left[1 + 2g(\alpha_{ann})\right]\left[1 + 300g(\alpha_{ann})\right]\rho_g U_{gs}^2}{(\rho_l - \rho_g)g}$$

$$- \frac{\frac{.0025}{CD_{tube}(1-\alpha_{ann})^3}\rho_l U_{ls}^2}{(\rho_l - \rho_g)g} \tag{9}$$

where

$$C = \frac{1}{\pi}\left[\left(\frac{P_t}{D_{tube}}\right)^2 - \frac{\pi}{4}\right] \tag{10}$$

and

$$g(\alpha_{ann}) = \frac{\left[1 + 4C(1 - \alpha_{ann})\right]^{0.5} - 1}{2} \tag{11}$$

The transition occurs at the intersection of Equations 8 & 9 where $\alpha_{churn} = \alpha_{ann}$, and this defines the locus of the U_{gs}, U_{ls} pairs, at which transition takes place. The intersection of code predicted data with the transition curve for the OTSG shows the slug-to-annular point for the OTSG.

$$\alpha_{S-A}(OTSG) = 0.63 \tag{12}$$

TUBE BUNDLE HEAT TRANSFER CORRELATIONS

The accuracy of predicted heat transfer coefficients in flow boiling is important for the design and optimization of heat exchange equipment and the prediction of steady state and transient behavior of steam generators. There are various correlations proposed for flow boiling. Most of these correlations are based on experimental results inside tubes. The heat transfer correlations used in RELAP underpredict the heat transfer coefficients for tube bundle flow. Much larger boiling coefficients have been obtained on the secondary side of tube bundles in the Semiscale steam generator (Boucher 1987). Measurement-derived secondary heat transfer coefficients were as high as 62,346 W/m²-K (3.0 BTU/sec-ft²-°F), whereas the Chen correlation predicted 13,703 W/m²-K (0.66 BTU/sec-ft²-°F). The Chen correlation was developed primarily from data for flow inside an externally heated tube. Flow mechanisms are different for flows inside internally heated tube bundles. It is believed that the bundle geometry causes the flow behavior to be significantly different from flow inside tubes. Studies of boiling heat transfer in a horizontal tube bundle in upward crossflow with R-113 also indicate the need to develop new correlations for tube bundle geometry (Jenson and Hsu 1987). Bubble rise velocities are greater in tube bundles. In addition, it has been observed that few bubbles move in the space between rods but migrate to the open area that exists within an array of 4 rods (Venkateswararao 1981). This "sweeping" or "sliding" of bubbles from the rod walls to the open area in the cell induces circulation and increases turbulence. This results in heat transfer enhancement. Furthermore, it is postulated that heat transfer will also be enhanced by the additional turbulence created in the tube bundle flow by the tube support plates. Accordingly, understanding the basic mechanisms of tube bundle flow is of great importance in the design and analysis of more efficient heat exchangers.

The RELAP5/MOD2 code-predicted heat transfer coefficients calculated from the correlations for single phase forced liquid convection, subcooled nucleate boiling, and saturated nucleate boiling were reviewed and modified for "tube bundles".

RELAP5/MOD2 uses the Dittus-Boelter correlation to calculate heat transfer coefficients for single phase forced liquid convection

$$h = C\frac{k_f}{D_e}Re_f^{0.8}Pr_f^{0.4} \tag{13}$$

where C = 0.023. This correlation was originally derived for smooth flow in tubes. Weisman (1959) has studied available heat transfer data for water (single-phase) flowing parallel to tube bundles. The data was correlated using the form of the Colburn equation as a basis. The constant C in Equation 13 was replaced by a function of the pitch-to-diameter ratio (P_t/D_{tube}) and for the OTSG triangular pitch arrays is given by

$$C = 0.026\frac{P_t}{D_{tube}} - 0.006 \tag{14}$$

Evaluating this for a typical OTSG, C = 0.0304, which is a 32% increase over the Colburn value of 0.023. The RELAP5/MOD2 code was modified so that when a volume's pitch was not equal to zero, it replaced the constant 0.023 in Equation 13 with the constant predicted by Equation 14. However, since single phase forced liquid convection flow was never predicted in the OTSG tube bundle region, this modification had no effect on the predicted temperature profile.

The Chen correlation is used in RELAP5/MOD2 for subcooled and saturated nucleate boiling (Chen 1963).

$$h = h_{mac} + h_{mic} \tag{15}$$

$$h_{mac} = 0.023\frac{k_g}{D_e}Re_f^{0.8}Pr_f^{0.4}F \tag{16}$$

$$h_{mic} = 0.00122\frac{k_f^{0.79}C_{pf}^{0.45}\rho_f^{0.49}}{\sigma^{0.5}\mu_f^{0.29}h_{fg}^{0.24}\rho_g^{0.24}}\Delta T_{sat}^{0.24}\Delta P_{sat}^{0.75}S \tag{17}$$

The parameter F is the Reynolds number factor $(Re_{TP}/Re_f)^{0.8}$, and has a purely hydrodynamic nature; it takes into account the enhancement of heat transfer due to an increase in vapor quality (mixture quality) and was derived from tube flow data. The parameter S is the suppression factor due to the ratio of effective-to-wall superheat, which takes into account the nucleate boiling suppression by forced convection because of the reduction in the thermal boundary layer thickness. Currently, RELAP5/MOD2 calculates F from

$$F = 1.0 \qquad X_{tt}^{-1} \leq 0.1 \tag{18}$$

$$F = 2.35(X_{tt}^{-1} + 0.213)^{0.736} \quad X_{tt}^{-1} \geq 0.1 \tag{19}$$

where X_{tt}^{-1} is the Martinelli flow parameter

$$X_{tt}^{-1} = \left(\frac{\alpha_g\rho_g V_g}{(1-\alpha_g)\rho_f V_f}\right)^{0.9}\left(\frac{\rho_f}{\rho_g}\right)^{0.5}\left(\frac{\mu_g}{\mu_f}\right)^{0.1} \tag{20}$$

The RELAP5/MOD2 code was modified to choose a different heat transfer correlation if the volume had a pitch not equal to zero. The first modification was to insert the Weisman correlation (Equation 14) into Equation 16. The result was a superheat increase of 1.1°C (2°F).

The Reynolds number factor, F, can be described with a two-phase friction multiplier through the use of a momentum analogy, with the resulting expression for F given by

$$F = \left(\phi_L^2\right)^{\frac{m}{2-n}} \tag{21}$$

where ϕ_L^2 is the liquid-only two-phase friction multiplier, m is the Reynolds number exponent in the single phase convective heat transfer correlation, and n is the Reynolds number exponent in a Blasius-type friction correlation for the tube bundle. An expression was developed for ϕ_L^2 based on the data from a variety of tube banks (Ishihara 1980):

$$\phi_L^2 = 1 + \frac{8.0}{X_{tt}} + \frac{1.0}{X_{tt}^{2.0}} \tag{22}$$

The Reynolds number factor F, was modified with various combinations of constants and exponents to increase heat transfer coefficients to the range determined experimentally by Boucher. A simple equation for F has been derived which predicts heat transfer coefficients similar to that determined experimentally by Boucher.

$$F = \left[1 + \frac{20.0}{X_{tt}} + \frac{1.0}{X_{tt}^{2.0}}\right]^{0.75} \tag{23}$$

Note that for a typical OTSG, X_{tt}^{-1} ranges from 0.2 to 50.0 in the nucleate boiling region.

Figure 3 compares the base case (RELAP5/MOD2 with no modifications) tube bundle temperature profile with the profile obtained when using the combined modifications to the flow regime maps and the heat transfer correlations. These changes have produced an increase in superheat by 8°C (15°F). This figure shows that typically the first volume, or node, is subcooled, followed by saturation conditions until the aspirator location is reached. Critical Heat Flux or burnout is then achieved as indicated by a marked temperature increase above the saturation line. This point is also observed in the primary flow by the large change in slope in the temperature profile. It is believed that the drop in temperature in the last node of the secondary side is due to incorrect predictions of interfacial drag; subsequently, temperature decreases as the code attempts to "dryout" this volume.

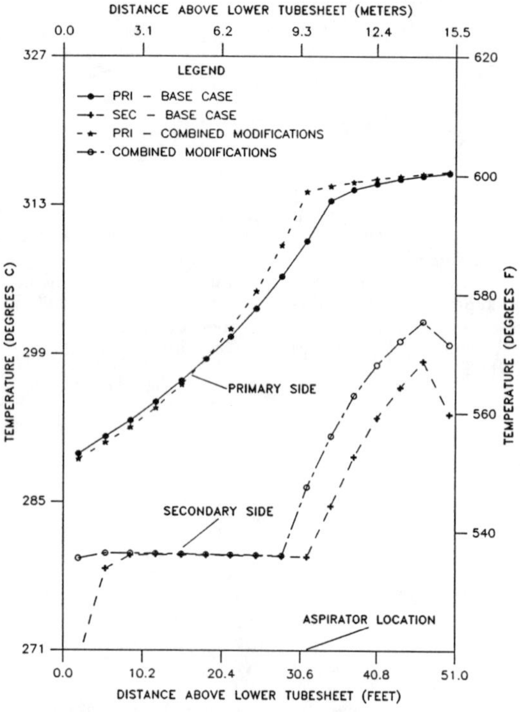

Figure 3 Base Case Temperature Distribution Compared With Combined Modifications

CONCLUSION

An accurate, realistic RELAP5/MOD2 model for the Once Through Steam Generator has been developed from technical drawings and specifications. Parametric studies were conducted which concluded that there was little effect on the predicted temperature distribution due to aspirator placement or due to the different junction geometry options allowed by the code. It was determined that underprediction of the heat transfer in the nucleate boiling flow can be mitigated (or corrected) by reducing the hydraulic diameter through the use of the small distance between the tubes, increasing tube heat structure surface area or by increasing inlet feedwater temperature. Literature searches have shown that tube bundle flow differs from the tube flow that RELAP5/MOD2 was developed for. RELAP5/MOD2 has been modified to "recognize" a tube bundle geometry and to choose a flow regime map and heat transfer correlation appropriate for that geometry. A new flow regime map for flow in bundles was developed and implemented in the code. This new flow regime map predicts better transition for bubble–to–slug and slug–to–annular flow for the OTSG. Consequently, improved saturated conditions for the fluid flow at the entrance to the boiler were obtained. The essential point is that these flow regimes have been shifted downward towards the tube bundle inlet, hence, we see the major effect that geometry plays in boiling heat transfer.

In addition, heat transfer correlations have been developed to produce similar heat transfer coefficients obtained experimentally in a scaled U–tube steam generator. This new correlation has caused superheat values to be increased by 8°C (15°F). Comparisons between the temperature profile test data for the 19–Tube Integral Economizer OTSG (Hassan 1988) and the RELAP5/MOD2 predicted values for both a base case and a combined modifications run on a 19–tube RELAP5/MOD2 model were performed. Better agreement is obtained.

REFERENCES

BAKER,O. "Multiphase Flow in Pipelines", Pipeline News, June 23, (1958).

BERGLES,A.E.; J.P. ROOS, and J.G. BOURNE, "Investigation of Boiling Flow Regimes and Critical Heat Flux", NYO–3304–13, Dynatech Corporation, Cambridge, Massachusetts, (1968).

BOUCHER,T.J., "Scale Model Test Results for an Inverted U–Tube Steam Generator With Comparisons to Heat Transfer Correlations", EG&G Idaho, Inc., ASME Winter Meeting, Boston, Mass., December 13–18, (1987).

CAREY,V.P. and G.D. MANDRUSIAK, "Annular Film–flow of Liquids in a Partially Heated Vertical Channel with Offset Strip Fins", International Journal of Heat and Mass Transfer, Volume 29, No. 6, (1986).

CHEN,J. "A Correlation for Boiling Heat Transfer to Saturated Fluids in Convective Flow", ASME Paper No. 63–HT–34, (1963).

COLLIER,J.G., "Convective Boiling and Condensation", 2nd ed., McGraw–Hill Publishing Company, New York, (1981).

DUKLER,A.E. and Y. TAITEL, "Flow Pattern Transitions in Gas–Liquid Systems: Measurement and Modeling", Multiphase Science and Technology, Volume 2, Hemisphere Publishing Corporation, New York, (1986).

HASSAN,Y.A., "Assessment of Boiling Heat Transfer Correlations for Once Through Steam Generators", Nuclear Technology, Volume 81, No. 3, (June 1988).

ISHIHARA,K.; J.W. PALEO, and J. TABOREK, "Critical Review of Correlations for Predicting Two–Phase Flow Pressure Drop Across Tube Banks", Heat Transfer Engineering, Volume 1, (1980).

JENSEN,M.K. and J.T. HSU, "A Parametric Study of Boiling Heat Transfer in a Tube Bundle", Proceedings ASME–JSME Thermal Engineering Joint Conference, Hawaii, March 22–27, (1987).

RANSOM,V.H.; R.J. WAGNER, J.A. TRAPP, L.R. FEINAUER, G.W. JOHNSON, D.M. KISER, and R.A. RIEMKE, "RELAP5/MOD0 Code Description," Idaho Engineering Laboratory, CDAP–TR–057, (May 1978).

RANSOM,V.H.; R.J. WAGNER, J.A. TRAPP, L.R. FEINAUER, G.W. JOHNSON, D.M. KISER, and R.A. RIEMKE, "RELAP5/MOD1 Code Manual," NUREG/CR–1826, EGG–2070, EG&G Idaho, Inc., (November 1982).

RANSOM,V.H.; R.J. WAGNER, J.A. TRAPP, L.R. FEINAUER, G.W. JOHNSON, D.M. KISER, and R.A. RIEMKE, "Code Structure, Systems Models, and Solution Methods", RELAP5/MOD2 Code Manual, Volume 1, Idaho Falls, Idaho, (August 1985).

VENKATESWARARAO,P., "Flow Pattern Transition for Two-Phase Flow in a Vertical Rod Bundle Array", Ph.D. Thesis, University of Houston, Houston, Texas, (1981).

WEISMAN,J. "Heat Transfer to Water Flowing Parallel to Tube Bundles ", Nuclear Science Engineering, Volume 6, (1959).

WILLIAMS,C.L. and A.C. PETERSON,Jr., "Two Phase Flow Patterns with High-Pressure Water in a Heated Four-Rod Bundle", Nuclear Science & Engineering, Volume 68, (1978).

Simulators VI
© 1989 By The Society for Computer
Simulation International
ISBN 0-911801-51-0

On comparison of models for simulation of transients in a PWR pressurizer

M. Massoud and F.J. Munno
Dept. of Chemical & Nuclear Engineering
University of Maryland
College Park, MD 20742

ABSTRACT

A qualitative comparison is made on various models for simulation of transients in a PWR pressurizer based on the features included in each model. For this purpose, various transport processes in the pressurizer are identified, then different models are evaluated and the reason for developing alternate models is addressed. Finally, the advantages and drawbacks associated with each model are presented. Based on this comparison, it is concluded that for off-line analysis and design, elaborate models utilizing the state-of-the-art data and correlations to maximize accuracy are recommended. However, for the purpose of on-line simulation, those models must sacrifice accuracy so as to optimize computation time.

INTRODUCTION

Thermal hydraulic analysis of a pressurizer has dual importance. In design, it provides a basic tool for determination of pressurizer dimensions to accommodate system transients. In operation, it provides the means to support and enhance the data acquisition system. The diversity of methods proposed for the analysis of the pressurizer requires a systematic comparison of models in order to identify and highlight the advantages and shortcomings of each method.

BACKGROUND

Pressurizer modeling, has evolved from a crude approach which has gradually been replaced by more refined models to achieve more detailed information and enhanced accuracy.

Design requirements of a pressurizer for a Pressurized Water Reactor (PWR) call for a vapor region to act as a compressible region during an insurge process which may be followed by the action of the spray system to reduce vapor pressure. Conversely, in the case of an outsurge process, sufficient supply of liquid is required to provide for the outsurge which is then followed by the action of heaters to maintain vapor pressure. It is further required that water level during transients remains well below a relief valve and well above the heaters location.

TRANSPORT PROCESSES IN A PRESSURIZER

During a PWR transient, mass, momentum, and energy are exchanged in the pressurizer. Of interest, however, are the mass and energy transfers. The momentum equation is applied only to the safety and relief valves (SRVs) in the form of critical (choked) flow. Due to their importance, mass flow rates and heat transfer processes are identified and discussed next.

Energy Transfer In Pressurizer

The energy exchanged is generally associated with heat, work and convective energy transfer. The heat transfer term includes the exchange of heat between solid-fluid, liquid-liquid, and liquid-vapor.

Solid-Fluid Heat Transfer - includes generation of bubbles by the action of the heater and the wall heat transfer. The latter includes heat transfer associated with change of phase such as vapor condensation on the cold wall or formation of bubbles in the liquid adjacent to the hot wall, during an outsurge. It also includes heat transfer by natural convection and radiation. Conduction exists axially and radially in the pressurizer wall. While all these processes might coexist, it is the magnitude of each process which determines the level of influence on the transient outcome.

Liquid-Liquid Heat Transfer - occurs during an insurge between the cold incoming flow and warmer pressurizer inventory. It also occurs between spray droplets and bubble liquid upon entering the bulk liquid.

Liquid-Vapor Heat Transfer - occurs between spray droplets and bulk vapor as well as vapor bubbles and bulk liquid.

Vapor-Vapor Heat Transfer - occurs between vapor bubbles generated in the liquid and bulk vapor upon entering the bulk vapor.

Mass Flow Rates In Pressurizer

Mass flow rates in pressurizer can be considered as those crossing the pressurizer physical boundary and those contained inside the pressurizer (Figure 1). The former includes insurge, outsurge, spray, and SRVs mass flow rates. The latter includes such flows as wall condensation, wall boiling, and heater boiling (solid-liquid interaction), spray condensation, interface condensation, interface evaporation, (liquid-vapor interaction), rainout and flashing (bringing metastable states to thermodynamics equilibrium). There are also mass flow rates associated with liquid-liquid and vapor-vapor interactions such as spray droplets upon entering bulk liquid and vapor bubbles upon entering bulk vapor. Further mass flow rates may exist if the presence of noncondensable gases (hydrogen, nitrogen, and fission gases) cannot be ignored.

EXISTING PRESSURIZER MODELS

Prediction of the pressurizer response to transients requires selection of appropriate fluid control volumes (CV) and solution of the conservation equations, written for these control volumes, in conjunction with the equation of state. Therefore, evaluation of various publicly available models, was based on the number of control volumes utilized in each model.

1CV Model

Simplicity of analysis, in the early pressurizer modeling, dictated assumptions such as the homogeneous equilibrium model (HEM). Selection of

one control volume to represent the whole pressurizer, requires both phases to be at the same pressure and temperature throughout transients. It also eliminates many details such as those associated with interphase interactions (Clark and Campble 1982).
Advantages - include simplicity and applicability to real-time simulation, where computation speed is at a premium.
Disadvantages - stems from its physical limitations. For example, in an actual insurge transient, the cold insurge coolant compresses and superheats the vapor. The vapor temperature and the pressurizer pressure increases. However, the homogeneous model predicts that the cold insurge would result in a pressure reduction (Kao 1984).

2CV Model

The 2CV model has been the formulation of most interest in the literature. The reason for development of a 2CV model has been the obvious shortcomings of the 1CV model when applied to rapid transients. Notwithstanding the existence of liquid in the bulk vapor and bubbles in the bulk liquid, the geometrical simplicity of two distinct bulk phases coexisting in the pressurizer has led investigators to adopt a deformable control volume for each of the two bulk phases. This allows the possibility of thermal nonequilibrium conditions. Early 2CV models used simplifying assumptions such as an isentropic process for bulk vapor. Bosley, et.al. 1957 indicated that such an assumption could be approached only by very rapid transients. Drucker and Tong 1961 eliminated the isentropic assumption by solving a set of simultaneous conservation equations, including a simple model for wall conduction. Radfield et.al. 1967 included the pressure control system. It has become customary, after Nahavandi et. al. 1967 to determine four thermodynamic states for the bulk liquid and the bulk vapor by comparing their corresponding enthalpies with the saturated liquid and saturated vapor enthalpies at the pressurizer pressure. These possible states, by permutation, are ($h_L<h_f$; $h_V=h_g$), ($h_L=h_f$; $h_V=h_g$), ($h_L>h_f$; $h_V=h_g$), and ($h_L>h_f$; $h_V>h_g$). Nahavandi and Makkenchery 1970 derived explicit equation for the rate of change of pressure in terms of water physical properties and mass flow rates for each of the four aforementioned states. Pressure as a function of time was then defined by numerical integration. Baron 1973 and Sami 1986 applied the same model to obtain fairly close prediction of data. Among the 2CV models developed as an integral part of a reactor coolant system code are those of Kao 1984 and Studovic and Stevanovic 1985. The former model is, however, superior with respect to inclusion of physical phenomena, mathematical modeling, and numerical techniques.

Various 2CV models differ mainly in the constitutive relations and by a lesser degree in the solution technique. As an example for the constitutive relations consider the case of the metastable condition such as superheated liquid which might exist if water is pure and the pressure reduction process is slow. Since the 2CV model only accounts for four possible states within the pressurizer, therefore metastable conditions; superheated liquid and subcooled vapor, must necessarily lead to liquid flashing and vapor rainout, respectively. Nahavandi 1970, Baron 1973, Geffray 1980, and Baltra 1981 have explicitly correlated the rainout and flashing mass flow rates to the void fractions in bulk liquid and bulk vapor. As a result, neither an insurge without spray nor an outsurge without the heater action can be associated with rainout and flashing, respectively. Maeck 1976 on the other hand, utilized a steam drum model in which rainout and flashing mass flow rates are correlated to the rate of change of pressure, determined by using an isentropic assumption. Abdallah et al. 1982 account for flashing and rainout processes by explicitly solving for thermodynamic equilibrium qualities in the bulk liquid and bulk vapor. Kim 1984 derives analytical expressions for these processes, as does Kao by utilizing the continuity and energy equations in the absence of spray or heater action.
Advantages - increased application range and enhanced information.
Disadvantages - requirement of several constitutive equations and increased computational time.

3CV Model

This is an extension of the 2CV model in which stratification in the bulk liquid, due to the cold insurge flow is taken into account (Baggoura and Martin 1983), (Kim 1984), (Back et al 1986). The most detailed 3CV model is derived by Kim 1987 which uses a total of seven control volumes; three for bulk fluids, three for the pressurizer wall facing the corresponding bulk fluids, and one for noncondensible gases (Figure 1). Kim, however, assumes that the vapor phase remains saturated at all times. The mass and energy exchange at the bulk liquid interface takes place only by mixing which is correlated to the insurge flow by a distribution factor.

At the bulk vapor-bulk liquid interface heat and mass transfer are ignored in the Kim model if the penetration depth of the insurge is sufficiently small to disturb the interface. Otherwise, Kim uses convection heat transfer and the latent heat to determine the mass transfer. Baggoura and Martin, however, compare the vapor saturation pressure to the pressurizer reference pressure in order to determine if condensation on the interface or evaporation from the interface takes place. They compared their 3CV model with data as well as with those predicted by a 2CV model, and found that the latter overpredicted the measured water level in an outsurge, whereas the former closely predicted the data.
Advantages - more accurate prediction of transient especially, for an outsurge after insurge transient.
Disadvantages - are indeed minimized since the addition of an extra control volume for fluid doesn't introduce undue calculational efforts.

4CV Model

This model (Todreas 1986) is perhaps the most elegant of all reviewed in which one control volume is allocated to each of the following, bulk liquid (L), vapor in bulk liquid (v), bulk vapor (V), and liquid in bulk vapor (l). Three types of interface are defined, (LV), (Ll and Vv), and (Lv and Vl), Figure 2. Such an extensive formulation provides the maximum amount of information (45 unknowns) about processes occurring during transients. There are a total of eight conservation equations, fourteen equations of state and one volume constraint. On the otherhand, it requires eight constitutive equations and ten jump conditions which are instantaneous balance equations at the aforementioned boundaries. Since shear work is neglected, expression of work in terms of volume change has added four additional equations to obtain a closed set. Still, a number of simplifying assumptions are made. For example, kinetic and potential energies are neglected, as is the case in all other pressurizer modeling. Flow through SRVs and the presence of non-condensible gases are included. Furthermore, wall heat transfer is only accounted for in the bulk vapor. Work and

heat transfer rates are included only across selective boundaries, and ignored across others (work and heat transfers are assumed negligible across interfaces Ll or Vv and heat transfer is neglected across LV interface). The formulation, however, is such that these effects could be incorporated. It can be shown that the 4CV model is reducible to 2CV model by combining the conservation equations of each bulk fluid and applying their related jump conditions. It is important, to notice that the 4CV model introduces additional heat and work terms inside each bulk region which will loose their significant by smearing out and combining conservation equations of each bulk fluid. The 4CV model has not yet been integrated in a computer software package to access its capability in predicting data nor its shortcomings. Therefore, the advantages and disadvantages are speculation.
Advantages - additional information to be obtained during transients which very likely would lead to enhanced accuracy.
Disadvantages - requirement for several constitutive equations, larger computer memory size, and increased computation time.

CONCLUSION

Several models for simulation of transients in a pressurizer were evaluated. A qualitative comparison was made based on this evaluation. The models were classified depending on the number of control volumes used for pressurizer fluid inventory. This resulted in 1CV, 2CV, 3CV, and 4CV models. It was concluded that the 1CV model offers simplicity and even sufficient accuracy under circumstances in which thermodynamic equilibrium exists. In general, however, the 1CV model must be used with caution, because it may lead to erroneous results if applied to rapid transients. The 2CV model which is perhaps the most popular model offers some versatility in which thermodynamic nonequilibrium conditions can be simulated, yet memory size and computation time are small enough to allow real time calculation. This is very important especially when the pressurizer is part of an integrated reactor coolant system code. It has been shown, however, that the prediction of the 2CV model is not satisfactory in insurge transients which are followed by an outsurge, because there is no temperature gradient in a given control volume. This led to the development of a 3CV model in which liquid stratification is treated explicitly. Recently, the 4CV model has been devised which has not yet been tested. An even more rigorous treatment than the 4CV model would perhaps be a 5CV model to take into account liquid stratification. However, it is to be seen whether the advantages to be gained by increasing complexity outweigh the obvious disadvantages. Such a conclusion can only be reached if various models are examined quantitatively in a consistent and systematic manner over a wide range of application.

ACKNOWLEDGMENT

The assistance of Professor Neil E. Todreas in providing many of the references as well as helpful comments on the original work are greatly acknowledged.

REFERENCES

Abdallah, M.A. et al. 1982. "Pressurizer Transients Dynamic Model." Nuclear Engineering and Design 73, 447-453

Baek, S.M. et al. 1986. "A Nonequilibrium Three-Region Model For Transient Analysis of Pressurized Water Reactor Pressurizer." Nuclear Technology, vol 74, 260-266: (Sep.)

Baltra Aedo G. 1981. "Design Of A Coordinated Plant Control System For A Marine Nuclear Propulsion Plant." N.E. Thesis, Dept. Of Nuclear Eng., MIT

Baggoura, B. and W.R. Martin. 1983. "Transient Analysis Of The Three Mile Island Unit 2 Pressurizer System." Nuclear Technology, Vol. 62: (Aug.)

Baron, R.C. 1973. "Digital Model Simulation Of A Nuclear Pressurizer." Nuclear Science and Engineering: 52, 283-291

Bosley et al. 1957. "A Fundamental Approach To The Analysis Of Steam Surge Tank Transients." ASME paper 57-A-269

Clark, R.N. and B. Campbell. 1982. "Instrument Fault Detection In A Pressurized Water Reactor Pressurizer." Nuclear Technology, Vol. 56: 23-32 (Jan.)

Drucker, E.E. and K.W. Tong. 1961. "The Compression Of Initially Saturated Vapors." Syracuse University Research Institute Technical Report: ME761-790A

Geffray, C. 1980. "Nuclear Reactor (PWR) Pressurizer Real Time Modeling For Sensor Validation.", M.S. Thesis, Dept. of Nuclear Engineering, MIT

Kao, S.P. 1984. "A Multiple-Loop Primary System Model For Pressurized Water Reactor Plant Sensor Validation." Ph.D. Thesis, Dept. of Nuclear Engineering, MIT

Kim, S.N. 1984. "An Experimental Model Of A PWR Pressurizer During Transients." Ph.D. Thesis, Dept. of Nuclear Engineering, MIT

Kim, S.N. 1987. "PWR Pressurizer Modeling." Nuclear Engineering and Design:102, 199-209

Moeck, E.O. and H.W. Hinds. 1976. "A Mathematical Model Of Steam Drum Dynamics." In Proceedings of the 1975 Summer Computer Simulation Conference (San Fran., CA, Jul. 21-23)

Nahavandi, A.N. et al. 1967. "A Comparison Of Equilibrium And Nonequilibrium Thermodynamic Model In A Water Reactor Pressurizer." Transaction of ANS: (Winter Meeting)

Nahavandi, A.N. and S. Makkencherry. 1970. "An Improved Pressurizer Model With Bubble Rise And Condensate Drop Dynamics." Nuclear Engineering and Design:12, 135-147

Redfield, J.A. et al. 1967. Nucl. Appl., 4, 173

Sami, S.M. 1986. " A Dynamic Model For Predicting CANDU Pressurizer Performance." Nuclear Technology Vol. 72: (Jan.)

Studovic, M. and V. Stevanovic. 1985. "Nonequilibrium Pressurizer Model." In Proceedings of Third International Topical Meeting on Reactor Thermal Hydraulics (Newport, RI, Oct. 15-18)

Todreas, N.E. 1986. "Personal Communication." Dept. of Nuclear Engineering, MIT

a: $\dot{m}_{isu}$
b: $\dot{m}_{osu}$
c: $\dot{m}_{ei}$
d: $\dot{m}_{wb}$
e: $\dot{m}_{hb}$
f: $\dot{m}_{fl}$
g: $\dot{m}_{ie}$
h: $\dot{m}_{nc}$
i: $\dot{m}_{sp}$
j: $\dot{m}_{sc}$
k: $\dot{m}_{wc}$
l: $\dot{m}_{ic}$
m: $\dot{m}_{ro}$
n: $\dot{m}_{srv}$
o: $\dot{m}_{sp}$

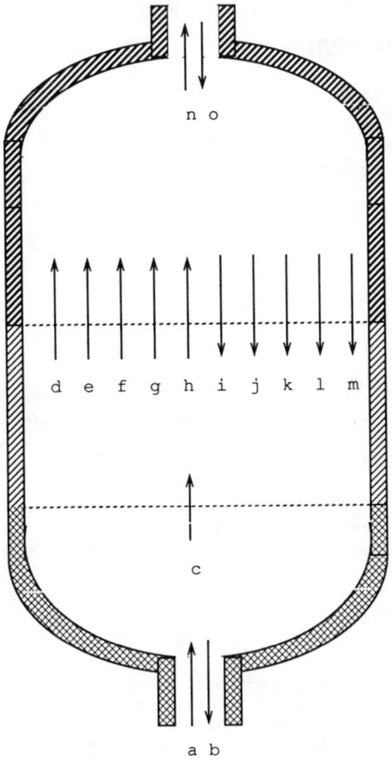

Figure 1 Mass Transfer Between Contol Volumes In A 3CV Pressurizer Model

NOMENCLATURE

h: enthalpy
l: liquid in bulk vapor
L: bulk liquid
m: mass flow rate
v: vapor in bulk liquid
V: bulk vapor

Subscripts

f: saturated liquid
fl: flash
g: saturated steam
hb: heater boiling
ic: interface condensation
isu: insurge
L: bulk liquid
nc: noncondensable gases
osu: outsurge
sc: steam condensation
sp: spray
srv: safety relief valve
wb: wall boiling
wc: wall condensation

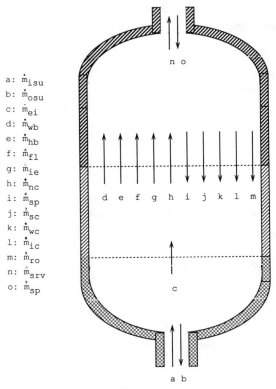

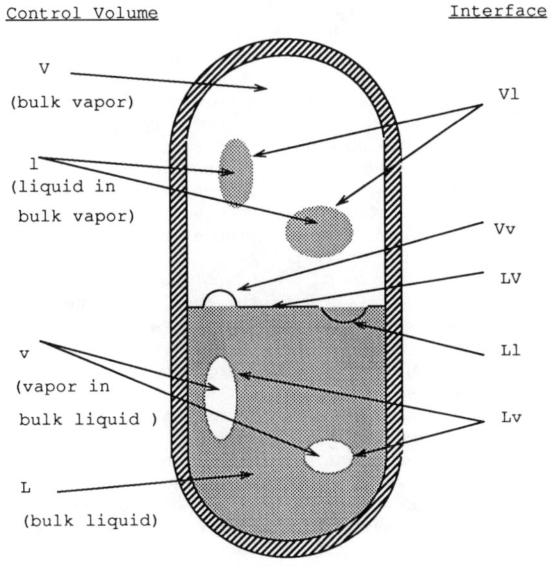

Figure 2 Control Volumes and Corresponding Interfaces For 4CV Pressurizer Model

Simulators VI

ISBN 0-911801-51-0

Simulation of natural circulation cooldown in pressurized water reactors

Farrokh Seifaee and Solieman Kashanian
Computer Simulations Corporation
P.O. Box 173
Colonia, NJ 07067

Abstract

Simulation of natural circulation in the primary side of the pressurized water reactors is critical for training reactor operators on full-scope nuclear power plant training simulators. One-dimensional conservation equations of mass, energy and momentum are applied to the reactor coolant system which is divided into seven elements. The system's pressure is calculated based on the pressurizer pressure. The thermal calculations are performed using the implicit Euler integration at the nodes of the various elements.

The plant data and the simulated results were compared for the hot leg temperature, cold leg temperature and reactor core flow rate during natural circulation cooldown due to loss of off-site power. This comparison reveals that the simulation model for the reactor core flow rate and the temperatures of the hot and cold legs, closely simulates the transient behavior of the reactor coolant system during the single phase natural circulation cooldown.

Introduction

It is widely accepted that nuclear power plant simulators play an essential role in training the reactor operators. The full-scope nuclear plant training simulators are primarily used as a training device to provide initial and requalification training for power plant operators. Recent incidents at nuclear power plants in the U.S. and abroad have underscored the need to accurately predict and simulate the various plant conditions. Accomplishing this will enhance the reactor operators' ability to react to incidents promptly and accurately.

Natural circulation may occur under a wide variety of pressurized water reactors (PWR) accident conditions whenever an appropriate heat sink (steam generator) is available. These accidents may include cold leg break and loss of off-site power. In the case of a cold leg break, according to operating procedures the reactor coolant pumps (RCP) will be turned off if the subcooling margin in the RCS is lost and the reactor coolant becomes two-phase. With the loss of off-site power, the electric power to the RCPs is cut off. Incidents such as the loss of off-site power, would stop force convection in the reactor core due to the trip of the reactor pump. Natural circulation through the core and the removal of core decay heat must then be established. The accident at Three Mile Island and the tripping of the reactor coolant pumps, underscores the need for further study of natural circulation cooldown in the reactor coolant system.

There are a number of theoretical and experimental studies on natural circulation which present data obtained in small and large scale test facilities. Most of the data on natural circulation cooldown with applications to nuclear reactors is related to two-phase flow instabilities. Wissler et al. [1] studied experimentally and theoretically the behavior of the flow in natural circulation loop. They demonstrated that the flow rate in the loop is directly related to the temperature difference of the heated section of the loop. Boure et al. [2] reviewed the state of the art of two-phase flow instabilities. They presented heat transfer coefficients and circulation flow rates for different flow regimes. Rothe et al. [3] studied the uncertainties in modeling steady, two-phase flow in hot legs in a PWR of the once-through steam generators. They analyzed the uncertainties due to the effects of gas-liquid slip (flow regime), friction, and flashing between full-scale and in-scale models. They found that the uncertainties in flow and pressure drop characteristics of the full-scale hot leg are great.

A simplified treatment of a single phase loop of a nuclear reactor was presented by Lewis [4] in order to obtain an estimate of a steady state flow rate and core temperature difference. Zvirin et al. [5] investigated analytically and experimentally on natural circulation loops related to pressurized water reactors. They employed a one-dimensional model where the only spatial coordinate encircles the circulation loop. By comparing a one-dimensional analysis with the results of the experiments and available plant data, they demonstrated that a simple analytical modeling method is capable of describing the steady state and transient behavior. Adams et al. [6] presented natural circulation cooling characteristics during cold leg breaks in PWRs. They provided data from several PWR accident simulations in the Loss-of-Fluid Test (LOFT) pressurized water reactor. The study concluded that natural circulation cooling is sufficient for removing the decay heat from the reactor core during an accident as long as there are no practical limitations on the secondary system to reject heat from the reactor core.

The objective of the present paper is to present the subcooled natural circulation results from the full-scope specific plant simulator and to compare these results with the available plant data. The analysis is based on existing modeling methods for natural circulation cooldown.

Description of the Model

One dimensional conservation equations of mass, energy, and momentum are applied to the reactor coolant system. The reactor coolant system is simulated by dividing it into seven elements as shown in Figure 1: the reactor core and lower plenum, upper plenum, hot legs, primary side of the steam generators, and the reactor coolant pumps. The pressurizer system is simulated separately and merged with the reactor coolant system.
The following assumptions are made in different control volumes:

a) homogeneous flow exists in the reactor loop until phase separation occurs in the loop
b) perfect mixing exists when streams of water converge at the thermal node
c) reverse flow is allowed everywhere throughout the loops.

The temperature and other fluid properties, such as the density of each node, are calculated based on the pressure and enthalpy of the node.

Overall mass balance in the reactor coolant loops, including search flow, interface makeup flows, let down flows, and possible high pressure injection and low pressure flow rate results in the change of mass inventory in the reactor coolant system. Pressure of the reactor coolant system is calculated at nodes along the loops at several points. The pressurizer pressure and upper plenum pressure are calculated explicitly. The other pressures are compared based on the pressure drop from the momentum balance equation. Each control volume has an average pressure which is a function of frictional losses and elevation.

Natural circulation in PWRs is possible as long as some requirements are met: 1) a heat source is available to produce low density water; 2) a heat sink is available to produce high density water; 3) a flow path is available connecting the warm and cold water; 4) the high density water is above the low density water. This last requirement involves a concept called thermal center (Figure 2). The thermal center is the point in the core or the steam generator where the primary water is at average temperature.

The rate of natural circulation depends on the following actors:

a) the friction (resistance to flow) of the piping and components through the circulating path
b) the strength of the heat source, i.e., the available decay heat power which is a function of post power history and time since the reactor tripped
c) the strength of the heat sink, the colder the heat sink, the more it will be able to cool the primary coolant via the steam generators
d) the difference in height between the core and the steam generators thermal centers, the larger this difference, the more natural circulation flow will result.

The natural circulation volumetric flow rate can be obtained from Zvirin et al. [5] studies.

Description of the Transient

To examine the fidelity of the model for natural circulation cooldown, a series of tests were performed on the Arkansas Nuclear One, Unit-One, full scope training simulator. The referenced plant is a 2568 MWt pressurized water reactor (Babcock and Wilcox design) with two Once-Through Steam Generators (OTSGs). The simulator fully simulates the power plant control room and is equipped with three Gould SEL computers in parallel operation. The simulator is utilized for training the reactor operators of the referenced plant. The software which drives the simulator includes models for real-time simulation of the entire system of the actual power plant.
Comparisons were made between the simulator results and the plant data.

The actual plant data was obtained due to a loss of off-site power [7]. Upon loss of off-site power, the feedwater condensate pumps were tripped causing a loss of the main feedwater pumps due to low suction pressure. The emergency feedwater system was automatically initiated when the main feedwater pumps were lost. The emergency feedwater system automatically feeds both generators up to 50% of the operating range level at the maximum rate. Plant data indicates that natural circulation was achieved within several minutes of loss of off-site power.

Simulation Results

Comparisons were made for key parameters between the simulation results and the plant data.

Figure 3 shows the primary flow rate through the reactor core after all reactor coolant pumps are tripped. The results indicate that the simulation model predicts the core flow rate close to the plant data. In the first 100 seconds after the RCPs trip, the pumps' speed were coasting down, therefore some force convection still exists in the primary loops. After about thirty minutes into the transient, the core flow rate is about 7% of the total core flow rate before the RCPs are tripped. The flow oscillation demonstrates that as the temperature difference between hot leg and cold leg becomes smaller, the primary flow rate reduces, which in turn causes higher hot leg temperature. Subsequently, higher hot leg temperature increases the primary flow rate through the core.

Figure 4 compares the hot leg temperature obtained by the simulation model with the plant data. A sudden drop in the hot leg temperature in the first minute after the RCP's trip, is due to the drop of the reactor thermal power. Later on, hot leg temperature is gradually being reduced after the natural circulation has been established. The simulation results match the plant data. The results are in good agreement when natural circulation effects begin to dominate the flow characteristic of the primary site.

Figure 5 shows the comparison between the plant data and the simulation results for the cold leg temperature. The simulation results demonstrate that the cold leg temperature prediction of the reactor coolant system is close to the plant data during the natural circulation establishment. The cold leg temperature of the flow exiting the primary side of the steam generator is close to the saturation temperature of the steam generator pressure.

Figure 6 compares the reactor coolant pressure between the plant data and the simulation results during the loss of off-site power. The results show that the simulation model closely predicts the reactor's pressure. During loss of off-site power, the main feedwater pumps to the steam generators trip. Therefore, the flow to the steam generators is lost and consequently the reactor temperature increases. This increase in reactor temperature causes the reactor volume to swell and the pressure of the reactor coolant system initially increases. However, after the reactor trip, the reactor thermal power reduces to decay heat level and the pressure of the reactor coolant is reduced. Once the reactor pressure is reduced to about 1800 psia, the high pressure injection system is activated and the pressure is gradually increased to avoid the loss of subcooling margin and the reactor coolant system pressure stays in a subcooled condition.

Conclusion

The simulation results demonstrate that the present model for natural circulation cooldown in the real-time domain can closely predict the plant data. Simulation results for the core flow rate, reactor coolant pressure, and the hot and cold leg temperatures were close to the actual plant data during loss of off-site power. As natural circulation is delivered in the RCS, the cold leg temperature will be about equal to the saturation temperature in the steam generators. The hot leg temperature will be increased as is necessary to develop the driving head required for flow in the reactor core. The simulation results show that as the natural circulation flow rate will regulate itself. That is, as the decay heat reduces, the difference between the hot and the cold leg temperature will decrease and the flow rate will decrease.

The simulation results of natural circulation demonstrate that the core flow rate is sufficient for removing the decay heat from the system and reducing the temperature difference across the core. Being able to simulate natural circulation on full-scope training simulators is crucial for training operators in responding to conditions relating to natural circulation and the conditions in which cooldown can be established.

References

1. Wissler, E.H., et al., "Oscillatory Behavior of a Two-Phase Natural Circulation Loop," AIche Journal, 2, 157-162, 1956.
2. Boure, J.A., et al., "Review of Two-Phase Instability," Nuclear Engineering and Design, 25, 165-192, 1973.
3. Rothe, P.H., et al., "Scaling of Two-Phase Flow During Natural Circulation in a PWR Hot Leg," EPRI-NP-4854, Nov. 1986.
4. Lewis, E.E., "Nuclear Power Reactor Safety," Wiley, New York, 1977.
5. Zvirin, Y., et al., "Experimental and Analytical Investigation of a PWR Natural Circulation Loop," EPRI-NP-1364-SR, March 1980.
6. Adams, J.P., et al., "Natural Circulation Cooling Characteristics During PWR Accident Simulations," EGG-LOFT-5430, April 1981.
7. Nesbit, S.P., "ANO-1 Natural Circulation Cooldown Analysis," Arkansas Power and Light Company, Unit Transient Report, June 1980.

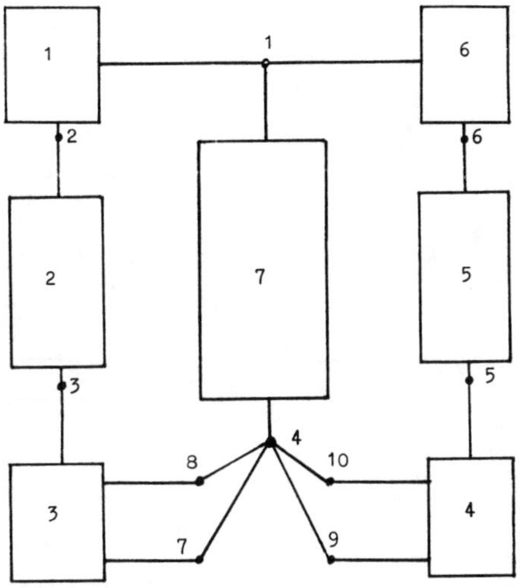

FIGURE 1 - SCHEMATIC DIAGRAM FOR CONROL VOLUMES AND THERMAL NODES OF THE PRIMARY SYSTEM

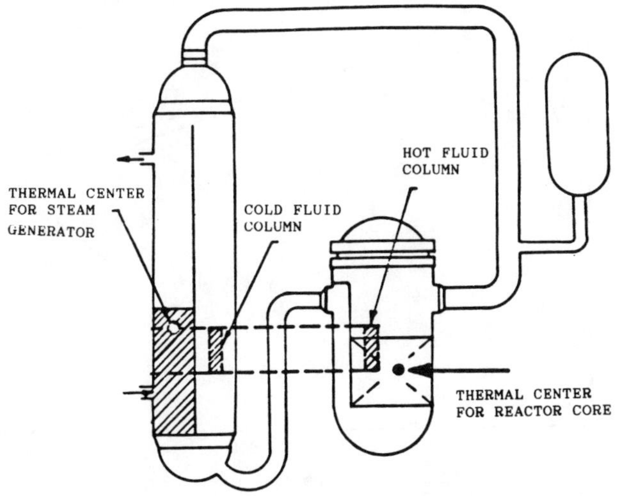

FIGURE 2 - SCHEMATIC DIAGRAM FOR NATURAL CIRCULATION DRIVING HEAD

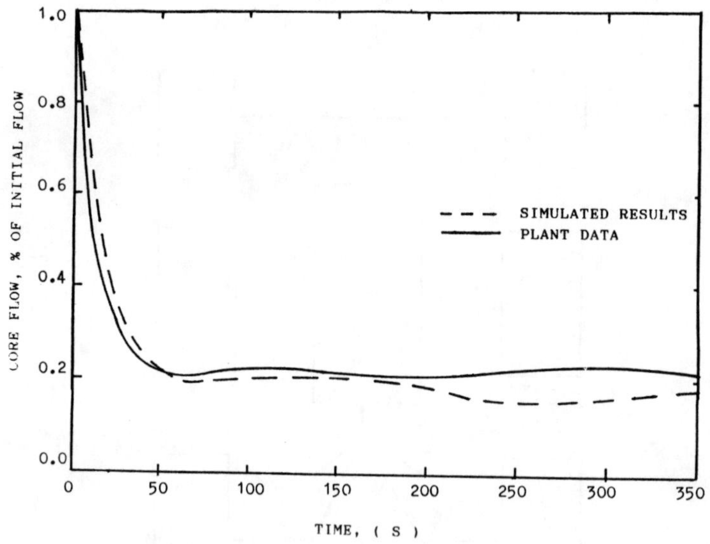

FIGURE 3 - PRIMARY FLOW AFTER LOSS OF OFF-SITE POWER

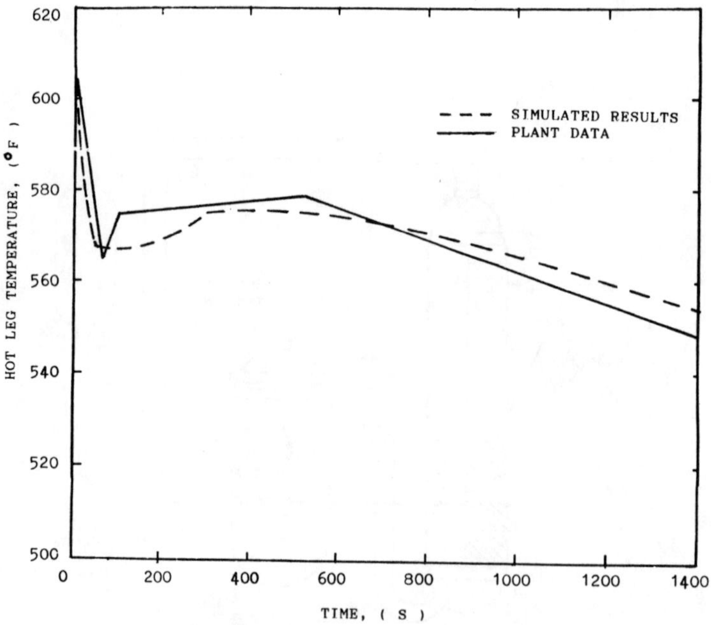

FIGURE 4 - COMPARISON FOR HOT LEG TEMPERATURE AFTER LOSS OF OFF-SITE POWER

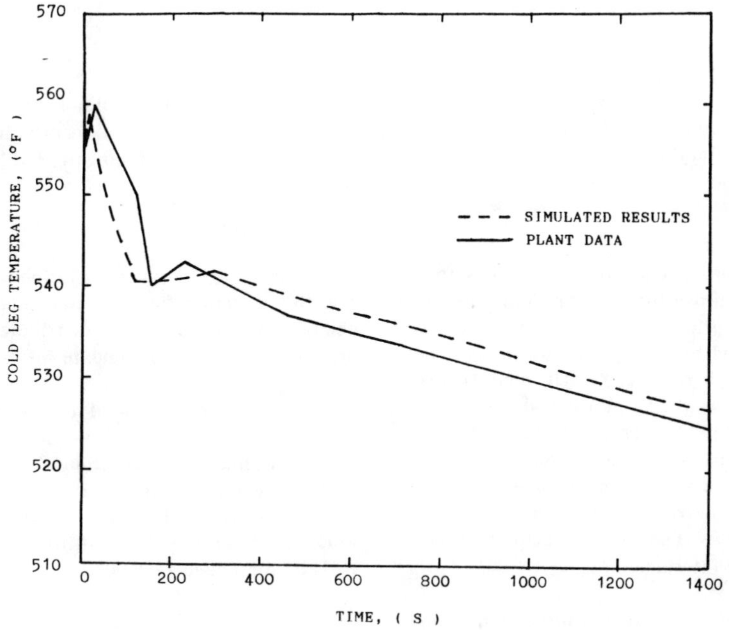

FIGURE 5 - COMPARISON FOR COLD LEG TEMPERATURE AFTER LOSS OF OFF-SITE POWER

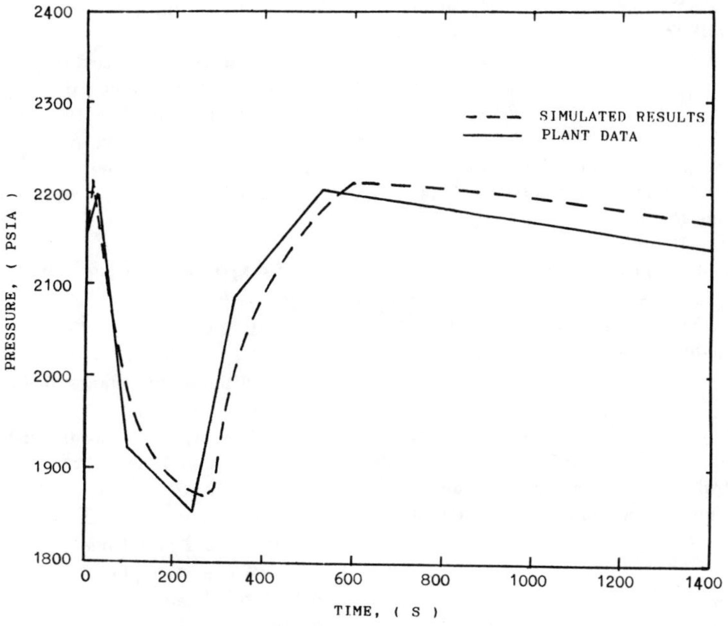

FIGURE 6 - COMPARISON FOR PRIMARY SYSTEM PRESSURE AFTER LOSS OF OFF-SITE POWER

Simulators VI

ISBN 0-911801-51-0

Enhancement of training simulator
Part 1: Advanced man machine interface

F. Mahjouri, PhD   M. R. Fakory, PhD
Singer Link-Miles Simulation Corporation
Columbia, Maryland 21045

J. Olmos Sc.D.
Southern California Edison Co.
San Clemente, CA 92672

ABSTRACT

The availability of low cost but powerful workstations opens a wide horizon to improve the man machine interface. These workstations, with a price tag of less than $20K, have an 8 MB main memory and are equipped with at least one large mass storage peripheral (130 MB and above). Connecting these workstations via an industry standard local area network (i. e., build-in Ethernet interface) offers a powerful, distributed and open-ended computer architecture. The UNIX operating system environment, with sophisticated graphics capabilities of software/hardware such as pop-up windows, multiple bit planes and on-line help, facilitates advanced the man machine interface.

This paper will explore the potential utilization of high speed (25 MHz), 32-bit microprocessors with "Megapixel" display and sophisticated graphics technology for dedicated computer intensive applications as represented by various microcomputer manufactures. CRT-based simulation approach will be introduced. The concept of Computer Aided Exercise Program (CAEP), Trainee Performance Review (TPR), Validation and Verification (V&V), and Auto Testing will be discussed. This discussion will focus on simulator requirements as described in ANSI/ANS 3.5 - 1985, Appendix B.

INTRODUCTION

Realistically, the history of computing shows that the demand for more computing power has always outstripped the supply. If the past is any guide to the future, the availability of more computing power will only open up real-time applications requiring greater functionality, thus exacerbating the timing problems. There is no substitute for intelligent deployment of finite resources. The availability of low cost but powerful microcomputers facilitates open-ended computing power architecture.

The new distributed and dynamic computing environment offers unlimited computing power. The software engineer is relieved from hardware constraints and can exercise the sound principal of system engineering by developing a system that [1]:

- o Meets the user's needs
- o Interfaces with and complements the operation of other related systems
- o Functions over the real range of imposed environmental and operating constraints
- o Is adaptable; is capable of adapting to future changes in needs, environments and interfacing requirements.

Because of the incorporation of features which allow selective system refinement and modification in response to changing requirements, the distributed software and hardware architecture can accommodate future changes.

The new generation of microcomputers such as NeXT, Silicon Graphics, Sun, Masscomp, etc. represent true price and performance breakthroughs in computing power. The multiprocessing architecture of IRIS 4D/240 developed by Silicon Graphics Inc. [2] demonstrate the ability of a workstation to sustain 80 Million Instructions per Second (MIPS) for under $100,000.

HARDWARE CAPABILITY

The daily introduction of new products leads us right into the mainstream of sophisticated graphics technology with a level of computational power that provides the highest performance in both graphics and general computing which is needed for the simulation industry at an affordable price.

Silicon Graphics released its IRIS Series, a series of high end multiprocessor systems with supercomputing server last October. The entry level of this new product is based on a powerful 32 bit CPU and an optional floating point co-processor (see Table 1). The processors run at 12.5 MHz and delivers 10 MIPS for a price of less than $20,000.

- o 12.5 MHz 32-bit RISC CPU
- o 10 MIPS
- o 8 MB RAM
- o 8 color bit planes
- o 4 additional bit planes dedicated to windows, overlay, and underlay
- o 170 MB SCSI Winchester disc drive
- o 19" diagonal 1280 X 1024 color monitor
- o Optical 3 button mouse
- o Ethernet port
- o Two RS-232 serial port
- o One Centronics port
- o One SCSI port
- o One VME slot
- o Audio Ports: In, Out, Mic
- o Price $19,990.00

Table 1 : Personal IRIS System Standard Configuration.

Steve Jobs, the former CEO of Apple Computers, introduced the NeXT computer also in the same time [3]. The soul of his new machine is the 68030 microprocessor, with its built-in memory management unit, from Motorola Inc. The basic configuration with 8 MB of memory, an optical 256 MB disc drive, and an optional 660 MB Winchester disc drive priced about $10,000. These machines are just the beginning of a new area of affordable supercomputing power.

The NeXT Generation

The story of the Apple computer and the success of Macintosh lead us to believe that NeXT will be the machine for the nineties. The CPU board of NeXT is built around Motorola's latest 68030 processor and 68882 math co-processor, both running at 25 MHz. The standard hardware has 8 MB of memory and is expandable to 16 MB (see Table 2).

- o 25 MHz-32 bit 68030 CPU
- o 10 MPIS
- o 8 MB RAM
- o 660 MB SCSI Winchester disc drive
- o 256 MB Optical Disc Cartridge
- o 17" diagonal 1120 X 832 monochrome monitor
- o Optical mouse
- o Two Ethernet channels
- o One serial channel
- o One DSP channel
- o One printer channel
- o One video channel
- o Two Audio Ports
- o Two disc channels (one for the magneto-optical drive, one for SCSI hard disc drive)
- o Price $10,500.00

Table 2 : NeXT Standard Configuration.

A read/write magneto-optical drive serves as mass storage device. This peripheral fits into a 5.25 inch full-height bay and has a slot to accept an optical cartridge. The cartridge is removable through a software actuated eject mechanism using an internal motor.

The optical cartridges resemble overgrown 3.5 inch floppy discs. Steve Jobs claims the drive is more reliable than a Winchester hard disc drive, although access time can be as much as 50-60 milliseconds; two to three times slower than that of Winchester drives. Each 256 MB optical cartridge costs about $50.

Another impressive feature of NeXT is its built-in Ethernet interface chips, which work with electronic-mail and voice-mail software. A Digital Signal Processor chip (DSP) provides stereo output with compact-disc quality, as well as speech recognition. The DSP56001 is linked to Motorola's 68030 making NeXT's machine the first workstation with a built-in voice synthesizer. The DSP is clocked at 20 MHz, and instructions execute every two clock cycles to give the chip an execution rate of 10 MIPS.

The power supply will work in any country, automatically decoding what kind of current is being provided. A single monitor cable supplies both video and power from the computer box. The computer case is made of magnesium for heat dissipation.

Ease of use is enhanced through now-standard icon-and-window layout, but with a few twists. Rather than a trash can, for example, it has a "black hole" that swirls when something is thrown away. The menus "tear off" from the menu bar and can be pasted anywhere on the screen. To prevent users from losing control by overlaying too many icons, on screen icons can be placed in a "dock" at the side that slides down and out of sight.

HARDWARE/SOFTWARE TRADEOFF

Trading off hardware components for software elegance is new to most program managers. Designers have always accepted whatever complement of computer hardware was provided and implemented the necessary software. Many applications can trade off to save hardware by making the software more complex. Sometimes designers have compromised and developed unnecessarily complex code to achieve a better man machine interface. Even in these cases, the software designer has been at the mercy of the skills of the human factor engineer.

In the simulation industry, the proper choice of the boundary line between hardware and software is an important decision. In very high volume production the elimination of a single inexpensive hardware component may justify the expenditure of several thousand dollars in engineering time. On the other hand, when production volumes are in the "onesy-twosy" range, hardly any useful component is too expensive, since it will reduce the development time and cost for the project.

The choice of the optimum boundary line is further complicated as more and more complex ICs become more available. Simultaneously, designers are tackling harder and harder projects for which interfaces have never before been designed. Some of new ICs for controlling video displays, floppy discs, keyboards, and communications channels make the design of discrete circuitry impractical. These new components are also inexpensive and so powerful that both production and engineering costs go down dramatically.

The distinction between hardware and software is very fuzzy and probably will become more so in the future. Hardware is generally a physical entity that is mechanical or electronic in nature. Software on the other hand is a conceptual entity and to some extent abstract in nature.

A computer is a piece of hardware, however, it has no functionality by itself. The programs stored within and executed add functionality to the computer. Software consists of an algorithm and the detailed step by step instructions to be conducted by the computer to implement the algorithm. It gives the computer a functional purpose. Thus, software is conceptual rather than a physical entity.

Considering the software world for a moment, there are various types of software that exist:

Higher Order Language - This type of software divorces the developer from the hardware, such as FORTRAN, C, Pascal, etc.

Assembly Language - This is the basic language recognized by the computer when converted to binary form. It is very hardware dependent and not a preferred means to develop software.

Microcode - Microcode is a hardware level language used by computer manufacturers to implement the computer instruction set (the assembly language). It rarely is used for application software implementation because it generally requires a hardware designer to implement.

Firmware - Software is normally stored in volatile memory within a computer; by volatile, it can be altered by over writes or by cycling of power. Where software is stored in non-alterable, non-volatile memory it is referred to as firmware. Generally, an IC has to be replaced to alter the firmware. Many imbedded computers use this technique where the applications are typically control, interface, etc.

To add to the confusion, microcode, assembly language or Higher Order Language types of software can be firmware if it meets the characteristics delineated above.

Hardware and software can be blended together to create entities which fall into neither class. Given the growth of chip complexity, it is likely that these entities may have to be classified as software.

There is no "cookbook" method for determining the optimum, however, software can have a longer life due to the ease of change. On the other hand, the very ease of changing software creates a serious problem in controlling the design. Thus, the need exists for tight configuration control of software.

SOFTWARE DEVELOPMENT

The fascination of simulation is magnified through the instructor's station window. This window, a powerful man machine interface, opens the world of simulation to the user. One touches the correct icon on a screen, and a display comes to life, showing things that never were nor could be. It becomes real in the sense that it moves and works, producing visible outputs separate from the construct itself. It prints results, draws pictures, and captures trends.

Of course the technological base on which one builds is always advancing. As soon as one freezes a design, it becomes obsolete in terms of its concepts, but implementation of real products demands phasing and quantizing. The obsolescence of an implementation must be measured against other existing implementations, not against unrealized concepts. The challenge and the mission are to find solutions to real problems on the actual schedules with available resources and within the budget.

The present software development environment promotes modular block building systems. Database packages, display managers, communication managers, and report generators are just a few tools with bounded boundaries. The challenge for today's programer is interface management and selection of suitable "blocks" to form a new entity.

Real-Time Operating System

The operating system is the focal point for the development of real-time simulators. It must provide basic support for guaranteeing real-time constraints, support fault tolerance and distribution, and integrate time-constrained resource allocations and schedule across a spectrum of resource types. Given that the system is distributed, the designer faces a complicated end-to-end timing analysis problem [4]. In other words, time constraints are applied to the collection of cooperating tasks and not only to individual tasks.

Real-Time Database

The characteristics of a real-time database are distinct from commercial database systems. A real-time database is a dynamic system, a large amount of data is continuously updated, and it must satisfy stringent timing requirements.

In a real-time database system the synchronized and sequential access to data is the key. A significant portion of data is often highly perishable in the sense that it has value to the mission only if used quickly. Satisfying the timing requirements involves two issues:

The degree of concurrence in transaction must be increased;

Concurrence control protocols and real-time scheduling algorithms must be integrated.

We believe the UNIX operating system will grow and advance with technology. The simplicity of its structure, cleverness of its design and help rather than hindrance features make the UNIX system unique.

Above all, the UNIX system provides an environment for tool-using and tool-building. No matter what the application, the UNIX operating system supplies an extensive set of tools to assist these processes. Just about any tool the user needs is there. If it isn't, he will find that it is very easy to construct the process he wants by connecting together existing tools [5].

Human-Imposed Requirements

The efficiency of a man machine interface is judged by its response to the user demand. An operator wants to interact with the simulator in a straight forward manner. Therefore, the communication media forms the systems' backbone upon which predictable, stable, and extensible subsystems are built.

To be successful, the real-time communication subsystem must be able to satisfy individual message-level timing requirements. These requirements are driven not only by an applications' interprocess communication, but also time-constrained operating system functions and peripheral performance invoked on behalf of application processes.

Software engineering practices complimented by powerful hardware will continue to advance the man machine interface.

CRT-based Simulator

The concept of a CRT-based simulator is not new. In the Electric Utility Industry, supervisory control has been used for more than two decades [6]. In its most complex form, referred to as a Supervisory Control And Data Acquisition (SCADA) system, it is used to control all generation, transmission, and distribution over a wide geographical area, from one centralized location.

There were undoubtedly many methods of remote control invented by early pioneers in the supervisory control field, and long since forgotten. For sure, SCADA did not begin with touch screens, optical mice, electronic sensors, and analog to digital converters; but with a person reading a measurement and taking some mechanical control action as a result of that measurement.

In the simulation industry we can march towards panel-less simulation technology risk free. The path is paved by a front runner in the Electric Utility Industry.

A pictorial library represents the physical contour and movement pattern of panel devices. User selects instrumentation such as meters, controllers, and switches from this library to build a drill session and places them in any location of screen or if necessary multiple screens. Then he binds these mimics to their representative model variables from the database.

Once one verifies the completeness and correctness of a configuration and its interfaces, a simulation scenario can be executed remotely from simulator mechanical control and indication hardware. This configuration can be captured and stored on electronic media and shared or used as a training tool in any compatible workstation.

Thus, the pictorial and instrumental simulation of panels provides the ability to exercise control over a specific device, and to confirm its performance in accordance with the directed action without physical integration or existence of instrumentation in the simulation environment.

Computer Aided Exercise Program

The Computer Aided Exercise Program (CAEP) gives capability to a user to develop, initiate, and execute a previously composed scenario. These scenarios can be developed on any workstation to build a drill library and and moved to any other compatible system. Each scenario may contain any number of executable commands.

The various steps within a particular exercise will be capable of being triggered manually by instructor, automatically, or based on delay times associated with each command. A trainee will be able to work at his own workstation assuming that the station is armed with the CRT-based simulator software and database.

Trainee Performance Review

The Trainee Performance Review (TPR) supports the instructor to evaluate trainees performance. Sets of parameters to be monitored during TPR and their limits can be chosen before running a drill and maybe combined with the CAEP scenario. The actions performed by a student will be recorded during the exercise for later review. This action can be segregated into separate reports based on the section of the simulator on which activities are monitored.

Validation and Verification

Appendix B of ANSI/ANS-3.5-1985 provides the basis for validation of a nuclear power plant simulator by comparison of its performance with the best available data. Annually, the response of the simulator shall be compared to the actual plant response or best estimated plant response annually.

A user oriented system facilitates performance testing and minimizes the effort of data entry [7]. The user selects parameters to be compared and enters the best available data into a designated file system. A digitizing tablet is used for transient data entry. Calculated data from the simulator is collected directly from the simulator.

The performance comparison module can be initiated after data collection is completed. The results of the comparison are formulated into a designated file system, ready for the report generation module.

Auto Testing

Integration of CAEP, TPR, and V&V functions will generate an automated testing environment with no operator follow-up action. The test procedure including operator action will be stored as a CAEP drill. The performance of the simulator and selected parameters will be recorded in a TPR file. And finally, the V&V system will compare simulator computed values obtained from the TPR file against reference plant data. The result of this exercise can be used as a performance evaluation of the whole system!

Expert System

The success of the Auto Testing function depends on operator expertise. Once the evaluation criteria is outside the operator's head, more people can work at refining it, and as it is fine-tuned, simulation moves from art to science.

The benefit of this Expert System is that once the knowledge has been captured in code, it can be protected and shared [8]. If instructor is too busy to teach younger operators, a CAEP/TPR scenario can help by serving as a training tool.

Many people can, in effect, become apprentices to a few experts. People who are afraid to ask questions because they are expected to know the answer can consult with a CRT-based simulator in private. And the experienced operator can benefit by seeing how another expert approaches the maneuver by reviewing auto testing records.

CONCLUSION

The availability of affordable microcomputers with a platform ranked at more than 10 MIPS for under $10,000, or under $1,000 per MIPS, suggests the implementation of microcomputers in the simulation industry. Experts foresee the introduction of powerful workstation by 1992 offering 100 MIPS for $10,000, with optical disc drive, fiber optical networking, voice, and video capabilities.

UNIX will be the operating system of choice. The competitive battles between operating systems will be around the new feature. Nevertheless, full ANSI C will be the srtandard language of UNIX with mapped files and dynamic linking for shared libraries as its minimum feature.

The hardware cost will be reduced further by introduction of CRT-based simulators. This platform combined with the advanced man-machine interfaces such as CAEP, TPR, V&V, and Auto Testing will build an expert system, which is a foot in the door to artificial intelligence.

REFERENCES

[1] R. Forsch, "The Emerging Shape of Policies for the Acquisition of Major Systems", Marine Technology, July 1969, pp. 231-236.

[2] SiliconGraphics Computer Systems, "The Personal IRIS", A Technical Report, October 1988.

[3] T. Thompson, N. Baran, "The NeXT Computer", Byte, Vol. 13, November 1988, pp. 158-175.

[4] J. Stankovic, "A Serious Problem for Next-Generation Systems", IEEE Computer, Vol. 21, October 1988, pp. 10-18.

[5] H. McGilton, R. Morgan, "Introducing the UNIX System", McGraw-Hill Book Company, 1983.

[6] IEEE Power Engineering Society, "Fundamentals of Supervisory Control Systems", IEEE Tutorial Course, 81 EHO 188-3-PWR, 1981.

[7] F. Mahjouri, R. Felker, "Verification and Validation Package for Nuclear Power Plant Simulators", Proceedings of the SCS Simulators Conference, 1988, Vol. 19, October 1988, pp. 422-426.

[8] D. Leonard-Barton, J. Sviokla, "Putting Expert Systems to Work", Harvard Business Review, March-April 1988, pp. 91-98.

Simulators VI
© 1989 By The Society for Computer
Simulation International
ISBN 0-911801-51-0

SERT-I-FI-KA-SHUN

Thomas A. Suttner
Singer Link-Miles Simulation Corporation
8895 McGaw Road
Columbia, Maryland 21045

ABSTRACT

Certification of nuclear power plant simulators, now required by Government regulations, has become a pressing issue for all Utilities. This paper addresses one method of achieving certification. The approach discussed will meet the requirements of the regulation yet can be implemented with minimum resources. The scope can be expanded to meet individual Utility internal requirements as required.

The process described in this paper is an all-encompassing coordinated approach designed to cover hardware, software, testing, database, evaluation, correction, re-verification and submission of certification.

"SERT-i-Fi-KA-SHUN"

Sounds like the old military saying "Yesterday I kudn't spell instructor and now I are wun". Perhaps Webster is trying to tell us we should concentrate on pronunciation and meaning rather than worry about exact spelling. The same philosphy can be applied to the interpretation and meaning of NUREG 1258. Instead of looking for the "exact spelling" or hidden agenda items of the regulation, more concentration should be given to the meaning and general requirements. The words "certify" and "certification" are in all our minds since the publication of NU REG 1258. Instead of certification may be we should look at the synonym "authenticate." Submission of the NRC Form 474 indicates the authenticity of the simulator to replicate a referenced plant in that it looks like, feels like and acts like your plant. If this criteria is met, your simulator can be used as an effective tool in both the training and licensing of operators. The real question is how do you authenticate your simulator to meet the requirements of NU REG 1258.

As with any government regulation, NUREG 1258 is concise and to the point and gives clear direction to the user. It is like a saying that is prevalent around Washington D.C., "Elect a lawyer to write laws in a manner that requires the user to hire a lawyer to interpret them". Job security. I have been involved in the Modification and Services area at Singer for the past four years and have followed the certification process from the beginning. The process described in this paper is based on conversations with Utilities, as well as my interpretation of the requirements of the regulations and their association guides. As with any regulation, interpretation lies within the mind of the reader.

Last August I was privileged to witness the NRC audit of the Maine Yankee Simulator. The simulator certification was accepted during the exit interview on 1 September 1988, the first in the industry. I have discussed with many utilities the certification process and the methods they used achieve certification and today would like to pass on to you a summation of those discussions.

Certification Process

All agree the first step is to develop a plan. Although there are various views of what should be in this plan, the points most identified were schedule, procedures, milestones and resources.

The main driver to the schedule is how the simulator has been maintained to date. If the configuration has been properly maintained in all areas, the schedule can be very short. If not, you may need until March 1991 to submit the Form 474. The creation of procedures is also linked to your past. If good configuration control procedures are in place, a major hurdle has been overcome. Procedures identifying methods of controlling the simulator to ensure that it matches the plant are a must in the certification process. The areas that need to be addressed in procedures are evaluation of plant modifications for incorporation into the simulator, current data base reflecting the simulator, discrepancy corrections, hardware upgrades, ability to operate the simulator using the plant's operating and emergency procedures, student feedback and the documentation to support these areas.

The meat of the entire plan is the tasks or milestones that must be defined. These milestones must act as check and review points during the entire process to verify each requirement of NUREG 1258 is met. Typical milestones are verification of a current up-to-date data base, a review of all plant updates after the original data freeze during simulator construction, verification that the Final Specifications and Documentation reflect the data base, a detailed simulator hardware comparison review against the plant's control room, creation and execution of the operability test, a review and testing of all relevant LERs, both Industry and the referenced plant, and a review of all documentation to support changes that have been made to the simulator. Each of these items must then be subjected to an evaluation to determine if the requirements of the regulation are met. If the requirement is not met, a decision must be made to determine if an upgrade or rework is require. These items then must be scheduled for correction dependent upon their licensing or training requirement. Items that may impact licensing must be scheduled for correction prior to submitting the Form 474. NUREG 1258 directs itself to the licensing use of the simulator. You may want to correct training deficiencies at the same time. Minor shortcomings should be identified and rationale provided as to why you are not correcting them at this time or why you do not intend to correct them.

Resources

To develop and implement a certification plan will require dedicated human resources. The training and re-qualifying requirements of today often tax a Utilities resources to the point of no return. In this case, you may have to enlist the assistance of outside help. Since certification is designed to be a one time event, you may want to consider this approach if your resources are limited.

A typical simulator management team concept could consist of the following as a minimum for the certification process of the simulator:

1. Simulator Manager - Responsibilities include the evaluation of the recommendations submitted by the various members of the staff and develop priorities for their impelementation and scheduling. This individual would also be upper management's contact point pertaining to simulator status, effective use and budgeting considerations. Recommendations would be made on the use, upgrade and certification of the simulator to where it meets all the requirements of existing, and in some cases, proposed regulations.

2. I&C Hardware Specialist - This person would verify that correct instrumentation is installed in the simulator and would also attend training courses on the compter complex and the I/O system. After delivery, the I&C specialist would be responsible for tracking the plant hardware changes and making recommendations for their future implementation in the simulator. In addition, this individual would make sure that hardware or wiring changes are completed and in-house efforts are reflected in the documentation. Accurate documentation is critical to ensure that the simulator configuration is tracking with the plant design changes.

3. Software Systems Engineer - This individual is also important in the initial procurement as well as in follow-on work. Being in on the initial procurement allows the engineer to become totally familiarize himself with the modeling techniques used for the simulator development. If this is not possible, it may be prudent to investigate a training course by the vendor of the simulator. Having this engineer resident as a full time asset enables this individual to assist in the tracking and evaluation of plant modifications and assessing their impact on the trainer. Involvements in this area would assist in the engineer's development and implementation of the required systems software modifications required. Additionally, the engineer would be able to identify the approximate time to install the mod and evaluate any impact that could result to the training schedule. The responsibility of maintaining the software data base and updating of the FDSs to reflect the current simulator software configuration would also fall to this individual.

4. Software Analyst Engineer - During the initial procurement, this individual could follow the development of a system from start to finish as well as attend training courses offered by the vendor. This puts the engineer in the position to implement future modifications undertaken by the Utility on a scale deemed feasible by his management. Additionally, this person would monitor spare computer time and memory remaining and identify the possible need for a computer upgrade. The Analyst could further evaluate changes to systems in the plant and assign priorities for including them in future modifications of the simulator. The Analyst would also assume joint responsibility with the Software System Engineer for the software data base and FDS updating.

5. Simulator Operations Specialist - This individual would be responsible for conducting all testing of the simulator, including discrepancy correction verification, modification testing, LER testing and the annual certification operability tests. The operator would act as the liason between the simulator management team and the training department. Feedback from the training department or the students would be passed through the Operator to the simulator management team. This individual would be responsible for seeing that information on all changes to the simulator and its performance were passed on to the instructors utilizing the simulator. The Operations Specialist would also coordinate training schedules for the most effective use of the simulator, working with the training department in identifying their needs. Additionally, this person could be responsible for scheduling and establishing time windows for modifications.

Implementation

After the plan has been developed and approved, implementation begins. If the resources are available, most of the phases of the plan can be conducted in parallel, such as the data base update and comparison to the FDSs, the hardware comparison, the verification of the procedures processes, and the testing of the simulator, both operability and procedure-wise. Each of these phases need a final report with recommendations issued. A review board can then study the reports and make the decision where and how to move. Any changes or modifications that result from these decisions will need to be incorporated utilizing the approved procedures ensuring a tight configuration management.

The establishing and scheduling of windows for modifications is of a prime concern for all the members of the simulator management team. An analysis of the type of modification to be implemented must be undertaken in depth, outlining its impact on scheduling, hardware, modeling and possible computer impact.

After the analysis has been completed, the projected time to complete the modification must be estimated. At this point you are ready to prepare a specification for potential vendors can be generated if necessary.

Modifications fall into a number of categories, some of which are as follows:

1. Advanced models
2. New plant systems
3. Remote operating panels
4. Additional peripheral panels
5. Emergency response facility simulation
6. Hardware changes
7. Computer upgrade
8. Verification and Validation Testing Program

Any modifications that take place as a result of the trainer's evolution during the certification process must follow the procedures developed to support the certification. This will ensure that all documentation, records, and testing are conducted properly and verified. A final report on each modification, whether done in-house or using an outside vendor should be required at the completion.

Submission of Certification

After all reports have been evaluated and resulting corrections implemented, preparation of the certification package can commence. As a minimum this package should contain a short history of the simulator, a list of exceptions and supporting rationale, a hardware disparity list, a discrepancy status report, a data package with the operability and LER test results, a report on the limitations of the simulator, copies of the procedures used to conduct this certification, and a plan to support the required 4 year certification process defined in NUREG 1258. The final step before submittal is to complete the Form 474.

Summary

To summarize the certification process as defined in NUREG 1258 need not be a harrowing experience. If the configuration procedures are detailed, well written, and followed, the job will be easier. Once a data base has been established and verified, keep it up-to-date. As corrections are made, record and file the test results. As LERs occur, verify that the simulator is capable of recreating the events. Keeping the simulator up-to-date will make the job easier and more rewarding, and thus avoid the "Oh Oh Better Call Macco" syndrome.

Simulators VI

ISBN 0-911801-51-0

Efficient matrix procedures for the simulation of coupled processes

George Zyvoloski
Earth and Space Sciences Division
Los Alamos National Laboratory
Los Alamos, NM 87545

Abstract

An improved method which reduces the degree of freedom in coupled flow problems is described. The method, termed IRDOF, prefactors a 2N by 2N matrix into a N by N matrix by neglecting some off diagonal terms. After solving the reduced system, the full solution is easily recovered. The solution is then enhanced by taking two successive over relaxation cycles in coupled form. Compared to the fully coupled solution, the IRDOF method showed marked improvement in speed and storage.

Introduction

Coupled processes exist in every discipline which is characterized by flow in porous media. Oil Recovery, Geothermal Energy Extraction, and Chemical and Nuclear Waste Isolation are some of the areas of current research which require complex partial differential equations to represent the physics of the flow problem. Finite Difference Methods (FDM) or Finite Element Methods (FEM) are used to discretize the differential equations. These equations are usually solved implicitly because of the large time scales involved in the physical processes. In addition, because of the nonlinearity of the constitutive relations, the system of equations resulting from the application of the FDM or FEM are nonlinear. Several methods are available to solve these equations, the most popular is the Newton-Raphson method. This method requires the solution of a linear set of equations at each iteration to obtain a correction to the independent variables. The matrix associated with this linear system is called the Jacobian matrix and its sparsity structure determines the computer cost of the code. It accounts for between 50-90 percent of the total CPU time of the code. As a consequence much work has been directed to the efficient solving of linear equations.

The most popular method used recently is the Preconditioned Conjugate Gradient Method (PCG). The reader is referred to the many references available.[1,2,3,4] Incomplete factorization is the most popular preconditioner and the one used for the work reported herein. For an account of Incomplete Factorization the reader is referred to Reference 5. In comparison to direct methods, CPU times have been decreased by two orders of magnitude and storage requirements decreased by an order of magnitude. Large 3-D problems, despite these improvements, are still limited by storage and CPU times. The Adaptive Implicit Method (AIM)[6,7] has attempted to improve the solution of equations generated by the Newton-Raphson method. The approach of AIM is to decrease the number of unknowns in multiple degree of freedom problems by identifying areas of the numerical grid where variables are changing slowly. Some variables in these areas may be treated explicitly thereby reducing the number of implicit equations. These remaining equations are then solved using the PCG method. The AIM technique was developed for use on black oil simulators. Here the independent variables are pressure and saturations of oil and water. Nodes are placed in either an active or passive group depending on the magnitude of the pressure or saturation changes. In the active cells the equations are solved fully implicitly, in the passive cells, the pressure is solved implicitly while the saturations are solved explicitly. This is known as the IMPES procedure (Implicit Pressure, Explicit Saturation). Some complicated bookkeeping is necessary to formulate the matrix equations correctly. It is important to note that for the nodes using the IMPES method, the degree freedom has been reduced from three to one. Typically, about 20 percent of the nodes run fully implicitly with about a 30-50 percent decrease in CPU time realized. The results are sensitive to the inputted values of the norms of the pressure and saturation changes necessary for defining the active and passive sets.

The method described herein is similar to the AIM method in that it attempts to reduce the degree of freedom of the Jacobian matrix, but is strikingly different in many other aspects. We run all the nodes in a modified degree of freedom reduction and then attempt to recouple the solution afterwards.

General Degree of Freedom Reduction Method

The development of the AIM method was fostered by a need in the petroleum industry. As stated earlier, the method was originally used to improve the performance of black oil simulations. Subsequently, the method was also applied to thermal recovery computer codes.[8]. The method presented here was developed out of a need to simulate heat and mass transfer in porous media. The results are applicable to a wide variety of porous flow problems, but the theory will be presented for this specific case. The equations which describe the flow of heat and mass in a porous media may be written:

$$\nabla \cdot (D_m \nabla p) + q_m + \frac{\partial}{\partial y}(D_{m\ell}\rho_\ell + D_{mv}\rho_v) + \frac{\partial A_m}{\partial t} = 0$$

$$\nabla \cdot (D_e \nabla p) + \nabla \cdot (K \nabla T) + q_e + \frac{\partial}{\partial y}(D_{e\ell} + D_{ev}\rho_v) + \frac{\partial A_e}{\partial t} = 0 \quad (1)$$

where the accumulation terms, A_m and A_e are given by:

$$A_m = \phi(S_v\rho + S_\ell\rho_\ell)$$

$$A_e = (1-\phi)\rho_r u_r + \phi(S_v\rho_v u_v + S_\ell\rho_\ell u_\ell)$$

and where the transmissibilities are defined as

$$D_m = D_{m\ell} + D_{mv}$$

$$D_e = h_\ell D_{m\ell} + h_v D_{mv}$$

$$D_{m\ell} = \frac{kR_\ell\rho_\ell}{\mu_\ell}, \quad D_{mv} = \frac{kR_v\rho_v}{\mu_v}$$

The terms are defined in Table I. It is important to note here that the pressure is represented in derivative terms while the enthalpy occurs only in the D_e terms. This will facilitate the simplification of the solution matrix described later in the paper.

Table I. Definition of Terms

p	- pressure
h	- enthalpy
k	- medium permeability
R	- relative permeability
S	- saturation
u	- internal energy
T	- temperature
ρ	- density
μ	- viscosity
t	- time
Subscripts	
ℓ	- refers to liquid phase
v	- refers to vapor phase
r	- refers to medium (rock)

These equations are discretized using a finite element method. A fully implicit formulation is used and a Newton-Raphson iteration is used to solve the resulting set of nonlinear equations. The system of linear equations which must be solved at each iteration has the form:

$$\begin{pmatrix} \frac{\partial F_{mi}}{\partial P_1} & \frac{\partial F_{mi}}{\partial h_1} & \frac{\partial F_{mi}}{\partial P_2} & \frac{\partial F_{mi}}{\partial h_2} & \cdots & \frac{\partial F_{mi}}{\partial h_n} \\ \frac{\partial F_{e1}}{\partial P_1} & \frac{\partial F_{e2}}{\partial h_1} & \frac{\partial F_{e1}}{\partial P_2} & \frac{\partial F_{e1}}{\partial h_2} & \cdots & \\ \frac{\partial F_{m2}}{\partial P_2} & & \cdots & & & \\ \vdots & & & & & \\ \frac{\partial F_{en}}{\partial P_1} & \cdots & & & & \frac{\partial F_{en}}{\partial h_n} \end{pmatrix}^k$$

$$\begin{pmatrix} \Delta P_1 \\ \Delta h_1 \\ \Delta P_2 \\ \Delta h_2 \\ \\ \\ \Delta P_n \\ \Delta h_n \end{pmatrix}^{k+1} = - \begin{pmatrix} F_{m1} \\ F_{e1} \\ \\ \\ \\ \\ F_{mn} \\ F_{en} \end{pmatrix}^k \quad (2)$$

where F_{mi} and F_{ei} refer to the mass and energy equation residuals respectively and P_i and h_i refer to the pressure and energy variables. The energy variable is temperature for single phase and saturation for two phase.

This set of equations is solved with a PCG method suitable for nonsymmetric equations. It uses incomplete factorization for a preconditioner and the GMRES orthominimization technique.[9] Incomplete factorization offers flexibility which is useful when a variety of easy and difficult problems are solved. For easy problems, a factorization consisting of terms only in the spots occupied by the original nonzero matrix elements, is appropriate. This factorization is called ILU (0). For difficult problems it may be important to include terms which arise from the elimination of the original matrix elements. These additional terms are labelled first order and the resulting factorization is called ILU (1). By continuing this process higher order factorizations may be obtained. The higher order factorizations are better approximations, but require more storage and are more time consuming to generate. The solution is carried out in 2 by 2 block form. That is, instead of solving the 2N by 2N system depicted by Eq. 2, a N by N system is solved with each matrix element now being a 2 by 2 submatrix. Instead of simple additions and multiplications, matrix additions and multiplications must be performed. The block form of the matrix enhances stability[1] and saves storage on the pointer system which identifies nonzero matrix elements. For a description of the general connectivity solver used here, the reader is referred to reference 5. In this paper the Newton-Raphson iteration is terminated if the initial residual is decreased by a factor of 10^{-6}. If the energy variable (ie temperature or saturation) is changing more slowly than the pressure, than the off diagonal derivatives with respect to this variable may be neglected in the Jacobian Matrix, Eq. 2. For clarity in the discussion that follows, Eq. 2 may be rewritten as follows:

$$\begin{pmatrix} \frac{\partial F_m}{\partial p} & \frac{\partial F_m}{\partial h} \\ \frac{\partial F_e}{\partial p} & \frac{\partial F_e}{\partial h} \end{pmatrix}^k \begin{Bmatrix} \{\Delta p\} \\ \{\Delta h\} \end{Bmatrix}^{k+1} = - \begin{Bmatrix} \{F_m\} \\ \{F_e\} \end{Bmatrix}^k \quad (3)$$

where $[\partial F_m/\partial P]$ is a N by N matrix which contains the derivatives of the nodal mass equation residuals with respect to the nodal pressures. The other matrices are defined similarly. All of the results reported in this paper were run using the Los Alamos code FEHM.[11]

To obtain a computationally efficient scheme for solution the derivatives of the transmissibilities with respect to pressure and enthalpy are neglected. With this important modification the matrices $[\partial F_m/\partial h]$ and $[\partial F_e/\partial h]$ become diagonal while $[\partial F_m/\partial p]$ and $[\partial F_e/\partial p]$ are banded. This simplification means that the equations for the correction $\{\Delta h\}$ and $\{\Delta p\}$ can be separated, giving the equation

$$\{\Delta h\} = \left[\frac{\partial F_e}{\partial h}\right]^{-1}\left\{ -\{F_e\} - \left[\frac{\partial F_e}{\partial p}\right]\{\Delta p\}\right\} \quad (4)$$

and

$$\left[\left[\frac{\partial F_m}{\partial p}\right]-\left[\frac{\partial F_m}{\partial h}\right]\left[\frac{\partial F_e}{\partial h}\right]^{-1}\left[\frac{\partial F_e}{\partial p}\right]\right]\{\Delta p\}$$

$$= -\{F_m\}+\left[\frac{\partial F_m}{\partial h}\right]\left[\frac{\partial F_e}{\partial h}\right]^{-1}\{F_e\} \qquad (5)$$

As a consequence of the diagonal nature of $[\partial F_m/\partial h]$ and $[\partial F_e/\partial h]$, Eq. (5) represents an unsymmetric banded system of equations which is solved using the PCG method, once $\{\Delta p\}$ is obtained by direct evaluation using Eq. (4). Although there is an approximation made in the solution process by neglecting the derivatives of the transmissibilities with respect to p and h it is important to note that this involves no approximation in the final solution of Eq. (2). The coefficient matrix and the right-hand side of Eq. (2) are updated at each iteration using the latest information to calculate transmissibilities and other quantities.

The algorithm as just described has worked well on many geothermal energy problems for the last decade.[10,11] We refer to this algorithm as the RDOF algorithm. It works because, while the Jacobian matrix is altered, and more Newton-Raphson iterations occur in the modified scheme, these iterations are more than offset by the reduced computations per iteration. This was true when a banded direct solver was used for solving the linear equations. When PCG methods are used, this is not always the case (see the results section) and a new algorithm was designed. After some experimentation, a refinement scheme was added to the just described RDOF scheme. The refinement consists of taking one or two cycles of a successive over relaxation scheme (SOR) after the correction is obtained from the RDOF method. The SOR iteration may be described as follows. Representing the matrix in Eq. (2) as $A = L + D + U$. One cycle of SOR is equivalent to solving the system:

$$[M] = \left[\frac{1}{\omega}D + L\right]\left[\frac{1}{\omega}D^{-1}\right]\left[\frac{1}{\omega}D + U\right]\begin{pmatrix}\{\Delta P\}\\ \{\Delta h\}\end{pmatrix}^{k+1}$$

$$= -\begin{pmatrix}\{F_m\}\\ \{F_e\}\end{pmatrix} \qquad (6)$$

where the right hand side of Eq. (6) represents the right hand side of Eq. (2). It is important to note that no additional storage is necessary to perform the operations indicated in Eq. (6). A value of ω=1.2 was used throughout this study.

In all of the tests, this algorithm uses a few more iterations than the fully implicit method (FIM). In terms of computer speed, the method was up to three times as fast!

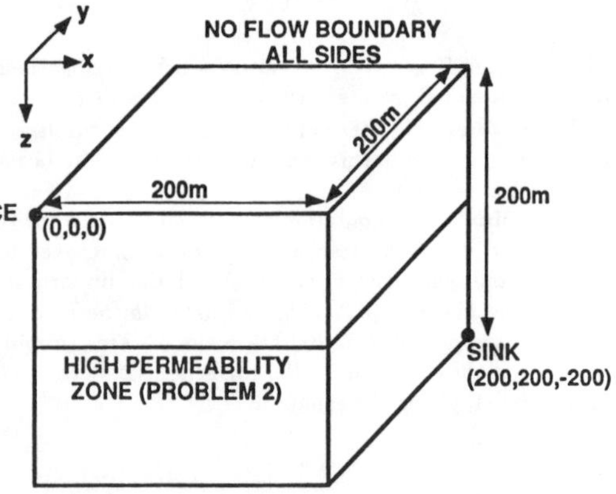

Fig. 1. Description of problem geometry for test problems 1, 2, and 3.

Examples and Discussion

To determine the utility of the IRDOF algorithm, several different problems were run. They are all 3-D problems ranging from 250 unknowns to 6750 unknowns, and from relatively easy to difficult. All of the problems are based on the cubic domain given in Fig. 1. The physical parameters of the problems and input parameters are listed in Table II. The first test case is a single phase heat and mass transfer problem with uniform properties where injection takes place at one corner of the cube and extraction at another corner. The finite element solution utilized 8 node brick elements and provided upwind weighting for the enthalpy and relative permeability terms. Details can be found in Reference 11. The problem was solved on three different grids: 5 by 5 by 5, 10 by 10 by 10, and 15 by 15 by 15. A histogram plot of CPU time vs total number of nodes, for the FIM method, the RDOF method and the IRDOF method, is given in Fig. 2. The IRDOF method is clearly superior, reducing CPU time by as much as 50 percent in running the code. All problems were run on a CRAY-1. Because of complex thermodynamic relations, and a high overhead for assembling the finite element equations, a greater improvement was not seen in the total running time of the code. Also in Fig. 1 are comparisons on CPU times for solving the Jacobian system only. Here the IRDOF really shines. On the largest grid, the IRDOF method was almost three times as fast as the FIM method. It should be noticed here that the solutions obtained by the various methods differed by less than 2%. This compares with up to 5% reported with the use of the AIM method.[4] It is also interesting to note that while we rate this as an easy problem, standard iterative methods or direct methods would cost orders of magnitude more on the larger dimension grids. In fact the ILU(0) used on the problem was averaging over 20 iterations per Newton iteration indicating it was being tested severely. The second problem was more difficult than the first. The problem differs from the first problem by the inclusion of a high permeability zone midway in the cube. See Fig.1. The permeability in this zone was 1000 times greater than the rest of the problem. The FIM method required an ILU (2) factorization to solve the problem with no time step reduction. The RDOF and the IRDOF methods, using ILU (2) in the single degree of freedom solver, were also able to complete the problem. The results are presented in Fig. 3. The computer times are lower than Problem A. This is a result of the ILU(2) factorization used. The figure shows clearly that the IRDOF works well on difficult problems. The figure also shows that the RDOF method showed no advantage over the

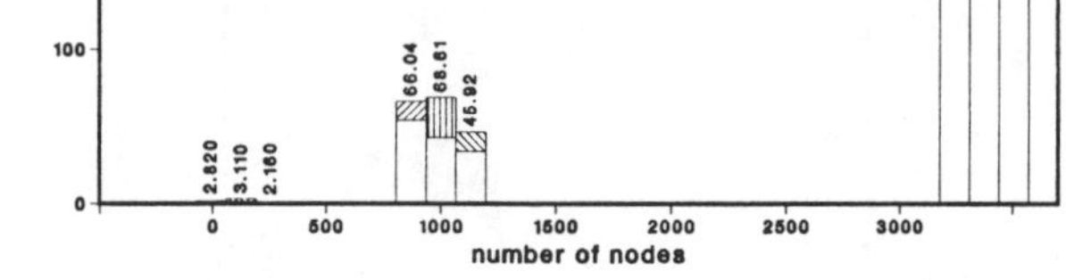

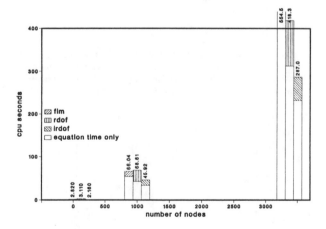

Fig. 2. Comparison of CPU times for the first test problem.

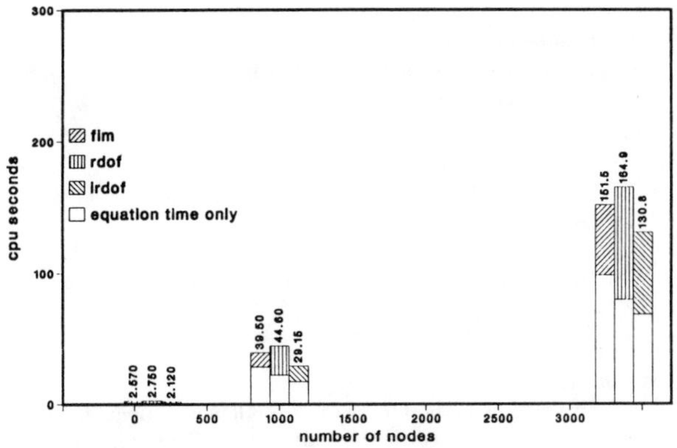

Fig. 3. Comparison of CPU times for the second test problem.

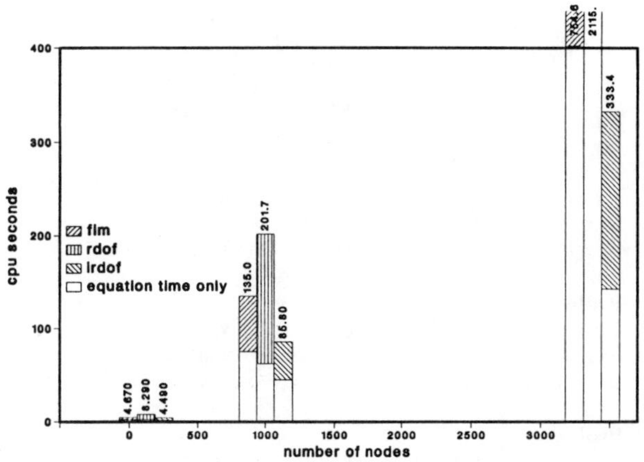

Fig. 4. Comparison of CPU times for the third test problem.

FIM on this problem. The CPU advantage of the IRDOF over the FIM varied between 13% and 26% for the total code cost, and between 30% and 40% for the cost of solving equations only. While the speedup was only 13% for the largest problem size the mass and energy balances were 10 times better for the IRDOF method than the FIM method. With adjustments more speed is available. The third problem had, once again, the same geometry as the first problem. The problem is one involving two-phase flow with a condensing front. The domain is initially at a liquid saturation of 0.8. With the injection of cold fluid (20° C) a condensation front propogates from the source. This a good test problem because the phase change requires under-relaxation on the Newton-Raphson iteration.[8] Because of the phase changes, the time step multiplier was invoked differently for the FIM and IRDOF runs making the simulation times different for the two runs. The IRDOF method required more iterations on an average per time step but rarely exceeded the iteration limit (15). The FIM method required less iterations in general but went over the limit several times. When this occurred, the time step was halved. Different simulation times for the methods resulted. The CPU times were normalized by the simulation times. An ILU(0) factorization was used. The results are presented in Fig. 4. Again, the IRDOF method is clearly superior to the other algorithms. Compared to the FIM method, a CPU reduction between 36 % and 56% is seen for the total running time of the code, and between 40% and 64% for solving the equations only.

To evaluate the robustness of the IRDOF algorithms the total iteration for the simulation was compared. Table III provides a breakdown of Newton-Raphson iterations for the three methods by problem and grid size. The iteration count for the IRDOF method was nearly that of FIM for Problem 1. For Problem 2, the iteration count was higher for the IRDOF method, but the method also produced better balance errors (10^{-4} instead of 10^{-3}). In the third problem, the IRDOF method had more iterations than the FIM method, but ran smoother and with a larger average time step. Overall, the results show the IRDOF algorithm to be robust. The results reported in this paper are for a reduction in the degrees of freedom from two to one. The AIM method, as applied to black oil problems, reduces the degrees of freedom from three to one. On such problems, it is expected that when using the IRDOF much larger CPU reductions would occur. This is because the number of nonzero matrix terms increases by a factor of 9/4 from the two degree of freedom problem to the three degree of freedom problem. Because there are never any explicit nodes, fully implicit 2nd-order time stepping schemes are available.[12]

Table II. Parameter Specifications for Test Problems

Problem 1

Geometry:
Dimension of cube 200 m/side
Cell size (3 grids): 50 m, 22.22 m, 14.29 m

Rock Properties:	
Permeability	10^{-14} m^2
Porosity	0.1
Rock Density	2700 Kg/m^3
Thermal Conductivity	3.0 w/(M °C)
Specific Heat	1000. J/(Kg °C)

Boundary Conditions:
No fluid or heat flow on all faces of the cube

Initial Conditions:	
Pressure	2.0 MPa
Temperature	150°C
Source/Sink	
Injection (0, 0, 0)	10.0 (5.0 for the largest problem) Kg/sec
Production (200, 200, -200)	Constant pressure (2 Mpa)
Time Step Size	
Initial	0.1 days
Maximum	10 days
Multiplier	1.5

Problem 2:

Add high permeability zone (k=10^{-11} m^3) at plane z=-100 m

Injection (0, 0, 0)	2.0 Kg/sec
Time Step Size	
Initial	0.01
Maximum	2.0

Problem 3:

Permeability	10^{-13} m^2
Initial Pressure	2.0 MPa
Production at (0,0,0)	25.0 Kg/sec
Initial saturation	0.8
Initial time step size	0.05 days
Maximum stime step	10.0 days

Table III. Newton-Raphson Iteration Count For the FIM, IRDOF, and RDOF Methods

	FIM	RDOF	IRDOF
Problem 1			
5 x 5 x 5	40	40	82
10 x 10 x 10	51	60	161
15 x 15 x 15	90	85	194
Problem 2			
5 x 5 x 5	40	40	73
10 x 10 x 10	44	56	130
15 x 15 x 15	79	101	148
Problem 3			
5 x 5 x 5	87(89.1)*	101(81.6)	201(74.09)
10 x 10 x 10	208(44.6)	222(64.52)	336(20.25)
15 x 15 x 15	230(20.38)	294(43.53)	393(7.90)

* Indicates completed simulation time (days)

Storage Considerations

One of the benefits of using an adaptive implicit method is the saving in computer storage. Table IV gives a summary of of storage requirements for the FIM, IRDOF, and RDOF, in addition to the storage needed for the original linear system. The RDOF and IRDOF methods show storage requirements that approach half the FIM method. The RDOF requirements are actually smaller because only the diagonal members of the $\left[\frac{\partial F_m}{\partial h}\right]$ and $\left[\frac{\partial F_e}{\partial h}\right]$ matrices need ever be formed. The reduced storage of the RDOF and IRDOF methods make them attractive for use on a workstation or personal computer.

Programming the IRDOF Method

The IRDOF method can be easily implemented in an existing code. The matrix manipulations described by Eq. 2 can be coded and called before any single degree of freedom solver is called and likewise the complete solution extracted after returning from the solver. No pointer system, as in the AIM method, is required. Even codes with direct solution of the linear equations will benefit from the IRDOF method.

Conclusions

The IRDOF method presented in this paper has been shown to be greatly superior to the fully implicit method (FIM) and the reduced degree of freedom method (RDOF).The advantages may be summarized as follows:

1. Reduction in CPU time of up to 50% for problems tested.
2. Reduction in CPU time for solving of the linear equations of up to 64% for problems tested.
3. Reduction of computer storage of almost 50% over FIM method.
4. Easy to program. Can be retrofitted to existing codes.
5. Can maintain second order accuracy in the time differencing because no nodes are treated explicitly.
6. Can be generalized to higher degree of freedom systems.

Table IV. Storage Requirements for FIM, IROOF, and RDOF Schemes

	Factorization	GMRES
Problems 1 and 3 (ILU(0))		
FIM	7 x 4 x N	(North + 1) x 2 x N
IRDOF	7 x 1 x N	(North + 1) x 1 x N
RDOF	7 x 1 x N	(North + 1) x 1 x N
Problem 2 (ILU(2)		
FIM	18* x 4 x N	(North + 1) x 2 x N
IRDOF	18* x 1 x N	(North + 1) x 1 x N
RDOF	18* x 1 x N	(North + 1) x 1 x N

N = number of nodes
North = number of orthogonalizations in GMRES
* estimated from actual computer storage

Acknowledgement

This work is supported by the Los Alamos National Laboratory which is operated by the University of California for the U. S. Department of Energy. Helpful comments by Bryan Travis are gratefully acknowledged.

References

1. Behie, A., and Vinsome, P. K. W., "Block Iterative Methods for Fully Implicit Reservior Simulation, " *SPEJ*, October 1982, pp 658-668.
2. Meijerink, J. A., and van der Vorst, H. A., "Iterative Solution Method for Linear Systems of Which the Coefficient Matrix is a Symmetric M-matrix, " *Math. of Comp.*, January 1977, pp 148-162.
3. Stoer, J., "Solution of Large Linear Systems of Equations by Conjugate Gradient Type Methods," in *Mathematical Programming. The State Of The Art*, edited by A. Bachem, M. Grotschel and B. Korte, Springer-Verlag, 1983.
4. Manteuffel, T. A., "An Incomplete Factorization Technique for Positive definite linear systems," *Math of Comp.*, Vol. 34, 1980, pp 473-497.
5. Zyvoloski, G., "Incomplete Factorization for Finite Element Methods,"
6. Forsyth, P. A., Jr., and Sammon, P. H., "Practical Considerations for Adaptive Implicit Methods in Reservoir Simulation," *J. Comp. Phys.*, February 1986, pp 265-281.
7. Bertiger, W. I., and Kelsey, F. J., "Inexact Adaptive Newton Methods," *Eighth SPE Symposium on Reservoir Simulation*, Dallas, February 1985, pp49-60.
8. Behie, G. A., Forsyth, P. A., and Sammon, P. H., "Adaptive Implicit Methods Applied to Thermal Problems," *SPEJ*, November 1987, pp 596-598. *IJNME*, Vol 23, 1986, pp 1101-1109.
9. Saad, Y., Shultz, M. H., "GMRES: A Generalized Minimal Residual Algorithm for Solving Nonsymmetric Linear Systems," *Siam J. Stat. Comput.*, July 1986, pp 856-869.
10. Zyvoloski, G. A., O'Sullivan, M. J., and Krol, D. E., "Finite Difference Techniques for Modelling Geothermal Reservoirs," *Int. J. Num. Anal. Meth. Geomech.*, Vol. 3, 1979, pp 355-366.
11. Zyvoloski, G., "Finite Element Methods for Geothermal Reservoir Simulation," *Int. J. Num. Anal. Meth. Geomech.*, Vol. 7, 1983, pp 75-86.
12. Richtmyer, R. D., and Morton, K. W., *Difference Methods for Initial-Value Problems*, Interscience Publishers, Wiley, 1967.

Simulators VI
© 1989 By The Society for Computer
Simulation International
ISBN 0-911801-51-0

Enhancement of training simulator
Part II: Advanced Models

M.R. Fakory, PhD, F. Mahjouri, PhD and R.A. Felker
Singer Link-Miles Simulation Corporation
Columbia, Maryland 21045

J. Olmos Sc.D.
Southern California Edison Co.
San Clement, CA 92672

ABSTRACT

Following the release of 10CFR55 "Operator Licenses" which specifies the requirements for simulation fidelity and control of nuclear power plant training simulators, many utilities have focused on procuring new certifiable plant specific simulators as well as enhancing their existing plant reference simulators. Enhancing fidelity of existing simulators to the level required by the guideline, includes, among other activities, 1) upgrading the simulator's man machine interface and 2) installation of advanced models. These advanced models utilize state-of-the-art mathematical tools, requiring a special computer complex and computer memory compatible with the existing simulator computer system. This paper illustrates some of the shortcomings associated with the existing simple models. The necessity and effects of advanced models to improve fidelity of training simulators are demonstrated.

INTRODUCTION

The considerable attention to train nuclear power plant operators on plant specific simulators has prompted the needs to equip the referenced plant simulators with real-time advanced thermal hydraulics and neutronics models. To enhance fidelity of nuclear training simulators, it is necessary, as a minimum, to equip the simulator with advanced models for simulation of critical systems [1]. Reactor coolant system (RCS), pressurizer, reactor core physics, steam generator, main steam supply and condensate/feedwater systems are among the main critical systems within the simulator software. Simulation of the nuclear steam supply system (NSSS) with advanced models plays a critical role in enhancing the fidelity of simulators, since some major malfunctions (e.g., LOCA, full rod ejection, partial rod ejection, PORV stuck open, hydrogen release) which are encountered during emergency operation of power plants directly affect this system. Therefore accurate real-time simulation of the thermal hydraulic and nuclear phenomena within NSSS is necessary to achieve the simulation fidelity required for certification. Also, since the advanced models are based on first principle laws of physics, once the advanced models are properly installed and operational, modification of the software to accommodate the plant design changes on the simulator is possible without major software modifications.

SHORTCOMINGS OF THE OLD MODELS

In the past, many training simulators were designed to be equipped with models which utilized simple numerical techniques compatible with capabilities of the economically available real-time mini computers. As a result, many old simulators designed by past vendors are equipped with a reactor core model which demonstrate shortcomings in many areas of training scenarios. These models have been designed to calculate the neutron flux for a bare reactor and then synthesized the results through coupling coefficients to obtain the flux values at several (ranging from four to 48) nodes. Some of the shortcomings associated with those models are summarized as follows:

- The rod worth determination accommodated the conditions that no more than a few (about three to four) rods total were misaligned at a time.
- The core neutron reflection and specifically the thermal shields were not correctly simulated.
- A single control rod group worth curve was used to present all full length rod group worth curves.
- Rod shadowing effects were not explicitly calculated. Therefore, in using malfunctions, misaligning nearest neighbor CRAs was prevented, which if not prevented could show somewhat greater control rod effects than what would be in the referenced plant under the similar conditions.
- The simulated rod worths were first-order approximations. Therefore, mixing both "in" and "out" misalignments such that the net reactivity worth difference was very small could produce a trajectory opposite to that which could be experienced in the actual plant.

The reactor core geometry and boundary conditions strongly affect the neutron distribution in the core. The reactor core flux distribution is a function of neutron generation, leakage and destruction rates. However, the neutron leakage through the reactor core boundaries can be described by,

$$n(\text{leakage}) = (1. - a) * w$$

where a is the neutron albedo and w is the neutron transport probability. A higher albedo represents a core boundary with less neutron moderation and reflection. Figure 1 shows the sensitivity of core flux distribution along the core vertical axis as a function of core albedo variations. The parameters aH and aV are albedos in horizontal and vertical directions, respectively. As shown, increasing vertical albedo raises the neutron flux at core boundaries while increasing the horizontal albedo flattens the neutron flux. Therefore, actual core boundary conditions must be closely simulated for accurate calculation of neutron flux distribution in the core.

NEW MODELING TECHNIQUES

Singer has developed, installed and verified the fidelity of "Real-Time Advanced Core and Thermal-Hydraulics" (RETACT) and "Space Time Kinetics" (STK) neutronic models to overcome the shortcomings associated with the old conventional models. Singer's STK core model is capable of calculating the reactor neutronic flux at a predetermined number of macronodes simultaneously. The STK core model is a neutron kinetic model which has the capability to simulate both PWR and BWR cores and is equipped with advanced techniques for prediction of the neutron transport probabilities.

Implementation Of STK Core Neutronics and RETACT Models Into SONGS Unit 2/3 Simulator

A) Original Reactor Core, RCS, and SG Simulator Models

The San Onofre Nuclear Generating Station Unit 2/3 simulator was delivered by Singer to Southern California Edison in 1983. Its original computer configuration consisted of two Gould 32/7780 computers. The models implemented for the Reactor Core neutronics, RCS and SG thermal hydraulics were typical industry-wide for the simulator delivered at that time. Their modeling scope was severely limited by the amount of economically available real-time minicomputer processing power.

Since original simulator acceptance testing, certain major deficiencies were recognized for these models. The limitations in the original Reactor Core model were inherent to the utilization of a single-node point-kinetics formulation to calculate the neutron population for the entire core. From this bare single-node neutronic flux, a 12-node (4 quadrants, 3 axial positions) flux distribution was further synthesized. The 12-node flux calculation attempted only to account for local variations of xenon and iodine concentration.

The original simulation models of RCS and SG were essentially limited to a single-phase multi-node formulation, with allowances made for simulation of saturated steam regions in the steam generator, pressurizer and reactor upper vessel head area. Because of the limitations, many important phenomena observable in a PWR NSSS during transient and accident conditions could not be properly simulated. These phenomena include coolant voiding throughout the RCS and SG, two-phase heat transfer in the reactor core, two-phase flow natural circulation including SG tube reflux boiling phenomena; countercurrent flow of liquid and gas phases, accumulation of noncondensable gases and steam voids in specific regions of the NSSS; and drain down of the RCS.

B) Reactor Core, RCS and SG Advanced Model Upgrade of SONGS Unit 2/3 Simulator

In the fall of 1986 Singer performed an upgrade of the SONGS simulator computer complex. The SONGS simulator computer processing capacity was nearly tripled with the addition of a Gould 32/97-80 computer. As shown schematically in Figure 2, communication between the 32/97-80 "turbo" computer and the 32/77-80 "master" and "slave" computers was accomplished through a Gould Multiprocessor Shared Memory System. Synchronization of the turbo computer CPU and IPU simulation executive tasks was achieved through a hardware interrupt line between the master and turbo computers.
The substantial increase in the throughput capacity achieved on installation of the Gould 97-80 computer was needed to accommodate the following contemplated software enhancements:

1. Plant Monitoring System

The Gould PACE system was installed on SONGS Units 2 and 3 during their last refueling outages (fall of 1987 and summer of 1988 respectively). For the actual plant, the PACE PMS processing requirements per unit amounted to 85% of Gould 32/97-80 throughput capacity. Southern California Edison's simulator staff implemented in-house the PACE system over a year period from May 1987 to May 1988. The performance of PACE on the simulator comprises all its major functions including the Combustion Engineering (CE) Core Operating Limit Supervisory system. The only major function excluded is the Historical Data Retrieval System. Moreover, by selecting a simulation approach, rather than the stimulation of PACE, SCE achieved a reduction from 85% to 15% 32/97-80 throughput capacity requirements (300 msec/sec CPU time).

2. Reactor Core Space-Time Kinetics (STK) Neutronic Model

In the spring of 1988 Singer installed the STK neutronic core model on the SONGS 2/3 simulator. STK is a macronode based space-time dependent neutron kinetic model. The reactor core data required by STK mainly consists of separate B-constant parameters for each assembly fuel type. STK was found to require 15% of the turbo computer capacity (300 msec/sec 32/97-80 IPU time) on the SONGS simulator.
The SCE simulator staff evaluated the performance of the STK on the SONGS simulator [3]. Significant improvements were observed in various training areas including
(a) Axial shape Index (ASI) - Transient effects on ASI due to changes in moderator temperature and boron concentration, as well as axial Xenon oscillations due to control rod insertion were observed and verified.
(b) Excore Instrumentation - Safety, control and startup channel excore signals are now evaluated by STK as a function of the neutron flux calculated for the fuel assemblies in the proximity of the excore instrumentation. Downcomer coolant density effects, rod control shadowing and shape-annealing effects are also included.
(c) Incore Instrumentation - Local neutronic and thermal-hydraulic effects on neutron incore detector and core exit thermo-couple readings were verified. Thus, neutron flux and coolant temperature asymmetries resulting from CEA insertion and Xenon imbalances are now observable in the simulator incore instrumentation.
(d) Core Processor Calculators (CPCs) and Core Operating Limit Supervisory System (COLSS) - An accurate 3-dimensional core power distribution calculation in the

simulator permits proper evaluation of Peak Linear Heat Rate and Minimum Critical Heat Flux Ratio. STK provides adequate inputs for the simulation of the CPC and for the PMS COLSS function.

3. RCS and SG Two-Phase Flow Thermal-Hydraulic RETACT Model

The upgrade of the RCS and SG of SONGS 2/3 simulator models to Singer's advanced two-phase RETACT code (Real-Time Advanced Core and Thermal-Hydraulics) is currently under way and is planned to be completed by February of 1990. RETACT's thermal-hydraulic model is based on the multi-phase conservation equations for fluid mass , energy and momentum which are integrated numerically, in space and time, over a large number (about 50) of fluid cell control volumes. The code also integrates conservation equations for boron and liquid- and gas-carried radioactivity, and the energy conservation equations for heat conduction in the fuel, steam generators and pipe walls. A widely accepted drift flux model is used to calculate the relative flow of gas and liquid phases, respectively [3].

CONCLUSION

A nuclear power plant training simulator must be equipped with models which are designed to meet the performance standards needed for certification or the NRC may not proceed to conduct operator examinations on the simulator. ANS 3.5 Standard criteria specifies that "simulator computed values of critical parameters shall agree with plus or minus 2% of the reference plant parameters and shall not detract from training" [4]. The shortcomings associated with simple old models have been discussed. As demonstrated, simplified models can generate a simulator response opposite to that experienced in the actual plant. The results of present study agrees with an INPO report which noted that significant improvements are needed in simulator fidelity and modeling capablities [5]. Studies show that limited instructor options (malfunctions) and limited capablities/fidelity can hamper the variety and realism of simulator exercises. Therefore, equipping training simulators with advanced models is inevitable. The results experienced at SCE's SONGS simulator demonstrate that significant improvements in simulator fidelity are achieved on installation of Singer's advanced models. The results also demonstrate that with the available computer facilities, it is possible to equip the existing simulators with the advanced models for critical systems.

REFERENCES

[1] M.R. Fakory and F. Seifaee "Transient Response of a Five Region Nonequilibrium Real-Time Pressurizer Model", Transactions of American Nuclear society, June 1987.

[2] M.A. Kelley "Simulator Core Upgrade Test Results", Sothern California Edison, San Onofre Nuclear Generating Station Interim Report, August 1988.

[3] E.K. Lin, C.L. Jen, S. Fabic and P. Anderson "Advanced Thermalhydraulic Modeling for Power Plant Simulators", The Institution of Nuclear Engineers Conference on Simulation for Nuclear Reactor Technology, Cambridge, England, April 1984.

[4] "American National Standard, Nuclear Power Plant Simulators for Use in Operator Training", American Nuclear Society, ANSI/ANS-3.5, October 1985.

[5] R.M. Wyatt and T.M. Muschara "Observations of Transient Training for Operator Using Full Scope Simulators", Institute of Nuclear Power Operations (INPO), Proceedings of Anticipated and Abnormal Transients in Nuclear Power Plants, American Nuclear Society Topical Meeting, April 1987.

Figure-1 Sensitivity to vertical albedo

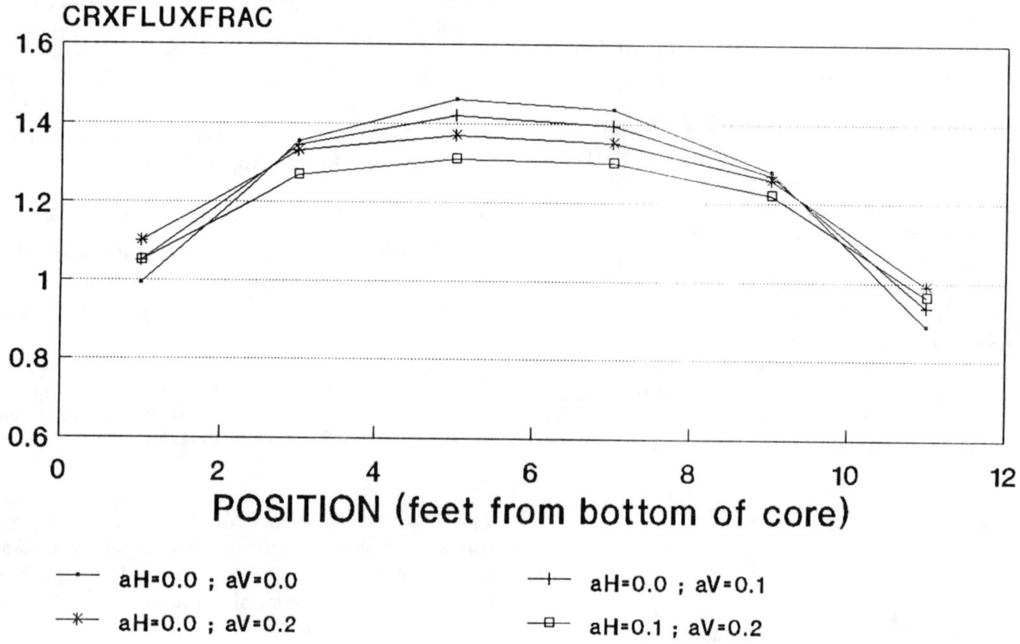

Figure-2 SONGS Computer Complex

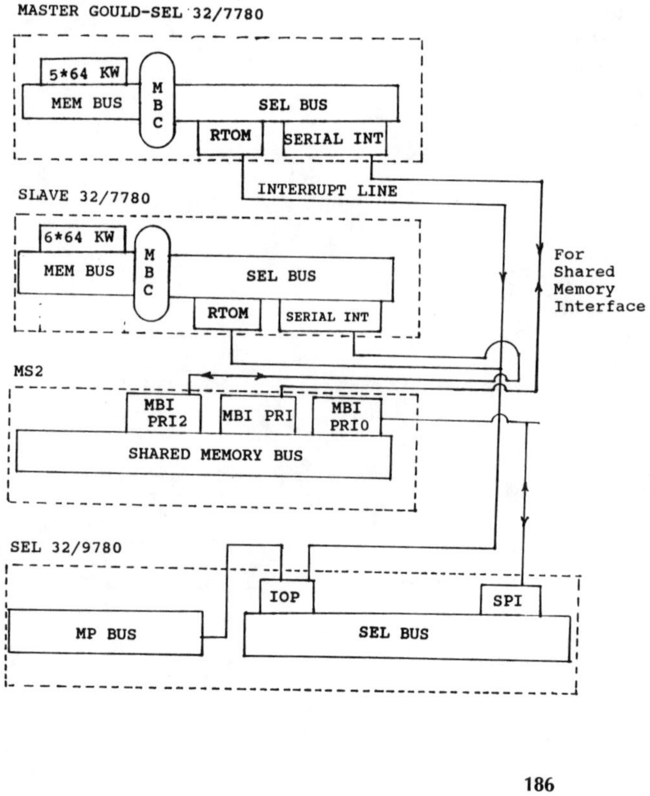

Simulators VI

ISBN 0-911801-51-0

Low cost portable Radar/DRLM simulator for shipboard training

Robert S. Hartman
Simulation Technologies Inc.
170 Wilbur Place
Bohemia, NY 11716

ABSTRACT

The use of a Radar/Landmass Simulator on board ship is a superior training technique having the advantage of training the radar operator in his own system environment. This approach greatly improves operator proficiency and effectiveness. Training is further enhanced when the simulator is capable of presenting a wide range of situation scenarios. Accuracy, high resolution, and realistic video display qualities are important attributes for the simulator. Modular design, miniaturization, and high reliability are essential. Finally, the simulator design must have the ability to interface to a wide variety of different ship's systems. This paper presents a description of a Portable Radar/DRLM Simulator designed to meet the above requirements at low cost and in a small package.

INTRODUCTION

Traditionally, we are accustomed to seeing a radar target generator and a digital radar landmass (DRLM) generator employed in a landbased ship bridge simulator or in a stand-alone radar trainer. Here, the radar simulator system (RSS) realistically simulates typical X-band or S-Band shipboard radar characteristics and generally interfaces these signals to operational shipboard radar display consoles. Ships signals normally received by these radar display consoles are simulated. For the radar, these are antenna position, triggers and acknowledge pulses, operator range switch position selection, and video. For ship subsystems, these signals consist of gyro compass (heading) and speed log. When these signals are received at the simulator and/or radar display indicator, all necessary data is received to allow digital target generation and digital radar landmass generation. Additionally, all necessary data is received by properly equipped radar display indicators, to effectively present training scenarios for Heads-up, North Stabilized, True Motion, or ARPA exercises.

PERFORMANCE

There are no simulator performance penalties or reduced training capabilities because of a requirement for a portable design. Modern electronics, miniaturized packaging and recent microprocessor technologies are combined to reduce size, weight, and complexity to give a reasonable package which can be carried on board ship.

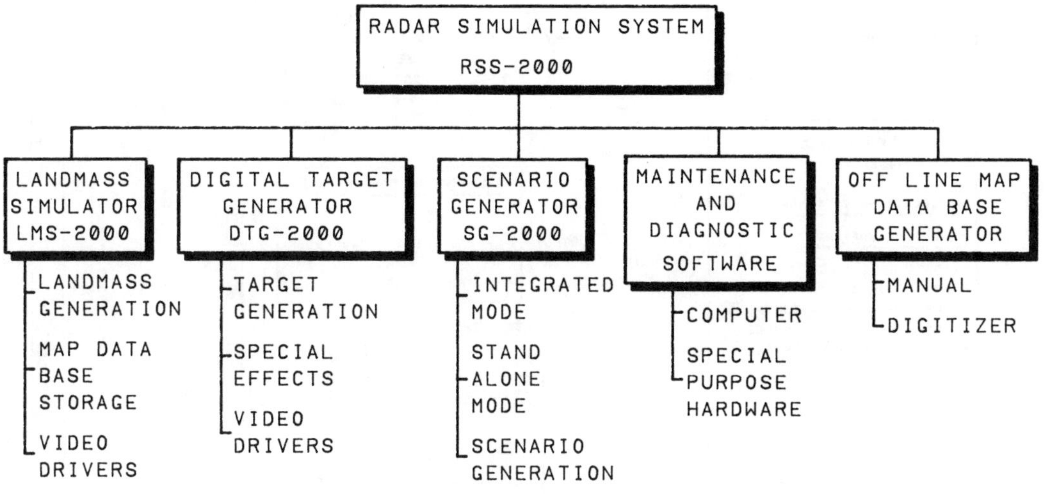

Figure 1 - Family Tree

The Family Tree of Figure 1 and the high level Block Diagram of Figure 2 are applicable to both a fixed-site or portable radar simulator. In either case, the radar simulator must provide the following as a minimum to achieve effective training:

- High resolution and accuracy
- Realistic modeling of Own Ship and target dynamics.
- Realistic imaging and occulting
- Accurate simulation of operation and procedures for radar features and controls.
- Realistic limits on performance caused by environmental and other effects.

RADAR CHARACTERISTICS

The "Performance" discussion above starts with a requirement for high resolution and accuracy. These are given below along with other pertinent radar characteristics to be simulated.

A. Range Resolution: 1/128 NM= 16 Yds.

B. Pulse Width:

1. 0.1 to 1.4 usec 0.1 usec increments.
2. Pulse width decoded from Radar Range Select Switch position of indicator.

C. Positioning Accuracy: 1/256 NM=8YDS.

D. Maximum Range: 256 NM

E. Number of In-Beam Targets: Up to 255

F. Azimuth Resolution: 0.35 degrees

G. Antenna Characteristics

1. Antenna RPM: Up to 30 RPM; Default to 20 RPM
2. Horizontal Beamwidth: 3 degrees nominal, setable for specific radar
3. Vertical Beamwidth: Up to 90 degrees, setable for a specific radar.

H. Output Video

1. Target, Trigger Video: Adjustable 0-10 Volts, positive or negative polarity.
2. Drive Capability: 30 Meters with 75 OHMs

I. Cloud and Clutter

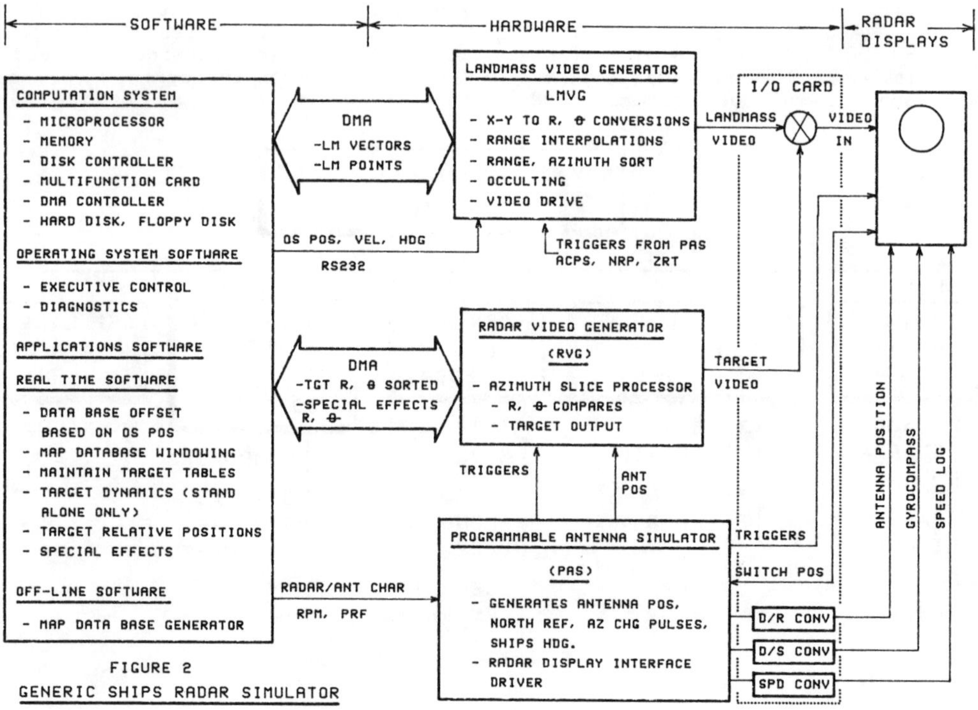

FIGURE 2
GENERIC SHIPS RADAR SIMULATOR

TARGET CHARACTERISTICS

A. Number of Targets: 0-20

B. Surface Target Characteristics: Same as own ship

C. Air Target Characteristics: 0-20 (optional)

D. Aspect angle simulated for surface targets

E. Surface Targets range limited by line of sight and target size (detectability)

OWN SHIP (OS) CHARACTERISTICS

Variations in Own Ship characteristics may be selected to match a training requirement. The variables which may be inserted are radar band X or S, ship size and length, speed range, turn rate, antenna height, and antenna blind sectors.

ENVIRONMENT AND SPECIAL EFFECTS

Moving weather, wind, clouds, clutter, sea return and jamming are effects which may be simulated to add realism and target detection training problems. For the most part, however, these effects are relegated to advanced training and to simulation of special problems and are generally optional.

SIMULATOR CONTROL TERMINAL

In a typical land based simulator, keyboard/CRT terminals are generally used for control and data display. These devices allow the exercise of fully interactive operations. For the portable simulator, there has been some use of a small handheld terminal containing function and numeric keys and a single line alphanumeric display. This is adequate for running simple problems, but this type of terminal does not provide sufficient display or command/control ease. A superior control terminal for the portable simulator is one of the small portable lap-top computers which are presently available. These devices are available in small size and light weight (approximately 5 to 6 pounds). More importantly, they can provide a full range of keyboard inputs and 80 column by 25 line displays for excellent interactive operations and display pages for rapid initialization and control of the simulator. A typical display page for Target data is shown in Figure 3. The lap top, with its shorter display height, will compress the vertical dimension of the page shown.

REALISTIC IMAGING AND OCCULTING

The gaming area for landmass should cover a minimum of 32 x 32 nautical miles, with some problems running to 200 x 200 nautical miles. When the accuracy and resolutions given above are achieved, fine correlation will exist between the radar simulator video display, a wide screen visual system, and map coordinates.

Realistic landmass and in-water navigation marker displays are important for training effectiveness. Radar simulators displaying an entire map and all its in-water points regardless of range, do not give effective training. They merely show a map image which differs from the image a radar

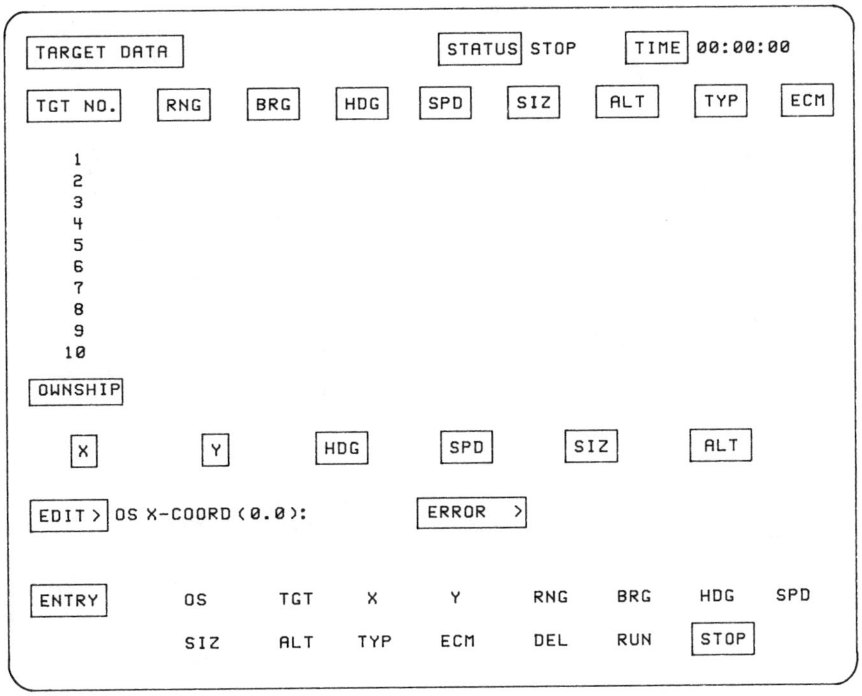

Figure 3 - Display Page

will display by "seeing around the bend" or through objects. The real world radar will not see around the bend, and will not see in-water points at some distance from own ship. For realism, the displayed range of landmass returns and in-water navigation objects should be limited by line of sight and size. When this is done, harbor entry and restricted water navigation training can be very effective. Landmass returns will be restricted for land behind land or around the bend when a real world radar would also restrict visibility of these areas. As the ship travels beyond a bend or other blocking areas, the radar image should continuously uncover or restrict new areas. In-water points, being low and small, have a radar visibility of perhaps six miles, and new points will appear and older points will drop out as the ship progresses along a channel.

The following formula for managing landmass, cultural objects, and in-water objects has been followed with success.

Primary Landmass is that landmass basically at sea level or "first seen" and is generally visible up to approximately 17 to 24 nautical miles depending upon antenna height. It has several levels of intensity each followed by pseudo-random noise to depict landmass beyond the point of initial landfall. Primary landmass generally will occult primary landmass.

Secondary Landmass is interior landmass. It is visible up to 25 to 35 nautical miles depending upon own ship's antenna height. Secondary landmass will generally occult secondary landmass.

In-Water Points represent buoys, channel markers, etc. These are visible to a range of 5 or 6 nautical miles.

On-Land High Points represent cultural objects, towers, etc. These are visible to a range of 25 to 35 or more nautical miles.

Cultural Objects are visible to either 17.3 NM or 25 NM. The 17.3 NM objects occult primary landmass and the 25 NM objects occult secondary landmass.

ACCOMMODATING SHIP'S VARIABLES

The most difficult aspect of accomplishing a shipboard installation is the necessity for the simulator interface to accommodate the wide variations that exist from ship to ship. These variations exist between radar systems, gyrocompass systems and ships speed log systems of different manufacturers, between old and new installations even for the same manufacturer, and between the various sizes and classes of ships.

A typical illustration of these variations are the antenna position transmitter which may be resolver, synchro, 50-60 HZ, 400 Hz, or pulse position encoders. Gyrocompass signals may be transmitted by synchro, or by different voltage and polarity levels of stepper switches ranging from 28 V, 35 V, 50 V, and 90 V levels. Ship's speed log data, although connected to the ARPA indicator, may also be inserted manually for ARPA training. Because of this, it is not usually added for training.

In order for the simulator to accommodate the majority of these variations, it is necessary for the simulator hardware and software interface design to be highly modular. Indeed, the basic simulator design configuration must be approached from this point of view from the very beginning. A practical approach, presently in production, is shown in the high level block diagram shown in Figure 2. Here, a ship's interface is accommodated by an I/O Module which has the specific data converters and drivers needed for that installation. The simulator design, other than the I/O module, remains unchanged.

GRADUATED COST/TRAINING/COMPLEXITY MATRIX

As had been stated, realism of display must be presented for effective training. Realistic depiction of landmass, surface targets, in-water points and stored scenarios are part of that given minimum requirement. After this, training level verses the cost and complexity of the installation must be considered.

Table 1, presents a matrix of factors related to training levels which can be achieved. the first installation (No. 1 in Table) is the simplest and lowest cost approach which gives Heads Up, North Up, and limited ARPA training. In this installation, antenna position is detected passively for use by the simulator. This is accomplished by connecting to the electrical terminals at which the antenna position transmitter enters the display indicator. The correct position converter circuit in the simulator I/O section must, of course, be used. Trigger and video connections can be conveniently made by coaxial connectors. In this installation, no simulator connection is made for gyrocompass. North-Up display may be initiated from the simulator keyboard and generated by software rotation of the displayed image. The ships gyrocompass, which actually remains connected, is an incremental output device and will not significantly flavor results while the ship is tied dockside. Effective ARPA training can be obtained but will be limited to cases where Own Ship course is not changed. This "simplest and lowest cost" installation approach may give all the training which is necessary for many purposes.

Method No. 2 provides an active injection of simulated antenna position signals when it is not feasible to use the first method. However, this method adds some installation inconvenience and cost. The third installation method is the most likely next level to be employed. Here simulated gyrocompass signals are actually generated and injected into the display indicator. ARPA training can be obtained without limiting Own Ship course changes. The method again adds some installation and cost, but may be justified by training need.

TABLE I - INSTALLATION METHODS

SHIP'S CONNECTION or SIGNAL INJECTION	ADVANTAGES	DISADVANTAGES
1. Antenna kept rotating (no RF transmission dockside). Antenna position is obtained by passively connecting to Antenna Synchro/Resolver/Pulse transmitter. Simulated signals limited to Antenna position, trigger, pulse width and landmass video. Gyrocompass is not input.	1.1 Simplest installation, lowest cost. No rewiring of ships cabling. 1.2 Provides Heads Up, North Up, & limited ARPA training.	1.1 ARPA training restricted to straight line courses.
2. Antenna position generated by Simulator and injected into indicator in place of ship's antenna transmitter. Simulator generates trigger, pulse width, and video, but not Gyrocompas signals.	2.1 Provides training itemized in 1 above.	2.1 ARPA training restricted to straight line courses 2.2 Simulator cannot drive lines at same time that antenna drive is connected. Therefore antenna drive wires must be disconnected and simulator wires substituted. 2.3 Addition of a permanent junction box will expedite simulator connection after rewiring. 2.4 More costly approach
3. Simulated Gyrocompas Signal generated by Simulator (as well as Ant Pos in 2 above) and injected into indicator instead of ships compass signals.	3.1 Provides Heads Up, North Up, and full ARPA training allowing course changes by Own Ship.	3.1 Requires disconnection of ship's Gryo-compass and substitution of simulated Gyro-compass lines. 3.2 May require changing of Compass Adapter strapping. 3.3 Addition of a permanent junction box will expedite connection. 3.4 More complex installation.

Simulators VI
© 1989 By The Society for Computer
Simulation International
ISBN 0-911801-51-0

Vessel resources management with full-mission simulation

Doward G. Douwsma
Grafton Group
P.O. Box 592
Dayton, Ohio 45405

Harry J. Crooks
Maritime Training & Research Center
1 Maritime Plaza
Toledo, Ohio 43604

ABSTRACT

The professional mariner works in an increasingly complex environment composed of dynamic and interrelated technical and social systems. Vessel safety has long been the mariners primary responsibility and until recently was assumed to be the logical result of finely tuned technical skills known as seamanship. But seamanship alone does not give the mariner the knowledge and skills necessary to manage the interrelated technical and social systems.

Vessel Resources Management is the effective utilization of hardware, software, and liveware to achieve safe and efficient vessel operation. Following carefully crafted, real-time scenarios, vessel officers learn to simultaneously manage both systems. The full-mission bridge and engineroom simulators of the Maritime Training and Research Center (Toledo, Ohio) are coupled in such a way that deck and engineroom officers must coordinate their efforts, communicate their decisions, mutually "trap" errors, and monitor their crew's efforts to achieve a safe "voyage".

Variations of Vessel Resources Management have now been developed for, and presented to, mariners of the United States Coast Guard, the U.S. inland waters, and the Great Lakes. Preliminary results indicate that this application of simulator technology will have a significant impact in the safety of vessel operations (including accident reduction) and in the efficiency of vessel operation (including fuel consumption and maintenance costs).

INTRODUCTION

The professional mariner works in an increasingly complex environment composed of dynamic and interrelated technical and social systems. Vessel safety has long been the mariner's primary responsibility and until recently was assumed to be the logical result of finely tuned technical skills known as seamanship. But seamanship alone does not give the mariner the knowledge and skills necessary to manage the interrelated technical and social systems.

Come aboard a complex modern vessel as she enters a busy port. From the ship's bridge we can see the "environment". There are bridges, piers, docks, other vessels in motion and vessels at anchor. There are small boats, large boats, ferry boats and sail boats. There is wind and tide and current and daylight or dusk or dark.

The vessel itself is a complex technical system. There are engines and rudders and thrusters for movement and control. There are charts and receivers and loran for navigation. There are short range and long range radios for communication. There are gyros and repeaters and signaling devices for stability. And there is radar to see what is and to predict what will be.

On the bridge is a part of the ship's social system. There is a captain and a watch officer, a pilot and a helmsman. Each is a polished expert at his job. The captain knows his vessel and her characteristics. The watch officer is backup to the captain and keeps careful note of his vessel's position in relation to the environment. The pilot knows the local waters, this harbor, its uniqueness and its dangers. The helmsman responds to commands quickly and accurately.

There are other parts to the social system: the engine room officers and crew, the galley officers and crew, the deck hands, and others. Each is highly skilled, each is separate, each is interrelated to the whole.

The radar screen is a point where the technical and the social systems interact. Marine radar shows not only the shoreline and other vessels. It plots the right now and predicts, for six minutes hence, the location of other vessels, large and small, underway or still. It is truly a magic black box to show the social system what "will be". It is an invaluable tool in close quarters maneuvering. It requires formal coursework, much practice, and careful thought to master the modern ARPA display.

The radar is a frequent stop as the captain and the pilot bring our vessel into harbor. The radar keeps the social and technical systems placed within the environment. It helps maintain the separation needed for safe maneuvering.

In a now famous case, the radar screen went blank. No longer was there a picture and a prediction. The watch officer, the pilot, and the captain all gathered around the now dark screen. They discussed possible causes, they fiddled with the controls, they focused all their attention on a breakdown of the technical system. The helmsman continued to maintain his course and the engineroom crew continued to maintain the last called for speed.

This vessel and its crew with finely tuned seamanship skills ran into another vessel. There were injuries but no loss of life. There was damage but neither ship sank. The cargoes were saved but both ships required extensive repairs.

Mr. C. P. Srivastava, the Secretary-General of the International Maritime Organization (of the United Nations) said in his annual address on World

Maritime Day: "It would, of course, not be realistic to expect that maritime accidents can ever be completely eliminated. The fury of the elements knows no bounds and some casualties will occur. Unfortunately, some of these accidents cause the loss of precious human lives, apart from the loss of ships themselves and their cargoes. We have, in the past year or so, been deeply shocked and greatly saddened by several tragic maritime casualties which have occurred in many parts of the world.

"As enquires into maritime casualties show, most maritime accidents are caused by *human error.* (The IMO has) agreed that something more can, and should be done ... it has been agreed that special attention should be focused on *shipboard management-* ... (emphases added) (IMO News, 3:88)

VESSEL SYSTEMS

The explosive growth of technology has not bypassed the maritime industry: electronic vessel controls, loran with its pinpoint navigational accuracy, and the ARPA radar are quick illustrations. New communication tools allow ship owners to speak with captains anywhere in the world. Loading and unloading is now done in hours where not many years ago it took days and sometimes weeks for vessel "turnaround". And ships are big and bigger as materials and hydrodynamics work together in new ways.

But the social system is much unchanged. The captain is by maritime law and tradition, the master. Watch officers, engineroom officers, galley officers, and the entire crew follow his lead and respond to his direction. And each, as an individual, is assumed to have those highly polished single person skills.

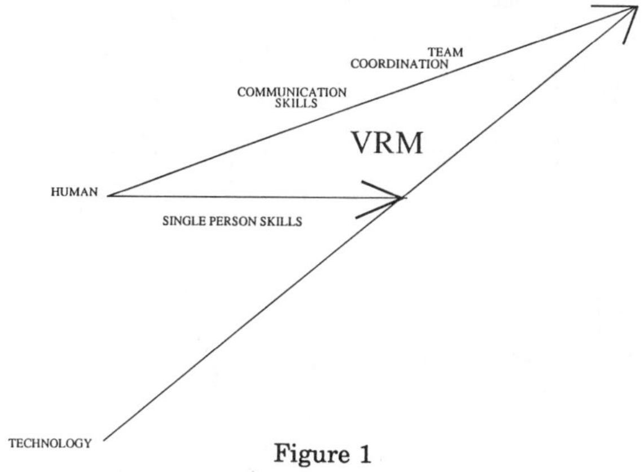

Figure 1

When the technical systems were simpler, the strength of a vessel was its social system and each person's seamanship skills. The human skills could successfully manage the technology.

But as Figure 1 indicates, the technologies have grown to the point where individual skills are no longer adequate. The single person skills need to be augmented with team coordination and communication skills. And these new skills must be practiced and honed and developed with the same care as the old seamanship skills.

Vessel Resources Management is the means by which these new skills can be taught. VRM is both a learning program and a perspective for todays professional mariner.

Vessel Resources Management is part of the response Mr. Srivastava describes. The purposes of VRM are to improve vessel safety and to increase the efficiency of vessel operations. The methodology is to develop new shipboard management skills on the part of the captain, the chief engineer, and the entire crew. Vessel resources management is the process that matures the social system skills so those skills can again manage the continuing advances in the technical system; to reduce the gap that imperils vessels and their crews.

Many times the maritime social system does not accept a statement such as; "Captain, this does not look right." As we sailed into harbor, surely the helmsman saw the other vessel. But the captain, the watch officer, and the pilot were otherwise engaged so nothing was said. The technical need for ARPA radar and its failure to function, caused shipboard management to miss the human error.

Had the captain and crew been trained in vessel resources management they would have acted much differently. Recognizing the ARPA radar failure as a challenge, the captain would have followed the paradigm shown in Figure 2. The captain would have framed the challenge, raised questions concerning it, solicited ideas and suggestions, and finally articulated his decision and the attendant responsibilities of each person. He would have established processes and set up control mechanisms to permit safe maneuvering without the ARPA. And had one cycle failed to trap the error of "everyone watching the broken radar", the VRM trained helmsman would have framed the challenge of the impending collision without fear of retribution.

Vessel Resources Management

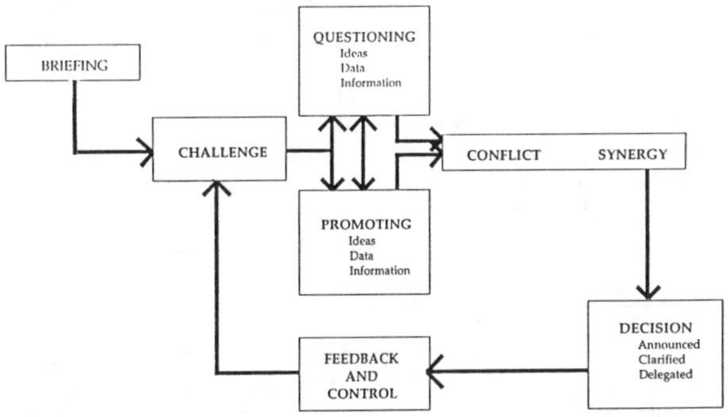

Figure 2

The vessel resources management skills are triggered by a challenge to the status quo, the challenge may come from outside: weather, other vessels, the shipowner - or from the vessel itself: equipment failure, accident, or human performance failure. The challenge may be stated by any member of the crew. Questioning and promoting are currently under- used shipboard management skills. VRM supplants the old "individual knowledge" with team communication and information generating which results in more knowledgeable and correct decisions made by the captain.

Many times a vessel is put in jeopardy when a subordinate is afraid to frame a challenge or promote an alternative to a senior officer. The helmsman may "know" that the captain does not tolerate being interrupted or being "told how to operate" his vessel.

CONFLICT

Ideas, data, and information generated this way may develop conflict. There may be more than one acceptable alternative. The sources of information may not agree. The pilot may feel that radar is not required for safe passage, the watch officer may feel that immediately coming to anchor is the safest practice. Conflict leads to the potential for synergy - a better solution than any single person could have produced.

The decision belongs to the captain; the responsibility continues to be his. But VRM adds to his decision responsibility a requirement to announce the decision to all concerned. VRM trained crews do not accept decisions which are not clearly stated so that each person is fully aware of the "captain's intent". VRM trained crews expect to be free to seek clarification if they do not understand intent or their assigned tasks.

Finally, VRM demands that a feedback and control structure be established to assure that the challenge is resolved. Simple, standardized structures work best but creative and unique structures are sometimes required. A failure in the monitoring process becomes a new challenge to the vessel crew.

Resources management is a conscious process. It requires reaching out and tapping into all the available resources; hardware, software, and liveware. It requires the recognition that the maritime technical system is too complex for a single person to know it all. It requires that each crew member learn to suggest alternatives, to identify potential errors, and to reach to other resources. It opens the door in the social system for a subordinate to offer an idea, a suggestion, or a warning.

The Vessel Resources Management syllabus includes these team coordination and communication skills: situation analysis, communication, problem solving, decision making, delegation, motivation, error trapping, team development, stress management, leadership, followership, conflict, synergy, and performance observation and critique. The training course is five days and four evenings of intensive learning and hands-on practice in the simulator.

MARITIME SIMULATION

Maritime simulators have been used extensively for developing these finely honed individual skills. The speed, safety, and stop-action capabilities of the simulators encourage repetitive drills of critical seamanship skills. Docking, undocking, turning, changing speeds, sailing a course, and identifying lights are all necessary skills that capitalize on the capabilities of a simulator.

This use of a simulator is akin to baseball's batting practice. It keeps one's hands and eyes and mind sharp. It can develop and maintain a high level of individual skill. But batting practice is not the same thing as playing a real game.

Vessel Resources Management requires a different kind of simulation. Captains, and chief engineers, and officers learn the VRM skills when they experience the actual shipboard management of the technical and social systems. These new coordination and communication practices begin to make sense when there is visible success based upon the use of these practices on a "voyage". VRM skills need to be practiced in a more "real life" setting than the stop-action of simulated docking. And these skills can be learned through both personal practice and through observing the practices of others; batting practice is only of marginal help to the observer.

Learning and practicing new skills requires a full complement of personnel in both the engineroom and the bridge. People need to become helmsmen, and oilers, and watch officers, and captains by performing the duties of those positions. They need to frame challenges, promote ideas, help develop alternative responses, and then carry out the captain's decision. VRM demands new social system skills and a session of batting practice does not meet that need.

The key to VRM success has been the capability at the Maritime Training and Research Center (MTRC) simulator to couple the bridge and the engineroom in real time. What happens in the engineroom is reflected on the bridge. The challenges facing the bridge also impact the engineroom. The speed and accuracy with which the framed challenge is communicated to engine room or bridge becomes a clear measure of VRM learning.

FULL MISSION/BRIDGE SIMULATOR

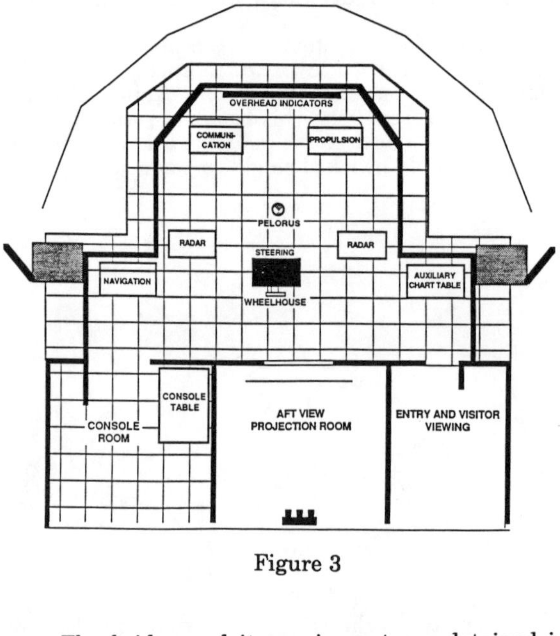

Figure 3

The bridge and its equipment are detained in Figures 3 and 4. The equipment is typical of a modern vessel in both content and layout. The physical size of the bridge is large enough to permit a full complement of personnel plus observers. The Remote Monitoring Console (Figure 5) provides enough space for additional observers and staff to monitor the progress of the "voyage".

The engineroom display (Figure 6) and control room (Figure 7) also conform to the typical modern vessel in content and layout. Again, there is sufficient size to include a full complement of chief engineer, watch officer, oiler, and observers. The control room offers additional space for observers of the "voyage".

VISUAL SCENE

- Full Color
- 182° Horizontal Field of View Forward
- 26° Horizontal Field of View Aft
- 26° Vertical Field of View
- 3.1 Arc Minutes Pixel Resolution
- Rear Projection
- Matches Radar Display Within 0.2 ft.
- Objects Approached to 0 ft.
- 30 Hertz Screen Refresh Rate
- Very High System Reliability
- Excellent Brightness
- Excellent Linearity
- Allows Accurate Visual Bearing Taking
- Object Occulting
- Good Range Light Sensitivity
- Accurate Aids to Navigation with IALA Flash Patterns
- Over 400 Lights at Night with Silhouettes

Figure 4

Remote Monitoring Console

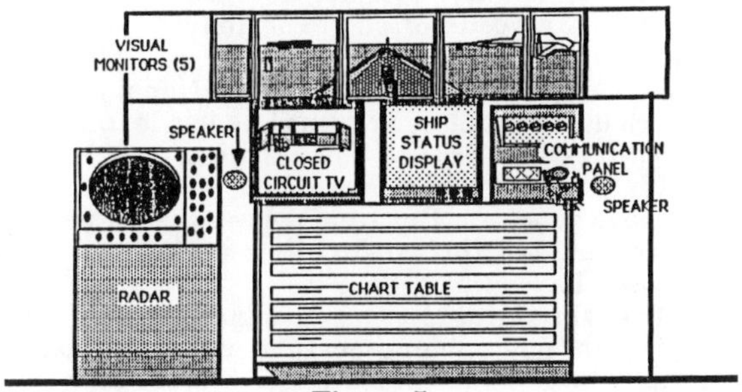

Figure 5

Bridge requirements for speed and direction are repeated to the engineroom for execution. Basic engineroom activities such as engine RPM are repeated to the bridge. Sound phone and regular phone communications are available. Conversations on the bridge and in the engineroom are broadcast to both the control stations. And the control stations are in continuous voice contact.

Participants in the VRM programs "sail" carefully crafted scenarios. Each scenario is written so that one or more of the VRM skills is emphasized during the voyage. Each scenario includes both simple and complex challenges. Simple challenges are those which can be resolved with the resources available; complex challenges require that the vessel crew work around that challenge for the rest of the voyage.

The specific challenge and the timing of the challenge are written into the script. However, the instructional staff has the option of not introducing a challenge, or changing the timing of the challenge, based on the performance of the learning team. Challenges are designed to be resolved; there are no impossible missions. The fundamental learning philosophy is success, not failure.

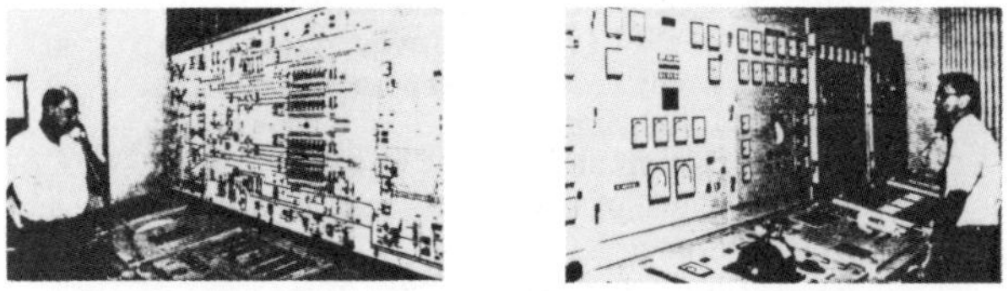

Figure 6

Figure 7

ELEMENTS OF VRM

There are three elements to VRM learning. First is the classroom which is used to describe and define the VRM skills. The classroom process includes lectures, discussions, exercises, and role plays. The simulator phase focuses on solving real problems in real time. Normal, abnormal, and emergency conditions are included as part of the challenge scripting. Focused observation is a critical part of the simulation phase as there are learner observers in the engineroom, on the bridge, and at both control stations. The final phase is feedback. Team and individual self-critique focus on the skills employed "well" and the application potential in "real life". Peer critique from the observers is focused on the entire VRM paradigm - that is, the use of all the VRM skills during the voyage.

The typical VRM course is made up of an equal number of captains and chief engineers or deck and engineering watch officers. The experience level is usually high with over twenty years' service the norm but with some participants having had fewer than ten years' service.

Each scenario is conducted as in actual practice. A vessel team will consist of a captain, a chief engineer, a deck watch officer or two, a helmsman, an engine watch officer or two, and an oiler. There will be assigned observers on the bridge, in the engineroom, and at the control stations. "Playing the position" can be difficult since the vessel captain and helmsman are both "real captains". But, usually after the first few minutes of the voyage each participant plays his position to the learning advantage of all.

Each voyage starts with a captain's briefing. Captains are expected to inform everyone, including at least one member of the engineroom team, of at least the following information:

* position and type of vessel
* nature of voyage (to and from where)
* planned navigational route
* weather, tide, and current
* speed
* personal preferences (repeated orders, etc.)

The Chief Engineer is also expected to brief the captain on this minimum list:

* limitations of engine machinery
* maximum speeds and turn rates available
* on-going maintenance during the voyage
* availability of anchoring equipment

Each 'voyage' is planned to take about fifty minutes. The initial briefings usually take about ten minutes and personal preparation such as watch officer chart familiarization also takes about ten minutes. An early concern was that these voyages would be too short for learning and practicing the VRM skills. Experience has shown that these fifty minutes are intensive learning periods. Longer periods tend to either be repetitive or to cause the teams to revert to their former communication and coordination patterns.

DEBRIEFING AND FEEDBACK

After each voyage, the observers hold a debrief of the team's performance. The focus of the debrief is on the use of the VRM model and the results of the VRM practices. Recrimination, finger-pointing, and put-downs are not encouraged; sometimes the staff has to step in and control the debrief. Critiquing captains and chiefs is not a typical maritime practice but has been well accepted in these courses. Self-critique has also been better received than we had anticipated.

All voyages are videotaped at the bridge control station. All bridge activity and conversation, communications with the engineroom, and all non-vessel radio links are included on the tape. These tapes are used during the debrief/feedback session and are then presented to the captain for his disposal.

Error trapping, capturing the chain of human error, before an incident or an accident is a primary emphasis of VRM. We use both canned and live exercises to teach error trapping.

In the classroom we use video tape re-creations of maritime accidents to practice. These re-creations clearly demonstrate the lack of team coordination, the use of ill-conceived problem solving models, and a generalized "individual skill" approach to resolution. After exposure to the VRM concepts, errors seem to pop off the screen. Groups sometimes even talk to the actors - yelling out, "No, not that way!"

It is on the voyages that error trapping becomes a new skill. The VRM paradigm encourages the helmsman to wrench the captain from the blank ARPA radar and demands that he maneuver away from the approaching vessel. The chief engineer no longer agrees that all is "ok" when in fact all steering control has been lost. The third mate speaks up when hitting a bridge piling is still a far-off probability. And the captain still makes the decisions, is still the master.

PRELIMINARY RESULTS

Preliminary results of vessel resources management have been encouraging. Captains, chief engineers, and company managers have told us that there is a new level of communication aboard vessels with some VRM training. The deck and engine departments have initiated coordination. One vessel team found a way to maintain a critical machine and still provide all the "up and available" time needed. Conversations between officers now include concerns of communication and coordination in addition to "sailor talk".

Some captains are beginning to see their function in a much broader perspective. No longer locked in on the all-knowing master role, they are discovering the thrill of delegation. As subordinates assume more complex responsibilities, the captains discover they can be shipboard managers.

We have forecast fuel savings of $60,000 or more for one VRM trained fleet. This savings will come from better coordination between captain and chief as they plan vessel speeds and voyage timing. The same fleet expects reductions in its repair and maintenance costs for all VRM trained crews.

The full-mission coupled simulators are the critical capability in the introduction of VRM skills to the maritime industry. Neither classroom nor real life can duplicate controlled experiences in team coordination and communications. In real life, each mariner reverts to his finely tuned individual skills to resolve challenges unless and until he has learned and mastered the VRM process and practices.

It's always easy to say:"This is what he/they should have done----." But what we want is *not* to have to go back and say this is what they should have done for they will have already done it.

The simulator creates a significant cultural change with new communication and coordination patterns which changes the social system and thus also changes the social-technical dynamics and interface. No longer does one person have to remember all the information and every piece of operating data. No longer does one person have to rely on his own knowledge, skills, and experience.

We are developing new sets of seamanship skills to join those finely tuned individual skills: we are adding team coordination and team communication.

Initial classes in Vessel Resources Management are meeting our expectations. Major great lakes, deep sea and US government fleets have committed to VRM as an operation procedure and as a means to improved vessel safety and operating efficiencies. Training is now being conducted regularly at the Maritime Training and Research Center in Toledo, Ohio.

References

Orlady, H.W. and Foushee, H.C. (Eds.) *Cockpit Resource Management Training* (NASA CP-2455). Moffett Field, CA: NASA-Ames Research Center, May, 1986. (NTIS No. 86-87038).

---- "Shipboard Management Guidelines Will Help Implementation". IMO NEWS, Number 3: 1988. International Maritime Organization: London, 1988.

Simulators VI

ISBN 0-911801-51-0

Distributed microcomputer systems for Naval and Merchant training and research simulators

Ian R McCallum
Maritime Dynamics Ltd
Llantrisant House, Mid Glamorgan CF7 8BS UK
and
Department of Maritime Studies
University of Wales College of Cardiff
Colum Place, Cardiff CF1 3EU, UK

ABSTRACT

The changing demands of the marketplace and the development of new, powerful microcomputers and networking systems enables new cost-effective marine simulators to be designed which are able to achieve the same sort of performance as was possible only with very large systems a few years ago. As the maritime world emerges from the prolonged recession of the eighties, the availability of such tools enables a range of training and research activities to be undertaken which would have been impracticable using older technologies. This leads to new realisations of the role of simulators in the fields of training, and particularly in port design and operational evaluation.

MARINE SIMULATOR REQUIREMENTS FOR THE LATE EIGHTIES

With a reported shortfall of 300-400 trained junior officers per annum for the UK flagged marine fleet alone, (Shaw, 1988), the prolonged shipping recession of the early part of the decade may be said to be truly over. A resurgence of marine activity is observable throughout the world, with much of the activity centred around the Pacific Basin. Applications for places at maritime colleges are running in some cases at up to ten times the capacity of the colleges, and there is a resurgence of building and re-equipping at maritime colleges worldwide.

This activity takes place at a time of continuing interest in efficient shipping operations. The trend of increasing ship size is apparent in all trades but the VLCC market, with new container ship tonnage being too wide to pass through the Panama Canal, and 230,000 dwt ore carriers being built with manoeuvring characteristics being designed around particular ports, (Elzinga and Sellmeijer 1987). As the most cost effective ship design for a given trade is frequently a large ship with high freeboard, powered by a single Slow Speed Diesel engine with fixed pitch propeller and no thrusters, there is a premium on being able to ascertain, before a given trade is contemplated, or before extensive port works are undertaken, that the ship is able to enter and leave the port safely, in a range of operational conditions.

The combination of large, relatively unmanoeuvrable ships, using ports with minimal operational margins places increasing reliance on the ability of pilots to control their ships with increasing skill, and on port engineers to design channels with adequate, but not over-generous margins. Conventional training methods for ships' officers and pilots will in general not equip them well for operations with totally new ship types in ports with marginal clearances, and there is an emerging awareness of the ability of simulation aids to assist in the training of pilots and ship's officers.

The role of marine simulators in the design of channels and ports is now well established. Over a decade of development by simulator operators and suppliers, coupled with a greatly enhanced appreciation of the abilities of simulation techniques by regulatory authorities, have led to the situation where, in many countries, it is now the norm, rather than the exception, to commission a ship manoeuvring study as part of the port design process. For many years, it has been usual to model port developments, by either physical or mathematical methods, to determine the current flows and wave loadings on proposed structures, but the port users have been left with an area of uncertainty in the effects of these currents and wave loadings on ships actually using the port. If it is possible within the normal budget of a feasibility study to examine the effects on a ship manoeuvring in a range of conditions, then this will tend to be done as part of most studies.

This ability to carry out a range of inexpensive feasibility studies requires the ready availability of inexpensive simulators, which are sufficiently simple to operate and flexible enough in their ship and environmental math modelling abilities, to be able to be used within the normal timescale of such a study. The US Coastguard has, during the past year, commissioned studies on the manoeuvres of a number of pushtow combinations, to determine whether it is possible to model ship behaviour with a knowledge of only the principal dimensions and operational particulars of that particular ship. Preliminary results would tend to indicate that, within the accuracy required of most port design studies, the process of predictive modelling is now achievable using present technologies.

The requirements for naval operator training are similarly undergoing a pronounced change. With the trend towards ships with very much reduced crew numbers, and a consequent reliance on automation, there are far fewer seagoing training billets, but a significantly greater training requirement. Engine control consoles are significantly more complex, with a greater information content than was the norm even a few years ago, with a very much greater reliance on automated operations. Paradoxically, this can result in a greater training requirement, as the operator needs to be able to diagnose a range of faults from the information presented to him on a screen or on a row of dials. At present, the level of automation in naval and merchant power plants is such that the operator is denied many of his sensory inputs by placing him in a sealed control room, while presenting him with many hundreds of indicators, often poorly designed from an ergonomic point of view, from which he is expected to deduce the plant's state, in both normal and failure conditions.

With the reduced seatime available to trainee naval officers, there is a greater reliance on simulators for shiphandling, Officer of the Watch training, and for Operations Room training, both tactical and procedural. The costs of the traditional methods of providing these types of Ops room trainers is such that few navies are prepared to afford them. However, the trends towards the greater use of microcomputers and non Milspec equipment for shore based training have transformed the situation to the extent that the smaller navies can now think in terms of procuring a full range of shore based simulation equipment for their training needs.

HARDWARE DEVELOPMENTS IN TRAINING AND RESEARCH SIMULATORS

Two developments which have transformed simulator design over the past decade have been the increasing availability of cheap, sophisticated microcomputers, able to be networked in a flexible, adaptable manner, and the increasing trend of shipboard equipment to resemble computer equipment.

The basic design of a ship simulator requires a number of simulation tasks to be undertaken simultaneously. For a bridge trainer, these will include:

- Representation of the visual scene
- Calculation of own and target ship motions
- Representation of radar and a range of navaids
- Calculation of a range of human factor measures, or Steering Quality Indices.

While it has been the norm for many years to consider the representation of the visual scene as a separate task, to be done in a separate series of computers, for most simulators all the other tasks were carried out in a single large computer. This carried a large overhead in terms of first cost, lack of adaptability, maintenance costs, and the provision of special computer rooms. A typical annual maintenance charge for a world class bridge simulator of the traditional design can be as much as $200,000.

Current simulator designs use a network of microcomputers to carry out all the computing tasks, with the requirement to represent the visual scene being considered as just one of these tasks. The provision of an adequate level of visual validity for most marine simulation needs is achievable now by a single graphics workstation or engine per visual channel, which can be attached to a network computer for linking purposes. A typical design for a networked microcomputer based bridge simulator is shown in Fig 1, where each computing task is assigned to a separate computer. Because each computer is cheap to acquire, relatively simple to program, and may be easily networked to the others, the cost of the complete simulator can be significantly reduced, both from a first cost and running cost point of view.

The networking requirements of such a simulator are fairly stringent. Computers of several different manufacture, employing different operating systems may have to be networked in such a way that the memory of one can be accessed by any of the others. It is found that many networks cannot operate adequately in this manner, being designed mainly for fileserver based operations. It has been found necessary to develop a network specially for this type of task, which:

- is inexpensive to install in each computer
- will operate for a range of computers of different makes and operating systems
- will allow the contents of memory to be passed to another computer
- has a fast enough data rate for the required information to be passed.

The inherent serviceability of microcomputers is extremely high, so that the maintenance of the complete simulator can be addressed in a totally different manner to that which is usual for simulators using a single main computer. An appropriate method for ensuring an adequate availability is to have sufficient spare computers and other major units to enable any defective ones to be replaced from the spares stock. This may be done using local staff, so that the downtime for the simulator can usually be maintained at under two hours. Often simulators using distributed microcomputers have no permanent maintenence staff at all, relying on regular planned maintenance visits and local repair by replacement.

The trend towards microcomputer based simulators was initiated mainly by manufacturers and users of part task facilites. As the capacity of microcomputers becomes larger, the design philosophies are being extended to larger and more sophisticated facilities. There is no hard upper limit on the size of such a facility. The network of Fig. 1 can be extended at will, both in the direction of more computers, (and hence more facilities) inside each own-Ship, and in the direction of more Own-Ships. The upper limits on the extent of the simulator which can be designed in this way is set in the main by the capability of the Instructor or Researcher to cope with the information and control requirements of his task.

There is no immediate correlation between the physical size of a marine simulation facility and its level of sophistication and comprehensiveness. Indeed, in some areas such as the mathematical modelling of Own Ship, some small port design simulators need to be at least as comprehensive as some of the largest world class facilities.

THE COST/REALISM PROBLEM

During their infancy, the design of marine

simulators was to a great degree influenced by that of the larger aircraft simulators, particularly in the perceived requirement for a high degree of realism on the bridge. There is now, for most marine requirements, a large and increasing divergence between the physical realism of the simulator and that of the real world, at a time when the producers of aircraft training simulators are making ever more attempts at greater realism.

The requirement for realism in the cockpit is usually justified in aircraft simulators by expressions of the type that the training "must be better" for more realism, and that is it "important for the trainee to feel all the cues". While an aircraft simulator is likely to cost upwards of $25M, its usage rate is such that it can pay for itself in under two years, and so it may be argued that, if the operators are uncertain about whether all that realism is worth the cost, it doesn't matter too much provided there are customers to pay for it.

The current trends in marine simulators are in precisely the opposite direction. The main constraint on the purchase or operation of a civil marine simulator is that of obtaining sufficient funds for its continued operation. Because there is at present no mandatory requirement for simulator training in bridge operations for marine personnel, the training market for civil simulators is fragmented and not well funded. The main, and increasing market for civil marine simulators is for the investigation of port designs, and in feasibility studies for new ports or the introduction of new ship types into existing ports. These studies are very cost and time sensitive. There is a large and increasing market for studies which can be completed within the time and cost constraints of a civil engineering feasibility study. The funds available for the ship manoeuvring aspects of this type of study may be measured in tens of thousands of dollars, but rarely greater. Additionally the study is usually expected to be completed in a few weeks at the most, such a timescale to include the production of ship and port databases, and the conduct and analysis of several tens or a few hundred runs. There is a very small, and perceivably decreasing market for large, well funded studies of ship manoeuvres of the type carried out so well by CAORF over the past decade, (Puglisi et al, 1987).

In order to satisfy this new market, simulators have to be designed and operated to totally different standards of performance. In order to comply with the cost and time constraints imposed by the market, the simulator must be designed exceptionally flexibly, but with adequate sophistication and realism in the provision of the visual cues and in the mathematical modelling of the ships involved. It is in the determination of what is adequate in this sense that guides much of the current research into civil marine simulator development.

In an early study at CAORF, (McIlroy, Eda & Shizume, 1982), it was found that the provision of a greater field of view, a coloured visual scene, (vs. a black and white one), or a daylight as opposed to a nocturnal scene, in no cases produced greater training gains. While a variety of reasons was evinced for the lack of training gains, there does not emerge a clear confirmation of the "More is Better" argument. The author regularly uses a small port design simulator, (Fig. 2), which has been specifically designed for addressing the smaller port design and ship operations tasks referred to above. The provision of visual cues is rather elementary in this machine compared with the type of visuals currently used in most aircraft situations, but the experience of a large number of port desgn studies is that the pilots carrying out the investigations can obtain adequate positional information from the limited visual fidelity available. What appears to be required is for the key visual cues, such as leading marks, jetties and buoys, to be viewable in their correct spatial relationship. The provision of a large colour range, a high update rate, and a high level of visual realism for shore features does not appear to be essential for the type of task for which the simulator is used. A continuing programme of research is being undertaken at the University of Wales to attempt to obtain formal, quantitative guidelines on what is an effective degree of visual realism for the port design task.

One feature which is seen as essential for adequate port design simulation is the ability to view stern leads, and most ship simulators now being designed offer this facility. In the simulator of Fig. 2 this is achieved by the pilot being able to switch the angle at which the three visual screens are looking to any position around the ship, giving all round cover.

Because the simulator is being used almost exclusively by fully qualified pilots, it is not seen as important to give it a high degree of bridge face validity. It is perceived that there could be an inverse relationship between the level of training or experience of the simulator operator and the level of face validity required. However, it can equally be argued that for preliminary training, the presence of too many distractions can be counter productive.

NAVAL TRAINING SIMULATORS - DESIGN METHODOLOGIES

The predominant requirement for naval simulators, in marked contrast to the civil requirements is for training aids. With the present worldwide squeeze on training budgets, the provision of large bridge trainers is not large. In the UK, there has been a perceived need for a naval world class bridge trainer for at least six years, but at no time have the funds for such a facility been forthcoming. It is only in the past two years that the US Navy has been able to procure a large bridge training facility, at Newport Rhode Island, (Guest and Miller 1987).

A major reason why more navies do not have such facilities has to date been the cost of such a facility. The two main cost determinants have been the perceived requirement for very high fidelity visual systems in a naval bridge trainer, coupled with the provision of Milspec "Real" equipment on the bridge. In a number of cases, it is possible to provide a design of simulator which fulfils the those navies which have to date been unwilling or unable to afford the more expensive systems.

The requirement for actual, as opposed to synthesised hardware can cause a naval training simulator to cost between thre and ten times the price of a facsimile device with an adequately high face validity. Figs 4 and 5 show a small simulator whcih recently entered service with the Royal Navy for training helmsmen in steering procedures. The simulator is based on a network of personal computers, with the large numbers of I/O devices required being interfaced directly to a computer in each student console. A near 100% level of face validity is achieved, although no preliminary reearch was carried out to determine whether this level of face validity was in fact required from a training point of view. Normal commercial standards of design and manufacture were used, with a very substantial cost saving. In a design exercise for another Commonwealth Navy for an Ops Room trainer, representing a complete ship's Ops Room, the provision of a complete simulator using a network of over 50 separate microcomputers coupled with non-Milspec equipment enabled a two thirds saving to be made over the normal type of provision. In a multi-million dollar procurement, this type of saving is seen as being significant.

It should be stressed that the cost advantages of non-Milspec procurement using networks of microcomputers are not made at the expense of serviceability or sophistication. The computing power attainable with networks of microcomputers is greatly in excess of anything which was available in a mainframe computer even five years ago, and the level of serviceability obtainable from non-Milspec equipment is fully adequate for most shore based training requirements.

Precisely the same arguments can be advanced for the development of engine room trainers for naval applications. Fig. 6 shows the computer schematic diagram of an engine room trainer for a four engined Fast Patrol Boat, powered by four turbocharged diesel engines. The simulator is designed to mimic the control rooms for the engines, generators, auxiliary and damage control rooms. Each major item of equipment is represented by its own separate computer, with additional computers for the Instructor Room, Student Learning Centre, and an Offline Development Centre. Again, no attempt would be made to incorporate a high level of Milspec equipment, reliance being placed on provideing a good facsimile to commercial standards.

CONCLUSIONS

Some examples have been shown of new types of ship simulator, for both research and training applications in naval and merchant scenarios. The use of networks of linked microcomputes are considered to have considerable advantages in terms of cost, flexibility and maintainability. The use of these techniqes has been instrumental in developing a range of new markets for marine simulation, as new applications which could not be addressed on cost or time grounds become available.

It is seen that the use of these techniques enables simulators to be designed without sacrificing either sophistication of mathematical modelling or comprehensiveness of provision. Nor need there be any significant lack of realism in the provision of consoles. One factor which considerably aids the designer of marine simuators is the increasing trend of equipment manufacturers to make their equipment look like computer screens. The new generation of raster scan radars can be very simly emulated, and it is necessary to think carefully before deciding to incorporate a real radar as opposed to a facsimile one in new simulators.

An area which remains inadequately researched in that of defining the degree of provision in a simulator which is necessary for the accomplishment of a range of tasks. The temptation to provide exscessive realism should be resisted if costs come into the calculation at all, and indeed there may be occasions when excessive realism is counter-productive in a training environment, and certainly unnecessarily costly in many research or design roles.

REFERENCES

Elzinga, Th. and R. Sellmeijer. "The use of Simulators in Judging Manoeuvring Characteristics of a Bulk Carrier". In Proceedings of the RINA International Conference on Ship Manoeuvrability, Gatwick, London, 29 Apr. - 1 May 1987, Paper 30.

Guest, F.E. and E.R. Miller. "MarineSafety International Shiphandling Learning Center at Newport, Rhode Island, Proceedings MARSIM 87, Trondheim, June 22-24 1987, 146-165.

McIlroy, W., H. Eda and P Shizume. "Validation Procedures for Ship Motion and Human Perception". International Marine Simulator Forum Documentation Handbook, Section 18-1. IMSF Secretariat, TNO/IWECO, PO Box 29 2600 AA Delft.

Puglisi, J.J. et al. "The Proposed Plan for Widening of the panama Canal and Application of Simulator Techniques for the Development and Validation of the Proposed Solution". Proceedings MARSIM 87, Trondheim, June 22-24 1987, 166-192.

Shaw, P, MP. 1988. "Future for the Merchant Navy". Seaways, (Journal Nautical Institute), December 1988, 3-4.

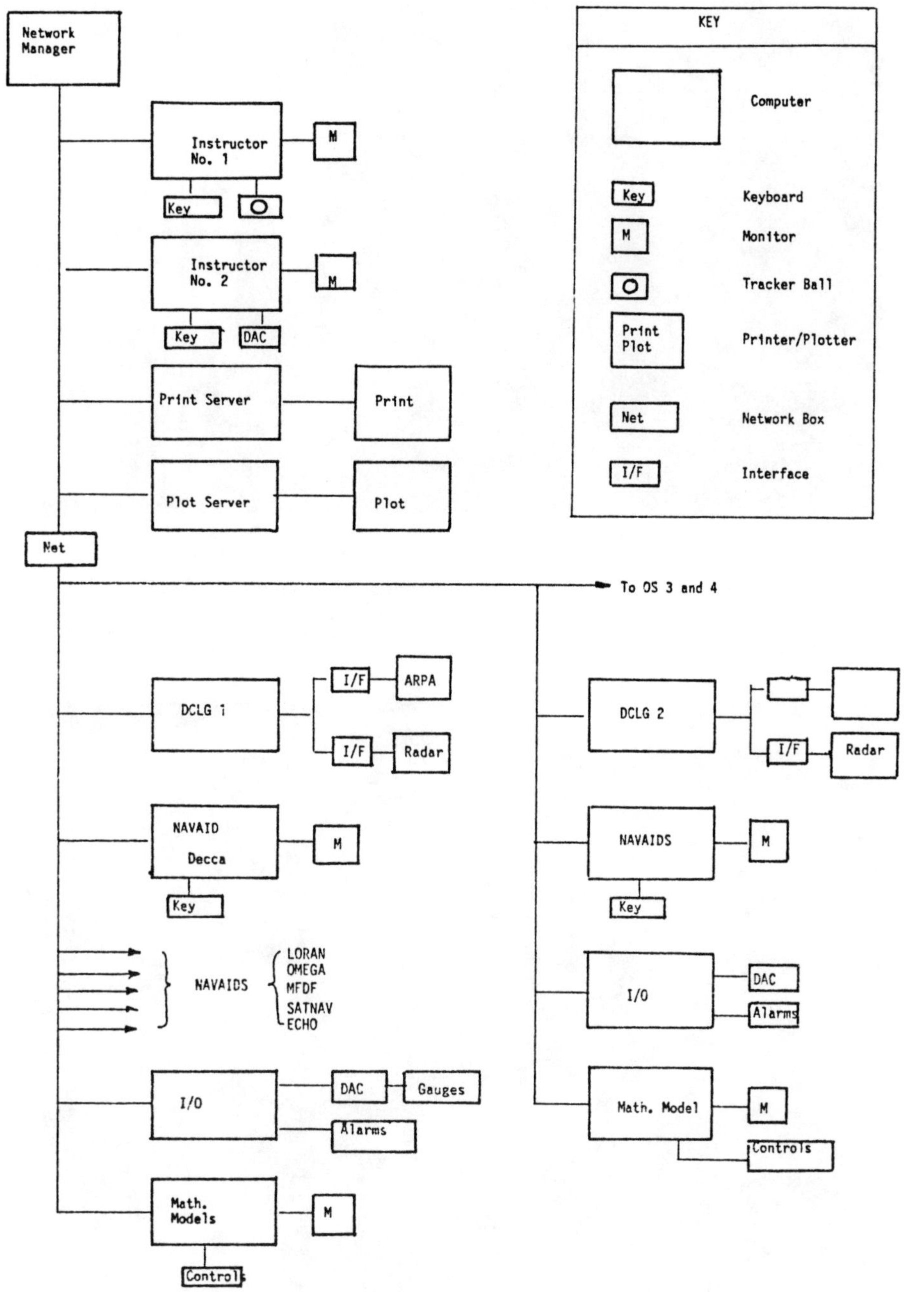

Fig. 1. Typical Computer Network, Microcompuer Based Simulator

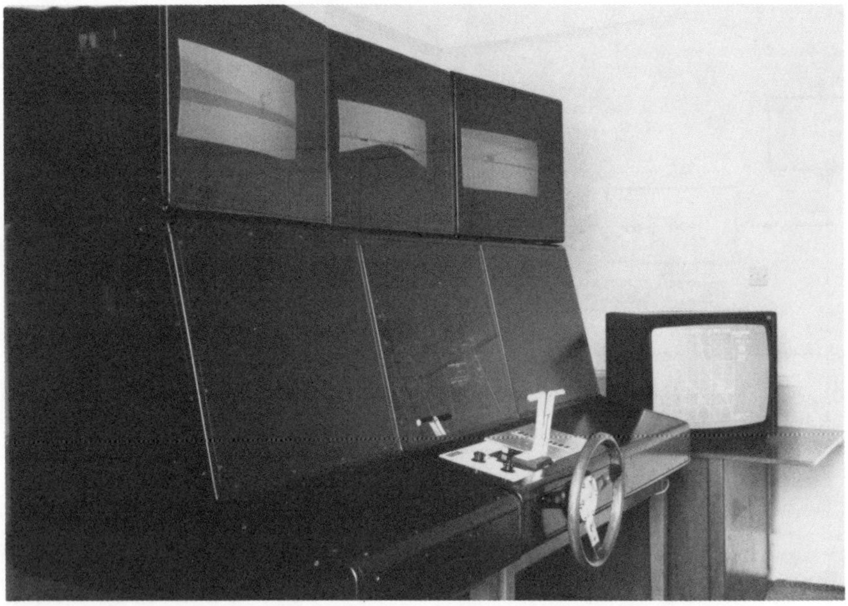

Fig. 2. MARDYN Port Design and Ship Operations Simulator

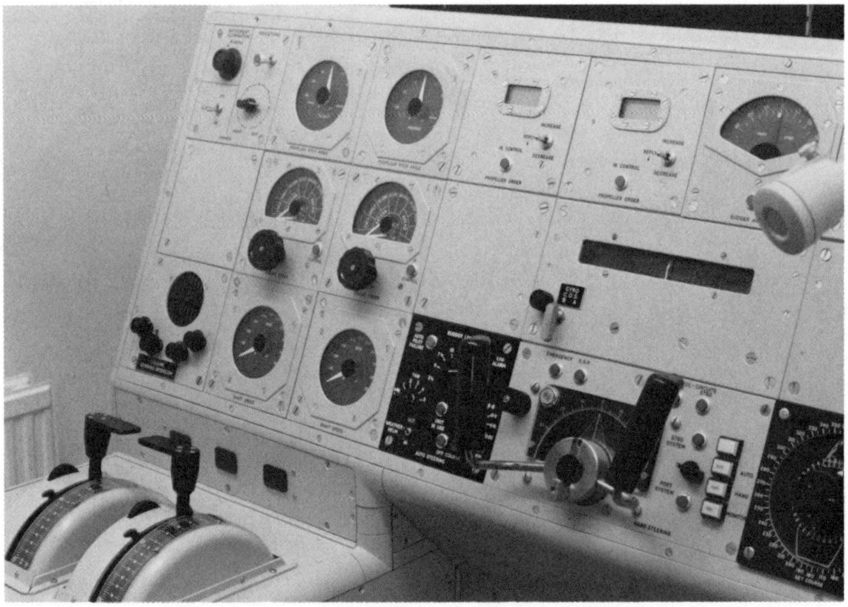

Fig. 3. Royal Navy Helmsman Trainer - Control Panel Detail

Simulators VI
© 1989 By The Society for Computer
Simulation International
ISBN 0-911801-51-0

Modeling multiphase flow in oil reservoirs

Frank S. Kovarik and Dae G. Huh
New Mexico Petroleum Recovery Research Center
New Mexico Institute of Mining and Technology
Socorro, New Mexico 87801

ABSTRACT

This paper provides a brief description of the current level of development of the modeling of multiphase flow in oil reservoirs with emphasis on enhanced oil recovery (EOR) processes. The field of research is summarized, with emphasis on carbon dioxide miscible flooding. This paper is written for engineers and scientists who work in the area of simulation but are not familiar with the petroleum field.

Enhanced oil recovery (EOR) is frequently separated into three research areas (Taber 1985): high-pressure gas flooding, chemical flooding, and thermal recovery methods. Between 1973 and 1980, thermal methods accounted for the steady growth in enhanced oil recovery in the U.S. Since 1980, the growth in thermal recovery projects has stabilized; chemical EOR and gas injection (primarily miscible) methods are responsible for the recent increases in enhanced recovery. The growth in the chemical flooding area has been provided by polymer-augmented waterflooding. CO_2 flooding has been the fastest growing gas injection process; however, hydrocarbon miscible gas projects have been expanding. In recent years, three large pipelines, which deliver CO_2 to the west Texas Permian Basin and also eastern New Mexico, have been completed, and CO_2 flooding projects have almost tripled from 1982 to 1986. CO_2 flooding is expected to increase at a fairly rapid rate (if the oil price is above $20/barrel) in the U.S.

The EOR perspective throughout the world is similar, but with much less emphasis on CO_2 and polymer flooding methods. Most of the EOR activity in the world is accounted for by thermal recovery. However, miscible gas projects have been increasing rapidly. Both miscible and immiscible nitrogen injection has become more popular recently because of favorable cost and availability in more remote areas. A majority of planned EOR projects outside the U.S. have been scheduled to use the hydrocarbon miscible gas process (based on 1984 data).

A brief history of reservoir simulation is given in this paper, then a short introduction to the field of enhanced oil recovery. Next, the simulation of miscible gas flooding is discussed in more detail, followed by brief, general descriptions of various reservoir models. Current model formulations and equation solving methods are presented. Examples are given of the new mechanistic models that are being developed and are now starting to be used in conjunction with the large, three dimensional, field-scale reservoir simulators in order to enable improved prediction of the performance of oil recovery projects. Indeed, these mechanistic models, based on engineering fundamentals, can help predict performance at the laboratory-scale and are being used to define new mechanisms that effect reservoir-scale displacements.

We will examine some of the reasons why simulation models are used, i.e., what questions need to be answered regarding projected reservoir performance, and then conclude with our view of the future of the simulation of multiple phase flow in oil reservoirs.

INTRODUCTION

As in all papers of this sort, we make no claims at universality, but hope the reader's interest will be held by what is included and his/her curiosity piqued by what is left out or partially described. For those of you who have not already done so, a brief tour of a prior review (Coats 1982), which this introduction is, in part, based upon, would be worthwhile. We have categorized the contents here primarily on the basis of what we consider to be the important new frontiers in reservoir simulation. A brief look at the history of reservoir simulation follows.

Reservoir simulation is the utilization of mathematics to predict oil recovery (reservoir performance) and also to compare the economics of alternate recovery methods. Before 1960, Buckley-Leverett calculations, analytical methods, and zero-dimensional material balances, were the state of the art.

The 1960's brought forth the development of sophisticated computer programs which could solve large sets of finite difference equations describing three-dimensional, transient, multiphase flow in porous media. Reservoir simulation was primarily concerned with two-phase gas/water and three-phase, three-component (oil, water, gas) problems, and the recovery methods modeled were usually pressure maintenance or depletion. The main concern was the matching of production history not the correct representation of recovery process physics.

During the 1970's, simulation methods spread to enhanced recovery processes such as miscible flooding, especially CO_2 flooding, as well as chemical flooding, steam flooding, and in-situ combustion. Individual models were assembled for each complex recovery scheme. Difficult problems addressing the physics of oil displacement needed to be tackled, such as the influence of chemical agents (e.g., interfacial tension reduction and emulsification), reaction kinetics, and complex multicomponent phase behavior on oil recovery.

A reservoir simulation model can be described in the simplest manner as a set of material balance equations which are combined with Darcy's Law (modified to include relative permeability) and subjected to a number of constraints, capillary pressure relations, and equilibrium conditions. Reservoir properties and fluid properties are generally considered uniform throughout a grid block, but can vary from one block to another. Fluid properties can also vary with time. Some causes of the complexity of the model are (1) reservoir heterogeneity, (2) the nonlinearity of relative permeability and capillary pressure as a function of saturation, and (3) the nonlinearity of fluid PVT properties.

Types of input required for the model include reservoir description data and fluid PVT properties, as well as well locations, perforated intervals, rate schedules, and productivity indices. Output includes spatial fluid pressures and saturation distributions, injection/production rate for each well, and producing GOR (gas-oil ratios) and WOR (water-oil ratios).

<u>ENHANCED OIL RECOVERY</u> (Baily 1984)

Enhanced oil recovery, defined by the National Petroleum Council (Baily 1984), is the "incremental ultimate oil that can be economically produced from a petroleum reservoir over that which can be economically recovered by conventional primary and secondary methods." Primary recovery relies upon natural reservoir energy to drive the oil out of the reservoir through the production well. As this natural energy dissipates over a period of time, additional energy is needed in order to continue to produce oil; and so, water or gas are added, under pressure, to the reservoir in secondary recovery processes. Waterflooding is a very successful method for improving oil recovery.

The EOR processes, commonly known as tertiary recovery methods are broadly classified into three areas: (1) miscible flooding, (2) chemical flooding, and (3) thermal recovery. Conventional primary and secondary recovery methods are expected to recovery only about one-third of the original oil that is in the reservoir. Thus, the potential impact of EOR processes on domestic oil production is significant.

Miscible EOR methods (Taber 1985) include the use of nitrogen, CO_2, and hydrocarbon gases as miscible solvents and have the ability to recover lower viscosity oils. Carbon dioxide flooding should make the largest contribution to oil recovery by miscible enhanced methods in the future. And indeed, CO_2 flooding has been the fastest growing gas injection method in recent years, with around 70 active projects in the United States. CO_2 flooding projects almost tripled between 1982 to 1986, and recent surveys indicated a continued rapid growth in the United States (provided the oil price is above \$20/barrel).

Chemical EOR includes surfactant (micellar-polymer or microemulsion) flooding, alkaline flooding, and polymer flooding methods. Surfactant flooding has received the greatest attention in recent years in research centers because of the excellent potential for improving low-to-moderate viscosity oil recovery. However, it is a complex process where a significant (and detailed) laboratory effort is necessary for field project design.

Thermal EOR includes in-situ combustion, cyclic steam injection, and steam flooding. Steam processes have been used the most in the field (the most advanced EOR method) and, thus, have the least uncertainty in predicting field performance. Steam floods are frequently applied in reservoirs, in place of primary or secondary methods, to recover viscous oils or tars. In-situ combustion has not proved economically successful to date.

<u>RESERVOIR SIMULATION OF MISCIBLE FLOODING PROCESSES</u>

The reader is referred to Stalkup (1983), Katz and Stalkup (1982), Coats (1982), and Stalkup (1982) upon which most of this section is based.

One of the key weaknesses in reservoir simulation is in the area of reservoir description. Spatial macroscopic permeability and continuity within the oil zone, as well as locations of faults, fractures, and shale barriers, initial fluid saturations, well productivity and injectivity, and other rock properties need to be described in the model. History matching, whereby the reservoir description is consistent with past performance can also be of help, but only gives a gross picture and is, in our opinion, used far too much in reservoir studies.

The reservoir pressure must be above the minimum miscibility pressure (MMP) in order to achieve miscible displacement. Besides pressure distribution, an efficient miscible gas sweep of the oil zone is affected by the size and type of miscible solvent slug as well as the drive fluid used to displace the solvent slug, the mobilities of the reservoir fluids, and reservoir heterogeneity. Volumetric sweepout can be influenced by gravity tonguing, viscous fingering, and channeling. Multiphase flow effects on sweep efficiency, the residual oil to a miscible flood, and solid phase precipitation should all be evaluated. Other important considerations tied to miscible sweepout are the optimal WAG (water-alternate-gas) injection system which is believed to reduce solvent mobility over continuous gas injection, the effects of gravity segregation, and the extent of oil trapping.

Not all oil displaced in a miscible flood is recovered, and the residual oil saturation left after contact by a miscible solvent (unit displacement efficiency) depends on complex phase behavior, rock properties, and the degree of dispersion. As an oil bank is displaced some of the oil is lost to crossflow into stagnant zones, and production wells should be positioned such as to capture and produce the maximum amount of contacted and displaced oil. Immiscible displacement mechanisms (oil swelling and viscosity reduction, vaporization of hydrocarbons, etc.) must be accounted for when the reservoir pressure drops below the miscibility pressure.

The relative permeability of fluids in a reservoir can be reduced by bypassed oil behind a solvent front as well as by immobile phases caused by complex system phase behavior (e.g. CO_2/oil systems). Accurate relative permeability and capillary pressure functions are necessary for any predictive technique.

A general finite difference simulator that represents all the important process physics in miscible and near-miscible displacements, has not been developed; however, the main ones currently applicable to miscible flooding include the modified black oil simulators (Todd and Longstaff 1972) and compositional simulators (Coats 1980). Several types of modified black oil simulators and compositional simulators have been proposed. In general, neither type of simulator accurately predicts the effect of physical dispersion on oil displacement and recovery.

Large grid blocks average-out the fine structure of a viscous finger-dominated displacement front. The initial displacement front perturbation and nonlinear growth cycles should be described in detail by a predictive model. The relative velocity that exists between the solvent and oil fingers is neglected in the diffusion-convection simulator (Peaceman and Rachford 1962) and other modified black oil simulators; the solvent and oil are assumed to be well-mixed in the grid block and to flow at a uniform velocity, which causes optimistic sweepout calculations.

A mixing parameter model (Todd and Longstaff 1972) was developed in order to improve the predicted sweepout and oil recovery in viscous finger-dominated floods where omega, the mixing parameter, is used to calculate solvent and oil component viscosities. Omega equalling one corresponds to complete mixing, and omega equalling zero corresponds to negligible mixing within the grid block. The model is critically limited, however, because omega is effectively only a fitting parameter.

Compositional models describe the hydrocarbon content of a reservoir as an N-component mixture. Equilibrium K-values and gas/oil phase behavior are determined from correlations or from equations of state (usually cubic). Physical dispersion terms are generally not included in the mass balance equations.

Some advantages of compositional simulation over black oil include: (1) predicting near-miscible displacement performance where compositionally-dependent condensation, vaporization, and swelling are important, (2) including the effect of composition on interfacial tension which in turn helps determine residual oil saturation, (3) considering the effects of complex phase behavior, dynamic (multiple contact) miscibility, and composition dependent viscosity and density on reservoir fluid recovery efficiency. Calculation of phase behavior can be extremely difficult in near-to-fully miscible displacements because phase composition paths travel through the critical point region. Compositional simulators should be tuned against continuous phase equilibrium data and also one-dimensional, slim tube data in the range of interest.

Numerical dispersion (spatial truncation error) in finite difference simulations, in physical terms, is exhibited through smeared solvent fronts in miscible flooding, and usually results in early gas breakthrough. Smaller, and greater numbers of, grid blocks reduce numerical dispersion, however, computing time and storage constraints are generally exceeded before the dispersion is eliminated. An unreasonable number of grid blocks is usually necessary to achieve dynamic miscibility over a few feet in the reservoir (scaled to match the laboratory data). Numerical dispersion also affects the (1) mixing of transition zone fluids resulting in erroneously predicted multiple phases and (2) the dilution of solvent slugs which causes errors in optimum slug size calculations.

Computational speed, storage, and vectorization have improved dramatically over the last decade (Coats 1982). Vector processing capabilities enable the coding of more efficient simulators, e.g., vectorization of code can reduce computing time by one to two orders of magnitude. So, larger, fully compositional, reservoir studies are becoming more feasible. However, three-dimensional, field simulations have been infrequent because of cost and complexity. Two-dimensional areal and vertical cross section schemes frequently are used to study sensitivity to reservoir and process variables and also to predict final performance.

MODEL TYPES

A mathematical model of a petroleum reservoir is an expression of the physical system translated into mathematical equations, a set of partial differential equations (PDE). Mathematical models of petroleum reservoirs can be divided into four different groups according to the mechanisms associated with recovery methods: the black oil (or β) model, the compositional (or miscible) model, the chemical, and the thermal model. In this section, basic governing equations are introduced for each mathematical model.

Black oil model (Aziz and Settari 1979)

The black oil model is the simplest model, in which only two hydrocarbon components are considered in addition to the water component: a non-volatile component (=black oil) and a volatile component (=gas). The basic flow equation in a black oil model is a diffusivity equation. This is a combination of the mass continuity equation for each phase for each grid block and the Darcy's equation representing the phase flow rate between each grid block. As an example, consider a control volume in a one-dimensional multi-phase fluid flow. The continuity equations for the three phases (water, oil, and gas) are:

$$-\nabla \cdot \left(\frac{U_w}{B_w}\right) = \frac{\partial}{\partial t}\left(\frac{\phi S_w}{B_w}\right) + q_w \tag{1}$$

$$-\nabla \cdot \left(\frac{U_o}{B_o}\right) = \frac{\partial}{\partial t}\left(\frac{\phi S_o}{B_o}\right) + q_o \tag{2}$$

$$-\nabla \cdot \left(\frac{R_{sw}U_w}{B_w} + \frac{R_{so}U_o}{B_o} + \frac{U_g}{B_g}\right) = \frac{\partial}{\partial t}\left[\phi\left(\frac{R_{sw}S_w}{B_w} + \frac{R_{so}S_o}{B_o} + \frac{S_g}{B_g}\right)\right] + R_{sw}q_w + R_{so}q_o + q_g \tag{3}$$

And the Darcy's equations are:

$$U_w = -\frac{kk_{rw}}{\mu_w}(\nabla p_w - \gamma_w \nabla z) \tag{4}$$

$$U_o = -\frac{kk_{ro}}{\mu_o}(\nabla p_o - \gamma_o \nabla z) \tag{5}$$

$$U_g = -\frac{kk_{rg}}{\mu_g}(\nabla p_g - \gamma_g \nabla z) \tag{6}$$

Combining these equations, the final forms are:

$$\nabla \cdot [\lambda_w(\nabla p_w - \gamma_w \nabla z)] = \frac{\partial}{\partial t}\left(\frac{\phi S_w}{B_w}\right) + q_w \quad (7)$$

$$\nabla \cdot [\lambda_o(\nabla p_o - \gamma_o \nabla z)] = \frac{\partial}{\partial t}\left(\frac{\phi S_o}{B_o}\right) + q_o \quad (8)$$

$$\nabla \cdot [R_{sw}\lambda_w(\nabla p_w - \gamma_w \nabla z) + R_{so}\lambda_o(\nabla p_o - \gamma_o \nabla z) + \lambda_g(\nabla p_g - \gamma_g \nabla z)]$$
$$= \frac{\partial}{\partial t}\left[\phi\left(\frac{R_{sw}S_w}{B_w} + \frac{R_{so}S_o}{B_o} + \frac{S_g}{B_g}\right)\right] + R_{sw}q_w + R_{so}q_o + q_g \quad (9)$$

with the transmissibility $\lambda_j = \frac{kk_{rj}}{\mu_j B_j}$

In order to solve the above three PDEs, the following constraint equations are needed:

$$S_w + S_o + S_g = 1 \quad (10)$$

$$Pc_{ow} = P_o - P_w \quad (11)$$

$$Pc_{go} = P_g - P_o \quad (12)$$

In the black oil model, there are basically three diffusivity equations and three constraint equations with six unknowns (P_o, P_w, P_g, S_o, S_w, S_g). Three PDEs are discretized into finite difference equations (FDE) and solved by the finite differences method or the finite element method. These discretized methods are explained in the next section, Model Formulation.

Compositional Model (Coats 1980, Nghiem et al. 1981)

The compositional model differs from the black oil model in that the oil and gas phases are represented by multicomponent mixtures, rather than two components. This model contains N_c hydrocarbon components in addition to the water phase.

A compositional simulator has significant advantages over a black oil model when the situation involves compositional-dependent mechanisms such as vaporization, condensation, and oil swelling. The diffusivity equations for the compositional model are:

$$\nabla \cdot [T_w(\nabla p_o - \nabla p_{cow} - \gamma_w \nabla z)] = \frac{\partial}{\partial t}[\rho_w \phi S_w] + q_w \quad (13)$$

$$\nabla \cdot [T_g y_i(\nabla p_o + \nabla p_{cgo} - \gamma_g \nabla z)] + \nabla \cdot [T_o x_i(\nabla p_o - \gamma_o \nabla z)]$$
$$= \frac{\partial}{\partial t}[\phi Z_i(\rho_o S_o + \rho_g S_g)] + q_i \qquad \text{for} \quad i = 1...N_c \quad (14)$$

where $T_j = \frac{kk_{rj}\rho_j}{\mu_j}$

Besides these equations, there are thermodynamic equilibrium equations:

$$fu_i^o = fu_i^g \qquad \text{for} \quad i = 1...N_c \quad (15)$$

$$Z_i = Lx_i + Vy_i \qquad \text{for} \quad i = 1...N_c \quad (16)$$

$$V = \frac{\rho_g S_g}{\rho_g S_g + \rho_o S_o} \quad (17)$$

$$L = \frac{\rho_o S_o}{\rho_g S_g + \rho_o S_o} \quad (18)$$

Also, the constraint equations are:

$$\sum_{i=1}^{N_c} x_i = \sum_{i=1}^{N_c} y_i = 1 \quad (19)$$

$$S_w + S_o + S_g = 1 \quad (20)$$

In a compositional model, there are $3N_c$+6 equations with $3N_c$+6 unknowns (x_i, y_i, Z_i, P_o, S_o, S_g, S_w, L, and V).

Equilibrium compositions of the phases co-existing in each grid block are determined from flash calculations using K-value correlations or from solving equations of state at the thermodynamic equilibrium condition of equal fugacity of a given component in each phase.

Thermal Recovery Model (Coats 1980)

The thermal recovery methods are used mainly in heavy and/or high viscosity oil reservoirs. In these reservoirs, generation of heat reduces the reservoir flow resistance by reducing the viscosity of the crude oil. Thermal recovery methods include hot water flooding, steam drive, cyclic steam injection, and in-situ combustion (wet or dry, and forward or backward).

In this model, there is one more constituent equation in addition to the mass balance equations. This is the energy balance equation. Coats developed a simulator which models four phases (j=1 for water, j=2 for oil, j=3 for gas, and j=4 for solid coke) and N_c components. The N_c components are as follows:

<u>N_c</u>
1 - water
2 - oil (heavy oil)
3 - gas
4 - coke
5 to N_c - gas or oil components

The constituent equations are:

a) Mass Balance equations

$$\frac{\partial}{\partial t}(\phi\sum_{j=1}^{N_p}\rho_j S_j x_{ij}) = \sum_{j=1}^{3}\nabla\cdot[T_j x_{ij}(\nabla p + \nabla p_{cj} - \gamma_j \nabla z)] - q_i + \sum_{r=1}^{N_R} q_{ir} \quad (21)$$

for $i = ...N_c$

where $T_j = \frac{k k_{rj}\rho_j}{\mu_j}$

b) Energy Balance

$$\frac{\partial}{\partial t}[\phi\sum_{j=1}^{N_p}\rho_j S_j E_j + (1-\phi)M_f(T - T_{in})]$$

$$= \sum_{j=1}^{3}\nabla\cdot[T_j H_j(\nabla p + \nabla p_{cj} - \gamma_j\nabla z)] + \nabla\cdot(k_t\nabla T) \quad (22)$$

$$+ \nabla\cdot(k_t\alpha_3\nabla T^4) - Q_H - Q_{HL} + \sum_{r=1}^{N_R} H_r$$

And the constraint equations are:

c) Saturation constraint

$$\sum_{j=1}^{N_p} S_j = 1 \quad (23)$$

d) Mole fraction constraints

$$\sum_{i=1}^{N_c} x_{ij} = 1 \qquad \text{for } j = 1...N_p \quad (24)$$

Chemical Model (Pope & Nelson 1978)

Chemical flooding can be broadly classified as any EOR process which uses chemicals in order to reduce the mobility of the displacing fluid, or to lower the interfacial tension between oil and water. These include low and high tension flooding, polymer flooding, and alkaline flooding.

A chemical model, in general, uses N_c material balance equations. For example, a one-dimensional compositional chemical simulator used N_c continuity equations to model several major processes such as phase behavior, interfacial tension effect on residual saturation, and increased polymer viscosity with concentration. This model included three phases (water, oil, and microemulsion) and six components (water, oil, surfactant, polymer, total anion, and Ca^{++}ion).

The continuity equations for the component i and the Np phases are:

$$\frac{\partial}{\partial t}(C_i + \hat{C}_i) + \frac{q}{A\phi}\frac{\partial}{\partial x}\sum_{j=1}^{N_p} f_j C_{ij} = 0 \quad (25)$$

for $i = 1...N_c$

where $f_j = \frac{k_j/\mu_j}{\sum_{j=1}^{N_p}(k_j/\mu_j)}$

This can be discretized by the explicit finite difference method. Using dimensionless terms, this equation becomes:

$$(C_i + \hat{C}_i)_{\Delta Q_D + Q_D} = (C_i + \hat{C}_i)_{Q_D}$$

$$+ \frac{\Delta Q_D}{\Delta X_D}\sum_{j=1}^{N_p}[(f_j C_{ij})_{X_D - \Delta X_D} - (f_j C_{ij})_{X_D}]_{Q_D} \quad (26)$$

with $X_D = \frac{x}{l}$ and $\partial Q_D = \frac{q}{lA\phi}\partial t$

constraint equations are:

$$C_i = \sum_{j=1}^{N_p} S_j C_{ij} \quad (27)$$

and

$$\sum_{j=1}^{N_p} S_j = 1 \quad (28)$$

In this model, the "Hand" plot (Treybal 1963) is used for the numerical representation of the phase diagram of the binodal curve and the distribution curve.

MODEL FORMULATION (COATS 1982)

The general simulation model is a set of partial differential equations. These partial differential equations are discretized into finite difference equations implicitly or explicitly. The most frequently used formulation (numerical model) in multiphase flow is the IMPES™ method. This method denotes implicit pressure and explicit saturation. IMPES uses old time level values of relative permeabilities in the interblock flow terms. Solution of a single pressure equation is followed by an explicit updating of fluid saturations and compositions in each grid block (Coats 1982). This formulation becomes unstable if the volumetric flow through a grid block in a time step exceeds a small fraction of the block pore volume. A more stable formulation than IMPES is the sequential method, in which solution of fluid saturation equations using implicit values of relative permeabilities follows the pressure equation solution. However, the implicit method is the most stable method. The implicit formulation (or SS formulation) solves the N_c equations simultaneously.

Computer time per time step increases from the IMPES to the sequential to the implicit formulation when the time step size is constant. However, the overall computing time depends upon the time step size for each formulation.

Most of the petroleum reservoir simulators have been written in a finite difference formulation which utilizes a semi-regular distribution of grid points. The finite element method is also used, but results in increased computer time. Advantages of the finite element method over the finite differences method are the relative ease with which the boundary conditions of the problem are handled and the variational treatment of grid blocks. For the discretization from PDE to the finite difference equation, the Taylor series expansion is usually used. There are two ways to discretize equations in 2-dimensional space. One is the five-point finite difference method, and the other is the nine-point finite difference method. Nine-point finite difference schemes have four more diagonal points than the ordinary five-point. Using the nine-point scheme, the grid-orientation effect can be reduced (Coats 1982).

SOLUTION TECHNIQUES

After the PDEs are discretized, the resulting finite difference equations are linearized. These linear equations should then be solved either by the direct method (Gaussian elimination or Gauss-Jordan) or the iteration method.

In the direct method, LU factorization and Gaussian elimination are used. The form of the resulting matrix depends on the ordering of equations. In order to reduce the computer time and storage, a D4 ordering scheme is often used. D4 matrix-banding is an alternating diagonal ordering scheme and is explained in detail by Price and Coats (1973). It is more economical to use the iteration method in a multidimensional simulation. The most frequently used iteration methods are:

SIP (strongly implicit)
SOR (successive over relaxation)
ADIP (Alternating direction iteration).

Other iteration methods are Jacobi and Gauss-Seidel methods.

The finite difference equation in the single phase 2-D case with a regular ordering scheme can be written as:

$$a_{ij}U_{i,j} + b_{ij}U_{i-1,j} + c_{ij}U_{i+1,j} + d_{ij}U_{i,j-1} + e_{ij}U_{i,j+1} = f_{ij} \quad (29)$$

where a, b, c, d, e, f are coefficients and U is a dependent variable.

Using the Jacobi method, this becomes:

$$U_{ij}^{(k+1)} = -\frac{1}{a_{ij}}[b_{ij}U_{i-1,j}^{(k)} + c_{ij}U_{i+1,j}^{(k)} + d_{ij}U_{i,j-1}^{(k)} + e_{ij}U_{i,j+1}^{(k)} - f_{ij}] \quad (30)$$

Using the Gauss-Seidel method:

$$U_{ij}^{(k+1)} = -\frac{1}{a_{ij}}[b_{ij}U_{i-1,j}^{(k+1)} + c_{ij}U_{i+1,j}^{(k)} + d_{ij}U_{i,j-1}^{(k+1)} + e_{ij}U_{i,j+1}^{(k)} - f_{ij}] \quad (31)$$

The SOR method is a modified Gauss-Seidel method:

$$U_{ij}^{(k+1)} = (1-\omega)U_{ij}^{(k)} - \frac{\omega}{a_{ij}}[b_{ij}U_{i-1,j}^{(k+1)} + c_{ij}U_{i+1,j}^{(k)} + d_{ij}U_{i,j-1}^{(k+1)} + e_{ij}U_{i,j+1}^{(k)} - f_{ij}] \quad (32)$$

When $0 < \omega < 1$, this method is called under-relaxation and when $\omega > 1$, it is called over-relaxation or SOR (successive over relaxation). The SOR method accelerates the speed of convergence. If the optimum relaxation factor (ω) is obtained, the rate of convergence is accelerated.

In order to explain the ADIP method (Aziz and Settari 1979), Eq. 29 is rewritten in the following form by grouping it into three terms:

$$(a_1x_{ij}U_{i,j} + b_{ij}U_{i-1,j} + c_{ij}U_{i+1,j}) + (a_2y_{ij}U_{i,j} + d_{ij}U_{i,j-1} + e_{ij}U_{i,j+1}) + (g_{ij}U_{i,j}) = f_{ij} \quad (33)$$

If this equation is written in a matrix form:

$$(H + V + \Sigma)u = d \quad (34)$$

$$(H + \frac{1}{2}\Sigma + rI)u = (rI - V - \frac{1}{2}\Sigma)u + d \quad (35a)$$

$$(V + \frac{1}{2}\Sigma + rI)u = (rI - H - \frac{1}{2}\Sigma)u + d \quad (35b)$$

$$\{(H + \frac{1}{2}\Sigma) + r^{(k+1)}I\}u^* = \{r^{(k+1)}I - (V + \frac{1}{2}\Sigma)\}u^{(k)} + d \quad (36a)$$

$$\{(V + \frac{1}{2}\Sigma) + r^{(k+1)}I\}u^{(k+1)} = \{r^{(k+1)}I - (H + \frac{1}{2}\Sigma)\}u^* + d \quad (36b)$$

where H = matrix of horizontal direction derivative
V = matrix of vertical direction derivative
Σ = matrix of time derivative
r = iteration parameter chosen to accelerate convergence of the iterative process.

First Eq. 36a is solved for u^*, then Eq. 36b is solved for $u^{(k+1)}$. This process is continued until convergence is obtained.

In the SIP method (Aziz and Settari 1979), the general matrix form of Au = d can be rewritten as:

$$(A + N)u = (A + N)u - (Au - d) \quad (37)$$

so that A + N is easily factored into L and U matrices which are sparse. Hence the equation becomes:

$$(LU)u^{(k+1)} = (LU)u^{(k)} - (Au^{(k)} - d) \quad (38)$$

or $(LU)\delta^{(k+1)} = -R^{(k)}$ where $\delta^{(k+1)} = u^{(k+1)} - u^{(k)}$ and $R^{(k)} = Au^{(k)} - d$. After the elements of LU are computed, $U\delta^{(k+1)}$ is calculated and then $\delta^{(k+1)}$ is solved.

MECHANISTIC MODELING

Fractured Reservoirs

Petroleum reservoirs are often fractured, either naturally, or by artificial stimulation, or even by having excessive pressure applied during injection of fluids in EOR flooding operations. Large fractures provide conduits through which flow readily occurs, but the majority of the reservoir fluid is generally stored in the pore space of the intact matrix. Thus, in the extreme case of a highly fractured reservoir, a gas or waterflooding operation may effectively sweep only the fractures and leave much of the oil bypassed. Therefore simulation of fluid flow in fractured reservoirs is of great interest to the petroleum industry.

Most of the fractured reservoir simulations have been based on a dual porosity concept, in which a reservoir is represented by homogeneous matrix blocks separated by continuous fractures. Thomas et al. (1983) described the dual porosity, fractured reservoir model. The flow equations in this model are essentially the same as those in the conventional black oil model except for the matrix/fracture transfer terms.

The flow equations in fracture are

$$\nabla \cdot [\lambda_i(\nabla p_i - \gamma_i \nabla z)] - q_i + \lambda_i^{mf}(p_{im} - p_i) = \frac{\partial}{\partial t}(\phi S_w / B_w) \tag{39}$$

for i = oil &water, and

$$\nabla \cdot [\lambda_g(\nabla p_g - \gamma_g \nabla z)] + \nabla \cdot [\lambda_o R_{so}(\nabla p_o - \gamma_o \nabla z)] - q_g - R_{so} q_o$$
$$+ \lambda_g^{mf}(p_{gm} - p_g) + \lambda_o^{mf} R_{so}(p_{om} - p_o) = \frac{\partial}{\partial t}(\phi S_g / B_g + \phi R_{so} S_o / B_o) \tag{40}$$

for gas phase

The matrix/fracture flow equations for three phases are

$$-\lambda_w^{mf}(p_{wm} - p_w) = \frac{\partial}{\partial t}(\phi S_w / B_w)_{matrix} \tag{41}$$

$$-\lambda_o^{mf}(p_{om} - p_o) = \frac{\partial}{\partial t}(\phi S_o / B_o)_{matrix} \tag{42}$$

$$-\lambda_g^{mf}(p_{gm} - p_g) - \lambda_o^{mf} R_{so}(p_{om} - p_o) = \frac{\partial}{\partial t}(\phi S_g / B_g + \phi R_{so} S_o / B_o)_{matrix} \tag{43}$$

where $$\lambda_w^{mf} = \sigma \left(\frac{k k_{rw}}{B_w \mu_w} \right)_{matrix} \tag{44}$$

$$\lambda_o^{mf} = \sigma \left(\frac{k k_{ro}}{B_o \mu_o} \right)_{matrix} \tag{45}$$

$$\lambda_g^{mf} = \sigma \left(\frac{k k_{rg}}{B_g \mu_g} \right)_{matrix} \tag{46}$$

σ is the geometric factor that accounts for the surface area of the matrix blocks per unit volume and a characteristic length associated with matrix/fracture flow.

Also the constraint equations are:

$$S_w + S_o + S_g = 1 \tag{47}$$

$$p_{cow} = p_o - p_w \tag{48}$$

$$p_{cgo} = p_g - p_o \tag{49}$$

for both fracture and matrix.

Viscous Fingering in Porous Media

Viscous fingering, the frontal instability of a displacement, occurs when the mobility of a displacing fluid is greater than the mobility of the displaced fluids. Viscous fingering is very common, both in immiscible displacement of water flooding of high viscosity oils and in miscible displacement due to the low viscosity of solvents (gases). There have been many mathematical treatments of unstable miscible displacements with unfavorable mobility ratios. Some of these are listed below.

Peaceman & Rachford (1962) developed a system which takes into account the influence of gravity, the spatial distribution of permeability, diffusion, and fluid viscosities and densities. A small random variation of permeability using the following equation was used to initiate the finger growth.

$$k_{ij} = k_{av}(1 + k_s \beta_{ij}) Z \tag{50}$$

where β_{ij} is a random number,
Z is a correction factor, and
k_s is a specified standard deviation

For the effect of viscous fingering on displacement efficiency, Koval (1963) developed the K-factor method similar to the Buckley-Leverett calculations.

In his K-factor method, the oil recovery and solvent cut are easily calculated by the following equations with K as the parameter:

$$N_{pv} = \frac{2(K V_{pi})^{1/2} - 1 - V_{pi}}{K - 1} \tag{51}$$

$$f_s = \frac{K - (K/V_{pi})^{1/2}}{K - 1} \tag{52}$$

where K represents the multiplication of the heterogeneity factory H and the effective viscosity ratio E.

In this calculation, he assumed the fractional flow equation describing miscible displacement as the following equation:

$$f_s = \frac{1}{1 + \frac{1 - S_s}{S_s}(1/H)(1/E)} = \frac{KS}{1 + S(K - 1)} \tag{53}$$

where $$E = \frac{\mu_{oe}}{\mu_{se}} = [0.78 + 0.22(\mu_o/\mu_s)^{1/4}]^4 \tag{54}$$

Vossoughi et al. (1984) used a method similar to Koval's whereby they modified the convection-dispersion equation to reflect viscous fingering:

$$D \frac{\partial^2 S_1}{\partial x^2} - U \frac{\partial f_1}{\partial x} = \frac{\partial S_1}{\partial t} \tag{55}$$

Converting into dimensionless terms, this equation becomes:

$$\frac{\partial^2 C_D}{\partial x_D^2} - N_{pe} \left(\frac{\partial f_1}{\partial S_1} \right) \left(\frac{\partial C_D}{\partial x_D} \right) = \frac{\partial C_D}{\partial t_D} \tag{56}$$

with $$f_1 = \frac{(\mu_2/\mu_1) - [S_1 + (1-S_1)(\mu_2/\mu_1)^{1/\gamma}]^\gamma}{(\mu_2/\mu_1) - 1} \qquad (57)$$

$$C_D = \frac{C}{C_{in}}$$

$$x_D = \frac{x}{l}$$

$$t_D = \frac{tD}{l^2}$$

$$N_{pe} = \frac{Ul}{D}$$

and γ is an empirical parameter

Todd and Longstaff (1972) developed a miscible displacement model using the gas and oil relative permeabilities under the assumption of complete miscibility between oil and gas (= solvent). Therefore, $P_{cgo} = 0$.

Considering the reduction of area available for one component by the presence of another component, the relative permeabilities are

$$k_{ro} = \frac{S_o}{S_n}(k_{rn})$$

and $$k_{rg} = \frac{S_g}{S_n}(k_{rn}) \qquad (58)$$

where $S_n = S_o + S_g$

A mixing parameter (ω) is used to determine the effective viscosities of the miscible components. The two limiting viscosities are the pure component viscosity (μ_o, μ_g) and the viscosity when the entire block is occupied by the dispersed zone (μ_m),

where $$\mu_m = \frac{\mu_o \mu_g}{\left(\frac{S_g}{S_n}\mu_o^{1/4} + \frac{S_o}{S_n}\mu_g^{1/4}\right)^4} \qquad (59)$$

Then the effective viscosities are expressed by following equations after the mixing parameter model proposed by Lee and Claridge (1964).

$$\mu_{oe} = \mu_o^{1-\omega}\mu_m^\omega$$

with $0 < \omega < 1$ (60)

$$\mu_{ge} = \mu_g^{1-\omega}\mu_m^\omega$$

Todd and Langstaff applied the same concept to the density calculation

$$\rho_{oe} = \rho_o \left(\frac{S_o}{S_n}\right)_{oe} + \rho_g \left[1 - \left(\frac{S_o}{S_n}\right)_{oe}\right] \qquad (61)$$

$$\rho_{ge} = \rho_o \left(\frac{S_o}{S_n}\right)_{ge} + \rho_g \left[1 - \left(\frac{S_o}{S_n}\right)_{ge}\right] \qquad (62)$$

Here the effective fractional saturations are obtained by rearranging the equation (59):

$$\frac{S_o}{S_n} = \frac{M^{1/4} - \left(\frac{\mu_o}{\mu_m}\right)^{1/4}}{M^{1/4} - 1} \qquad (63)$$

$$\left(\frac{S_o}{S_n}\right)_{ge} = \frac{M^{1/4} - \left(\frac{\mu_o}{\mu_{ge}}\right)^{1/4}}{M^{1/4} - 1} \qquad (64)$$

$$\left(\frac{S_o}{S_n}\right)_{oe} = \frac{M^{1/4} - \left(\frac{\mu_o}{\mu_{oe}}\right)^{1/4}}{M^{1/4} - 1} \qquad (65)$$

with $M = \frac{\mu_o}{\mu_g}$ and $\frac{S_g}{S_n} = 1 - \frac{S_o}{S_n}$

When M = 1, they use the following simple equations

$$\rho_{oe} = (1-\omega)\rho_o + \omega\rho_m \qquad (66)$$

$$\rho_{ge} = (1-\omega)\rho_g + \omega\rho_m \qquad (67)$$

where $\rho_m = \rho_o\left(\frac{S_o}{S_n}\right) + \rho_g\left(\frac{S_g}{S_n}\right)$

The value of $\omega = 1$ corresponds to complete mixing of oil and solvent, while $\omega = 0$ corresponds to no mixing. A value in the range of 0.5 - 0.7 is frequently used. In this model, the wetting phase is water and oil, and the gas phases are non-wetting phases.

In Homsy's (1987) review of viscous fingering, he concluded that the viscous fingering experienced a cyclic process: shielding, spreading, and splitting. At the beginning of fingering initiation, a single finger is dominant because it runs slightly ahead of the other fingers and shields them from further growth. This dominant single finger spreads while advancing due to surface tension (immiscible case) and dispersion (miscible case). When fingering width exceeds a critical value (the accurate value of this critical finger width is not known, but is considered to happen at $[(12\mu U/\sigma)(\ell/b)^2 \approx 10^3]$), the tip of the finger becomes unstable and splits into two or more fingers.

In order to study the initiation and development of viscous fingers and gravity tongues, Chang (1988) has performed three-dimensional numerical simulations for horizontal displacements. The system is a bed of unconsolidated sand having a uniform porosity and a uniform permeability. The mass density of the fluid phase is a weak linear function of the concentration of the displacing fluid.

The dimensionless governing equations are written as:

$$\nabla \cdot \bar{v} = 0 \qquad (68)$$

$$\nabla \hat{p} - Gw\bar{b} + \frac{\hat{\mu}}{k}\bar{v} = 0 \qquad (69)$$

$$\phi \frac{\partial w}{\partial t} + \tilde{v} \cdot \nabla w + \nabla \cdot \tilde{j} = 0 \quad (70)$$

where $$\tilde{j} = -\phi(D_d + a_t \mid \tilde{v} \mid)\nabla w - \phi(a_l - a_t)\frac{\tilde{v} \cdot \nabla w}{\mid \tilde{v} \mid}\tilde{v}$$

In order to reduce the numerical diffusion and to obtain a high degree of accuracy, the flux-corrected transport method is used to find the concentration field. The pressure field is obtained by using the alternating direction implicit procedure with successive over-relaxation.

For $N \neq 1$ and $M = 1$, the calculations do not show any instabilities even with macroscopic perturbations to the system at the injection face. For $M \neq 1$ and $N = 1$, fingers appear when the system has been perturbed macroscopically at the injection face. Numerical errors are not sufficient to trigger the fingers. For $N \neq 1$ and $M \neq 1$, instabilities can be triggered both by numerical errors and by macroscopic perturbations to the system at the injection face.

Two different seeds of the random number generator are used for macroscopic perturbations to the system. When the seed of the random number generator is changed, the manner in which the fingers grow changes, with the larger finger sometimes developing off-center. The results of the simulations clearly are dependent on the form of the perturbations used to trigger the instabilities.

Front Tracking

The major problems in a miscible flood simulation include: numerical dispersion in the finite difference method, oscillating solutions for convection-dominated flow, and the grid orientation effect. As mentioned in a previous section, the grid orientation effect can be minimized by using a nine-point finite difference scheme. Numerical dispersion is usually used to model physical dispersion, and it is a major source of error in an unstable miscible flood.

In order to suppress numerical dispersion and include physical dispersion explicitly, Hatziavramidis (1987) introduced the psuedospectral method. He used Chebyshev polynomial expansions to approximate the spatial derivatives. The direction of the displacement is divided into elements whose boundaries and size change as the approximate location of the front evolves in time. The method of collocation is used to project the equations from physical into spectral space. This results in finer resolution of the areas of interest.

First, the approximate position of the displacement front is calculated at every time step by

$$X_f^k = X_f^{k-1} + U_f^{k-1}\Delta t \quad (71))$$

where

X_f = dimensionless front position

U_f = dimensionless front velocity

Then, the regions in front of and behind the interface are divided into subdomains, and local Chebyshev polynomials are used to approximate the derivations of the functions in the axial direction to suppress the oscillating solution.

When the points at which the solution is calculated are chosen as the extrema of the Nth order Chebyshev polynomial, a denser distribution of points close to the boundaries are obtained, and the approximation of the derivatives is carried out according to the method of collocation points.

The procedures of the psuedospectral method are as follows:

When the collocation points are $x_j = \cos[\pi(j-1)/N]$, for $j = 1 \ldots N+1$, the first two derivatives of the function to be estimated, $F(x)$, can be approximated by

$$F'(x_j) = \sum_{l=1}^{N+1} \hat{G}_{j,l}^{(1)} F(X_l) \quad (72)$$

$$F''(x_j) = \sum_{l=1}^{N+1} \hat{G}_{j,l}^{(2)} F(X_l) \quad (73)$$

with $$\hat{G}^{(k)} = TG^{(k)}\hat{T} \quad \text{for} \quad k = 1,2 \quad (74)$$

and $$G^{(2)} = G^{(1)}G^{(1)} \quad (75)$$

Here, T, $\hat{T}$ and $G^{(1)}$ are matrices with the following elements:

$$T_{ij} = \cos\left[\frac{\pi(i-1)(j-1)}{N}\right] \quad (76)$$

$$\hat{T}_{ij} = \frac{2}{NC_iC_j}\cos\left[\frac{\pi(i-1)(j-1)}{N}\right] \quad (77)$$

with $C_1 = C_{N+1} = 2, \quad C_i = 1$ for $1 < i < N+1$

$$G_{ij}^{(1)} = \begin{cases} 0 & \text{, if } i \geq j \text{ or } i+j \text{ even} \\ \dfrac{2(j-1)}{\overline{C}_i} & \text{, } (\overline{C}_1 = 2, \overline{C}_2 = \overline{C}_3 = \ldots = 1) \text{ otherwise} \end{cases} \quad (78)$$

Foam Flow in Porous Media

Due to the poor sweep efficiency of the enhanced oil recovery methods using gas injection, the use of a foaming agent for profile modification becomes increasingly important. It is not an easy task to simulate the flow of foam through porous media because the flow behavior of gas and the foaming solution may be a combination of continuous gas flow, continuous liquid flow, and breaking/reforming foam continuous liquid flow, and breaking/reforming foam flow. The effect of trapped gas saturation also should be included.

A mathematical model of foam viscosity in smooth capillaries was developed by Hirasaki and Lawson (1985). They modeled the foam flow through smooth capillaries, accounting for three dynamic changes at gas-liquid interfaces. These changes are 1) resistance caused by liquid slugs between gas bubbles, 2) interface deformation due to the viscous and capillary force against the restoring force of surface tension, and 3) the surface tension gradient. This model should be expanded further, before being applied to flow in a porous media because the authors assumed that the foam exists either as bulk foam or as a chain of bubbles, which may be true only in smooth capillaries.

The apparent viscosity contribution of the three dynamic changes are:

$$\frac{\mu_{app}}{\mu} = L_s n_L + 0.85\frac{n_L R}{r_c/R}(3\mu U/\sigma)^{-1/3}[(r_c/R)^2+1] + (n_L R)(3\mu U/\sigma)^{-1/3}\sqrt{N_s}\frac{(1-e^{-N_L})}{(1+e^{-N_L})} \quad (79)$$

where L_s = length of liquid slug
n_L = number of equivalent lamellae/unit length
R = capillary radius
r_c = radius of curvature of gas-liquid interface

U = velocity of bubble
σ = surface tension
μ = viscosity of water

$$N_s = -\frac{1}{(p)_c\mu}\frac{d\sigma}{d\Gamma}\frac{\Gamma_o}{\alpha}\frac{1}{r_c} = \frac{\beta}{r_c} \quad (80)$$

$$N_L = \frac{[2/(p)_c][L_B/r_c][3\mu U/\sigma]^{-1/3}}{([1/(p)_c][1/\mu][d\sigma/d\Gamma][\Gamma_o/\alpha][1/r_c])^{1/2}} \quad (81)$$

where L_B = length of thin film portion of bubble
$(P)_c$ = coefficient from constant integration
Γ = surface excess concentration
Γ_o = equilibrium concentration
α = mass transfer rate constant
β and $2/(P)_c$ should be determined from the experiment

The first term of the right-hand side is due to the liquid slug, the second term is due to the shape deformation, and last term is due to the surface tension gradient.

The population balance approach was used to model foam flow by Fall et al. (1986). The usual conservation equations are coupled with balances on the densities of flowing and stationary bubbles in the foam. Mass conservation equations for one-dimensional, two-phase, incompressible flow are:

$$\phi\frac{\partial S_w}{\partial t} + U_t\frac{\partial f_w}{\partial x} = 0 \qquad \text{for water phase} \quad (82)$$

where $$f_w = \frac{1+\frac{k}{U_T}\lambda_{rg}[\partial p_c/\partial x + g(\rho_w-\rho_g)\sin\alpha]}{1+\lambda_{rg}/\lambda_{rw}}$$

and λ_r is relative mobility

and

$$\phi\frac{\partial(S_g X_f n_f)}{\partial t} = -\nabla\cdot(U_g n_f) + G_f \quad (83)$$

for gas phase

where $U_g = -\lambda_{rg}(n_f, X_f \ldots) k\nabla\Phi_g$

and $$G_f = \begin{cases} \dfrac{N_n}{\dfrac{a_1}{P_c^*-P_c}+\dfrac{b_1}{v_g}} & \text{, if } P_c < P_c^* \text{ and } t_{form} < t_{conv} \\ 0 & \text{, otherwise} \end{cases}$$

This approach takes into account the number and size distribution of the foam bubbles (foam texture). It was assumed that capillary snap-off was the only mechanism changing bubble density.

SUMMARY

Reservoir simulation (Coats 1982) estimates recovery for a given producing operation, evaluates the differences in oil recovery from altered operating methods (e.g., alternative enhanced oil recovery processes), and compares the economics inherent to different recovery programs. The main types of simulators used for miscible displacement, modified black oil and compositional, have been considered along with other specialized models. Methods of prediction were shown to be influenced by many factors, including reservoir description, nonlinear relative permeability and capillary pressure functions, nonlinear fluid PVT properties, well injectivity and productivity, numerical dispersion, pressure distribution, crossflow of displaced oil, etc.

Errors inherent to finite difference approximations and cell size, i.e., numerical dispersion and grid orientation, were discussed. Some of the other causes of calculation uncertainty in miscible and immiscible performance predictions include the poor representation of displacement front instabilities, crossflow-and-dispersion/phase behavior interactions, transition zone (dynamic) miscibility, diffusional-mass-transfer recovery of oil trapped by water, and in general, a less than satisfactory representation of the physical mechanisms by which oil is mobilized and recovered.

The degree of error that remains under the most optimistic conditions is estimated to be around ± 25 percent for ultimate recovery predictions and much greater for producing rate predictions. Predicting future performance and developing methods which increase the ultimate oil recovered are the primary concerns for reservoir simulation study. Some examples of the types of questions that we can attempt to answer through a reservoir simulation study are (Aziz and Settari 1979):

> How should a field be developed and produced (for example, well pattern and spacing, producing rate, etc.) in order to maximize profit?
>
> How and when should the best enhanced recovery method be implemented at the field?
>
> What laboratory data are necessary and what is the sensitivity of the model to process parameters? What are the most important parameters to follow in the field application of an enhanced recovery process?
>
> How can laboratory results be scaled up for field application?
>
> What part of the reservoir is being depleted of oil?

Some Thoughts on the Future of Reservoir Simulation

We have been moving toward larger and larger field studies, i.e., using more grid blocks for better reservoir definition or characterization, with the advent of increased computer speeds, storage capabilities, and vectorized codes (Coats 1982). There will be a continued development of hardware and improved user interface (Aziz 1987). Research is continuing on the development of single, generalized simulators capable of modeling most recovery methods of interest (Coats 1982). Different types of specialized, "limited" compositional simulators are also being developed. Front-tracking models, important in EOR processes, are being actively researched.

The complicated physical processes present in the EOR methods are poorly understood and not adequately represented in reservoir simulators. Laboratory-scale mechanistic models which characterize pore-level process mechanisms present in EOR systems, and also in fluid diversion treatments for improved sweep efficiency, are continuing to be developed, probably more so on the academic side. These mechanistic models enable prediction of oil recovery performance at the laboratory-scale and are being used to define the critical parameters that affect reservoir-scale displacements.

Modeling physical processes as the system is scaled up from the laboratory to the field, i.e., representing scale-up parameters, is another challenge for reservoir simulation developers. Reservoir description, which is poorly accounted for in current models, can influence predictions at each scale, especially in EOR processes. Techniques need to be developed which incorporate reservoir information at scales above and below the scale of the grid block (Aziz 1987). Detailed field studies also need to be conducted with unusually well-characterized reservoirs to enable the coupling of complex physics to various length scales of heterogeneity.

NOMENCLATURE

a_1	constant
A	cross sectional area
a_ℓ	dimensionless longitudinal dispersivity
a_t	dimensionless transverse dispersivity
B	formation volume factor
b_1	constant
b	thickness of porous medium or Hele-shaw model
b	unit vector in the direction of gravity
C_i	total concentration of component i in mobile phase
$\hat{C}_i$	total concentration of component i in rock (= adsorption)
D	dispersion coefficient
D_d	dimensionless effective diffusion coefficient
E	internal energy
f	fractional flow
fu	fugacity
g	gravitational acceleration
G	dimensionless quantity characterizing the ratio of the excess gravitational forces attributable to the density difference between the displacing fluid and the displaced fluid to the viscous forces
H	enthalphy
H_r	heat of reaction r
$\vec{j}$	dimensionless effective mass flux vector
$\vec{J}_D$	flux of bubble due to hydrodynamic dispersion
k	permeability
$\hat{k}$	dimensionless permeability
k_{av}	average permeability
k_{ij}	permeability in 2-D space
k_r	relative permeability
k_s	standard deviation in permeability
k_t	thermal conductivity
ℓ	length (of system)
L	mole fraction of liquid phase
M	the ratio of the viscosity of the displaced fluid to the viscosity of the displacing fluid
M_f	reservoir rock heat capacity
n	density of bubbles in the gas phase
N	the ratio of the density of the displacing fluid to the density of the displaced fluid
N_c	number of components
N_p	number of phases
N_R	number of chemical reactions
P	pressure
$\hat{P}$	dimensionless modified pressure
P_c	capillary pressure
P_{cj}	phase j capillary pressure, Pj - P
q	sink or production (negative for source or injection)
Q_H	production rate of enthalphy

Q_{HL} heat loss rate to overburden

q_{ir} rate of creation of component i due to reaction r

R_s solution gas-oil (water) ratio

S saturation

t time

T temperature

T_{in} initial temperature

T_j transmissibility

U Darcy or superficial velocity vector

v interstitial velocity

V mole fraction of vapor phase

$\tilde{v}$ dimensionless velocity of the fluid

w normalized mass fraction

x distance

X_f fraction of gas phase flowing

x_i mole fraction of component i in oil phase

x_{ij} mole fraction of component i in phase j

y_i mole fraction of component i in vapor phase

z depth (vertical downward direction)

Z_i overall mole fraction of component i

α dip angle

α_3 ratio of radiation to heat conduction

β_{ij} constant from random number

γ specific weight

λ_r relative mobility

λ transmissibility

μ viscosity

$\hat{\mu}$ dimensionless viscosity

ρ molar density

σ interfacial tension

ϕ porosity

ω relaxation factor

Φ flow potential

Differential operator

$$\nabla = i\frac{\partial}{\partial x} + j\frac{\partial}{\partial y} + k\frac{\partial}{\partial z}$$

SUBSCRIPT

app apparent
e effective
f flowing gas phase
g gas
i component
in initial
j phase
m mixture
n non wetting phase
o oil
s solvent
t total
w water
1 displacing fluid
2 displaced fluid

SUPERSCRIPT

o oil
g gas
k iteration number
mf matrix/fracture

ACKNOWLEDGEMENTS

The authors wish to thank Joe Taber for his help on the introduction, Eric S.H. Chang for his contribution to the viscous fingering section and for his assistance in proofreading the manuscript, Phil Johnson for insights into fractured reservoir modeling, and Carol Dotson for typing this manuscript.

This work was supported, in part, by the U.S. Department of Energy, the New Mexico Research and Development Institute, and a consortium of major oil companies including the Abu Dhabi National Reservoir Research Foundation, Amoco, ARCO, Cities Service, Conoco, Chevron, Marathon, Sohio, Petro-Canada, JNOC, and Texaco.

REFERENCES

Aziz, K. and Settari, A.: Petroleum Reservoir Simulation, Applied Science Publishers, London, 1979.

Aziz, K.: "From the CMG Panel on the Future of Reservoir Simulation," GMG Advances, June, 1987.

Baily, R.E. et al.: Enhanced Oil Recovery, National Petroleum Council, June, 1984.

Chang, Shih-Hsien: "Stability of Miscible Displacements in Porous Media,": PhD dissertation, Northwestern University, Evanston, IL (1988)

Coats, K.H.: "In-Situ Combustion Model," SPEJ (December, 1980) 533-554.

Coats, K.H.: "An Equation of State Compositional Model," SPEJ (October, 1980) 363-376.

Coats, K.H.: "Reservoir Simulation: State of the Art," JPT (August, 1982) 1633-1642.

Falls, A.H. et al.: "Development of a Mechanistic Foam Simulator: The Population Balance and Generation by Snap-Off," paper SPE/DOE 14961 presented at the SPE/DOE 5th Symposium on EOR, Tulsa, April 20-23, 1986.

Gardner, A.O., Peaceman, D.W., and Pozzi, A.L. (1964) Soc. Pet. Eng. J., March.

Hatziavramidis, D.T.: "A New Computational Approach to the Miscible Displacement Problem," paper SPE 16004 presented at the 9th SPE Symposium on Reservoir Simulation, San Antonio, February 1-4, 1987.

Hirasaki, G.J. and Lawson, J.B.: "Mechanisms of Foam Flow in Porous Media: Apparent Viscosity in Smooth Capillaries," SPEJ (April, 1985) 176-190.

Homsy, G.M.: "Viscous Fingering in Porous Media," Ann. Rev. Fluid Mech., 19, (1987) 271-311.

Katz, M.L. and Stalkup, F.I.: "Oil Recovery by Miscible Displacement," 11th World Petroleum Conference, London, July, 1983.

Koval, E.J.: "A Method for Predicting the Performance of Unstable Miscible Displacement in Heterogeneous Media," SPEJ (June, 1963) 145-154.

Nghiem, L.S. et al.: "Compositional Modeling with an Equation of State," SPEJ (December, 1981) 687-698.

Peaceman, D.W. and Rachford, Jr., H.H.: "Numerical

Calculation of Multidimensional Miscible Displacement," SPEJ (December, 1962) 327-339.

Pope, G.A. and Nelson, R.C.: "A Chemical Flooding Compositional Simulator," SPEJ (October, 1978) 339-354.

Price, H.S. and Coats, K.H.: "Direct Methods in Reservoir Simulation," paper 4278 presented at the 3rd Numerical Simulation Symposium, Houston, January 11-12, 1973.

Stalkup, F.I., "Status of Miscible Displacement," presented at the International Petroleum Exhibition and Technical Symposium of the SPE, Bejing, China, March, 1982.

Stalkup, F.I., Miscible Displacement, Monograph 8, SPE of AIME, New York, 1983.

Taber, J.J.: "Enhanced Oil Recovery by Gas Miscible Flooding," presented at the EOR Symposium of the International Energy Agency Collaborative Research Program, Tokyo, Japan, October, 1985.

Thomas, L.K. et al.: "Fractured Reservoir Simulations," SPEJ (February, 1983) 42-45.

Todd, M.R. and Longstaff, W.J.: "The Development, Testing and Application of a Numerical Simulator for Predicting Miscible Flood Performance," J. Pet. Tech., July, 1972.

Treybal, R.E.,: Liquid Extraction, 2nd Ed., McGraw Hill Book Co., Inc., New York, (1963) 37.

Vossoughi, S. et al.: "A New Method to Simulate the Effect of Viscous Fingering on Miscible Displacement Processes in Porous Media," SPEJ (February, 1984) 56-64.

Simulators VI

ISBN 0-911801-51-0

Tools in transition

Thomas W. Jenkins and Robert A. Felker
Singer Link-Miles Simulation Corporation
8895 McGaw Road
Columbia, Maryland 21045

INTRODUCTION

In 1972, when Consolidated Edison specified the first utility owned plant reference simulator for Indian Point 2, a hand-held calculator was $400 without memory and had four arithmetic functions. Power plant simulators were in their infancy, as were EMS and SCADA systems. Life cycle issues were primarily hardware maintainability issues. Assembly language was predominate and acceptable (and often fun). However, more applications meant more assembly language to manage. The concept of software packages was not yet conceived. In 1972, who would have believed that by 1988 you would have a computer in your home, buy packages of software, and possibly never see assembly language again.

The changes in the next 15 years will be more illusive to predict than the previous years. However, we believe todays' tools and technologies, available for real time software, are well designed and field proven to support the certification needs of nuclear power plant simulators and the restructuring of fossil simulator products.

BRIEF HISTORY OF POWER PLANT SIMULATION

While EMS and SCADA systems evolved in response to cost effectiveness, the simulator systems were slower to advance in technology, due to subjectivity of training value. Training programs to satisfy licensing requirements were developed originally by nuclear steam system suppliers. The first simulators were designed and operated by the NSSS vendors. Demands for more simulator availability rose as more power plants were sold. Reliability, accuracy, and real time response would be issues as more and more users identified their particular needs. As a result, Consolidated Edison purchased their own trainer from a simulator company, Link Division of The Singer Company (now Singer Link-Miles Simulation Corporation).

The technology underwent a shift from the NSSS suppliers to the simulation companies who could apply power plant physics within the simultaneous constraints of real time execution and very little computer power (by today's standards). The renaissance that followed in the mid-seventies could be characterized by 90% physics and 10% art or, more appropriately, software artwork (or some would call it black magic).

On March 29, 1979, the TMI accident would change the operator training requirements and cause two distinct reactions in the nuclear training industry. First, INPO would be created and provide feedback to utilities on training programs. Second, the Nuclear Regulatory Commission endorsed the American Nuclear Society 3.5-1981 Standard, and required simulator certification by March 1991 (in accordance with NUREG 1258, "Evaluation Procedure for Simulation Facilities Certified under 10CFR55.45(b)", 26 May 1987).

These new regulations focus on keeping the simulator training program closely tied to plant operations and modifications. They address fidelity/accuracy of simulators as well as scope of the training program. As a result, simulators require major software and hardware upgrades, including total software replacement at some facilities.

In the simulation technology arena, SLMSC advanced from the renaissance directly to the space age. We have taken advantage of increased computer capacity to provide engineering emulations in real time of the reactor core neutronics, thermal hydraulics, and containment dynamics (i.e., no black magic left). This technology was developed by two former NRC personnel from the reactor analysis department and the SLMSC R&D department utilizing the best physics available. This product, RETACT (Real Time Advance Core and Thermohydraulics), was first delivered to GPU Nuclear Corporation for the TMI-1 simulator.

Engineering emulations and other advancements would have been difficult to implement if the supporting software engineering tools had not been developed. Software tools have replaced hard coding with automatic code generation, so that engineers can concentrate on the configuration requirements of the modeling and less, or not at all, on the programming techniques which were so important in the early simulators. The primary benefit is the application of more sophisticated physics with less software maintenance (i.e., no artwork).

TECHNOLOGY AND TOOLS

To appreciate the evolution of the tools and technology, it is useful to establish several points of reference for the currently installed full scope nuclear simulator base. We believe the industry has already passed through two periods which can be arbitrarily defined as "infancy" (1972 through 1978) and "adolescence" (3/29/79 through 1986), and which has recently entered the "maturity" era.

Attributes of the technology utilized within the infancy period can be summarized as follows:

- Computer Architecture
  - Single or multiple processors limited by memory and execution speeds.
  - Fixed point arithmetic, floating point hardware was generally viewed as an option.
- NSSS Simulation Techniques
  - Single node point kinetics core model.
  - Use of a synthesis model for flux distribution profiles.
  - Rudimentary heat transfer simulation.
  - Limited discrete malfunctions.
- BOP Simulation Techniques
  - Plant logic was frequently lumped.
  - Significant assumptions and simplifications were incorporated into the design.
  - Entire systems were excluded.
  - Limited dynamics based primarily on curve fits.
- Input/Output System
  - Typically included only the inner ring panels (5,000 to 10,000 points).
  - Completely host computer software dependent.
  - Very difficult to modify after initial installation.
- Instructor Station
  - 20 initial conditions.
  - Less than 100 discrete malfunctions.
  - Supported FREEZE, RUN, RESET, and BACKTRACK.
  - Very cumbersome and difficult to use.
- Process Computers
  - Small quantity of points.
  - Small subset of nuclear programs.
  - I/O performed primarily using typers and pushbutton panels.

Attributes of the tools utilized within the infancy period can be summarized as follows:

- Languages
  - Primarily assembly language for both logic and dynamics.
  - Transition began late in the phase to FORTRAN dynamics, although inline assembly was still prevalent.
- Programming Aids
  - Rudimentary and based exclusively on the computer vendors supplied tools.
- Software Environment
  - Non-existent, the programmers workbench concept had not yet arrived.
- Testing
  - Model tests were conducted on individual systems prior to integration.
  - Pre-acceptance and acceptance test durations were approximately three months.
- Hardware Support
  - I/O test functions were offline from simulation and basically performed go/no-go tests.
- Documentation
  - Manually generated and frequently did not correlate with the installed software

Attributes of the technology utilized within the adolescence period can be summarized as follows:

- Computer Architecture
  - Multiple monolithic computers tied through common memory to increase execution time and memory.
  - Increasing computer simulation fidelity.
  - First introduction of specialized processors.
- NSSS Simulation Techniques
  - Development of axial and radial nodalization for core design.
  - Use of a vector processor to solve the array based solutions of the core nodalization.
  - Introduction of generic malfunctions.
- BOP Simulation Techniques
  - Plant logic software is generally developed on a 1:1 basis using the equivalent reference plant schmatic and elementary diagrams.
  - Fewer assumptions and simplifications.
  - Secondary and tertiary systems were brought into the scope of simulation.

- Dynamics still primarily based on converging pressure vs. flow calculations.

- Input/Output System

  - Back panels and remote shutdown panels are usually included within the scope of simulation (10,000 to 15,000 points).

  - Application software is isolated from the I/O by the use of intelligent hardware mapping.

  - Modifications and extensions were easier to implement.

- Instructor Station

  - 50 initial conditions.

  - 100 to 150 malfunctions including both generic and variable types.

  - Addition of training scenario tools (I/O Overrides, Record/Replay,CAEP, TPR, etc.).

  - Color CRT's utilized to convey additional information to the instructor.

  - Use was still cumbersome and not instructor friendly.

- Process Computers

  - Extensive simulations of very complex display systems.

  - Large quantity of points (5,000 to 10,000).

  - Extensive peripheral complements.

Attributes of the tools utilized with the adolescence period can be summarized as follows:

- Languages

  - Primarily FORTRAN for both logic and dynamics.

  - Assembly language used in special applications.

- Programming Aids

  - Simulator vendor developed aids as extension to the computer vendor supplied tools (i.e., symbolic debuggers).

  - Introduction of parallel simulation to augment software development.

- Software Environment

  - Introduction of a total lifecycle software environment to support all aspects of development, test, maintenance and documentation of the software product.

  - Integrated data base structure with specialized language pre-processors.

  - Development of software libraries and reuseable software modules.

- Testing

  - Extensive integrated systems tests with a decreasing emphasis on stand alone non-integrated testing.

  - Pre-acceptance and acceptance test durations were approximately three to five months.

- Hardware Support

  - Stand alone test and diagnostic capability embedded within the I/O and severed from the host computer.

- Documentation

  - Semi-automatically generated through the existence of a software enviornment, however most drawings are still manually prepared.

  - Hardware documentation is generally not included within this framework.

Attributes of the technology utilized within the maturity period can be summarized as follows:

- Computer Architecture

  - Powerful, distributed real time market targeted computer systems without upper end execution or memory limits based upon additive network elements.

  - UNIX workstations with sophisticated graphics techniques (windows, multiple bit planes, etc.) for the instructor man machine interface.

  - Use of high speed (25MHZ) thirty-two bit microprocessors for dedicated compute intensive applications.

- NSSS Simulation Techniques

  - Development of true three dimensional nodalization using actual reload fuel data and core generated data as inputs to a standarized software package.

  - Solution of eigenvalue problems in real time.

  - Sophisticated engineering code level flux distribution Techniques (FLARE B approach); thermohydraulic code based upon first principles physics, and sophisticated heat transfer regime correlations (i.e., conservation of mass, energy, and momentum).

  - Implicit predictive capabilities within both the core and thermohydralics models.

- Eliminate the need to preplan malfunction break points (i.e., faults can be introduced in any node).

- Capability to simulate loss of core geometry and fuel failure scenarios.

• BOP Simulation Techniques

  - Use of Automatic code generators to develop FORTRAN logic code based upon CADD system pinlists.

  - Addition of optical scanning/character recognition technology to produce compatible CADD drawings for the code generators: Elements of the system include:

    1) Digitizing engine to scan the drawings and convert the result to a bit mapped raster image.

    2) Vectorization and recognition engine to vectorize the bit mapped image, use of Artificial Intelligence techniques to perform symbol recognition and reduce the drawing to a series of interconnected function blocks, and generate a CADD pinlist.

  - All secondary systems included within the scope of simulation.

  - Use of automatic code generator to develop FORTRAN dynamics code based upon simultaneous pressure versus flow matrices solutions (i.e., FLOWNET).

• Input/Output System

  - Use of commercially available, intelligent I/O equipment capable of supporting 25,000 points.

  - Software linearization, scaling, and change of state routines embedded within the I/O system to offload the host computer and standarize CPU processing applications.

  - Modifications and extensions are "sysgened" using microprocessor technology within the hardware.

  - Online error detection and replacement of faulty input cards without powering the system down (i.e., greater training availability).

• Instructor Station

  - Initial conditions only limited by available bulk storage capacity.

  - Thousands of possible malfunctions through the use of global component failures.

  - Automatic test and validation tools for use when the simulator is unattended.

  - High resolution CRTs with windows, touch screens, and voice actuation to relive the instructor of burdensome manual operations.

  - Introduction of "expert systems" to challenge individual students based upon their actual simulator performance.

• Process Computers

  - Complete stimulations of all control room display systems via an industry standard local area network (i.e., ETHERNET).

  - All field input points are dynamically simulated.

  - Actual plant system peripherals in emergency centers (TSC and EOF) can be switched to the simulator via the LAN to support E-Plan drills.

Attributes of the tools utilized withing the maturity period can be summarized as follows:

• Languages

  - FORTRAN will continue as the language of choice for simulation processes.

  - High Order Languages (HOL) will be used in specialized applications:

    1) 'C' for instructor station, executive, and display applications.

    2) HOL microprocessor languages for I/O and computationally intensive applications.

• Programming Aids

  - Extensive use of autocode generators in all aspects of simulator software development to produce correct, consistent, and standardized code while minimizing engineering resources.

  - Simulator vendor tools will become computer vendor independent through the use of shells and kernels.

• Software Environment

  - Extensive integration and use of commercially available third party software packages for data base management, debug, self test, and documentation.

  - Maturity of plant component software libraries.

• Testing

  - Automatic component model testing prior to integration.

- Extensive stand alone testing with a decreasing emphasis on systems testing.

- Reduced pre-acceptance and acceptance test durations.

- Automatic, non-attended performance and operability testing to support regulatory requirements.

• Hardware Support

- On-line error reporting down to the I/O point level to the instructor during training scenarios.

- Complete independence from the host computer for all maintenance activities.

• Documentation

- Use of a fully integrated document processor to generate text, graphics, drawings, and all specific hardware/software information for simulated plant systems.

IMMEDIATE USES

The burden of NUREG 1258 requirements on the industry will be born more heavily by the utilities than by the simulator vendors. Downtime of simulators on their sites, coupled with administrative burdens of NRC audits, will make the utilities' tasks more difficult than the original simulator procurements.

The utilities' needs for efficient on-site production of software will determine their schedule effectiveness, as well as their final NRC Form 474 submittal. Some simulators, where the tools are non-existent, will opt for full simulator replacement to avoid interruption of current training schedules.

SUMMARY

By the year 2000, computers will be structured differently than today. They will include voice actuation as primary input devices, video and graphics will be output, and computers will provide reasoning "cells" and learn from mistakes. Artificial intelligence and expert systems concepts will likely be redefined.

The power industry will benefit from full computer control with embedded physics emulation and fault tolerant recovery action. Plant availabilities will reach new highs as control concepts are redesigned to capitalize on new instrumentation techniques as well as embedded emulation and artificial intelligence. The simulation industry will expand more to plant applications in addition to training.

SLMSC will be providing the tools and technology embedded in new computer architectures. ISC software packages like RETACT, S3, and STK Core are available today for off-the-shelf purchase. Future products will be available through modem dial-up accounts.

The software tools will allow the industry to bridge the gap between available technology and the expense to apply it. More and better software products will be usable by more engineers with shorter implementation schedules and little or no maintenance.

BIBLIOGRAPHY

TVA's Action Plan for Simulator Configuration and Validation

Van N. Miller, TVA
Singer Link-Miles User's Conference, March 1988

"Nuclear Power Plant Simulators for Use in Operator Training"

ANSI/ANS 3.5 1985, American National Standards Institute/American Nuclear Society, LaGrange Park, Illinois 60525

Artificial Intelligence Optimizes Boiler Performance

GWKOZLIK, K. W. Bleakley and B. C. Skinner
Northern Indiana Public Service Co.
Power Engineering, February 1988

Evaluation Procedure for Simulation Facilities Certified
under 10CFR55

J. Wachtel, K. R. Langhery, C. Plott
Division of Human Factors Technology
Office of Nuclear Reactor Regulation
U. S. Nuclear Regulartory Commission
Washington, D. C. 20555

Nuclear Plant Simulators and Analizers

Dr. Dino Zanobetti
University of Bologna, Bologna, Italy
September 1987

Simulators VI
© 1989 By The Society for Computer
Simulation International
ISBN 0-911801-51-0

Computer based training system in use at Newgrade Energy, Inc.

Douglas W. Watt, P.E.
Autodynamics
100 Willowbrook Road
Freehold, NJ 07728

and

Ennio L. Mastracci
NewGrade Energy Inc.
9th Avenue North
Regina, Saskatchewan S4P 3JB

INTRODUCTION

Autodynamics shipped a training system to NewGrade Energy Inc. NewGrade Energy (NEI) is presently using the system to teach their plant operators the new start-up shutdown, and emergency procedures for their new refinery processes, prior to these units coming on-stream.

BACKGROUND

Four new refinery processes are being brought on-line at NEI to further enhance the crude oil upgrading at their facility. With the addition of these units, the resulting Upgrader/Refinery complex will produce an upgraded synthetic crude oil. The refinery will make gasoline and diesel fuel from this upgraded crude oil, and ship any surplus upgraded oil to refineries in Eastern Canada. Byproducts of the process include high-grade coke for use in aluminum processing, metals and liquid sulphur.

Autodynamics developed training simulation programs for NEI's ARDS Unit, DHU, Sulfur, and Hydrogen Plants.

The ARDS Unit performs the primary upgrading function at NEI. The heavy oil residuum and hydrogen gas, under high pressure and high temperatures, pass through huge vessels containing catalysts. The sulfur and nitrogen contaminants in the oil react with the hydrogen, forming hydrogen sulfide and ammonia. The metals are deposited on the catalyst, and some of the heavier portion of the feedstock is broken down into lighter material.

The DHU is a downstream processing unit. Again, under high pressure and temperature, hydrogen is added to lighter liquids which were previously separated from the heavy oil. The purpose is to further improve the quality of the oil, so that top quality diesel fuel can be made.

The Sulfur Plant transforms the hydrogen sulphide and ammonia formed in the ARDS process, to ensure that they will not be released into the air as pollutants. The sulfur is recovered and sold.

The Hydrogen Plant provides the hydrogen used in the ARDS and DHU processes. Hydrogen is produced here by combining natural gas with steam - a process called reforming.

SIMULATOR OBJECTIVES

NewGrade Energy approached Autodynamics to provide a simulator that would fulfill the following objectives:

- Train the unit technicians for the start-up, shutdown, normal, and emergency operating conditions associated with the new plants.
- Familiarize the unit technicians with the Taylor MOD 300 Distributed Control System instrument configuration for each unit.
- Test the control and shutdown logic systems for the new plants.
- Test the various unit procedures for feasibility and logistics.

ACTION

Cognizant that Autodynamics offered many off-the shelf proprietary process simulation programs, NEI recognized that custom simulation programs had to be developed in order to meet the simulator objectives.

The custom simulation programs of NEI's process units were based on the same design data from which the actual process units were built. This data included:

- The plant heat and material balance.
- Plant instrument and logic diagrams.
- Equipment specification sheets.
- Tray-to-Tray material balances for each distillation column.
- Process reaction kinetics.

When actual plant data is used to develop a process simulation, a high degree of simulation fidelity is achieved.

- The plant heat and material balance reveals a wealth of process data. From this data comes information on stream flow rates, composition, temperature, specific heat, latent heat of vaporization, and vapor-liquid equilibrium. This plant operating condition is also reflected in the "design start" initial condition for each of the process simulations.

- The plant instrument diagrams and instrument specification sheets provides process data by showing the control signal paths, valve directions, vessel connections, and line sizes. The instrument diagrams also provided process logic data.

- Equipment specification sheets are examined so that vapor and liquid hold-up within vessels are faithfully modeled. Attention is also given to instrument tap locations on process drums and vessels. This ensures that vessel liquid levels are accurately modeled and faithful process dynamics are achieved. The liquid vapor hold-up for each piece of equipment also provides the basis for the rate of change of drum composition as the composition of the drum feed changes. The same is true for pressure changes. As the size of the drum or vessel increases, the rate of composition, level, pressure, etc., decreases.

- Process licensors were contacted to provide data regarding the kinetics of their units. This information was included in the simulation programs so that off-design simulation performance would be as faithful as process operations near the unit's normal operating conditions.

SIMULATOR DETAILS

To further increase the effectiveness of the simulator training, Autodynamics interfaced the simulation software with one of CE-Taylor's MOD-300 Operator Stations.

The simulation software was designed to operate on a DEC MicroVax II. The simulation software then communicated with the Taylor MOD 300 Operator Station via Taylor's console gateway and DEC's Ethernet link module. A block diagram of the training system's data flow is shown in Figure 1.

Many high fidelity details have been included within the simulated processes. A short description of these details follows.

TAYLOR MOD 300 DIRECT CONNECT BLOCK DIAGRAM

FIGURE 1

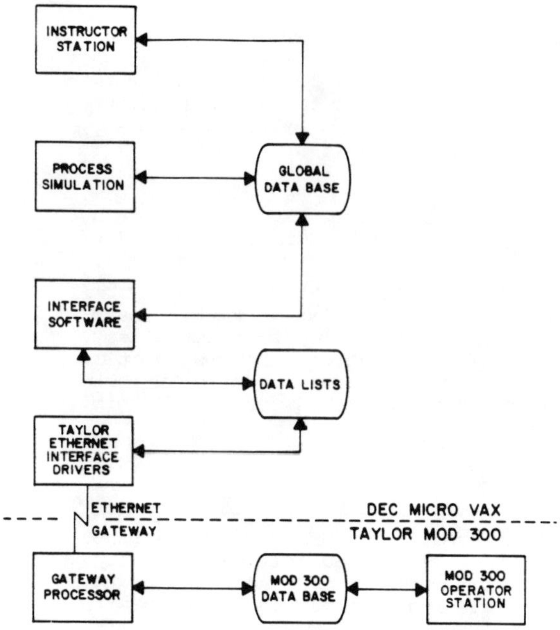

Atmospheric Resid Desulfurization

The ARDS simulation included the simulation of one desulfurization reactor train with full preheat integration, reactor effluent heat recovery, gas separation and recycle gas compression.

The primary training objectives of this program are to:

- Develop an understanding of the ARDS process and the effects of rigorous heat integration.

- Start-up and shutdown of the ARDS process.

- Proper operation of the fractionator column.

- Familiarize the unit technicians with the advanced control system and logic interlocks.

In order to meet these goals, the ARDS simulation program concentrated on the following equipment:

- Residue feed and recycle gas pre-heat exchangers and heaters.

- The desulfurization reactors.

- High and low pressure flash drums.

- Recycle gas compressor.

The heat exchanger exit temperatures are dynamically calculated as a function of inlet stream flow rates, temperatures, physical and thermodynamic properties, overall heat transfer coefficients and mean temperature driving forces. Partial condensation of the tubeside hydrocarbon is simulated. The heat transfer coefficients are calculated as a function of shell and tube side flows.

Gas Fired Heaters. The recycle gas heater and the resid feed heater are gas fired, with four tube passes. The simulation considered each pass in detail. As with the resid feed heater, all four tube passes and the firebox were modeled in detail.

ARDS Reactor Section. The hydrocarbon stream passes through a catalyst bed where desulfurization, deoxygenation, denitrogenation and olefin saturation occurs. These processes remove the impurities from the oil by converting the sulfur, nitrogen and oxygen in the feed to hydrogen sulfide, ammonia and water.

The inlet to each reactor and to the guard chamber is controlled by adjusting the amount of recycle gas injected in the feed of each bed which acts as a quench. Inlet quenching is required due to the exothermic reactions that occur.

In the simulation, reaction rates are dependent on the partial pressure of hydrogen, reactor residence times, and catalyst poisoning. Catalyst poisoning occurs if the wash water is lost and the ammonia concentration is allowed to increase.

Reactor temperatures are dynamically calculated as a function of inlet stream temperature, flow rate and reaction rate.

High and Low Pressure Flash Drums. In the simulation, pressure, temperature, gas and liquid compositions and liquid and vapor inventories are dynamically calculated. The vapor-liquid equilibrium are dynamically calculated as a function of vessel pressure, temperature, inlet composition and thermodynamic properties. The pressure is determined by performing a vapor material balance around the drum. Similarly, a liquid material balance is used for the calculation of level. Absorption of the hydrogen into the liquid phase and gas flow through the level control valve is simulated.

ARDS Recycle Gas Compression. The recycle gas compressor is simulated in detail. The steam turbine and the compressor share a common shaft. In the simulation, the shaft speed is calculated by balancing the horsepower supplied by the turbine with the horse power used by the compressor.

Dynamic pressure calculations are incorporated in the suction and discharge of the recycle gas compressor. The flow through the compressor is a function of polytropic head developed, compressor speed and mechanical losses. Polytropic head developed is calculated from the gas compressibility, suction temperature, compression ratio and polytropic efficiency. The compressor performance closely follows the vendor provided performance curve.

Distillate Hydrotreater Unit Process Simulation

The DHU consists of reaction and fractionation sections. The reaction section includes feed preheat, treating and cracking reactors, reactor effluent heat recovery, and reactor effluent separation. The fractionation section includes the fractionator, naphtha splitter, debutanizer and support equipment including the off-gas compressor.

The specific training objectives of the program are centered on the operation of:

- Feed heating system
- Reactors
- Recycle compressor
- Plant logic systems.

Reactor Feed Heating System. The Reactor Feed Heating System was simulated in detail. Four passes were modeled on the reactor charge heater. The heat balance model included tube skin temperature and thermal lag. On the firebox side, combustion calculations, heat balance, and draft profile were simulated.

DHU Reactors. The hydrocracking reactor converts distillate boiling range material into naphtha and lighter products. The reactions are exothermic.

The reactor conversion is a function of many parameters, most importantly feed quality, hydrogen partial pressure, catalyst bed temperature, and catalyst age. Empirical data was used to calculate the conversion of feed to products and hydrogen consumption in the reactors as a function of current process conditions.

For all effluent heat exchangers, exit temperatures are dynamically calculated as a function of inlet stream flow rates, temperatures, physical and thermodynamic properties, overall heat transfer coefficients and mean temperature driving forces. The heat transfer coefficients are calculated as a function of shell and tube side flows.

DHU Recycle Gas Compressor. The scope of the DHU Recycle Gas Compressor is similar to the ARDS Recycle Gas Compressor.

Hydrogen Generation Section

The Hydrogen Generation Section consists of the feed preheat, reformer, and the HT and LT shift converters. The specific training objectives of this program, the HGS simulation program, provides NEI with the capability to train operators on the proper operation of:

- Reforming furnace (including shutdown conditions)
- ID and FD fans
- Effluent waste heat boilers
- Steam drum
- HT and LT shift converters.

The program will provide training in unit start-up, normal operations, unit shut-down, and emergency conditions. Simulation of the unit logic system is included.

Reforming Furnace. The reaction kinetics for the reformer calculate the composition of the streams leaving the reactors. The methane reforming reaction was assumed to reach equilibrium conditions, whereas the water shift reaction was assumed to have a 30 degree F approach to equilibrium.

Draft pressures, air registers, the ID and FD fans are modeled. Both the main and auxiliary reformer furnace burners are modeled. Burner instrumentation and logic is included.

The other reforming system equipment, such as the combustion air preheater, combustion air steam preheater, the reformer waste heater boiler, and BFW a circulating pumps is included in the simulation.

Steam Drum. A simplified shrink and swell model is included in the boiler simulation. This model calculates the volume of bubbles in the boiler liquid pool. The volume of the bubbles will vary as a function of temperature and pressure. The shrink and swell model provides realistic boiler training. Shrink and swell is normally included with all Audy simulations and is indicative of Audy's attention to detail to meet training objectives.

Shift Converters. In the HTS converter, the bulk of the carbon monoxide produced in the reformer reacts with steam to produce carbon dioxide and hydrogen. The HTS converter was divided into three sections. The reaction rate in the HTS converter is calculated as a function of gas composition and temperature. This rate is used to calculate the composition and temperature of the gas leaving each section of the converter. The inlet and outlet temperature in each catalyst bed section is calculated.

The carbon monoxide concentration is further reduced in the LTS converter. The LTS converter is also divided into three sections. The extent of the shift reaction is used to calculate the composition and temperature of the gas leaving each section of the converter.

Sulfur Recovery Unit

The specific training objectives of the program are centered on the operation of:

- Reaction Furnace
- Waste Heat Boiler
- Reheaters
- Claus Reactors
- Sulfur Condensers.

Reaction Furnace, Waste Heat Boiler-Steam Drum. The reaction furnace temperature is calculated dynamically as a function of the acid gas and the air streams, their corresponding temperatures and specific heats, the heat of reaction, and the radiation losses to the atmosphere. Provisions are made in the program for the start-up air and natural gas lines.

In the steam drum the three element boiler feed water control is included. The emergency shutdown conditions associated with the reaction furnace are also included in the simulation.

Sulfur Condensers. The sulfur vapor produced by the reaction between H2S and SO2, is condensed in the sulfur condensers and the liquid sulfur is drained to the various sulfur pits. The water level in the sulfur condensers are calculated dynamically based on the unsteady state mass and the energy balance equations. These levels are controlled as in the actual plant. The steam produced is sent to the steam header. The outlet temperatures of the process streams are calculated and controlled. Sulfur condensation is modeled.

Converters. The reaction between hydrogen sulfide and sulfur dioxide takes place in the converters in the presence of catalyst to produce sulfur and water vapors. The reaction kinetics for each converter is used to calculate the composition of the streams leaving the reactors and the heat generated by the reaction.

Reheaters. The temperature of the process gas stream leaving the condenser is raised by the reheaters. The reheater outlet temperatures are calculated dynamically and controlled. Outlet gas O_2 and CO concentrations are modeled.

RESULTS

The training system developed by Autodynamics has already had an immediate benefit us at NewGrade Energy. By using the simulator, the plant process control system has been tested, and improved where design weaknesses existed.

It was demonstrated that one of the control schemes planned for the plant plainly would not work. This control scheme was redesigned and installed in the plant prior to the unit coming on stream. More often, we found that the controller tunings incorporated in the plant control system were to tight for unit stability. These controller tuning parameters were also changed prior to the start-up of the process units.

The plant logic has also been tested and validated. The most severe plant logic problem encountered was the plant alarm system. There were too many critical alarms sounding the alarm announciator. Many of the instrument loops were configured with critical process variable deviation alarms. The process deviation alarms were configured with a +/- 3% tolerance. With all of these signals triggering the alarm announciator, the plant operators began to show a tendancy to ignore the plant alarms. We changed many of the deviation alarms to the "non-critical" type, which does not trigger the alarm announciator. Now proper attention is given to the critical plant alarms.

The plant start-up procedures were also fully tested on the simulator. We found portions of the procedures were too vague, and these procedures were augmented prior to the actual unit start-up.

Another direct benefit of the Autodynamics' Training System was that we were given a chance to live with the distributive control system configuration while in the training phase. We were then in a position to identify improvements in the instrument loop layout to allow for faster plant control responses, and for improved presentation of plant information.

The initial phases of operator training has been completed. Each of the plant operators have had at least 100 hours of training on starting up our new units. Each of the master operators have had at least 24 hours of training on their units. They now are able to draw on their training to start-up the units in a confident and safe manner.

Simulators VI
© 1989 By The Society for Computer
Simulation International
ISBN 0-911801-51-0

MAAP-GRAAPH: A nuclear power plant accident simulation tool

A. Sharon, J. L. Crocker and R. E. Henry
Fauske & Associates, Inc.
16W070 West 83rd Street
Burr Ridge, Illinois 60521

ABSTRACT

Increasing emphasis is placed on training operators and accident management teams to recognize and promptly respond to severe accident conditions in a nuclear power plant. An essential part of any comprehensive training program is a simulation tool for such accidents. The MAAP-GRAAPH package, described here, offers an efficient, economical and well proven approach for meeting this need. It is based on the MAAP computer program that was extensively benchmarked against data from plant accidents and experimental programs. The graphical enhancement makes it easy to understand the accident progression and examine the effect of various operator actions on mitigating the accident.

INTRODUCTION

The accidents at Three Mile Island Unit 2 (TMI-2) and Chernobyl Unit 4 have demonstrated the importance of the "human factor" in severe accidents of nuclear power plants. Both accidents occurred due to wrong interpretation of the plant status and to the lack of operator training in severe accident phenomena. Hence there is a growing realization that operators and accident management teams should be trained in severe accident phenomena and uderstand the system behavior that may lead to an accident and, if faced with an accident, how to terminate it safely and bring the plant back to a controlled, coolable state.

Such a training tool, called MAAP-GRAAPH was developed by Fauske & Associates, Inc. and is described in this paper. MAAP-GRAAPH is a hardware-software package based on the Modular Accident Analysis Program (MAAP) computer code. The second part of the name, GRAAPH, stands for Graphically Represented Accident And PHenomena.

MAAP is a severe accident thermal-hydraulic and fission product analysis code for the nuclear steam supply system, the containment and the auxiliary (reactor) building. Development was funded by the industry sponsored IDCOR program which included all U.S. reactor vendors, architect engineering firms, most U.S. utilities and several foreign utilities. With the end of IDCOR, development and maintenance efforts have been transferred to EPRI and an independent MAAP user's groups.

The mainframe version of MAAP is currently in active use by approximately 30 organizations, mainly for PRAs and development of emergency exercise scenarios. However, recently with the development of a PC version and the graphical enhancement package GRAAPH, it is being used for training and verification of emergency operating procedures.

As a severe accident simulator, MAAP calculates all the relevant thermal-hydraulic conditions and fission product concentrations throughout the plant. It allows for a large variety of operator actions by extensive modeling of the engineering safeguards systems in the plant. EPRI has funded a V&V effort by independent organizations and various benchmarking activity to gain confidence in the code and the physical models. The code is capable of running much faster than real-time and hence is useful for all kind of training requirements.

DESCRIPTION OF MAAP-GRAAPH SOFTWARE

The physical models in MAAP-GRAAPH are identical to those used in the mainframe version of MAAP. To this foundation, MAAP-GRAAPH adds a sophisticated user interface which greatly enhances the ability of the user to perform operator actions and interpret the results. The latter is particularly important, since severe accidents can involve a very large number of phenomena which interact in subtle ways. The features of the user interface are as follows.

The primary element of the user interface is a full-color, graphical display which depicts the primary system, containment, and engineered safeguards. When viewed as a whole, this display indicates water levels in various parts of the plant, the status of engineered safeguards, and valve positions. By using a mouse, valve positions and pump status can be changed during the run by placing a cursor over the desired equipment and pushing a button on the mouse. The colors of the equipment and associated piping change to reflect their new state.

A key feature of the display is the ability to "zoom". A particular region of the plant can be selected by placing a box around the region with the mouse. This area can then be scaled to fill the entire display. Alternatively, a "windows" mode can be activated which allows several zoomed views to be displayed simultaneously. When areas of the plant are expanded, pressurizer gas temperature, shell temperature, hydrogen and fission product masses, and spray flowrate could be shown. The user can display any of the variables from a list of approximately 5000 calculated plant parameters. These parameters are not visible in the unexpanded view. In this way, only desired information need be displayed.

To assist in viewing trends, at any time the user can call up an extensive library of plotted parameters. Included in this library are a user-defined set of plots which could be used, for example, to display information from a Safety Parameter Display System. If desired, the user can restrict the plots only to show those quantities which can actually be read in the control room.

A hard-copy of plots can be obtained on a variety of output devices: dot matrix printers, laser printers, or plotters. Since the package has all the capabilities of the mainframe version of MAAP, the ability to obtain report-quality figures allows MAAP-GRAAPH to be used for PRA studies, emergency scenario development, etc., when it is not being used for training.

DESCRIPTION OF MAAP-GRAAPH HARDWARE

At present, the MAAP-GRAAPH package can be run on super-microcomputers and minicomputers or on enhanced personal computers (PCs). This paper will focus on the latter.

In the PC version, the package actually executes on a coprocessor card that is installed in a slot in the PC. This card provides computational power approaching that of a VAX 11/780 and 4b megabytes of memory for minimal cost. When installed in a personal computer, this gives the user the ability to perform state-of-the-art severe accidents simulations at speeds much faster than real-time in a package that resides on his/her desktop. For example, a 40 hour station blackout transient executes in approximately 5 hours. Attached to the coprocessor card is a companion video card which drives a dedicated high-resolution monitor at high speed.

ILLUSTRATION OF GRAPHICAL CAPABILITIES

MAAP-GRAAPH was developed for various nuclear power plants:

- A Westinghouse PWR with a large dry containment is shown in Figure 1.
- A Westinghouse PWR with an ice condenser is shown in Figure 2.
- A BWR with a Mark I containment is shown in Figure 3.
- A BWR with a Mark II containment is shown in Figure 4.

Also available is a B&W primary system. Other plants such as BWR with a Mark III containment or a CE primary system are modeled in MAAP but the graphical enhancements were not yet developed.

All of the above pictures show a full view of the plant and the status of the engineering safeguard systems. A red color is used for a disabled system, a green color for a stand-by system and a blue color for an active system. An example of an expanded "zoomed in" view of some of these systems is shown in Figure 5 (PWR, ice condenser).

Different colors are also used for indicating the hydrogen concentration. Yellow for H_2 mole fraction below 10^{-3}, purple for a molar concentration above 10^{-2} and orange for an intermediate concentration). Figure 2 shown low H_2 concentrations in the hot legs and the pressurizer.

The core conditions are illustrated by several colors and representative coolant channels. Core regions with temperatures below 1200 K are colored in white while gray is used for core regions above 1200 K. Yellow is used for core regions with temperatures exceeding 1850 K and red for core regions that reached the core material melting point (2500 K). The transition temperatures of 1200 and 1850 K correspond to different cladding oxidation rates. An expanded core status during a severe accident is shown in Figure 6. Note that changes in the core geometry due to the melting process are clearly displayed.

The ability to simultaneously display the overall plant view and an expanded view of the steam generator and pressurizer is illustrated in Figure 7.

When "zooming in" on a particular portion of the plant, key variables that represent the thermal-hydraulic conditions in that regions becomes visible. This is illustrated in Figure 8 which shows the wetwell floor in a BWR Mark II after core material had reached the reactor vessel. The cooled core material is spread on the floor and is covered by water. The pressure, water and gas temperature in that region are shown for the wetwell.

An overall plant process monitor for a PWR with an ice condenser containment is shown in Figure 9. It displays the most important thermal hydraulic conditions in various parts of the plant including the primary system, two steam generators, the pressurizer, the core and in five different containment compartments. The status of various systems and components are also highlighted in the display. For example, "CR OK" indicates normal core conditions.

SUMMARY

As increasing emphasis is placed on training operators and engineers to recognize and manage beyond design based accidents, a simulation training tool is needed. The MAAP-GRAAPH package illustrated here offers an efficient, economical and well-proven approach for meeting this need. Its graphical capabilities makes it easy to follow and understand the accident progression and to explore the effect of the operator actions on the accident outcome.

REFERENCES

1. IDCOR. 1987. "Tasks 16.2 and 16.3", MAAP Users Manual. Available from EPRI.

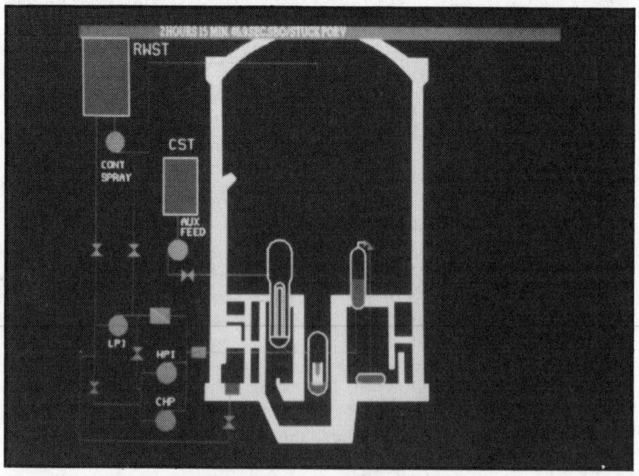

Figure 1: MAAP-GRAAPH illustration of a severe accident in a PWR with a large, dry containment (Zion like plant).

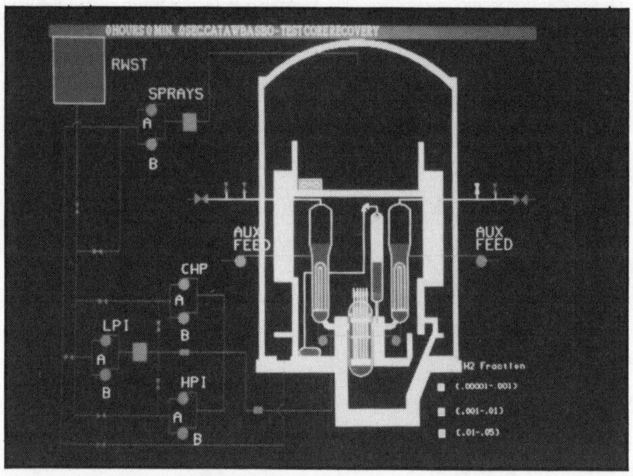

Figure 2: MAAP-GRAAPH illustration of an accident in a PWR with an ice condenser plant (Sequoyah like).

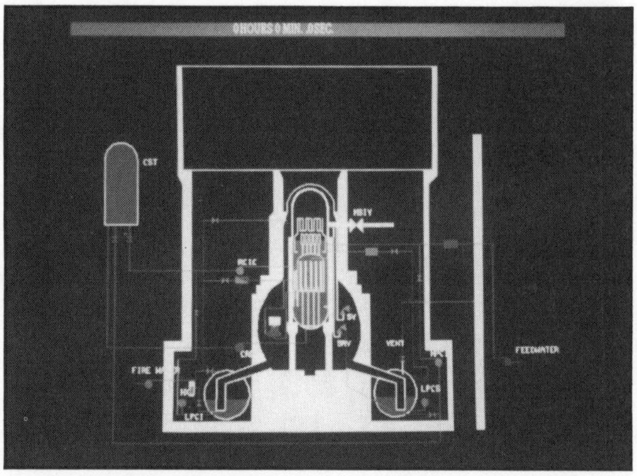

Figure 3: MAAP-GRAAPH illustration of a BWR with a Mark I containment.

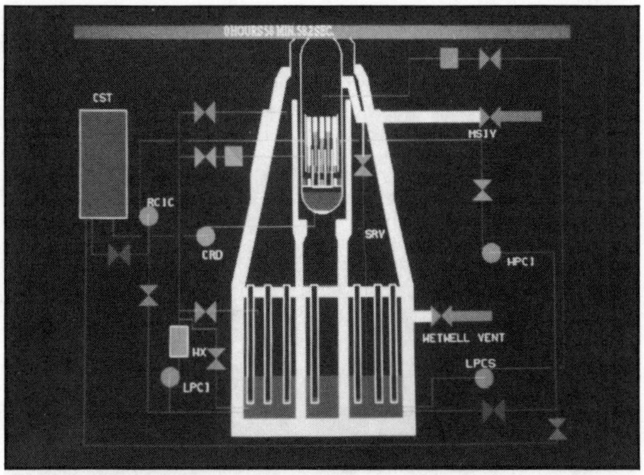

Figure 4: MAAP-GRAAPH illustration of severe accident BWR with a Mark II containment.

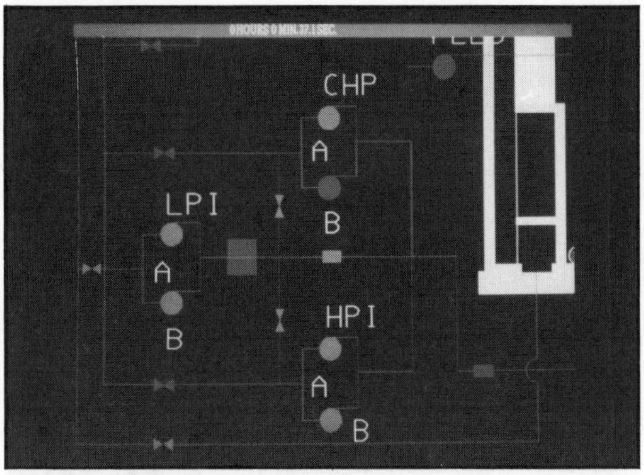

Figure 5: Expanded ("zoomed in") view of some of the engineering safeguard systems in a PWR with an ice condensed containment.

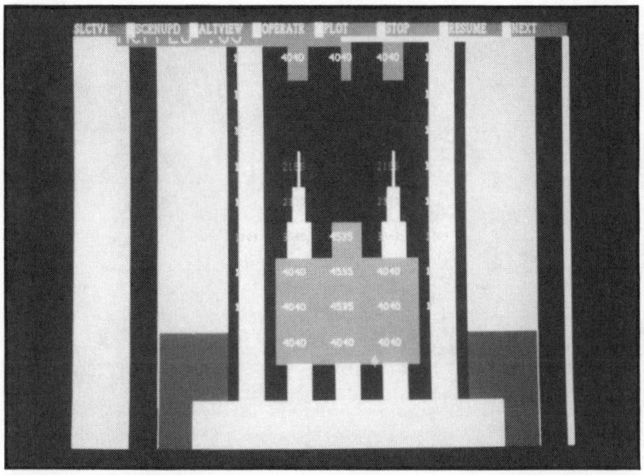

Figure 6: Expanded view of the core conditions status during a severe accident.

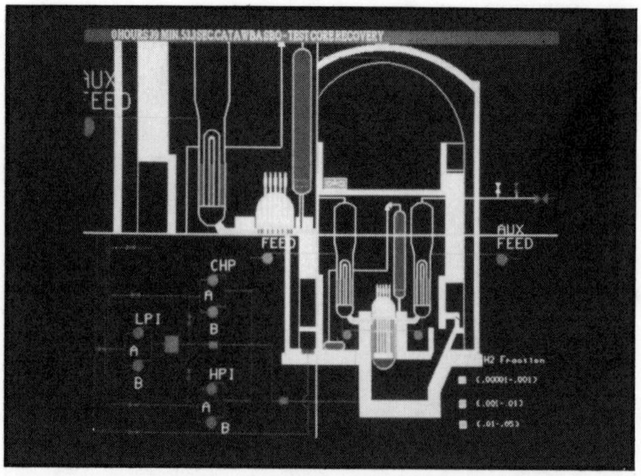

Figure 7: Simulatous display of the overall plant picture and an expanded view of the pressurizer and steam generator.

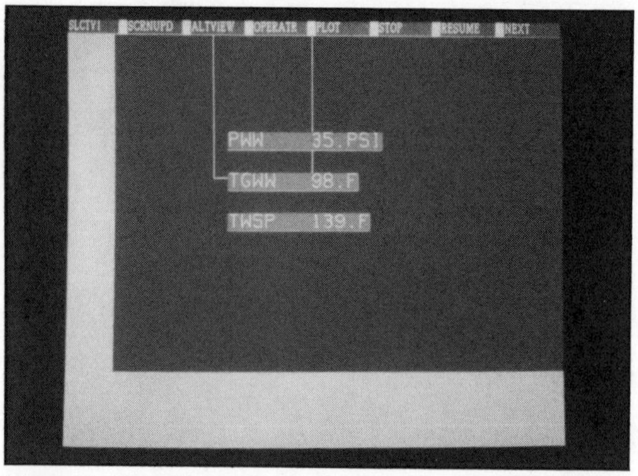

Figure 8: Expanded view of the drywell in a BWR Mark II after core material that was ejected from the vessel had spread on the floor.

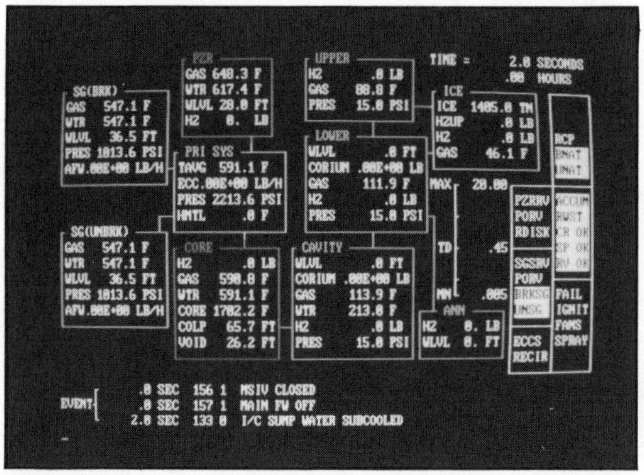

Figure 9: Overall plant process monitor for a PWR with an ice condenser containment.

Simulators VI
© 1989 By The Society for Computer
Simulation International
ISBN 0-911801-51-0

Simulations of the recent LaSalle-2 incident with the BNL plant analyzer

H. S. Cheng, A. N. Mallen, and W. Wulff
Department of Nuclear Energy
Brookhaven National Laboratory
Upton, New York USA 11973

ABSTRACT

This paper presents the results of simulations of the recent power oscillation incident at the LaSalle-2 Nuclear Power Plant using the BNL Plant Analyzer. The causes of the oscillation were investigated and the sensitivity of the oscillation to key parameters was studied. It is concluded that the observed power oscillation was caused by boiling instability (i.e., density wave oscillation) reinforced by the reactivity feedback in neutron kinetics, and that the density wave oscillation resulted from flow reduction due to recirculation pump trip and feedwater temperature reduction due to partial loss of feedwater heating capabilty as well as power peaking.

INTRODUCTION

On March 9, 1988, an Instrument Maintenance (IM) technician at LaSalle Unit 2, while performing a functional test on a differential pressure switch, caused both recirculation pumps to trip off due to a valving error (Diederich 1988). Because of the large and rapid power reduction, feedwater heater high level alarms caused a partial isolation of feedwater heaters, resulting in a reduction of 51 °F in feedwater temperature. Approximately 5 minutes into the event, the local power range monitor (LPRM) up- and downscale alarms began annunciating and the average power range monitors (APRM) were observed to be oscillating with an ~2.3 s period. Realizing the unit's unfavorable location on the power/flow map, the operating staff was preparing to scram the reactor manually, when an automatic scram occurred on high-flux trip (118% trip on APRM). Prior to the scram, the operators attempted to remedy the situation by trying to restart the recirculation pumps, but failed.

The growing power oscillation observed in this incident raises concerns about the stability of BWRs. The important questions are: Why did the oscillation occur? Was there a possibility for divergent oscillations? What if the operator did restart the recirculation pumps? What if the Main Steam Isolation Valves (MSIV) were inadvertently closed right after the pump restart? Brookhaven National Laboratory (BNL) was asked by the USNRC to simulate the LaSalle-2 event with the BNL Plant Analyzer (BPA) (Wulff 1984 and Cheng 1986). This paper reports the results of the BPA simulations as well as the important findings of the present analysis.

*Work performed under the auspices of the U.S. Nuclear Regulatory Commission.

EVENT DESCRIPTION

After the control systems had been ruled out as the cause of the instability by using the BPA, it was postulated that the observed growing power oscillation was caused by a nuclear thermal hydraulic instability brought about by the recirculation pump trip and the partial feedwater heater loss plus power peaking.

The transient was initiated from the 85% power and 75% flow condition by a recirculation pump trip followed by a partial feedwater heater loss. Table 1 summarizes the sequence of events for the transient.

Table 1

Sequence of Events

Event/Action	Time (m)
1. Steady state at 85% power and 75% flow	-5.0
2. Recirculation pumps tripped	0.0
3. Reactor power dropped to 37%	0.4
4. Core flow reached natural circulation (29%)	0.5
5. Feedwater heaters partially isolated	1.0
6. Reactor power reached 45% & "beat" phenomena began	2.0
7. Modulated limit cycle oscillations continued	5.2
8. Enhanced limit cycle oscillations began	5.9
9. Growing oscillations started	7.3
10. Reactor power reached 118%, and reactor tripped	8.1
11. End of transient	9.0

THE BPA SIMULATION

The proper initial conditions are essential for the analysis of this event. A steady-state run was first made to obtain the desired initial conditions. The initial conditions obtained by the BNL Plant Analyzer are summarized as follows:

1.	Reactor Power	2808 MWt
2.	Core Inlet Flow Rate	10,210 kg/s (81 Mlb/h)
3.	System Pressure	69.5 MPa (1007 psia)
4.	Steam Flow Rate	1424 kg/s (11.3 Mlb/h)
5.	Feedwater Flow Rate	1424 kg/s (11.3 Mlb/h)
6.	Recirculation Drive Flow Rate	3641 kg/s (28.9 Mlb/h)
7.	Recirculation Pump Speed	1590 rpm
8.	Core Average Void Fraction	41.7 %
9.	Core Average Fuel Temp.	601°C (1113°F)
10.	Core Average Coolant Temp.	285°C (545°F)
11.	Core Inlet Subcooling	11°C (20°F)
12.	Feedwater Temperature	206°C (402°F)

Reactivity feedback plays an important role in a BWR for both the steady-state and transient analyses. The feedback coefficients used in the BPA simulation were obtained from the earlier work on the void feedback (Cheng 1977) and the Doppler feedback (Cheng 1978). Axial power distribution is known to affect the core instability of a BWR (Yokomizo 1987). The axial power profile used in this work is a typical bottom-peaked power shape with an axial peak of 1.38.

The results of the BPA simulations are presented in Figures 1 through 9. Figure 1 presents the simulated power oscillation which shows a remarkable resemblance to the actual APRM traces (Kaufman 1988). The zoomed display of the power oscillation just prior to the automatic scram is shown in Figure 2, which shows a period of oscillation of ~2.8 s as compared to ~2.3 s as observed in the actual event. That the power oscillation is the result of the density wave oscillation is clearly demonstrated by the oscillatory void behavior as shown in Figure 3.

Figure 4 presents the simulated core flow response and Figure 5 shows the zoomed display of the core flow oscillation with the same period of ~2.8 s as the power oscillation. The core flow quickly reaches the natural circulation condition within a minute due to the recirculation pump trip as shown in Figure 6 for the recirculation pump speed and in Figure 7 for the recirculation drive flow.

Figure 8 shows the feedwater flow response and Figure 9 presents the feedwater temperature response along with the actual plant data. The temperature response shows good agreement with the plant data except for the value at 1 min.

SUMMARY AND CONCLUSIONS

The BPA has been used to simulate the recent LaSalle-2 power oscillation incident. Extensive sensitivity studies were performed. The simulation results support the following conclusions:

1. The best-estimate conditions for LaSalle-2 led to limit cycle oscillations only.

2. The LaSalle-2 conditions within the uncertainty envelope produced growing oscillations leading to automatic scram as actually observed in the event.

3. The cause of the LaSalle-2 event was the coupled nuclear thermal-hydraulic instability originated by the density wave oscillations and reinforced by the reactivity feedback. The instability was brought about by the combination of:

   - Power peaking (especially radial peaking),
   - Flow reduction due to the recirculation pump trip,
   - Feedwater temperature reduction due to the partial feedwater heater loss.

4. The amplitude of the power oscillation remains bounded even after a postulated scram failure.

5. Reactor should be scrammed when LaSalle-type power oscillations occur.

6. These studies reinforce the importance of continued monitoring and controlling of peaking factors.

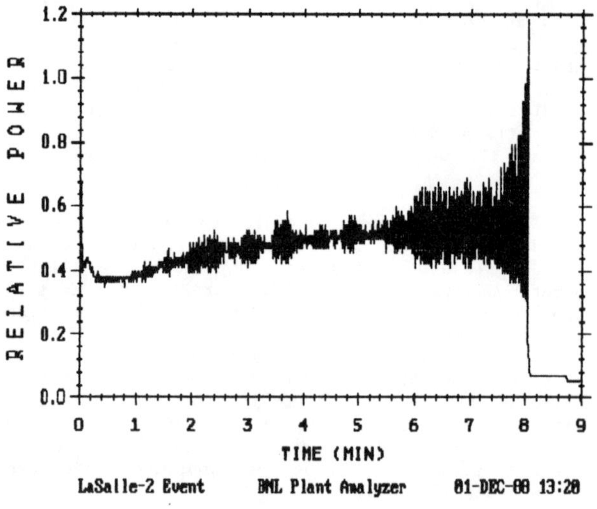

Figure 1 Simulated Reactor Power Oscillation for the LaSalle-2 Event.

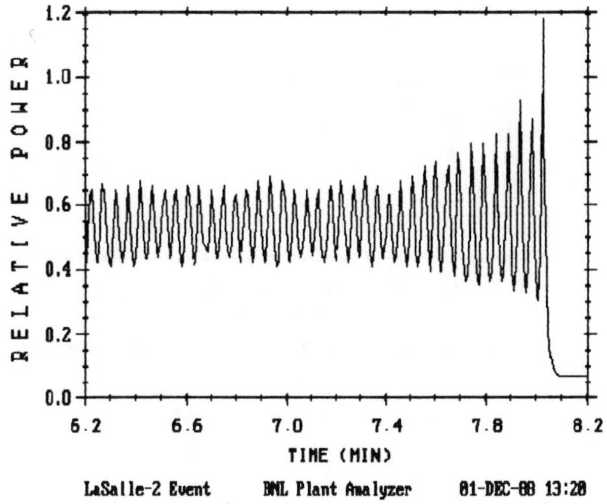

Figure 2 Zoomed Display of the Power Oscillation.

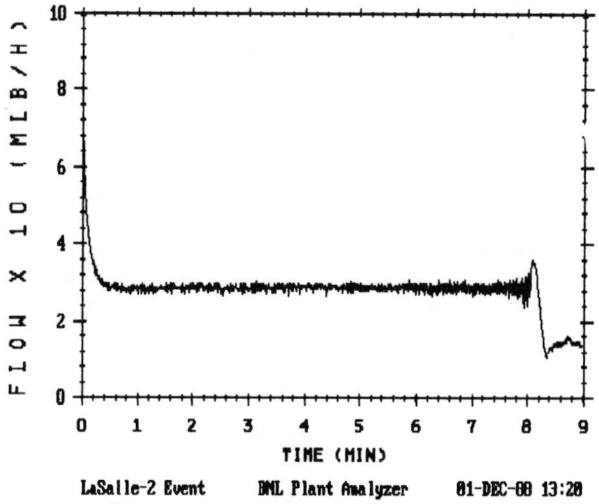

Figure 4 Simulated Core Flow Response for LaSalle-2 Event.

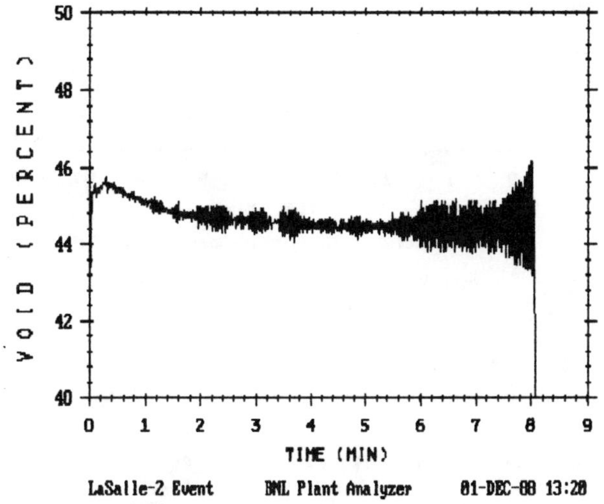

Figure 3 Oscillating Behavior of Core Average Void Fraction.

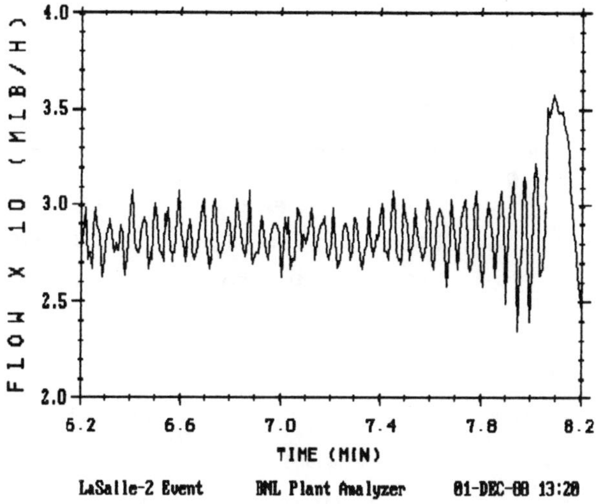

Figure 5 Zoomed Display of the Core Flow Oscillation.

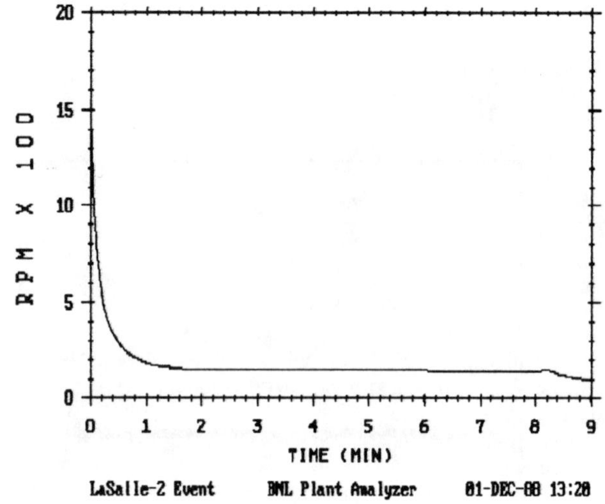

Figure 6 Recirculation Pump Speed Response.

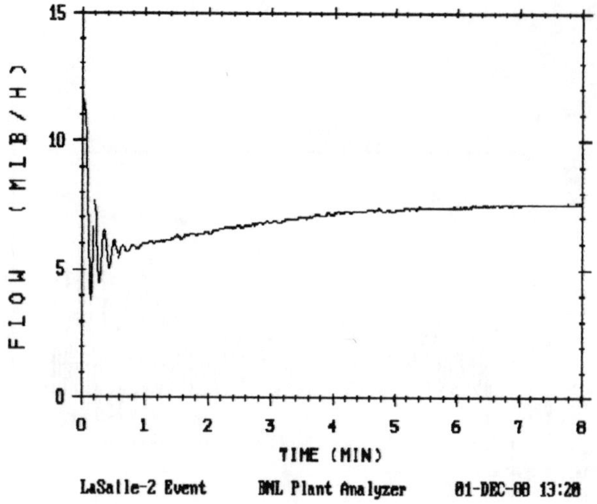

Figure 8 Simulated Feedwater Flow Response for the La-Salle-2 Event.

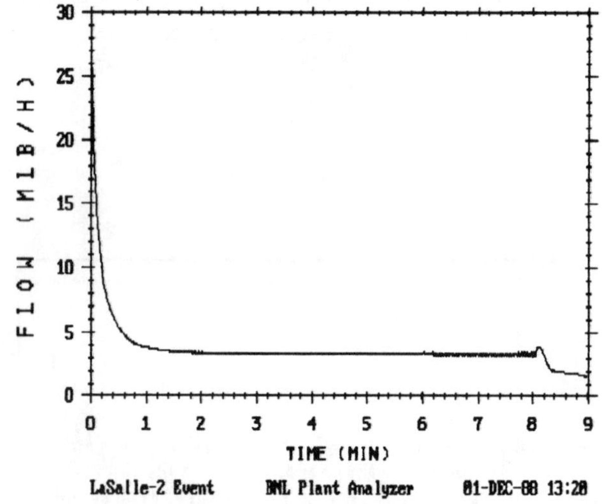

Figure 7 Recirculation Drive Flow Response.

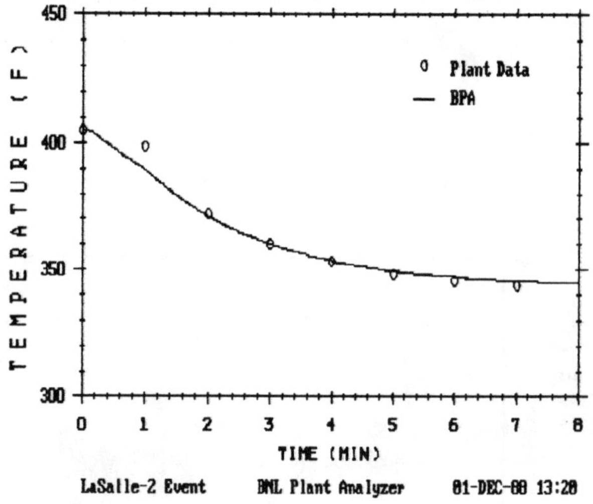

Figure 9 Feedwater Temperature Response for the LaSalle-2 Event

REFERENCES

Cheng, H. S. et al. (1977), "A Space-Time Analysis of Void Reactivity Feedback in BWRs," Brookhaven National Laboratory, BNL-NUREG-23501.

Cheng, H. S. et al. (1978), "BWR Doppler Feedback - Effect of Voids, Control Blades, Gadolinia, and Exposure," Brookhaven National Laboratory, BNL-NUREG-24433.

Cheng, H. S. (1986), "Boiling Water Reactor Plant Analyzer Development at Brookhaven National Laboratory," Nucl. Sci. Eng., 92, 144-156, January 1986.

Diederich, G. J. (1988), "Potentially Significant Event: Unit 2 Scram Initiated by Valving Error," LaSalle County Station, Letter to N. Kalivianakis, March 11, 1988.

Kaufman, J. and Lanik, G. (1988), "Private Communication," Division of Analysis and Evaluation of Operating Data, The U.S. Nuclear Regulatory Commission, May 6, 1988.

Wulff, W. et al. (1984), "The BWR Plant Analyzer," Final Report, Brookhaven National Laboratory, NUREG/CR-3943, BNL-NUREG-51812.

Yokomizo, O. et al. (1987), "Space-Dependent Analysis of BWR Core Nuclear Thermal Hydraulic Stability," Proceedings of ANS Topical Meeting on Anticipated and Abnormal Transients in Nuclear Power Plants, Vol. 3, VII-9, Atlanta, Georgia, April 12-15, 1987.

Simulators VI
© 1989 By The Society for Computer
Simulation International
ISBN 0-911801-51-0

Simulation Software Support (S³) system

D. Burgess F. Mahjouri, PhD
Singer Link-Miles Simulation Corporation
Columbia, Maryland 21045

ABSTRACT

In any significant software development effort the software development environment used is an important element. The size and complexity of modern nuclear power plant training simulators requires a powerful software organization system.

This paper will discuss the software database and a set of integrated support programs in use on a large number of real-time power plant simulators. Contents, usage and control of the software database, automated development and documentation aides, testing and real time execution environment, integration of trainer features, and expectation of continued modification will be explored.

INTRODUCTION

The Simulation Software Support System (S3) provides an integrated software development environment for FORTRAN simulation software on nuclear power plant simulators. A controlled central database of software elements and an extensive family of support programs are the central components of the S3 system. This central database serves as the software configuration manager. The system includes the background programs used to build, modify, control, and extract information from the software database as well as an execution environment including loader, debugging, and executive programs.

The S3 system was created approximately 7 years ago. Since that time the system has been utilized for over 20 nuclear power plant simulators plus a few other training simulator projects. S3 is used on the GOULD CSD CONCEPT 32 line of computers with the MPX operating system.

THE SOFTWARE DATABASE

The software database consists of all data which is directly related to the simulator software load. The principal components of this are the global data definitions and the software modules. Additional components include the simulator panel I/O interface information, initial condition sets, and standard building blocks for common software modules. Design document data and reference data tracking are only loosely coupled with the S3 system.

MASTER DATA DICTIONARY

Full information on all simulator data symbols (variables, constants, and parameters) is maintained in the S3 Master Data Dictionary (MDD). To allow liberal incorporation of mnemonic and plant component identification in symbol naming conventions a symbol length of 16 characters is used. In order to maintain consistent data availability for documentation, debugging, and logging virtually all program symbols are required to be defined in the MDD. The software database includes space for a lengthy description of each symbol and has separate fields for units, system code, default display format, and default value.

The types of symbols defined in the master data dictionary consists of variables, constants, and parameters. All variables and constants are assigned addresses in global common partitions. Global offsets may be optionally specified by the user, however, for most usages the database support programs take care of address assignments. For cases where the "equivalent" symbols are needed or a series of data points must be placed in a common buffer, a multilevel sub-partitioning tree structure is used. The support programs take care of enforcing the bounding requirements of different data types and ensuring that addresses of data items and arrays do not overlap.

The S3 system automatically maintains cross-reference information identifying every software module which references each symbol. This information is immediately available for software engineers inquiry and is used to mark modules for automatic propagation of the effects of changes to symbol definitions to all effected object code.

PROGRAM MODULES

The S3 system tracks software modules in its Module Specification File (MSF). Each module is preprocessed before being compiled. Actions of the preprocessor include resolution of all symbols, enforcement of a few restrictions imposed as good programming practices, output formatting, and automatic equation annotation with descriptions of the variables used. After compilation, a post processor is executed to produce a listing incorporating any error messages from the compiler with the S3 program listing, log the compilation and program revision, and store the new program object and cross-reference information. Cross-reference information is automatically maintained for each symbol referenced and each subroutine call.

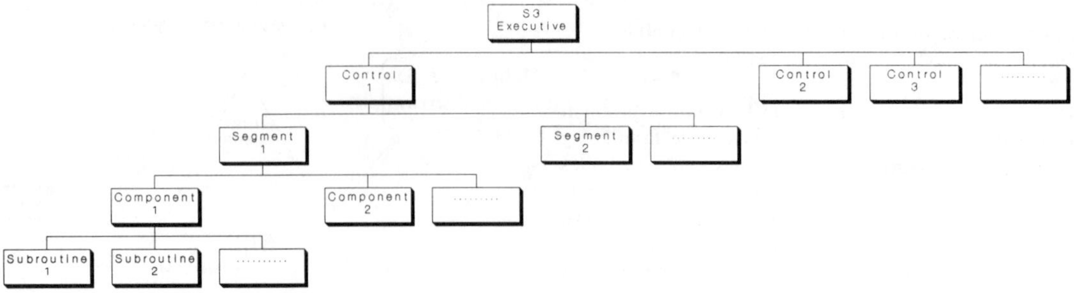

Figure 1 : Simulator Software Support Module Hierarchy

The S3 system defines program types "Control", "Segment", "Component", and "Subroutine" to provide high visibility to four levels of program hierarchy (See Figure 1). S3 "Control" modules are the top level of the math modeling software for each plant system. Executive loading and cyclic schedule are specified by control module. "Segment" modules are called by control modules and loaded with the control module which calls them. Segments are used to divide the program code for each simulated system into logical sections and modules whose size is easy to work with. The bulk of the specific code for each simulated system is normally located in its segment modules. "Component" modules are principally for instances of common instrument types such as pumps, valves, or controllers. "Subroutine' modules are the lower levels of program hierarchy and are typically used for common mathematical operations.

The S3 database maintains strict control of all object code and accepted source versions. The module specification file also records whether or not each object is consistent with the current state of the Master Data Dictionary. The supporting software includes abilities to report status information about all modules and to automatically submit modules for compilation.

PANEL INPUT OUTPUT DATABASE

The S3 system fully supports simulator input/output (I/O) interface integration for the Singer Distributed I/O system and Computer Products Inc. (CPI) Advanced Simulation Linkage System (ASLS). This includes software for the creation and maintenance of a database defining the simulator I/O and correspondence of software symbols to hardware signals and for on-line execution of the I/O interface. Simulator features closely related to the panel I/O which are incorporated in the I/O control software include switch check, I/O override, record/replay, and fast response to digital input state changes.

The S3 system includes an Input Scanning Activation System (ISAS) to provide fast response to changes in digital input states. The I/O database allows the designation of a "Component" module subroutine and activation option for each digital input. Fast response to digital input states is achieved by scanning all digital inputs every real-time pass and calling these components out of their normal turn on detection of DI changes. The activation options are to call the module when the DI changes from off to on, on to off, either transition, or continuously at the overall maximum cycle rate as long as the DI is true. This provides complete flexibility for the software to respond immediately to the input and normally includes the complete logic appropriate to the simulated instrument.

INITIAL CONDITION SETS

Initial condition sets (IC) consist of global images including all simulator state data for the snapshot and reset functions required on simulators. The initial condition sets are part of the software database. Usages of the initial condition sets beyond the simulator reset function include a list function to make the information readily available to off-line users, simulation of the plant condition in the software testing environment and the capability to update ICs to correspond to changes in the Master Data Dictionary (MDD).

COMPONENT DEVELOPMENT SYSTEM

S3 includes a Component Development System (CDS) for automated generation and maintenance of building block modules through a macro expansion process. The definition for a common type of module is called a generic component. Instances where a generic component definition and argument list are used to create a component module is a specific component. Typical usages of this system would include general definitions and many specific instances of air, motor, or solenoid operated valves, pumps, and circuit breakers.

Both the "Generic Component" definitions and "Specific Component" instances are treated as database components for controlled development and maintenance. When a generic component definition is modified the support software will automatically propagate the effects of this change by regeneration of all effected specific components.

CROSS-REFERENCE DATABASE

Accurate and complete cross reference information contributes greatly to the ease of software modification. The cross-reference information consists of the following lists:

- Which modules reference each data symbol
- Which data symbols are used by each module

- Which other modules are called by each module
- Which other modules call each module.

When a software engineer goes to look into a problem in a system with which he or she may have little familiarity the ability to quickly identify all usages of specific variables and constants is critical to their being able to modify equations with confidence and avoid unforseen side effects. The cross reference data provides immediate access to which modules reference any given data item. The list capability is extended to extract the specific statements referencing given symbols to fully automate the process of looking at how a variable is used.

The cross-reference data is also used to identify which modules must be modified and/or recompiled when the address or other attributes of a data item are changed. Whenever any change is made to a data point definition which may effect the modules which reference it, all referencing modules are marked as "inconsistent" with the database. Recompilation of inconsistent modules is then fully automated.

The cross-reference data is also used to provide fully automated system interface lists. The interface from one system to another is defined as those variables defined by the first and referenced by the other. This is easily identified by automatic analysis of the cross-reference information.

Cross-reference data is also used by the interactive symbolic debugger to provide automated display of all variables referenced by a given module and to provide the long database names for memory references in patch mode disassembly output.

S3 DATABASE LEVELS

The S3 approach to configuration management starts with the definition of three levels of the simulator software (See Figure 2). These are called the "TRAINING SYSTEM", "OFFICIAL DEVELOPMENT SYSTEM" (ODS), and "USER DEVELOPMENT SYSTEM" (UDS) levels.

The "Training System" level is defined as an accepted simulation load for use in training. This level is only subject to change through replacement by an accepted "Official Development System".

The "Official Development System" (ODS) is a complete set of simulator software which is protected from unauthorized modification but may include recently integrated and partially tested modifications.

The "User Development System" (UDS) level is a partial set of simulator software treated as amendments to an (ODS). There may be many user development systems (typically one for each user). All modifications to the simulator software are initially entered at this level. When prospective changes have been sufficiently tested at this level a restricted merge process is used to integrate the changes into the ODS.

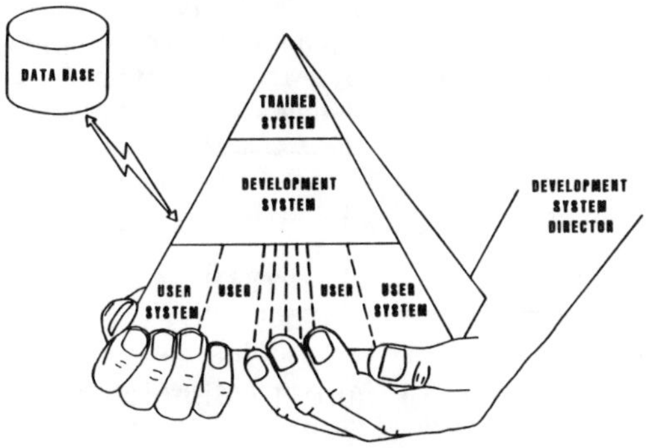

Figure 2: The S3 Approach to Configuration Management

The three database levels are applied to all elements of the software database. Engineers performing software modifications to the simulator enter and test all changes at the user (UDS) level. Mulitple users may perform software modification and testing at this level without interfering with each other nor with simulator testing nor with real-time operation of the simulator. The ODS can only be modified through the restricted merge process.

Extended tracking of changes to the (ODS) performed as part of the merge process is used to provide a full history of software modifications to the simulator.

TESTING AND EXECUTION ENVIRONMENT

The S3 system execution environment includes loader, debugger, and executive tasks. Most of this software is common between on-line execution for real-time simulation and off-line software testing.

REAL-TIME CONTROL

The Master Synchronization Task (MST) performs overall software control functions for the real-time execution of simulator software. Activities of the MST include initialization operations such as activation and loading of the executive tasks, simulator auxiliary tasks, and initialization of global common areas and the simulator panel I/O system. During real-time operation of the simulator the MST performs the clock update and status processing, initiates frame processing of the real-time executives, enforces timing constraints, performs the snapshot/reset disc I/O, and controls the simulator panel I/O system. When multiple CPUs are used to execute the simulation load a Slave Synchronization Task (SST) performs as proxy for MST in the additional computers.

EXECUTIVE TASK

The S3 executive tasks serve as host for FORTRAN simulation modules. The executives principal duty is to schedule the modules loaded into it. Additional executive duties consist of error interception and reporting, and interfaces to support the loader and debugger programs. The S3 executive program has two forms. The interactive executive (IEXEC)is designed for independent or off-line testing of modules at background priority levels. The real-time executive (RTEXEC) is designed for real-time execution as part of a full training simulator load. The two forms of the executive provide largely identical interfaces for module execution and for software engineers using the loader and debugger.

Real-time executive tasks (RTEXEC) are activated and controlled by MST and SST programs. RTEXEC executes at foreground priorities and is constrained to operate in real time by MST. Shared global common memory is used for communication throughout the real-time system.

The interactive executive (IEXEC) provides a background module testing environment highly equivalent to the real-time module execution environment. The interactive executive is activated by the loader and controlled through the interactive symbolic debugger. The IEXEC does not share memory with other tasks and executes at time sharing priorities. Clock and status processing activities of the MST are simulated locally by the IEXEC and controlled from the debugger. Using the IEXEC, multiple engineers may execute software tests without interfering with each other nor with real-time usage of the simulator.

LINKING LOADER

The Linking Loader (LLD) is used to load simulation programs into the executive tasks. The loader provides very simple commands for the user to specify the executive load and scheduling. LLD is integrated with the software database system to locate the appropriate object codes to load and to verify that the objects being loaded are consistent with the current state of the database. LLD uses the module type identifications unique to S3 to produce a load which highlights the module hierarchy.

INTERACTIVE SYMBOLIC DEBUG

The Interactive Symbolic Debugger (ISD) provides services for simulation software engineers to control, monitor, and debug modules executing in the real-time environment. ISD executes as an independent task from that being debugged and provides a variety of monitor and patch capabilities. ISD communicates with the executive entirely through operating system message services and provides essentially identical interaction with interactive and real time executives. ISD accesses the S3 software database to extract load map information from LLD, and various forms of data definition information. In addition to monitor and patch functions the ISD provides control of simulation status, module scheduling, time modes, and snapshot/reset functions normally performed from the simulator instructor station. Extended features of ISD include two forms of breakpoints, capabilities of monitoring and patching any task executing in the MPX environment, trend data collection, and dynamic data modification.

CONCLUSION

This paper has presented a summary of the scope and organization of the S3 Simulation Software Support System. The software used on power plant training simulators is expected to require maintenance and modification throughout the life of the simulator to reflect reference plant changes and demands for increased simulation realism. The primary value of the S3 system is to provide the organization and software configuration management to make this continuing task as simple and trouble free as possible. It is believed that the sizable initial design and implementation effort combined with long term control and enhancement has produced a system which well serves the diverse software support needs of real time simulation.

The S3 system will continue to provide an integrated software environment for development and enhancement of nuclear power plant training simulators. The system will continue to receive enhancement to serve the convenience of the engineers utilizing it and the training features of the simulators on which it is used. Two major directions expected for future development of the S3 system are to produce a more portable system and to simplify integration of the S3 system onto simulators initially developed without it.

Simulators VI

ISBN 0-911801-51-0

Simulation of pump locked rotor resistance in a model B&W reactor

M. Massoud
Dept. of Chemical & Nuclear Engineering
University of Maryland
College Park, MD 20742

ABSTRACT

An analysis is performed to determine the flow resistance parameter of the UMCP (University of Maryland at College Park) model reactor operating in the natural circulation mode. The analysis includes both the absence and the presence of the B&W prototype primary pump with locked rotor. The intention of this analysis is to determine the amount of additional resistance required to satisfy the scaling criteria under steady-state, single-phase, and symmetric operational condition. This analysis indicates that a thin-plate orifice, 2 inches in diameter installed in each one of the four cold legs matches the resistance of the prototype locked-rotor pump, at the design flow rate.

INTRODUCTION

The UMCP 2x4 loop is a test facility designed to investigate the thermal hydraulic behavior of the TMI type Babcock & Wilcox (B&W) nuclear plants (Hsu 1987). One of the major objectives of the UMCP testing is to provide data for computer code assessment. Major components of the facility include the vessel, two steam generators, and one pressurizer. The vessel is consisted of the core utilizing electrically heated rods, downcomer, lower plenum, upper plenum, and the upper head. Hot fluid enters the steam generators through two candy-cane type hot legs. It, then returns to the vessel through four cold legs. Heat is transferred to the secondary-side and eventually dumped in the cooling tower.

Prior to the installation of the primary pumps, a series of testes were conducted to evaluate natural circulation under single-phase and two-phase flow conditions. In these tests, the resistance introduced to the flow by the locked rotor of the prototype primary pump had to be accounted for. Therefore, the flow resistance in the prototype was scaled down and built into the system as explained in this report.

FORMULATION

The similarity between the model and the prototype for pressure drop is derived from the integral momentum equation

$$\oint \frac{\partial}{\partial t}\left(\frac{\dot m}{A}\right) ds = \oint \frac{1}{A}\frac{\partial}{\partial s}\left(\frac{\dot m^2}{\rho A}\right) ds - \oint f \frac{\dot m\,|\dot m|}{2\rho g_c D A} ds - \oint K^* \frac{\dot m^2}{2\rho g_c A^2} + \oint \rho g \underline{e}_s \cdot \underline{e}_z ds + \Delta p_{pump} \qquad (1)$$

Equation (1) can be simplified to get (Massoud 1987)

$$\Sigma\left(\frac{L}{A}\right)\frac{d\dot m_{HL}}{dt} + \Sigma\left(\frac{L}{A}\right)\frac{d\dot m_V}{dt} = -\frac{1}{2} R \frac{\dot m_{HL}^2}{\rho g_c} + \beta\rho_o \frac{g}{g_c} l_{th}\,\Delta T \qquad (2)$$

Equation (2) can be further simplified for steady-state conditions as

$$\frac{1}{2g_c} R\, Q_{HL}^2 = \beta\rho_o \frac{g}{g_c} l_{th}\,\Delta T \qquad (3)$$

where R, the flow resistance parameter in Equation (3) is given by

$$R = R_{HL} + \frac{R_{SG}}{N_{SG}^2} + \frac{R_{CL}}{N_{CL}^2} + R_V N^2 \qquad (4)$$

Individual flow resistance parameters in Equation (4) are related to skin friction and form losses by:

$$R = \sum_i \left[f \frac{L}{D}\frac{1}{A^2} + \frac{K^*}{A^2}\right]_i \qquad (5)$$

Core temperature ΔT, in Equation 3 can be replaced by the core power due to the steady-state energy balance. The resulting equation may be applied to the model and prototype, the ratio of which becomes

$$\frac{R_M}{R_P} = \frac{\beta_M}{\beta_P}\,\frac{\rho_P}{\rho_M}\,\frac{(c_p)_P}{(c_p)_M}\,\frac{(l_{Th})_M}{(l_{Th})_P}\,\frac{P_M}{P_P}\left(\frac{(Q_{HL})_P}{(Q_{HL})_M}\right)^3 \qquad (6)$$

In order to determine R_M in terms of flow resistance of the prototype, the values on the right-hand side of Equation (6) are evaluated at the design condition. The most notable of these values are the system thermal length and the flow resistance parameters which are approximated as follows.

Thermal length is approximated by (Massoud 1987)

$$l_{Th} = \left(\frac{L_{SG} - L_C}{2} - Z_{SG}\right)$$

where L_{SG}, L_C, and Z_{SG} are the steam generator tube length, core height, and the elevation difference between the steam generator lower tube sheet and the core inlet, respectively.

Flow resistance parameters of individual components, calculated at design flow rate (6825 lbm/hr for model and 2.695×10^{-6} lbm/hr for prototypes, respectively) per Equation (5), are presented in Table 1.

Equation (6) can now be used to determine the ratio of the flow resistance parameter by providing ratios of; water physical properties, thermal length, decay power, and volumetric flow rate at design condition. Power ratio is determined by using the decay curve at 3.5% of the nomial power for prototype and 200 kW for model. The flow ratio is obtained by noting that the model is volume scaled by 1/500 with the time scale being equal to unity. Therefore, Equation (6) yields

Table 1

Flow Resistance Parameters (ft^{-4})

Component	Model	Prototype
V	215	0.015
HL	346	0.012
SG(tube side)	369	0.074
CL	872	0.057
P	*	0.465**

* to be calculated
** Larson 1987

$$\frac{R_M}{R_P} = \frac{0.797\text{x}10^{-3}}{2.36\text{x}10^{-3}} \times \frac{42.37}{53.65} \times \frac{1.51}{1.08} \times \frac{2.8}{19} \times \frac{0.2}{93.4} \times \frac{1}{500}$$

or

$$\frac{R_M}{R_P} = 14617$$

The prototype flow resistance parameter is calculated as 0.2784 ft^{-4}, therefore, that of the model becomes 4069 ft^{-4}. Since the model flow resistance parameter per Equation (4), not including the pump, is 1793 ft^{-4} therefore the additional resistance to be introduced becomes 2276 ft^{-4}. This amounts to a pressure drop of 0.592 lbf/ft^2 which should be introduced to each cold leg. This pressure drop is provided by a thin plate orifice whose diameter is determined from Figure 1 (Fox 1978) and (Bean 1971) in which K* is given as

$$K^* = \frac{h_l}{V_t^2/2g}$$

which can alternatively be written as

$$K^* = \left(\frac{2g(\Delta p/\rho)}{(Q/A_{CL})^2}\right)\lambda^4 \qquad (7)$$

where λ is the ratio of the orifice to the cold leg diameter.

Substituting values for parameters inside the bracket in Equation (7) and plotting the result on Figure 1, the answer is found by locating the intersection with the plot of thin plate orifice.

This procedure for the desired Δp of 0.592 lbf/ft^2 leads to λ = 0.686 resulting in an orifice diameter of 2 inches. Experimental data (Figure 2) support the calculated quantity.

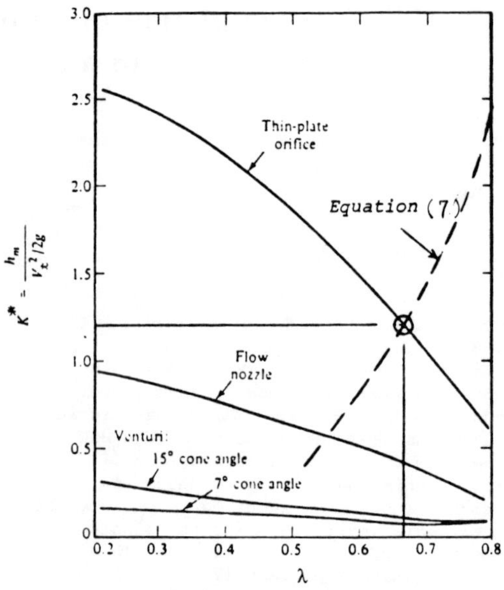

Figure 1 Nonrecoverable Head Loss In Bernoulli Obstruction Meters

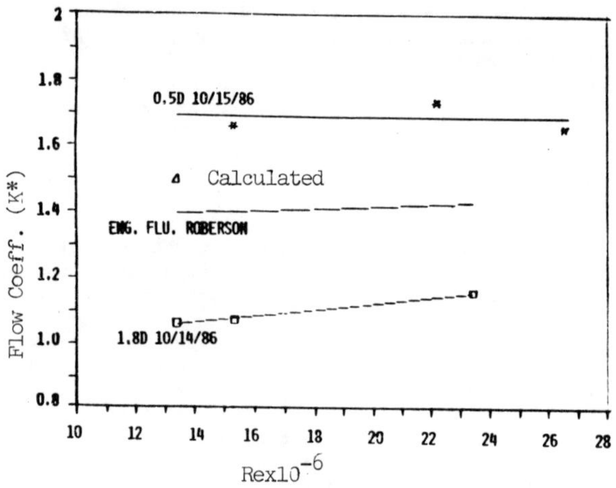

Figure 2: Flow Coeff. (K*) V.S. Renolds No. For One Cold Leg Orifice

SUMMARY

An integral momentum balance was applied to the thermosyphon loop in order to determine the required nonrecoveralbe head loss to be introduced to the flow by utilizing a thin plate orifice. The non-recoverable head loss simulates flow resistance of the prototype locked pump rotor. The calculated result is in good argument with test data.

REFERENCES

Bean, H.S. (ed.) 1971. "Fluid Meters; Their Theory And Application." 6th Ed., ASME, New York

Fox and Mcdonald. 1978. "Introduction to Fluid Mechanics." 2nd Ed., J. Wiley

Hsu, Y.Y., Massoud, M., et al. 1987. "University of Maryland at College Park (UMCP) 2x4 Loop Test Facility." NUREG/CR-4843, Vol. 1 (Mar.)

Larson, T.K. 1987. "An Investigation of Integral Facility Scaling and Data Relation Methods." NUREG/CR-4531 (Feb.)

Massoud, M. 1987. "An Analytical And Experimental Investigation of Natural Circulation Transients In A Model Pressurized Water Reactors." NUREG/CR-4788

NOMENCLATURE

A:	flow area, ft^2
C_p:	specific heat, Btu/lbm-°F
D:	diameter, ft
e:	unit vector
f:	friction factor
g:	gravitational acceleration, ft/sec^2
K*:	form loss factor
l_{th}:	thermal length, ft
L:	component length alongside the flow, ft
$\dot{m}$:	mass flow rate, lbm/sec
N:	number of active loops in the thermosyphon system
p:	pressure, lbf/ft^2
P:	power, MW
Q:	volumetric flow rate, ft^3/sec
R:	flow resistance parameter, ft^{-4}
s:	element of length, ft
t:	time, sec
T:	temperature, °F
V:	velocity, ft/sec
Z:	elevation, ft

Greek

∂:	differential operator
Δ:	difference
Σ:	summation
ρ:	density, lbm/ft^3
β:	volumetric expansion coefficient, $°R^{-1}$
λ:	ratio of orifice to cold leg diameter

Subscript

C:	core
CL:	cold leg
HL:	hot leg
l:	minor or form loss
M:	model
P:	prototype
P:	Pump
SG:	steam generator
t:	throat
V:	vessel
o:	reference

Simulators VI

ISBN 0-911801-51-0

Future uses for simulators in human factors research

Christpoher Plott
Micro Analysis and Design
Boulder, Colorado

ABSTRACT

Human factors criteria and measures of human performance typically applied to the nuclear industry are often difficult to assess and evaluate. Largely, they are the result of work conducted in the laboratory or in other industries that is being generalized to nuclear applications. In order to make these criteria and measures more relevant and useful, it is necessary to reevaluate their utility in nuclear power plant operational settings. The nuclear power plant simulator is a valuable tool for performing this evaluation. This paper discusses the potential application of simulators for achieving this purpose and outlines some of the potential benefits.

THE PROBLEM OF HUMAN FACTORS CRITERIA AND MEASURES

The recent National Research Council report "Human Factors Research and Nuclear Safety" (Moray, 1988) strongly advocates the need for better measures and models of human performance within the nuclear industry. This is particularly true in the areas of training, licensing, human reliability, and causal models of human error. The purpose of this paper is to discuss the role of nuclear power plant simulators in supporting these efforts. Some of the benefits to industry that will result from human factors research using the simulators will also be discussed.

The experience of many nuclear power professionals in dealing with human factors issues has been, to say the least, less than satisfying. Most people agree that having a work environment and work methods which enable people to do their jobs safely, effectively, and efficiently is, without question, very desirable. Unfortunately, when people begin to review and apply human factors principles, measures, and criteria, they make some discoveries which they find disturbing. Included among these discoveries are that many of the principles and criteria are:

1. simple common sense (e.g., remove tripping hazards);

2. not applicable in the current context (e.g., trackball criteria);

3. measured using units or methods which are not applicable or practical in the operational setting (e.g., defining colors in terms of their spectral frequency);

4. placing what seem to be unreasonable limits on the tasks, systems, or environment under consideration (e.g., the fifth percentile female should be accommodated).

The concern over these discoveries is well justified. If the criteria or methods are inappropriate or are applied incorrectly they may result, at best in the unnecessary expenditure of resources, and at worst in degrading system performance. Both of these outcomes are the very opposite of the intended purpose of the criteria and methods.

There are some problems in using many of the existing criteria and measures, human factors "cookbooks," and in extrapolating from existing data because it is "common sense." This information was generally developed for other industries and often in the laboratory rather than real world settings. Little or no consideration was given to the special concerns and problems of nuclear power technology and operations. The result is that such "boiler plate" criteria and measures may not be entirely applicable to the nuclear industry.

In the laboratory, controlled experiments are run in contrived environments to develop criteria. Experimenters observe changes in human performance that are said to be due to systematic changes of environmental, task, or system variables. The results of these experiments allow the investigators to develop predictions or descriptions of human performance. These results can also define the range of values for these experimental variables which may include the point at which human performance is optimal and the points at which it begins to degrade. Criteria are then based on these optimal and minimally acceptable points. These criteria are limited however, in that they are truly applicable only under the experimental conditions in which they were developed.

To overcome the limitations of laboratory developed criteria and measures many industries have moved the experiments into operational or near operational settings. This type of activity can be seen in the aerospace industry. New human interface design characteristics and performance measures are progressively applied to the different levels of operational systems (e.g., static mock-ups, functional mock-ups, simulators, flight tests). It can also be seen in the computer industry with the application of techniques such as rapid prototyping. In both cases, the final test of the utility of a design or measure is performed on an operational or near operational system when the actual system is not suitable or available. In this way they replicate the conditions in which the criteria or measure will be applied and avoid the problems of generalizability from laboratory data. However, system specificity is then the basic limitation of these criteria and measures.

While many of the criteria and measures developed in the laboratory and in other industries can be generalized to the nuclear industry with some caution, there are also many which cannot. As discussed above, the experimental conditions or the specific nature of the tasks for which the criteria and measures were developed create limitations are what cause problems with their application to the nuclear industry. In order to develop valid measures and criteria for the nuclear industry it is essential to test those which cannot be generalized on the same or similar operational system to which they will apply.

THE ROLE OF SIMULATORS

For the nuclear industry, the full-scope plant referenced simulator provides the nearest form of operational reality available for many operating scenarios. Conducting human performance research on an actual plant is both unsafe and uneconomical. The simulator provides a realistic operational environment which is safe and economical. It also provides a controlled environment in which systematic, replicable research can be done. These characteristics make the simulator a critical tool for the development of valid human factors criteria and measures for nuclear power plant control room operations.

Significant human factors research has recently been conducted using nuclear power plant simulators. For example, Horst et al (1988) recently completed a study investigating the effect of control room lighting levels on operator performance. They used a simulator to run controlled operational tests at systematically manipulated lighting levels. Their results clearly showed that lighting levels had little effect on operator performance until levels fell below 10 foot candles. The implication of this research is that the current control room lighting requirements of 40 - 100 foot candles may not be necessary for operators to perform their functions.

In another application, Worledge (1988) has recently reported on the interim results of operator reliability studies using simulators. While it is not yet possible to draw definite conclusions from these studies, it is expected that they will provide new insight into the nature of operator reliability and into the validity of reliability measures now in use. Improved human reliability data will, in turn, improve the reliability and risk assessment analyses for overall plant performance.

THE BENEFITS TO INDUSTRY

Before discussing the benefits to industry for supporting human factors research using simulators, it needs to be acknowledged that industry cooperation will be essential if these research efforts are to become a reality. Industry owns and operates almost all of the plant referenced simulators in the country. The argument can be made that the industry purchased and built these simulators to support their training programs and not human factors research. However, the benefits should be considered before supporting such a position.

The discussion of the benefits has been divided into specific and general benefits. Specific benefits are those which directly affect plant operations. General benefits are those which do not such as public image or political benefits. Each of the benefits are discussed briefly below.

Specific Benefits

Control Room and System Design and Redesign. Objective measures which relate design characteristics to improved operator performance would provide support for sound, justifiable decision making by the utilities. Such measures allow those responsible for design decisions to support their arguments with scientifically based engineering requirements. These arguments can be used effectively in presentations to both upper management and the regulators.

Operator Training and Testing. Objective measures of operator performance are critical for ensuring that the desired training has occurred. While simulators are already an integral part of most training programs, further research aimed at defining valid, reliable measures of operator performance would increase their utility. These measures could also be used in the performance of transfer of training studies to help determine the amount and nature of simulator fidelity required to train various skills. For example, the measures could be applied in determining what kinds and how much training are appropriate for part-task or limited scope simulators with the full-scope plant referenced simulator being used as a baseline. The incorporation of systematic data collection on these operator performance measures within the training program could eventually lead to their incorporation into the operator examination program. In recent years the NRC has endeavored to make exams more closely tied to industry initiated efforts in this area.

Procedure Technology and Content Evaluation. Over the last several years simulators have been used to validate the symptom based procedures which were developed as part of the response to the TMI accident. In the future, simulators will continue to play an important role in procedure validation as new technologies and formats for presenting procedural information are introduced. The technology for computer-based interactive procedures is currently available and provides a potentially powerful medium for procedure presentation. Along with this is the introduction of alternative formats for this presentation. Features such as flow charts, high resolution graphics, automated checklists, and operator queries may all be used to enhance the procedures. They may also be misused and create problems for the operator. The simulator provides the ideal test bed for the evaluation of the technologies and presentations.

General Benefits

Industry Access and Use of Data. Industry's participation ensures the availability of good human performance data which could prove to be invaluable in addressing emerging technical and safety issues, regulatory initiatives, or generic concerns.

Public Image. By supporting this kind of research, industry would be able to point to an area which would not have been possible without their support. In terms of public image, examples of helping to enhance the public safety and health can be very valuable. Supporting research into improving the performance of the human component of the system could go a long way in this regard.

CONCLUSION

The nuclear power plant simulator can be a valuable tool for conducting future human factors research. There are many ways, both technical and non-technical, in which the industry could benefit from providing this support. Among them are safer operation, improved training, improved procedures, more enlightened and less adversarial regulation, and enhanced public image. It is strongly encouraged that industry consider both supporting and initiating the use of simulators for human factors research in nuclear power operations.

REFERENCES

Horst, R.L., Kershner, R.L., Silverman, E.B., Mahaffey, D.L., Parris, H.L. (1988). "Research Study on the Effects of Illumination on the Performance of Control Room Tasks" Proceedings of the IEEE Fourth Conference on Human Factors and Power Plants, Monterey, CA.

Moray, N. P., Ed. (1988). Human Factors Research and Nuclear Safety. National Academy Press: Washington, D.C.

Worledge, D. (1988). "Interim Results and Conclusions from EPRI Experimental Operator Reliability Program" Proceedings of the IEEE Fourth Conference on Human Factors and Power Plants, Monterey, CA.

Simulators VI
© 1989 By The Society for Computer
Simulation International
ISBN 0-911801-51-0

Training benefits of research on operator reliability

D. H. Worledge
Electric Power Research Institute
Nuclear Power Division
3412 Hillview Avenue
Palo Alto, CA 94304

and

V. Joksimovich, A.J. Spurgin
Accident Prevention Group, Inc.
11545 West Bernardo Court, Ste. 100
San Diego, CA 92127

ABSTRACT

The purpose of the EPRI Operator Reliability Experiments (ORE) Program is to collect data for use in reliability and safety studies of nuclear power plant operation which more realistically take credit for operator performance in preventing core damage. The three objectives in fulfilling this purpose are: (1) to obtain quantitative/qualitative performance data on operating crew responses in the control room for potential accident sequences by using plant simulators; (2) to test the Human Cognitive Reliability (HCR) correlation; and (3) to develop a data collection analysis procedure. This paper briefly discusses the background to this program, data collection and analysis, and the results of quantitative/qualitative insights stemming from initial work. Special attention is paid to how this program impacts upon simulator use and assessment of simulator fidelity. Attention is also paid to the use of data collection procedures to assist training departments in assessing the quality of their training programs.

BACKGROUND AND INTRODUCTION

The comprehensive treatment of human interactions is deemed to be a key to the adequate understanding of various accident sequences and their relative importance in public safety considerations. There is an abundance of evidence to support the notion that humans play a dominant role in both causing and terminating accidents at various industrial facilities. Such evidence comes in the form of actuarial data (e.g, Chernobyl, TMI 2, numerous precursors) or results from various generic and plant-specific probabilistic risk assessment (PRA) studies.

In view of the importance of human interactions, EPRI has sponsored a series of research projects over the past six years to increase understanding and improve techniques for analyzing them. Although the principal aim of this research was to support PRA, the results and insights derived from it have proved to have applications in operator training, emergency operating procedures development, human factors considerations and expanded roles for simulators. This paper discusses how the use of complex quantitative evaluations of crew responses can be applied to operator training and simulator operations. In addition, the paper describes the scope and results of initial work in the form of time-reliability curves of crew responses to key human interactions.

ORE PROGRAM

The program's initial work is mainly concerned with the testing of the human cognitive reliability (HCR) correlation (Spurgin, et al., 1984). The HCR correlation is intended to represent the behavior of crews performing tasks in nuclear power plant control-rooms. The HCR correlation is a form of time-reliability curve which quantifies the probability of non-response of a control room crew within a specified time. Key features of the HCR correlation are reflected in the several hypotheses listed in Table 1. The testing of the HCR correlation entails carrying out experiments using large plant simulators, developing data collection and analysis methodology and examining the analyses to see if the basic HCR hypotheses are confirmed and to suggest modifications to HCR if necessary. The status of HCR hypotheses testing is seen in Table 1. Additional program work comprises refining of the HCR and applications of the refined correlation.

Table 1

STATUS OF HCR HYPOTHESIS TESTING

Hypothesis	Status
1. Time Dependence	Valid
2. Single Parameter Does Normalization	Valid
3. Median Performs Well	Valid
4. Discrete Correlation Groups Appear	Valid ?
5. S, R, K Characterize Groups	?
6. Weibull and/or Lognormal	Valid
7. PSFs impact quantifiable	Invalid Thus Far

+Median of measured response times for all crews at each plant.

*Standard deviation of normalized response times for each plant where normalized times equal actual times divided by the median response.

Simulator Facilities Used For ORE

Modern control room training simulators provide a considerable potential for making measurement of operator performance to improve understanding of the basic models and to provide support for human reliability estimates. This was fully recognized during development of the HCR model; the use of simulators for validation purposes became an obvious choice. Furthermore, experiments on simulators can take advantage of requalification training sessions with only minor perturbations to the utility. Currently, six U.S. utilities are participating in the program: Commonwealth Edison (La Salle), Pacific Gas and Electric (Diablo Canyon), Wisconsin Public Service (Kewaunee), Philadelphia Electric (Limerick), Pennsylvania Power & Light (Susquehanna), and Duke Power (Oconee). Electricite de France (EDF) (Bugey and Paluel) and EPRI are collaborating closely in their respective programs of operator experiments including the design of the experimental method, statistical analysis of data and interepretation of qualitative observations.

It should be pointed out that EDF has pioneered the use of simulator experiments for emergency procedure and safety panel validation. A large number of experiments has been conducted since 1983 employing simulators at the three training centers: Bugey, Paluel and Caen. This background of experience provided a stepping stone for the EPRI project. The collaborative agreement provides cross-fertilization between the two programs. The two programs, if fully combined, would constitute the largest source of human reliability simulator data in the world, from which numerous nuclear safety insights could be derived.

The U.S. participants typically: a) make the full-scale plant simulators, with the associated equipment together with the operating crews, available for the conduct of experiments (typically in conjunction with scheduled requalifications sessions); b) have close involvement in defining accident scenarios; c) perform programming of scenarios and assist in the conduct of experiments; d) share the information and insights being generated; and e) provide guidance via a steering group. This process often involved the collaboration of utility PRA groups and training staff.

ORE Status

The status of EPRI ORE data collection is summarized in Table 2. Two or more scenarios were observed at each simulator with several crews being exposed to the same (or essentially the same) scenarios. Each scenario spans several pre-defined "key" human interactions for which timing data is collected and analyzed. Preliminary data are reviewed (qualified) to assure that each HI measurement is representative of the population of licensed control room operators and is unaffected by simulator problems or trainer interference. To date, over 1,000 qualified data points have been collected.

Data collected during simulator retraining sessions with control room-crews is performed by observer teams collecting response times of crews augmented by simulator records, such as data loggers, and video recordings. In addition to time data, post-transient interviews are also carried out to help define insights into operator decisions, such as which plant variables or alarms are used by the crews in given circumstances. This latter information is used along with information on operator experience and education to determine the influence of various performance shaping factors (PSFs).

Table 2

STATUS OF SIMULATOR DATA COLLECTION

Simulator	# of Scenarios	# of Crews	# of HIs	Total # of Qualified Data Points
PWR 1	3	10	10	95
BWR 1	2	18	10	137
BWR 2	7	3-6*	13	125
PWR 2	7	6	30	167
PWR 3	8	5-7*	12	130
BWR 3 II	6	9	15	125
PWR 1 II	6	16	16	250

* Scenario Dependent Total = 1029

Statistical measures are used to characterize crew responses to key interactions. Principal measures are a central point estimate (mean or median response time), and an estimate of spread or variability (variance or standard deviation). Voluminous raw response time data are reduced to a small set of statistical measures and subjected to preliminary evaluation for consistency and trend. The data was further organized and analyzed to test the HCR correlation. The seven hypotheses listed in Table 1 were examined using various analysis techniques. Later, data was aggregated in several ways to develop interim positions on the HCR correlation.

RESULTS

Results are reported for the ORE program to date. Project work is continuing, with additional and updated results forthcoming in the near term.

Hypotheses

For the HCR correlation to be valid, the seven hypotheses have to be confirmed. Table 1 shows the current state of investigation for each hypothesis. The majority of the key hypotheses are confirmed. Hypotheses 1, 2, 3, and 6 are clearly confirmed. Hypothesis 4 can be viewed as partially confirmed.

The crew responses are clearly time dependant (Hypothesis 1) and are shown to fit either Weibull or lognormal distributions (Hypothesis 6). Hypotheses 2 and 3 relate to normalization by dividing actual response times of the crews by the median value (T 1/2) of response times for all crews. This produces a set of dimensionless response times. This process can be illustrated by showing that very similar human interactions with different actual times can yield close standard deviations after normalization. Table 3 shows two examples from the results. The corresponding curves for the

PWR results are shown in Figure 1. These results indicate that underlying cognitive behavior for these HIs is similar (i.e, the shape of the curves are very close) and despite the existing plant-specific differences among the PWRs, the response curves moved closer together once normalized.

Hypotheses 4 is partially verified because data do suggest the presence of groups, but they overlap considerably. It has been found that the preliminary interpretation of skill(s), rule (R) and knowledge (K) based attributes for the human interactions involved (hypothesis 5) do not map the interactions unambiguously into one of the observed interaction groups. Further work is underway to find good labels for these interaction groups. Testing of hypothesis 6 is not complete and is continuing.

Table 3

COMPARISON OF RESPONSE TIME PARAMETERS FOR SIMILAR HUMAN INTERACTIONS FOR DIFFERENT PLANTS

HI	Plant	Median Response+ (Seconds)	Normalize Sigma Value*
BWR			
ATWS:	A	79	0.71
Suppress. Pool	B	145	0.74
Cooling Initiation	C	138	0.85
PWR			
MSLB/SGTR:	A	323	0.24
SG Isolation	B	766.5	0.30

+ Median of measured response times for all crews at each plant.

* Standard deviation of normalized response times for each plant, where normalized times equal actual times divided by the median response.

QUALITATIVE OBSERVATIONS

In the course of participating in the experiments, the observer teams made qualitative observations relative to the responses of the crews. Records taken during the experiments provide not only information for use in the program, but also provide a useful data base for trainers, operators, procedure developers and human factors personnel. Observations below are grouped into five categories: Simulator Limitations, Training, Human Factors, Procedures, and Crew Structure and Communications.

Actual Time Lognormal

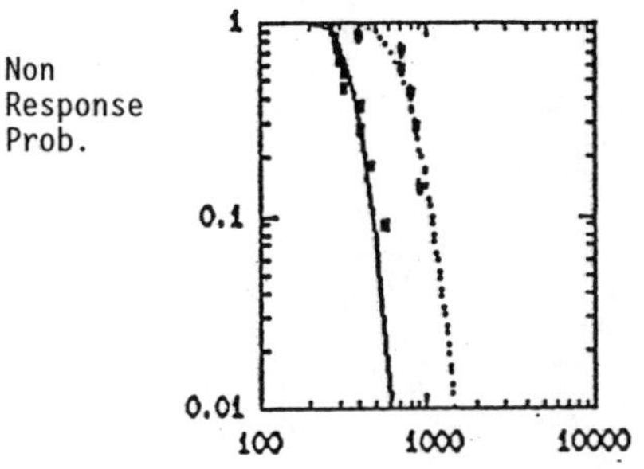

Normalized Time Lognormal

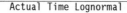

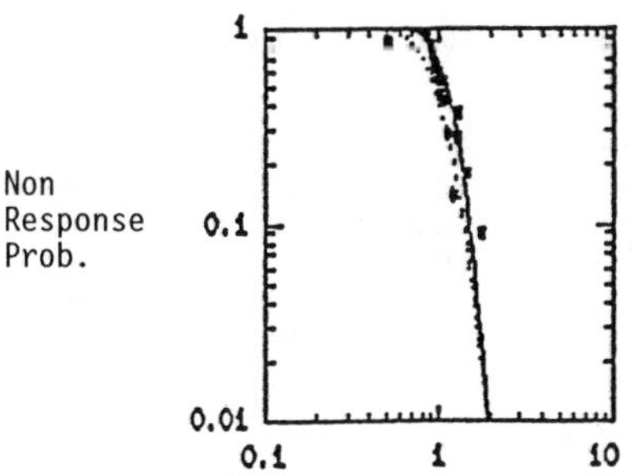

Figure 1. Time Reliability Curves of Non-Normalized and Normalized Data For Isolation of Faulty Steam Generator in a SGTR for Two PWRs.

Simulator Limitations

A simulator's capacity to accurately model actual plant conditions is crucial to the collection of comprehensive and reliable data. While testing the scenarios it was observed that some simulators could not model all scenario variables. In addition, as the model of the plant is upgraded, older digital computers may be incapable of modeling the plant correctly.

Areas which need attention in PWRs are mainly associated with thermal-hydraulic modeling. These cover modeling of void formation, hot leg behavior from "bubbly" flow to high void, and reflux cooling in the steam generator. Some steam generator models seem to be in need of improvement. One area that seemed to be particularly deficient in the minds of the crews was the modelling of auxiliary operators by the trainers. There did not appear to be consistent criteria applied to the time taken by the auxiliary operators in performing tasks. Also, there were no criteria for when they could be expected to be successful. EPRI expects to examine the potential for including actions of auxiliary operators and maintenance technicians outside the main control room in the same quantitative framework as the HCR model in the near future.

Training Aspects

Use of Scenarios. The scenarios used in the operator experiments have been designed so as to pose varying levels of complexity to the crews. At some simulators the experiments were the first PRA-oriented scenarios experienced by the crews. These crews were unused to dealing with the more complex scenarios. However, the training staff noted that the crews became very comfortable with complex scenarios over the course of the experimental program. On the whole, crews were generally favorable toward the challenges afforded by such scenarios.

Training Program Evaluation. By and large, training staffs evaluate the crews on qualitative performance measures such as application of correct procedures and intra-crew and extra-plant communications. It is believed that routine timing of crews on key human interactions in simulator scenarios along with commentary to characterize the crew response with respect to use of procedures, slip/errors made and recovered, and other factors could provide a means under utility control to evaluate training effectiveness. Crew response times for human interactions could be used as one indication of training effectiveness for time-critical tasks. Reduction in median response time could be used as an indication of crew improvement and training effectiveness. Such records and trending of the crew's performance would enable objective evaluations to be made of all of the crews' performance. The training group could then evaluate how to improve the training program or suggest what improvements should be made to the procedures or control-room displays.

Human Factors

Control room design reviews and task analysis programs have, or seem to have, obviated most human factors deficiencies. During the EPRI experiments, however, observers noted several items that seemed to affect the crew response time and accuracy. This suggests utilities should encourage training and operating staffs to use simulator training as another means to identify potential problems. Typical human factor items identified by observers were: a) Instrument Location; b) Instrument/Panel Design; c) Control Handle Location and Labelling; d) Display Characteristics and Design; e) Alarms/-Annunciator Design; and f) SPDS Validity and Reliability.

Crew Structure and Communications

Organization. Training practices of augmenting crews and/or random personnel absences resulted in variability in crew structure during the respective experimental series, although the latter is viewed as representative of actual plant practice. Essentially constant across the plants is the use of at least two licensed reactor operators (RO) who manipulate controls; one PWR uses three RO's. Also constant is the assigned responsibility of one licensed Senior Reactor Operator (SRO) to be in charge of executing Emergency Operating Procedures. Beyond these two areas of responsibility, crew size and organization varies significantly from plant to plant. The quality of the response seemed mainly to depend on the quality of the procedure reader (SRO) and his ability to see where the plant was headed and what the procedures said. It is not clear what crew size and organization is optimal from these experiments.

Communications . During training at all simulators, intra-crew communications are emphasized and evaluated as part of the requalification exercises. What is observed, however, is that crews often do not communicate in the desired fashion during the first time back on the simulator; after being reminded in trainer critiques, most crews attempt to follow the desired style even while noting that to do so is "acting" for them. Those who express some resistance note that they know their crew members well and are able to communicate well in their "normal" mode.

The human factors form used during scenario observations asks to characterize the crew leadership style on a five-point scale ranging from "authoritarian" to "democratic". Qualitatively, it appears that the most efficient crews, in terms of response times, tend to be more "authoritarian" so long as the true leader understands the plant state and does not force the crew to make poor decisions. Most crews, however, are characterized as "participative" in which the ultimate decision maker is clearly understood but crew members feel free to challenge the SRO as a way of checking the diagnosis.

Procedures

The emergency operating procedures (EOPs) provide the backbone of crew responses to accident scenarios. The current vintage of both BWR and PWR EOPs are considered to be "symptom based" so that crews may react as dictated by the EOPs to various symptoms indicated by displays and instrumentation. (It is noted, however, that the PWR procedures tend to be a hybrid of symptom-and-event based.) In general these procedures, which help diagnose and make decisions, are intended to evoke "pure" rule-based cognitive behavior on the part of the crews. The results tend to confirm that responses in general are biased to rule-based and show that the procedures are accomplishing their desired objective.

The observer records quite clearly show where the crews have difficulties with the procedures and how many of the crews suffer from these problems. Training staff and the procedure developers can help resolve these problems.

QUANTITATIVE OBSERVATIONS

Aggregated Curves

Data aggregation in the ORE program means that operator response times for individual HIs among various scenarios, various plants or types of plants are combined (pooled) in various ways. Data aggregation is performed to enhance the statistical database, and provide bases for comparison of results at different levels of aggregation for between-plant comparisons of BWRs to all PWRs results.

Figure 2, for example, shows the respective aggregate curves for all-BWR and all-PWR date. It also shows the aggregate of these two as the "all-data" curve. The results indicate that aggregated curves correspond roughly to "rule-based" behavior with the PWR curve slightly to the left and the BWR curve slightly to the right of the "all-data" curve.

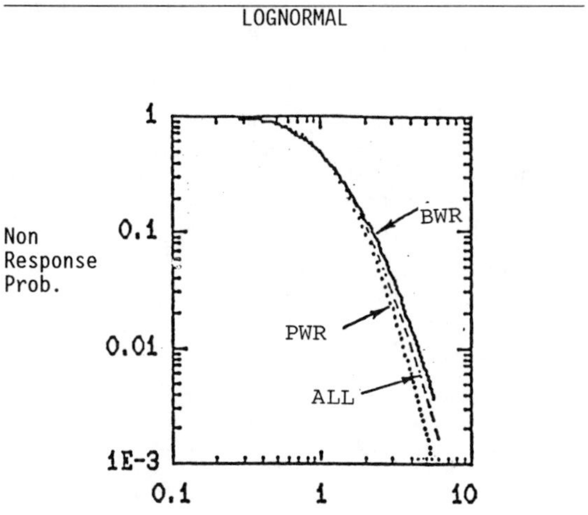

Figure 2. Aggregate Time Reliability Curvews for all PWR and BWR Data.

Analysis

In general, the responses of crews are grouped close to specific ORE curves and large deviations from such a curve may indicate differences in the performances of groups of crews or individual crews. For example, crews may implement different strategies in response to an event and this shows in the shape of the curves. The differences in strategies may be due to differences in cues/indications that crews act upon or the order of tasks that they perform. Often the trainers are only peripherally aware of these different strategies and do not usually know the effects on performance. The operations group may wish to selectively modify how the crews carry out the tasks based on this information, since one strategy may be considered more risky than another.

The average (or median) time spent by crews on various HIs differ significantly. This may be due to differences in plant response to different transients, although there are often marked differences between median response times for similar transients at different but similarly designed plants. The latter may be due to familiarity with the actions, degree of complexity of specific procedures, etc. The measured crew median response times on various HIs could yield useful perspective to trainers, procedure developers and human factors persons. In general, a small number of operator errors (slips/mistakes) was observed. These will be further examined later in the program. The results suggest that crew experience does not have a significant effect on crew response. This is intuitively puzzling, but could be due to the fact that all the operating crews undergo similar training/requalifications and use the same procedures.

SUMMARY

The combination of a quantitative method for collecting performance data together with a systematic method for recording qualitative data relating to aspects of crew performance (such as communications) can build an information base to help utilities refine training programs and plant operations. It can provide information on how training programs impact on crew performance. It can be used to provide information evaluating how successfully changes in training programs improve crew performance. Simulator fidelity in crew operations can be assessed using the data base to compare obtained results to expected results. The data can also provide information on which parts of plant procedures cause difficulties which affect crews, and on difficulties individual crews have with some aspects of plant operations.

We expect the results of these experiments have far reaching effects, not only on risk estimates, but also on how training effectiveness and simulator fidelity is measured and monitored. EPRI's research program is turning to these issues. It appears that the area of operator training can benefit greatly from focused R&D that has the goal of improving the operators ability to respond to accident situations. The qualitative steps that the industry has taken in these technical areas are already yielding quantitatively measurable performance improvements. Increased crew performance improvements are to be expected as this methodology expanded to encompass simulator operations and operator training programs.

REFERENCES

Joksimovich, V. and D. H. Worledge, 1988. "Using Simulator Experiments to Analyze Human Reliability for PRA Studies. " Nuclear Engineering International, (January).

Rogers, K. C., 1988. "Nuclear Plant Simulators from a Regulatory Point of View." Address to Power Simulation Users Conference. (Anapolis, MD, March).

Spurgin, A. J., G. W. Hannaman, Y. Lukic and D. H. Worledge, 1984. "Impact of a Behavior Model of the Control-Room Crew on Plant Transient Analysis," Paper Presented at the International Conference on Power Plant Simulation. (Cuernavaca, Morelos-Mexico, November).

Simulators VI
© 1989 By The Society for Computer
Simulation International
ISBN 0-911801-51-0

Non-training uses of simulators

John M. Fahley and Robert W. Colley
Electric Power Research Institute
Nuclear Power Division
3412 Hillview Avenue
Palo Alto, California 94303

ABSTRACT

The use of simulators for plant operator training is well established, especially in the nuclear power industry. The use of training simulators for non-training purposes is becoming more extensive and is showing that simulators can be useful and cost effective tools in performing a variety of applications and evaluations. This paper discusses historical and evolving uses of training simulators for Research and Development (R&D) projects other than power plant operator training. These alternative R&D uses of simulators include:

- evaluation of engineering design modifications,
- testing and evaluation of control systems,
- development, verification, and modifications of procedures,
- human factors studies,
- human reliability studies,
- testing and evaluation of operator aids.

NON-TRAINING USES OF THE DCPP TRAINING SIMULATOR

Diablo Canyon Power Plant (DCPP) is owned and operated by Pacific Gas and Electric Company (PG&E) of San Francisco, California. DCPP uses a pair of Gould 32/87 real time minicomputers for the operator training simulator. One machine is dedicated to training and used with the full scope control room training facility. The other machine, referred to here as the development machine, is primarily for software maintenance and other activities in support of training.

The development machine has been found to be a vital and necessary component in maintaining and improving the operation and fidelity of the training simulator. The majority of time spend on the development machine is for revising discrepancies found during training exercises and to change the simulation models in order to keep the simulator up to date with plant changes. Upgrades to newer and more advanced simulator models, improvements in the instructor interface, and upgrades in the simulator's operating system have all been facilitated by performing initial evaluation on the development machine before transfer over to the training machine. Other, non-training related uses of the development machine have been supported and are described below. It should be pointed out that the following uses would probably not have been supported if only one simulator computer was available.

Plant Network SPDS Development

A local area network has been implemented at the DCPP. This network connects into several data sources and provides a highway for passing plant data to over a 1000 PC based terminals located around the site. The intersystems computer group at DCPP has been pursuing connecting many of the onsite computer systems into the network so data may be made available in many locations. One data source of interest was the Safety Parameter Display System (SPDS). Before proceeding with this however, the development simulator (which has a functioning SPDS model), was connected onto the network to provide SPDS data in a realistic fashion. This connection assisted the intersystems computer group in developing and testing network communications and PC terminal screens which would later be used on the network when the plant SPDS system was connected. In this instance, the simulator was used as a data source for developing and testing an application that would eventually be implemented on the plant network.

Alarm Processing System

PG&E is working with the Electric Power Research Institute (EPRI) in developing an Alarm Processing System (APS). The thrust of this work is to apply expert system technology onto the plant annunciator located in the control room. The annunicator provides visual and audible signals to alert operators on plant conditions. During plant transients, the control room operator is deluged with numerous alarms from the annunciator, which may consequently result in useful information being overlooked or result in important details being masked. The Alarm Processing System will seek to improve plant operator interaction with the annunciator system by providing programmed reasoning in the presentation of alarms. A prototype APS is being developed for implementation and evaluation on the DCPP training simulator. Evaluation of the system will be performed during operator training exercises. For this case, the simulator is being used to assist in the evaluation of an new operator aid, and more generally, is being used to help evaluate the application of expert system technology for improving plant operations.

Evaluation of the RETRAN Code

PG&E has been developing a RETRAN model specifically for evaluation of the two DCPP units. RETRAN is a large mainframe based computer code for performing evaluation of plant transients and safety analysis. To assist in this development, data from the simulator has been recorded and used to review the modeling selected for use in RETRAN. This review has lead to changes and subsequent improvements in the DCPP specific RETRAN model. This use of the simulator could be categorized as assistance in the development of engineering analysis. Iteratively, the DCPP specific RETRAN model, when completed, will be used to evaluate and qualify the fidelity of the simulator required by the NRC.

Plant Operations Analysis

The simulator has also been used for the evaluation of plant operations. DCPP, in co-operation with Westinghouse, performed an evaluation of possible temperature stratification in the pressurizer surge line. This issue was of concern in relation to possible temperature shock effects on the surge line metal. The DCPP simulator was used to assist in evaluation of temperature and flow conditions in the surge line and was later used to evaluate changes in plant operating procedures for addressing this issue. This use of the simulator was in essence for engineering evaluation of plant conditions, and for evaluating changes to the plant operations procedures in support of the engineering analysis.

OTHER EXAMPLE NON-TRAINING USES OF SIMULATORS IN THE U.S.

Indianapolis Power and Light has purchased a power plant simulator for the Petersburg unit number 4. In addition to training, the simulator has been used for several engineering studies such as to evaluate and modify startup and shutdown procedures for reducing startup and shutdown times. It has also been used to develop a procedure to speed elbow replacement during an outage, and assist engineering personnel with modifications of plant feedwater systems (Piskorowski and Stevens 1988). Separately, TVA, EPRI, and Westinghouse developed and performed evaluation of a new digital feedwater control system for nuclear power plants. A prototype system for evaluating the digital control system and new signal validation algorithms was evaluated using TVA's Sequoyah plant simulator (Cain and Sun 1987).

EXAMPLE NON-TRAINING USES OF SIMULATORS OUTSIDE THE U.S.

Britain's Central Electricity Generating Board (CEGB) developed a pair of simulators in support of a single power plant. One simulator is located on-site, the other is at a training facility. The off-site facility is used for a variety of non-training activities such as plant commissioning (evaluating instrument and control layouts), procedure validation, and testing of ergonomic design changes in the control room. Another proposed non-training use is in the development and evaluation of software for a plant process computer, where a simulator could be used as a testbed for testing new or revised plant computer software. This can lead to reduced development and debugging time before implementing the software in the plant. This type of evaluation is most effective if the plant software can be directly transferred from evaluation on the simulator testbed to implementation on the plant computer (Fry and Gow 1983).

Full scale simulators often include a model for the simulation of the plant computer. This model could be used for evaluation and debugging software for a plant computer or a plant computer replacement. In this instance, the simulator would be a data source for evaluating the software rather than a software testbed.

The Halden project in Norway has developed a full scope simulator specifically for R&D. This facility is used for evaluating training programs, computerized operator support systems, plant design changes, and computerized control systems (Karppinen et al. 1983).

In addition to training, the Loviisa Nuclear Power Station full scope training simulator in Finland is also used extensively for other purposes. The use of the full scope simulator for R&D was motivated by cases where a simulation of the complete process of operating the plant was important. Some of the R&D activities performed at Loviisa include: research on a means to restrict the number of activating alarms in plant transients (similar to the Alarm Processing Project described above); study of plant operational practices to help assist in identifying operator decision making methods and the reasons for operational errors; evaluation of a Critical Function Monitoring System for assisting plant operators; evaluation of emergency procedures; and testing of a new concept unit block controller. Further work in the areas of emergency procedures, alarm reduction and operator decision making were considered (Rintilla and Heimburger 1983).

Ontario Hydro found their plant replica simulators to have advantages beyond the use of training. They have experimented with the use of their training simulators to study station problems, verify proposed design changes, and develop new operating procedures. It was found that simulator tested designs and procedures had significantly fewer installation and commissioning problems than are generally associated with such projects. Evaluations were performed on an uprating of the nuclear units from 890 to 940 megawatts, and improvements to the deaerator level and pressure control systems. Both of these projects successfully used the training simulator to develop and test a control strategy which was subsequently installed at the station, resulting in time and cost reductions. Encouraged by the success in the use of training simulators for concept validation and verification, Ontario Hydro is developing a low cost central facility for use in all aspects of the design process. The facility will incorporate software from the training simulators and a user friendly generic interface which will enable designers to configure and operate it. (Sharway et al. 1988).

Taiwan Power Company, in collaboration with EPRI, has implemented and evaluated an Emergency Operating Procedures (EOP) tracking system on a plant training simulator. This EOP system provides assistance to plant operators in the performance and management of emergency procedures during plant transients. Real time notification of emergency procedure steps, on-line explanations of messages, priority filtering, and checking of data quality are provided. Initial evaluation of the EOP tracking system on the simulator has been completed, with additional evaluation planned in 1989. In this situation, the training simulator has been used to evaluate several items: computer assistance in the performance of emergency procedures; use of expert systems technology in control rooms; and human factors improvements on operator response to plant conditions. (Divakaruni 1987), (Cheng et al. 1989).

CONCLUSION

Training simulators have been found to be a useful tool in performing a variety of tasks outside of their primary purpose of training. This paper has described several examples of the use of training simulators for purposes such as evaluation of new designs, computer based operator aids, control systems, expert system technology and human factors issues. In many cases it was found that use of a training simulator resulted in a cost and time savings. In some cases, the success and cost effectiveness of using simulators for non-training purposes justified the development of a separate engineering simulator. In any event, the number and types of non-training uses of simulators appears to be on the increase and the usefulness of training simulators for additional purposes is becoming well established.

REFERENCES

Cain, D. G., 1987. Emergency Operating Procedures Tracking System. EPRI Research Report NP-5250M. Electric Power Research Institute, Palo Alto, California (June).

Cheng, J.F.; Chiang, R.; Spurgin, A. J.; Cain, D. C.; Sun, B. K.-H. and C. Christiansen, 1989. "Evaluation Of An Emergency Operating Procedure Tracking Expert System By Control Room Operators", Paper to be presented at the EPRI Seminar on Expert System Applications for the Electric Power Industry (Orlando, Florida, June 5-9).

Divakaruni, S. M. and B. K.-H. Sun (1987). Advanced PWR Steam Generator-Feedwater Digital Control System. EPRI Research Report NP-4919-LD. Electric Power Research Institute, Palo Alto, California (April).

Fry, J. P. and R. S. Grow, 1983. "Use of Simulators for Training, Plant Testing, Validating Operating Procedures and In Plant Emergency Situations". Nuclear Power Plant Training Simulators, IAEA/NPPCI Specialists Meeting (Espoo, Finland, September 12-14).

Karppinen, J.; Stokke, E. and E. Rinttila, 1983. "A New Dedicated Simulator for Man-Machine Systems Research", ibid.

Rinttila, E. and H. Heimburger, 1983. "Experiences of Using the Loviisa Training Simulator for Research and Development", ibid.

Sharawy, P. S.; Kennard, J. R. and Q. B. Chou, 1988. "Design and Use of an Engineering Simulator for Power Plant and Training Simulator Updates". Presented at the EPRI Conference on Power Plant Training Simulators and Modeling (Charlotte, North Carolina, June).

Simulators VI
© 1989 By The Society for Computer Simulation International
ISBN 0-911801-51-0

Investigation of the accuracy of simulator fidelity necessary for operator training

Catherine D. Gaddy Mark S. Pellechi
General Physics Corporation
6700 Alexander Bell Drive
Columbia, MD 21046

and

Robert Colley
Electric Power Research Institute
3412 Hillview Avenue
Palo Alto, CA 94303

ABSTRACT

The purpose of this study is to determine the accuracy of simulator fidelity required for nuclear power plant operator training. Operator response data is needed to determine the degree of parameter variability necessary before the operators' mental model of the plant state changes. In order to have fidelity with the simulator environment but also have the required experimental control, the method involves use of small-scale simulation tests followed by qualification of the data in a full-scope simulator. The results will include parameter-specific error tolerances. This information will be used to provide a quantitative basis for the American National Standard that at present provides general, qualitative guidelines. The approach taken in this study may have applicability in other simulation environments in which decisions must be made regarding the functional fidelity of simulation necessary for training.

INTRODUCTION

The purpose of this study is to determine the accuracy of simulator fidelity required for nuclear power plant operator training. The current investigation is focused on requirements for functional fidelity of the simulator, as opposed to physical fidelity; and on steady-state operation, as opposed to operation under transient conditions. The results of the study will be provided to an American National Standard (ANS) working group that is revising the standards for simulator fidelity. The current, applicable portion of the standard states that simulator computed values for critical parameters should agree within ± 2% of the reference plant parameters; non-critical parameters have a tolerance of ± 10. This guidance is viewed by some as being too strict for certain critical parameters, and perhaps not precise enough in a few instances.

In order to provide more specific guidance, operator response data is needed to determine the degree of parameter variability necessary before an operator decides the plant is no longer in a steady-state configuration. The selection of a data collection approach to meet this need was based on several criteria:

- Ability to change parameter readings by parameter and across power levels, so operators respond to randomly presented parameter sets and are not overly attentive to subtle changes
- Ability to collect a large number of operator responses
- Ability to generalize to diverse designs of simulators representative of all four nuclear steam supply system (NSSS) vendors.

Based on these criteria, data will be collected using a small-scale simulation, and in the full-scope simulator. A small-scale simulation will be used first to remove simulator-specific cues, and to determine what variation in the absolute value operators will detect without benefit of the above-mentioned cues. Then, the operators will walk through the same parameter changes in a full-scope simulator, and the previously reported tolerances will be modified if they are beyond an alarm limit, or beyond the point at which a physical display change would cue the operator. In this way, the maximum allowable error tolerance for absolute values of the parameters will be identified.

Literature Review

The literature review focused on two areas: critical parameters in commercial nuclear power plant operation, and methodological considerations in designing studies on operator information processing using small scale-simulations.

The list of potential critical parameters was compiled based on the American National Standard (1985) and a Regulatory Guide from the U.S. Nuclear Regulatory Commission (NRC) (1983). Then, literature related to groupings of parameters based on plant safety functions was used to review the parameter list for omissions. This literature included descriptions of: safety functions developed by each of the four NSSS vendors as part of development of emergency procedure guidelines (vonHerrmann, 1983); safety functions used for safety parameter display system (SPDS) and disturbance analysis and surveillance system (DASS) development (Meyer, Long, Harmon, & Spurgin, 1983; Spurgin, Cain, & Long, 1982); and operator functions, including consideration of normal operations, developed for the NRC crew task analysis project (Burgy et. al., 1983).

Finally, literature related to small-scale simulation tests of operator information processing was used to develop the methodology for small-scale tests of critical parameters (e.g., Morris & Rouse 1985; Rasmussen, 1986, Spettell, 1986; Spurgin, Lukic & Hannaman, 1986; Woods & Roth, 1986; and Woods, Roth & Pople, 1987).

Based on the literature review, the experimental approach was developed further. The primary hypothesis is that operators will make consistent decisions regarding plant state based on parameter readings. The independent variable is the set of critical parameters that will be varied in accordance with algorithms for each of three reactor power levels. The dependent variable is operator responses to the parameters. Operators will be asked to indicate whether parameter readings are indicative of steady-state operation or otherwise.

METHOD

Three types of data collection included in this study are described: the utility survey, small-scale simulation tests, and full-scope simulation walkthroughs.

Utility Survey

The first step in the data collection process involved collection of information from electric power utility companies about critical parameters for nuclear plant control room operations training. This information will be compiled and used to develop the set of critical parameters for the small-scale simulation tests.

Participants. The written survey was mailed to simulator or training managers at electric power utility companies that have nuclear facilities in the United States, and are currently members of the Electric Power Research Institute.

Materials. The written survey was developed based on the list of critical parameters provided in the current American National Standard and supplemented with parameters from other sources. Separate surveys were developed for the two major types of commercial reactors: boiling water and pressurized water. Eighty-eight potential critical parameters were listed for boiling water reactors; 111 were listed for the pressurized type.

Procedure. Participants were asked to indicate which parameters should be considered critical. The definition of critical was "those parameters that require direct and continuous observation to operate the power plant under manual control, and input parameters to plant safety systems" (American Nuclear Society, 1985). They were asked to go through a list of the parameters considering steady-state operational conditions. They were then asked to reconsider the list of critical parameters from the perspective of transient conditions. Examples of representative transients to consider were presented (Kraje, Smith, Donovan, & Bucheit, 1985). For boiling water reactors, the transients were: turbine trip and loss of feedwater, recirculation pump shaft seizure, small loss-of-coolant accident (LOCA), and closure of all main steam isolation valves with failure of rod insertion. The transients for pressurized water reactors were: loss of feedwater followed by a stuck-open pressure-operated relief valve (PORV), a steam generator tube rupture with stock-open PORV, shaft seizure in a reactor coolant pump, small LOCA, and the Three Mile Island accident scenario.

Participants returned the surveys in prepaid envelopes, and the results were compiled. These results were used to develop the set of critical parameters for the small-scale simulation tests. The remainder of this paper focuses on the approach used for data collection related to steady-state operation.

Small-Scale Simulation Tests

The second portion of this study involves data collection based on operator responses to a personal-computer-based, small-scale simulation of the full-scope simulator displays. This data will be used to evaluate what parameter fluctuations affect the operator's mental model of the plant state.

Participants. Licensed reactor operators will be the participants. Reactor operators (ROs) and senior reactor operators (SROs) undergo simulator-based training as part of their annual requalification requirements by Federal law.

Operators licensed on plants representative of the four nuclear steam supply system (NSSS) vendors will be included. The four NSSS vendors are General Electric for BWRs; and Babcock and Wilcox, Combustion Engineering, and Westinghouse, for PWRs. Operators who have a range of operating experience will be included. Twelve operators each will be targeted from two different plants of each of the four NSSS vendor types (i.e., eight sites total). Background information will be collected on the experience and training of the participants.

Materials. Four displays are under development - one for each of the four NSSS Vendors' plants. Each NSSS-vendor-specific display will be an overall plant mimic presented on a personal computer. In addition to the mimic of major plant components and process lines, parameter values will be listed in digital form with engineering units next to a descriptor of the parameter. The parameter values will be displayed in close proximity to the associated component or process line on the mimic.

The mimic will be used to provide an organizational context for the parameters and to minimize the tedium of looking at tabularized lists of parameters. Display formats such as those in full-scope simulators (meters, chart recorders, indicator lights, annunciators) were not incorporated in the small-scale simulation for two reasons. First, these display formats vary considerably across plants (even of the same NSSS type). Second, digital information is needed to develop a quantitative standard. Some simulators do not have digital displays for certain parameters.

To drive the displays, software has been developed that uses parameter-specific algorithms to change parameter values. Only one parameter will change per screen, and some screens will remain unchanged. The specific parameter that changes will be varied randomly, however all operators will see the same randomized presentation. When one parameter changes, all others will be set at a steady-state value. The parameter-specific algorithm will increase or decrease a value continuously, so different values of a particular parameter will not be presented randomly. For example, an operator might see a steady-state value for feedwater flow on several consecutive screens. Then the operator would see the value increased by two percent; several screens later he or she would see an increase of four percent, and so forth.

Procedure. Data will be collected for each of three reactor power levels separately: 25%, 75%, and 100%. Operators will be told which power level to consider for that portion of the test.

As each screen is presented, operators will be asked to indicate whether the plant state has changed from steady-state for the particular power level, upon what parameter(s) he or she based the judgment, and the degree of confidence in the judgment (in percentage). The presentation time of each screen will be controlled by the operator.

Full-Scope Simulation Walkthroughs

After the small-scale simulation data has been collected and compiled, operators will walk through their respective simulators with the data collection team. The operators will be asked to indicate the displays they use to monitor the critical parameters. Information on annunciator or alarm setpoint values, values associated with noticeable meter or chart recorder deviations, and meter banding/color coding or other physical cues to the operator that the plant state has changed will be documented. This information will be used to qualify the data collected during the small-scale simulation. Specifically, for situations in which the reported digital change is greater than the parameter precision necessary to affect a physical cue change in the simulator, the error tolerance for the parameter will have to be made more stringent. In this way, the maximum allowable error tolerances for absolute values of the critical parameters will be identified.

RESULTS AND DISCUSSION

Data from the utility survey will be compiled to develop the critical parameter set. Data from the small-scale simulation tests will be presented for each of the NSSS vendors. For each NSSS vendor, data will be presented by power level and parameter. For each parameter, the values selected by a statistically significant number of operators as indicative of other than steady-state will be presented in quantitative form and as a percentage. Correction factors based on the simulator walkthroughs will be shown. For example, at the 100% power level, feedwater flow might vary .3 million pounds per hour beyond the steady-state value before a significant number of operators indicate confidence that plant state has changed. This number would be qualified based on the information gathered during the simulator walk through.

These results will be provided to the American National Standard working group that is currently revising the standard for simulator fidelity. The data will be used to develop parameter-specific tolerances for the fidelity of training simulators. This approach may be useful in other simulation applications in which decisions must be made about "how good is good enough" for training simulator fidelity.

REFERENCES

American Nuclear Society Standards Committee Working Group ANS-3.5. 1985. "American National Standard, nuclear power plant simulators for use in operator training." ANSI/ANS-3.5-1985. American Nuclear Society, La Grange Park, IL.

Burgy, D.; C. Lempges; A. Miller; L. Schroeder; H. VanCott; and B. Paramore. 1983. "Task analysis of nuclear power plant control room crews." Technical Report NUREG/CR-3371. U.S. Nuclear Regulatory Commission, Washington, D.C.

Kraje, B.; L. Smith; M. Donovan; and B. Bucheit. 1985. "Analytic simulator qualification methodology." Technical Report NP-4243. Electric Power Research Institute, Palo Alto, CA.

Meyer, O.R.; A. B. Long; D. L. Harmon; and A. J. Spurgin. 1982. "The Safety Parameter Display System: A progress statement." Technical Report 82-NE-36. The American Society of Mechanical Engineers, New York.

Morris, N.M. and W. B. Rouse. 1985. "The effects of type of knowledge upon human problem solving in a process control task." *IEEE Transactions on Systems, Man, and Cybernetics*, SMC-15: 698-707.

Rasmussen, J. 1986. "Development and testing of a model for simulation of process operator response during emergencies in nuclear power plants." In *Proceedings of the International Topical Meeting on Advances in Human Factors in Nuclear Power Systems*, 443-451.

Spettell, C.M. 1986. "The application of laboratory data from small-scale simulators to human performance issues in the nuclear industry." In *Proceedings of the International Topical Meeting on Advances in Human Factors in Nuclear Power Systems*, 217-221.

Spurgin, A.J.; D. G. Cain; and A. B. Long. 1982. "Decision-making aid for operational crews: Status of the EPRI DASS project." In *Proceedings of an International Symposium on Nuclear Power Plant Control and Instrumentation*. International Atomic Energy Agency, Vienna, Austria, 111-129.

Spurgin, A.J.; Y. D. Lukic; and G. W. Hannaman. 1986. "Analysis of small scale tests." In *Proceedings of the IEEE Conference on Systems, Man, and Cybernetics*.

U.S. Nuclear Regulatory Commission. 1983. "Instrumentation for light-water-cooled nuclear power plants to assess plant and environs conditions during and following an accident." Regulatory Guide 1.97. U.S. Nuclear Regulatory Commission, Washington, D.C.

vonHerrmann, J.L. 1983. "Methods for review and evaluation of emergency procedure guideline, Volume 1: Methodologies." Technical Report NUREG/CR-3177. U.S. Nuclear Regulatory Commission, Washington, D.C.

Woods, D.D. and E. M. Roth. 1986. "Models of cognitive behavior in nuclear power plant personnel." Technical Report NUREG/CR-4532. U.S. Nuclear Regulatory Commission, Washington, D.C.

Woods, D.D.; E. M. Roth; and H. Pople. 1987. "Cognitive Environment Simulation: An artificial intelligence system for human performance assessment." Technical Report NUREG/CR-4862. U.S. Nuclear Regulatory Commission, Washington, D.C.

Simulators VI

ISBN 0-911801-51-0

Fundamentals and main features of the German NPA project ATLAS*

D. Beraha, T. Voggenberger

Gesellschaft für Reaktorsicherheit (GRS) mbH

Forschungsgelände, D-8046 Garching

Federal Republic of Germany

ABSTRACT

The paper gives a survey of the nuclear plant analyzer ATLAS (ATHLET Analysis Simulator). It is designed as an engineering simulator for analyses of reactor transients and accidents, the investigation of operational and accident procedures and the validation of diagnosis systems, information displays and control systems.

ATLAS uses the system codes ATHLET and TRAC/PF1 as process models for the simulation of thermohydraulics. Balance of plant systems are simulated by both a detailed model package and the high level simulation language GCSM.

As front-end to the user ATLAS incorporates a communication system including a picture generator, various graphic output displays and an interactive operation surface for controlling the simulation process. ATLAS is implemented on a mainframe with two full-graphic workstations.

Work is in progress on the user interface in order to facilitate data handling, in the extension of on-line simulation support, the improvement of computing performance and the installation of ATLAS on a distributed computer architecture.

DEVELOPMENT GOALS

The rapid increase of computer power and the availability of fast computer graphics within the last years render possible the on-line simulation of complex technical systems or processes with detailed physical models by use of interactive simulators.

There is extended experience in nuclear industry with the use of training simulators for nuclear power plants. This kind of simulators is mainly used for training of operators and other technical staff. Especially the real time requirement usually limits the range of application to operational transients or incidents.

In nuclear safety technology multiple sophisticated codes and models have been developed for various kinds of applications in reactor analysis. Usually those codes are running on mainframes in batch mode with a low level of operating comfort and result representation. The international development of nuclear plant analyzers intends to upgrade the simulation environment of those codes to increase efficiency of analysis and understanding of plant behavior.

The nuclear plant analyzer project ATLAS has been started in 1985 as a joint project between Gesellschaft für Reaktorsicherheit (GRS) and Siemens/KWU with an intensive planning of the main development goals. In order to provide a flexible simulation tool with a wide spectrum of applications some basic requirements were defined:

- Full graphic system
- Software standardization
- Portability (hardware independence)
- Flexible interfaces (multiple model software)
- Interactive user support
- Plant independence
- Detailed simulation degree

Paying attention to these requirements various analyses and engineering tasks may be performed by applying this plant analyzer. The range of application covers the analysis of operational transients, incidents and accidents in nuclear power plants (LWR), the investigation and improvement of operational and accident procedures and the development and validation of diagnosis systems, information displays and control systems.

Although real time performance is not compulsory for engineering simulators, minimization of computing time has been one of the important aspects during the development. Work is in progress for further improvements in this field, especially in order to support on-line analysis of severe accident questioning.

SIMULATION MODELS

The ATLAS simulator includes the two system codes ATHLET /1/ and TRAC/PF1 /2/ as process models for the simulation of reactor thermohydraulics and neutronics. For the modelling of Balance of Plant (BOP) systems (e.g. control-, safety-, auxiliary systems) a detailed model library related to a reference PWR developed at Siemens/KWU is available. For general purpose BOP simulation a continuous system simulation language, the General Control System Module (GCSM) /3/ is used.

The basic structure of ATLAS is shown in fig. 1. The system codes are coupled to the BOP models and the communication program (graphics and interactive control) by sophisticated interfaces such that changes within these codes are kept to an absolutely necessary mimimum. Thus the high standard of validation of both codes also applies to the versions implemented into the plant analyzer. The minimization of program changes facilitates the implementation of improved versions of the codes; the general interfaces reduce the effort in coupling of additional process models, because no structural

* Work sponsored by the German Federal Ministry for Research and Technology

changes in the basic architecture of the simulator are necessary.

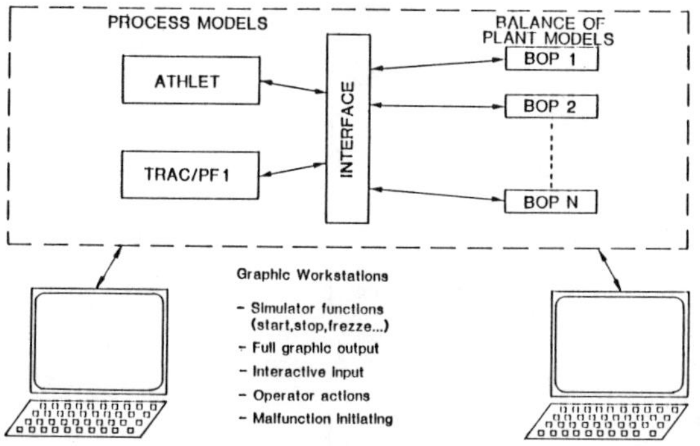

Fig. 1. Basic structure of the nuclear plant analyzer ATLAS

Process models

TRAC/PF1 is implemented as a reference code with worldwide use for the simulation of threedimensional fluiddynamic effects. For a detailed code description see /2/. Interfaces are realized to graphics and interactive control including malfunction simulation, but not to the BOP models. Because computational speed lies far beyond real time the application of TRAC is limited to some few special analyses.

Thus in the ATLAS project emphasis is shifted towards ATHLET and present and future work is concentrated exclusively on this code. ATHLET is being newly developed at GRS incorporating the transient analysis code ALMOD /4/, the LOCA code DRUFAN /5/, and the refill and reflood code FLUT /6/ into a modular network structure with a uniform input deck. Connection of basic modules for thermofluiddynamics, heat conduction and neutron kinetics to a thermohydraulic network allows the flexible simulation of a nuclear power plant. According to the desired application one can choose between several fluiddynamic options reaching from the description of thermodynamic and kinetic nonequilibrium up to a fast running homogeneous model with integrated mass- and momentum balance enabling real time simulation in some cases. In addition to these general flow models there are special models for components available such as pressurizer, steam generator, valves, pumps etc. Neutron kinetics simulation is possible by applying a point-kinetics model or a 1-D-model, the implementation of a simplified 3-D-model /7/ considering Xenon dynamics and control rods influence is under work. For further details of the models within ATHLET see also /8/.

BOP-models

Because of the high degree of automation in German nuclear power plants and the presence of elaborate limitation systems in addition to the plant protection and safety system special emphasis is put on the systems controlling the process.

For the 1300 MW KONVOI reference plant (most recent Siemens/KWU design) a set of approximately 40 BOP models simulating all important control- and auxiliary systems, e.g. reactor power control, interlock system, main condensate system, is available. These models have a very deep degree of simulation close to the functions of the original systems, but are coded in fixed structure such that adaptation to other plants, especially BWRs, is difficult.

For enhanced flexibility future BOP simulation will concentrate more and more on GCSM, which allows the modelling of any ordinary nonlinear differential equation system by input data. By combining basic standard elements such as switches, function generators, integrators etc. to a network describing the desired system, an easily changeable model may be defined and no recompiling is required. Another important feature of GCSM is the sophisticated coupling to the implicit thermohydraulic integration method, that ensures a satisfactory accuracy and guarantees optimal computational speed.

Simulation of interactively controlled malfunctions or operator actions is performed by a special failure-function-module allowing the replacement of model calculated values by user defined ones. This module supports the simulation of system failures and operator actions, e.g. the thermic drift of an amplifier or a system shutdown.

A very detailed description of BOP modelling within ATLAS is given in /9/.

COMMUNICATION SYSTEM

The communication system in ATLAS consists of two parts: a graphics editor (APG, a picture generator), which is used in an off-line mode to generate dynamic pictures, and the monitor, into which the generated pictures are integrated and provided with process data. All graphics is based on the GKS (Graphic Kernel System) -Standard. Thereby, portability to a wide variety of actual and future high-performance workstations is insured. At the time being, the 2b-level of GKS is used which does not allow for asynchronous input (i.e., events or interrupts generated by the graphic devices such as mouse, keyboard or digital tablet); in future, this limitation will be overcome. Fig. 2 depicts the functional connection between the picture generator and the monitor. The interface between the two systems is provided by the APG-metafile. This metafile is used to input already generated pictures into APG for further modification, and to store the pictures. The metafile is read by the monitor and subsequently processed as described below.

The picture editor

The design of the APG aimed at the generation of dynamic pictures and ease of picture modification. It allows the interactive construction of static and dynamic objects, which may be stored on the APG-metafile in an object library. These objects can be inserted in a picture (which in itself is defined as an object), undergoing transformations such as shifting, scaling and rotation.

Initial information such as the user surface icon as depicted in fig. 2 or possibly a picture to be modified are read in from the APG-metafile containing all graphics commands needed for redrawing the desired objects. The graphics commands contain the GKS-commands (e.g. drawing primitives and its attribute settings, workstation control, segment generation) and enhanced functions in form of APG-

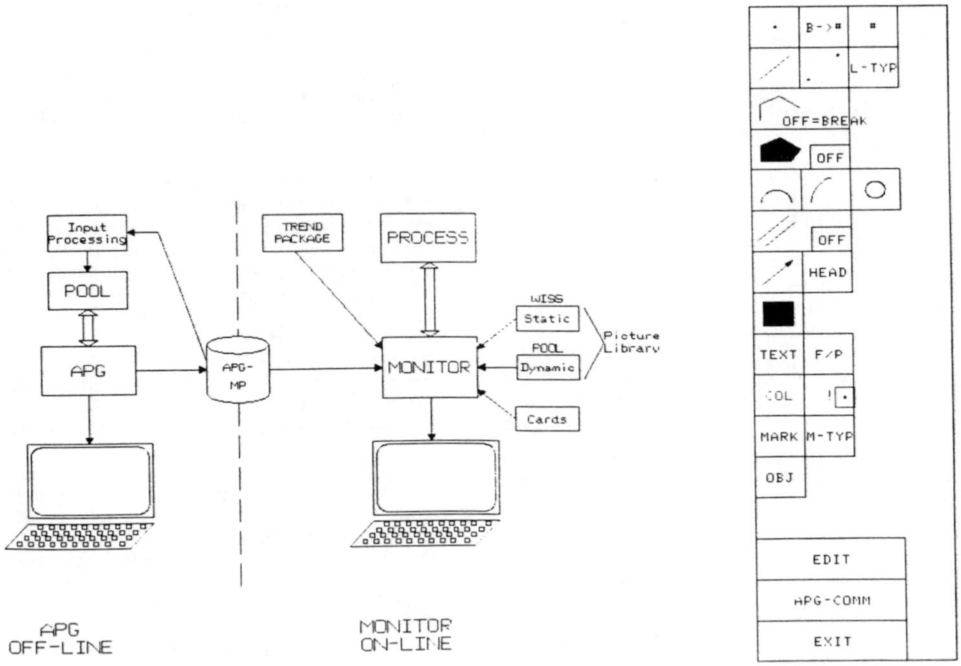

Fig. 2. Generation and management of picture data

commands (e.g. symbols such as valve, pump, vessel). The metafile is read into a main storage area named pool, which is structured as a doubly linked list. An interpreter retrieves the commands from the pool and calls the corresponding graphic function. Graphic commands in the pool may be modified either by interactive graphic devices or by directly editing the pool. Facilities for inserting and modifying are provided by a pool editor.

In GKS, the graphic commands are grouped into segments. Segments accept only a limited set of dynamic changes; in general, the segment has to be deleted and redrawn if changes occur. To enable animation of segments, dynamic changes are defined by variations of command parameters. With each parameter, a flag can be set indicating the address where the parameter value to be used in consecutive segment updates can be retrieved. The scope of this dynamic parameter setting extends to all GKS and APG-commands, which gives the user a large variety of possible dynamic changes. Provisions are made for updating segments only when necessary to reduce picture regeneration time. At the end of the interactive session, the pool is dumped on the APG-metafile which is then processed by the monitor or another APG-session.

The monitor

Visualisation of the model output and control of the model software (simulation of operator actions and malfunction initiation) is done by the monitor. The monitor is connected to the model software by means of either direct access files or a fast data link (hyperchannel). The model software transmits physical data which are processed in the monitor to produce the graphic data for update, such as scaling, conversion of data to color indices of a given color scale, and transformation of data into text formats. From the monitor, control commands are sent back to the model software as described before.

At initiation of the monitor, the graphics data are read in from the APG-metafile. The monitor recognizes static and dynamic objects. Static objects are kept in the Workstation Independent Segment Storage (WISS) for fast retrieval, dynamic objects are kept in the pool for picture updates. In addition, a software package for trend display is included in the monitor. Trend pictures can be set up by card input. The trends specified there are held in local storage to improve response time. However, all process data from the model software may be displayed as trends at run-time, as well as their name and value in the monitor, by interactive choice with graphic devices. The history of those values is retrieved from a file which stores past data up to a user-defined time interval. During monitor execution, the operator may change the time-window of the trends and the range of the y-axis.

Actually the monitor contains about 20 pictures. Interactive functions are provided for managing these pictures in windows (GKS-windows which are independent of the operating system), such as creating, moving and deleting windows, window operations to change the display priority and a zoom function. The control bar is displayed on the right side of the screen (see fig. 3).

Simulator control

Control of the simulator refers to the simulator functions and the initiation of operator actions and malfunctions. Simulator functions include those specified for training simulators (e.g. start, stop, freeze, backtrack, replay). Operator actions and malfunctions have identical effect on the model software and are treated as one subsystem of the monitor. As one of the main design requirements consisted in enabling many different (eventually non-nuclear) dynamic simulation codes to be run on the monitor, a data base has to be set up containing the monitor-specific names of the incoming process variables, information about their minimum and maximum values for trend display and scaling, and information on the mode of action possible on them (if the values can be changed by user provided ones). This is referred to as the monitor keyword list.

Malfunctions and operator actions are initiated by interactive input. Several types of time-functions (steps to extrema, ramps with a definable gradient) may be chosen interactively by pop-up menues.

Examples of graphic output

Fig. 3 and 4 show two examples of pictures in the monitor. The first one is displayed as entry and gives the synopsis of the plant state for two loops. Along the primary loop, several values such as temperatures, pressures and voids may be displayed in form of color shadings along the loop in an appropriate color scale. Maxima and minima of the color scale as well as the colors to be used can be chosen by the user at run-time. Also, the picture can be interactively switched from one such value to another. Further dynamics available at the moment refer to the water levels in steam generator and pressurizer, indicators for spraying and heating in the pressurizer, and alphanumeric display of important process parameters. More information will be included in this picture as indicated by user demands.

Instead of referring to this synopsis as a code-independent picture, a user may be interested in the exact nodalization of the plant and its parameters. In this case, a nodalization picture as shown in fig. 4 may be chosen. It is generated directly from the ATHLET-input and included in the

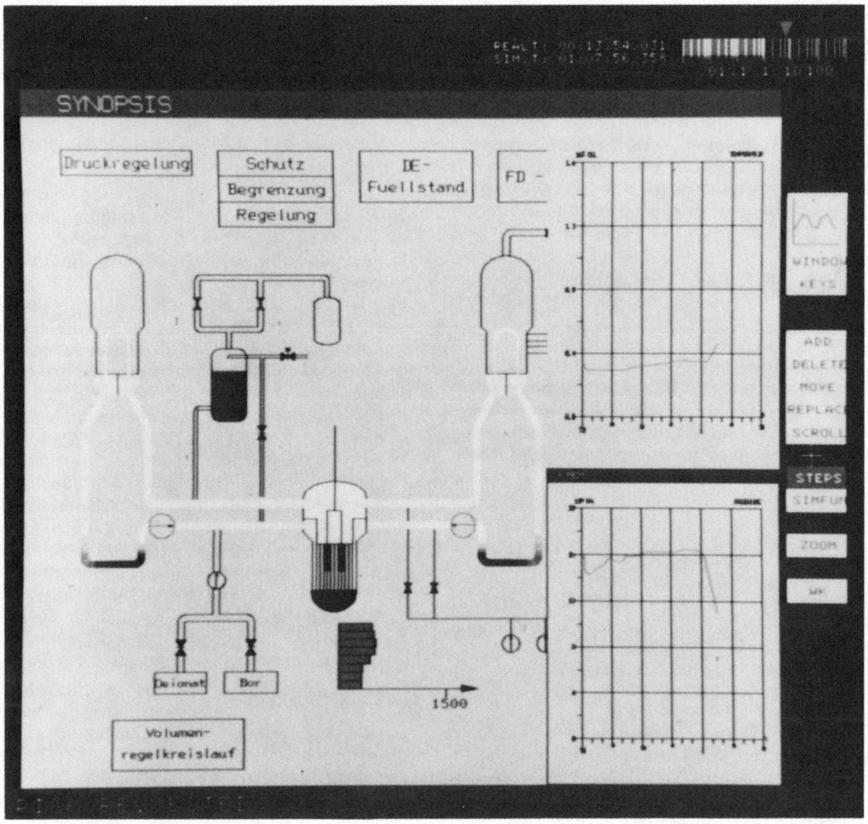

Fig. 3. Graphic windows display (plant synopsis and trend curves)

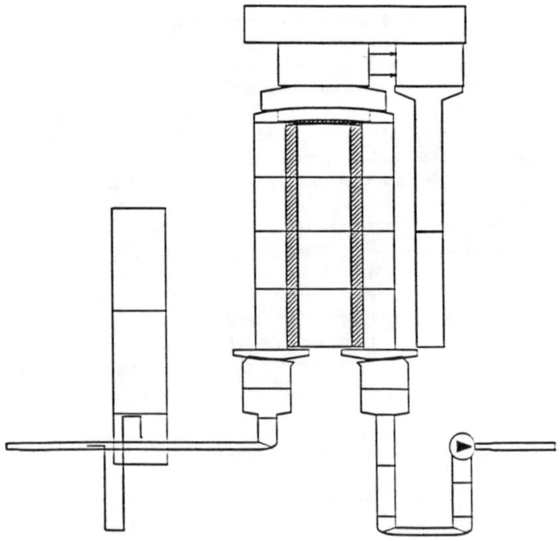

Fig. 4. Graphic display of ATHLET nodalization

monitor for dynamic output display. The nodes are colored according to the color scales also used in the synopsis with the same dynamic values available.

These displays makes allowance for the many applications and user requirements envisaged, which range from the code developer, interested in the exact reproduction of the code output, to training purposes, where code-specific information is of secondary importance.

COMPUTER ARCHITECTURE AND IMPLEMENTATION

ATLAS is actually implemented on a mainframe. However, a project is under way with the aim of constructing a test control room, with a distributed computer architecture suited to the requirements of fast simulation and application of ATLAS for the purposes stated in the introduction, with emphasis on the analysis of operating procedures for accident management.

Mainframe implementation

The model software and the monitor are installed on an AMDAHL 5870 with two IBM 5080-workstations (1024x1024 pixels, 128 colors) connected by channel. Mode software and monitor are run in two sessions or jobs as depicted in fig. 5. The communication between the sessions is done by direct access files, which are written and read in both directions. The intent of using direct access (DA) files lies mainly in portability issues. Instead of using DA-files, a hyperchannel may be used in an intra-host mode, reducing the large IO overhead encountered with file communication. Synchronization goes along with both types of data transfer between monitor and process in the sense, that the subsequent calculation of the process session is interrupted, if the display of the previous sent data has not been finished in the monitor.

As GKS on mainframes is not yet available on the 2C-level, which offers asynchronous (event-driven) input capabilities, an interrupt is necessary for enabling graphic input from the monitor. This is done by another session which continually reads an alphanumeric terminal for input. The communication is similar to the one used for communication of models and monitor.

As the monitor is able to handle several workstations, both IBM 5080's may be used for display and graphic input. The workstations are double-buffered (two frame buffers), which is a prerequisite for fast dynamic picture update without disturbing regeneration effects on the screen.

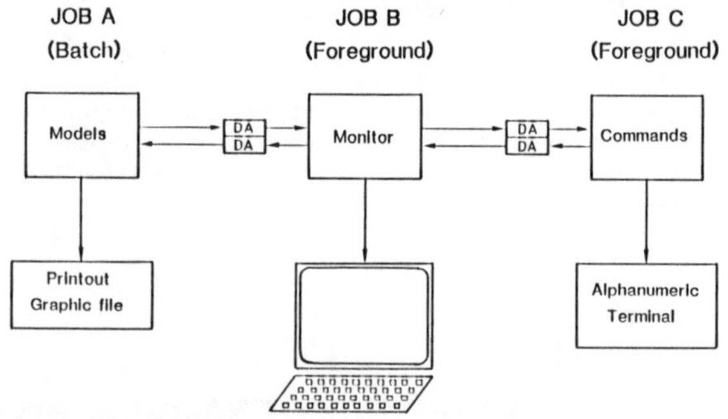

Fig. 5. ATLAS software organization and data flow on a mainframe

Test control room

The schematics of the test control room are shown in fig. 6. In this configuration, the mainframe is freed of the burden of the monitor system and is used exclusively for ATHLET. Investigations are under way concerning the replacement or enhancement of the general purpose mainframe by powerful parallel computer architectures to speed up the model software. The monitor is run on a process computer, which acts as host for the attached workstations (five workstations in the first project phase) and which is connected to the mainframe by a hyperchannel for fast data transfer. As the experience with GKS was very satisfactory, particularly with respect to the scope of the (two-dimensional) graphic functions and its portability, this standard will apply also for the test control room. However, efficient implementations of GKS on distributed systems are not yet generally available. In a joint development with a GKS software supplier, a GKS kernel is being developed with an interface to CGI, the Computer Graphics Interface (a forthcoming standard), which is capable of operating in an ETHERNET network. Thus, hardware independence is conserved, provided that CGI is available on the workstations. The workstations to be used in the first phase are based on a VME-bus architecture operating under UNIX, with a double frame buffer. The process computer will further be used to run applications which obtain data from the simulator and produce their own output displays such as plant information systems, diagnostic and operator support systems, as well as for general program development and software maintenance.

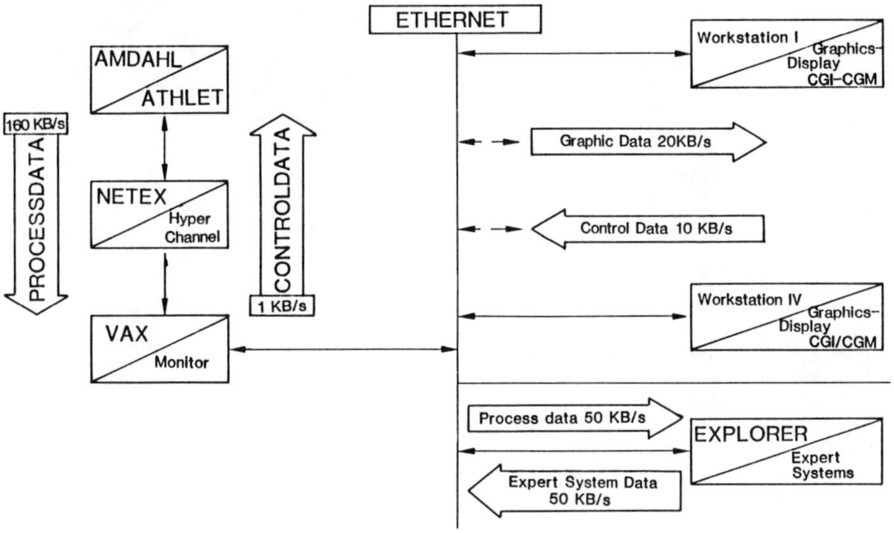

Fig. 6. Configuration of the test control facility

DEVELOPMENTS IN PROGRESS

Experiences in using the ATLAS simulator and continuously increasing requirements posed on the system by applicants have shown some important points to be improved. Thus it is desirable to extend the range of application, to speed-up the overall computational performance, to reduce the effort in input data generation and to improve the user support during simulation.

Model software upgrades

For the extension of the simulation range to severe accidents the implementation of ATHLET-SA, being developed at GRS and IKE/Stuttgart to model severe core damages and melting, Zirconium oxidation and fission product transportation, and additionally the containment model RALOC /10/ into ATLAS is planned.

Concerning the simulation of other nuclear power plants than KONVOI, especially BWR, the number of BOP models has to be enlarged, some special models (e.g. steam separator) are to be developed and integrated with appropriate input data into the plant analyzer.

As simulation time is well beyond real time especially for LOCA analyses, work is in progress in enhancing the simulation range of fast running model options, the improvement of numerical solution algorithms and the ATHLET code structure with respect to parallel computer architectures. All this work is done in code development projects at GRS in close connection with the simulator development.

Simulation support

This point covers various user aids during preparation of analyses, on-line analyses and post-analyses.

An important aspect is the time consuming and erroneous generation of code input in form of subsequent input cards with alphanumeric data. Good experiences have been made with the graphic display of nodalization data enabling the user to check geometry and network configuration.

Thus an intelligent and interactive user environment for input generation is in development based on an expert system shell providing graphic aids and on-line retrieval of plant data bases. In a first step GCSM data preparation has been chosen, because frequent data updates are necessary due to plant design changes in BOP systems and effort in this case is rather high. The input tool will graphically support the connection of basic GCSM elements to a block diagram, the design modification and the visualization of system parameters. The system also will include help functions, error handling and interactive run tests.

Besides the graphic display of results during a simulation additional on-line support will be helpful to facilitate the interpretation of results and the control of simulation, e.g. according to operation guidelines or component design values. Thus an expert system based information tool, will be established, allowing the access to plant data, reference manuals, system layout diagrams, operation and accident procedures and supplementary information or experience gained from previous analyses.

For post-analyses it is useful to provide comparison capabilities to previous calculations and measured data of nuclear power plants or test facilities. It is intended to store relevant pyhsical data in a data base system that can be accessed by an appropriate interface to the communication program on user's request.

CONCLUSIONS

The implementation of the thermohydraulic system codes TRAC and ATHLET into the nuclear plant analyzer ATLAS has been completed successfully. Numerous graphic displays with dynamic result presentation and the interactive control of simulation considerably increase the effectivity and quality of reactor safety analyses. Standard software and generalized interfaces guarantee hardware independence and minimize the effort of including additional model software.

Taking into account the intended range of simulation capabilities up to the analysis of severe accident procedures and the experiences gained by current applications several major extensions are necessary. The basic requirements for development are improving the model software with respect to simulation range and computational time, increasing the overall performance by advanced computer systems and enhancing the user support by involving expert system based tools and data base systems.

REFERENCES

/1/ Wolfert, K.; Lerchl, G.; Miró, J.E.; and Sonnenburg H.G.
"The GRS Thermalhydraulic System Code ATHLET for PWR and BWR Analyses". In Proceedings of 3rd International Topical Meeting on Nuclear Power Plant Thermalhydraulics and Operation (Seoul, Corea, 14-17 Nov., 1988)

/2/ Lies, D.R. et al.
"TRAC-PF1/MOD1 An Advanced Best-Estimate Computer Program for PWR Thermal Hydraulics Analysis", NUREG/CR-3858, 1986

/3/ Graf, U.; Miró, J.E.; Schaefer, A.; and Voggenberger, T.
"ALMOD4/MOD1 Code Description Basic Models and Methods", GRS-A-1316/III, Dec. 1986

/4/ Schaefer, A.; Miró J.E.; Höppner, G.; Frisch, W.; Meissner, R.; and Gaal, U.
"ALMOD4 Advanced PWR Transient Analysis Code".
In proceedings of the ANS Topical Meeting on Anitcipated and Abnormal Plant Transients in Light Water Reactors.
(Jackson, USA, 26-29 Sept., 1983)

/5/ Steinhoff, F.
"DRUFAN 02, Interim Program Description". GRS Reports. Part 1: GRS-A-685, March 1982, Part 2: GRS-A-714, May 1982

/6/ Hora, A.; Michetschläger, C.; Sonnenburg, H.G.; and Teschendorff, V.
"Analysis of Reflood Phenomena by the Two-Fluid Code FLUT". In Proceedings of Advances in Two-Phase Flow and Heat Transfer,
M. Nijhoff Publ. (The Hague, 1983)

/7/ Lupas, O.
"3-D Real-Time Core Model for Digital Control" In proceedings of the VIII International School on Nuclear Physics, Neutron Physics and Nuclear Energy
(Varna, Bulgaria, 19-28 Nov., 1987)

/8/ Austregesilo, H.; Jakubowski, Z.; Miró, J.E.; and Voggenberger, T.
"Modelling of a Pressurized Water Reactor within the German Nuclear Plant Analyzer ATLAS". Proceedings of the 1989 Eastern Multiconference/Simulators VI.
(Tampa, USA, 28-31 Mar., 1989)

/9/ Austregesilo, H.; and Voggenberger, T.
"Simulation of Control and Safety Systems within the German NPA"
5th Summer School on Heat Transfer
(Lappeenranta, Finland, Aug. 1988)

/10/ Jahn, H.L.
"RALOC-MOD1, A Computer Program for the Determination of Local Gas Concentration in Subdevided Vessels"
GRS-A-333, Aug. 1979, NRC Translation 796

AUTHOR INDEX

AUTHOR INDEX